MACHINE
TOOL
METALWORKING

PRINCIPLES AND PRACTICE

Second Edition

JOHN L. FEIRER

McGraw-Hill Book Company

New York   St. Louis   San Francisco   Dallas   Düsseldorf   London
Mexico   Panama   Rio de Janeiro   Singapore   Sydney   Toronto

ABOUT THE AUTHOR

JOHN L. FEIRER majored in metalworking at Stout State College, where he was given the Eichelberger Scholarship for three years. He has had several years' teaching experience in Midwestern junior and senior high schools and colleges. During World War II, he served as head of the Aviation Metalsmith School, Norman, Oklahoma. Dr. Feirer is now Professor and Head of the Industrial Education Department at Western Michigan University at Kalamazoo. He is active in industrial education and has written widely for the field. His *General Metals* is one of the McGraw-Hill Publications in Industrial Arts. He is also the coauthor of *General Shop,* another book in this series.

Library of Congress Cataloging in Publication Data

Feirer, John Louis.
  Machine tool metalworking.

  1. Machine-tools. 2. Metal-work. I. Title.
TJ1185.F4   1973   684'.09   72-10166
ISBN 0-07-020369-5

MACHINE TOOL METALWORKING: Principles and Practice

PREFACE

Machine Tool Metalworking is an introductory text on the machining of metals. It is designed to be used wherever a beginning machine-shop class is taught in industrial education.

The author has based his coverage on the results of recent research concerning students who have graduated from machine-shop programs. This research has shown that certain operations students learn are of much value and are used frequently. Other operations are less often used, while some of the more advanced techniques are not used at all by new graduates. In this text, primary emphasis is given to the important areas of benchwork, measurement, drilling, and turning. Somewhat less emphasis is given to milling and grinding operations.

Since students remember comprehensive information longer and use it more often than the detailed knowledge of a large number of unrelated operations, the author has emphasized broad concepts in regard to all machine tools. A great deal of space is devoted to such topics as how machines operate, what cutting tools are used and how they shape metal, how to determine speeds and feeds, and the essentials of mechanics. In addition, all new words and terms have been defined so students can quickly develop the vocabulary of the trade.

New features of this edition include the following:

The Metric System. The United States will eventually convert to the metric system. Therefore, the machinist should become acquainted with this measuring system and the tools used. The dual system of measurement—namely, the English and the metric systems—is included whenever applicable.

Precision Measuring Tools. These are funda-mental to all machine operations. In this revision, information pertaining to precision measurement has been greatly expanded.

Band Machining. The band machining process is utilized in most metal industries and is included for the first time in this edition.

Vertical Milling Machine. Since this popular type of milling machine is often found in the small job shop and educational laboratory, more attention has been given to the processes that can be performed on it.

Materials. Additional emphasis has been placed on the kinds of materials that are used and how they are heat-treated, inspected, and tested.

New Machining Techniques and Equipment. A large number of new machining techniques for specialized uses have been developed in recent years. While it is not the intention of this text to provide students with in-depth instruction in these new techniques, the techniques are covered to the extent that the students will be acquainted with them. Included are such significant developments as numerical control and electrical machining (EDM, ECM, and ECG).

The author greatly appreciates the generous cooperation of the numerous companies in supplying both illustrations and technical assistance. A special note of appreciation should go to Mr. William Brown of the Clausing Corporation for many of the illustrations that appear in Sections 5 and 6, to the Superior Electric Company for materials used in Unit 101, and to the Brown & Sharpe Manufacturing Company for use of materials from their manual, *The Young Machinist's Handbook.*

John L. Feirer

CONTENTS

ACKNOWLEDGMENTS

Acknowledgment is sincerely given to the following companies for providing helpful suggestions, data, and illustrations:

Acco Wilson Instrument Division, Allis-Chalmers; Aluminum Company of America; American Iron and Steel Institute; The American Tool Works; Armstrong Bros. Tool Co.; Astro Broaching Corp.; John Bath & Company, Inc.; Bethlehem Steel Corp.; The Billings and Spencer Co.; The Black & Decker Mfg. Co.; Boeing Company; Boston Gear Works; Bridgeport Machines, Inc.; Brown & Sharpe Mfg. Co.; Cadillac Gage Co.; Carborundum Co.; Casting Specialities Co.; Caterpillar Tractor Co.; CEJ Gage Co.; Challenge Machinery Co.; Chicago Latrobe; Chicago Tool and Engineering Co.; Chrysler Corp.; Cincinnati Inc.; Cincinnati Lathe and Tool Co.; Cincinnati Milacron, Inc.; Clark Instrument, Inc.; Clausing Corp.; The Cleveland Twist Drill Co.; Columbian Vise & Mfg. Co.; Covel Mfg. Co.; Cross Co.; DeVlieg Machine Co.; W. C. Dillion & Co., Inc.; DoAll Co.; The duMont Corp.; Eastman Kodak Co.; EHCO Tool & Machine Co., Inc.; Elox Corp. of Michigan; Ex-Cell-O Corp.; Federal Product Corp.; Fellows Corp.; Fosdick Machine Tool Co.; Gaertner Scientific Corp.; Gem Vises—J. E. Martin Machine Co.; General Electric Co.; General Motors Corp., Giddings & Lewis-Bickford Machine Co.; Gorton Machine Co.; C. A. Gray Co.; Greaves Machine Tool Co.; Greenfield Tap and Die, United-Greenfield Division of TRW, Inc.; Gulf Oil Corp.; Hammond Machinery Builders, Inc.; Henry L. Hanson Co.; Heald Machine Co.; The Hill Acme Co.; Houdaille Industries; Index Machine & Tool Co.; Industrial Fasteners Institute; International Nickel Co.; Johnson Gas Appliance Co.; Jones & Lamson Division of Waterbury Farrel; KMS Industries, Inc.; Kalamazoo Manufacturing Co.; Kearney & Trecker Corp.; Kempsmith Machine Co.; Kennametal, Inc.; Kysor Industrial Corp.; L-W Chuck Co.; Landis Tool Co.; LeBond; Lufkin Rule Co.; Magnaflux Corp.; Mattison Machine Works; McDonnel Douglas Corp.; Mesta Machine Co.; Metra-Tech Corp.; Mohawk Tools, Inc.; Moore Special Tool Co., Inc.; Morse Twist Drill & Machine Co.; NATCO Products Corp.; National Aeronautics and Space Administration; National Twist Drill & Tool Co.; New Departure—Hyatt Bearings Division of General Motors Corp.; The New England Machine & Tool Co.; Nicholson File Co.; Norton Co.; Tinius *Olsen* Testing Machine Co.; Palmgren Steel Products; Peerless Machine Co.; Portage Machine Co.; Powder Metallurgy Parts Association; Republic Steel Corp.; Racine Hydraulics and Machinery, Inc.; Ready Tool Co.; Rockwell Manufacturing Co.; Sheldon Machine Co., Inc.; The Shore Instrument & Manufacturing Co., Inc.; Sipco Tool & Die Co.; J. T. Slocomb Co.; South Bend Lathe; Standard Gage Co., Inc.; Stanley Tool Division, The Stanley Works; The L. S. Starret Co.; Steel City Testing Machines, Inc.; Sun Oil Co.; Sundstrand Corp.; The Superior Electric Co.; Texaco, Inc.; Timesavers, Inc.; The Timken Co.; Union Twist Drill Co., Butterfield Division; United Aircraft Corp.; The U. S. Burke Division, Machine Tool, Cincinnati Manufacturing Corp.; United States Steel Corp.; Universal Vise & Tool Co.; Van Norman Co.; The Walton Co.; The Warner & Swasey Co.; Wells Manufacturing Corp.; Western Electric Co.; J. H. Williams & Co.

The cover photograph is courtesy of Alfred Herbert Ltd.

TO THE STUDENT

This book was written to help you learn about the field of machine tool metalworking. Many of you may some day want to earn a living as a machinist, tool and die maker, draftsman, technician, or engineer. If you do, a knowledge of basic machine shop practice is necessary. There is fun in "watching the chips curl off the metal," but this alone is not enough. You must learn about machinery, about cutting tools, and about processes. To do this you will have to study and read, as well as work in the shop.

This textbook will help you. Here are some other things that will help you:

1. *Get in the habit of using a dictionary.* Learning the new words and terms in machine shop is very important. You should learn to speak the language of the machinist, draftsman, and engineer. Instead of asking for a "thingamajig" or a "what-cha-call-it," a "doodad" or a "gizmo," use the correct name of each part, tool, or process. Most of the new words and terms are defined in this book. You should also use a standard dictionary and a dictionary of technical terms whenever necessary.

2. *Learn to use handbooks.* In every important field of learning there are handbooks that contain the detailed technical information that would be impossible to include in a textbook. These handbooks are usually thick and complicated-looking "bibles of the trade." They may frighten you at first. However, once you learn to use the index you will be able to find any special information you need. Two excellent handbooks in the metalworking manufacturing field are (a) *The New American Machinist's Handbook;* and (b) *Machinery's Handbook.*

3. *Read trade magazines.* Besides the popular technical magazines, there are trade magazines in each field that tell about new products, processes, and machinery. You'll find that these trade magazines can be a great help to you in keeping up with a field. They'll give you the latest information on how things are done in industry. If you plan to earn a living in a field related to metalworking, you should enjoy reading these trade magazines. Most libraries have a good trade magazine in each field.

4. *Apply mathematics.* Sometimes you may wonder why you need to learn so much about mathematics. You'll find part of the answer in your machine shop classes. You'll find a day-to-day use for it in every step in making a project, from reading the drawing or print to measuring the finished product.

5. *Review science as it applies to the machine shop.* In the machine shop you'll find many examples of applied science. As you learn to use machines, grind cutting tools, and make projects, review in your mind the basic scientific principles involved. Which pair of pulleys will produce the greatest speed? Why must a cutting tool be clamped securely? Why is steel different from cast iron? How can the chisel be made hard and tough? You'll find that science provides the answer to each of these questions.

Most of all, learn to work safely, quickly, and intelligently. Remember that it's not enough to work only with your hands. More and more, our repetitive hand-skill jobs will be done by machine. Knowing the "why" will be just as important as knowing "how." This book will get you off to a good start in both respects.

INTRODUCTION TO MACHINE SHOP

UNIT 1. Machine Tools Today— The Five Basic Machines

Machining is one of the four major metal manufacturing methods. The other methods are hot forming, cold forming, and casting (Fig. 1-1). Machining is done when a very accurate and smooth surface is needed. The metal is shaped by cutting away chips, with either cutting tools or abrasives (Fig. 1-2). In the machining process, metal is turned, shaped, milled, cut, or otherwise reduced or changed by removing chips with machine tools to produce the desired shape and dimension.

MACHINE TOOLS: MEASURE OF MAN'S PROGRESS

Henry Ward Beecher said, "A *tool* is but the extension of a man's hand, and a *machine* is but a complicated tool." To understand this statement fully, it is necessary for you to know how tremendously machine tools have affected our lives.

Since man first picked up a rock to use as a hammer, his progress has been governed by the kind of tools he has developed. Today, every product known is a product of machine tools. If not used directly in the manufacture of a product, machine tools are required to produce the material and equipment necessary for its processing or growth.

● Without machine tools, the population of the world could not feed or clothe itself.

● Without machine tools, modern man would cease to exist.

● Without machine tools, modern civilization could not exist.

We have modern conveniences only because today's machine tools can cut and form metal to extremely close limits of accuracy at high rates of speed.

Millions of cars operate because machine tools produce in quantity all those intricate metal parts from which these vehicles are made (Fig. 1-3). Chairs, tables, beds, and bookcases are made by saws, drills, planes, sanders, and other tools that are assembled from parts made by machine tools (Fig. 1-4). The farm output of the

A

B

C

D

Fig. 1-1.   The four basic manufacturing methods are: (A) *cold forming*, production of parts at low or cold temperatures; (B) *hot forming*, formation of metals by heating them to a high temperature and then applying pressure; (C) *casting*, formation of metals by pouring liquid metal into a form; and (D) *machining*.

Fig. 1-2.   All machining operations produce chips.

Fig. 1-3. A car of the future. Without machine tools, products such as this would not be possible.

Fig. 1-4. Machine tools are needed to make the machines used in woodworking.

Fig. 1-5. Modern farming methods require sophisticated equipment made on machine tools.

Fig. 1-6. Complicated machine tools are needed to produce modern means of transportation.

United States has increased many fold because of tractors, combines, cultivators, grain millers, chemical fertilizers, threshing machines, and other supplies and equipment made either by machine tools or by machinery that was made by machine tools (Fig. 1-5). Railroad locomotives, freight cars, airplanes, ships, and trucks are possible only because of machine tools (Fig. 1-6). The mills, refineries, processing plants, and other production facilities that turn out steel, aluminum, paper, chemicals, textiles, petroleum products, plastics, and food rely directly on machine tools for the construction of production and processing equipment, and some of these products require machine tools in their manufacture (Fig. 1-7).

In this age of electronics, atomic power, and rockets, machine tools remain the key to man's progress (Fig. 1-8). They open the door to methods and techniques that permit man to translate his dreams into realities that raise his standard of living (Fig. 1-9).

Fig. 1-7. Modern industry needs precision equipment of all types, and machine tools must build it.

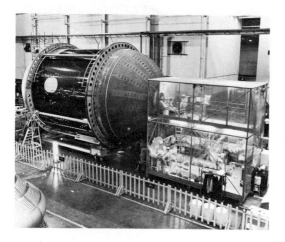

Fig. 1-8. Men working in space will need a sky lab that is produced with machine tools.

Fig. 1-9. Man could not have reached the moon without machine tools.

The real wealth of our nation is in what we make to meet our needs and wants. What good would money be if there were no automobiles, television sets, or the thousand and one other things we use everyday? Can you imagine what a car would cost if only a few were produced every year? When Henry Ford first made his Model T in 1909, he produced about 10,000 the first year. By 1915, Ford was producing, with machine tools, about a quarter of a million (250,000) cars each year. The price of each car was only about one-half the price it was 6 years earlier. The more goods we produce, the more there are to distribute among us. Also, the cost will be lower, and our standard of living will be higher. It is only through the use of machine tools that we are able to increase the production of things we need in our everyday life.

A *hand tool* is one that is skillfully used and guided by the hand alone. Hammers, screwdrivers, files, and chisels are examples of hand tools (Fig. 1-10). *Machine tools* include power-driven machines of many types and sizes. They are capable of cutting and forming metal into parts we want to make. Electric motors do the work of driving the machines and moving the different parts automatically (Fig. 1–11). Thus, machine tools are a powerful substitute for human strength and skill.

WHAT MASS PRODUCTION MEANS

When the name of Eli Whitney is mentioned, most of us are reminded of the cotton gin. Whereas this invention was important, it in no way compares with the contribution he made to the development of *mass production*. Before Eli Whitney's time, a gunsmith had to make and fit each part of a musket individually. He made one gun at a time, and each gun differed a little from all the others. This, as you can see, took much time and required a great deal of skill and patience. In 1798, Eli Whitney wrote to the Secretary of the Treasury of the United States offering to produce 10,000 muskets in 2 years. Whitney's idea was to use "specialized labor." This meant that he would have one man who was only fairly skilled make just one part of the

Fig. 1–10.   A screwdriver is a simple machine even though it is called a hand tool.

musket. All these parts would then be the same, and each part would then fit into any of the muskets. He also decided that each part had to be standardized and made as accurately as pos-

Fig. 1–11.   A modern, numerically controlled machine tool.

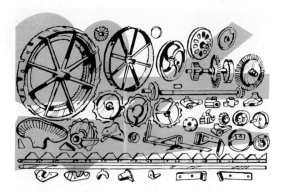

Fig. 1-12. Whitney's methods were used by many inventors, including Cyrus McCormick who developed and invented a reaper in 1831. This great time- and labor-saving device consisted of a number of mass-produced parts.

sible so that hand-fitting could be eliminated. Whitney was given the contract.

At the end of the first year, Whitney had produced very few muskets. As a result, he was called to Washington to explain. You must remember, in those days people had no idea that it would be possible to mass-produce an item such as a musket. They thought that Whitney would hire enough skilled craftsmen to *hand-produce* the muskets at the rate of 16 a day. Whitney took with him to Washington several boxes containing parts for 10 muskets. He placed these parts neatly in piles on a table and asked an official to pick out a part from each pile. From these he quickly assembled a musket. He also assembled nine other muskets from the other parts. In doing this, Whitney demonstrated the most important single idea of modern industrial production, that is, the idea of "interchangeable parts" (Fig. 1–12). This demonstration convinced the officials that Eli Whitney could produce the muskets in any quantity. Whitney, however, had to spend most of the first year "tooling up." This meant doing three things:

1. He had to build special machines to do the metal cutting or machining on the parts. Consequently, Whitney is credited with having invented the first plain milling machine in 1818.

2. He had to design and make special tools such as drill jigs and fixtures. A *drill jig* is a work-holding device or tool which holds a workpiece to be drilled. Hardened steel bushings are used to guide the drills. Holes drilled with a "jig" will be in the same exact location in each part. The story goes that one of Whitney's assistants developed this device to hold one of the parts and guide the drill for making the hole. When Whitney asked him what it was, he said, "Oh, it's a thing-a-ma-jig." This was later shortened to jig.

A *fixture* is another type of work-holding device or tool. It holds one or several parts in an exact position while cutting tools machine them to size. Fixtures are usually permanently attached to a machine tool, while jigs are not.

3. He had to develop a system for measuring the parts, for each part had to be accurate enough to be interchanged with any of the other parts. You must remember that in those days there was no standard of measurement such as we have today.

This, then, was the first example of mass production. There were no power tools on that first production line. Foot-operated lathes, hand-operated drilling presses, and a crude milling machine, which Whitney himself designed, were the machines available. Whitney assigned each part of the musket to one workman or a group of workmen who soon became specialists in its fabrication. The workmen used simple template drill jigs and profiling fixtures, establishing standards through snap gages. Their measurements were crude by modern standards, with tolerances of about $\frac{1}{100}$ in. But these were sufficient for that time, and an important new principle was established. It was the beginning of a system that today is used to manufacture everything from typewriters to tremendous road graders.

Interchangeability, made possible by machine tools, is a primary requirement of modern manufacture. Today, parts are so accurately mass-produced by machine tools that formerly expensive luxuries are now relatively inexpensive necessities. Because of machine tools, the quality of workmanship which makes interchangeability possible is just as available to a plant employing only a few men as one employing thousands. The economies of mass production, possible only because of machine tools, have made thousands of products available to

Fig. 1-13. Such diverse products as cooking equipment and cameras are available to everyone because of machine tools.

everyone at moderate cost and have provided jobs for millions of workers in cities and towns throughout the country (Fig. 1-13).

BASIC ELEMENTS OF MACHINING

Basic to the machining process are the following four elements:

Machine Tools. The most common machine tools are lathes, milling machines, drilling machines, shapers, and grinders. There are many varieties of special-purpose machines used in manufacturing which are adapted from one or more of the basic machine tools.

Many of the machines of industry are similar to those found in the school shop except that they are larger and more complex. They have many electronic and hydraulic controls. Some pieces of more highly automatic equipment feature numerically controlled operations.

Cutting Tools. The cutting tool used on a machine tool can be a single-point tool like that used on the engine lathe, shaper, or planer; a multiple-point cutting tool like a milling-machine cutter; a drill, reamer, and broach (a kind of planing machine); or a grinding wheel used on a grinder (Fig. 1-14). Cutting tools are

Fig. 1-14. A lathe utilizes a single-point cutting tool, and a milling machine has a multiple-point cutting tool.

made from high-speed steel, stellite, carbide, diamond, ceramics, or abrasives (including silicon carbide and aluminum oxide).

Materials. Materials from which parts are machined include standard bar stock, forgings, and castings (Fig. 1-15). Bar stock may be carbon steel, tool steel, stainless steel, aluminum, a copper-based alloy, or any of the more unusual metals such as magnesium or titanium.

Jigs and Fixtures. Different fixtures are designed and developed for holding parts for machining. Jigs are built to hold parts and to control cutting tools in drilling.

WHAT IS A MACHINE TOOL?

According to the National Machine Tool Builders' Association, "a *machine tool* is a power-driven machine not portable by hand, used to shape or form metal by cutting, impact, pressure, electrical techniques, or a combination of these processes."

Thus, it is obvious that machine tools can be built in a wide variety of types. Basically, however, there are two main categories. The first is the cutting-type machine tool, which shapes metal to size and contour by cutting away the unwanted portions. The second is really an assortment of machine types, all rather recent in origin. By controlling the characteristics and forces of chemicals, electricity, magnetism, liquids, sound, light, and even gunpowder, it is possible to shape materials into products that are often beyond the capabilities of conventional equipment.

Some authorities include a third category of machine tool. Machine tools in this group shape metal by shearing, as paper is sheared with scissors, or by hammering or squeezing it into the desired shape. Only the first two categories of machine tools will be discussed in this book.

For the various operations that must be performed in the metalworking shop, there are many different types of machines, each designed to do work of a specific nature. Actually, there are over 500 different machine tools, each built in a variety of sizes and forms. For each type and size of machine tool, there are many special work-holding devices called *attachments*.

There are special machine tools that are

Fig. 1-15.   Forging of a valve. The one on the right is only partly machined.

built to perform successive operations, once the workpiece has been loaded into place. The operator literally does not touch the work from the beginning to the end of the succession of machining steps. Such equipment is referred to as *automated* or *transfer machinery*.

Precision of operation is the most outstanding characteristic of today's machine tools. Dimensional accuracies during the past 50 years have progressed from one-thousandth of an inch, to one ten-thousandth of an inch, and now approach a millionth of an inch. This is about one three-hundredths the thickness of a human hair! Such precision makes it possible and feasible to produce hundreds of identical parts, all so much alike that they may be freely interchanged or substituted in assembly or repair, without hand-fitting.

FIVE BASIC TECHNIQUES

The variety and combinations of machine tools today are almost unlimited. Some are small enough to be mounted on a workbench. Others are so large they require special buildings to house them. They range in cost from a few hundred dollars to hundreds of thousands of dollars. Others, such as transfer lines, will extend for hundreds of feet through a plant.

Large or small, inexpensive or costly, machine tools can be categorized into five major classifications, identified as the five basic techniques of shaping metal. These basic operations

Fig. 1-16. A drill press used for drilling.

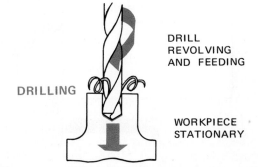

DRILLING

DRILL
REVOLVING
AND FEEDING

WORKPIECE
STATIONARY

include drilling and boring (including reaming and tapping), turning, milling, planing (including shaping and broaching), and grinding (including honing). Regardless of the simplicity or complexity of a machine tool, it performs one or more of these operations. Variations of the five basic techniques are employed to meet special situations. There are, for example, machines that combine two or more of these techniques, as in a boring, drilling, and milling machine; a stamping, punching, and shearing press; or a combination milling and planing machine. Some people add metal forming (including shearing, stamping, pressing, and forging) as a sixth basic technique. However, these processes do not involve metal removal in the form of chips. Therefore, they are not included in this text.

In addition to the five basic techniques, there are newer metal shaping methods developed during the past two decades that employ the disintegrating, corrosion, erosion, and force characteristics of chemicals, electricity, magnetism, liquids, explosives, sound, and light.

Drilling and Boring. Drilling is a basic machine-shop technique dating back to primitive man. It consists of cutting a round hole by means of a rotating drill (Fig. 1-16). Boring, on the other hand, involves the finishing of a hole already drilled or cored by means of a rotating, offset, single-point tool (Fig. 1-17). On some boring machines, the tool is stationary and the work revolves; on others, the reverse is true.

Under the classification of drilling and boring, there are included two other types of machining techniques; reaming and tapping. *Reaming* consists of finishing a hole already drilled, usually to very close tolerances (Fig. 1-18). *Tapping* is the process of cutting a thread inside a hole so that a cap screw may be used in it.

Turning. The lathe, as the turning machine is commonly called, is the father of all machine tools. Its principle has been known since the dawn of civilization, probably originating as the potter's wheel. The piece of metal to be machined is rotated and the cutting tool is advanced against it (Fig. 1-19).

A turret lathe differs from an engine lathe in that it is equipped with a multisided tool holder (turret) to which a number of different cutting tools are attached. The turret makes it

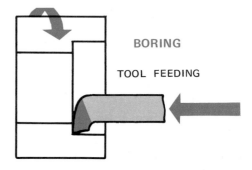

WORKPIECE REVOLVING

BORING

TOOL FEEDING

Fig. 1-17.   Boring a hole.

Fig. 1-18.   Reaming can be done on many machines including the drill press and the lathe.

Fig. 1-19.   An engine lathe.

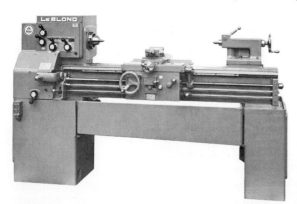

TURNING

WORKPIECE REVOLVING

TOOL
TRAVELING
OR FEEDING

possible to bring several different cutting tools into successive use and to repeat the sequence of machining operations over and over again without resetting the tools.

When the number of identical parts to be turned is increased from a few to hundreds or thousands, single- and multiple-spindle automatics are used. These machines perform as many as six or eight different operations at one time on as many parts. They are entirely automatic, and once set up and put into operation, they relieve the operator of all but two duties, monitoring the operation and gaging the accuracy of finished parts.

Planing and Shaping. Planing metal with a machine tool is a process somewhat similar to planing wood with a carpenter's hand plane. The essential difference lies in the fact that the machine tool is greater in size, that it is not portable, and that the cutting tool remains in a fixed position while the work is moved back and forth beneath it (Fig. 1-20). Planers are usually large pieces of equipment; sometimes large enough to handle the machining of surfaces 15 to 20 feet wide and twice as long. A shaper differs from a planer in that the workpiece is held stationary and the cutting tool travels back and forth (Fig. 1-21).

Slotting is an operation similar to the operation performed on a shaper. Slotting, however, is performed vertically. Slotters, or vertical shapers, are used principally to cut certain types of gears (Fig. 1-22).

Broaches may be classed as planing machines. The broach has a multiplicity of cutting teeth, each cutting-edge a little higher than the one before and graduated to the final size required. The broach is pulled or pushed over the surface to be finished. It may be applied internally, for example, to finish a square hole; or it may be applied externally to produce a flat surface or a special shape.

Milling. Milling consists of machining a piece of metal by bringing it into contact with a rotating cutting tool which has multiple cutting-edges (Fig. 1-23). There are many types of milling machines designed for various kinds of work. The planer type, for example, is built like a planer, but has multiple-toothed revolving cutting tools. Machines using the milling principle, but built especially to make gears, are called *hobbing machines*.

Some of the shapes produced by milling machines are extremely simple, like the slots and flat surfaces produced by circular saws. Other shapes are more complex and may consist of a

Fig. 1-20. On a planer, the tool remains stationary while the work moves back and forth.

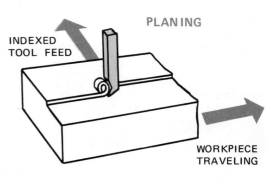

PLANING

INDEXED TOOL FEED

WORKPIECE TRAVELING

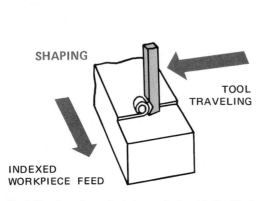

SHAPING

TOOL TRAVELING

INDEXED WORKPIECE FEED

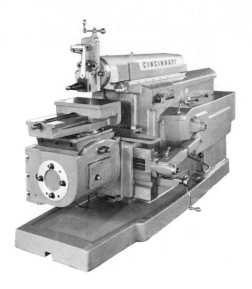

Fig. 1-21.   On a shaper, the tool moves back and forth while the work remains stationary.

INDEXED WORKPIECE FEED

TOOL TRAVELS UP AND DOWN

SLOTTING

HAND FEED

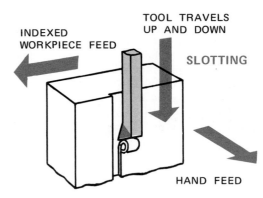

Fig. 1-22.   A slotter or vertical shaper milling machine.

Fig. 1-23.   A milling machine.

MILLING

CUTTER REVOLVING

WORKPIECE FEEDING

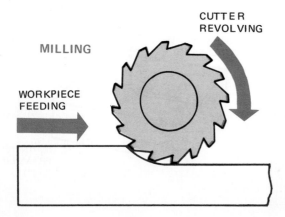

variety of combinations of flat and curved surfaces, depending on the shape given to the cutting-edges of the tool and on the travel path of the tool.

Fig. 1-24.   A surface grinder.

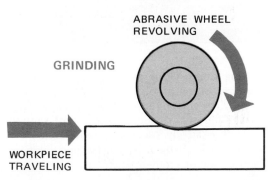

ABRASIVE WHEEL REVOLVING

GRINDING

WORKPIECE TRAVELING

Grinding. Grinding consists of shaping a piece of work by bringing it into contact with a rotating abrasive wheel (Fig. 1-24). The process is often used for the final finishing to close dimensions of a part that has been heat-treated to make it very hard. This is because grinding can correct distortions that may have resulted from heat treatment. Grinders may be used on external cylindrical surfaces, in holes, for flat surfaces, and for generating threads (Fig. 1-25). In recent years, grinding has also found increased application in heavy-duty metal removal operations. This process is referred to as *abrasive machining*.

Lapping is another operation which falls under the classification of grinding. Lapping entails the use of abrasive pastes or compounds and is limited in its use to extremely small amounts of stock removal and to instances where a high degree of precision and surface finish is desirable.

OTHER MACHINING PROCESSES

There are many other machining processes that are closely related to the ones just described. Often these can be done on one or more machines.

Band Machining. *Band machining* is a method of cutting stock to size and shape on a specially designed band saw. This machine will produce many shapes both on internal and external surfaces (Fig. 1-26). Whereas the horizontal band saw is used primarily to cut stock to length, the vertical band saw is more commonly used for more accurate machined parts. This tool is usually used as a first step in a machining process. If a complicated part must be made, the large masses of material are removed by band machine; and then the part is finally finished to accurate size by milling or grinding. The same type of vertical band saw can also be used for *machine filing*.

Countersinking and Counterboring. *Countersinking* is a way of cutting a cone-shaped recess on the outer edge of the end of a hole. This process can be done on the drilling machine or lathe and also on certain types of milling machines.

Counterboring is a method of partially re-

Fig. 1-25. A cylindrical grinder.

Fig. 1-26. Band machining is done with a vertical band saw.

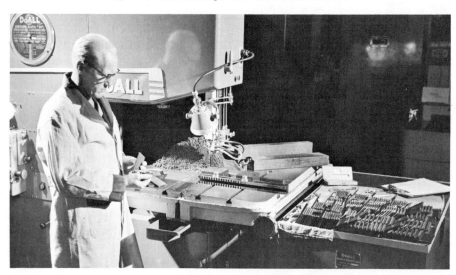

boring a cylindrical hole, thus enlarging it for part of its length. The larger hole that has been bored forms a shoulder in relationship to the smaller one. Counterboring can also be done on a drilling machine or lathe, and sometimes on a milling machine. It can also be done on certain types of grinders.

Cutting Gears. Gears can be cut on a milling machine; but in production, they are more frequently cut on a machine called a *gear hobbing machine.* Any machining method of cutting gears is relatively expensive; therefore, many smaller gears are made by powder metallurgy or from plastic or synthetic materials.

UNIT 2. Metal Cutting and Cutting Fluids

If you have ever watched machine tools cut metal, you know that the metal isn't actually cut at all. Rather, chips are shorn away from the workpiece by the machine tool. Sometimes you see short, small chips (Fig. 2-1). Other times the chips will be longer and will curl as they come off the metal (Fig. 2-2). When you understand what happens when metal is being cut, you will be better able to use all machine tools more intelligently.

Most of the machining we do in a machine shop is done with cutting tools. A *cutting tool* is a hardened piece of metal or other material, such as a grinding wheel, with a cutting-edge that cuts the metal. Four things determine the way a machine tool cuts metal:

1. *The kind of material in the workpiece.* As you will soon learn, each material has various

Fig. 2-2. A continuous chip coming from a part being turned on a lathe.

characteristics such as toughness, malleability, brittleness, and ductility which affect the ease or difficulty of machining it (machinability of the material). Some metals are easy to machine; others are not. Molybdenum steel, for example, is only half as machinable as low-carbon, free-cutting steel. Table 2-1 provides a useful index of the relative machinability of common steels. A complete explanation of the numbering system used in this table is found in Unit 6.

2. *The kind of material in the cutting tool.* Most of the cutting tools you will use are made of high-speed steel (steel alloyed with tungsten for higher cutting speeds). Industry makes wide use of various tungsten carbide and ceramic tools that can operate at extremely high speeds.

3. *The shape of the cutting tool.* All cutting with a sharp edge, whether it is with the thin blade of a slicing knife or the almost square edge of a closely supported carbide tool, is basically a wedging-apart action. Obviously, the first essential to any wedging tool is a penetrating edge. It is also obvious that the narrower the blade the less force or power will be required to "wedge" it through the material to be cut. Therefore, when cutting soft materials with a cutting tool made of a much harder and stronger substance, the blade can be sharpened to a long thin edge. As the hardness of the material to be cut increases, however, the strength of the cutting-edge must also be increased. Cutting a soft-iron nail, for example, will cause a fine steel

Fig. 2-1. Discontinuous chips coming from a block of cast iron.

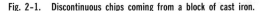

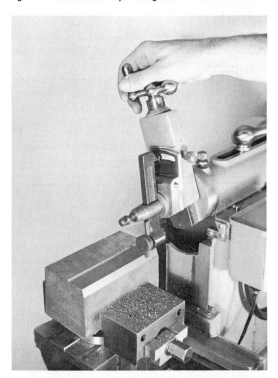

Table 2-1. Approximate machinability of SAE and AISI steels.

Kind of Steel			Relative Machinability Based on 1112 as 100%
Free Machining Steels		1112	100
		1113	135
		1115	81
		1120	78
		1212	100
		1213	135
Carburizing Steels	Carbon Steels	1020	63
		1015	53
		1010	53
		1025	53
	Alloy Steels	3115	53
		3120	53
		5120	51
		2317	51
		4615	51
		4620	51
		8617	51
Heat Treating Steels	As Rolled	1030	62
		1035	62
		1040	60
		1045	48
		1050	45
		3130	41
		3135	38
		2330	35
		3140	32
		2345	30
	Annealed for Machin-ability	1045	60
		4340	58
		1050	57
		4130	55
		3130	55
		4140	50
		3135	48
		4150	45
		3140	45
		2330	45
		3145	43
		5140	42
		3150	40
		6150	40
		9260	40
		5150	40
		2340	38
		2345	37
		1095	30
		52100	30

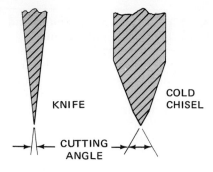

Fig. 2-3. Cross section of a knife and a cold chisel showing the difference in cutting angles. Cutting tools for metal machines must have a cutting angle that is great enough to take the heavy stresses.

blade to dull immediately, even though the steel in the blade is harder than the metal being cut. If you were to examine the edge of this blade under a glass, you would see that it is either bent or broken. The shape of a cutting tool, then, helps to determine the strength of a cutting-edge. This explains why a knife edge will dull almost upon contact with metal while the more obtuse cutting-edge of a cold chisel will stand up to continuous pounding into metal (Fig. 2-3).

The cutting-edge of any metal-cutting tool must be strong and well supported. Remember that a tremendous force is exerted against a cutting-edge during the machining process. Pressure against cutting tools as great as 250,000 pounds per square inch (psi) has been measured on large metal-cutting lathes.

4. *The action of the cutting tool on the material being cut.* This is most important because it is the action of the cutting tool on the material being cut which determines the kind of chip that will be formed. Chips show whether a machine is being operated correctly. They also show whether the cutting tool is correctly ground to the shape and sharpness required for the job.

WHAT HAPPENS IN METAL CUTTING

Many people still compare the cutting action of a cutting tool to what happens when an axe or knife splits wood (Fig. 2-4). This, of course, is not a good comparison. In cutting wood, the axe

Fig. 2-4. A knife cutting a piece of wood. This comparison is often used incorrectly to illustrate the action of a metal-cutting tool.

or knife splits the wood fibers. By contrast, the metal-cutting process takes place as follows:

1. When the workpiece or the cutting tool moves, the face of the cutting tool compresses (squeezes together) the metal being cut.

2. This compressed metal tries to escape from the face of the cutting tool. It does so in a manner known as *plastic flow*. Although we think of metals as hard materials, they are actually made up of many minute particles. If some of the particles are pushed hard enough, they will make the other particles move also. Thus, a part of the metal moves. It does not spring back into place like an elastic band when you stretch it and then let go. Rather, it remains deformed, very much like a piece of molded

clay. With softer metals like lead or copper, you can demonstrate plastic flow by denting them easily with a hammer.

3. As the cutting-edge moves forward, the metal often compresses too much. The metal is strained at the cutting-edge by what is known as a *concentration of stress* (force).

4. The concentration of stress at the cutting-edge causes a chip to shear (break by force) from the workpiece. The chip flows over the face of the cutting tool.

KINDS OF CHIPS

There are three kinds of chips that result from metal cutting:

1. *Discontinuous* (*segmental*) *chips* (like fish scales). Brittle metal such as cast iron or hard bronze produces small chips, each one separate from the previous one. The metal compresses in front of the cutting-edge of the tool until it breaks away and the chip leaves the face of the tool. This happens over and over again as long as the cutting continues (Fig. 2-5). This type of chip is most easily disposed of. The finish of the workpiece is good when the pitch of the segments is small.

2. *Continuous Chip.* Metal is compressed in front of the cutting-edge. Then the metal begins to escape as a continuous (unbroken) chip. There is no "buildup" in front of the cutting-edge. Because a better finish results, this is the

Fig. 2-5. How a discontinuous chip is formed. The edge of the cutting tool in *A* and *B* is compressing the metal. The chip in *C* and *D* is breaking away from the metal. The chip in *E* is completely separated. The initial compressed layer passes off with each chip segment.

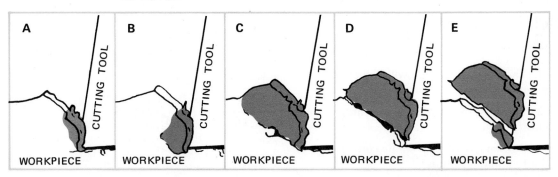

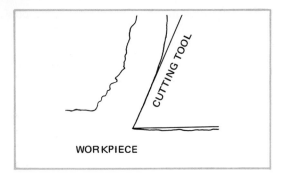

Fig. 2-6. A continuous chip produced while machining a ductile metal. This is the ideal chip from the standpoint of quality of finish on the workpiece, temperature of the tool point, and the amount of power consumed to do the job.

ideal chip on ductile materials (those which can be hammered or drawn out thin), (Fig. 2-6).

3. *Continuous chip with built-up edge next to tool face.* First, the metal directly in front of the cutting tool becomes compressed. Soon the chip begins to form and flow away. Then small particles of metal from the workpiece anchor or lodge on the very point of the cutting tool. As the compressed metal on the cutting-edge builds up, this edge becomes larger and larger and is more easily moved. Thus, a built-up edge is produced. Finally this edge breaks away from the cutting tool. The fragments from the built-up edge are torn off and escape with both the chip and the workpiece. Since some of the fragments attach themselves to the workpiece itself, the surface becomes rough. This action goes on all the time while the cutting takes place. Soft or mild steel usually forms a continuous chip with a built-up edge when machined with high-speed steel-cutting tools (Fig. 2-7).

GOOD MACHINING

Good machining depends on three things:

1. The ease or difficulty with which the chip is removed from the workpiece

2. The ease or difficulty with which a good finish is obtained

3. The amount of wear on the cutting-edge of the tool during cutting

CUTTING FLUIDS

Cutting fluids are used in machining to do five things: (1) cool the workpiece and the tool, (2) reduce friction, (3) protect the work against rusting, (4) control the amount of the built-up edge, and (5) wash away chips.

When metal surfaces rub together, they get hot. This heat is produced by *friction* (the resistance of motion between two objects in contact with each other). You will note that Fig. 2-8 indicates three zones of friction. The first is the area where the front of the tool touches the workpiece. The second is the area between the top of the tool and the chip. The third is between the workpiece and the chip that is being removed.

In using a cutting fluid, it is important to get the fluid to the correct place. Too often the beginner allows the cutting fluid merely to drop on the top of the workpiece. This isn't much

Fig. 2-7. A continuous chip with a "built-up" edge. Note how pieces of the chip tend to pressure-weld to the face of the tool, producing a built-up edge. This built-up edge keeps breaking off and re-forming, resulting in a rough surface. If the built-up edge is small and sharp, it increases the effective angle and lowers the required cutting force. It also helps to protect the cutting-edge of the tool.

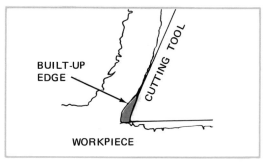

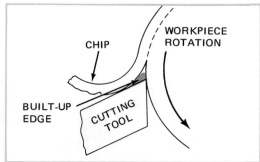

Table 2-2. Recommended cutting fluids for various metals.

Material	Drilling	Reaming	Turning	Milling	Threading
Aluminum	Kerosene Kerosene Lard oil Soluble oil	Kerosene Soluble oil Mineral oil	Soluble oil	Soluble oil Lard oil Mineral oil Dry	Soluble oil Kerosene Lard oil
Brass	Dry Soluble oil Kerosene Lard oil	Dry Soluble oil	Soluble oil	Dry Soluble oil	Lard oil Soluble oil
Bronze	Soluble oil Lard oil Mineral oil Dry	Soluble oil Lard oil Mineral oil Dry	Soluble oil	Soluble oil Lard oil Mineral oil Dry	Lard oil Soluble oil
Cast iron	Dry Air jet Soluble oil	Dry Soluble oil Mineral-lard oil	Dry Soluble oil	Dry Soluble oil	Sulfurized oil Mineral-lard oil
Cast steel	Soluble oil Mineral-lard oil Sulfurized oil	Soluble oil Mineral-lard oil Lard oil	Soluble oil	Soluble oil Mineral-lard oil	Mineral-lard oil
Copper	Soluble oil Dry Mineral-lard oil Kerosene	Soluble oil Lard oil	Soluble oil	Soluble oil Dry	Soluble oil Lard oil
Malleable iron	Dry Soda water	Dry Soda water	Soluble oil	Dry Soda water	Lard oil and soda
Monel metal	Lard oil Soluble oil	Lard oil Soluble oil	Soluble oil	Soluble oil	Lard oil

Steel:
  Alloys
  Forgings
	Soluble oil
	Sulfurized oil
	Mineral-lard oil
		Soluble oil
		Mineral-lard oil
		Sulfurized oil
			Soluble oil	Soluble oil
				Mineral-lard oil
					Sulfurized oil
					Lard oil

Steel, manganese (12 to 15%)	Dry				
Steel, mild	Soluble oil Mineral-lard oil Sulfurized oil Lard oil	Soluble oil Mineral-lard oil	Soluble oil	Soluble oil Mineral-lard oil	Soluble oil Mineral-lard oil
Steel, tool	Soluble oil Mineral-lard oil Sulfurized oil	Soluble oil Lard oil Sulfurized oil	Soluble oil	Soluble oil Lard oil	Sulfurized oil Lard oil
Wrought iron	Soluble oil Mineral-lard oil Sulfurized oil	Soluble oil Mineral-lard oil	Soluble oil	Soluble oil Mineral-lard oil	Soluble oil Mineral-lard oil

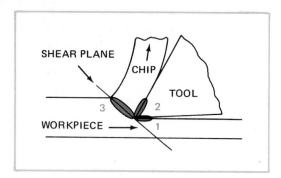

Fig. 2-8. Sources of heat: (1) 10 percent from the tool work zone, (2) 30 percent from the chip tool zone, and (3) 60 percent from the sheer zone.

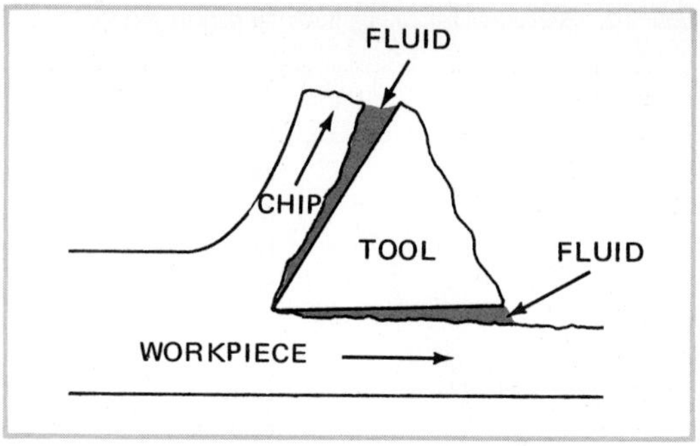

Fig. 2-9. Cutting fluids have two ways of reaching the cutting-edge; between the chip and the tool, and between the workpiece and the tool.

help. Cutting fluids have only two paths for getting into the areas where they will do some good, between the front of the cutting tool and the workpiece and between the top of the cutting tool and the chip (Fig. 2-9).

There are many types of cutting fluids used in the machine shop. Some of the most common are:

1. *Mineral oils,* which are light oils made from natural petroleum products.

2. *Lard oils,* which are animal oils and one of the best cutting fluids available.

3. *Mineral-lard oils,* which are a combination of lard and mineral oils. These oils are less expensive than pure lard oil and are considered very good cutting fluids.

4. *Sulfurized oils,* which are mineral or mineral-lard oils to which sulfur has been added.

5. *Soluble oil,* which is an emulsion (liquid mixture) of a soluble oil and water. Together they form a white or colored liquid widely used for many machining operations.

Table 2-2 shows the recommended cutting fluid for various kinds of metals. The cutting fluids recommended are for high-speed steel tool bits. (A cutting fluid is seldom used when machining steel or cast iron with carbide cutting tools, due to the tendency of the carbide to chip from intermittent cooling.) From this table you should learn that there is a particular type of cutting fluid to be used for certain metals and operations. Be sure to use the correct one.

UNIT 3. Mechanics of Machines

An adequate machine for a job is one that is large enough to hold a workpiece, is strong enough to resist cutting forces without excessive deflection, provides sufficient torque to rotate the tool or work, and is equipped with a drive having sufficient power to supply the required energy (Fig. 3-1).

A *machine* is a device that performs work. *Work* is done when a resistance is overcome by a force acting through a measured distance. A *force* is a push or pull exerted on or by an object. The size of the force is commonly measured in weight-type units such as pounds or tons. A force has both size and direction. To produce work, *energy* is necessary, since energy is the capability for doing work. When work is accomplished, energy is expended.

A machine shop generally contains many different kinds of machines (lathes, milling machines, shapers, etc.). A hammer or screwdriver is also a machine, since a machine is any device

Fig. 3-1. This heavy-duty lathe has all the characteristics of an adequate machine tool. It is made up of many simple machines.

that helps you to do work. It may help by changing the amount of force or the speed of action required to do a job. Machines are also used to transform energy. For example, the traditional machine tool transforms electrical energy to mechanical energy. Machines are also used to transfer energy from one place to the other. On a lathe, for example, gears, belts, and pulleys transfer energy from the motor to the headstock spindle and to the carriage. Machines are also used to change the direction of force. For example, in the shaper the direction of force is changed from rotating to back-and-forth (reciprocating) motion.

KINDS OF SIMPLE MACHINES

While some of the machines you see in the machine shop look quite complicated, they are all made up of "simple machines." There are six basic simple machines; the lever, the wheel and

Fig. 3-2. The six basic machines.

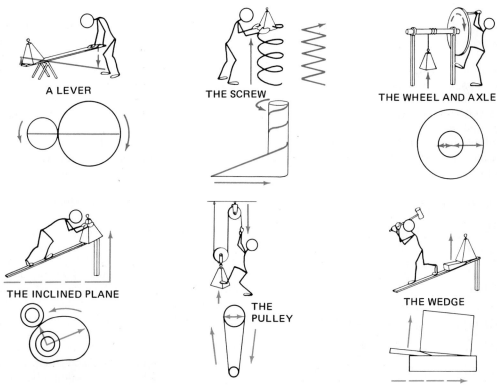

A LEVER

THE SCREW

THE WHEEL AND AXLE

THE INCLINED PLANE

THE PULLEY

THE WEDGE

axle, the pulley, the inclined plane, the screw, and the wedge. It is important that you understand the construction and principle of each of these simple machines (Fig. 3-2).

The simplest machine is the *lever*. A teeter-totter is a familiar example of a lever in which one weight balances the other. When a small child sits on one end of the board and a large boy on the other, the small child goes up and the large boy goes down. However, if the large boy moves close enough to the center of the board, the small child will be able to go down and raise the large boy off the ground. This example of leverage (mechanical advantage) is used in many types of machines and machine tools.

There are three basic parts to all levers, the fulcrum *f*, the force *e*, and the resistance *r*. Three classes of levers are shown in Fig. 3-3. The location of the *fulcrum* (the fixed or pivot point with relationship to the resistance or weight) and the effort (force) determine the lever class. The teeter-totter is an example of a first-class lever. A second-class lever has the fulcrum at one end while the effort is applied to the other end. The third-class lever has the effort applied between the fulcrum and the resistance.

A *wheel and axle* is often just a wheel fastened to a rod. The steering wheel of an automobile is a good example. Actually it is a special form of lever in which the weight or resisting force is applied to the axle while the effort is applied to the rim of the wheel.

Pulleys are used on machinery to transmit motion and power. Various speeds may be obtained by the use of large and small pulleys.

Have you ever watched a delivery man move a heavy round object such as a barrel from a truck? He extends a plank or platform from the truck to the ground and rolls the barrel down. The use of this plank or platform, called an *inclined plane,* makes the job easier. The principle behind the inclined plane can be used to explain the operation of a cam. A *cam* is a device for changing rotary motion into irregular rotary or reciprocating motion. Cams are connected to levers or rods to obtain the required movement of parts.

A *wedge* is a kind of an inclined plane. The difference is in the way in which it is used. A wedge is pushed or forced under a load to move it. Cutting tools, such as an axe, a wood-working plane, and a chisel, act like wedges. A taper center for a lathe is a type of wedge.

A *screw* is nothing more than an inclined plane cut around a rod or cylinder. The simplest example is a nut and bolt. A jack screw is capable of lifting a great weight because the incline of the screw threads is small compared with the length of the lever that must be used to turn the screw.

Study the construction of a metal-cutting lathe or any other machine tool in the shop. You will find many examples of the simple machines we have just described.

KINDS OF MACHINE TOOLS

Machine tools are made up of a number of mechanical principles or combinations of the simple machines you have just studied.

Broadly speaking, there are three types of machine tools. The first shapes metal by *cutting* it. This type of machine tool may be defined as a power-driven machine, not portable by hand, and used for the purpose of removing metal in the form of chips.

The second type of machine tool shapes metal by *shearing* it, as we cut paper with scissors, or by *hammering* or *squeezing* it into shape. This type is known as a *metal-forming machine tool.* It may be defined as a power-driven machine, not portable by hand and used to press, forge, emboss, hammer, or shear metal.

The third category of machine tool consists of an assortment of machining devices of unusual and, for the most part, recent origin. Included in this group are machines for electric discharge machining (EDM) and electrochemical machining (ECM). By controlling the charac-

Fig. 3-3. The three classes of levers.

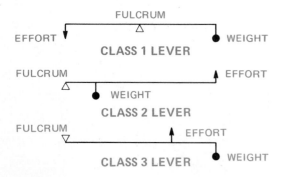

teristics and forces of chemicals, electricity, magnetism, liquid, sound, light, and even gunpowder, it is possible to shape materials in ways that are often beyond the ability of conventional machines.

PULLEYS AND BELTS

Pulleys and belts are widely used to transmit power and provide a means of changing speeds on machine tools.

In a simple belt drive where two pulleys are belted together, one of the pulleys is always the *driver,* while the other is the *driven.* A pulley mounted on the shaft of an electric motor would be the *driver pulley.* The pulley it is belted to would be called the *driven pulley.* If both driver and driven pulleys are the same size (have the same diameter), both will turn at the same speed. However, if the driver pulley is twice the size of the driven pulley, then the driven, or smaller pulley, will turn at twice the speed of the larger, or driver pulley. From this example, we obtain the general rule that the smaller the pulley the faster it turns, and the larger the pulley the slower it turns (Fig. 3–4).

Another interesting fact about pulley size concerns the amount of power transmitted between driver and driven pulleys. For example, when a small driver pulley is belted to a larger driven pulley, it is possible to obtain much more power at the driven pulley.

There are three common types of pulley and belt drives used on machine tools. They are:

1. *Flat pulleys and belts.* This is the oldest and simplest type of pulley and belt. The pulley may be a single pulley, or it may have three or four different diameters. A one-piece pulley having three or four diameters is called a *cone pulley* (Fig. 3–5). Actually the pulleys are not flat. They are tapered slightly so that the diameter of the pulley is a little larger at its center. We call this a *crowned pulley.* The pulley is made larger in diameter at the center because a flat belt will always climb to the highest part of a pulley. The crown ensures that the belt will run in the center of the pulley (Fig. 3–6).

2. *V-belts and pulleys.* This type of pulley has a V-shaped groove cut around its circumference. A V-shaped belt fits accurately into this groove.

Fig. 3–4. A pulley and belt drive on a lathe: (A) belt-tension release lever, (B) V-belt adjustment, and (C) flat-belt tension adjustment.

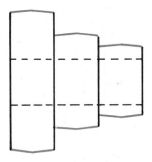

Fig. 3–5. A three-step cone pulley for a flat belt.

Fig. 3–6. A small flat pulley (crowned to keep the belt in the center).

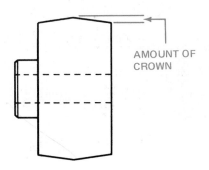

AMOUNT OF CROWN

V-belts are endless belts (made in one piece) that contact the side of the pulley rather than the bottom. They run quieter than flat belts and are used a great deal on machinery requiring high speeds (Fig. 3-7).

3. *Variable-speed pulleys.* This type of pulley makes it possible to change the speed between driver and driven pulleys without stopping the pulleys or the machine. In fact, the speed should be changed only while the machine is running. The driver pulley of a variable-speed drive is made of two V-shaped sides. By means of an adjusting screw attached to a crank wheel, one side of the pulley may be opened or spread apart from the other side. As it spreads apart, the belt moves inward toward the smaller diameter, producing a slower speed to the driven pulley, also made of two parts. As the sides of the driver pulley are brought together, the belt is forced outward toward the large diameter, which increases the speed of the driven pulley (Fig. 3-8).

GEARS

Gears, like pulleys and belts, are used to transmit *positive* motion and power from one revolving shaft to another (Fig. 3-9). A *gear* is actually a wheel with very accurately shaped teeth. These teeth mesh with the teeth of another gear to provide a positive-motion drive. This means that when one gear turns, the gear it meshes with must also turn.

The opposite of a positive drive is a friction drive. Understanding the difference between a positive drive and a friction drive will be of help in understanding gear drives. A simple friction drive might be shown by two round disks placed so that one is in contact with the other on the circumference. As one disk turns (revolves), the other also turns. When the resistance becomes greater than the friction between the disks, one slips over the other. Motion is thus lost or stopped altogether by one of the disks. By cutting teeth on the disks so they mesh accurately, we obtain positive motion and there is no slippage. The size of a gear is expressed by the number of teeth not by the diameter in inches.

Gear Trains. Two or more gears in mesh are often called *gear trains*. The gears that transmit power

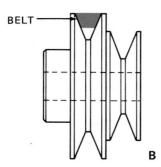

BELT

B

Fig. 3-7. (A) V-pulleys are used in many machine tools. (B) Note that the belt rides on the side rather than the bottom of the V.

Fig. 3-8. The mechanical arrangement on the drill press using a variable-speed drive.

Fig. 3-9. This headstock assembly shows how belts, pulleys, and gears are utilized in providing power to the headstock spindle and to the lead screw.

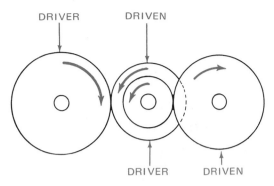

Fig. 3-11. A compound gear train.

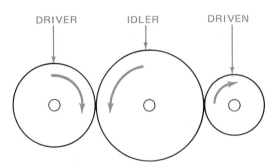

Fig. 3-10. A simple gear train.

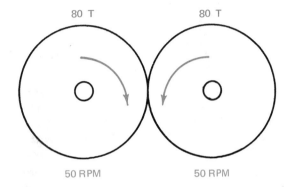

Fig. 3-12. Direction and speed of equal-size gears.

are called *drivers,* or *driving gears,* and the others are *followers,* or *driven gears.* There are two common types of gear trains.

1. A simple gear train consists of two or more gears in mesh, with each gear mounted on a separate shaft (Fig. 3-10).

2. A compound gear train consists of four gears, with two of the gears mounted on one shaft giving two driver gears and two driven gears (Fig. 3-11).

Idler Gears. When two external gears mesh, they rotate in opposite directions. This can be avoided by putting a third gear, called an *idler,* between the driver and the driven gear. The idler gear doesn't change the gear ratio at all. It merely makes the driver and the driven gear turn in the same direction.

Idler gears may be used with either a simple or a compound gear train. More than one idler gear may also be used if necessary.

Size, Speed, and Direction of Rotation. Two gears in mesh having the same number of teeth will revolve at the same rate of speed (rpm), but in opposite directions (Fig. 3-12). If, however, one gear has 40 teeth and the other 80, a size ratio of 1 to 2 (1:2), the 40-tooth gear will make two turns for every one complete turn of the 80-tooth gear. The relationship between the speeds of gears and the numbers of teeth is an *inverse* one. This means that the size ratio of two gears in mesh is just the opposite of the speed ratio. If the size ratio is 1:2, then the speed ratio would be 2:1 (Fig. 3-13).

As stated above, two gears in mesh will rotate in opposite directions. If we place an idler

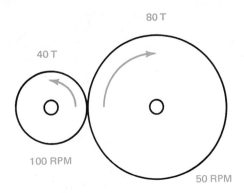

Fig. 3-13. Size ratio is inverse to speed ratio.

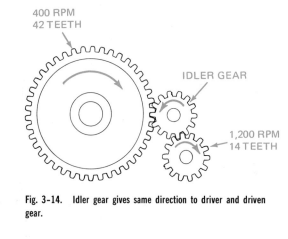

Fig. 3-14. Idler gear gives same direction to driver and driven gear.

gear between the two gears, however, both driver and driven gears will rotate in the same direction. Thus, we get a general rule that an even number of gears in mesh, such as 2, 4, and so on, will give an opposite direction between driver and driven, and an uneven number of gears in mesh, such as 3, 5, and so on, will give the same direction of rotation between driver and driven gears (Fig. 3-14).

TYPES OF GEARS

Gears and gearlike devices are commonly used in machine tools to transmit power, to change speeds, to change direction of rotation, to change shaft direction, and to provide a positive nonslip drive. You should have a knowledge of the various types of gears and know the purpose of each (Fig. 3-15).

1. *Spur gears.* Spur gears have teeth cut straight and parallel to the axis of the shaft rotation. They are used to transmit power between shafts that are parallel. With spur gears, not more than two teeth are meshed at one time. Thus, the load is rapidly transmitted from one tooth to another. For this reason, spur gears are usually used at only low speeds.

2. *Helical gears.* Helical gears are like spur gears except that the teeth are cut at an angle across the face of the gear. Helical teeth contact along the line across the profile. They are used to transmit power between shafts. Helical gears operate more quietly than spur gears and also have greater strength and durability.

3. *Herringbone gears.* Herringbone gears are actually double helical gears. On many herringbone gears, the right- and left-hand rows of teeth are separated by a narrow gap at the center. This provides greater accuracy and better meshing. Herringbone gears are used on high-speed units where a great reduction in speed ratio is necessary. The shape of the teeth provides for both a smooth and quiet drive.

4. *Bevel gears.* Bevel gears are used when rotary power is to be transmitted from one shaft to another, both of which form an angle. Bevel gears with straight teeth are used for right-angle drive. They are often called *miter gears* when the gear ratio is 1:1. To obtain the advantages of the helical gear operation, the spiral bevel gear was developed. It can be used where the shafts to be connected are not at right angles. Hypoid gears resemble spiral bevel gears except that the axis of the pinion gear is above or below the axis of the driven gear.

5. *Worm gears.* A worm-gear drive consists of a *worm* (driver) and a *worm gear* (driven). The worm looks like a screw thread, and the worm gear resembles a spur gear. With a worm-gear drive, it is possible to obtain large speed reduction at a right-angle drive. The action of worm gears is unlike that of any other type of gear. The worm is actually a screw which drives the worm gear.

6. *Rack and pinion.* A rack and pinion consist of a spur gear and a flat piece of metal having teeth cut into it. This unit is used to change rotary (revolving) motion into reciprocating

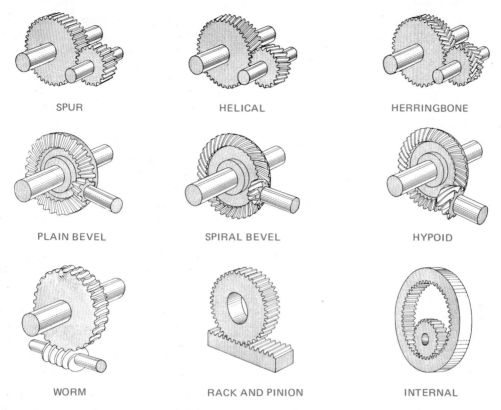

SPUR   HELICAL   HERRINGBONE

PLAIN BEVEL   SPIRAL BEVEL   HYPOID

WORM   RACK AND PINION   INTERNAL

Fig. 3-15. Principle types of gears.

(back-and-forth) motion. In some machines, the gear may roll over the rack, and in others the rack may be moved by the gear. The rack and pinion are used on a lathe when moving the carriage by hand.

7. *Internal gears.* Internal gears have teeth cut on the inside of the rim. An internal gear drive is more compact, runs more smoothly, and has stronger teeth than an external spur gear.

TAPERS

A piece of work that increases or decreases uniformly in diameter or width is said to be *tapered.* A cone is a good example of a taper. In machine-shop work many of the machine tools have spindles with tapered holes. The drill press, for example, may have a tapered hole for holding taper-shank twist drills and other taper-shank tools.

The purpose of a taper is to locate and hold tools or attachments centrally in relation to

some other part of the machine. For example, a lathe center which has a taper shank, when properly placed in the tailstock spindle, will locate the point of the center so it will be in true alignment with the axis of the lathe. At the same time, it will hold the center firmly in place because of the wedgelike action of the taper (Fig. 3-16).

Fig. 3-16. Parts of a taper.

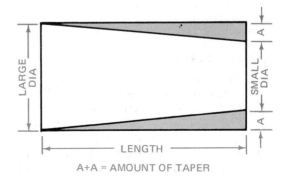

LARGE DIA   A   SMALL DIA   A

LENGTH

A+A = AMOUNT OF TAPER

27

There are five standard taper systems widely used in machine-shop work. The difference between each of these systems should be clearly understood. They include four types of tapers which are "self-holding" and one which is "self-releasing."

Self-holding Tapers. The name "self-holding" is applied to the smaller tapers because the angle of the taper, which is only 2 or 3 degrees, can be so firmly seated or wedged into the socket or mating part that the holding force is usually sufficient to resist any force that may cause the parts to slip.

Each of the systems of tapers has a name which has a definite meaning to a machinist. Each taper system differs from the other. A taper from one system cannot be used with the taper from another system. We call these *standard taper systems*. In each, the amount of taper varies. The amount of taper is the difference between the large and small diameters. The amount of taper may also be stated as the *taper per inch* (tpi) or the *taper per foot* (tpf), which means the rate, or amount, the taper increases or decreases in diameter for each inch or foot of length. The self-holding taper systems include:

1. *Brown and Sharpe tapers* are used mostly on milling and grinding machines and on the tools and attachments for these machines. The sizes of the tapers are expressed by a number from 1, the smallest, to 18, the largest. The tpf is approximately $\frac{1}{2}$ in. for all sizes except No. 10, which has a tpf of 0.5161 in. A machinist is not expected to memorize the dimensions for each size of taper, but he should know how to find the sizes in a table of tapers.

2. The *Morse standard taper* is largely used for drilling machines and drilling tools such as twist-drill shanks. Many lathes also use this taper. In this system, the tpf is approximately $\frac{5}{8}$ in. There are eight sizes of tapers numbered from 0, the smallest, to 7, the largest. Each size varies slightly from the $\frac{5}{8}$-in. taper per foot, and it is necessary to use a taper table to determine the actual sizes for each taper number (Fig. 3-17).

3. The *Jarno taper* is the simplest of all the tapers to calculate. This taper has a tpf of 0.600

Fig. 3-17. A Morse self-holding taper-shank twist drill.

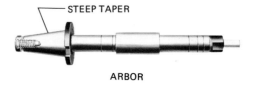

Fig. 3-18. A self-releasing or steep taper on a milling machine arbor.

in. It is used on various types of machine tools, especially diemaking machines. No table of sizes is needed for this system of tapers because the diameters and length of the taper can be calculated directly from the number of the taper. The large diameter is found by dividing the number of the taper by 8. The small diameter is found by dividing the number of the taper by 10. The length is found by dividing the number of the taper by 2. For example, a No. 8 Jarno taper would have a large diameter equal to 1 in., a small diameter equal to $\frac{8}{10}$ in., and a length of 4 in. The advantage of the Jarno taper is that only one number is needed to figure all the sizes necessary for machining the taper.

4. *American Standard (self-holding) Machine Tapers* are a series of self-holding tapers used for small tools and machine parts. It consists of 22 sizes. The 3 smallest sizes have a tpf of 0.5020 in., 8 sizes are selected from the smaller tapers in the Morse and Brown and Sharpe systems, and 11 larger sizes have a tpf of $\frac{3}{4}$ in. A No. $4\frac{1}{2}$ taper fills the gap between the Morse No. 4 and No. 5 tapers.

Self-releasing Tapers. For many years the Brown and Sharpe taper was used on milling-machine spindles, arbors, and adapters. (*Arbors* and *adapters* are attachments that hold cutting tools on a milling machine.) Because of the small amount of taper, 0.500 tpf, it was difficult and time-consuming to remove arbors from the machine spindle. In 1927, the milling-machine taper, also known as the American Standard (steep) Machine Taper, was designed. It is now used on all present-day horizontal milling machines. It has a tpf of $3\frac{1}{2}$ in. and comes in 12 sizes. Because of the steep angle of the taper, it is not self-holding. A shank having this type of taper must be held in the spindle holes by means of a cam lock or a draw-in-bolt arrangement. It is easily and quickly assembled or taken apart, and the taper serves only to locate and align the parts (Fig. 3-18).

BEARINGS

A bearing is a support for a revolving shaft or a moving part on a machine. A good understanding of the various types of bearings and how they are used is an important part of a machinist's job. Some of the more common types of bearings used in machinery follow:

1. *Ways* are flat bearing surfaces used to guide and support moving parts of machine tools. Ways may be flat, V-shaped, or dovetailed (Fig. 3-19).

2. *Plain or sleeve bearings* are widely used in many slower-running machines and electric motors (Fig. 3-20). They are generally made from bronze because it wears well as a bearing material. We might describe this kind of bearing as a simple bushing having an inside and outside diameter and a length. The inside is machined very accurately and smoothly to fit a shaft, and the outside is machined to fit a hole into which the bearing is to be placed. The part of the shaft that revolves in the bearing is called a *journal*. These bearings must be kept well oiled. Journal bearing surfaces on shafts are commonly ground to size and to a mirrorlike finish known as *super finish*. This ensures a long-lasting and smooth-running bearing surface (Figs. 3-21 and 3-22).

3. *Ball bearings* are precision-made bearings which make use of the principle that "nothing rolls like a ball." A number of steel balls are held between an inner race, or bearing surface, and an outer race (Fig. 3-23). A retainer ring keeps the balls spaced equally between the races. Ball bearings, often called *antifriction bearings,* are excellent for use in high-speed machinery where work loads are not too heavy. Ball bearings require proper lubrication with the correct grade of oil or grease. Careful handling is also necessary.

Fig. 3-19. Flat and V-ways on a lathe bed (above). Dovetail ways on a cross slide (below).

4. *Roller bearings* are also antifriction bearings (Fig. 3-24). They use hardened steel rollers, instead of balls, between the races of the bearing. They are capable of carrying very heavy loads and are widely used on locomotives and railroad cars of all types. Small sizes of roller bearings, as used on automobiles, are often called *needle bearings*. Roller bearings may be of either the straight type or the tapered type (Fig. 3-25).

LUBRICANTS

All moving parts of machinery and machine tools require lubrication. *Lubrication* is the oil-

29

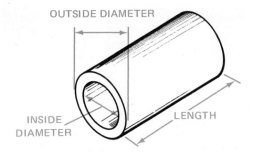

Fig. 3-20.   A plain circular (round) bearing.

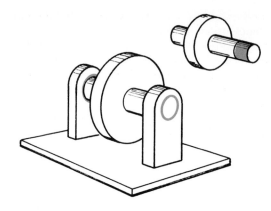

Fig. 3-21.   Journal bearing.

Fig. 3-22.   Superfinished lathe spindle and bearing.

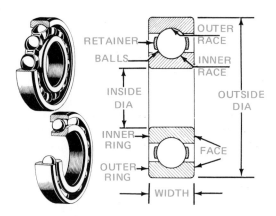

Fig. 3-23.   Construction and parts of a ball bearing.

Fig. 3-25.   A tapered roller bearing.

Fig. 3-24.   A straight roller bearing.

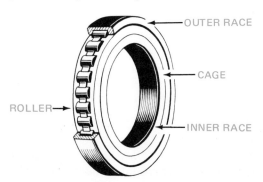

ing or greasing of parts that move or rotate. If you own a bicycle, motorcycle, or car, you probably already know something about the value of lubrication (Fig. 3-26). There are several reasons why proper lubrication of machinery is so important:

1. The lubricant fills space between metal parts and acts as a cushion.

2. The lubricant prevents excessive wear because a film of oil between parts reduces metal-to-metal contact.

3. The lubricant helps to overcome friction within the moving parts by allowing one part to slip over the other more easily.

4. The lubricant serves as a cooling agent by carrying away some of the heat produced by friction.

5. The lubricant protects bearing surfaces from rust and corrosion.

Machine tools cost a great deal of money because they are so accurately made. But they would soon lose their accuracy and value unless they were properly lubricated at regular periods. Some parts of a machine tool require daily lubrication. Other parts of the same machine may need to be lubricated only every 2 or 3 months. A good machinist always keeps an oilcan handy and knows when and where to use it.

We use both oil and greases to keep machinery operating properly. Lubricating oils are generally refined mineral oils made in several different grades or thicknesses. For example, No. 10 oil is a light oil, and a No. 30 oil is a heavy oil. Greases are made from a mixture of petroleum lubricating oils and fats. They are thicker than oils and generally nonliquid. Grease is made in different grades, such as light, medium, and heavy. It is most important to use the correct type and grade of lubricant in the right place. For example, high-speed spindle bearings on a grinding machine require a light oil since heavy oil might ruin the bearings.

LIMITS, TOLERANCES, AND FITS

You will remember that parts are manufactured so they are interchangeable. In other words,

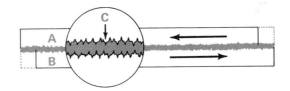

Fig. 3-26. A lubricant, when placed between two solid surfaces, tends to keep the two surfaces apart. If the metal body (A) is moved to the left and the metal body (B) is moved to the right, the teeth of both surfaces cannot cling to each other because they are held apart by the fluid (C). Thus lubrication reduces friction.

each part of a machine or mechanism is made to a certain size and shape so it will fit into any other machine or mechanism of the same type. To make the part interchangeable, each individual part must be made to a size that will fit the mating part in the correct way. It is not only impossible, but also impractical to make many parts to an *exact size*. This is because machines are not perfect, and the tools become worn. A slight variation from the exact size is always allowed. The amount of this variation depends on the kind of part being manufactured. For example, a part might be made 6 in. long with a variation allowed of 0.003 (three-thousandths) in. above and below this size. Therefore, the part could be 5.997 to 6.003 in. and still be the correct size. These are known as the *limits*. The difference between upper and lower limits is called the *tolerance*.

When the tolerance is in both directions from the basic size, it is known as a *bilateral tolerance* (plus and minus). Sometimes the limit is allowed in only one direction. This is known as a *unilateral tolerance*. For example, a hole may have to be 2 in. minus 0.000 in., or plus 0.005 in. This means that the hole must not be smaller than 2 in., but can be as large as 2.005 in.

FACTS ABOUT FITS

In machine construction, many of the parts bear such a close and important relation to one another that a certain amount of hand-fitting is essential. If the surfaces in contact are to move on each other, the fit is classed as a sliding or running fit. If the surfaces are to make contact with sufficient firmness to hold them together under ordinary use, the fit is classed as either a driving, shrink, or forced fit.

Sliding Fits. Under this head may be classed the fitting of cross and traversing slides of lathes, milling machines, drilling machines, boring machines, grinding machines, and planers. These fits are usually obtained by scraping. In most of these fits the moving and stationary parts are held in contact with each other by means of adjustable contact strips or gibs. In some cases, such as the tables of grinding and planing machines, the weight of the parts is sufficient to maintain close contact.

Running Fits. When surfaces in contact move on each other, the fit is classed as a *running fit*. Journal bearings of spindles, crank shafts, line shafting, and other parts are contained under this heading.

Forced Fits and Shrink Fits. Under this head are classed those fits where the separate parts must act in use as if they were a single piece. For example, the crank pins and axles in locomotive driving wheels or the cutter heads and spindles of numerous woodworking machines. A forced fit is obtained by pressing one piece into another. A shrink fit is obtained by heating the outside piece, bringing it into proper relationship with the inside piece, and allowing it to shrink into position as it cools.

Limits. In the case of both running and sliding bearings, a certain amount of hand-fitting is necessary to obtain desired results. The limiting requirements are usually those of alignment and contact. It is essential with journal and flat sliding bearings that accurate contact between the surfaces be made. Also, a limit of alignment with other machine parts may be required. For example, the ways and the cross slide of a lathe's tool carriage must be parallel to or at right angles to the axis of the spindle within set limits. In engine lathe construction, the limit set per foot length is 0.001 in.

In making shrink and forced fits, limits are usually those of size and pressure. In forcing the axles into locomotive driving wheels, specifications may limit pressure to between 100 and 150 tons.

Amount to Leave. Where pins, spindles, and the like are to be forced into holes, or where collars, hubs, flanges, and other machine parts are to be shrunk onto spindles, it is customary to make the diameter allowance upon the spindle rather than upon the hole. The amount added to the spindle or shaft diameter must of necessity vary with the length and diameter of the hole, the metals used, and the form of the surrounding hub. Table 3–1 shows the tolerances used by one manufacturer.

LIMITS OF TOLERANCE

Whereas it is possible to produce machine parts with measurements refined to almost any degree of accuracy, extreme precision may prove too costly in certain cases. The following rules define the degree of accuracy to be expected in those cases where specifications and drawings do not call for greater precision than the rules provide.

1. Full information regarding the limits of tolerance should be clearly shown on drawings submitted, or be definitely covered by written specifications to which reference must be made by notation on the drawings.

2. Where dimensions are stated in common fractions ($\frac{1}{2}, \frac{1}{4}, \frac{1}{8}$, etc.) with no limits of tolerance specified, it is assumed that a considerable margin for variation from figured dimensions is allowable. Unless otherwise ordered, the supplier will proceed according to the dictates of his best judgment as to what limits should be taken.

3. For all important dimensions, decimal figures should be used and limits clearly stated on detail drawings. If decimal figures are not used for such dimensions, a notation referring to the degree of accuracy required must be placed prominently on the drawing.

4. When it is necessary to reduce fractions to decimal equivalents, and limits are not specified, it will be assumed that a limit of ±0.001 is permissible.

5. Where dimensions are stated in decimal figures but with limits not specified, the amount of variation from stated dimensions depends

Table 3-1. Allowances for different classes of fits.

Class	Nominal Diameters	Up to $\frac{1}{2}$ in.	$\frac{9}{16}$-1 in.	$1\frac{1}{16}$-2 in.	$2\frac{1}{16}$-3 in.	$3\frac{1}{16}$-4 in.	$4\frac{1}{16}$-5 in.
			Tolerances in Standard Holes*				
A	High Limit	+0.0002	+0.0005	+0.0007	+0.0010	+0.0010	+0.0010
	Low Limit	−0.0002	−0.0002	−0.0002	−0.0005	−0.0005	−0.0005
	Tolerance	0.0004	0.0007	0.0009	0.0015	0.0015	0.0015
B	High Limit	+0.0005	+0.0007	+0.0010	+0.0012	+0.0015	+0.0017
	Low Limit	−0.0005	−0.0005	−0.0005	−0.0007	−0.0007	−0.0007
	Tolerance	0.0010	0.0012	0.0015	0.0019	0.0022	0.0024
			Allowances for Forced Fits				
F	High Limit	+0.0010	+0.0020	+0.0040	+0.0060	+0.0080	+0.0100
	Low Limit	+0.0005	+0.0015	+0.0030	+0.0045	+0.0060	+0.0080
	Tolerance	0.0005	0.0005	0.0010	0.0015	0.0020	0.0020
			Allowances for Driving Fits				
D	High Limit	+0.0005	+0.0010	+0.0015	+0.0025	+0.0030	+0.0035
	Low Limit	+0.0002	+0.0007	+0.0010	+0.0015	+0.0020	+0.0025
	Tolerance	0.0003	0.0003	0.0005	0.0010	0.0010	0.0010
			Allowances for Push Fits				
P	High Limit	−0.0002	−0.0002	−0.0002	−0.0005	−0.0005	−0.0005
	Low Limit	−0.0007	−0.0007	−0.0007	−0.0010	−0.0010	−0.0010
	Tolerance	0.0005	0.0005	0.0005	0.0005	0.0005	0.0005
			Allowances for Running Fits†				
X	High Limit	−0.0010	−0.0012	−0.0017	−0.0020	−0.0025	−0.0030
	Low Limit	−0.0020	−0.0027	−0.0035	−0.0042	−0.0050	−0.0057
	Tolerance	0.0010	0.0015	0.0018	0.0022	0.0025	0.0027
Y	High Limit	−0.0007	−0.0010	−0.0012	−0.0015	−0.0020	−0.0022
	Low Limit	−0.0012	−0.0020	−0.0025	−0.0030	−0.0035	−0.0040
	Tolerance	0.0005	0.0010	0.0013	0.0015	0.0015	0.0018
Z	High Limit	−0.0005	−0.0007	−0.0007	−0.0010	−0.0010	−0.0012
	Low Limit	−0.0007	−0.0012	−0.0015	−0.0020	−0.0022	−0.0025
	Tolerance	0.0002	0.0005	0.0008	0.0010	0.0012	0.0013

*Tolerance is provided for holes, which ordinary standard reamers can produce, in two grades, classes A and B, the selection of which is a question for the user's decision and dependent upon the quality of the work required; some prefer to use class A as working limits and class B as inspection limits.

†Running fits, which are the most commonly required, are divided into three grades, class X for engine and other work where easy fits are wanted, class Y for high speeds and good average machine work, and class Z for fine tool work.

upon the customary practice of individual manufacturers. There are no universally accepted tolerance standards. The following were used in one particular instance and cannot be considered as anything more than representative:

Two-place decimals	±0.005
Three-place decimals	±0.0015
Four-place decimals	±0.0005
Five-place decimals	±0.0002

6. Where close dimensions, such as the location of holes from center to center in jigs, fixtures, machine parts, and other exact work of like character are required, detail drawings should be prominently marked "ACCURATE" and plus or minus limits clearly indicated.

7. The dimensions of internal cylindrical gages, external ring gages, snap gages, and similar work specified to be hardened, ground, and lapped, will be obtained as accurately as the best mechanical practice applying to commercial work of the particular grade specified will permit.

8. When holes to be drilled are from 0.002 to 0.015 in. (and, in some cases, even more), greater than the size of the drill to be used, they should be reamed, ground, or lapped after boring. Detail drawings should bear appropriate notations.

UNIT 4. Safety in the Machine Shop

The saying, "A good worker is a safe worker," is especially true in the machine shop. Here you will be working with both hand tools and power-driven tools or machines. None of these tools and machines is unsafe. There are only unsafe people.

You must learn to use the equipment in the machine shop in a correct and safe manner. Most accidents are caused by doing the wrong thing, or by not following carefully the instructions given. Short cuts, shop nonsense, and horseplay result in accidents. To prevent accidents, follow the ABC of safety: "Always Be Careful." The best way to do this is to follow carefully the instructions in each unit of this book. You will find safety suggestions throughout.

Here are some general safety suggestions:

1. *Dress correctly.* Machinists in most shops wear either an apron or a shop coat. In other shops where the work is rough, they may wear work trousers and close-fitting shirts with short sleeves.

You should never wear loose-fitting clothing. Anything loose, such as a sweater or necktie, may be caught in the moving parts of a machine and injure you. Remove your necktie, or tuck it into your shirt close to your collar (Fig. 4-1). Remove all jewelry such as rings and wrist watches. A ring can catch on a turning part of a machine and pull your finger off. Keep your hair cut reasonably short, or tie it back out of the way.

2. *Always protect your eyes.* Wear safety glasses or an eyeshield. In a machine shop there

Fig. 4-1. This student is dressed correctly.

is always danger from flying chips or particles from grinding wheels. Be wise and protect your eyes. For 100 percent eye protection at all times, many shops require everyone to wear safety glasses. Safety glasses are more comfortable than glass eyes (Fig. 4-2)!

3. *Remember: A shop is a place to work.* Always attend strictly to business and keep your mind on what you are doing. Daydreaming and talking can cause serious trouble. Do not allow others to be near a machine you are working on. One moment of carelessness may mean a lifetime of sorrow.

4. *Always be neat and clean.* Do your part in the necessary shopkeeping. Remember, there is a place for everything, and you must keep everything in its place. Keep the area around machines clean and free of oil. Keep tools properly arranged.

5. *Know your job and follow instructions.* After you have been given instructions, don't try to be different "just this once" (Fig. 4-3). If you lose a finger or an eye, you will always be different. Don't guess at the correct way to do a job. Go over the instructions carefully, and if you still don't understand, ask your instructor. Asking another student is not the safe way.

6. *Know your machine.* Make sure the guards are in place, especially after repairs have been made. Make certain that all clamps holding the work are tight. Always stop a machine before making any adjustments or taking measurements (Fig. 4-4). Be sure keys and wrenches are removed before starting a machine. Knowing how to stop a machine is just as important as knowing how to start it.

7. *Keep your hands away from all moving parts.* You must resist the temptation to "feel" the machined surface of the work while the machine is running. Fingers have been lost this way. It is never necessary to rub your fingers over a finished surface, and to do so is a dangerous habit.

8. *Never try to remove chips with your fingers.* Metal chips have many razor-sharp edges. They will cut your fingers or become imbedded in your skin, and they may be the cause of an infection. Always use a brush, a piece of metal,

Fig. 4-2. You have one pair of eyes that can never be replaced. Protect them at all times by wearing safety glasses or goggles.

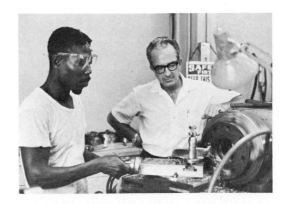

Fig. 4-3. This student is learning to follow directions.

Fig. 4-4. Here's a good safety practice: Stop the machine before attempting to measure work.

Fig. 4-5. Chips are razor sharp. Always use a brush and never your hands to remove them.

Fig. 4-7. Is the wrench this worker using the correct size? Always use a wrench that fits the nut snugly. Using misfit wrenches for tightening nuts will ruin the machine.

Fig. 4-6. A dangerous kind of chip. It's too long; never handle these with your bare hands.

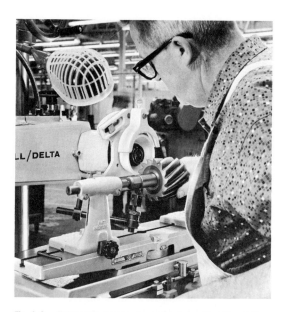

Fig. 4-8. Unless this operator is careful, he could easily cut his thumb on the sharp edge of the milling-machine cutter.

or a stick to remove chips. Never use your hands (Fig. 4-5).

9. *Keep the floor around your machine clear of metal chips and waste pieces of stock.* Scrap pieces and long curly chips are tripping hazards. Put them in a waste can provided for such chips, and place the stock where it belongs. Sharp chips can cut through the thin soles of your shoes and cause an injury.

10. *Learn how to grind and adjust cutting tools so the chips will be short.* There is a way to grind cutting tools so the chips they form will break off short. Long, sharp chips are dangerous and usually unnecessary (Fig. 4-6).

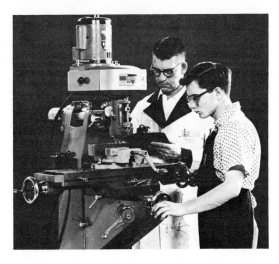

Fig. 4-9. This student is learning to operate a machine properly.

11. *Use and care for hand tools correctly.* Never carry sharp-pointed tools in your pocket. Make sure that files and screwdrivers have handles. There is a correct use for each hand tool. Accidents and injuries result when they are used incorrectly (Fig. 4-7).

12. *Take care of cuts and bruises, no matter how small.* Report every accident to your instructor. Make sure that you have cuts, burns, and bruises taken care of by someone who knows first aid. An accident report form may be necessary on some types and degrees of injuries. Your instructor will show you how to make one out (Fig. 4-8).

13. *Always shut off the power before making any adjustment.* Wait for the machine to stop before leaving it *for any reason.* Never attempt to clean or oil a machine while it is in motion. When setting up the workpiece or removing it from the machine, make sure that there is plenty of space so that your hand will not strike against the cutting tool or other machine parts.

14. *Learn before working.* Never attempt to run a machine until you have had a demonstration and proper instructions. Do not touch, turn on, or attempt to operate the controls on any machine without instructions (Fig. 4-9).

UNIT 5. Using Mathematics

A machinist works with figures constantly. Mathematics is probably his most used tool and one he couldn't do without. All blueprints that he follows in his work are filled with figures showing dimensions or sizes. If the machinist failed to follow the dimensions given, the products made from these blueprints would be worthless. A careless machinist loses both time and money for himself and his employer.

Every machine-shop job requires the use of shop mathematics. The mathematics you need to know is quite simple. Of course, the more mathematics you know, the more interesting and less difficult your work will be. Also, your opportunities for advancement will be greater.

For the time being, all you need to use is simple arithmetic, such as adding and subtracting fractions and decimals, changing fractions to decimals, and solving simple formulas. However, you must be able to do these things rapidly and accurately.

LINEAR, OR STRAIGHT-LINE, MEASUREMENT

In the United States, the standard unit of measurement is the *inch* (in.). The inch is divided into fractional parts for finer measurements.

The English system divides the inch into common fractions, such as $\frac{1}{2}$, $\frac{1}{4}$, $\frac{1}{8}$, $\frac{1}{6}$, $\frac{1}{32}$, and $\frac{1}{64}$. The decimal system divides the inch into decimal fractions, such as 0.01, 0.001, and 0.738.

Two numbers are necessary to express a common fraction, such as $\frac{5}{8}$. The *numerator* (top number) shows how many of the parts (5) are expressed. The *denominator* (bottom number) shows the size of the parts (8ths).

A *decimal* (from the Latin word meaning 10) is a fraction that always has a denominator of

10, or a power of 10 (such as 100, 1,000, 10,000). The numerator alone is written, and a decimal point (.) is used to determine the denominator. The denominator is always 1, with one zero added for each figure in the decimal. For example, 0.75 is read $\frac{75}{100}$ (seventy-five-hundredths), because there are two places in the decimal. One-tenth may be written $\frac{1}{10}$ or 0.1. One-thousandth may be written $\frac{1}{1,000}$ or 0.001. Table 5–1 shows how to read decimals.

CHANGING COMMON FRACTIONS TO DECIMALS

When figuring dimensions, it is often necessary to change common fractions to decimals (Table 5–1). To change a fraction to a decimal, divide the numerator by the denominator. To divide a smaller number by a larger number, place a decimal point after the smaller number, then add as many zeros as you need, either to make the decimal come out even or to give the desired number of decimal places (tenths, hundredths, thousandths, or ten-thousandths).

Here is an example of how a fraction may be changed to a decimal:

Problem. Change $\frac{15}{32}$ to a decimal.

Solution. Divide 15 by 32.

$$
\begin{array}{r}
0.46875 \\
32\overline{)15.00000} \\
12\,8 \\
\hline
220 \\
192 \\
\hline
280 \\
256 \\
\hline
240 \\
224 \\
\hline
160 \\
160 \\
\hline
\end{array}
$$

A person not connected with shopwork would read the answer as forty-six thousand eight hundred seventy-five hundred-thousandths, because there are five places in the decimal. A machinist, however, would read it as four hundred sixty-eight and seventy-five hundred-thousandths. The last two figures, 75, are actually three-fourths of another thousandth. If he

Table 5-1. How to read decimals.

Millions	Hundred-thousands	Ten-thousands	Thousands	Hundreds	Tens	Units	Decimal point	Tenths	Hundredths	Thousandths	Ten-thousandths	Hundred-thousandths	Millionths
0	0	0	0	0	0	0	.	0	0	0	0	0	0
7	6	5	4	3	2	1	.	1	2	3	4	5	6

were interested in the dimension to the nearest thousandth only, then he would drop the last two figures, 75, and add 0.001 to the 0.468, giving 0.469.

In machine-shop work it is common practice, when working to thousandths of an inch, to carry out the decimal to four places (ten-thousandths). Then, if the fourth figure in the decimal is 5 or greater, you add one more thousandth (0.001) to the third figure in the answer.

Good machinists remember most of the commonly used decimal equivalents so they don't have to waste time looking them up. You

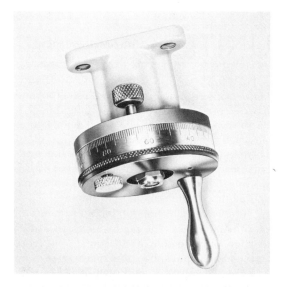

Fig. 5-1. The dials on most machine tools read in thousandths. If, for example, a movement of $\frac{1}{8}$ in. is specified, the handle must be turned one complete revolution (0.100) plus an additional one quarter (0.025) for a total of 0.125 in.

Table 5-2. Decimal equivalents of common fractions.

Fraction	Decimal		Fraction	Decimal
$\frac{1}{64}$	0.015625		$\frac{33}{64}$	0.515625
$\frac{1}{32}$	0.03125		$\frac{17}{32}$	0.53125
$\frac{3}{64}$	0.046875		$\frac{35}{64}$	0.546875
$\frac{1}{16}$	0.0625		$\frac{9}{16}$	0.5625
$\frac{5}{64}$	0.078125		$\frac{37}{64}$	0.578125
$\frac{3}{32}$	0.09375		$\frac{19}{32}$	0.59375
$\frac{7}{64}$	0.109375		$\frac{39}{64}$	0.609375
$\frac{1}{8}$	0.125		$\frac{5}{8}$	0.625
$\frac{9}{64}$	0.140625		$\frac{41}{64}$	0.640625
$\frac{5}{32}$	0.15625		$\frac{21}{32}$	0.65625
$\frac{11}{64}$	0.171875		$\frac{43}{64}$	0.671875
$\frac{3}{16}$	0.1875		$\frac{11}{16}$	0.6875
$\frac{13}{64}$	0.203125		$\frac{45}{64}$	0.703125
$\frac{7}{32}$	0.21875		$\frac{23}{32}$	0.71875
$\frac{15}{64}$	0.234375		$\frac{47}{64}$	0.734375
$\frac{1}{4}$	0.25		$\frac{3}{4}$	0.75
$\frac{17}{64}$	0.265625		$\frac{49}{64}$	0.765625
$\frac{9}{32}$	0.28125		$\frac{25}{32}$	0.78125
$\frac{19}{64}$	0.296875		$\frac{51}{64}$	0.796875
$\frac{5}{16}$	0.3125		$\frac{13}{16}$	0.8125
$\frac{21}{64}$	0.328125		$\frac{53}{64}$	0.828125
$\frac{11}{32}$	0.34375		$\frac{27}{32}$	0.84375
$\frac{23}{64}$	0.359375		$\frac{55}{64}$	0.859375
$\frac{3}{8}$	0.375		$\frac{7}{8}$	0.875
$\frac{25}{64}$	0.390625		$\frac{57}{64}$	0.890625
$\frac{13}{32}$	0.40625		$\frac{29}{32}$	0.90625
$\frac{27}{64}$	0.421875		$\frac{59}{64}$	0.921875
$\frac{7}{16}$	0.4375		$\frac{15}{16}$	0.9375
$\frac{29}{64}$	0.453125		$\frac{61}{64}$	0.953125
$\frac{15}{32}$	0.46875		$\frac{31}{32}$	0.96875
$\frac{31}{64}$	0.484375		$\frac{63}{64}$	0.984375
$\frac{1}{2}$	0.5		1	1

numerator and denominator by the same number. In this case both numerator and denominator can be divided by 125. Consequently, 125 divided by 125 equals 1, the numerator, and 1,000 divided by 125 equals 8, the denominator, giving a common fraction of $\frac{1}{8}$.

ADDING COMMON FRACTIONS AND DECIMALS

It is often necessary to add common fractions and decimals to get a total dimension of a piece of work. In Fig. 5-2, for example, to find the total length of the part, it would be necessary to add $1\frac{7}{8}$, $\frac{3}{4}$, and 3.286 in. The easiest way to do this is to change the common fractions to a decimal: $\frac{3}{4}$ equals 0.750 and $\frac{7}{8}$ equals 0.875. In adding decimals you must always keep the decimal points one under the other. The figures would be set down in this manner:

$$
\begin{array}{r}
1.875 \\
0.750 \\
3.286 \\
\hline
5.911
\end{array}
$$

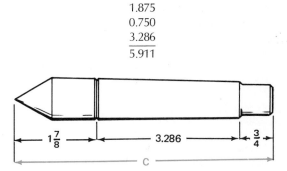

Fig. 5-2. Can you find the overall length *C* of this lathe cutter?

should start by memorizing the decimal equivalents of such common fractions as $\frac{1}{2}$, $\frac{1}{4}$, $\frac{1}{8}$, $\frac{1}{16}$, $\frac{1}{32}$, and $\frac{1}{64}$. As you use the other decimal equivalents shown in Table 5-2, you will find yourself remembering more and more of them.

CHANGING DECIMALS TO COMMON FRACTIONS

Sometimes it is necessary to change a decimal to a common fraction. This can be done easily by first writing the decimal as a fraction. For example, if we wish to change 0.125 to a common fraction, we write the fraction $\frac{125}{1,000}$, because three places in the decimal indicates thousandths. Then we reduce this fraction to its lowest terms. This is done by dividing both the

ADDITION OF DECIMALS

In adding decimals, tenths are written under tenths, hundredths under hundredths, etc. When this is done, the decimal points fall in a straight line. The addition is the same as in adding whole numbers (Fig. 5-3). Consider the following example:

$$
\begin{array}{r}
2.18 \\
34.35 \\
0.14 \\
4.90 \\
\hline
41.57
\end{array}
$$

Adding the first column on the right gives 17 hundredths or 1 tenth and 7 hundredths. As with

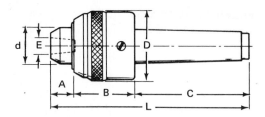

SHANK SIZE	A	B	C	D	d	E	L
# 2MT	0.35	1.73	2.68	1.69	0.75	0.43	
# 3MT	0.55	1.89	3.35	2.05	0.98	0.55	
# 4MT	0.71	2.36	4.25	2.60	1.34	0.71	
# 5MT	0.63	3.03	5.32	3.58	1.97	1.10	
# 6MT	1.06	3.94	7.36	4.80	2.72	1.50	
# 7MT	1.42	4.76	10.4	5.83	3.35	1.89	

Fig. 5–3. Can you find L for each different shank size?

FINDING ONE-HALF OF A COMMON FRACTION

On many jobs in the shop, it is necessary to find one-half of a certain fraction. Simply stated, we merely divide the fraction by 2. To a beginner in shopwork this is not quite as simple as it sounds. It becomes simple, though, once you understand how it is done. Let's assume that we have to lay out a circle having a $\frac{7}{8}$-in. diameter on a piece of metal. For this job it is best to use a divider. A *divider* is a tool having two sharp-pointed legs that can be set for different dimensions by using a steel rule. It is used to draw circles or space dimensions on metal parts. We must set the divider to one-half of $\frac{7}{8}$. We can calculate this by multiplying $\frac{1}{2} \times \frac{7}{8}$, thus $\frac{1}{2} \times \frac{7}{8} = \frac{7}{16}$, which is correct. The solution to this same problem could also be found without a pencil and paper. Since there are 2 sixteenths in every eighth, one-half of $\frac{1}{8}$ would equal $\frac{1}{16}$. Then one-half of $\frac{7}{8}$ would equal $7 \times \frac{1}{16}$, or $\frac{7}{16}$. Another method worth remembering is to keep the same numerator and multiply the denominator by 2. In this example, $2 \times 8 = 16$, the denominator. The correct answer would then be $\frac{7}{16}$.

whole numbers, we write the 7 under the hundredths column and add the 1 to the tenths column (the column of the next higher order). The sum of the tenths column is 15 tenths or 1 unit and 5 tenths. The 5 is written under the tenths column and the 1 is added in the units column. If the decimal points are kept in a straight line, that is, if the place values are kept in the proper columns, addition of decimals is the same as addition of whole numbers. Note that the decimal point in the sum falls directly under the other decimal points.

SUBTRACTION OF DECIMALS

We subtract decimals column by column, as with whole numbers. Notice that the place values in the following example are directly under the corresponding place values. Notice also that this causes the decimal points to be aligned.

$$
\begin{array}{r}
45.76 \\
-31.87 \\
\hline
13.89
\end{array}
$$

CALCULATING ADDITIONAL DIMENSIONS ON DRAWINGS

A blueprint usually gives all the basic dimensions needed to make a part. Often a machinist finds it necessary to calculate additional dimensions to make or check the part. In most cases you can add or subtract certain dimensions to get the dimension needed. For example in Fig. 5–4, let's assume you wish to know the thickness of the spacing collar. To find this dimension, subtract the inside diameter from the outside diameter and divide the result by 2.

$$
\begin{array}{ll}
1.388 & \text{outside diameter} \\
0.868 & \text{inside diameter} \\
\hline
0.520 & \text{double thickness}
\end{array}
$$

Single thickness:

$$
\begin{array}{r}
0.260 \\
2\overline{)0.520}
\end{array}
$$

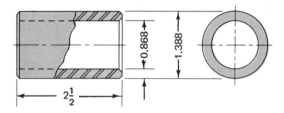

Fig. 5-4.   Can you find the thickness of the spacing collar?

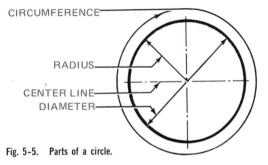

Fig. 5-5.   Parts of a circle.

Table 5-3.   Solving geometric figures.

TO FIND	FORMULA
Circumference of a circle	Multiply the diameter $\times 3.1416$ Multiply the radius $\times 6.283185$
Diameter of a circle	Multiply the circumference $\times 0.31831$ Multiply the square root $\times 1.12838$
Radius of a circle	Multiply the circumference $\times 0.159155$ Multiply the square root $\times 0.56419$
Area of a circle	Multiply the square of the diameter $\times 0.7854$ Multiply the square of the circumference $\times 0.07958$ Half the circumference by half the diameter
Area of surface of a ball (sphere)	Multiply the square of the diameter $\times 3.1416$
Volume of a ball (sphere)	Multiply the cube of the diameter $\times 0.5236$
Area of an ellipse	Multiply the long diameter by the short diameter $\times 0.78540$
Side of a square inscribed in a circle	Multiply the diameter $\times 0.7071$
Side of a square equal in area to a given circle	Multiply the diameter $\times 0.8862$
Diameter of a circle equal in area to given square	Multiply a side of the square $\times 1.12838$
Diameter of a circle equal in area to given square	Multiply a side of the square $\times 1.12838$
Side of a hexagon inscribed in a circle	Multiply the diameter of the circle $\times 0.500$
Diameter of a circle inscribed in a hexagon	Multiply a side of the hexagon $\times 1.7321$
Side of an equilateral triangle inscribed in a circle	Multiply the diameter of the circle $\times 0.866$
Diameter of a circle inscribed in an equilateral triangle	Multiply a side of the triangle $\times 0.57735$
Area of a square	Multiply the base by the height
Area of a rectangle	Multiply the base by the height
Area of a triangle	Multiply the base by $\frac{1}{2}$ the perpendicular height
Area of a trapezoid	Multiply $\frac{1}{2}$ the sum of the parallel sides by the perpendicular height
Area of a regular hexagon	Multiply the square of one side $\times 2.598$
Area of a regular octagon	Multiply the square of one side by 4.828
Area of a regular polygon	Multiply $\frac{1}{2}$ the sum of the sides by the inside radius

SOLVING GEOMETRIC FIGURES

Many machinery parts are made up of simple geometric figures such as squares, circles, triangles, hexagons, and similar shapes. A machinist must often find one dimension of a geometric figure when another is given. For example, suppose the diameter of round bar stock is known, and the circumference is needed. To find the circumference of the bar stock, a circle, multiply the diameter by 3.1416, (π). If the diameter of the stock is 4 in., then the circumference would be 4 times 3.1416, or 12.5664 in. (Fig. 5–5). Common formulas used with geometric figures are listed in Table 5–3.

OTHER FORMULAS USED IN MACHINE SHOP

The machinist uses other formulas for figuring such things as cutting speed, feed, thread depth, and amount of taper. Consult the index for these and other formulas.

UNIT 6. Selecting Metals

Many different kinds of metals (stock) are used in machine-shop work (Fig. 6-1). The kind of metal used for making a part depends upon what the part is to be used for and whether or not the part is to be heat-treated. *Heat-treating* means that a metal is made harder and tougher by heating it and cooling it in different ways. Some metals can be heat-treated and some cannot.

Some parts require a hard, tough metal and others may be made of softer metals. It would be foolish and wasteful of time, effort, and material to make a cutting tool for the wrong kind of steel, only to find it useless after spending hours of work on it. It is very important, then, that you learn how to select the correct metal *before* you start a job.

In machine shop we use metals in three basic forms:

1. *Castings.* Cast parts can be purchased for many kinds of machine-shop projects (Fig. 6–2).

2. *Forgings.* The forging method is used to produce parts that require great strength and rigidity (Fig. 6–3). Most forgings must be machined before they can be used.

3. *Bar stock.* This is the most common form of materials for machining. Bar stock is made in standard shapes and is available in many different sizes (Fig. 6–4).

SHAPES OF STOCK

In your machine-shop course you will, for the most part, use metals which are purchased in the form of long bars. We call this *bar stock*. Bar stock is made in five standard shapes (Fig. 6–5).

There is a correct way to specify the dimensions or sizes of these shapes. Round stock has only two dimensions, diameter and length. Flat stock has three dimensions, thickness, width, and length. Square stock also has three dimensions, but both widths are the same. Note that the sizes of hexagon and octagon shapes are specified according to the distance across the flats and length.

The way in which stock is specified is more or less standard in most shops. For example, when requesting round stock, you should give the diameter first then the length. For flat stock, you would first give the thickness, then the width, and finally the length in that order. For square stock you could state the width twice, as $\frac{1}{2}$ by $\frac{1}{2}$, or you could say, "$\frac{1}{2}$-in. square," then add the length. For hexagon (six-sided) or octagon (eight-sided) shapes, you would give the distance across the flats first, then the length.

Most suppliers have the following common shapes and sizes in stock:

1. Rounds (shafting) in diameters from $\frac{3}{16}$ to 9 in.

2. Squares from $\frac{1}{4}$ by $\frac{1}{4}$ in. to $4\frac{1}{2}$ by $4\frac{1}{2}$ in.

3. Flats (rectangular shapes) from $\frac{1}{8}$ by $\frac{5}{8}$ in. to 3 by 4 in.

Fig. 6-1. A white-hot billet of steel is shown emerging from the heating furnace as it begins its trip through the bar mill at a steel plant.

Fig. 6-2. This casting is being checked for accuracy.

Fig. 6-3. Many hand tools and machine parts are made by forging.

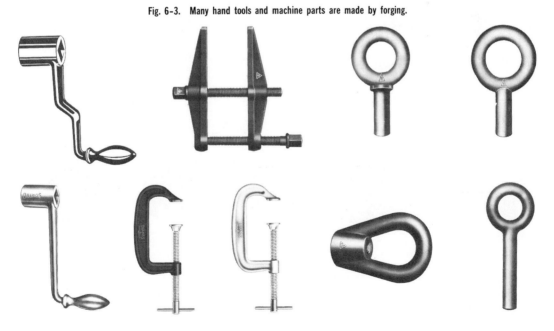

4. Hexagons from $\frac{1}{4}$ to 4 in.

5. Octagons from $\frac{1}{2}$ to $1\frac{3}{4}$ in.

METALS

Metals are divided into two general types—ferrous and nonferrous. *Ferrous* metals are those which contain iron. *Nonferrous* metals are those which do not contain iron. However, some nonferrous metals may contain a small amount of iron as an impurity.

FERROUS METALS

Steel and cast iron are the most common ferrous metals in general use. *Steel* is an alloy containing chiefly iron, carbon, and certain other elements in varying amounts. A wide range of physical properties may be obtained in steel by control-ling the amount of carbon and other alloying elements and by subjecting the steel to various heat treatments.

Alloying Elements in Steel. Plain carbon steels usually contain, besides iron and carbon, small amounts of silicon, sulfur, phosphorus, and manganese. Alloy steels are formed by the addition of one or more of the following elements: nickel, chromium, molybdenum, vanadium, tungsten, manganese, silicon, and small amounts of other alloying elements.

Carbon. Carbon is by far the most important alloying element in steel. It is the amount of carbon present which largely determines the maximum hardness obtainable. The higher the carbon content, the higher the tensile strength and the greater the hardness to which the steel may be heat-treated.

Low-carbon steels are usually used for low-strength parts requiring a great deal of forming. Medium-carbon steels are used for forgings and other applications where increased strength and a certain amount of ductility are necessary. High-carbon steels are used for high-strength parts such as springs, tools, and dies. The following list is a classification of ferrous materials according to their carbon content.

Ferrous Material	Carbon Content
Wrought iron	Trace to 0.08%
Low-carbon steel	0.04 to 0.30%
Medium-carbon steel	0.30 to 0.60%
High-carbon steel	0.60 to 1.70%
Cast iron	1.70 to 4.50%

Fig. 6-4.   Bar stock is made in a wide variety of shapes and sizes.

Fig. 6-5.   Shapes of bar stock and dimensions.

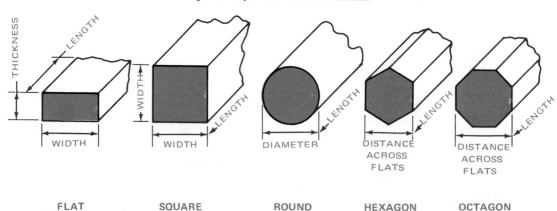

FLAT   SQUARE   ROUND   HEXAGON   OCTAGON

Wrought iron is almost pure iron. It is the choice for a great deal of ornamental ironwork. It is not frequently found in the school shop because of its high cost. It forges well, can easily be bent hot or cold, and can be welded.

Carbon steels are classified by the amount of carbon they contain. This amount is given in *points* (100 points equals 1 percent) or by percentage.

A. *Low-carbon steel,* often called soft or mild steel, contains 0.04 to 0.30 percent carbon (4 to 30 points). It does not contain enough carbon to be hardened. This type of steel is available as black-iron sheet, band iron, bars, and rods. Because it is easily welded, machined, and formed, low-carbon steel is suitable for products and projects in which an easily worked metal is needed. It is used for most bench metal and ornamental ironwork.

B. *Medium-carbon steel* has 0.30 to 0.60 percent carbon (30 to 60 points). It is used for many standard machine parts. In the school shop it is used for projects like hammer heads and clamp parts.

C. *High-carbon steel* contains 0.60 to 1.70 percent carbon (60 to 170 points). The best kind for school shops contains 75 to 95 points. It is used for making small tools or for any item that must be hardened and tempered.

Alloy steels have special properties determined by the mixture and the amount of other metals added. To the *metallurgist,* a scientist who works in metal mining and manufacturing, steels containing very small quantities of elements other than carbon, phosphorus, sulfur, and silicon are known as *alloy steels.* Each alloy steel has a personality of its own. A car is made of about 100 different kinds of alloy steel.

Some of the common alloying elements are described below:

● *Manganese.* Manganese helps to reduce certain undesirable effects of sulfur by combining with the sulfur. It also combines with carbon to increase hardness and toughness. Manganese possesses the property of aiding in increasing the depth of hardness penetration. It also improves the forging qualities by reducing brittleness at rolling and forging temperatures.

● *Silicon.* Silicon does not normally occur in steels in excess of 3.00 percent. A small amount of silicon improves ductility. It is used largely to increase impact resistance when combined with other alloys.

● *Sulfur.* Sulfur is generally regarded as detrimental to the hot working of steel and to the impact properties of steel treated to high tensile strength. However, sulfur is an invaluable aid to machining, and steels are often resulfurized to as high as 0.30 percent to gain advantage of this property.

● *Phosphorus.* Phosphorus has an undesirable effect on steel in that it imparts brittleness. There is some evidence that a small amount of phosphorus, less than 0.05 percent, increases tensile strength.

● *Nickel.* Nickel dissolves easily in molten steel. It is present in the common nickel steels in a proportion of 0.40 percent up to 5.00 percent. The addition of nickel increases strength, yield point, hardness, and ductility. It also increases the depth of hardening. Nickel steels are less susceptible to warping and scaling than most other steels. Nickel increases corrosion resistance and is one of the major constituents of the "stainless" or corrosion-resisting steels.

● *Chromium.* Addition of chromium imparts hardness, strength, wear resistance, heat resistance, and corrosion resistance to steels.

● *Molybdenum.* Molybdenum, even in extremely small amounts, has considerable effect as an alloying element on the physical properties of steels. Molybdenum increases elastic limit, impact strength, wear resistance, and fatigue strength. Molybdenum steels are readily heat-treated, forged, and machined.

● *Vanadium.* Vanadium is usually used in amounts of less than 0.25 percent. As an alloying agent, vanadium improves fatigue strength, ultimate strength, yield point, toughness, and resistance to impact and vibration. Chromium-vanadium steels have good ductility and high strength.

● *Tungsten.* Tungsten is used largely with chromium as a high-speed tool steel which contains 14.00 to 18.00 percent tungsten and 2.00 to 4.00 percent chromium. This steel possesses the characteristic of being able to retain a sharp cutting-edge even though heated to redness in cutting.

Tool-and-die steels are a large group of steels used when careful heat-treating must be done. These steels are used for parts such as chisels, hammers, screwdrivers, springs, and tools and dies used to cut and form metals.

Tool steels with certain alloying elements are designed for specific uses. There is a special American Iron and Steel Institute, AISI, numbering system for these materials. Each company also uses specific brand names to identify their products. The most common kinds of tool steels include:

- High-Speed Tool Steels
  Symbol M: Molybdenum types
  Symbol T: Tungsten types

- Hot Work Tool Steels
  Symbol H: Chromium types
  Symbol H: Tungsten types

- Cold Work Tool Steels
  Symbol D: High-carbon, High-chromium types
  Symbol A: Medium-alloy, Air-hardening types
  Symbol O: Oiled-hardening types
  Symbol S: Shock-resisting tool steels
  Symbol P: Mild-steels

- Special-Purpose Tool Steels
  Symbol L: Low-alloy types
  Symbol F: Carbon-tungsten types
  Symbol W: Water-hardening tool steels

Rolled steel, which includes bar, rod, and structural steels, is produced by rolling the steel into shape, much as clothes are squeezed through a wringer. *Hot-rolled steels* are formed into shape while the metal is red-hot. The metal passes through a series of rollers, each a little closer to the next one. As the steel passes through the last rollers, hot water is sprayed over it, forming a bluish scale. This steel is fairly uniform in quality and is used for many different kinds of parts. Hot-rolled bars of the best quality are used to produce cold-finished steels. *Cold-finished steels* are used when great accuracy, better surface finish, and certain mechanical properties are needed. There are several ways of producing cold-finished bars. The most common results in what is called *cold-worked steel.* After the scale from the hot-rolled bars is removed, one of two techniques is employed. (1) The bars are cold-drawn, that is, drawn through dies a few thousandths smaller than the original bar. (2) The steel is cold-rolled, that is, rolled cold to the exact size.

Drill rod is a grade of high-carbon tool steel or high-speed steel. It is finished by grinding and polishing so that the outside is smooth and very accurate in size. You can identify drill rod by its shiny surface, which is much smoother than any of the other steels used in the shop. Drill-rod bars are generally made in 3-ft lengths and come in round, hexagonal, and square shapes. Drill rod is more expensive than most other steels.

Cast iron is used for the heavy parts of many machines. It is the most common material for making castings. Cast iron is low in cost and wears well. It is very brittle, however, and cannot be hammered or formed. It contains 2 to 4 percent carbon. The basic kinds of cast iron are white iron, gray iron, and malleable iron. Malleable iron is a particular kind of cast iron, made more malleable by an annealing procedure. Malleable-iron castings are not so brittle or hard. They can stand a great deal of hammering. Many plumbing fixtures are made of malleable iron. *Nodular iron* is a kind of cast iron that is even better for withstanding shocks, blows, and jerks.

NONFERROUS METALS

Copper is one of the most important nonferrous metals. It has an excellent resistance to saltwater corrosion.

Zinc is used as an alloying ingredient in making brass and some bronzes. It is also often used as a protective coating on steel sheets, which are then called *galvanized sheets.*

Tin is seldom used except as an alloying ingredient. Alloyed with lead, it makes a soft solder. Alloyed with copper, it produces bronze.

Nickel is a hard, malleable, and ductile metal. It is resistant to corrosion and is, therefore, often used as a coating on other metals.

Combined with other metals, its effect is to make the alloy hard, strong, and ductile. It also imparts greater resistance to oxidation and corrosion.

Brass is an alloy (mixture) of copper and zinc. There are many grades and kinds of brass. It can be identified by its yellow color. It is used for many parts that do not require great strength and where it is necessary to resist rust and corrosion. Bars can be purchased in standard shapes, including different thicknesses of sheet metal.

Bronze is produced when alloying elements (other metals) are added to copper. It is known as bronze because of the color. Bronze, then, is a broad term used for many copper-based alloys. It may look very much like brass, but is more difficult to machine. The addition of tin to copper makes a very tough bronze which is excellent for bearing material. It is highly resistant to rust and corrosion. In addition to bearings, it is used for gears, pump parts, springs, and welding rods.

Table 6-1. AISE-SAE steel designations.

General Type	Number Series	Description	Principal Alloy Content—%		
			Nickel	Chromium	Molybdenum
Carbon	1000	Plain carbon			
	1100	Free cutting (screw stock)			
	1200	Free cutting (screw stock)			
Manganese	1300				
Nickel	2300		3.50		
	2500		5.00		
Nickel-Chromium	3100		1.25	0.60	
	3300		3.50	1.50	
Molybdenum	4000				0.20–0.30
	4100			0.80–1.10	0.15–0.25
	4300		1.65–2.00	0.40–0.90	0.20–0.30
	4600		1.65–2.00		0.20–0.30
	4800		3.25–3.75		0.20–0.30
Chromium	5100	Low chromium		0.55–0.75	
	50100	Low chromium (bearing)		0.40–0.60	
	51100	Medium chromium (bearing)		0.90–1.15	
	52100	High chromium (bearing)		1.30–1.60	
Chromium-Vanadium	6100	.15% min. Vanadium		0.80–1.10	
Silicon Manganese	9200	1.2–2.2% Silicon		0.00–0.80	
Triple Alloy	8600		0.40–0.70	0.40–0.80	0.15–0.25
	8700		0.40–0.70	0.40–0.60	0.20–0.30
	9300		3.00–3.50	1.00–1.40	0.08–0.15
	9400		0.30–0.60	0.30–0.50	0.08–0.15
	9700		0.40–0.70	0.10–0.25	0.15–0.25
	9800		0.85–1.15	0.70–0.90	0.20–0.30

Aluminum is seldom used in its pure form. It is usually alloyed with other metals to form a strong, very lightweight metal. Aluminum is silvery in color and is made in many different alloys for specific purposes. Some of these alloys are best for making castings, and others can be made into bar stock of many different shapes and sizes. Aluminum is used extensively because of its light weight, easy workability, good appearance, high resistance to corrosion, and other desirable properties. When alloying elements such as magnesium, copper, nickel, and silicon are added, an alloy stronger than low-carbon steel can be produced.

IDENTIFYING STEELS

There are three basic methods of identifying steels, namely, the number system, the color-scheme method, and the spark-test method.

Number System. The Society of Automotive Engineers (SAE) and the American Iron and Steel Institute (AISI) have developed numerical systems for classifying steel. These systems are almost identical. The AISI system, however, is a bit more comprehensive since it includes a letter preceding the number which tells the kind of furnace in which the steel was made. (A = basic open-hearth alloy steel, B = acid Bessemer carbon steel, C = basic open-hearth carbon steel, D = acid open-hearth carbon steel, E = electric furnace steel.) The basic numbering system for steel includes four digits. The first digit indicates the type of steel to which the steel belongs. For example, 1 indicates carbon steel, 2 indicates nickel steel, and so forth. The second digit indicates the approximate percentage of the principle alloy and elements. The last two digits indicate the approximate carbon content in hundredths of 1 percent. For example, 2340 steel is a nickel steel containing approximately 3 percent nickel and 0.40 percent (sometimes called 40 points) carbon. If an A preceded this number, such as A2340, it would indicate

that this steel was made in a basic open-hearth furnace. In a few cases, five numbers are used. The last three numbers represent the carbon content in high-carbon chromium bearing steel. Table 6-1 lists the AISI and SAE steel designations along with the approximate percentage of alloying elements.

Color-scheme Method. Manufacturers and wholesalers often paint the ends of bar steel with different colors of paint to identify different types of steels. Most large machine shops use standardized colors to indicate each of the kinds of steel available.

Spark-test Method. To be effective, the person performing this test should have a considerable amount of experience in order to correctly judge the type of steel being tested. The test is made by observing the sparks given off as a piece of metal is held against a grinding wheel. The kind, frequency, position, and color of the sparks are all considered in making the identification. Figure 6-6 shows the types of sparks given off by various metals. Before attempting a spark test, make sure that the grinding wheel has been properly dressed.

Fig. 6-6. The spark test for common metals: (A) low carbon (machine), (B) high carbon (tool), (C) cast iron, and (D) stainless.

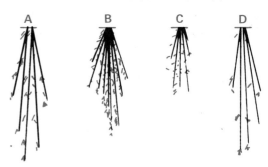

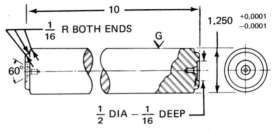

ALLOW 0.012 TO 0.015 FOR GRINDING

A

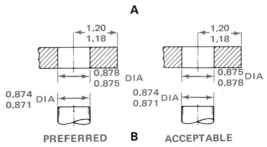

PREFERRED **B** ACCEPTABLE

Fig. 7-1. (A) The basic dimension is 1.250 in. (B) Showing tolerance by the limit dimensioning method.

UNIT 7. Reading a Drawing and Planning Your Work

In industry, designers and engineers design the complete product and each individual part that makes up the product. Draftsmen make an *assembly drawing* for the complete product and a *detailed drawing* for each part. The drawings are then reproduced in quantities and these copies are called *prints*. Prints are used by machinists who make the parts and by engineers and technicians who prepare the *work orders*, the *routing sheets* (where it is to go), and the *stock lists* (materials needed).

You should be able to do all these steps yourself. That is, you should be able to make a detailed drawing, read a print correctly, prepare a bill of materials, and plan the order of operations for making each part of a project. It is assumed that you have already had a course in mechanical drawing and are able to read a print. If you have not already studied mechanical drawing, it is suggested that you review one of the many good drawing textbooks available in your library.

SOME COMMON TERMS AND SYMBOLS

To be able to read machine drawings, there are a few common terms and symbols with which you should be familiar.

Limits. *Limits* are the maximum and minimum values prescribed for a specific dimension. A limit is included in the maximum or minimum dimension and indicates the variation from normal which the work must not exceed. For instance, if the nominal diameter of a hole is 1 in., and the limits of size are expressed as $\frac{0.999}{1.001}$, then any work not over 1.001 in. nor under 0.999 in. will be accepted.

Limits on dimensions not otherwise specified are:

Fractional dimensions	±0.010 in.
Decimal dimensions	±0.005 in.
Reamed holes	±0.0005 in.
Drilled holes	±0.002 in.

Tolerance. *Tolerance* represents the total amount by which a specific dimension may vary, and it is the total difference between the maxi-

mum and minimum limits. With a maximum limit of 1.001 in. and a minimum limit of 0.999 in., the tolerance would be 0.002 in.

Tolerances may be shown on drawings by several different methods. In the unilateral method, the minimum or the maximum measurement is used as the dimension figure, and the difference allowable is given as a plus or minus tolerance figure. In the bilateral method, the dimension figure indicates the plus or minus variation that is acceptable (Fig. 7-1A). In the limit dimensioning method, the maximum and minimum measurements are both stated (Fig. 7-1B).

Allowance. *Allowance* applies particularly to fits, as in the case of a hole and a shaft. It is the intentional difference between the maximum limits of mating parts to accomplish the desired fit. In other words, it is a minimum clearance or maximum interference of mating parts. There are forcing, driving, running, and sliding fits.

Fillets and Rounds. *Fillets* are concave metal corners added to a casting. Because rounded corners cool more evenly than sharp corners, fillets increase the strength of the metal and reduce the possibility of breakage. *Rounds,* or radii, are edges or outside corners that have been rounded to prevent chipping and to avoid sharp cutting-edges (Fig. 7-2).

Casting. *Castings* are objects made by pouring molten metal into a mold (usually sand) of a certain shape and allowing it to cool.

Forging. *Forging* is the process of shaping metal while it is hot or pliable by a hammering or pressing process either manually (blacksmith) or by machine.

Common Metal Conventions. A few of the more common metal conventions used in most foundries and machine shop drawings are illustrated in Fig. 7-3.

KINDS OF DRAWINGS

The position of parts when they are all in place is shown by an *assembly drawing* (Fig. 7-4A). Any dimensions that may be given are for purposes of assembling and erecting only. For reference, it is common practice to designate the part numbers of each part making up the assem-

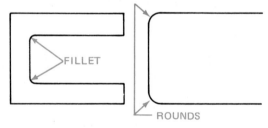

Fig. 7-2. Fillets and rounds.

Fig. 7-3. Simplified material conventions.

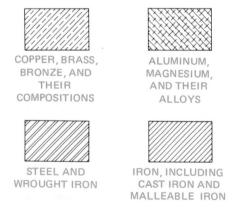

COPPER, BRASS, BRONZE, AND THEIR COMPOSITIONS	ALUMINUM, MAGNESIUM, AND THEIR ALLOYS
STEEL AND WROUGHT IRON	IRON, INCLUDING CAST IRON AND MALLEABLE IRON

bly. Sometimes an assembly drawing is made as an exploded pictorial (either isometric or perspective) drawing (Fig. 7-4B).

A *detail drawing* is a print illustrating a single component or part (Fig. 7-5A). It provides information regarding shape, size, type of material, type of finish, tolerance, necessary shop operations, and number of parts required.

For simple projects having only a few parts, both assembly and detail drawings are often shown on a single print (Fig. 7-5B). For larger projects having many parts, there should be an assembly print and a detail print for each individual part.

Section drawings are often prepared when it is necessary to show complicated parts or components (Fig. 7-6). By cutting away a portion of a part in one or more views, the interior construction of an object can often be more readily understood.

MEANING OF LINES

Various types of lines have certain meanings on drawings. Their use and meaning have become standard practice. Machinists and toolmakers must know the meaning of each type of line in order to read and understand drawings.

Each type of line is made thin or thick to indicate its purpose or use on the drawing. Sometimes a thin line is called a light line, and a thick line is called a heavy line. In either case, the meaning is the same, and both terms correspond to the standard for lines. Figure 7-7 shows the various types of lines used on shop drawings. Figure 7-8 shows how these lines are used.

DIMENSIONS

Dimensions tell the size of each of the various parts of an object or job to be made in the shop. A drawing that is correctly made contains all the dimensions necessary to make the part. Sometimes a machinist finds it necessary to calculate or add a dimension or two to make his job easier.

There are two common methods of dimensioning machine drawings. The method used depends upon the degree of accuracy required for the part to be made.

1. It is common practice to dimension drawings in inches and common fractions when the part to be made does not require a fine degree of accuracy (American National Standards Institute says only to tolerances of $\frac{1}{64}$) (Fig. 7-9). This method of dimensioning is followed for most of the projects in this book. Good judgment is necessary to fit parts together when only fractional dimensions are shown. As you gain experience, you will develop this judgment.

2. For parts that require precision measurements, dimensions are always given in inches and decimal parts of an inch. Most machine

Fig. 7-4. (A) An assembly drawing. (B) A pictorial assembly drawing.

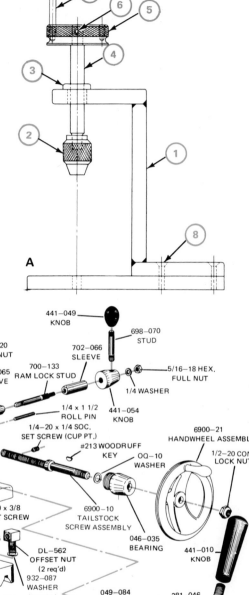

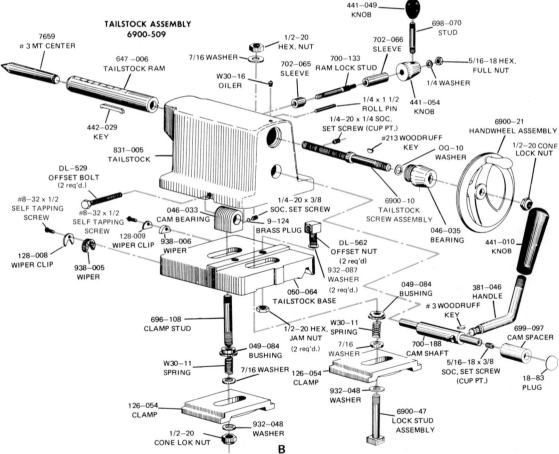

TAILSTOCK ASSEMBLY
6900-509

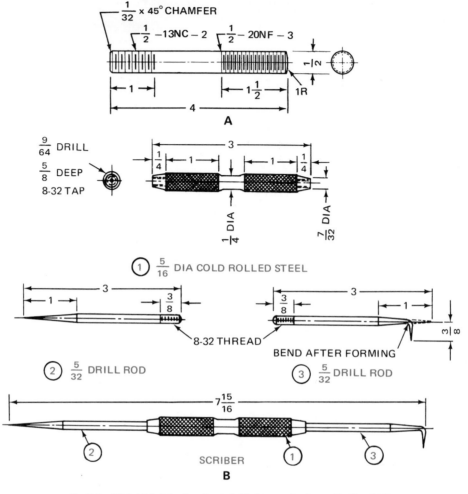

Fig. 7-5. (A) A detailed drawing of a stud. (B) An example of a combination detail and assembly drawing.

Fig. 7-6. A simple section drawing.

Fig. 7-8. Application of lines.

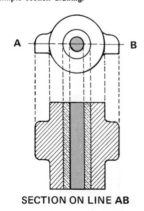

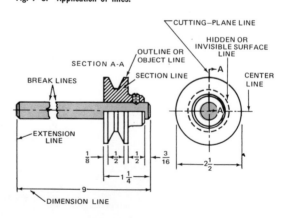

LINE STANDARDS

Type	Example	Description	Application
Solid lines		Solid lines are the most prominent lines on a drawing. They are heavy, dense, black lines approximately 1/32 in. wide, but the width may vary to suit the size of the drawing.	To show the visible edges of objects.
Hidden lines		Medium weight broken lines of approximately 1/8 in. dashes, closely and evenly spaced, less prominent than the solid lines.	To show hidden edges.
Center lines		Fine lines made up of long and short dashes alternately spaced and uniform in length; finer than the hidden lines.	To indicate centers.
Dimension, witness, leader, and work lines	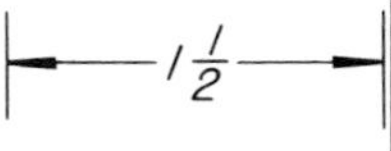 $1\frac{1}{2}$	Fine lines of approximately the same width as center lines; unbroken, except at dimensions.	To show dimensions, indicate the distance measured, as leaders for notes, and work lines.
Cutting-plane lines		Lines consisting of approximately 1/4 in. dashes evenly spaced; slightly heavier than the solid lines.	To indicate where a section is taken.
Cross-section lines	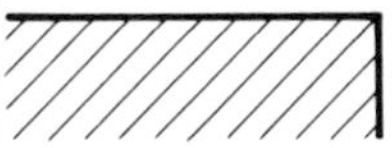	Fine parallel lines generally drawn at 45° angles, equally spaced, and proportionate to the size or mass of the section.	To show surfaces exposed by cutting a section.
Break lines	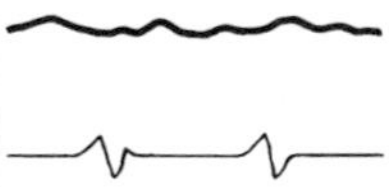	Heavy freehand lines for short breaks. Ruled fine lines and freehand zig-zags for long breaks.	To eliminate repeated detail when overall reference dimensions are shown.
Phantom lines		Fine broken lines consisting of one long and two short dashes alternately and evenly spaced.	To show adjacent parts, alternate positions, and lines of motion.
Arrowheads	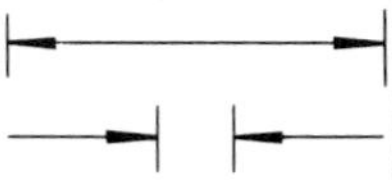	Arrowheads are small, sharply pointed, solid, and of uniform size; not extending beyond the witness lines.	To indicate points from which dimensions are taken.

Fig. 7-7. Various types of lines have certain meanings on drawings.

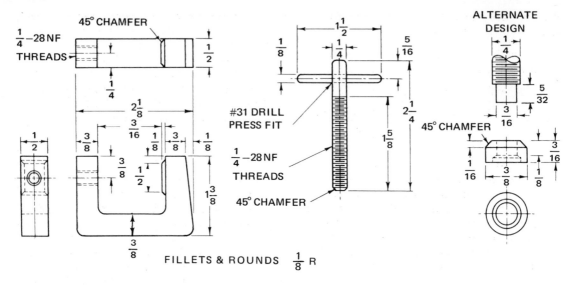

Fig. 7-9. A drawing dimensioned in fractions.

Fig. 7-10. (A) A steel block with dimensions shown in inches and decimal fractions of an inch. Notice the tolerance for each dimension. (B) If several similar parts are required, a table may be drawn to show the dimensions of various parts. Letters are drawn on the views and listed in the table so that the machinist can secure the necessary dimensions.

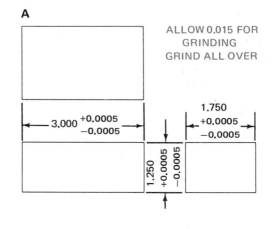

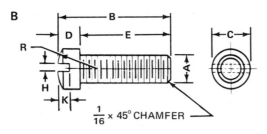

SCREW	A	B	C	D	E	H	K	R
$\frac{1}{4}$ – 20 NC	0.250 $\begin{smallmatrix}+0.000\\-0.005\end{smallmatrix}$	$\frac{23}{32}$	$\frac{3}{8}$	$\frac{7}{32}$	$\frac{1}{2}$	0.070	0.097	$\frac{13}{32}$
$\frac{5}{16}$ – 18 NC	0.3125 $\begin{smallmatrix}+0.000\\-0.005\end{smallmatrix}$	$\frac{3}{4}$	$\frac{7}{16}$	$\frac{1}{4}$	$\frac{1}{2}$	0.079	0.115	$\frac{9}{16}$
$\frac{3}{8}$ – 16 NC	0.375 $\begin{smallmatrix}+0.000\\-0.005\end{smallmatrix}$	$1\frac{1}{16}$	$\frac{9}{16}$	$\frac{5}{16}$	$\frac{3}{4}$	0.088	0.142	$\frac{11}{16}$
$\frac{1}{2}$ – 13 NC	0.500 $\begin{smallmatrix}+0.000\\-0.005\end{smallmatrix}$	$1\frac{13}{32}$	$\frac{3}{4}$	$\frac{13}{32}$	1	0.110	0.188	$1\frac{11}{32}$
$\frac{5}{8}$ – 11 NC	0.625 $\begin{smallmatrix}+0.000\\-0.005\end{smallmatrix}$	$2\frac{1}{32}$	$\frac{7}{8}$	$\frac{17}{32}$	$1\frac{1}{2}$	0.138	0.240	$1\frac{1}{8}$

drawings used in industrial plants are dimensioned in decimals. This method is used:

a. To obtain greater accuracy in making the part.

b. To help eliminate errors.

c. To make it easier to show the tolerances and allowances for each part and between the mating parts.

d. To show a machinist or toolmaker that dimensions must be measured with precision measuring tools, such as a micrometer or vernier instruments. These measuring tools measure directly in decimals. Dimensions that require precision are given in thousandths (0.001) or in ten-thousandths (0.0001) of an inch (Fig. 7-10).

SCALE SIZE OF DRAWINGS

Parts are sometimes too large or too small to be drawn to actual or *full size*. Very large parts must be drawn to a smaller size so the drawing will fit on a standard-size paper. Very small parts would be difficult to draw, and the print would be difficult to read if made actual size. Drawings that are made larger or smaller than the actual size of the part are called *scale drawings*.

The scale size is usually placed on a drawing in a section of the title block. When a drawing is full size, the scale would be given as 1 to 1 (1:1). When the drawing is made one-half the actual size, the scale would read 1:2. If the drawing is made twice the actual size, the scale would read 2:1. It is important to note that the dimensions always give the actual size of the finished part, regardless of the scale used.

SYMBOLS

Symbols are figures or simple drawings used to show certain things on industrial drawings. The use of symbols saves much time and simplifies a drawing. Two common symbols used on machine drawings are those that show *screw threads* and *finish* marks (Figs. 7-11 and 7-12). Screw-thread symbols may be either the regular or the simplified form. The simplified form is preferred because it saves time. The surface finish symbol is a sharp V that just touches the object line. It means that the surface on the workpiece must be machined or finished in some manner, such as grinding. The way the piece is to be finished, or the quality of surface finish desired, may be indicated by additional letters or numbers in the V, according to a company's code or standards. For example, if the surface required grinding, the symbol might read $\overset{6}{V}$. A newer symbol, $\overset{32}{\underset{16}{V}}$, is used when it

Fig. 7-11. Thread symbols: (A) regular and (B) simplified.

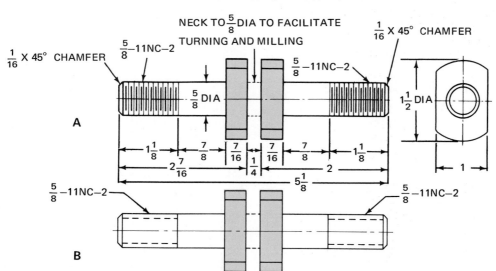

Table 7-1. Common abbreviations used on drawings.

Abbreviation	Meaning
,	Feet or minutes
"	Inches or seconds
°	Degrees
BRS	Brass
CBORE	Counterbore
CH	Caseharden
CI	Cast iron
CS	Carbon steel
CSK	Countersink
DI	Ductile iron 60-40-15
DI	Ductile iron 80-60-30
DIA	Diameter
FAO	Finish all over
GM	Gun metal
gpm	Gallons per minute
GR	Grind
HDN	Harden
HSS	High-speed steel
LH	Left hand
m	Meter
MI	Malleable iron
mm	Millimeter
MS	Machinery steel
N	National
NC	National coarse
NF	National fine
NS	National special
P	Diametral pitch
P_1	Circular (axial) pitch
psi	Pounds per square inch
R	Radius
RH	Right hand
RPM	Revolutions per minute
SC	Steel castings
SHI	Sheet iron
SMS	Soft machinery steel
SSC	Semisteel castings
T	Teeth
THD	Thread, threads
TS	Tool steel
UNC	Unified national coarse
UNEF	Unified national extra fine
UNF	Unified national fine
WI	Wrought iron

NEW FINISH MARK   OLD FINISH MARK

Fig. 7-12. Old and new finish symbols.

is necessary to control the surface quality. The numbers indicate maximum and minimum average roughness in microinches. A microinch, μin., is one-millionth of an inch (0.000001 in.).

ABBREVIATIONS

Many terms and words are so frequently used on drawings that considerable time can be saved by abbreviating them. Common abbreviations are shown in Table 7-1. As you use these terms from day to day, you should learn the meaning of each and the abbreviation, so you can use them in actual practice. A machinist often says *OD* and *ID* instead of *outside diameter* and *inside diameter*.

SPECIFICATIONS AND NOTES

Sometimes additional information cannot be shown directly on the views. It is added as notes or as information in the title block or record strip. Specifications include such information as the kind of material, kind of finish, heat treatment, special instructions for machining, and similar items.

PARTS LIST

A parts list may be required on a machine drawing. Usually placed on an assembly drawing, it gives the name, quantity, material, stock size or weight, stock number, or drawing number of each part. A column may be added for remarks. Usually the larger or more important parts are listed first, and the smaller or standard parts, such as screws, are listed last.

SURFACE ROUGHNESS

Surface roughness is now established as a qualitative standard of measurement. Detailed drawings usually indicate the degree of roughness allowed on finished surfaces. The American National Standards Institute recommends the unit of surface roughness to be μin. AA, which means microinch arithmetical average. A microinch is one-millionth of an inch.

The symbol used to indicate surface roughness is $\sqrt{}$. Frequently this symbol is abbreviated to $\sqrt{}$. If the symbol $\sqrt[16]{}$ appears on a particular surface to be machined, it means that any surface finish from dead smooth to 16 microinch AA is acceptable. Surface roughness may be evaluated by visual or factual comparison if roughness comparison specimens are available (Fig. 7-13).

READING A DRAWING OR PRINT

Figure 7-14 shows a typical project that you may make in the shop. Find the answers to these questions by reading the print:

1. How many parts (components) are there for this project?

2. What is the overall size of the clamp body? (Overall means all outside dimensions.)

3. What is the radius of the outside corners of the clamp body? Inside radius?

4. What is the threaded length of the screw?

5. What is the diameter in decimal fraction of the threaded section of the screw?

6. How many threads per inch are there on the screw?

7. Why is the hole in the screw for the handle a different size than the handle?

8. What is the overall size of the pad?

9. What is the difference in the decimal size between the hole in the pad and the small end diameter of the screw?

10. What is the overall size of the handle?

Fig. 7-13. Definitions of surface roughness.

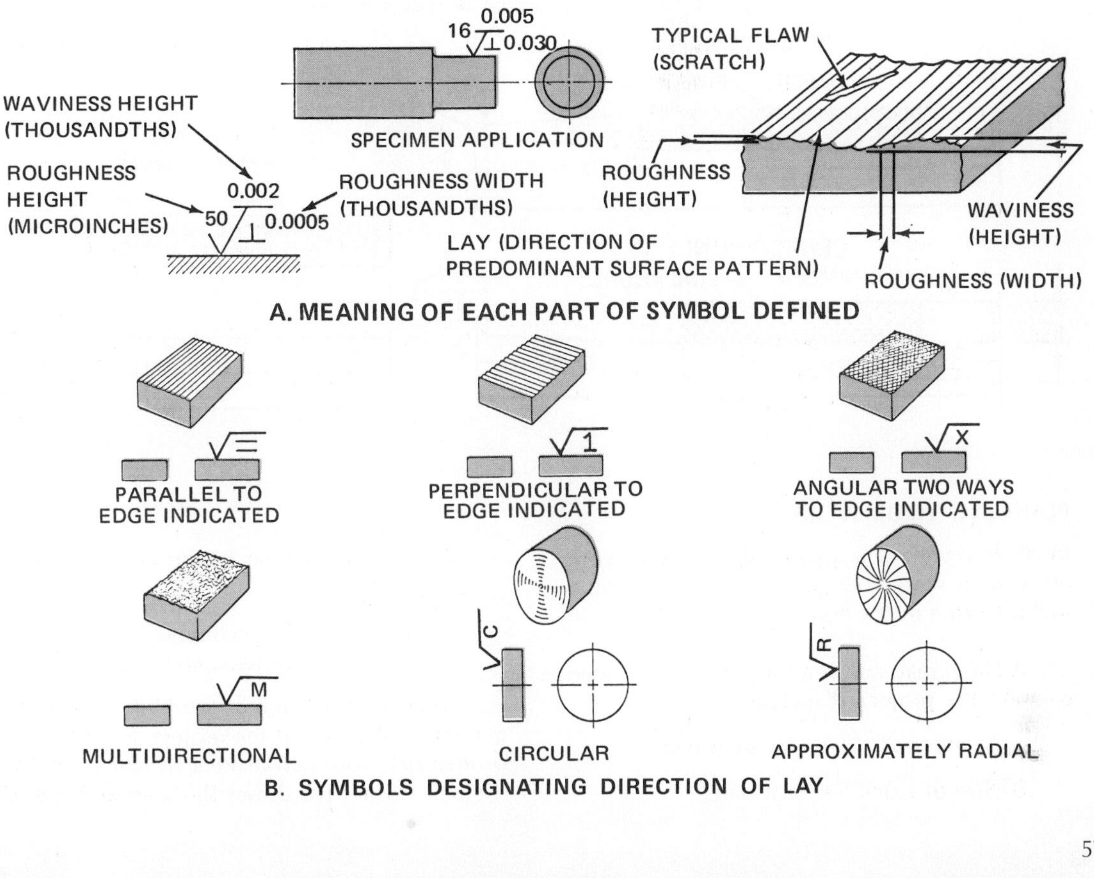

A. MEANING OF EACH PART OF SYMBOL DEFINED

B. SYMBOLS DESIGNATING DIRECTION OF LAY

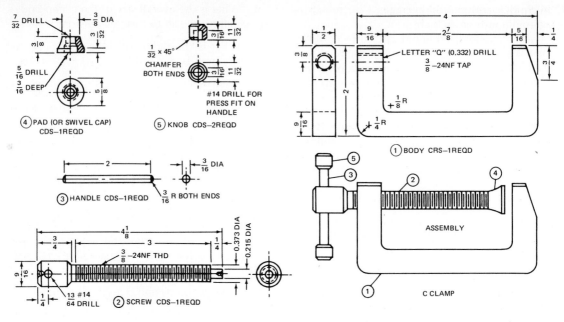

Fig. 7-14. An assembly and detail drawing of a C-clamp.

Fig. 7-15. Center and prick punches are made of tool steel.

PRICK PUNCH

$\frac{1}{16}$ × 45° CHAMFER   FINE KNURL

$\frac{3}{8}$

$\frac{3}{4}$ $2\frac{1}{4}$ 2

5

A

60°

CENTER PUNCH

$\frac{1}{16}$ × 45° CHAMFER   FINE KNURL

$\frac{3}{8}$

$\frac{3}{4}$ $2\frac{1}{4}$ 2

5

B

90°

TOOL STEEL
HARDEN & TEMPER

REF NO	PRICK PUNCH DIAMETER A	CENTER PUNCH DIAMETER B
1	$\frac{1}{16}$	$\frac{1}{8}$
2	$\frac{5}{64}$	$\frac{5}{32}$
3	$\frac{3}{32}$	$\frac{3}{16}$
4	$\frac{1}{8}$	$\frac{1}{4}$

PLANNING YOUR WORK

In all shopwork, it is a good idea to "plan your work, then work your plan." Your plan should include three major items:

1. A *bill of materials* is a list of items you need to make the project. It includes:

a. Number of pieces for each part

b. Size of stock for each part

c. Name of part

d. Kind of material (name and number if any)

e. List of standard or commercial parts, such as bolts, nuts, washers, and screws

You can list the bill of materials as you read and study the print of the project. From this bill of materials you then make a *stock-cutting list*. A stock-cutting list shows the kind and size of rough stock needed. For example, to make the center or prick punch shown in Fig. 7–15, the rough stock would have to be about $\frac{1}{8}$ to $\frac{1}{4}$ in. larger in diameter and about $\frac{3}{4}$ in. longer than the finished size.

A bill of materials should also list castings or forgings whenever they are required. A casting may be used for all kinds of irregular forms or shapes of parts. It is made in a foundry by pouring molten metal into a sand mold. A forging is a part of irregular shape or form that has been stamped out of red-hot metal by means of a forging machine or press. The hot metal is hammered or pressed between dies which shape it to the desired form and size. Small machine shops purchase castings and forgings or have them made to order.

2. A *plan of procedure* is a list of the steps needed to complete a project or job. These steps are called *operations,* and the *order of the operations* should be listed very carefully. There are certain operations on each job that must be done before others can be done. When you plan the procedure for doing a job, you must be able to see ahead. Make a list of what is to be done first, second, third, and so on. On some jobs it is quite possible to arrive at a dead end before the job is completed. This results in a waste of time, effort, and material, which could have been avoided by planning the order of operations. Operations cover such processes as:

    a. Cutting stock to correct length

    b. Locating and drilling center holes

    c. Mounting between centers in the lathe

    d. Rough-turning to size

The basic operations are described in detail in this book so that you can acquire a thorough knowledge and use this knowledge to make parts skillfully and efficiently.

In industry, the engineer or methods man in the planning department includes a similar list of operations when he makes up shop orders, work orders, or routing orders. The plan of procedure serves as a guide to the man in the shop when machining, assembling, and inspecting the completed product. It tells the order in which the operations are to be performed, and which machines and tools are to be used.

3. A *list of tools and equipment* needed will help you to get off to the right start. It saves you time by avoiding frequent trips to the tool crib. It also makes your working habits more efficient, which is one of the marks of a skilled worker.

UNIT 8. Cutting Off Stock to Length with Power Saws

Stock can be cut to length in seven basic ways: *abrasives, cold sawing, friction sawing, shearing, oxyfuel, hack sawing,* and *band sawing.* Each of these seven methods has certain advantages and disadvantages associated with it. These include:

1. *Abrasive cutting* (using a grinding wheel to cut to length) is particularly good when cutting hardened steel, mild steel, and stainless steel (Fig. 8–1). Because it leaves severe burrs on the edges, a deburring operation is necessary. Abrasive cutting does not lend itself to high production but is good for rough work.

2. *Cold sawing* is done by a variety of machines which use a circular saw blade similar to that used on a table saw for cutting wood. Blades are usually chrome-vanadium steel, but carbide insert tooth blades are also used. This method is excellent for cutting mild steel, stainless steel, aluminum, brass, and copper (Fig. 8–2).

3. *Friction sawing* is not an actual cutting operation but a burning process using a blade saw operating at high speed. It cannot be used to cut solid stock because too much heat builds

Fig. 8-1. Cutting pipe to desired length by use of an abrasive wheel.

Fig. 8-3. Cutting heavy sheet stock to size on a large shear.

Fig. 8-2. Cutting nonferrous metal with a circular saw mounted on a radial arm saw.

Fig. 8-4. Cutting heavy steel plate with a flame cutting torch. Plates over $1\frac{1}{2}$ in. thick are cut this way.

up in the blade. It is excellent, however, for the structural parts of mild steel and stainless steel.

4. *Shearing* is the fastest way to cut solid stock. It produces no chips (Fig. 8-3).

5. *Oxyfuel* is a cutting method using acetylene or other burning gases mixed with oxygen. It is the slowest and most uneconomical of the ways to cut stock to length (Fig. 8-4).

6. *Power hack sawing* (an adaptation of hand hack sawing) is one of the most common methods for cutting stock to length (Fig. 8-5).

7. *Band sawing* makes use of a continuous blade to do the cutting (Fig. 8-6).

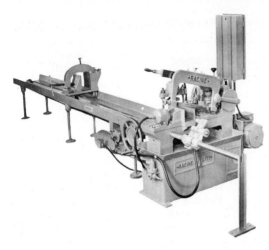

Fig. 8-5. This heavy-duty automatic hacksaw is an efficient machine for cutting multiple lengths of material.

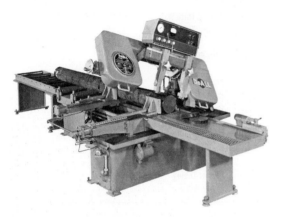

Fig. 8-6. A heavy-duty bandsaw with automatic cutting controls of the type used in industry.

Fig. 8-7. A power hacksaw with the parts named.

In most machine shops stock is rough cut to length with either a power hacksaw or a continuous-blade horizontal band saw. The power hacksaw is usually permanently mounted to the floor, and the band saw can be moved freely on casters.

POWER HACKSAW

The power hacksaw is a power-driven tool used for cutting off stock (Fig. 8-7).

Parts. The machine consists of a base with a worktable and vise on it. The vise can be adjusted for cutting stock at right angles and at several other angles. A saw frame holds the blade. In operation, the stock is fastened in a vise. The sawing takes place only on the forward, or draw, stroke. The frame lifts up slightly on the return stroke. A switch is used to turn on the power, and a clutch handle is used to start the saw operating. The size of the saw is determined by the largest diameter (or square) that can be cut. A common size is 3 by 3 in. Larger models have a coolant system attached.

Blades. Blades are made of carbon steel, high-speed tungsten steel, molybdenum steel, or high-speed molybdenum steel. They come in standard lengths, such as 12, 14, 16, 18, 24, and 30 in. Each blade has from 4 to 14 teeth per inch. These blades have a *raker set* (one unset tooth followed by two oppositely set teeth).

Blades with 4 teeth per inch are useful for cutting heavy solid bars of stock. The 6-tooth saws can be used for cutting machine steel, soft metals, and large section metals.

Blades with 10 teeth per inch are used for cutting high-speed steel, tool steel, heavy angle iron, thick wall pipe, cast iron, heavy structural shapes, and so on. For cutting tool steel, high-speed steel, light structural shapes, steel tubing, and pipe, blades with 14 teeth per inch can be used.

Installing a Blade. Loosen the thumbscrew and remove the old blade. Install the new blade with the teeth pointing toward the motor end of the machine. Tighten the blade until it is *taut* (gives off a clear note when tapped lightly).

61

CARE AND USE OF POWER HACKSAW

1. Select the right blade for the job (Table 8-1).

2. Be sure to insert with the teeth pointing in the cutting direction.

3. Keep close watch on blade tension, speed, and pressure.

4. Do not start a new blade in an old cut. It is better to reverse the work and start a new cut.

5. To increase the blade life, operate it at somewhat lower speed and lighter pressure at the start.

6. When cutting efficiency drops, insert a new blade rather than continuing with an old, worn blade.

7. Check the blade-holder pin frequently.

CUTTING OFF STOCK

1. Check the vise to make sure the jaws are at right angles to the blade. Most bar stock is sheared to length at the steel mill and the end is not perfectly square. If it is a new bar of stock, it is better to cut the end square before proceeding.

2. Open the jaws until the long bar or rod slips through under slight pressure. Support the outer end of the bar with a roller stand.

3. Push down on the handle of the frame until

Fig. 8-8. Cutting off stock with a power hacksaw.

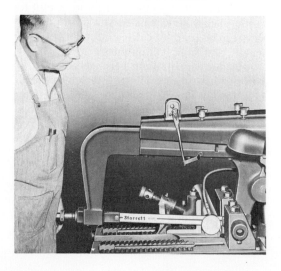

Table 8-1. Blade selection.

Material	Teeth Per Inch	Strokes Per Minute
FERROUS		
Drill Rod	10	90
Forging Stock, Alloy	4-6	90
Forging Stock, Mild	3-4-6	120
Iron, Cast	6-10	90-120
Iron, Malleable	6-10	90
Rails	6-10	60-90
Steel, Alloy	4-6	60-90
Steel, Carbon Tool	4-6	90-120
Steel, High Speed	6-10	60-90
Steel, Machinery	3-4-6	90-120
Steel, Stainless	3-4-6	60-90
Steel, Structural	6-10	90-120
Steel, Die Blocks	4-6	60-90
Steel Pipe	6-10	120
Tubing, Thick Wall	6-10	120
Tubing, Thin Wall	14	120
NON-FERROUS		
Aluminum	3-4-6	120
Babbitt	4-6	120
Brass Castings, Hard	4-6	90-120
Brass Castings, Soft	4-6	120
Bronze Castings	4-6-10	90
Bronze, Manganese	6-10	60-90
Copper Bars	3-4-6	90
Copper Tubing	10	120
Monel Metal	4-6	60-90

the blade just clears the top of the stock. Hold a steel rule against the right side of the saw blade, and move the bar of stock until the length from the blade is correct.

4. Tighten the vise securely.

5. Turn on the power. Push the frame handle down and pull on the clutch handle to start the saw frame moving (Fig. 8-8).

6. After the cutting is started, use a cutting fluid if one is available.

7. When the cut is complete, the machine stops automatically.

8. Most models have a stop rod that can be set when cutting several pieces to the same length.

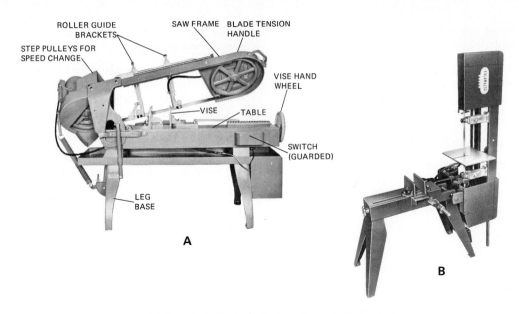

ROLLER GUIDE
BRACKETS

STEP PULLEYS FOR
SPEED CHANGE

SAW FRAME   BLADE TENSION
HANDLE

VISE HAND
WHEEL

VISE   TABLE

SWITCH
(GUARDED)

LEG
BASE

A

B

Fig. 8-9. (A) The horizontal bandsaw with the parts named. (B) Most bandsaws can also be used in a vertical position.

HORIZONTAL BAND SAW

The horizontal band saw is a small metal-cutting band saw that can be used with the blade in a horizontal or vertical position (Fig. 8–9).

Parts. The saw consists of a *base* with a *work-table and vise.* The *saw frame* is hinged at one end. On the frame are two wheels over which the continuous blade operates. Most of the blade is covered. Machine size is determined by the diameter of the wheels.

Cutoff Band Saw. Blades are purchased for each particular size of machine. These blades may have from 6 to 24 teeth per inch with raker set. They may vary in width from $\frac{1}{16}$ to 1 in.

Installing a Blade. Loosen the hand screw and slip off the old blade. Fold the blade. Install the new blade with the teeth pointing in the direction of blade rotation. Tighten the blade until it is taut. The amount of tension needed will vary with the blade width.

MAKING SQUARE CUTS

1. Check the vise jaws to make sure they are at right angles to the saw blade.

2. Mark the correct length on a piece of stock. If duplicate parts are to be cut, the stop gage can be set so that only the first piece needs to be marked (Fig. 8–10).

3. Place the stock in the vice and clamp it securely.

Fig. 8-10. Note that a stop gage is used to control the length of cut.

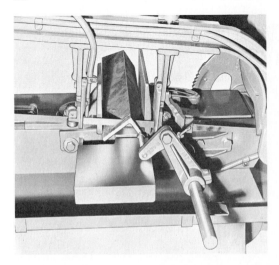

4. Adjust the blade guides so that they are only slightly wider than the stock that is to be cut.

5. Lower the saw frame until the blade just clears the work and check to make sure that the cut is at the desired point. Make sure that the work is so clamped that the cut will be made in the waste stock.

6. Turn on the power. Hold the handle of the saw frame with your right hand. In some machines, you must release a rachet lever with your left. This rachet lever allows the frame to be lowered. On other machines, a hydraulic unit controls the lowering of the saw frame.

7. Lower the blade slowly onto the stock to start the cutting. Never drop the frame quickly. On some machines, there is a weight on the frame that can be used to vary the pressure.

8. If required, use a cutting fluid.

9. The machine will turn off automatically when the cut is complete.

10. For angle cuts, adjust the vise jaws to the required angle.

UNIT 9. Discussion Topics and Problems

1. Why are machine tools so important?

2. What is meant by mass production?

3. What is a machine tool?

4. What are the five basic arts of metal cutting?

5. How does drilling differ from boring?

6. Explain the difference between shaping and planing.

7. Describe three kinds of chips in metal cutting.

8. What is the purpose of a cutting fluid?

9. Name the five simple machines.

10. Name five common types of gears.

11. What is a taper?

12. Name several standard tapers, and tell where each is likely to be used.

13. What is meant by a ball bearing?

14. Why must machines be lubricated?

15. What is meant by a tolerance?

16. Why is safety so important in a machine shop?

17. Why is mathematics so important in a machine shop?

18. How do you change a common fraction to a decimal?

19. What is the decimal equivalent of $\frac{3}{16}$ in.? $\frac{5}{8}$ in.? $\frac{13}{64}$ in.?

20. If the diameter of a circle is $3\frac{3}{16}$ in., what is the radius?

21. What is meant by a cold-finished steel?

22. Name three ways of identifying steels.

23. Explain an assembly drawing and a detail drawing.

24. How is the size of an object shown on a drawing?

25. What is meant by the scale size of a drawing?

26. When planning a project, what three things are necessary before you start to work?

27. Name two kinds of power saws for cutting stock to length.

SECTION 2

MEASURING AND GAGING

UNIT 10. Principles of Measurement

Measurement was one of the first activities engaged in by man. Cave dwellers had to make crude measurements to fashion tools and weapons. Beginning about 6000 B.C., man began to base measurements on the human body (Fig. 10-1). These standards were convenient and uniform enough to serve as a basis for measurement in early times.

RECENT HISTORY OF MEASUREMENT

After the Magna Charta was signed in the thirteenth century, King Edward I of England took a tremendous step forward in standardizing measurement. He ordered a permanent measuring stick made of iron to serve as a master yardstick for the entire kingdom. This yardstick, called the *iron ulna,* was surprisingly close to the length of our present-day yard. Because he realized that constancy and permanence were the key to standards, King Edward had the iron ulna made of the strongest and toughest material of the day. He also decreed that the foot

measure would be one-third the length of the yard and that the inch would be a thirty-sixth. This was the beginning of the English system of measurement still in use in the United States.

In 1793, when Napoleon was just beginning his rise to power, the French government adopted an entirely new standard of measurement called the *metric system.* This system was based on a unit called the *meter* (m). (For units of length, the official international spelling is *metre;* for units of volume, it is *litre.* In this text, however, we will use the spellings preferred in the United States, *meter* and *liter.*) The meter was supposed to be one ten-millionth part of the distance from the North Pole to the Equator when measured on a straight line running along the surface of the earth through Paris. The meter was just a little longer (39.37 in.) than the English yardstick.

All linear systems of measurements were based upon the meter. All units were multiples of ten. For example, there were 10 decimeters (dm) in a meter, 100 centimeters (cm) in a meter, and 1,000 millimeters (mm) in a meter. In the opposite direction, 10 meters were equivalent to 1 dekameter (dam), 100 meters to 1 hectometer (hm), and 1,000 meters to 1 kilometer (km).

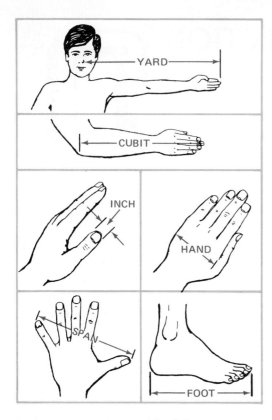

Fig. 10-1. Ancient people measured literally by "rule of thumb."

Table 10-1. SI base units.

Quantity	Unit	Symbol
Length	meter	m
Mass	kilogram	kg
Time	second	s
Electric current	ampere	A
Temperature	kelvin	K
Luminous intensity	candela	cd
Amount of substance	mole	mol

Both basic systems of measurement have survived to the present day, the English system in which length is measured in inches, feet, and yards, and the metric system in which length is measured in millimeters, centimeters, meters, and kilometers. Both systems make provision for measuring weight and capacity. In the customary system (English system), there are over 80 units of weights and measures from pounds to tons and inches to miles. The international system of units (SI Metric) has seven basic units (see Table 10-1). All other measurements are derived from these basic units. For example, the *liter* (l) is 1 cubic decimeter (dm^3). For all practical purposes, you will need to know only three common units; the meter for length, the liter for volume, and the kilogram (kg) for mass (weight). It is easy to remember these three measurements since the meter is somewhat longer than a yard, the liter is a little more than a quart (qt),

and the kilogram is somewhat more than twice the pound (lb). To convert the customary measurements into metric, the following are commonly used.

1. 1 in. equals 25.4 mm.

2. 1 qt equals 0.94 l.

3. 1 lb equals 0.453 kg.

All machine drawings are shown in millimeters. The millimeter is, of course, one-thousandth of a meter.

From the earliest days of our history as a nation, proposals have been made that our measurement system be changed to the metric system. In 1866, the use of the metric system was made legal in the United States, but not mandatory. With the advent of the space age, there has been great awareness on the part of industry and the general public as to the importance of measurement in science and technology. This has resulted in an increased pressure to change our system of measurement from the customary system to the metric system.

The best feature of the metric system is that all units are divided into ten parts (a decimeter is one-tenth of a meter, a centimeter is one-tenth of a decimeter, and a kilometer equals one thousand meters). Thus, it is a simple matter to compute smaller and larger units. This also applies when working with metric units of weight and capacity. Also, the metric system is consistent; that is, units of various quantities are so chosen that they work together with a minimum of mathematical juggling.

The United States is now the only major nation still using the customary system of measurement. If we are to compete successfully in international trade, we must convert to the metric system (Fig. 10-2). The reason for this is obvious. Our standard sizes do not even exist in the metric system. Take, for example, a $\frac{1}{2}$-in. bolt. It's metric system equivalent would measure 12.7 mm. A country or company using the metric system would not want a $\frac{1}{2}$-in. bolt. Instead, they would use a bolt that is 10 or 12 mm in diameter.

IMPORTANCE OF MEASUREMENT

Measurements involved in such manufactured items as automobiles and refrigerators are less exciting than for space rockets and missiles. However, our entire way of life and our economy are based on mass markets and mass production. In turn, mass production is based on specialization of manufacture and interchangeable parts. A piston made in Pennsylvania or a valve manufactured in California must, when assembled in Michigan, fit together and function in an engine. The typical manufacturer does not start with a pile of raw material at one end of the factory and end up with an automobile or a refrigerator at the other. Instead, he buys parts from manufacturers throughout the United States. These parts will fit into his final product only if they are produced to the same measurement standards as his own.

AMERICAN HISTORY OF PRECISION MEASUREMENT

Whereas Eli Whitney is thought of as the inventor of the cotton gin, he is really more important as the father of mass production. In the early 1800s, there were no national measurement systems, no national standards, and no gages or measuring techniques. Whitney produced the first standards for interchangeable parts by using crude measuring tools and by employing jigs, fixtures, and templates. The interchangeable part concept was quickly accepted in the United States. After Whitney's death in 1825, the use of

Fig. 10-2. Metric and English equivalent measures.

METRIC MEASURES

THE METRIC UNIT OF LENGTH IS THE METER = 39.37 IN.
THE METRIC UNIT OF WEIGHT IS THE GRAM = 15.432 GRAINS
THE FOLLOWING PREFIXES ARE USED FOR SUBDIVISION AND MULTIPLES:

MILLI = $\frac{1}{1,000}$ CENTI = $\frac{1}{100}$ DECI = $\frac{1}{10}$ DECA = 10   HECTO = 100   KILO = 1,000

MYRIA = 10,000

METRIC AND ENGLISH EQUIVALENT MEASURES

MEASURES OF LENGTH

1 METER	= 39.37 IN. OR 3.28083 FEET, OR 1.09361 YARDS
0.3048 METER	= 1 FOOT
1 CENTIMETER	= 0.3937 IN.
2.54 CENTIMETERS	= 1 IN.
1 MILLIMETER	= 0.03937 IN. OR NEARLY 1/25 IN.
25.4 MILLIMETERS	= 1 IN.
1 KILOMETER	= 1,093.61 YARDS, OR 0.62137 MILE

MEASURES OF WEIGHT

28.35 GRAMS	= 1 OUNCE AVOIRDUPOIS
1 KILOGRAM	= 2.2046 POUNDS
0.4536 KILOGRAM	= 1 POUND
1 METRIC TON	= 1.102 TONS (SHORT)
1,000 KILOGRAMS	= 2,204.6 POUNDS

MEASURES OF CAPACITY

1 LITER (1 CUBIC DECIMETER) =	61.023 CUBIC IN.
	0.03531 CUBIC FOOT
	0.2642 GALLON (AMERICAN)
	2.202 POUNDS OF WATER AT 62°F
28.317 LITERS	= 1 CUBIC FOOT
4.543 LITERS	= 1 GALLON (IMPERIAL)
3.785 LITERS	= 1 GALLON (AMERICAN)

this technique spread from the making of muskets to the making of clocks, sewing machines, and agricultural equipment. Today, it is the backbone of our technological economy.

Interchangeable parts, specialization of manufacture, a high-quality national measurement system, and mass marketing of products form the basis of our present economy. All these standards are based on the English system. The United States is faced with a decision that must soon be reconciled. While the rest of the world uses the metric system, the United States continues to follow the customary (English) system of measurement. It has been estimated that more than 20 billion measurements are made in this country every day. It is also estimated that the United States loses $60 billion annually in world trade because it is not on the metric system. In order to keep up with the rest of the world, this country must change from the English to the metric system of measurement.

It is wise for the beginning machinist to be acquainted with both English and metric systems of measurement. He should be able to convert from one system to the other (Fig. 10-3). He should also be able to read drawings in both systems (Fig. 10-4). He should learn to visualize how the two systems compare (Fig. 10-5).

DUAL DIMENSIONING

Since the inch and millimeter are both commonly used, a system of dual dimensioning has been developed which combines both dimensions on one drawing. With this system, the dimensions in decimal inches and in millimeters are shown. This eliminates the need to convert from one system to another. Therefore the

Fig. 10-3. (A) This metric conversion unit provides readings in inches and millimeters. The unit is accurate to ±0.001 in. and ±0.02 mm. (B) You can see here how this combination measuring unit can be used on machine tools. (C) The conversion unit installed on a vertical milling machine.

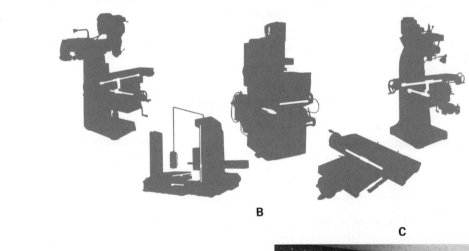

B

C

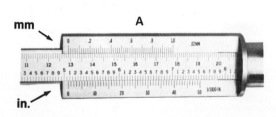

mm

A

in.

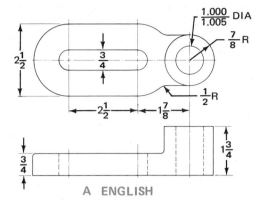

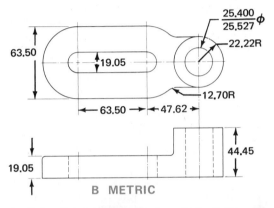

Fig. 10-4. (A) A simple machine drawing using the English system of measurement. (B) The same drawing using the metric system.

drawing can be used in any country in the world.

The standard units for dual dimensioning are the decimal inch and the millimeter (0.03937 in.). If the inch system is used as the basic dimensional procedure, then the millimeter equivalent should be placed in parentheses directly below or to the right of the dimension (Fig. 10-6A). In placing metric dimensions on a drawing, the following should be observed.

1. Millimeter values less than 1.0 should be shown as follows: 0.13.

2. Zeros should be added to the right of the decimal point in millimeter values as follows: 32.0.

3. When limit dimensions are used, show the minimum and maximum dimensions with the same number of digits following the decimal point. If necessary, add zeros for uniformity as follows:

$$\frac{25.00}{24.46}$$

4. When millimeter dimensions contain a unilateral tolerance, show both the plus and minus even though one may be zero.

5. When bilateral tolerance is used in which the tolerances are unequal, show the maximum and minimum tolerance as follows:

$$32.00^{+0.25}_{-0.10}$$

Fig. 10-5. (A) A comparison of the foot and yard with the meter, millimeter, centimeter, and decimeter. (B) A graphic picture of the comparison of measures of capacity and weight in the English and metric systems.

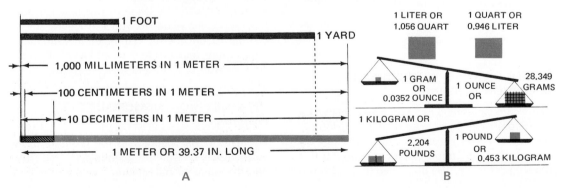

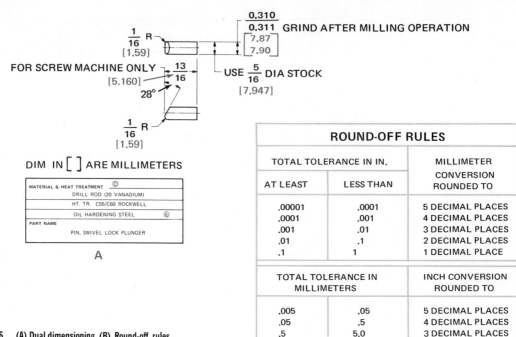

ROUND-OFF RULES

TOTAL TOLERANCE IN IN.		MILLIMETER CONVERSION ROUNDED TO
AT LEAST	LESS THAN	
.00001	.0001	5 DECIMAL PLACES
.0001	.001	4 DECIMAL PLACES
.001	.01	3 DECIMAL PLACES
.01	.1	2 DECIMAL PLACES
.1	1	1 DECIMAL PLACE

TOTAL TOLERANCE IN MILLIMETERS		INCH CONVERSION ROUNDED TO
.005	.05	5 DECIMAL PLACES
.05	.5	4 DECIMAL PLACES
.5	5.0	3 DECIMAL PLACES
5.0 AND OVER		2 DECIMAL PLACES

B

Fig. 10-6. (A) Dual dimensioning. (B) Round-off rules.

6. On existing drawings with dimensions in fractions, dual dimensions should be shown by adding the millimeter conversion adjacent to the fractional inch dimension as follows: $2\frac{7}{16} \pm \frac{1}{64}$ $\begin{matrix}(62.30)\\(61.52)\end{matrix}$

7. The symbol ∅ and the abbreviation DIA are the same. They indicate that a feature or tolerance is diametral. Either may be used in a dual-dimensioned drawing.

8. Symbolized tolerance notes for form and positional control should be dual-dimensioned as follows—⊕A ∅ .002 (0.051).

9. Roundoff rules for converting from inches to millimeters are shown in Fig. 10-6B.

MASTER DRAWING WITH SEPARATE DIMENSION DRAWINGS

Many companies who need both customary and metric drawings do not use dual dimensioning. Instead, a master drawing is made without dimensions. Then, photographic copies of this drawing are made. The draftsman then adds the metric dimensions to one or more drawings and the customary dimensions to the others. In this way, the same master drawing can be used for the part regardless of where it is to be produced. In some cases, although the drawing may be dimensioned in metric units, it may have notes and other information in Japanese. In other cases, the same metric drawing may have notes and other information in German.

COST OF CONVERTING TO THE METRIC SYSTEM

Figure 10-7 indicates the number of measuring instruments used by three of our major industries and their value. As you can clearly see, a change to the metric system of measurement will require reinvestment in all types of precision measuring tools and machine tools.

HOW PRECISION MEASUREMENT IS DONE

For many years, accuracy to the thousandth of an inch was considered adequate for industry, and the standard micrometer was considered a

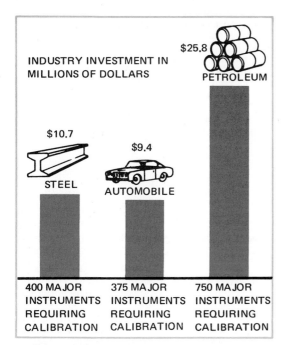

INDUSTRY INVESTMENT IN
MILLIONS OF DOLLARS

$25.8
PETROLEUM

$10.7
STEEL

$9.4
AUTOMOBILE

400 MAJOR INSTRUMENTS REQUIRING CALIBRATION	375 MAJOR INSTRUMENTS REQUIRING CALIBRATION	750 MAJOR INSTRUMENTS REQUIRING CALIBRATION

Fig. 10-7. Note the number of major measuring instruments needed by three of our largest industries. Converting to the metric system will be expensive.

very accurate measuring instrument. Toward the end of the nineteenth century, Carl Johansson, a young man working in a Swedish rifle factory, recognized the need for more accurate standards. He developed a very accurate set of steel gage blocks which were called *jo blocks*. These blocks were carefully and painstakingly made so that each of them was accurate to within a few millionths of an inch. Jo blocks are used with a flat disk of glass called an *optical flat*. In actual measuring practice, the optical flat is laid across both the Johansson gage blocks and the production gage being checked. When a special filtered light is allowed to pass through the optical gage and reflect back from the upper surface of the Johansson gage blocks, alternate bands of light and dark are seen. This is an indication that the jo blocks and the production gage are not the same size. A trained technician can analyze these bands and tell within a few millionths of an inch how much higher one is from the other. This process of measurement is known as *interferometry*. By using a ray of light, man can measure distances much too small to be seen even with the most powerful microscope.

Current manufactured parts are measured by a variety of techniques including the use of air and electronic gages. When a part is measured by air, for example, it is put into a fixture. Air is then blown through an opening in this fixture. The amount of air used registers on a gage and indicates the exact size of the part being measured. Electronic gages can be used to measure within ten-millionths of an inch. Today it is even possible to measure to within a billionth of an inch. This is done with the aid of a *spectroscope,* which is an optical instrument able to identify elements in a substance (Fig. 10-8).

Fig. 10-8. This gives you a picture of the history of accuracy.

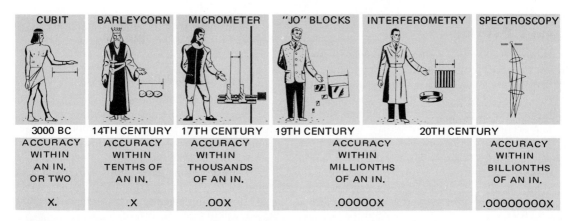

CUBIT	BARLEYCORN	MICROMETER	"JO" BLOCKS	INTERFEROMETRY	SPECTROSCOPY
3000 BC	14TH CENTURY	17TH CENTURY	19TH CENTURY	20TH CENTURY	
ACCURACY WITHIN AN IN. OR TWO	ACCURACY WITHIN TENTHS OF AN IN.	ACCURACY WITHIN THOUSANDS OF AN IN.	ACCURACY WITHIN MILLIONTHS OF AN IN.		ACCURACY WITHIN BILLIONTHS OF AN IN.
X.	.X	.00X	.00000X		.00000000X

THE INTERNATIONAL INCH AND METER

The international inch and meter are based on the wavelength of monochromatic light from krypton 86 gas. The length of a single wave is 0.0000238 in., giving us an absolute standard which never changes. Combine 42,016.807 of these light waves and you have the International Inch (Fig. 10-9).

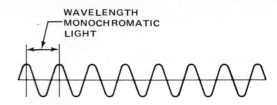

Fig. 10-9. A meter is defined as 1,650,763.73 wavelengths in vacuum of the orange-red line of the spectrum of krypton 86 gas.

UNIT 11. Basic Measuring Tools

Laying out a job is a common example of benchwork. Before you can lay out a job correctly, it is necessary to know how to measure accurately. This means that you must learn to read a steel rule and be able to use all measuring tools accurately and carefully.

In measuring any work, the degree of accuracy required definitely indicates the tool which should be used. A rule would not be suitable for measurements in thousandths or ten-thousandths of an inch, and an expensive and highly accurate electronic gage would be misused if used for measurements requiring a micrometer.

A tool must have greater inherent accuracy and be graduated finer than the accuracy required in the measurement. Table 11-1 lists a number of measuring tools, their finest readings, and the degree of accuracy inherent in each.

Table 11-1. Accuracy of measuring tools.

Dimensions in inches	Inherent Accuracy of Tool	Finest Tool Reading	Minimum Measuring Tolerance
For tolerances of 0.001 or greater Vernier Tools	0.0003	0.001	0.001
For tolerances of 0.0005 to 0.002 Micrometers (1")	0.0001	0.0001	0.0004
For tolerances of 0.0003 to 0.0005 Bench Micrometer Dial Snap Gages	0.0001 0.0001	0.0001 0.0001	0.0003 0.0003
Tolerances of .000001 to 0.0001 Electronic Comparator Electronic Gage Head	0.000001 0.000001	0.000001 0.000001	0.000001 0.000001

RULES AND THEIR USES

There are many different kinds of rules (scales) with various combinations of fractional and decimal graduations. Each is especially adapted to certain classes of work. By choosing the proper rule, it is easier for the mechanic to obtain accurate measurements.

Learning to measure accurately with a steel rule is one of the first steps toward becoming a skilled worker. Once you study and understand the different types of steel rules, how they are graduated or read, and how to use them correctly, you will be able to make measurements on any job quickly and easily.

TYPES OF STEEL RULES

1. The *plain or tempered steel rule,* made in 6-, 9-, and 12-in. lengths, is perhaps the most commonly used (Fig. 11-1). All steel rules have lines which divide each inch into either fractional or decimal parts. The lines are called *graduations.* Most steel rules are marked or graduated on all four edges. The first edge may be divided into eighths of an inch; that is, the

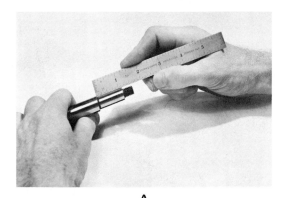

A

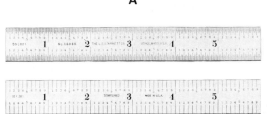

B

C

Fig. 11-1. (A) A 6-in. steel rule is used here to measure the length of a part of a shaft. The edge divided into sixteenths is used. Can you read the measurement? (B) A 6-in. steel rule with one side divided into 10 divisions per inch (0.100) and the other side divided into 50 divisions per inch (0.020). (C) Metric rules are available with metric or metric and English graduations.

Table 11-2. Brown and Sharp graduations for steel rules.

Graduation	No. 4	No. 6	No. 8	No. 9	No. 10	No. 11	No. 12
1st edge	8ths	10ths	32nds	16ths	32nds	64ths	50ths
2nd edge	16ths	50ths	64ths	32nds	64ths	100ths	100ths
3rd edge	32nds		10ths	64ths			
4th edge	64ths		100ths				

Fig. 11-2. Flexible steel rule.

distance between each of the graduated lines is exactly $\frac{1}{8}$ in. The second edge may be divided into sixteenths ($\frac{1}{16}$) of an inch, the third edge into thirty-seconds ($\frac{1}{32}$) of an inch, and the fourth edge into sixty-fourths ($\frac{1}{64}$) of an inch. The plain steel rule is generally graduated in this manner. Table 11-2 lists other graduations that are available.

2. The *flexible steel rule* is thinner and narrower than the plain rule. Because they are flexible, flexible steel rules can be curved to fit around a piece of work. They can also fit into a small space that would be difficult to measure with the thicker and wider plain steel rule (Fig. 11-2).

3. The *hook rule* has a single or double hook on one end which makes it convenient for measuring both inside and outside work. The hook serves as a reference point from which the measurement is taken. The hook makes it possible to locate the end of the rule to obtain an accurate measurement, even when you cannot see if the end is even with an inner surface. It acts as sort of feeler to tell you when contact has been made. It is also a good steel rule for setting an inside caliper (Fig. 11-3). Hook rules are made in both wide and narrow types. The narrow type is very useful for measuring through small-diameter holes.

4. The *rule depth gage* consists of a steel head or base through which fits a narrow steel rule. This rule is generally graduated in sixty-fourths of an inch. A nut provides a means of clamping the rule in place after the measurement has been made. Measurements are quickly and easily made. Simply loosen the nut and push the rule through the head to the required distance or depth, while holding the base against a surface of the work (Fig. 11-4).

5. The *caliper rule,* sometimes called a *pocket slide caliper,* is a handy measuring rule for both inside and outside measurements. It is generally made in 3-, 5-, and 6-in. sizes. Two lines on the fixed part are marked *in* and *out.* An inside measurement must be read from the *in* line. A measurement made on the outside would be read from the *out* line (Fig. 11-5).

6. *Keyseat rules* are necessary for laying off measurements or drawing lines parallel to the axis of cylindrical work such as measuring

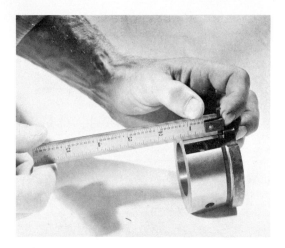

Fig. 11-3. Using a thirty-second ($\frac{1}{32}$ in.) hook rule to measure the distance from the groove to the end of the collar.

Fig. 11-4. Using a rule depth gage to measure the depth of a cylinder hole.

lengths for splining keyways on shafting. By means of keyseat clamps, any steel rule can be quickly converted into a useful keyseat rule (Fig. 11-6).

7. The *circumference rule* is a folding steel rule graduated in the normal way and also in

Fig. 11-5. A slide caliper.

Fig. 11-6. Keyseat rule.

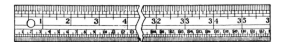

Fig. 11-7. Circumference rule.

Fig. 11-8. Shrink rule.

circumference inches. Both the diameter and the circumference of cylindrical work can be read directly from the same rule (Fig. 11-7).

8. *Shrink rules* are used for laying out casting patterns and core boxes. The contractions of various metals vary (cast iron, $\frac{1}{8}$ in. to each foot; brass, $\frac{3}{16}$ in. to each foot; and tin alloys, $\frac{1}{12}$ in. to the foot); hence, shrink rules are made oversize to allow for these contractions. The extra length is distributed uniformly throughout the rule. Double shrink rules are used when a working pattern is cast from a master pattern as in production molding and two shrinks must be provided for (Fig. 11-8).

HOW TO READ A STEEL RULE

Practice will make it possible for you to read a steel rule accurately and quickly. When you understand thoroughly the value of the lines or graduations and can add and subtract fractions without a pencil, you will be skilled at measuring with a steel rule.

Study the chart in Fig. 11–9 carefully. It illustrates the different fractional parts of the inch from $\frac{1}{2}$ to $\frac{1}{64}$ in. Note that the larger fractions, such as $\frac{1}{2}$ in., are indicated by long lines or graduations on the rule. The smaller fractional parts, such as $\frac{1}{32}$ and $\frac{1}{64}$ in., are shown by shorter lines or graduations. This helps in reading the rule and taking measurements quickly.

A good way to learn to read a steel rule is to draw a straight line about 6 in. long on a sheet of paper. Let this line represent 1 in. By eye, divide the line in half, and label "$\frac{1}{2}$ in." Proceed to divide the two half-inch spaces into halves and label these $\frac{1}{4}$ and $\frac{3}{4}$ in. Make these lines a

Fig. 11-9. This chart should help you read a rule. Notice that $\frac{8}{64}$ in. at line **F** is the same as $\frac{4}{32}$ in. at line **E**. This is the same as $\frac{2}{16}$ in. at line **D**, which is $\frac{1}{8}$ in. at line **C**.

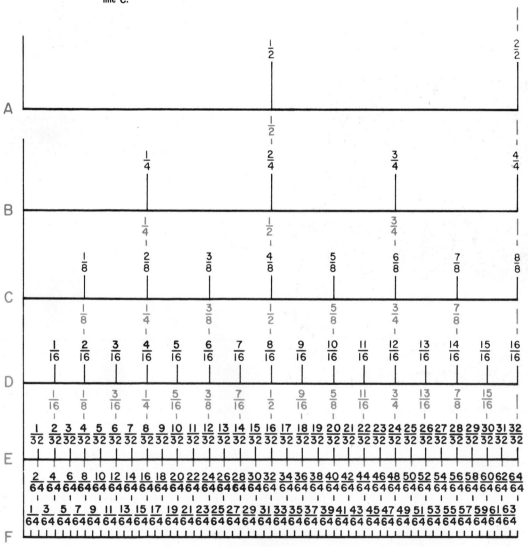

bit shorter than the $\frac{1}{2}$-in. line. Continue dividing the spaces into halves and labeling each set of lines until you complete the 64th line. If you make each set of lines a little shorter, your completed sketch will resemble the graduations on a steel rule. After working out this method, you will know exactly where to look on a rule to find any of the fractional parts of an inch. You will also know there are always two 64ths in $\frac{1}{32}$; two 32ds in $\frac{1}{16}$; two 16ths in $\frac{1}{8}$; two 8ths in $\frac{1}{4}$; two 4ths in $\frac{1}{2}$; and two halves in 1 in.

A machinist never says $\frac{2}{16}$ or $\frac{4}{8}$, but always reduces the fraction to its lowest terms. He knows that $\frac{2}{16}$ equals $\frac{1}{8}$, and that $\frac{4}{8}$ equals $\frac{1}{2}$, and so on. When measuring to 64ths or 32ds, he may use such terms as "$\frac{1}{64}$ over $\frac{3}{4}$" or "$\frac{1}{32}$ under $\frac{7}{8}$," rather than $\frac{49}{64}$ or $\frac{27}{32}$.

You now know that $\frac{1}{64}$ is the smallest graduation on a fractional rule. The decimal equivalent of $\frac{1}{64}$ is approximately 0.016 in. (read sixteen-thousandths). When measuring to 64ths, a skilled machinist can judge one-half or even one-fourth of this amount. Therefore, it is quite possible with practice to read a rule as close as 0.003 to 0.005 of an inch. Keep this in mind as you use a steel rule, and soon you will be able to do the same.

CARE OF STEEL RULES

A good steel rule is precision made and will serve for many years if properly used and cared for. Here are a few suggestions:

1. Always select the right type and length of rule for the job.

2. Keep the rule away from moving work or cutting tools.

3. Do not lay or drop tools or work parts on the steel rule.

4. Use your rule for measuring or laying out only. To use it as a screwdriver, for example, is a mark of carelessness.

5. You cannot measure accurately with a rule that is nicked or damaged.

6. Learn to take measurements from the 1-in. line or other major graduations rather than from the end.

7. Occasionally wipe off steel rules with an oily rag to prevent rust and stains.

8. Keep the 6-in. rule in your apron pocket when not in use.

9. Steel rules should never be thrown together in a drawer.

10. Occasionally clean your rule with fine steel wool. It will be easier to read.

SQUARES

Several types of squares are used by machinists and toolmakers. Squares are used to test the accuracy of two surfaces that must be square or at right angles to each other. They are also used for laying out lines that must be square or parallel to each other. Workpieces that must be machined square in a shaper or milling machine can be set up quickly and accurately by the use of a square.

The commonly used squares are as follows:

1. The *combination set* consists of three separate tools (square head, bevel protractor, center head) and a steel rule that may be used in each (Fig. 11–10A). The square head and rule is called a *combination square*. The combination set is useful for general work which does not require great accuracy (Fig. 11–10B).

The combination square head has both a 45-degree angle face and a 90-degree angle face. Because a 45-degree angle is so commonly used, this square is most useful. The combination square also contains a spirit level that can be used to check the levelness of a workpiece. It is not a precision level, however, and should not be used where extreme precision is required (Fig. 11–11).

For laying out dimensions or lines to fractional parts of the inch, the combination square is the best tool to use. The rule can be set a given distance from the head, and lines scribed at the end of the rule. The head is always held firmly against the surface from which the measurement is taken. Figure 11–12 shows several other applications.

The center head (sometimes called a *center square*) is a useful tool for finding the center on the end of a round shaft (Fig. 11–13).

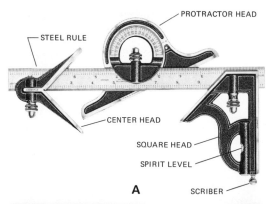

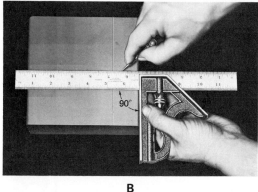

PROTRACTOR HEAD

STEEL RULE

CENTER HEAD

SQUARE HEAD

SPIRIT LEVEL

SCRIBER

90°

A

B

Fig. 11-10. (A) Parts of a combination set. (B) A combination square is the only square having both a 45 and a 90° face.

Fig. 11-11. Using the square to measure a part on a die.

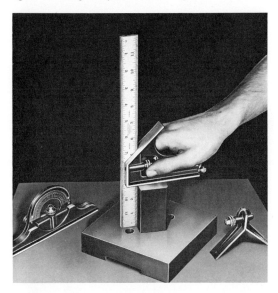

2. The *double square* consists of a parallel square head and a steel rule that can be moved through a slot in the square head. It is a good general-purpose square for work that does not require great precision. This square is provided with additional blades or rules made at certain standard angles for checking angular work, such as the angle of a drill point (Fig. 11-14).

3. A *try square* has a parallel square head and a fixed blade without rule graduations. It is a small square having a blade 4 to 6 in. long. Although it is very useful for general work, it is not considered a precision square (Fig. 11-15).

4. A *hardened steel square* is the most accurate square made. A square that has movable parts is quite satisfactory for general work. However, for precision work, that is, work that must be extremely accurate, the hardened steel

Fig. 11-12. Other uses of the combination set.

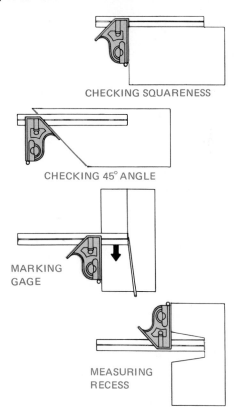

CHECKING SQUARENESS

CHECKING 45° ANGLE

MARKING GAGE

MEASURING RECESS

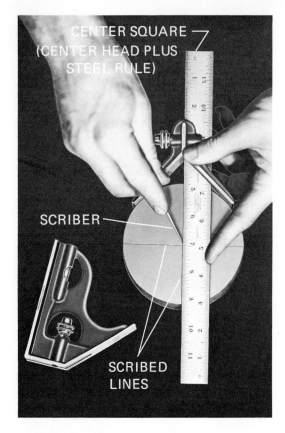

CENTER SQUARE
(CENTER HEAD PLUS
STEEL RULE)

SCRIBER

SCRIBED
LINES

Fig. 11-13. Finding the center of a round piece with the center square.

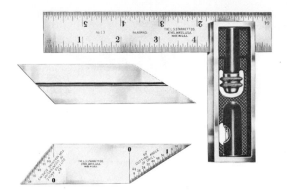

Fig. 11-14. A double square.

Fig. 11-15. A try square.

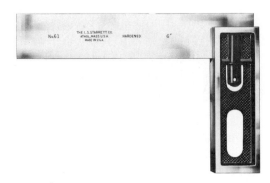

square is used. It is an expensive tool compared with other types of squares. It should never be used on rough work, or for work where other squares are satisfactory. Hardened steel squares must be handled very carefully. To drop one would destroy its accuracy. These squares are used by tool- and diemakers and inspectors for setting up and checking precision work on surface plates and machine tools (Fig. 11-16).

PROTRACTOR

One definition of an angle is that an *angle* is the space between two straight lines meeting at a common point. Another definition is that an *angle* is the difference in direction between two lines that either meet or would meet if sufficiently prolonged. In Fig. 11-17 the difference in direction between the lines *AO* and *BO* is the angle *AOB*. *AO* and *BO* are the sides, and

O is the vertex of the angle. In order to measure angles, the circumference of a circle is divided into 360 parts; each of these parts is called a *degree* (°). A degree is divided into 60 parts

Fig. 11-16. A precision hardened steel square.

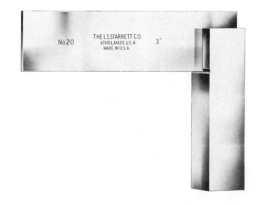

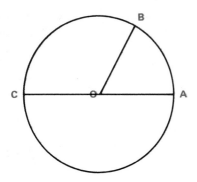

Fig. 11-17. Angle *BOA* is acute (less than 90°) and angle *BOC* is obtuse (more than 90°).

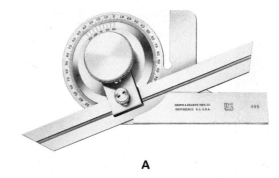

A

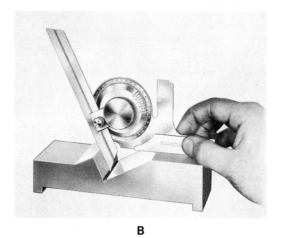

B

Fig. 11-19. (A) A universal bevel protractor. (B) Use of a universal bevel protractor to check an angle.

Fig. 11-18. A plain steel protractor.

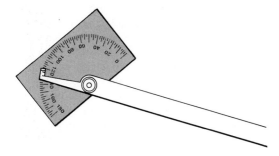

called *minutes* ('), and a minute is divided into 60 parts called *seconds* ("). Thus, when a circle is drawn about the vertex *O* (Fig. 11-17) the angle *AOB* will equal the arc *AB*.

A *protractor* is an instrument or tool used to lay out or measure angles. Several types are used by machinists and toolmakers. The best type to use depends upon the job and the accuracy required.

1. The *plain steel protractor* is useful for laying out and checking angles that do not have to be extremely accurate. It is also used to check cutting edge angles when grinding a twist drill. The protractor head has a scale graduated in whole degrees for a distance of 180° (half a circle). The blade can be set and tightened by a nut to hold it in place. This protractor is made of thin, flat metal, which makes it handy to use (Fig. 11-18).

2. A *bevel protractor* consists of a protractor head and a steel rule. The protractor head may be part of a combination set. The rule is adjustable and is held at any point by a thumb nut. The rule passes through the revolving turret or inner part of the protractor head. The turret is graduated from 0 to 180° (both left and right of the zero mark). Some bevel protractors have small spirit levels attached to their heads. Bevel protractors are graduated in whole degrees only. They are not intended for angular measurements that must be measured in degrees and minutes.

3. A *precision universal bevel protractor* with a vernier, often called a *vernier protractor,* is an instrument used to lay out, check, or measure an angle to an accuracy of 5 minutes ($\frac{1}{12}$ of a degree).

This protractor consists of a stock or base and a graduated dial in one piece. Inside the

Fig. 11-20. The zero line on the vernier is exactly at 17°. Notice that each of the No. 60 lines coincides with the lines above, making the reading an even number of degrees.

Fig. 11-21. The reading is 12 degrees 50 minutes.

graduated dial is a swivel plate having a vernier plate attached. The swivel plate is slotted to hold a 6- or a 12-in. blade. The heads can be rotated with the swivel plate to any angle desired. It can also be adjusted to any convenient length (Fig. 11-19).

It is important to know and understand the two separate and different scales on this instrument:

a. The protractor dial or outer scale is graduated in whole degrees, both to the left and to the right from 0 to 90°. Then the numbers run from 90 to 0° again, in such a manner that the entire circle is graduated. Every tenth line is numbered for quick and easy reading.

b. The vernier scale is a short fixed scale attached to the swivel. It has 12 lines or graduations, both to the right and to the left of the zero line. These lines represent minutes (60 minutes equals 1°). Therefore, each of the 12 lines represents 5 minutes ($\frac{1}{12}$ of $60 = 5$). Every third line from zero on the vernier plate is numbered 15, 30, 45, and 60 for easier reading.

Since both the protractor dial and vernier scales have graduations in opposite directions from the zero line, any size angle can be measured.

HOW TO READ A VERNIER PROTRACTOR

When the zero line on the vernier scale coincides or lines up exactly with a graduation on the protractor dial, the reading is always in exact or whole degrees, as shown in Fig. 11-20, which reads 17°. To check a reading that is an exact number of whole degrees, you will note that the number 60 graduated lines at each end of the vernier scale also line up or coincide with a line above on the protractor scale.

When the zero line on the vernier scale does not line up exactly with a line on the protractor scale, it means the reading must be in degrees and minutes. To find the angle, read directly on the protractor dial the whole number of degrees between zero on the protractor dial and zero on the vernier scale. Then count in the *same direction* (this is important) the number of divisions or graduations from zero on the vernier scale to the first line on the vernier scale that lines up or coincides with a line on the protractor dial. To get the number of minutes, multiply each of the divisions on the vernier scale by 5. For example, in Fig. 11-21 the reading is 12°50′ because the tenth line on the vernier scale lines up exactly with a line above on the protractor dial, and the zero line of the vernier scale is between 12 and 13° on the protractor dial.

UNIT 12. Using Calipers

A *caliper* is a tool used to measure a workpiece by contact. A great deal of skill is necessary to use it correctly. When using a caliper, hold it lightly in your finger tips so you can feel the lightest contact with the workpiece. With practice and experience you can make very accurate measurements.

A caliper is particularly useful for measuring distances between or over surfaces or for comparing dimensions with standards such as graduated rules. Because a caliper is often used for checking work in a lathe, a word of caution is in order. Calipers should never be used while the work is turning. There is always the danger of having the tool torn out of the hand with possible injury to the user. At best, the readings are inaccurate and misleading because the friction of the moving surface is sufficient to spring the legs or to draw the contact point away from the true diameter.

TYPES OF CALIPERS

The common types are the outside and inside calipers.

1. The *outside caliper* has two curved (bow) legs pointing toward each other. It is used for measuring workpieces such as the outside diameter or a cylinder. If the legs are jointed together at the top with a nut, it is called a *firm-joint caliper*. The legs must be opened and closed by hand pressure. Fine adjustments can be made by tapping one leg lightly on a bench top or the toolholder in a lathe. A *spring-joint caliper* has a heavy spring at the top of the legs which keeps spring tension on the legs. The opening and closing of the legs is controlled by a knurled nut (Fig. 12-1).

A caliper does not show a measurement. It is used with a steel rule or micrometer. To adjust or set an outside caliper, hold one leg over the end of a steel rule. Move the second leg until it just splits the graduated line desired on the rule (Fig. 12-2). When using the caliper, hold it square with the workpiece. To get an accurate measurement, the legs should just drag lightly over the workpiece. Do not force the legs over

the workpiece (Fig. 12-3). If the contact is correct, the weight of the calipers will be sufficient to move the legs over the workpiece when the caliper is held vertically.

Some persons have a sense of touch more highly developed than others. The degree to which their sense of "feel" is developed has a great affect on the accuracy of their work with the caliper. When used correctly, it is possible to measure within 0.002 to 0.005 in. of the exact dimension. Remember, use only the tips of the

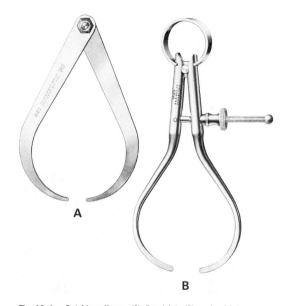

Fig. 12-1. Outside calipers: (A) firm-joint; (B) spring-joint.

Fig. 12-2. Setting the outside caliper. Note how the rule is held in one hand and the caliper in the other. The thumb and forefinger are used to adjust the knurled nut until the exact dimension is obtained.

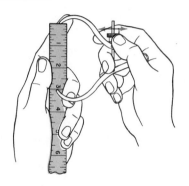

Fig. 12-3. Using an outside caliper.

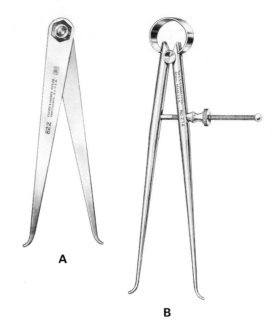

A

B

Fig. 12-4. Inside calipers: (A) firm-joint; (B) spring-joint.

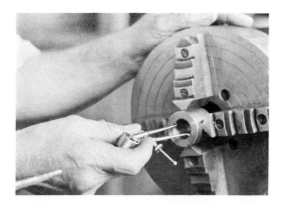

Fig. 12-5. In using the inside caliper, one leg is held firmly against the inside of the hole, while the other is swung back and forth to "feel" the largest diameter.

Fig. 12-6. Reading the inside dimension. One leg of the caliper and the end of the rule are held firmly against the machine surface as the other leg indicates the inside diameter reading.

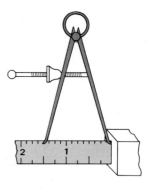

fingers to hold a caliper; never grip it too firmly. Relax the fingers to increase their sensitiveness to feel.

2. An *inside caliper* has two legs with feet that turn outward (Fig. 12-4). It is made with either a firm joint or a spring joint. It is used to measure the inside diameter of holes and it may also be used to measure the width of slots, grooves, and keyways.

The inside caliper requires a little more skill to use than the outside caliper. When checking a hole, care must be taken to hold the caliper just right. Hold one leg firmly against one side of the hole, then rock or swing the opposite leg. At the same time adjust it until it touches the

opposite side of the hole with a very light touch (Fig. 12-5). Any movement after this to the right or left should show a heavier feel or drag. This indicates that you have the largest diameter of the hole. To set an inside caliper, hold the end of a rule against a machined surface in a vertical position. Place one caliper leg against the surface and the rule. Then adjust the caliper until

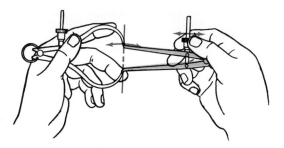

Fig. 12-7. Transferring measurements.

the other leg just splits the rule line for the dimension required (Fig. 12-6).

Here is an important point to remember when using calipers to measure work which is being machined. It is good practice to measure the work and always know how much more material is to be removed. It is not good practice to set calipers to a finished dimension and then try to turn or machine the work to fit the calipers.

TRANSFERRING A MEASUREMENT FROM ONE CALIPER TO ANOTHER

It is often necessary to make a shaft to fit a hole, or to bore a hole to fit a shaft. To do this, adjust the inside caliper to the hole size. Then, transfer this measurement to an outside caliper. Hold the inside caliper in your left hand and the outside caliper in your right hand. Place one leg of the inside caliper against a leg of the outside caliper, and use this as a pivot point. Then adjust the outside caliper until the other leg just drags across the opposite leg of the inside caliper (Fig. 12-7).

THE TELESCOPING GAGE

A *telescoping* gage is used somewhat like an inside caliper. Great accuracy can be obtained

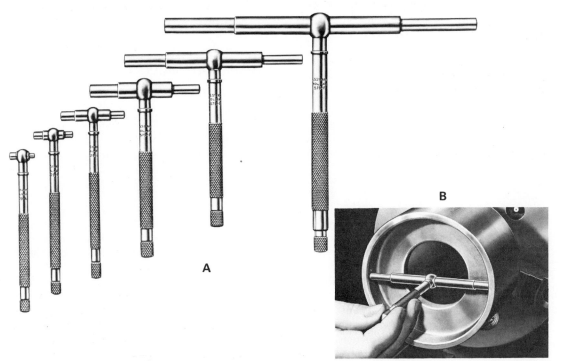

Fig. 12-8. (A) Several sizes of telescope gages. (B) Using a telescope gage.

A

B

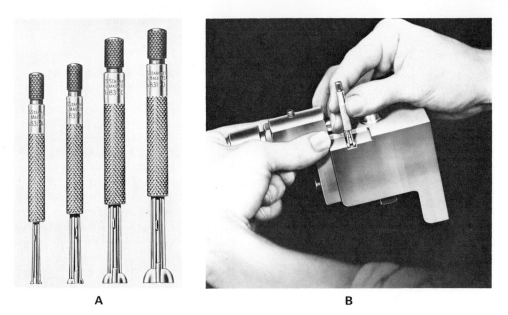

Fig. 12-9. (A) Several sizes of small hole gages, (B) Using a small hole gage to check a groove. The actual measurement is made with a micrometer or vernier caliper.

when the gage is used with a micrometer or vernier tool. Five different sizes are required to measure holes from $\frac{1}{2}$ to 6 in. The capacity of each is limited to a short distance. Each gage consists of two rods, one that slips inside the other. One part of the rod is fixed to a handle, while the movable part of the rod is forced outward by a spring. A screw through the handle acts as a lock clamp to hold the movable part in any location.

To measure an inside diameter, loosen the lock screw, compress the telescope pin, lock the clamp screw, and place the gaging head in the hole. Hold the handle parallel with the hole, and unlock the clamp screw so the telescoping pin can expand in the hole. Carefully align the handle, then tighten the lock screw. Check carefully for feel and contact before removing the gage. Measure across the two pins with a micrometer or vernier caliper (Fig. 12-8).

SMALL HOLE GAGES

Gages for measuring holes, slots, grooves, and recesses which are too small for telescoping gages are called *small hole gages*. They come in various sizes to measure 0.125 to 0.500 in. (Fig. 12-9).

UNIT 13. Reading and Using a Micrometer

A *micrometer,* or *mike* as it is often called, is a precision measuring instrument. One type is made to divide an inch into 1,000 equal parts. Another divides an inch into 10,000 parts. A machinist or toolmaker uses micrometers almost constantly in his daily work. He must be able to measure workpieces quickly and accurately, and he must be able to read the micrometer without making mistakes.

There is a great deal of difference between reading a micrometer and knowing how to use one. Only through constant use can a person acquire what is known as *feel* (just the right amount of pressure needed to get an accurate reading).

KINDS AND SIZES OF MICROMETERS

The common kinds of micrometers include:

1. The *outside micrometer,* used to measure the thickness of materials and parts and the diameters of workpieces (Fig. 13-1).

2. The *inside micrometer,* used to measure hole diameters, slots, and grooves (Fig. 13-2).

3. The *depth micrometer,* or *micrometer depth gage,* used to measure the depth of holes, slots, and distances of shoulders and projections (Fig. 13-3).

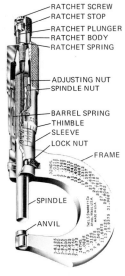

Fig. 13-1. Parts of an outside micrometer.

Fig. 13-2. An inside micrometer.

4. The *screw-thread micrometer,* used to measure the pitch diameter of screw threads (Fig. 13-4).

Micrometers are made in sizes up to 24 in. Micrometer sizes are classified as 0-1 in., 1-2 in., 2-3 in., and so on. A 1-in. micrometer is one that measures from 0 to 1 in.

PARTS

A standard micrometer has a U-shaped *frame,* an *anvil,* a *spindle,* a *sleeve, barrel* or *hub,* and a *thimble* (Fig. 13-5). The spindle has threads at the end which are attached to the thimble. Many micrometers have a *ratchet stop* at the end of the thimble. The ratchet stop enables begin-

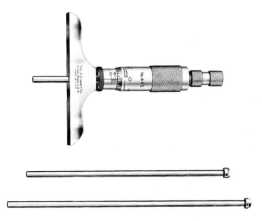

Fig. 13-3. A micrometer depth gage.

Fig. 13-4. A screw-thread micrometer used to measure pitch diameters of screw threads.

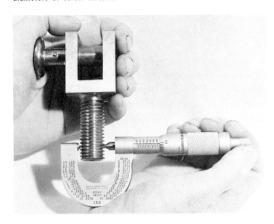

ners to obtain uniform pressure for accurate readings until they develop the sense of feel so necessary for accurate measurements. The *lock nut* is used to lock the spindle after the setting is made.

HOW THE MICROMETER WORKS

All micrometers use the screw-thread principle to obtain measurements. Most types have 40 threads per inch on the spindle screw. Therefore, each complete turn opens or closes the spindle a distance equal to the pitch (lead) of the screw, or $\frac{1}{40}$ in. Changing $\frac{1}{40}$ in. to a decimal equals 0.025 in. (twenty-five thousandths of an inch). There are 40 lines or divisions scribed upon the sleeve, all within a space of 1 in. Each time you turn the spindle one complete turn, you change the reading on the sleeve by one division. Every fourth division on the sleeve is marked 1, 2, 3, and so on, up to the tenth line. These represent 0.100, 0.200, 0.300 in., and so on. The tapered end of the thimble which turns with the spindle is divided into 25 equal parts or graduations. Since one complete turn of the thimble equals 0.025 in., turning the thimble $\frac{1}{25}$th of a turn will open or close the spindle exactly 0.001 in. Beginning with zero, every fifth line on the thimble is numbered 0, 5, 10, 15, and 20, making it easy to read the thousandths. Some of the newer micrometers have all the thimble graduations numbered.

READING THE MICROMETER

Each complete turn on the thimble represents 0.025 in. Each division on the thimble represents 0.001 in. Each division on the sleeve is equal to 0.025 in. Every four divisions are equal to 0.100 in. (4 × 0.025 = 0.100 in.). To read the micrometer:

1. Note the number of visible lines on the sleeve that show below the thimble, starting with zero. Count the number of 0.100 lines that show, then add to this the number of 0.025 lines, such as 0.025, 0.050, or 0.075. Then to this reading add the number of divisions on the thimble from zero to the line that coincides with the index line on the sleeve. The *index line* is the long line that runs lengthwise to the sleeve. All thimble readings are taken from the line on the

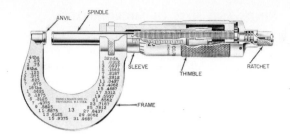

Fig. 13-5. Construction of a micrometer caliper.

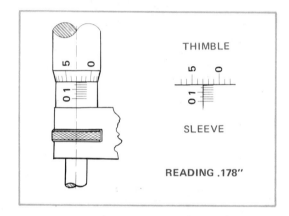

Fig. 13-6. The reading is 0.178 in.

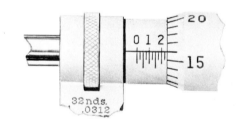

Fig. 13-7. The reading is 0.241 in.

thimble that lines up with or coincides with this index line.

2. In Fig. 13-6 you see three divisions past the Number 1 line on the sleeve, which makes seven full divisions from the zero line. This equals 0.175 (0.025 × 7 = 0.175) in. for the reading on the sleeve.

3. When the end of the thimble is somewhat beyond or in between the sleeve graduations, you must add the thimble reading from zero to

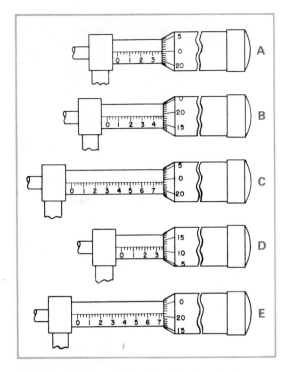

Fig. 13-8. Some additional examples of how to read a micrometer to 0.001 in.

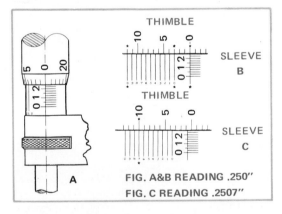

THIMBLE

SLEEVE B

THIMBLE

SLEEVE C

FIG. A&B READING .250"

FIG. C READING .2507"

Fig. 13-9. The reading on this ten-thousandths micrometer is 0.2507 in.

the sleeve reading to get the total reading. In Fig. 13-6 you see there are three divisions past the zero line on the thimble. This represents 0.003 in.

4. Add to the reading on the sleeve the reading on the thimble, or 0.175 + 0.003 = 0.178, the

total reading. Figure 13-7 shows a reading of 0.241 in. Other examples are shown in Fig. 13-8.

THE TEN-THOUSANDTH MICROMETER

For greater accuracy, a micrometer that reads to ten-thousandths of an inch can be used. This micrometer has an additional scale called a *vernier scale,* which makes it possible to read the number of ten-thousandths when the thimble lines do not coincide exactly with the index line. The vernier is located at the back of the sleeve. There are 11 lines numbered 0, 1, 2, 3, 4, 5, 6, 7, 8, 9, and 0, and 10 spaces, each of which represents 0.0001 in. (one ten-thousandth). This is equal to one-thousandth divided into 10 parts. When a line on the thimble does not line up exactly with the index line on the sleeve, look at the vernier. Find the numbered line of the vernier which lines up or coincides with a line on the thimble. This will be the number of ten-thousandths to be added to the reading in thousandths. For example, in Fig. 13-9 the reading is 0.2507 (0.250 + 0.0007) in.

CARE OF THE MICROMETER

1. Remember that a micrometer is a precision instrument. It must be handled and used with care, or the accuracy will be destroyed.

2. Keep your mike clean and occasionally put a drop of light oil on the screw threads. Wipe it with an oily cloth to prevent tarnish and rust.

3. Before using a micrometer, clean the face of the spindle and anvil. To clean them, close the spindle lightly on a piece of paper, then draw the paper out. Close the spindle gently, and note if the zero line on the thimble coincides with the zero on the index line. If it does not, loosen the cap at the end of the thimble. Reset the thimble to zero; then holding it carefully in position, tighten the cap.

4. When taking a measurement, use a very light pressure. Too hard a pressure will result in a wrong reading and may possibly strain the threads. This damages your micrometer.

5. When it is necessary to open or close a micrometer a considerable distance, hold it by the frame. Roll the thimble along your forearm or the palm of your hand.

USING THE OUTSIDE MICROMETER

In all machine-shop work it is important to develop a sensitive touch or feel. This is especially important when using precision measuring instruments such as the micrometer. Your sense of touch is very keen in your fingertips. Therefore, when adjusting the micrometer, use only your fingertips to set the measurement. Before you can acquire the proper sense of feel, it is necessary to hold and use a micrometer correctly.

1. To use a 1-in. micrometer:

   a. Hold it in your right hand with the frame in the palm, and with the third or little finger inside the frame. The thumb and forefinger should be used to turn the thimble (Fig. 13-10).

   b. Hold the workpiece in the left hand. Turn the thimble down until a light contact is made between the anvil and the spindle. If the micrometer has a ratchet stop, you may use it to obtain the correct feel or pressure. The ratchet should be clicked just once or twice for a correct reading. Moving the work slightly between anvil and spindle helps square and align it. At the same time, it tells you if the feel is correct.

   c. You may wish to tighten the lock nut before reading the mike, although this is not necessary unless you wish to preserve the setting for a purpose. If so, remove your thumb and forefinger from the thimble, without disturbing it, and tighten the lock nut slightly. You can then remove the mike from the workpiece.

2. When using larger micrometers, hold the frame in the left hand and locate the anvil against the workpiece. Then, holding the micrometer square, turn the thimble with the thumb and forefinger of your right hand. Move the micrometer slightly to the left and right as you turn the thimble. This will help you align or square the micrometer correctly on the workpiece (Figs. 13-11A and 13-11B).

USING AN INSIDE MICROMETER

An inside micrometer is used for measuring inside diameters of cylinders and rings, for setting

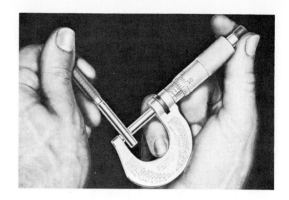

Fig. 13-10.   The correct way to hold a small micrometer.

Fig. 13-11.   (A) Measuring an inside dimension with an outside micrometer. (B) Squaring a large micrometer on the workpiece.

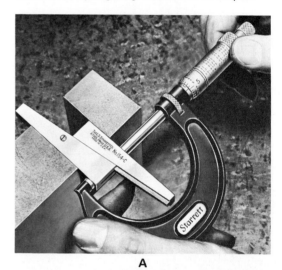

A

B

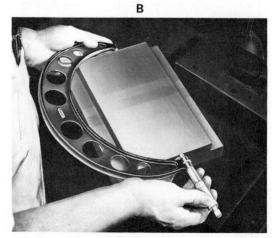

A

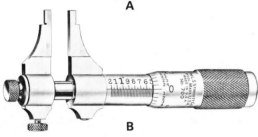

B

Fig. 13-12. (A) An inside micrometer used with a special holder to obtain an accurate reading. (B) An inside micrometer caliper.

Fig. 13-13. An inside micrometer used with extension rods.

calipers, comparing gages, and measuring between parallel surfaces (Fig. 13-12). Large distances are measured by using extension rods and gages (or collars) provided with each tool (Fig. 13-13).

1. To use an inside micrometer:

   a. Assemble selected measuring rod to micrometer head, making sure to wipe dirt from both rod shoulder and head. Align zero lines on rod and head.

   b. Hold assembled tool across diameter of work with one end contacting work.

   c. Screw micrometer head thimble until other end lightly contacts work. Be sure to rock gage slightly in different directions to "feel" true diameter of work. When using an inside micrometer, it is important to locate and guide the instrument carefully so that it will measure the largest diameter at the correct spot. Unless the micrometer is held square across the diameter, an accurate measurement cannot be made.

   d. Set tool to this true diameter, then take reading. Be sure to read correctly. Note that the graduations on the thimble and sleeve are in reverse order to those on an outside micrometer. Read the graduations under the thimble rather than the ones that are exposed.

   e. Add micrometer reading to rod length to obtain total measurement.

2. In addition to measuring rods, inside micrometers are furnished with one or more gages or spacing collars. These are assembled between the measuring rod shoulder and micrometer head to extend range of tool by $\frac{1}{2}$ or 1 in. depending on length of gage used.

3. Measuring rods can be individually adjusted to take up wear, and the micrometer head is also adjustable for wear on its screw. A knurled extension handle is available for obtaining inside measurements in hard-to-reach locations.

USING A MICROMETER DEPTH GAGE

A micrometer depth gage, as the name implies, is used to measure the depth of holes, slots, recesses, and keyways. The tool consists of a hardened, ground, and lapped base combined with a micrometer head. A measuring rod is inserted through a hole in the micrometer screw and brought to a positive seat by a knurled nut. It protrudes through the base and moves as the thimble is rotated. The screw is precision ground and has a 1-in. movement (Fig. 13-14A).

The reading is taken exactly the same as with an outside micrometer except that sleeve graduations run in the opposite direction (Fig. 13-14B). In obtaining a reading using a rod other than the 0-1-in. size, it is necessary to consider the additional rod length. For example, if the 1-2-in. rod is being used, 1 in. must be added to the reading.

Fig. 13-14. (A) A direct reading depth micrometer with extension rods. (B) Using a micrometer depth gage to measure the depth of a slot.

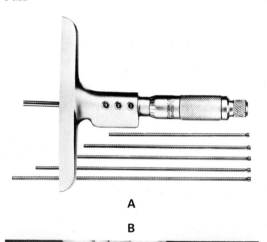

A

B

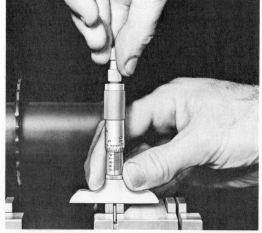

Before using the micrometer depth gage, wipe the base, end of rod, and work clean. Also make sure that the rod is properly seated in the micrometer head. Hold the base firmly against the work and turn the thimble until the rod contacts the bottom of the slot or recess. Tighten the lock nut and remove the tool from the work to read the measurement.

Adjustment to compensate for wear is provided by an adjusting nut at the end of each rod. Should it become necessary to adjust a rod, back off the adjusting nut one-half turn, then turn it to the new position.

USING THE DIGITAL READOUT MICROMETER

The digital readout micrometer differs from the conventional micrometer only in the system of reading a measurement. With the conventional micrometer, the measurement is read from graduated scales on the sleeve and thimble. Measurements with the digital mike are read directly from the numbers appearing in the three windows located on the frame. When numbers appear partially in view, use the number which shows the greater part of itself for reading to the nearest one-thousandth of an inch. The graduations on the thimble indicate tenths of a thousandth (Fig. 13-15).

HOW TO READ THE SPEEDMIKE TO TEN-THOUSANDTHS OF AN INCH

The speedmike differs from other micrometers in that its screw has 50 threads to the inch. The pitch of the screw being 50, one revolution of the thimble is one-fiftieth of an inch or 0.020 in. expressed decimally. There are 20 graduations on the bevel of the spindle. Each graduation, therefore, equals one-twentieth of a revolution ($\frac{1}{20}$ of 0.020 in.) or 0.001 in. expressed decimally. To use, read the measurement in thousandths and add the measurement indicated on the vernier scale which measures to a tenth of a thousandth of an inch (Fig. 13-16).

READING A MICROMETER GRADUATED TO MILLIMETERS

The customary pitch of the screw used in a metric micrometer is $\frac{1}{2}$ millimeter (mm). There-

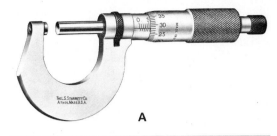

A

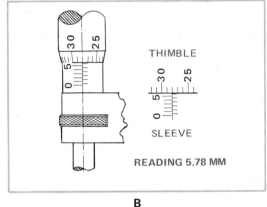

THIMBLE

SLEEVE

READING 5.78 MM

B

Fig. 13-17. (A) A metric micrometer. (B) Reading on a metric micrometer.

Fig. 13-15. This direct reading micrometer has a deep-throated frame. It is ideal for quick, accurate measurements of sheet stock.

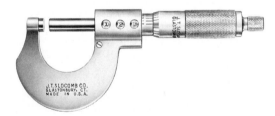

Fig. 13-16. This speedmike reads to ten-thousandths of an inch.

meters and the lower set divides each millimeter into $\frac{1}{2}$ mm). Then add the hundredths of a millimeter shown by the line on the beveled edge of the thimble that coincides with the horizontal line on the barrel (Fig. 13-17B).

Example.

Whole millimeter lines visible on barrel	5 = 5.00 mm
Additional half-millimeter line (lower) visible on barrel	1 = 0.50 mm
Line on thimble opposite long line on barrel	28 = 0.28 mm
Reading of measurement Total	5.78 mm

Millimeters may be easily converted into decimals with the aid of a table (Table 13-1). Also available are micrometers that indicate both decimals and millimeters. Thus, it is easy to compare measurements in the two systems (Fig. 13-18).

fore, one complete revolution of the measuring screw will equal $\frac{1}{2}$ mm. Two complete revolutions equal 1.00 mm. The beveled edge of a metric micrometer's thimble is graduated into 50 parts, each graduation representing one-fiftieth of a $\frac{1}{2}$ mm (a complete revolution of the thimble), or $\frac{1}{100}$ mm (Fig. 13-17A).

To determine a measurement, count the number of divisions visible on the barrel (the upper set of graduations show whole milli-

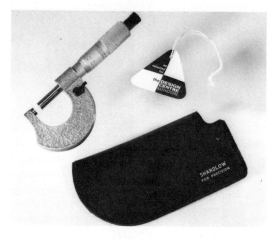

Fig. 13-18.   Combination metric and English micrometer. This micrometer is unique in being able to give measurements in both systems at the same time.

Table 13-1.   Decimal equivalents of millimeters.

mm	in.	mm	in.	mm	in.	mm	in.	mm	in.	mm	in.	mm	in.	mm	in.
0.1	0.00394	2.3	0.09055	4.5	0.17716	6.7	0.26377	8.9	0.35039	11.0	0.43307	13.1	0.51574	16.0	0.62992
0.2	0.00787	2.4	0.09448	4.6	0.18110	6.8	0.26771	9.0	0.35433	11.1	0.43700	13.2	0.51968	16.5	0.64960
0.3	0.01181	2.5	0.09842	4.7	0.18503	6.9	0.27165	9.1	0.35826	11.2	0.44094	13.3	0.52362	17.0	0.66929
0.4	0.01575	2.6	0.10236	4.8	0.18897	7.0	0.27559	9.2	0.36220	11.3	0.44488	13.4	0.52755	17.5	0.68897
0.5	0.01968	2.7	0.10629	4.9	0.19291	7.1	0.27952	9.3	0.36614	11.4	0.44881	13.5	0.53149	18.0	0.70866
0.6	0.02362	2.8	0.11023	5.0	0.19685	7.2	0.28346	9.4	0.37007	11.5	0.45275	13.6	0.53543	18.5	0.72834
0.7	0.02756	2.9	0.11417	5.1	0.20078	7.3	0.28740	9.5	0.37401	11.6	0.45669	13.7	0.53936	19.0	0.74803
0.8	0.03149	3.0	0.11811	5.2	0.20472	7.4	0.29133	9.6	0.37795	11.7	0.46062	13.8	0.54330	19.5	0.76771
0.9	0.03543	3.1	0.12204	5.3	0.20866	7.5	0.29527	9.7	0.38188	11.8	0.46456	13.9	0.54724	20.0	0.78740
1.0	0.03937	3.2	0.12598	5.4	0.21259	7.6	0.29921	9.8	0.38582	11.9	0.46850	14.0	0.55118	20.5	0.80708
1.1	0.04330	3.3	0.12992	5.5	0.21653	7.7	0.30314	9.9	0.38976	12.0	0.47244	14.1	0.55511	21.0	0.82677
1.2	0.04724	3.4	0.13385	5.6	0.22047	7.8	0.30708	10.0	0.39370	12.1	0.47637	14.2	0.55905	21.5	0.84645
1.3	0.05118	3.5	0.13779	5.7	0.22440	7.9	0.31102	10.1	0.39763	12.2	0.48031	14.3	0.56299	22.0	0.86614
1.4	0.05512	3.6	0.14173	5.8	0.22834	8.0	0.31496	10.2	0.40157	12.3	0.48425	14.4	0.56692	22.5	0.88582
1.5	0.05905	3.7	0.14566	5.9	0.23228	8.1	0.31889	10.3	0.40551	12.4	0.48818	14.5	0.57086	23.0	0.90551
1.6	0.06299	3.8	0.14960	6.0	0.23622	8.2	0.32283	10.4	0.40944	12.5	0.49212	14.6	0.57480	23.5	0.92519
1.7	0.06692	3.9	0.15354	6.1	0.24015	8.3	0.32677	10.5	0.41338	12.6	0.49606	14.7	0.57873	24.0	0.94488
1.8	0.07086	4.0	0.15748	6.2	0.24409	8.4	0.33070	10.6	0.41732	12.7	0.50000	14.8	0.58267	24.5	0.96456
1.9	0.07480	4.1	0.16141	6.3	0.24803	8.5	0.33464	10.7	0.42125	12.8	0.50393	14.9	0.58661	25.0	0.98425
2.0	0.07874	4.2	0.16535	6.4	0.25196	8.6	0.33858	10.8	0.42519	12.9	0.50787	15.0	0.59055	25.5	1.00393
2.1	0.08267	4.3	0.16929	6.5	0.25590	8.7	0.34251	10.9	0.42913	13.0	0.51181	15.5	0.61023	26.0	1.02362
2.2	0.08661	4.4	0.17332	6.6	0.25984	8.8	0.34645								

UNIT 14. Using Vernier Tools

The vernier scale, as described in the unit on micrometers, is also part of several other precision measuring tools. These tools, and instructions for their use, are presented in this unit.

THE VERNIER CALIPER

The *vernier caliper* is a precision instrument that is made to measure in thousandths of an inch (Fig. 14-1). Instead of using a screw like the micrometer, vernier tools have a sliding scale. The vernier caliper may be used for taking both inside and outside measurements. Graduations on one side are for inside measurements, and those on the opposite side are for outside measurements. The instrument consists of an L-shaped frame with a main scale engraved on the shank. The length of this main scale determines the size of the caliper. Smaller sizes are generally 6 in. Other commonly used sizes are 12 and 18 in., but they can be obtained up to 48 in. in length.

TWENTY-FIVE-PART VERNIER

The traditional vernier caliper consists of a 25-part vernier scale and a main scale which is divided into inches. Each inch is further divided into 40 parts. Each division on the main scale, then, is equal to 0.025 in. Every fourth division is numbered 1, 2, 3, and so on, indicating 0.100, 0.200, and 0.300 in. The vernier scale is attached to a movable jaw which slides along the main scale bar. The vernier scale has 25 divisions that equal 24 divisions on the main scale. The 24 divisions on the main scale are equal to a distance of 0.600 in. ($24 \times 0.025 = 0.600$). Thus, the value of one vernier division or space equals $0.600 \div 25 = 0.024$. Therefore, the difference between a space on the main scale (0.025) and a space on the vernier scale (0.024) is $0.025 - 0.024 = 0.001$. It is this difference in the spaces between the main scale divisions and the vernier divisions that makes it possible to measure to a thousandth of an inch.

HOW TO READ A TWENTY-FIVE-PART VERNIER

1. Read the number of full inches that show from zero on the main scale to zero on the vernier scale. In Fig. 14-2 this would be 1.000 in.

2. Read the number of divisions on the main scale beyond the last full inch to the zero of the vernier scale. Figure 14-2 shows 0.425. Note that the zero line of the vernier scale is between the 0.425 and 0.450 lines of the main scale.

Fig. 14-1. Parts of a vernier caliper. Notice that this view shows the scale for outside measurements.

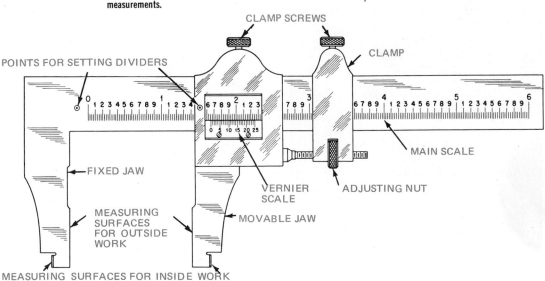

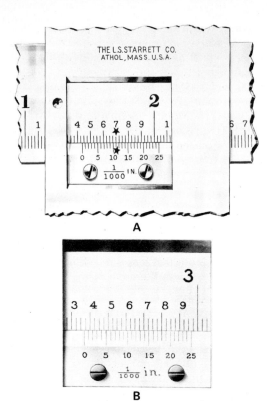

A

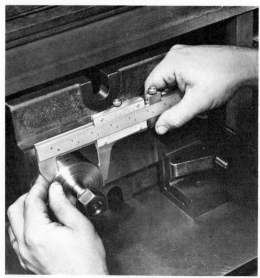

B

Fig. 14–2. (A) A reading of 1.436 in. (B) The reading on this scale is 2.368 in. Do you see how this was obtained? You cannot see the 2-in. mark on the rule; however, you can read directly 0.350 in., and on the vernier scale an additional 0.018 in.

Fig. 14-3. Using a fifty-part vernier caliper to measure an outside diameter. Notice how the caliper is held.

3. To read the vernier scale, read along the scale until you find a line that lines up exactly with a main scale line. In Fig. 14–2 the eleventh line is correct. This means that 0.011 is to be added to the main scale reading.

4. To get the total reading, add 1.000 + 0.425 + 0.011 = 1.436 in.

FIFTY-PART VERNIER SCALE

Modern vernier tools feature an improved big vernier with 50 instead of 25 divisions. The 50-division vernier scale has widely spaced, easy-to-read graduations in combination with half as many bar graduations as old-style instruments. This makes possible faster, more accurate, and greatly simplified settings and readings (Fig. 14–3).

HOW TO READ A FIFTY-PART VERNIER

The main scale on the bar (beam) of the tool is graduated in twentieths of an inch (0.050 in.). Every second division represents a tenth of an inch and is so numbered. The vernier plate is divided into fifty parts and numbered 0, 5, 10, 15, 20, 25, . . . , 45, 50. The fifty divisions of the vernier occupy the same space as forty-nine divisions on the bar. The difference between the width of one of the fifty spaces on the vernier and one of the forty-nine spaces on the bar is, therefore, one-thousandth of an inch ($\frac{1}{50}$ of $\frac{1}{20}$). If the tool is set so that the zero line on the vernier coincides with the zero line on the bar, the line to the right of the vernier zero will differ from the line to the right of the zero on the bar by $\frac{1}{1,000}$; the second line by $\frac{2}{1,000}$ and so on. The difference will continue to increase one-thousandth of an inch for each division until line 50 on the vernier coincides with line 49 on the bar.

To read the tool, note how many inches, tenths (0.100), and twentieths (0.050) the zero mark on the vernier is from the zero mark on the bar. Then note the number of divisions on the vernier from zero to a line which exactly coincides with a line on the bar (Fig. 14–4).

METRIC MEASURE

A vernier used for metric measure has a bar which is graduated in centimeters (cm), millimeters (mm), and $\frac{1}{2}$ millimeters. Its vernier gives a reading of $\frac{1}{50}$ of a millimeter (0.02 mm). For example, the vernier shown in Fig. 14-5 has been moved to the right 4 cm (40.00 mm) plus 1.00 mm plus 0.50 mm. Added together this equals 41.50 mm. The ninth line on the vernier coincides with a line on the bar as indicated by the stars. Therefore, 9 × 0.02 or 0.18 mm is to be added to the reading on the bar. The total reading, then, is 41.68 mm.

OTHER KINDS OF VERNIER MEASURING TOOLS

In addition to the vernier caliper, machinists find wide use for the following measuring tools:

1. The *vernier height gage* is a precision instrument used on a surface plate or another flat surface for laying out, checking, or inspecting work (Fig. 14-6). It consists of a *base,* an *upright bar,* a *sliding jaw* containing the vernier scale, and a *sliding clamp* connected to the sliding jaw for making fine adjustments. The sliding jaw has a clamp that holds a flat scriber or a dial indicator gage. The upright bar is graduated the same as a vernier caliper and is read in the same way. This tool may also be used as a vernier caliper.

2. The *vernier depth gage* (Fig. 14-7) is used for the same purpose as a micrometer depth gage. It is somewhat easier to use and, therefore,

Fig. 14-4. How to read a fifty-division vernier caliper.

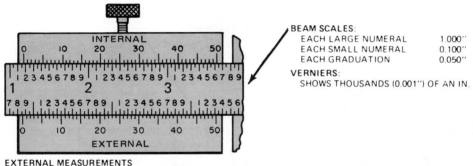

BEAM SCALES:
EACH LARGE NUMERAL   1.000"
EACH SMALL NUMERAL   0.100"
EACH GRADUATION   0.050"
VERNIERS:
SHOWS THOUSANDS (0.001") OF AN IN.

EXTERNAL MEASUREMENTS

USING THE LOWER VERNIER SCALE MARKED "EXTERNAL," READ FROM LEFT TO RIGHT:

VERNIER "0" HAS NOT PASSED AN IN. GRADUATION ON THE BEAM SCALE, SO READING INCLUDES NO IN.	0.000"
LAST BEAM SCALE NUMERAL PASSED BY VERNIER "0" IS "8" × 0.100" =	0.800"
PLUS INTERMEDIATE BEAM GRADUATION PASSED BY VERNIER "0" =	0.050"
PLUS VERNIER GRADUATION "20" WHICH COINCIDES WITH A BEAM GRADUATION =	0.020"
EXTERNAL READING IS	0.870"

INTERNAL MEASUREMENTS

USING THE UPPER VERNIER SCALE MARKED "INTERNAL," READ FROM LEFT TO RIGHT:

VERNIER "0" HAS PASSED INCH GRADUATION "1" ON THE BEAM SCALE, SO READING INCLUDES ONE IN.	1.000"
LAST BEAM SCALE NUMERAL PASSED BY VERNIER "0" IS "1" × 0.100" =	0.100"
PLUS INTERMEDIATE BEAM GRADUATION PASSED BY VERNIER "0" =	0.050"
PLUS VERNIER GRADUATION "20" WHICH COINCIDES WITH A BEAM GRADUATION =	0.020"
INTERNAL READING IS	1.170"

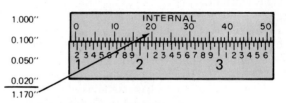

NOTE: IF VERNIER "0" AND "50" GRADUATION BOTH COINCIDE WITH SCALE GRADUATIONS, READING IS THE NUMBERED HUNDRED–THOUSANDTHS WITH WHICH THE VERNIER "0" COINCIDES OR THE EXACT FIFTY–THOUSANDTHS WITH WHICH THE VERNIER "0" COINCIDES.

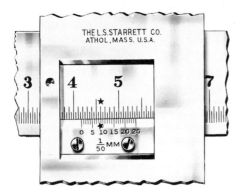

Fig. 14-5. The reading in metric measure is 41.68 mm.

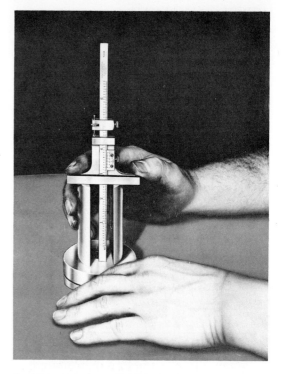

Fig. 14-7. A vernier depth gage.

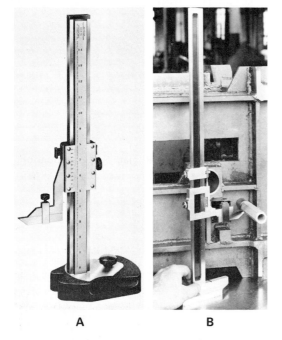

A   **B**

Fig. 14-6. (A) A fifty-part vernier height gage. (B) Using a vernier height gage to check a dimension. Surface plate and base of gage must be clean.

many machinists prefer it to a micrometer depth gage. These tools are ordinarily provided with a 6-in. blade (12-in. blades are available). The blade is graduated and read in the same manner as a vernier caliper. The blade slides in a slot in the base. The base contains the vernier scale. A clamp attached to the base contains a knurled nut for making fine adjustments. Clamp screws on the base and on the sliding clamp are for locking the blade in place.

USING VERNIER MEASURING TOOLS

There is a correct procedure for using vernier tools which makes it easier to obtain accurate readings and measurements:

1. Use a magnifying glass or toolmaker's eye loupe to avoid errors and prevent eyestrain when using a 25-part vernier.

2. Always locate or hold a vernier tool so that the light shines directly on the part you are reading (Fig. 14-8).

3. To set a vernier tool for a given dimension, loosen both clamp screws first. Then slide the movable jaw to the approximate position on the main scale, using the zero on the vernier as the index line. Always grasp the movable jaw by placing your fingers on each side of the main scale. Never pull on the end of the movable jaw. Tighten the screw on the sliding clamp. Set to correct reading by turning the adjusting screw. Then tighten the clamp screw on the movable jaw just snug enough to prevent its moving.

Fig. 14-8. Note how the operator is using the vernier height gage to make a layout. He is checking the dimension on the drawing.

4. To measure a workpiece with a vernier caliper for an *outside dimension,* open the caliper for a distance slightly greater than the workpiece. Tighten the movable clamp screw. Hold the tool square across the work with the solid jaw resting on the workpiece. As you turn the adjusting nut to bring the movable jaw into contact, move the caliper slightly to the right and left to square it properly. After locating the caliper exactly across the workpiece, move it in a slight arc as you adjust the nut for the final feel or setting. The jaws should just drag lightly across the workpiece for a correct reading. Then tighten the clamp screw on the movable jaw lightly. Recheck the feel or contact to see that it is the same.

To measure an *inside dimension,* place the fixed jaw against one side of the hole or slot. Lock the movable clamp in place with the screw. While turning the adjusting nut, move the caliper back and forth in a slight arc to help locate the true diameter or distance across the slot. When contact is made, lock the clamp screw lightly and recheck the feel.

5. To measure a dimension with a vernier depth gage, first loosen the two clamping screws. Hold the base firmly against the surface from which the measurement is to be made.

Slide the rod through the base to the part to be measured. Tighten the clamp screw lightly on the movable jaw and take the reading.

LAYING OUT A JOB WITH THE TWENTY-FIVE-PART VERNIER HEIGHT GAGE

The vernier height gage is used to lay out parts such as the fixture shown in Fig. 14-9. The drawing of this fixture shows that two holes are called for. Their centers are to be 3.750 in. above the base, ±0.003. Even though ±0.003 is allowed, the height gage should be set to the exact dimension given.

Once the casting has been machined on its surfaces, a layout of the holes can begin. A scribing attachment is first fastened securely into place on the height gage. This height gage is then adjusted by turning the adjusting screw until the zero index on the vernier scale coincides with the $3\frac{7}{10}$ index on the main scale, that is, 3.700. The screw is then turned until the zero index reaches two graduations more on the main scale. Properly set, the scales give the desired reading of 3.750 in. (3 in. from the main scale, 0.700 from the $\frac{7}{10}$ main scale graduation, and 0.050 from the two small main scale divisions of 0.025 each).

After tightening the lock screw and rechecking the reading, a line 3.750 in. up on the casting can be scribed. (Be sure that the base of the height gage, the bottom of the work, and the surface plate are thoroughly clean.) Scribe the line, being sure to maintain a firm contact as the base slides along the surface plate. The

Fig. 14-9. This drawing of a fixture will be used in making a layout.

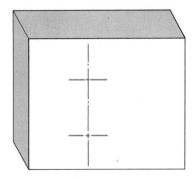

drawing (Fig. 14–8) also shows that the center of one hole is to be 1.250 to the right of the left-hand edge. Therefore, set the height gage to 1.250 and scribe the line (1 in. from the inch graduation, plus 0.200 from the tenths graduations, plus two divisions of 0.025 each).

The center of the second hole is to be 2 in. from the first one. Therefore, you must set the height gage at 3.250 in. (3 in. from the inch graduation, 0.200 from the tenths graduations, and two of the 0.025 divisions). Complete the job by scribing the final line (Fig. 14–10).

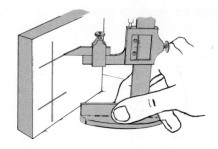

Fig. 14–10. The final line is being marked 2 in. beyond the first full mark.

UNIT 15. Dial Indicating Gages

One of the most widely used instruments today in layout, inspection, and quality control operations is the dial indicator. The dial indicator has precisely finished gears, pinions, and other working parts that make possible measurements from one-thousandth to fifty-millionths of an inch, depending on accuracy requirements.

Dial indicators are used to measure the dimensions of a workpiece or variations from some standard. The indicator is normally set at zero on the part or a standard of known size. When the part being measured is placed under the measuring point, the indicator hand shows the plus or minus variations of the part from standard dimension.

DIAL INDICATORS

Dial indicators are made in a wide variety of styles, types, and arrangements.

1. *Scales of measurement.* Dial indicators are available for both English and metric systems of measurements. Those using the English system of measurement generally have a scale reading in thousandths or ten-thousandths of an inch. Metric dials are available in scale divisions of 0.01 and 0.02 millimeter (mm).

2. *Types of operation.* The *plunger-type indicator* has a contact point at the end of a plunger which moves in a straight line to the surface being checked. Rack teeth on the spindle operate an amplifying gear train to move the handle. The *test-type indicator* has a contact point that extends from the side rather than the end. The point is attached to a lever which pivots about a bearing point and acts on a gear train.

3. *Types of dials.* Most indicator dials are of the *balanced-type.* These will indicate measurements in either direction from zero (Fig. 15–1). Balanced dial indicators are useful for checking plus or minus variations on a workpiece.

The *continuous-dial-type* indicator reads in only one direction (Fig. 15–2). A revolution counter is often included with this type of dial in order to register the number of revolutions made by the large hand of the indicator.

Fig. 15–1. Dial indicator of the balanced-type. Each small division is 0.0005 and every two divisions is 0.001.

Fig. 15-2. This dial indicating depth gage with extension points is a continuous-reading dial indicator. The large hand now shows 0.025. One complete revolution of the large hand (0.100 in.) will move the small dial hand one unit.

Fig. 15-3. A dial indicator with a hole attachment is used to check an internal opening to see if it is out of round.

DIAL GAGES

The principle or direct reading from a pointer and graduated dial provides both the accuracy and the speed of reading essential in many of today's inspection operations. The dial indicator has been incorporated in all types of special and standard gaging equipment, as well as in many machine tools (Fig. 15-3). Some gages are direct reading and others serve as comparators showing plus or minus variations in size.

DIAL COMPARATORS

The dial comparator is used for inspecting duplicate parts and various materials, either in bench inspection or on the production line. Such a comparator is shown in Fig. 15-4. It consists of a precision ground base which will accommodate all types of work as well as V-blocks and fixtures. The dial indicator itself is mounted on a vertical post.

DIAL TEST INDICATORS

The dial test indicator is a multipurpose tool used in layouts and inspections and on machine tools for truing up work, checking runout, con-

centricity, straightness, surface alignment, and transferring measurements (Fig. 15-5). Basically, it consists of a dial indicator mounted at the end of a movable horizontal arm which is fastened to an upright post. Various attachments are also available.

OTHER DIAL GAGES

Many specialized types of dial gages are available for use on a great variety of work. These include portable dial indicator hand gages, pocket gages, sheet gages, depth gages, inside gages, crankshaft or distortion gages, cylinder gages, and out-of-roundness gages (Fig. 15-6).

Dial Bore Gages. A dial bore gage is used for precision gaging of cylindrical bores (Fig. 15-7). The dial bore gage quickly inspects hole diameters and will detect and measure any variation from a true bore (out-of-round, bell-mouth, hour-glass, or barrel shapes). Basically, the gage consists of a contact head, an indicator housing, and a handle. An adjustable range screw plus two centralizing plungers give the gage a 3-point contact to ensure true alignment. The gaging contact actuates a nonshock dial indicator which reads in half-thousandth or ten-thou-

Fig. 15-4. The dial comparator is used for inspection operations in tool rooms and machine shops.

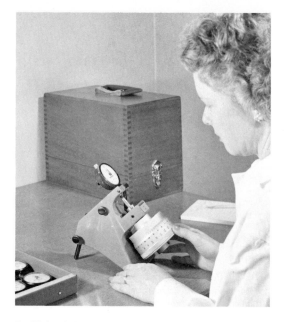

Fig. 15-6. A dial indicator comparator with a micrometer attachment for checking of precision parts.

Fig. 15-5. Using a dial indicator with a magnetic base to check a crankshaft.

Fig. 15-7. Inspecting bore size in a grinding operation.

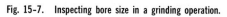

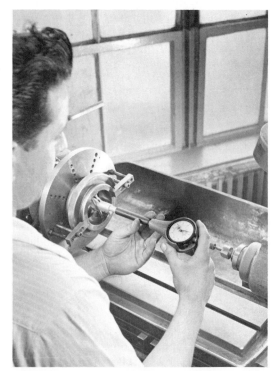

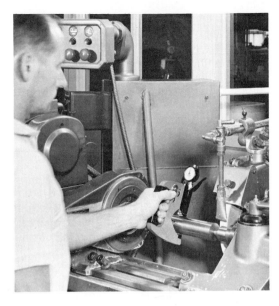

Fig. 15-8. Using a dial indicator snap gage to check work on a cylindrical grinder.

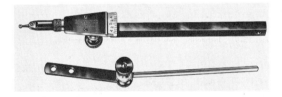

Fig. 15-9. A universal indicator and attachment. This instrument is used when setting up work on the lathe to make sure it is running true.

Fig. 15-10. Using a dial indicating micrometer to check the diameter of small parts.

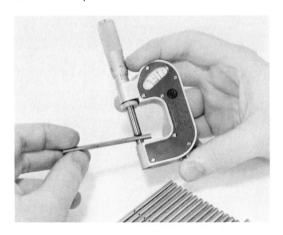

sandths of an inch. Models are available with ranges from 3- to $12\frac{1}{8}$-in. diameters and 6 to 7 in. bore depths.

Dial Indicator Diameter Gages. A dial indicator diameter gage is an extremely versatile instrument. It is adaptable to a wide range of gaging jobs and eliminates the need for many costly special-purpose gages. Uses include internal and external checking of shallow diameters, roundness, concentricity, grooves, recesses, shoulders, and tapers. Eight gage sizes are available to measure diameters from 12 to 60 in. in increments of 6 in. This type of gage has a rigid box-section beam and adjustable gaging contacts at each end. These contacts transfer work dimensions through a friction-free motion transfer mechanism to a direct-reading dial indicator. The indicator reads to 0.0005 in., but 0.001 and 0.0001 graduations are also available.

Dial Indicator Internal Groove Gages. A fast, accurate way to measure the inside diameter of grooves of all types is by means of the dial indicator internal groove gage. The gage has adjustments to handle a range of diameters from 0.375 to 6 in. It consists of a pistol-grip frame with a sensitive jaw and an adjustable reference jaw, both with hard chrome gaging contacts. The sensitive jaw is retracted by a thumb lever in order to insert the gage into the work. Dimensions are transferred through a motion transfer mechanism to a dial indicator reading in 0.0005 in.

Dial Indicator Snap Gages. Snap gages use a dial indicator for direct reading of variation in diameter of a thousandth of an inch (Fig. 15-8).

Universal Indicator Gage. A universal indicator gage (wiggler) is shown in Fig. 15-9. It consists of a long lever with a 10 to 1 (10:1) ratio. Small movement at the end or contact point will be amplified ten times at the indicator end. This type of gage can be mounted on a surface gage or fastened directly to a machine, for example, in centering stock in a four-jaw chuck.

Dial Indicating Micrometer. This instrument can be used as a micrometer or as a snap gage (Fig. 15-10). It contains a built-in dial indicator graduated in ten-thousandths of an inch.

UNIT 16. Gage Blocks and Gaging

Gaging refers to the operations involved in finding out if a dimension on a part has been made larger or smaller than the size required. Gages do not tell the exact size of parts. They merely tell whether a part is made within a certain *tolerance*. For this reason, gages are used by industry to make certain that parts will function correctly and will be interchangeable.

GAGE BLOCKS

The international inch and the international meter are now established in terms of the wavelength of monochromatic light (light having a single wavelength) emitted from krypton 86 gas. The length of a single wave from this gas is 0.0000238 in. and gives us an absolute standard which never changes. Light waves, of course, cannot be handled like a micrometer or vernier caliper. Instead, they are used to establish the length of physical standards having accuracy in millionths of an inch. These standards are called *gage blocks.*

Gage blocks are the industrial standards of length used for calibrating precision measuring instruments, verifying the accuracy of inspection gages and other types of masters (see below), checking accuracy of tools, setting gages and tools, laying out tools and fixtures, and inspecting parts. Essentially, they are blocks of a hard and stable material with measuring or gaging surfaces on each end. The measuring surfaces are ground and lapped to an overall dimension with a tolerance as close as plus or minus one millionth of an inch.

Gage blocks are made in several grades or degrees of accuracy. *Grand master blocks* control the accuracy of an entire manufacturing operation, and their principle use is to certify the accuracy of master blocks. Grand master gage blocks have a length tolerance of plus or minus one millionth of an inch. *Master blocks* are used to check the accuracy of the working blocks that are used in the shop. Master blocks designated as "AA" have a length tolerance of plus or minus two millionths of an inch. *Working blocks* are available in several grades ("A+" with a tolerance of plus four, minus two

millionths of an inch; "A" with a tolerance of plus six, minus two millionths of an inch; and "B" blocks for direct measuring).

Precision gage blocks are made from tool steel, chrome-plated steel, stainless steel, chrome carbide, and tungsten carbide (Fig. 16-1). They are machined and lapped to a high degree of accuracy. They are often called "*Jo*" *blocks* after C. J. Johansson, the first to develop an accurate series of blocks. Johansson's patent set contained 111 blocks in four series. They could be combined in form to make any length from 2 to 202 millimeters (mm) in steps of 0.001 millimeter. The standard set of gage blocks used in the United States contains 81 blocks and can be used to make 120,000 different length combinations.

Obviously, the use of gage blocks is a highly delicate and careful procedure. They can be easily ruined by improper handling. Grand master and master grades are never taken out of an environmentally controlled laboratory since heat and dust could interfere with their accuracy. When handling any grade of blocks, it is important to be sure that they are cleaned with a chamois. Also, avoid getting skin oil and perspiration on them.

USING GAGE BLOCKS

As seen in Table 16-1, there are 81 gage blocks in a set. The blocks are arranged in four series of step sizes. The first series is in ten-thousandths, the second in thousandths, the third in

Fig. 16-1. A complete set of precision gage blocks.

Table 16-1. Arrangement of sizes in an 81-block set.

First series: ten-thousandths—9 blocks									
0.1001	0.1002	0.1003	0.1004	0.1005	0.1006	0.1007	0.1008	0.1009	
Second series: thousandths—49 blocks									
0.101	0.102	0.103	0.104	0.105	0.106	0.107	0.108	0.109	0.110
0.111	0.112	0.113	0.114	0.115	0.116	0.117	0.118	0.119	0.120
0.121	0.122	0.123	0.124	0.125	0.126	0.127	0.128	0.129	0.130
0.131	0.132	0.133	0.134	0.135	0.136	0.137	0.138	0.139	0.140
0.141	0.142	0.143	0.144	0.145	0.146	0.147	0.148	0.149	
Third series: fifty-thousandths—19 blocks									
0.050	0.100	0.150	0.200	0.250	0.300	0.350	0.400	0.450	0.500
0.550	0.600	0.650	0.700	0.750	0.800	0.850	0.900	0.950	
Fourth series: inches—4 blocks									
1.000	2.000	3.000	4.000						

fifty-thousandths, and the fourth in inches. Assume that you must make a block measuring 3.4817 in. in length. First, select a block in the first series whose dimension ends in a 7 (since the last digit is 7). The first block selected, then, will be 0.1007. Next, subtract 0.1007 from the desired dimension. This leaves 3.381 in. Therefore, you must select a block from the second series that will subtract the 0.001. Before you do, however, look at the third series of blocks listed in Table 16-1. Note that they are available in multiples of fifty-thousandths, only. Therefore, block 0.131 in the second series is the only one that can be used. Now, select a 0.250 block from the third series, and a 3.000 block from the fourth series. A block measuring 3.4817 in. in length, then, can be made by stacking the following four blocks:

$$
\begin{array}{r}
0.1007 \\
0.1310 \\
0.2500 \\
\underline{3.0000} \\
3.4817 \text{ in.}
\end{array}
$$

As we have just seen, gage blocks of different lengths can be stacked or *wrung* together to obtain any length desired. The procedure for stacking is as follows: (1) Wipe each block with a soft, lint-free chamois. (2) Cover each block with a light film of lubricating oil for "cementing" action. (3) With a slight contact pressure, slide the blocks together and turn so that they are aligned. Good blocks, when wrung together, are so tightly held that they can support several hundred pounds (Fig. 16-2). There is no clear explanation as to why the wrung blocks hold together. However, it is generally thought that the combination of molecular traction and the cementing action of the oil is responsible for this tightness (Fig. 16-3).

As indicated earlier, gage blocks are used to check other measuring instruments (Fig. 16-4). This constitutes the major use of gage blocks in the average machine shop. Of course, working grades can be used directly to make setups or check spacing. However, this is only done when extreme accuracy is essential.

FIXED GAGES

Fixed-type gages are used to tell whether dimensions of a workpiece fall within required limits. For example, assume the diameter of a hole as given on a print is 1.250 in. ± 0.0005. This means that the hole cannot be smaller than 1.2495 or larger than 1.2505. To check the size of the hole, a plug gage with a "go" gage member on one end and a "no-go" gage member on the opposite end could be used. The "go" gage is always made to the low limit of the dimension because it must slide or fit into the hole. The "no-go" member is always made to the high limit of the dimension and must not fit into the hole. When the "go" gage will not fit into the hole, the hole is *too small*. When the "no-go"

Fig. 16-2. Precision gage blocks are so accurate that a number of them will adhere to each other when "wrung" together.

A

B

Fig. 16-3. Assembling gage blocks in combinations: (A) to check a dovetail and (B) to make a caliper by use of a constant pressure element. Without the constant pressure element, an unknown error of as much as 0.00014 could be present.

Fig. 16-4. Using gage blocks to check out an electronic comparator.

gage fits into the hole, the hole is *too large*. When the "go" gage fits into the hole and the "no-go" gage does not, the hole is within the specified limits.

PLUG GAGES

The most common type of gage is the plug gage which consists of a cylindrical plug of hardened steel, accurately machined to a specific size and mounted in a handle (Fig. 16-5). In sizes up to $2\frac{1}{2}$ in., it is usual practice to make these gages double ended. In larger sizes, there are usually separate "go" and "no-go" gages.

When using plug gages, it is important that the ends be inserted absolutely accurately; otherwise, they will jam or burr. To overcome this difficulty, there are several types of self-aligning plug gages. One type has a ball-bearing pilot end. Another has a chamfered end.

RING GAGES

"No-go" ring gages are used for checking outside dimensions of round parts (Fig. 16-5). In use, the gage should approach the work straight and be brought over it without twisting or turning. The "no-go" gage can readily be identified by its angular groove.

Taper ring gages are used for checking both the size and the angle of tapers. If the work cannot be shaken in the gage, the angle of taper is correct. When the small end of the work lines up with the limit mark, it is the correct size.

SNAP GAGES

Snap gages are designed for taking outside measurements. They are made in a wide variety of sizes and shapes (Fig. 16-6). The snap gage may be adjustable, fixed, or indicating. A commonly used adjustable-type is shown in Fig. 16-7. It has a large, flat anvil fixed on one jaw, and two gaging buttons in the other jaw. One, which is called the *"go" button*, is set at the maximum dimensions allowed by the tolerance specified for the work; the other, which is called the "no-go" button, is set for the minimum dimension allowed. The difference between the two is the tolerance allowed by the gage.

Snap gages should be used with care to reduce wear and to maintain accuracy. The cor-

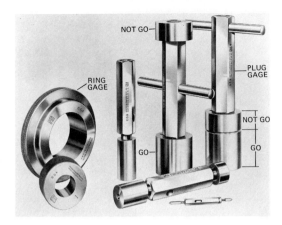

Fig. 16-5. Ring and plug gages.

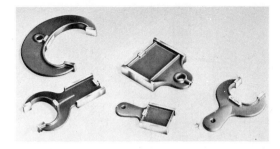

Fig. 16-6. Fixed snap gages.

Fig. 16-7. Adjustable snap gages. Adjusting the "go" and "no go" sizes with gage blocks.

rect way to gage a round piece is to place the anvil gently on the work; with a smooth, rolling motion, push the "go" button past the work. If the "go" button passes the work and the "no-go" button is stopped, the work passes inspection. If the "go" button does not pass freely, the gage should not be forced. Remember, the "go" button is set out as far as the tolerance will allow. Forcing it past an oversize part may damage the gage and render it useless for precision measurements.

Adjustable limit gages, such as snap gages, can be set to a precise dimension only through the use of master gages or precision gage blocks. Such adjustments are made in the gage control department of a manufacturing plant.

THREAD GAGES

Thread, plug, and ring gages used for checking threaded surfaces will be discussed in Unit 25.

INSPECTION OF GAGES

Mass production depends upon fixed gages for quick and accurate gaging of interchangeable parts. Constant inspection of products must be maintained to assure the precision required for interchangeability; and for this reason, fixed gages are the special tools of the inspector.

The gages employed for inspection must be used with the same care as those used for gaging work while it is being produced. Careful use is not enough. All gages must be checked periodi-

cally with master gages or gage blocks to determine their precision. One of the most important sections of a modern plant is the gage control or gage inspection department. Here all gages and other measuring tools are checked and adjusted.

ELECTRONIC GAGES

Electronic gages are used for ultraprecision gaging. Several types will read to ten-millionths of an inch (0.00001 in.). These gages can be used for identifying lengths, thickness, diameter, flatness, taper, and concentricity (Fig. 16-8).

AIR-OPERATED GAGES

Air-operated gages, utilizing the principle of air-jet sensing, are often used in industry (Fig. 16-9). Two basic systems are employed. In one, back pressure of air from the nozzle of the gage is measured. In the other, the actual flow of air across a surface is measured. These air-sensing gages can be used directly on machines to determine if cutting action is correct or if a part is being made to correct size.

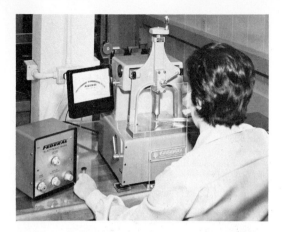

Fig. 16-8. Using an electronic gage to check small precision parts.

Fig. 16-10. A toolmaker using an optical comparator to check the dimensions of a part made with a punch and die.

Fig. 16-9. Checking the bore size of valves for engines using an air gage. This gage gives a direct reading to twenty-five millionths.

Fig. 16-11. A toolmaker's microscope. This is widely used in inspection and quality control. The object being measured is viewed through the microscope and enlarged 30 times. The part can be moved by means of a micrometer adjustment.

OPTICAL AND OTHER GAGES

Gages of this class rely upon some form of optical system or arrangement of lenses to magnify the work, or its shadow, for comparison with a magnified scale. Optical flats, toolmakers' microscopes, and optical comparators come within this category (Figs. 16-10 and 16-11).

Most pieces of optical equipment are not ordinarily used for production inspection. However, the optical comparator finds wide application for checking tools, gear profiles, first pieces produced on new tool setups, for experimental work, and complex profiles.

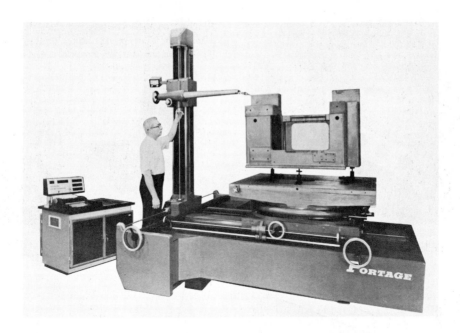

Fig. 16-12. A computer-controlled inspection machine that provides electronic read outs to .0001 in. All surfaces can be checked and given inspection. This is the kind of sophisticated equipment used by modern industry.

COMPUTER-CONTROLLED INSPECTION MACHINES

A *computer-controlled inspection machine* is, as its name implies, an inspection machine controlled by a computer (Fig. 16-12). A punched tape is read one block at a time by a computer which then guides an inspection machine probe from inspection point to inspection point. This type of machine produces both a hard copy printed record and a punched paper tape of the inspection results.

UNIT 17. The Sine Bar and Angle Gage Blocks

{ A *sine bar* is a precision tool used to measure angles accurately and to lay out work at a desired angle in relationship to a surface.}The sine bar is a hardened steel bar with two cylinders of equal diameter attached near the ends. The exact center between these cylinders is of a specific distance, usually 5, 10, or 20 in. (Fig. 17-1). Sine bars are made of tool steel hardened to extreme accuracy. They are used on surface plates and also on machines themselves to check angles or to make a setup to a specific angle.

USING THE SINE BAR

The sine bar is a relatively simple device which uses trigonometry to determine an unknown angle or a specific height setting. For example, in Fig. 17-2 height A divided by length L (it will be either 5, 10, or 20 in.) will determine the value of sine X. The sine of any angle is a constant value and can be found in such handbooks as

Fig. 17-1. A simple sine bar.

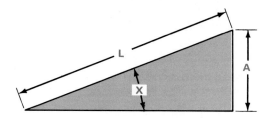

Fig. 17-2. The sine of angle X equals A divided by L.

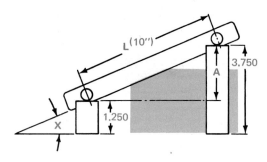

Fig. 17-3. Note how gage blocks are needed to raise the sine bar to determine angle X.

Fig. 17-4. (A) A plain sine table with a complete set of adjusting rods for very accurate settings. (B) Using a sine table. (C) Compound sine plate with permanent magnet top.

A

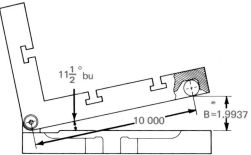

TO SET, FOR EXAMPLE, $11\frac{1}{2}°$ ANGLE WITH 10″ SINE TABLE (PLAIN OR COMB.) FIND SINE OF $11\frac{1}{2}°$, WHICH IS 0.19937.

MULTIPLY 0.19937 BY 10 IN. BY SIMPLY MOVING DECIMAL POINT ONE STEP TO THE RIGHT. RESULT: DIM. B = 1.9937.

USE GAGEBLOCKS OR SIMILAR TOOL EQUALING 1.9937 AND PLACE UNDER SINE BAR OF TABLE GIVING A CORRECT SETTING OF $11\frac{1}{2}$.

B

C

The New American Machinist's Handbook. If, for example, height A in Fig. 17-2 equals 3.50 in. and length L equals 10 in., the sine of angle X will be 0.350, which is equal to 20 degrees (°) and 30 minutes (′).

In many cases, it is impossible to rest the sine bar directly on a surface plate. Therefore, it must be raised a certain amount. For example, to get height A shown in Fig. 17-3, it is necessary to subtract the larger stack of gage blocks

Fig. 17-5. Angle gage blocks.

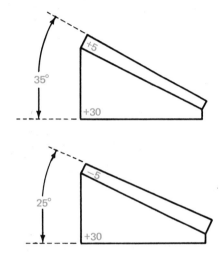

Fig. 17-6. A 30° and a 5° angle gage block can be used to obtain 25° and 35° angles.

Fig. 17-7. Using a dial indicator and angle gage blocks to check an angle.

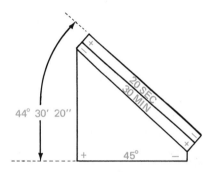

Fig. 17-8. Can you see how these three angle blocks are used to obtain a correct angle?

(3.750 in.) from the smaller stack (1.250 in.). Height A, therefore, would measure 2.50 in. By dividing this by 10, or the length L of the sine bar, you obtain the sine of the angle X which is 0.250. Checking a table of natural sines indicates that angle X equals 14°30′.

Sine plates (tables) are similar to sine bars except they are wider. Simple or plain sine plates are hinged at one end. Compound sine plates are hinged on one side and one end (Fig. 17-4). The latter permits accurate setting of work to one or two planes.

USING ANGLE GAGE BLOCKS

Angle gage blocks are simpler and easier to use than sine bars and plates. A set of angle gage blocks consists of only 16 blocks but can measure 356,400 angles (Fig. 17-5). These precision blocks are designed so that they can be used in either plus or minus positions. For example, to measure a 35° angle, you would simply take a 30° angle and add a 5° angle so that the plus ends are together. To get a measurement of 25°, you would use the same two blocks but "ring" them together so that the minus end of the 5° block is over the plus end of the 30° block (Fig. 17-6). Any size angle can be quickly and easily obtained in this manner (Fig. 17-7). For example, to adjust to an angle of 44 degrees (°), 30 minutes (′), and 20 seconds (″), add the plus end of the 45° block, the minus end of the 30-minute block, and the plus end of the 20-second block as shown in Fig. 17-8.

109

UNIT 18. Making a Layout

Laying out is a shop term which means making or marking lines, centers, or circles on workpieces to show the shape, size, and location of holes or openings to be machined. It is somewhat like a mechanical drawing. In making a layout, accuracy is the most important thing. An error at this point could ruin a job before it is started. To make a good layout you must:

1. Be able to read and understand drawings and blueprints.

2. Be able to select and use layout tools.

3. Be able to transfer carefully and accurately the measurements on the drawing to the metal itself (Fig. 18–1).

Fine and accurate laying out which paves the way for accurate working and finishing is one of the best examples of the precision worker's skill. Although mass production methods introduce wider use of jigs and fixtures for duplicate production of parts, laying out is far from diminishing in importance. Its value grows as the need for greater accuracy in the making of these jigs, fixtures, tools, and production machines increases.

Fig. 18-1. Making a layout. Notice that the work is being done on a surface plate.

LAYOUT TOOLS

1. The *bench vise* (machinist's vise) is used to hold many types of workpieces for layout purposes. Every machinist's or toolmaker's workbench is equipped with a bench vise. The bench vise has a swivel base so the vise and work can be located conveniently. The vise has two hardened steel jaws with faces that are serrated. *Serrated* means that the jaws have shallow teeth cut at an angle to each other. These teeth grip and hold the work from slipping. The teeth will also put marks into a piece of steel, which may spoil a finished job. To prevent this, a machinist always uses *vise jaw caps* made of soft metal such as copper, brass, aluminum, or lead, which can be placed over the hardened jaws (Fig. 18–2).

2. A *machinist's hammer* is used for striking, peening, shaping, and forming metal. There are two principal types of hammers used in machine-shop work: (1) hard and (2) soft.

There are three types of hard hammers: (1) ball-peen, (2) cross-peen, and (3) straight-peen. A ball-peen hammer is the most widely used for laying out, riveting and forming. The cross-peen and straight-peen hammers are used for heavier work, such as forging and shaping of hot metal (Fig. 18–3).

Fig. 18-2. This is the type of vise used by machinists. The soft jaws protect the surface of the work.

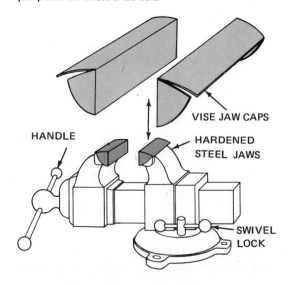

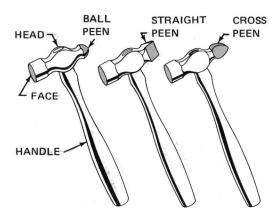

Fig. 18-3. Three kinds of peen hammers.

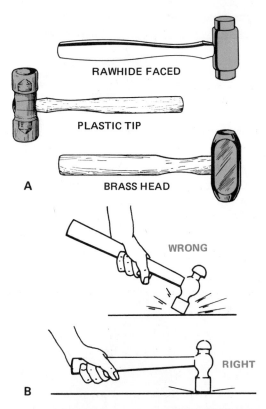

Fig. 18-4. (A) Three types of soft head hammers. Always use this type of hammer or mallet when pounding on machines or accessories. (B) The right and wrong way of using a hammer.

Fig. 18-5. A scriber. This one has replaceable points.

The size of a hammer is determined by the weight of the head, which varies from 4 ounces (oz) to 3 pounds (lb). A ball-peen hammer weighing 1 lb or less is best for layout work.

Soft-faced hammers having heads made of rawhide, brass, lead, or plastic should be used when it is necessary to strike finished parts or tap machine parts during repair or assembly work. Soft-head hammers are often called *mallets* (Fig. 18-4A).

When using a hammer of any kind, always grip it near the end of the handle, not near the head. This will allow better control. It is just as important to learn to hold and to use a tool correctly as it is to hold a ball bat or a tennis racket correctly (Fig. 18-4B).

3. A *scriber* is a sharp-pointed tool used for drawing or scribing lines on metal workpieces. It is an important layout tool. There are several types of scribers. A simple scriber is a slender tool-steel rod about 6 to 10 in. long having a sharp point at one or both ends. Sometimes one end is bent at a right angle to reach into difficult places. Most scribers have a knurled handle somewhat larger in diameter than the scriber itself for easier handling (Fig. 18-5).

A pocket scriber consists of a handle and a removable scriber point. The point can be reversed in the handle so the tool can be carried in your apron pocket. Never attempt to carry a sharp-pointed scriber in your pocket; it can cause serious injury.

The points of scribers must be hardened and tempered in order to cut or make a line on other metals. The point must be kept very sharp or it will not make a clean, sharp line. A dull point can be made needle-sharp by holding the scriber at a slight angle on an oilstone and rubbing it back and forth while you turn the point.

4. A *prick punch* is a layout tool used to mark the location of holes after the lines have been scribed. Sometimes prick-punch marks are placed along a layout line of irregular shape, or around a circle to be drilled. With these marks the machinist can readily tell if the work is being machined correctly. Even if layout lines rub off

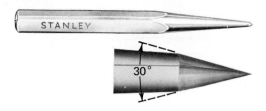

Fig. 18-6. A prick punch.

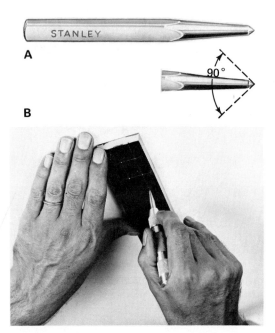

Fig. 18-7. (A) A center punch. (B) Easy one-hand precision center-punching is possible with the automatic center punch.

or are difficult to see, the line of small prick-punch marks will serve as a guide.

A prick punch has a sharp point ground to an included angle of from 30 to 60 degrees (°). It is the first punch used after laying out lines on the workpiece. The sharp point makes it easy to locate the intersection of lines, as for the center of a hole. The punch is tapped just enough to make a small indentation or prick-punch mark. The mark is then carefully checked by eye, or in the case of precision work, with a magnifying glass. The mark may be moved to correct an error by putting the punch point back

in the mark, slanting it in the direction the mark should go, and tapping the punch again. When the mark is correct, the punch is held straight up and down and tapped lightly to straighten the sides of the punch mark. If a deep punch mark were made first, it would be difficult or impossible to correct the error (Fig. 18-6).

5. A *center punch* is similar to a prick punch except that the point is always ground to an angle of about 90°. It is always used after the prick punch to enlarge the prick-punch marks so a drill can be started accurately and easily (Fig. 18-7).

6. A *surface plate* may be made from cast iron or a block of granite. They are made in many sizes. Small ones may be only 12 in. square. It is quite common to see surface plates 8 or 10 feet long and 4 feet wide. The top of a surface plate is machined and handscraped to an extremely smooth and flat surface (Fig. 18-8). A surface plate is a precision tool used mainly for layout and inspection of precision work. The work may be placed directly on the plate, or it may be placed on an angle plate, V-blocks, or parallel bars, which, in turn, are placed on the surface plate.

Surface plates are expensive precision tools and must receive excellent care. Never lay or drop tools such as files or hammers on these plates.

CAUTION

Never use the surface plate as an anvil on which work is hammered.

When not in use, it is correct practice to wipe the surface plate with an oily cloth and put the cover over it, if available.

7. A *surface gage* is basically a layout tool, but has many more uses in the average shop (Fig. 18-9). It can be used to level castings in a machine, to line up cutting tools or workpieces, and when an indicator is attached, to inspect and check machine spindles and workpieces.

It consists of a *base,* an *upright spindle,* and a *scriber.* The spindle is attached to a *rocker arm* that fits into the base. An *adjusting screw* on the rocker arm makes it possible to obtain fine adjustments after the approximate setting has been made (Fig. 18-10). The scriber is attached to the upright or spindle and can be moved or adjusted to any position around or along the spindle. A clamp holds it in place. The scriber point may be set to various dimensions for laying out lines by placing a combination square on the surface plate with the head set down against the plate. The square head holds the rule vertically, while the scriber of the surface gage

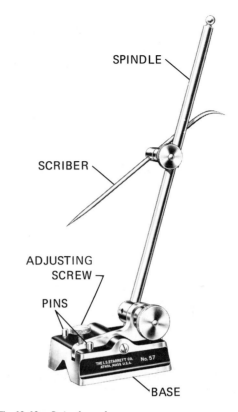

Fig. 18-10. Parts of a surface gage.

SPINDLE

SCRIBER

ADJUSTING SCREW

PINS

BASE

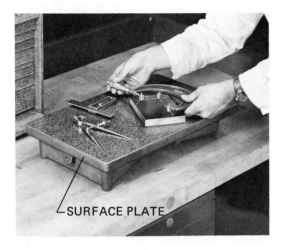

SURFACE PLATE

Fig. 18-8. A cast-iron surface plate.

Fig. 18-9. Using a surface gage to check the height of a workpiece.

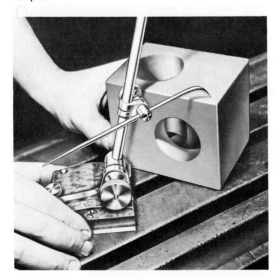

Fig. 18-11. Setting the surface gage to a dimension by use of the combination square.

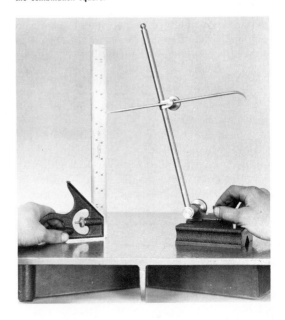

Fig. 18-12. A spring-joint divider.

angle to form the point desired. Finish by rubbing on an oilstone with the points still closed.

To set dividers, place one point in the inch mark of a steel rule. Open the other leg until you get the dimension you need (Fig. 18-13). Remember, a divider is always set to the radius of a circle, which is one-half of the diameter. To use the divider, place one leg in the prick-punch mark, tip the divider slightly, and make

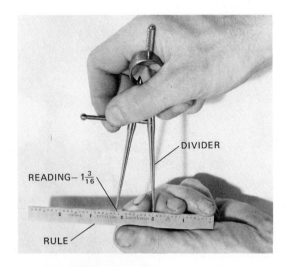

Fig. 18-13. Setting a divider. One leg is placed on the 2-in. mark and the other leg opened to a setting of $1\frac{3}{16}$-in. This will scribe a $2\frac{3}{8}$-in.-diameter circle.

is set to the rule. Then the dimension is transferred by the surface gage to the workpiece (Fig. 18-11).

With an indicator attached to the spindle, it is possible to inspect or check precision work. The indicator, of course, must first be set to a gage or precision gage blocks to obtain the dimension required. Then duplicate pieces may be checked to see if they are within the accuracy required. Parallelism of a part may be checked by merely moving the indicator back and forth along the workpiece while sliding the surface gage on the surface plate.

8. A *divider* is used like a compass to lay out circles or arcs and to space holes or other dimensions. It is used primarily to scribe the size and location of holes to be drilled. A spring-type divider, which can be opened or closed by a knurled nut, is the most widely used (Fig. 18-12).

The points of a divider should always be kept sharp and of the same length. It is impossible to do good work when the points are uneven or dull. It takes only a few minutes to put the points in good condition. First, close the points so they touch each other. Using the off-hand grinder, grind the ends to the same length. Then hold the points at an angle against the wheel. Rotating the divider, grind a nice long

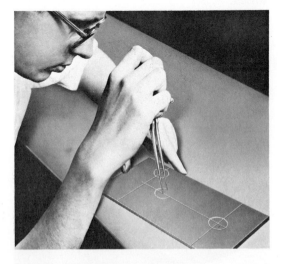

Fig. 18-14. Using a divider to scribe circles.

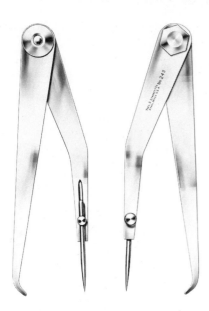

Fig. 18-15. Hermaphrodite caliper.

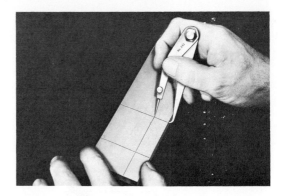

Fig. 18-16. Using a hermaphrodite caliper to lay out a line parallel to an edge.

one complete turn, which gives a clean line. Avoid turning the divider several times (Fig. 18-14).

⑨ A *hermaphrodite caliper* is a layout tool having one leg like an inside caliper and the other pointed like a divider (Fig. 18-15). It is used to locate the center of irregularly shaped stock or to lay out a line parallel to an edge (Fig. 18-16).

⑩ An *angle plate* is a precision tool having two surfaces at right angles to each other and opposite faces parallel. It is usually made of cast iron. After machining, it is ground or handscraped for accuracy. An angle plate is used as a fixture for holding work which is to be laid out, inspected, or machined. It is especially useful for holding work on a surface grinder so it can be ground very square. The angle plate is normally used in connection with a surface plate or a worktable on a machine tool (Fig. 18-17).

⑪ A *toolmaker's clamp* (parallel clamp) is used to hold parts together when making a layout. It is also used for machining operations, such as drilling. There is a slight knack to using this type of clamp. It is important to keep the jaws parallel while opening or closing them. This can be done very easily by holding the screw closest to the jaws in the left hand and revolving the clamp while holding the end screw (Fig. 18-18).

Fig. 18-17. An angle plate.

⑫ The *V-block* is a rectangular or square steel block in which V-slots having a 90-degree (°) angle have been cut (Fig. 18-19). V-blocks have many uses in a machine shop. An important use is holding round work for layout and machining operations. V-blocks are generally considered precision tools because they are hardened and ground very square and parallel, with the V-slot exactly centered.

⑬ A *trammel* is a layout tool used to measure the distance between two points, or to scribe large arcs or circles too large for ordinary dividers. It consists of a long, thin rod, called a *beam,* on which are mounted two sliding heads which hold the scribing points. The heads are adjustable and can be held firmly in place by means of a knurled nut. Extension rods can be attached to the main beam or rod when required (Fig. 18-20).

115

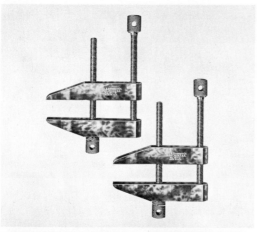

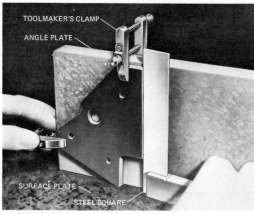

TOOLMAKER'S CLAMP

ANGLE PLATE

SURFACE PLATE

STEEL SQUARE

Fig. 18-18. Using toolmaker's parallel clamps to hold a workpiece to an angle plate.

Fig. 18-19. V-blocks.

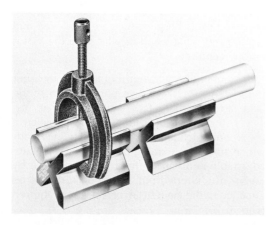

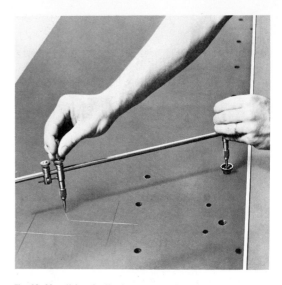

Fig. 18-20. Using the V-point on a steel-beam trammel to scribe an arc a precise distance from a hole.

Fig. 18-21. A vernier height gage.

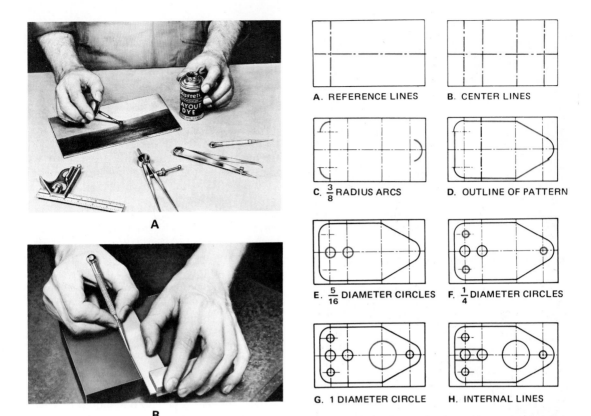

A. REFERENCE LINES　　**B. CENTER LINES**

C. $\frac{3}{8}$ **RADIUS ARCS**　　**D. OUTLINE OF PATTERN**

E. $\frac{5}{16}$ **DIAMETER CIRCLES**　　**F.** $\frac{1}{4}$ **DIAMETER CIRCLES**

G. 1 DIAMETER CIRCLE　　**H. INTERNAL LINES**

Fig. 18-22. (A) Coating metal with layout fluid before making a layout. (B) Using a steel square and scriber to lay out a line.

Fig. 18-23. Steps in making a layout.

14. A *vernier height gage* is an expensive precision instrument used to measure or lay out height dimensions to a thousandth of an inch (0.001). It is also used for inspecting and checking precision work after machining. The vernier height gage is always used on a precision surface plate or the table of a machine tool. The movable jaw holds a flat scriber point for laying out lines. An indicator may be attached for inspecting work (Fig. 18–21).

LAYOUT COLORING MATERIALS

Certain materials are used to color the surface of metals to make the layout lines stand out clear and sharp (Fig. 18-22A). Any of the following materials is satisfactory.

1. *Ordinary blackboard chalk* can be rubbed over the rough surface of cast iron or over the rough ends of a steel shaft for drawing lines to locate the center. It is not used on a smooth surface.

2. *Layout die* is a colored inklike fluid that can be spread over the metal with a brush. It dries quickly and leaves an even, blue-colored surface. Oil and grease should be cleaned from the metal first, or the layout fluid will rub off.

3. *Blue vitriol* is made by mixing 4 to 5 ounces (oz) of copper sulfate in a quart of water, and adding 4 or 5 drops of sulfuric acid. When blue vitriol is applied to a clean metal surface, the metal turns a copper color.

4. A *white coating* can be made by using powdered chalk or whiting mixed with alcohol. Alcohol is preferable to water because it dries more quickly and does not rust. It can be applied with a brush.

Fig. 18-24. Using the bevel protractor to check an angle.

Fig. 18-25. See how the combination square and steel rule are used to make sure the measurement is parallel to the edge of the workpiece. How many other measuring and layout tools can you name?

SCRIBING LINES

An important feature of scribers, dividers, scratch gages, trammels, surface gages, and similar marking tools is a nicely finished, well-tempered point, free from burr or distortion. Points should be checked frequently and ground or honed as required. The straight edges of rules, squares, and protractors should also be inspected for dents and nicks and checked for trueness from time to time against a master square (Fig. 18-22B). Since the location of centers for drilling and the intersection of lines are

marked with punched indentations, care in using a center punch is extremely important. Considerable practice is required to develop the knack of striking a single crisp tap or blow with a hammer to produce a deep or shallow dimple as desired. For fine work, an automatic center punch in which a built-in, adjustable spring provides the striking force is a great asset since both hands are available to steady the tool and it is not necessary to look away from the exact point of contact until the impression is made.

LAYOUT PROCEDURE

There are many possible methods of laying out machine-shop jobs. The correct method depends upon the accuracy required, the tools available, and the time allowed. However, there are certain procedures and skills that apply to the general run of jobs which require laying out (Fig. 18-23). Here are a few suggestions:

1. Remove all burrs with a file.

2. The ends of the stock should be made square, either by filing or by machining.

3. The surface to be laid out should be clean before layout fluid is applied.

4. When possible, always work from a given surface or a *base line*. A base line is one from which other required lines may be scribed. It also provides a checking point in case the work moves during the layout. Two base lines or reference lines may be needed.

5. Seat the work, especially flat and square work, on a surface plate so that all dimensions can be made from the surface plate. If this is not convenient, the work may be raised by placing parallel bars underneath.

6. When several parallel lines must be scribed, use a surface gage and surface plate.

7. To lay out the location of holes to be drilled, first scribe the center line along which the holes are to be drilled. Then scribe a line at right angles to the center line at the correct location for the first hole. Prick-punch the intersection. Use dividers to space the following holes. Prick-punch each intersection before proceeding with the next one so that the divider will not slip.

8. If angular lines must be laid out, do it in one of two ways:

a. Use a bevel protractor set to the correct angle (Fig. 18-24).

b. Mark off the correct dimensions of the angle from two edges of the work, or from two lines at right angles. Then connect the two points by using a steel rule or straight-edge and scribing along it to get the angle.

9. When a steel rule is used, make sure the rule is kept parallel to the workpiece so the exact length can be obtained (Fig. 18-25).

10. Hold the square firmly against the side of the workpiece. Mark a line across the workpiece. Turn or slant the scriber at a slight angle so the point will draw along the lower edge of the rule.

11. Good layout requires clean, sharp, *single* lines. Blurred or double lines are useless and indicate poor workmanship.

Fig. 18-26. (A) Making a layout for machining a V-block. (B) Steps in making the layout for a V-block.

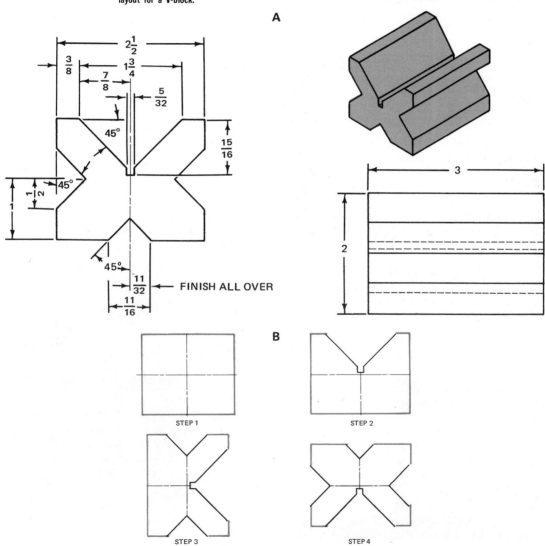

FINISH ALL OVER

LAYOUT OF A V-BLOCK

The following steps show how a V-block may be laid out (Fig. 18–26).

1. Select a piece of 2- by $2\frac{1}{2}$-in. AISI C1045 cold-finished steel. Cut off a piece $3\frac{1}{8}$ in. long.

2. Machine the ends square to the finished size.

3. Remove the burrs, clean the surface, and apply layout fluid to either end of the block.

4. Using a combination square with the rule set to the correct dimensions, or a surface gage on the surface plate, scribe vertical and horizontal center lines. (These will be used as reference or base lines.)

5. To lay out the large V-slot, which is $1\frac{3}{4}$ in. wide, set the rule of the square to measure $\frac{7}{8}$ in. from the vertical center line. Mark these points by scribing a short line.

Fig. 18-27. (A) A layout machine. (B) Note how the layout machine can be moved in three axes to cover all surfaces. (C) Scribing layout lines on a casting. The part is mounted on a rotary table so that it can be moved in a complete circle.

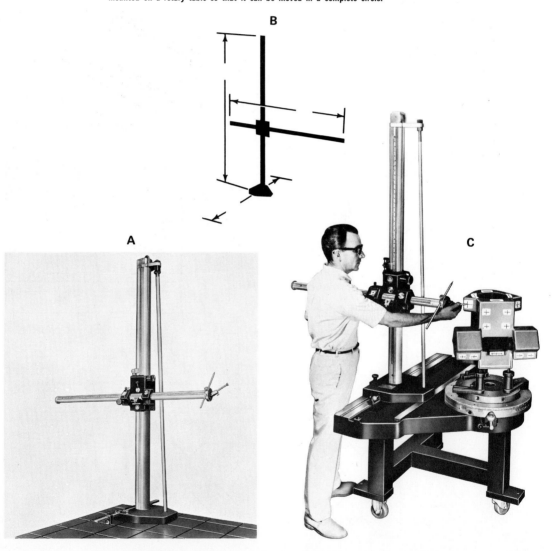

6. Set the square rule for $\frac{15}{16}$, and scribe the depth of the $\frac{5}{32}$-in.-wide slot.

7. On the horizontal center line, mark off the depth of the two V-slots on the sides of the V-block. Set the rule of the square to $\frac{1}{2}$ in., which is the depth of these slots. Scribe a short vertical line to indicate these points.

8. For the bottom V-slot, set the combination square rule for $\frac{11}{32}$ in. Mark this distance on the vertical center line.

9. Using the 45° face of a combination square, scribe the angular lines to form the V-slots, working from the depth and width marks. If a combination square is not available, use a bevel protractor set to 45°.

10. To lay out the width of the $\frac{5}{32}$-in. slot at the bottom of the large V-slot, set the square rule to $1\frac{1}{4}$ in. plus $\frac{5}{64}$ in. This is equal to one-half the width of the V-block (one-half of $2\frac{1}{2} = 1\frac{1}{4}$) plus one-half the width of the $\frac{5}{32}$-in. slot (one-half of $\frac{5}{32} = \frac{5}{64}$). Hold the square head against one side of the V-block, and draw a vertical line from the bottom of the slot to the V-slot. Place the square head against the opposite side of the V-block, and repeat to form the straight slot.

LAYOUT MACHINES

Industry uses a wide variety of layout machines for laying out and measuring parts (Fig. 18–27). These machines operate on three axes (X, Y, and Z) so that any type of layout or check can be done. Each axis has movable verniers, graduated in 0.005 in. Layouts calling for both straight and curved lines can be completed using this kind of machine.

UNIT 19. Discussion Topics and Problems

1. Describe the recent history of measurement.

2. What is the difference between the English and metric system of measurement?

3. What is the international inch?

4. Name three kinds of steel rules.

5. List the parts of a combination set.

6. Sketch the graduations on a steel rule in sixty-fourths of an inch for a distance of 1 in. Mark off the following dimensions in inches: $\frac{1}{4}$, $\frac{3}{16}$, $\frac{5}{32}$, $\frac{13}{64}$, $\frac{5}{8}$, $\frac{15}{16}$, $\frac{61}{64}$, $\frac{17}{32}$, and $\frac{45}{64}$.

7. Why should a caliper be held lightly with your fingertips when measuring a part?

8. For what is a hermaphrodite caliper used?

9. Describe how a micrometer can measure to one-thousandth of an inch.

10. Describe three kinds of micrometers.

11. What is a vernier caliper?

12. Describe the difference between a 25-division vernier caliper and a 50-division vernier caliper.

13. What is a dial indicator used for?

14. Explain how to use a dial indicator on a lathe.

15. What is the difference between gaging and measuring?

16. What is the use of gage blocks?

17. Who invented gage blocks?

18. What is the difference between a "go" and "no-go" gage?

19. Describe an electronic gage.

20. What is an optical comparator?

21. What are the common lengths of sine bars?

22. What is the difference between a sine bar and a sine plate?

23. How many blocks are there in a set of angle gage blocks?

24. What is meant by a layout? What are some of the requirements for a good layout?

25. Name and describe the various tools used for layout work.

26. Why are layout tools used?

27. What determines the method of layout to be used?

SECTION 3

BENCHWORK

UNIT 20. Cutting with a Hand Hacksaw

A hacksaw is used to cut off small bar stock, to saw away waste material from layout work, and for many other types of work that would otherwise require considerable time if done on a machine (Fig. 20-1). A hacksaw consists of a frame, a handle, and a blade. The frame itself may be a fixed type to take only one length of blade, or adjustable to take several lengths of blades (Fig. 20-2). Frames are made with straight handles or pistol-grip handles. The posts or clips that hold the blade in the frame can be turned or set at different positions or angles in relation to the frame.

BLADES

Here are some things you should know about hand hacksaw blades:

1. *Size*. The commonly used blades are made in 8-, 10-, and 12-in. lengths. They are approximately $\frac{1}{2}$ in. wide and 0.025 in. thick.

2. *Kind of material*. Blades are made from carbon steel, tungsten alloy steel, molybdenum steel, molybdenum high-speed steel, and tungsten high-speed steel. The type of blade to select depends upon the metal to be cut. High-speed steel blades last longer, but they are more expensive than carbon steel blades.

3. *Types of blades*. There are three types of blades in general use. These are *all-hard, semi-flex,* and *flexible back*. All-hard blades are made from a high grade of steel which is hardened and tempered. They are relatively brittle, however, and break easily. The flexible-back blade has only the teeth hardened, which leaves the back soft, making the blade less likely to break.

4. *Number of teeth*. The commonly used blades are made with 14, 18, 24, and 32 teeth per inch. This is often called the *pitch* of a blade. Pitch is actually the distance from the point of one tooth to the point of the next tooth. A blade having 32 teeth per inch is referred to by machinists as a 32-pitch blade. For cutting different materials the following blades are used (Fig. 20-3):

a. 14 teeth—for cutting soft steel, brass, and cast iron

b. 18 teeth—for cutting drill rod, light angle iron, and tool steels

c. 24 teeth—for cutting brass tubing, iron pipe, and thick-wall metal conduit

d. 32 teeth—for cutting thin-wall tubing and sheet metal

5. *Tooth set. Set* refers to how the teeth are bent or offset to one side or the other and to the amount of the offset. The set makes the cut or *kerf* wider than the blade itself so that the blade will not bind or stick. When the teeth are offset alternately to the right and left, it is called an *alternate set*. When several teeth are offset in one direction, and then several are offset in the opposite direction, it is called a *wavy set*. Blades with 14 and 18 teeth are made in the alternate set. Those with 24 and 32 teeth are made in the wavy set.

SAWING

1. Select the correct blade. Make sure that at least three teeth will be in contact with the

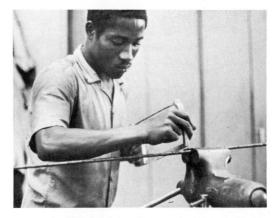

Fig. 20-1. Cutting a rod to length.

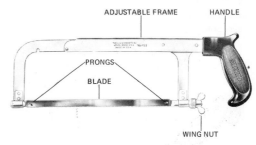

Fig. 20-2. Parts of a pistol-grip adjustable hacksaw.

Fig. 20-3. The life and service of hacksaw blades are dependent upon the use of the proper blade for the job. In selecting the correct blade, consider both the kind and shape of material to be cut. The coarser the tooth, the faster the saw cuts. The finer the tooth, the slower the cutting. Saws with fine teeth make cleaner cuts.

A. MILD MATERIALS IN LARGE SECTIONS	B. HARDER MATERIALS IN LARGE SECTIONS	C. UNUSUAL WORK SHAPES	D. PIPES, TUBING, CONDUIT

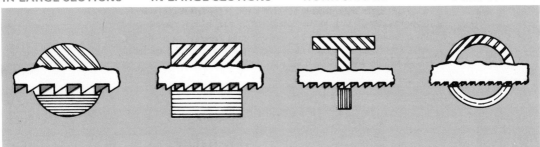

Choose coarse tooth blade to provide plenty of chip clearance and faster cutting.	Choose blade with finer teeth than in A to distribute cutting load over more teeth while still maintaining good chip clearing action.	Choose blade to always keep two or more teeth in contact with narrowest section. Coarse tooth blades straddle work and strip out teeth.	Choose blade with finest teeth per in. to keep two or more teeth in contact with wall. Keep inside of work free of chip accumulation.
HAND BLADES— 14 TEETH PER IN.	HAND BLADES— 18 TEETH PER IN.	HAND BLADES— 24 TEETH PER IN.	HAND BLADES— 32 TEETH PER IN.

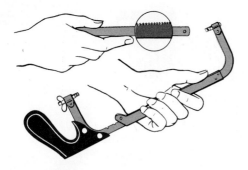

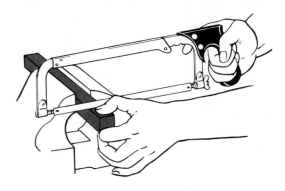

Fig. 20-6. To start an accurate cut, use the thumb as a guide and saw slowly with short strokes. As the cut deepens, remove your hand from the material; grip the front end of the frame firmly, and take full-length strokes.

Fig. 20-4. Make certain the frame is correctly adjusted for the length of the blade. Hold the blade with the teeth pointing away from the handle. Place the hole over the pin on the front stretcher. Then place the hole at the other end of the blade over the pin at the back. Make sure the teeth point away from the handle. The blade should be taut in the frame but not over strained. A properly strained blade when "thumbed" gives a clear, humming sound.

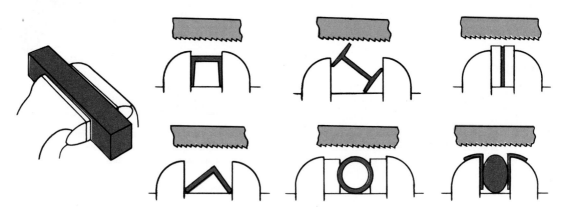

Fig. 20-5. Fasten the material to be cut in a vise. If the work is not square or rectangular, clamp it so as to allow cutting with as many teeth as possible. To hold oval or circular pieces, cover the vise jaws with wood, leather, or copper vise jaw covers. Sandwiching thin sheet material between pieces of scrap wood and cutting through both the wood and metal will make cutting easier and avoid stripping teeth.

metal at all times. Mount it in the frame with the teeth pointing forward from the handle (Fig. 20-4).

2. Tighten the wing nut or the handle until the blade is taut. It should be tightened in the frame just enough to keep it from buckling. If too tight, it may break while sawing.

3. Fasten the workpiece in the vise with the layout line as close to the end of the jaws as possible. If the material is extremely hard, file a small "nick" at one end of the layout line. Figure 20-5 shows the correct method of holding and sawing different shapes of metals.

4. Thin sheet metal can be sawed easily if it is placed between two pieces of scrap wood.

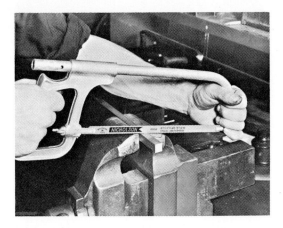

Fig. 20-7. This is the correct way to hold a hacksaw after the cut has been started.

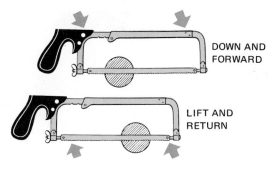

DOWN AND FORWARD

LIFT AND RETURN

Fig. 20-8. Apply enough pressure on the forward stroke to make the teeth cut. Don't allow the teeth to slip over the material. This dulls teeth and causes tooth breakage. Lift the blade slightly on each return stroke to avoid dulling the teeth, but do not lift the blade out of the cut.

5. Start the cut by guiding the blade with the thumb of your left hand, while taking one or two light strokes with the right hand (Fig. 20-6). Then grasp the end of the frame with your left hand (Fig. 20-7).

6. Apply pressure on the forward stroke only. Release the pressure on the return stroke (Fig. 20-8). A uniform speed of 40 to 60 strokes per minute is the correct speed for hack sawing. If you saw faster, you merely dull the blade.

7. As the cut is about to be completed, ease up on the pressure. Hold the material to be removed with your left hand. Make the last few cuts by operating the saw with the right hand only.

8. When making deep cuts that would cause the frame to strike the work, loosen the blade-tension nut and turn the blade at right angles to the frame.

UNIT 21. Cutting with a Cold Chisel

A *chisel* is a wedge-shaped cutting tool used to cut, shear, and chip metal. The cutting end is carefully hardened and tempered. In use, the chisel must be held properly against the work while it is struck with a hammer (Fig. 21-1).

KINDS OF CHISELS

There are four kinds of chisels used in machine-shop work (Fig. 21-2). These chisels are made in many different sizes from a high-grade carbon tool steel.

1. The *flat cold chisel* is a general-purpose chisel used for cutting or chipping metal. It is also used for splitting nuts or rivets when they have rusted or are difficult to remove.

2. The *diamond-point chisel* has a tapered square shape at the cutting end. The cutting-edge is ground diagonally from one corner to the opposite one, which leaves the cutting surface shaped like a diamond. It is used for chipping sharp corners and for cutting sharp grooves.

3. The *cape chisel* is forged with its cutting-edge slightly wider than the body. This is done to provide clearance for the body when the

Fig. 21-1. Cutting off rivet heads with a chisel. Notice how the chisel is held.

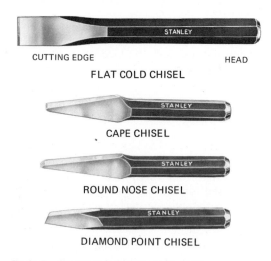

CUTTING EDGE   HEAD

FLAT COLD CHISEL

CAPE CHISEL

ROUND NOSE CHISEL

DIAMOND POINT CHISEL

Fig. 21-2. The four common types of cold chisels.

chisel is used to cut deep grooves. The cutting-edges may vary in width so that grooves of different widths can be cut.

4. The *roundnose chisel* is tapered to a round point with the cutting-edge ground to a single bevel. It is used for forming semicircular grooves

for flutes and oil channels and for chipping inside corners which have a fillet or radius.

HINTS FOR USING CHISELS

●   Always use a chisel that is big enough for the job.

●   Use a hammer that is heavy enough for the size of the chisel, the larger the chisel, the heavier the hammer.

●   Ordinarily, a chisel should be held in the left hand with the thumb and first finger about an inch from the upper end of the chisel. Hold the chisel with a steady but rather loose grip with finger muscles relaxed. That way, if you miss the chisel with the hammer and strike your hand it will slide down the chisel and lessen the effect of the hammer blow on your hand. The best thing to do, of course, is to not miss hitting the chisel.

●   When chipping metal, the depth of the cut is controlled by the angle at which you hold the chisel. Don't try to take too deep a cut. For rough cuts, one-sixteenth of an inch is enough, with half that much or less for finishing cuts.

●   Keep your eyes on the cutting-edge of the chisel. Swing the hammer in the same plane as the body of the chisel. Strike one or two light blows to check your swing, then increase the force as required.

●   If you are using a chisel on a small piece, clamp it rigidly in a vise. Chip toward the solid or stationary jaw of the vise. Chip in a direction away from, never toward, yourself.

●   To avoid marring or otherwise damaging finished surfaces on a piece which has to be clamped in a vise with roughened jaws, use copper jaw covers. These are frequently called *soft jaws* or *caps.*

SHARPENING A FLAT COLD CHISEL

The cutting-edge of a flat cold chisel is ground at an included angle of 60 to 70 degrees (°). The edge should be ground slightly curved instead of straight across (Fig. 21-3).

Use a fine or medium grinding wheel to sharpen the chisel. Hold one side of the cutting-edge against the face of the wheel. Move it back and forth in a slight arc. Cool the chisel frequently by dipping it in water. If the cutting-edge becomes overheated, the hardness will be destroyed, and the entire cutting end will have to be rehardened and tempered. Grind first one side then the other to form a sharp edge.

The body of a chisel is softer than the cutting-edge. Therefore, the head which is struck with the hammer will become *mushroomed* or flattened out; that is, the end will have a ragged edge. A mushroomed head is dangerous because small chips or particles often fly off at high speed when the chisel is struck. These chips may cause serious injury to you or someone working nearby (Fig. 21-4).

CAUTION

Always grind off the mushroom head and keep your chisels well dressed.

CUTTING WITH A FLAT CHISEL

1. Lay out the area to be cut away. Always wear safety glasses when using any kind of chisel.

2. Place the work on a soft metal plate.

CAUTION

Never attempt to use a surface plate for this kind of work.

3. Hold the chisel firmly in your left hand with the thumb and fingers around the shank of the chisel.

4. Place the cutting-edge on the layout line, and strike the chisel with a hammer. Keep your eye on the cutting-edge or work, not on the striking end of the chisel.

5. First, go over the entire layout line to get the chisel started (Fig. 21-5). Then start back and strike the tool with a harder blow to cut through the metal.

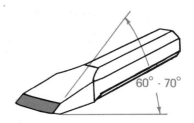

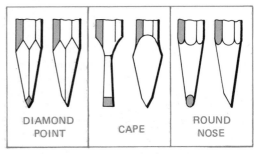

DIAMOND POINT   CAPE   ROUND NOSE

Fig. 21-3. (A) Grind the cutting edge angle as follows: 70° for cast iron, 60° for steel, 50° for brass, and 40° for copper and other soft metals. (B) The correct cutting-edges for other shapes of chisels.

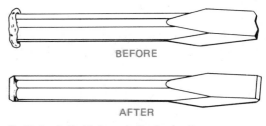

BEFORE

AFTER

Fig. 21-4. A chisel before and after dressing.

Fig. 21-5. Cutting with a cold chisel with the workpiece on a metal plate.

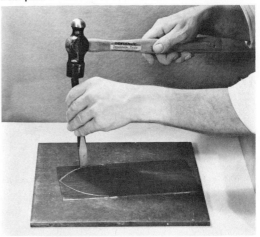

SHEARING METAL IN A VISE

1. Place the metal in a vise with the layout line just above the jaws of the vise.

2. Hold the cutting-edge of the chisel so that the lower bevel will be parallel with the surface of the vise jaw and at an angle of 30–35° (Fig. 21-6). If the head of the chisel is held too high, the cutting-edge will dig into the vise jaw. If the head is held too low, good shearing action will not result and the edge will be ragged.

3. Hold the chisel in your left hand and strike the chisel a firm blow. Work from one end of the vise jaw to the other, shearing the metal a little at a time with each blow of the hammer.

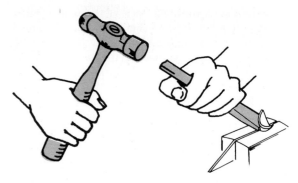

Fig. 21-6. Shearing with a chisel. Note the angle at which the chisel is held.

UNIT 22. Filing, Broaching, and Scraping

Filing is a hand machining process that shapes and smooths a metal surface by removing small chips. The file is one of the oldest tools known to man. Primitive man probably used a piece of granite or some hard stone for shaping his tools, patiently filing away until the tool was the shape he wanted.

Fig. 22-1. A good deal of filing was necessary to make this parallel vise. The machinist must have filing skill to be successful.

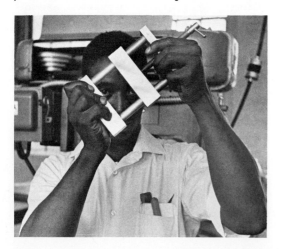

The ability to use the file efficiently is a most important asset of the truly skilled craftsman. Nothing can replace the light touch of a file in the critical fitting of parts. The tool-and-die maker, for example, uses a file for all precision work (Fig. 22-1). The lathe operator or machinist on a repair job must know how to use a file well. Every mechanic and repairman must know how to remove and shape stock with a file.

A process similar to filing is called *broaching* (Fig. 22-2). The broaching process consists of forcing a cutting tool, something like a file, through a hole or over a surface to change its shape. The cutting tool, called a *broach,* has multiple cutting-edges.

CLASSIFICATION OF FILES

Files vary in length, shape, type of cut, and coarseness of cut.

1. *Length.* Regular files vary in length from 4 to 18 in. A file 6, 10, or 12 in. long is the best for most work. Length is measured from the heel to the point (Fig. 22-3).

2. *Shape.* Common file shapes are rectangular, square, round, half-round, and triangular. The name given to a file often tells its shape. For example, a mill file is rectangular and a rattail file is round.

Fig. 22-2. By using a broach, you can change a cast or drilled round hole into a finely finished square or hex hole.

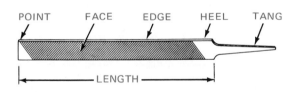

POINT   FACE   EDGE   HEEL   TANG

←——— LENGTH ———→

Fig. 22-3. Parts of a file.

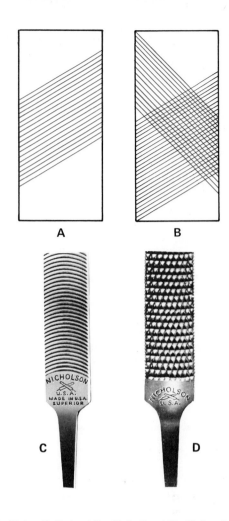

Fig. 22-4. (A) Single-cut file. (B) Double-cut file. (C) Curved-tooth file. (D) The rasp has sharp, narrow, chisel-like cutting teeth.

3. *Type of cut.* A *single-cut file* has teeth cut in one direction at an angle of 65 to 85 degrees (°) across its face. Single-cut files are usually used for finishing work (Fig. 22-4A). A *double-cut file* has two rows of teeth cut at opposite angles across its face forming sharp, diamond-shaped points (Fig. 22-4B). The double-cut file is used when a large amount of metal is to be removed. A *curved-tooth* file is used to file soft metal such as aluminum and copper, because its teeth do not clog easily (Fig. 22-4C). A *rasp* has a series of individual teeth, each shaped in the form of a chisel. This file makes an extremely rough cut for fast removal on aluminum and other soft materials (Fig. 22-4D).

4. *Coarseness.* Coarseness refers to the number of teeth on a file as compared to the length.

a. A *bastard-cut* file has coarsely spaced teeth. It is used for fast removal of stock and does not leave a smooth finish.

b. A *second-cut* file has a medium spacing of teeth and is used for general work.

c. A *smooth-cut* file has closely spaced teeth for finishing metal smooth.

Fig. 22-5. Common shapes and uses of machinist's files.

Cross Section	Name	Shape	Description	Use
	Flat	Rectangular	Tapered sides both in thickness and width	A good all-around file for doing heavy filing
	Hand	Thick rectangular	Edges parallel; one safe edge—no teeth; tapered in thickness	Filing flat surfaces
	Pillar	Almost square	Tapered in thickness —uniform width	Making slots and keyways
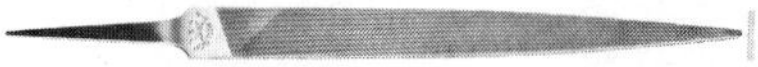	Warding	Thin rectangular	Sharply tapered width—thickness uniform	Making narrow openings for keys and the like
	Square	Square	Tapered or blunt	Enlarging square holes
	Round	Round	Tapered (rattail) or blunt	Shaping holes or curved surfaces
	Three-square	Triangular	Tapered or blunt	Filing sharp corners or grooves
	Half-round	Segment of circle	Tapered or blunt	Shaping concave or convex surfaces
	Knife	Knife shaped	Tapered	Filing sharp angles or corners

The fineness or closeness of the teeth on any file depends on both the cut and the length of the file. For example, an 8-in. bastard file has teeth closer together than a 12-in. bastard file.

TYPES OF FILES

Hand files can be divided into three groups, machinist's files, Swiss pattern files, and special-purpose files.

1. *Machinist's files*. These are the files most commonly used in machine-shop work. They will remove metal fast and are used whenever a smooth finish is not required. They come in nine standard shapes, as shown in Fig. 22-5. All machinist's files are double cut, except the very small round files and the back of the smooth-cut half-round files. In addition to these nine shapes, the machinist often uses a *mill file* (Fig. 22-6). The mill file is a single-cut file. It is used for drawfiling and for finish filing work in the lathe. It produces a very fine finish. The name comes from the fact that it was first used for filing mill saws.

2. *Swiss pattern files*. These are made to more exacting measurements than regular files. They are used primarily for precision filing by tool-and-die makers, jewelers, model makers, and instrument makers. While the cross sections of some Swiss pattern files are similar to the American pattern, the shapes differ. The points of Swiss pattern files are smaller, and the tapers are longer. The cuts of the teeth are also much finer (Fig. 22-7).

3. *Special-purpose files*. There are hundreds of special-purpose files designed for certain kinds of materials and work. A common one found in the average machine shop is the *long-angle lathe* file. It has teeth cut at a much longer angle than the teeth of a mill file. This produces a cleaner shearing action, eliminates scoring or tearing the metal, prevents chatter, and helps reduce clogging of the file. It is also a fast-cutting file and produces a very fine finish. Other special-purpose files are made for filing plastics, brass, lead, aluminum, and stainless steels (Fig. 22-8). These files are made in the same shapes and sizes as the general-purpose files.

Fig. 22-6.   A mill file.

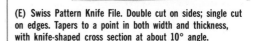

(A) Swiss Pattern Half-round File. Double cut on both flat and half-round sides.

(B) Swiss Pattern Square File. Double cut on all four sides. Narrower and longer tapered than comparative American pattern file.

(C) Swiss Pattern Round File (Tapered). Double cut. Narrower and longer tapered than conventional American pattern round file. Also made in blunt shape.

(D) Swiss Pattern Pillar Narrow File. Double cut on sides; edges "safe." Also made in regular and extra narrow pillar cross sections.

(E) Swiss Pattern Knife File. Double cut on sides; single cut on edges. Tapers to a point in both width and thickness, with knife-shaped cross section at about 10° angle.

(F) Swiss Pattern Three-square File. Double cut on sides; single cut on edges. Narrower and longer tapered than comparable American pattern sizes. Also blunt shape—used mainly for filing metal saws and sometimes called metal saw file.

Fig. 22-7.   The Swiss file comes in about 100 different shapes. The more common ones are shown here.

Fig. 22-8.   Extra soft metals such as lead and pure copper require coarse, short-angle, single-cut teeth to shear away the metal rapidly.

TAKING CARE OF FILES

1. Before using a file, always make certain that it is fitted with a good handle. It is dangerous to use a file without a handle, as the sharp tang can puncture your hand. Another reason is that you can control a file much better when it has a handle (Fig. 22-9).

There are two types of file handles. One type screws on and the other type is driven on. The screw-on type is preferred by most machinists because it cannot slip off while in use.

2. Keep the file clean. Brush the file in the direction of the teeth with a *file card*. A file card is a stiff wire brush mounted on a wooden handle. Small chips that remain in the file teeth are called *pinnings*. They should be pushed out with a metal *scorer* (a piece of wire flattened on the end), which comes with each file card. Any soft piece of metal may be used if a scorer is not available (Fig. 22-10).

3. When files are not in use, keep them separated. Don't throw files into a drawer or together on a bench. This will prevent their teeth from becoming dull. Files should be stored in a rack that keeps them separated.

4. Chalk the file teeth. Rubbing ordinary blackboard chalk across the face of the file will help to prevent metal from clogging or becoming wedged between the teeth. When teeth become clogged, pinnings produce deep scratches in your workpiece. This means you have to work harder and longer to produce a good job. It is especially important to keep your file clean and chalked when filing nonferrous metals such as copper, brass, and aluminum.

5. Keep your files away from moisture and water to prevent rust.

6. Never use a file for a pry bar. The tang is soft and bends easily. The body is hard and brittle, and a slight bending force can easily snap the file.

7. Never use a file as a hammer. Its brittleness may cause it to break and shatter.

8. The harder the metal to be filed, the finer the file teeth should be.

9. For filing nonferrous metals and plastics, greater speed and better results will be obtained

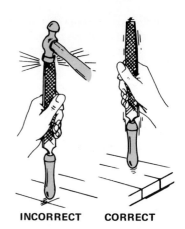

INCORRECT   **CORRECT**

Fig. 22-9. A file handle must be seated firmly on the tang. Hammering the file is dangerous and may break the blade. The correct method is to tap the handle on the bench until the tang is firmly seated.

Fig. 22-10. Using a file card to clean a file.

by using special-purpose files developed for this work.

STRAIGHT FILING

1. Place jaw caps on the vise jaws. Then clamp the workpiece in the vise. The workpiece should be held as close to the vise jaws as possible.

2. Correct position when filing is very important. Stand with your feet about 2 feet apart, with your left foot ahead of your right foot. You should be able to swing your arms and shoulders freely and comfortably.

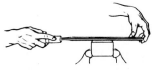

NORMAL FILING

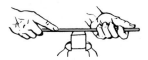

HEAVY STOCK REMOVAL

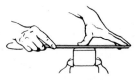

FLAT FILING

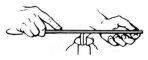

PRECISION WORK

Fig. 22-11. The position of the hands varies according to the work to be done. The principal change is in the position of the left hand.

Fig. 22-12. Drawfiling produces a smooth, flat surface and requires an entirely different technique of holding the file.

3. Grasp the handle of the file in your right hand with the thumb along the top and the fingers curled around the handle (Fig. 22-11).

    a. For heavy filing, grasp the tip of the file with the palm of your left hand.

    b. For normal filing, place the left thumb on the tip of the file and the next two fingers underneath.

4. Files cut only on the forward stroke. Apply pressure to the point at the start of the stroke. Then press with both hands as the center of the file crosses the work. Finally, apply pressure with the right hand as the end of the file crosses the work. Keep the pressure equalized from start to finish of each stroke. Move the file forward in a straight line. Do not rock it. Rocking the file produces a rounded surface. Press down only hard enough to make the file cut.

5. Lift the file slightly on the return stroke. When filing soft metal, you might allow the file to drag lightly to help clean and position it for the next stroke.

6. Work from one side or end of the work to the other by moving the file sideways to cover as much distance in one stroke as possible.

7. After every few strokes rap the file lightly on the bench to loosen the chips. Then brush the file teeth with a file card. Chalk the teeth before doing the final filing.

8. After you have filed a surface flat, a small burr or rough edge remains. Remove it by holding the file at an angle and moving it across the corner. This is called *breaking the edge*.

DRAWFILING

1. Drawfiling is done to remove rough file marks and dents and to obtain a very smooth finish and a flat surface. A mill file or a long-angle lathe file is usually used. If much metal must be removed, a second-cut or bastard-cut file may be used.

2. Drawfiling is different from straight filing. It is done by grasping the file at each end and pushing and pulling the file sideways across the work (Fig. 22-12).

3. Locate the file flat on the work. Hold it steady. Sometimes a file gives a better finish when held on a slight angle instead of at right angles across the work. As you push and pull the file, turn it slightly until you obtain the best cutting position. Use the cutting teeth near the tang.

4. Apply moderate pressure and try to keep the pressure the same throughout the strokes.

5. Move the file after a few strokes so you do not use the same teeth constantly. Exposing clean teeth will reduce the possibility of scratching the workpiece.

6. Clean the file frequently.

7. Always remove the sharp edge which results from drawfiling. To do this, hold the file at an angle and make a light stroke across the corners or edges.

FINE OR PRECISION FILING

1. Select the correct shape of file.

2. Hold the handle end of the file in your right hand. Hold the other end of the file between the thumb and forefinger of your left hand.

3. These files break very easily so apply only a little pressure on the forward stroke. In using the half-round and round file, apply a twisting movement as the cutting stroke takes place (Fig. 22–13).

BROACHING AT THE BENCH

After a hole has been reamed, it is often necessary to cut a keyway to a standard depth and width. This can be done at the bench with a set of broaching tools. The set includes cutting tools and bushings for use in various size holes (Fig. 22–14).

Fig. 22–13. Precision filing is often done by die-and-pattern makers.

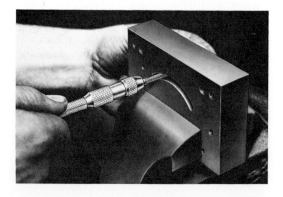

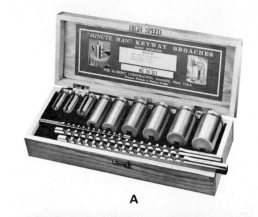

A

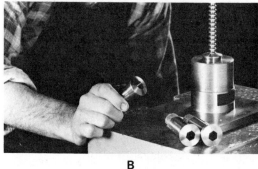

B

Fig. 22–14. (A) A standard set of broaches and bushings for cutting keyways. Broaches of many different shapes are available. (B) This machinist is using a special hexagonal broach to produce the opening for a collet.

To broach a keyway at the bench, follow these steps.

1. Select the right bushing for the hole. The sizes are plainly marked. Insert the bushing in the work.

2. Insert the broach. This is also plainly marked for size of keyway width.

3. Place the workpiece with bushing and broach in the arbor press (Fig. 22–15).

4. Lubricate with the correct lubricant (Fig. 22–16). Use white lead and lard oil for steel; use kerosene or thin cutting oil for aluminum. No lubricant is needed for most brass, bronze, and cast iron. However, always apply a little lubricant to the back of the keyway broach so that friction will be reduced.

5. Push the broach through the workpiece.

Fig. 22-15. Place the workpiece containing the bushing and broach in the arbor press.

Fig. 22-16. Lubricating the broach to do one-pass keyway cutting.

Fig. 22-17. Using a push-type keyway broach in an arbor or hydraulic press.

6. Make sure that the chips are kept clean by brushing away from the teeth.

7. Remove the broach. If additional depth is needed, a shim can be placed behind the broach, or a different size broach can be used. For production broaching, a push-type keyway broach can be used. This device does not require a bushing (Fig. 22-17).

USING A SCRAPER

Scrapers are used to make a surface more accurate than is possible by filing. They remove only a very small amount of material. Even though modern-day machining methods will produce very accurate surfaces, there are still times when hand scraping is necessary. Hand scraping requires a good deal of skill to remove high spots from the surface of work. Frequently, machine areas are scraped, such as the bed of lathes or the top of the knee of a milling machine.

KINDS OF SCRAPERS

The most common scraper is the *flat-type scraper*. The flat scraper is often made from an

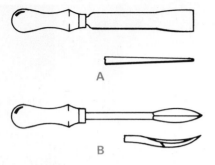

Fig. 22-18. Common shapes of scrapers and how to grind them: (A) flat and (B) bearing or half round.

Fig. 22-19. Handscraping the ways of a milling machine. Exceptionally long, wide-area ways are handscraped to assure perfect alignment for smooth operation.

old 10- or 12-in. file which is hardened and tempered to straw color after it is ground to the proper shape (Fig. 22-18). The tool can be kept sharp by honing on a stone.

The *bearing* or *half-round scraper* is a slender tool made of hardened steel especially shaped and curved. It is used for scraping a bearing surface so that a shaft will fit into it properly.

The *three-square scraper* is a hardened tool used to remove burrs and sharp internal edges from bushings.

The correct method of using a flat scraper is as follows:

1. Clean the work and surface plate with a solvent.

2. Apply a thin layer of prussian blue to the surface plate.

3. Place the work to be scraped face down on the surface plate and move it in a figure-eight pattern.

4. High spots will show in blue and must be removed by scraping (Fig. 22-19). Scraping is done by pushing the cutting-edge of the scraper across the high spots. Cutting is done on the push stroke. Cover only a small area at a time.

5. Repeat the process as often as necessary, covering with blue until the surface is completely flat.

FROSTING

Frosting or *flaking* is the process of decorating a scraped surface. It is done with a handscraper, making very light cuts, each in a different direction. Very short strokes of $\frac{1}{4}$ to $\frac{1}{2}$ in. are taken. Frosting results in a finished surface that is attractive in appearance.

SCRAPING A BEARING

A half-round bearing scraper is used to scrape a bearing. After applying a thin coating of bluing to the journal of the bearing, the bearing is put in place and revolved slightly. High spots show in blue. These are scraped away and the process is repeated until high spots no longer show. When necessary, the three-square or triangular scraper is used to get into corners and to remove sharp edges.

MEASUREMENT

Two Systems **Customary (English) units in inches, quarts, pounds, etc.**
SI (Metric) units in meters, liters, kilograms, etc.

Length

Customary: decimal inch such as
1.250 equals 31.75 mm

CENTIMETERS (cm)
MILLIMETERS (mm)

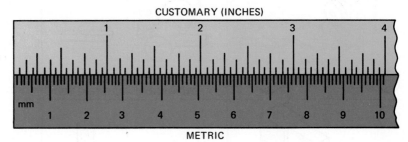

CUSTOMARY (INCHES)

METRIC

DUAL MICROMETER

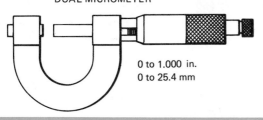

0 to 1.000 in.
0 to 25.4 mm

SAMPLE DUAL MICROMETER READINGS

mm	inches	inches	mm
1.0	0.039	0.125	3.17
5.0	0.197	0.250	6.35
10.0	0.394	0.375	9.52
15.0	0.590	0.500	12.70
20.0	0.787	0.625	15.87
25.0	0.984	0.750	19.05
25.4	1.000	1.000	25.40

Volume

LITER

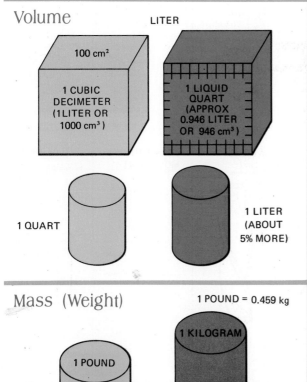

100 cm²

1 CUBIC
DECIMETER
(1 LITER OR
1000 cm³)

1 LIQUID
QUART
(APPROX
0.946 LITER
OR 946 cm³)

1 QUART

1 LITER
(ABOUT
5% MORE)

Mass (Weight)

1 POUND = 0.459 kg

1 KILOGRAM

1 POUND

Temperature

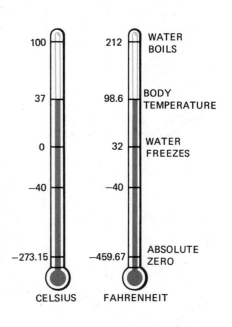

		WATER BOILS
100	212	
37	98.6	BODY TEMPERATURE
0	32	WATER FREEZES
−40	−40	
−273.15	−459.67	ABSOLUTE ZERO
CELSIUS	FAHRENHEIT	

TO FIND CELSIUS:
$5/9 (F−32) = C$

FIVE BASIC MACHINE TOOLS

MACHINE	PROCESS	TOOL	NORMAL MOVEMENT	
			WORKPIECE	TOOL
① Lathe	TURNING	SINGLE-POINT CUTTING TOOL	ROTATIONAL	STRAIGHT-LINE MOVEMENT
② Drilling	DRILLING	DRILLS	FIXED	ROTATIONAL AND VERTICAL
③ Milling — HORIZONTAL	MILLING	MULTITOOTH CUTTERS	STRAIGHT-LINE MOVEMENT	ROTATIONAL
VERTICAL	MILLING	MULTITOOTH CUTTERS	STRAIGHT-LINE MOVEMENT	ROTATIONAL AND VERTICAL

MACHINE	PROCESS	TOOL	NORMAL MOVEMENT	
			WORKPIECE	TOOL
④ Shaper-Planer 	WORKPIECE SHAPING		FIXED FOR CUTTING— STRAIGHT—LINE MOVEMENT AFTER CUT	STRAIGHT LINE FOR CUTTING
SHAPER				
PLANER	WORKPIECE PLANING	SINGLE—POINT CUTTING TOOL	STRAIGHT LINE FOR CUTTING	FIXED FOR CUTTING— STRAIGHT—LINE MOVEMENT AFTER CUT
⑤ Grinder				
SURFACE	GRINDING	ABRASIVE WHEELS	STRAIGHT LINE FOR CUTTING	ROTATIONAL
CYLINDRICAL			ROTATIONAL AND STRAIGHT—LINE	ROTATIONAL

NUMERICAL CONTROL OF MACHINE TOOLS

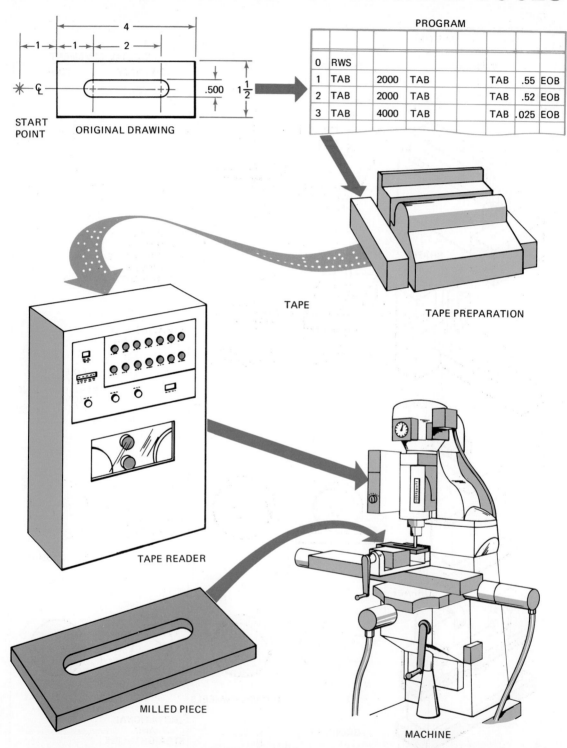

ORIGINAL DRAWING

START POINT

PROGRAM

0	RWS						
1	TAB	2000	TAB		TAB	.55	EOB
2	TAB	2000	TAB		TAB	.52	EOB
3	TAB	4000	TAB		TAB	.025	EOB

TAPE

TAPE PREPARATION

TAPE READER

MILLED PIECE

MACHINE

COMPUTER ASSISTED N/C PROGRAMMING

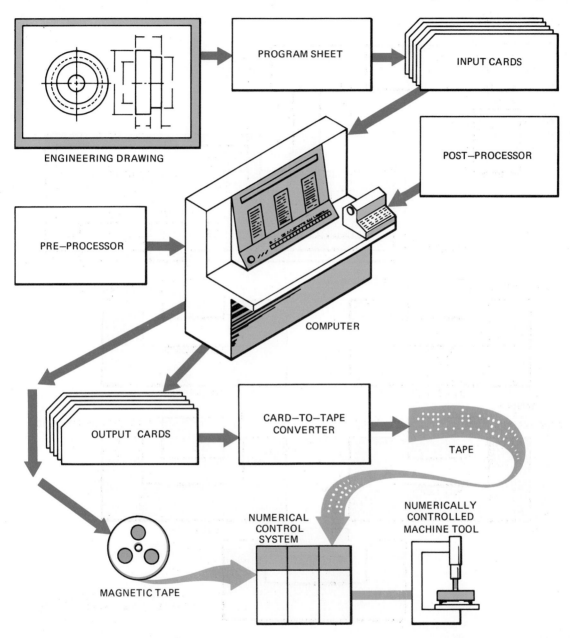

ENGINEERING DRAWING

PROGRAM SHEET

INPUT CARDS

POST—PROCESSOR

PRE—PROCESSOR

COMPUTER

OUTPUT CARDS

CARD—TO—TAPE CONVERTER

TAPE

MAGNETIC TAPE

NUMERICAL CONTROL SYSTEM

NUMERICALLY CONTROLLED MACHINE TOOL

The use of computers is becoming commonplace today. The computer must be primed with techniques to use before it can solve any problems put to it. These are called "pre-processor" routines, and they come with the computer.

Complete information on the machine tool—feeds, speeds, table travel, auxil-iary machining functions available, etc.—comprises the "post-processor" routines. Both of these routines come in the form of punched cards, mag-netic tape, or disks.

A logical description of the machining operations is written line-by-line on a program sheet and a data card is typed for each line. The computer then digests this data—using the processor routines—to generate a second deck of cards or a machine tape which con-tains the complete machining pro-gram. If cards are the output, then a control tape can be obtained from a card-to-tape converter to run the machine tool. Some systems will ac-cept the magnetic tape directly from the computer.

ELECTRICAL DISCHARGE MACHINING (EDM)

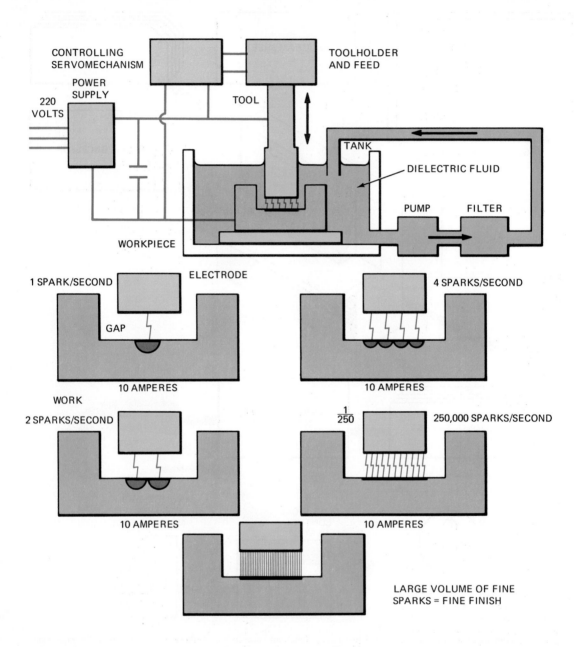

Electrical discharge machining (EDM) is the removal of metal by the energy of an electric spark that arcs between a tool and the surface of the workpiece. The tool and workpiece are immersed in a fluid such as oil that will not conduct electricity. The tool is positioned opposite the area of the workpiece to be machined and at a slight distance from it. Rapid pulses of electricity are delivered to the tool, causing sparks to jump from the tool to the workpiece. The heat from each spark melts away a small amount of metal. As the metal is removed, it is cooled and flushed away by the fluid being circulated through the spark gap. The spark removes material from the tool, so it is slowly consumed as machining progresses. The surface finish is proportional to the number of electrical discharges (cycles) per second.

THE LASER AS A PRODUCTION TOOL

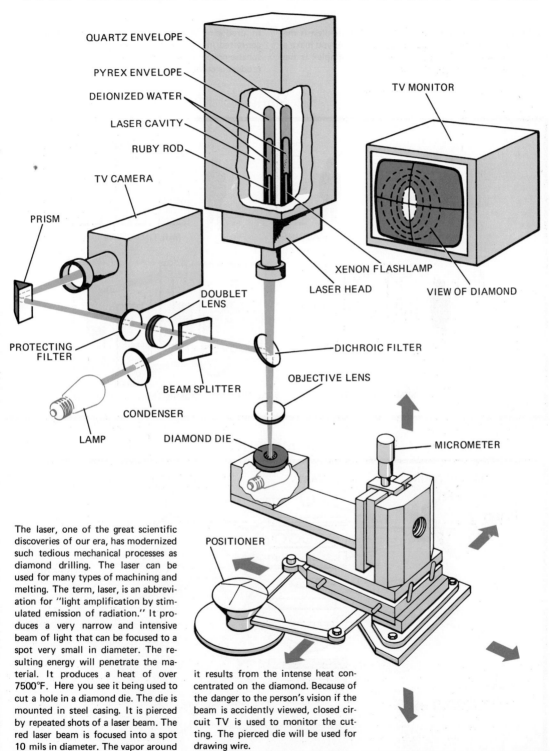

QUARTZ ENVELOPE

PYREX ENVELOPE

DEIONIZED WATER

LASER CAVITY

RUBY ROD

TV CAMERA

PRISM

TV MONITOR

XENON FLASHLAMP

LASER HEAD

VIEW OF DIAMOND

DOUBLET LENS

PROTECTING FILTER

DICHROIC FILTER

OBJECTIVE LENS

BEAM SPLITTER

CONDENSER

LAMP

DIAMOND DIE

MICROMETER

POSITIONER

The laser, one of the great scientific discoveries of our era, has modernized such tedious mechanical processes as diamond drilling. The laser can be used for many types of machining and melting. The term, laser, is an abbreviation for "light amplification by stimulated emission of radiation." It produces a very narrow and intensive beam of light that can be focused to a spot very small in diameter. The resulting energy will penetrate the material. It produces a heat of over 7500°F. Here you see it being used to cut a hole in a diamond die. The die is mounted in steel casing. It is pierced by repeated shots of a laser beam. The red laser beam is focused into a spot 10 mils in diameter. The vapor around it results from the intense heat concentrated on the diamond. Because of the danger to the person's vision if the beam is accidently viewed, closed circuit TV is used to monitor the cutting. The pierced die will be used for drawing wire.

METAL MANUFACTURING

There are five levels of manufacturing. The simplest is the handicraft activity similar to what you do when you make a metal product with hand tools. The most complex is the remotely controlled computer-operated plant.

In producing a product, the raw material must be first converted into parts. These parts are then put together as subassemblies and from these subassemblies the final product is produced.

Levels Of Manufacturing

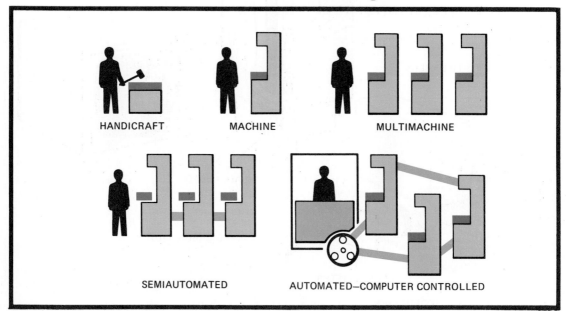

HANDICRAFT   MACHINE   MULTIMACHINE

SEMIAUTOMATED   AUTOMATED—COMPUTER CONTROLLED

Production Runs

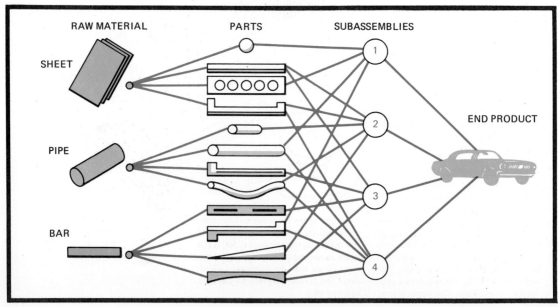

RAW MATERIAL   PARTS   SUBASSEMBLIES

SHEET

PIPE

BAR

1

2

3

4

END PRODUCT

UNIT 23.
Abrasives and Their Uses for Hand Polishing

An *abrasive* is a hard, sharp material used to wear away a softer material. In metalworking, each grain of abrasive is actually a cutting tool like a saw or chisel. For example, the average grinding wheel will bring to bear against a workpiece approximately 300 million abrasive cutting points during every minute of operation. If you were to look under a microscope at the dust produced when a piece of steel is ground, you would see tiny steel chips much like those produced by a lathe or drill.

Abrasives are used in the metalworking industry to grind, buff, polish, lap, and finish metal surfaces. They are an absolute necessity in the mass production of parts that must have the same size, shape, and finish. Abrasives are the only cutting tools that can be used on metals that have been hardened and tempered. Abrasives can be used to remove as little as one-millionth of an inch of material.

KINDS OF ABRASIVES

1. *Emery* is a natural hard mineral found in Greece, Turkey, Asia Minor, and certain parts of New England. It is dull black in color, hard, round, and rocky in shape. Very little emery is used in the metalworking industry today, except for polishing.

2. *Crocus* is a very fine abrasive cloth which is coated with red-iron oxide as the abrasive material. It is used to produce a very fine finish.

3. *Aluminum oxide* is the most widely used man-made or artificial abrasive. It was developed in 1897 by fusing the mineral bauxite with small amounts of coke and iron filings in an electric furnace. Reddish-brown in color and chunky in appearance, this abrasive is tough and durable. Even though it is not as hard or sharp as silicon carbide, its rugged toughness enables it to stand up to the most severe working conditions. Aluminum oxide is ideal for buffing and polishing steel, cast iron, and other metals.

4. *Silicon carbide* is the hardest and sharpest of all the abrasives. It was first made in 1891, while searching for a way to make artificial diamonds. It is produced by fusing sand and coke at high temperatures. It was first used for polishing diamonds and other gems. Silicon carbide is shiny and blue-black in color and is very close to industrial diamonds in terms of hardness and sharpness. This abrasive is well suited for use on soft nonferrous metals such as aluminum, copper, and brass and on nonmetalic materials such as plastics, glass, ceramics, lacquer, and enamel.

GRADING ARTIFICIAL ABRASIVES

Chunks of artificial abrasives are mechanically crushed to lump form, then fed through powerful jaw and roller crushers to be reduced to a usable grain size. The broken particles are then shifted into certain grit sizes by passing them over a series of accurately woven silk screens. The mesh of these screens, or number of openings per inch, ranges from No. 240 (very fine) to No. 10 (coarse). Flour sizes (grains finer than 240) are segregated by sedimentation or air flotation (Table 23-1).

KINDS OF ABRASIVE TOOLS USED IN INDUSTRY

Abrasive tools can be classified into four groups (Fig. 23-1).

1. *Coated abrasive products* are made by applying abrasive grains to an adhesive-coated backing. Some of the common coated abrasive products are sheets and rolls used for handwork and for pad sanders, disks for portable and stationary sanders, and belts for machine grinding, buffing, and polishing.

Most coated abrasive products are made with synthetic abrasives, either silicon carbide or aluminum oxide. Five kinds of backings are used: paper, cloth, paper-cloth combinations, fiber, and fiber-cloth combinations. An adhesive bond holds the abrasive to the backing. Four common adhesives are used for the purpose. These include hide glues, synthetic resins, modified glue, and modified resin. Resin-bonded products are used for rugged roughing and polishing applications. All waterproof coated abrasives are made with a resin bond.

Abrasives are added to a backing in two different ways. In *closed coating*, the abrasive

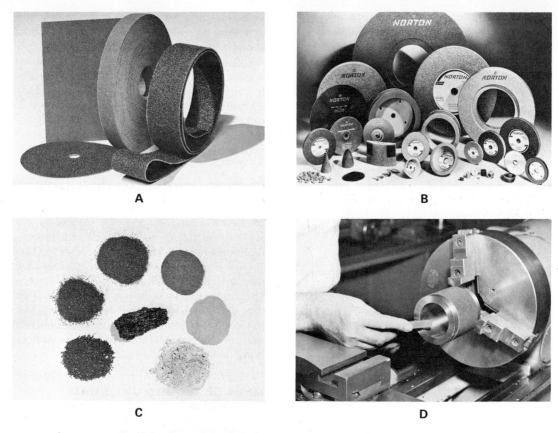

Fig. 23-1. Common forms of abrasives: (A) coated abrasive belts, sheets, and disks, (B) common shapes of grinding wheels, (C) various types of abrasive grain, and (D) breaking edges on a machine part with a bonded abrasive stick.

grains completely cover the surface of the backing. This dense coating lengthens the life of the abrasive on rugged operations. On *open coating,* individual grains are separated one from another at a definite distance, leaving bare spaces on the backing. These bare spaces keep the product from *loading up* when used on soft materials.

2. A *grinding wheel* is a disk made of abrasive grains held together with a bonding material or a binder. Each of the thousands of abrasive grain particles that make up a grinding wheel is actually a sharp cutting tool, each cutting away the surface of the material being ground.

Grinding wheels are held together with five kinds of bonds: vitrified, silicate, shellac, rubber, and resinoid. About three-fourths of all wheels are vitrified or closed bond. There are many shapes of wheels used in industrial grinding. One of the most common is the straight wheel,

Table 23-1. Grades of abrasives.

Coarse											Fine	Flour Sizes		
10		14		20		30		46		60		80		100		150		220		280		400		600
	12		16		24		36		54		70		90		120		180		240		320		500	

such as you would use on a grinder for sharpening tools. More information on grinding wheels can be found in Unit 93.

3. *Polishing grains* are made in a wide variety of grain sizes. They are used to coat hard wheels for polishing and buffing. Polishing grains are also made into a soft stick form that can be applied to a revolving wheel before buffing and polishing.

4. *Stones* and *sticks* are made of abrasive grains and bonding materials. They are molded into shapes for sharpening edged tools and for other industrial uses.

ABRASIVES FOR BENCHWORK

Abrasive cloth can be purchased in 9- by 11-in. sheets, or in rolls $\frac{1}{2}$ to 3 in. wide. Sheets may be purchased individually, by the quire (24 sheets) or per ream (20 quires). Abrasive cloth used in the shop comes in common grain sizes, such as 60 for medium-coarse work, 80 to 100 for medium-fine work, and 120 to 240 for very fine work. Abrasive grains, including the flour sizes, can be purchased in small quantities for special polishing jobs.

USING ABRASIVE CLOTH FOR
HAND POLISHING

1. Tear a strip of abrasive cloth from a roll or a sheet. When taken from a sheet, always tear the strip lengthwise to the sheet, not across. Determine how wide a strip is required before you tear it so there will be no waste. Abrasive cloth is quite expensive.

2. Wrap the strip around a flat stick or fold it over the end of a flat file. To rub abrasive cloth over the work with your thumb is a waste of time and indicates you do not know how to do the job right (Fig. 23-2).

Fig. 23-2. Wrap abrasive cloth around a file to smooth the metal surface.

3. Apply a few drops of oil to the metal surface. Lard cutting oil helps the abrasive to cut faster.

4. Rub the cloth back and forth in a straight line, applying pressure downward. If a flat surface is desired, do not rock the file. Locate the file flat on the work before you start and keep it that way.

5. Deep marks and scratches can be removed more easily if you use a coarse abrasive cloth first. Then change to a medium-grain size, and use a fine-grain size for the final finishing. If the workpiece has been drawfiled correctly, only a fine-grain cloth will be necessary.

6. After all the scratches have been removed, leave the oil on the surface. Reverse the cloth so the smooth backing will be against the work. Rub this smooth backing over the surface several times for a high polish.

7. Used abrasive cloth should not be thrown away unless it is completely worthless. It is excellent for touching up a polished surface that has become stained or needs to be repolished. A new piece of abrasive cloth would scratch a highly polished surface.

UNIT 24. Using a Bench or Pedestal Grinder (Offhand Grinding)

Every machine shop has one or more bench- or pedestal-type grinders for sharpening cutting tools. This type of grinding is called *offhand grinding* because the work is held in and controlled by the hands.

The *bench grinder* is a small grinder mounted on a bench. It consists of an electric motor with a shaft or spindle at each end. Grinding (abrasive) wheels are mounted on these shafts. One is usually a coarse wheel for fast grinding or removal of stock. The other is a fine-grained wheel for finish grinding (see Unit 93). The *pedestal grinder* is a larger machine which is mounted on a base and fastened to the floor (Fig. 24-1). The wheels of both bench and pedestal grinders are covered with a safety guard, except for the small area exposed for grinding.

Tool rests are an important part of offhand grinding machines. They provide a means of resting the work, so you can control the work-piece while it is held against the wheel (Fig. 24-2). *Safety-glass eyeshields* are placed over the working area to help protect your eyes. Always be sure to use them. Most grinders are also equipped with a waterpot for cooling the work, which becomes hot during grinding.

SAFETY

1. Always wear safety glasses or a face shield, even though the grinder is equipped with safety eyeshields.

2. Make sure the tool rest is set close to the wheel. It should be no more than about $\frac{1}{8}$ in. from the wheel for safety. Most accidents happen when the workpiece becomes wedged between the revolving wheel and the tool rest. This can break the wheel and cause serious injury to the operator.

3. Never let your fingers touch the wheels while they are turning. Remember, a grinding wheel is a cutting tool.

Fig. 24-1.   Parts of a pedestal grinder.

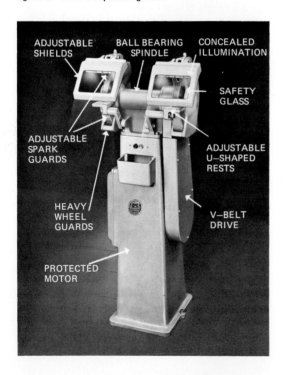

Fig. 24-2.   Make sure the grinder has tool rests that are properly adjusted.

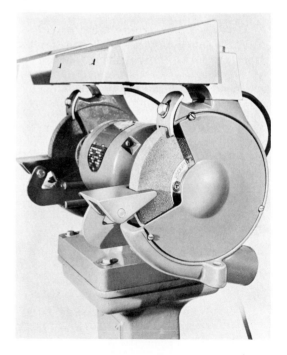

A   **B**

Fig. 24-3.   A loaded and glazed wheel: (A) before dressing and (B) after dressing.

A

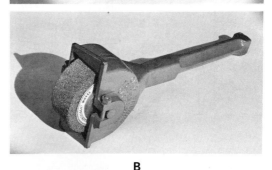

B

Fig. 24-4.   (A) Types of mechanical wheel dressers. (B) Wheel dressers made of abrasives.

HINTS FOR USING A GRINDER

1. Use only the face of the wheel, never the sides.

2. Keep the wheels dressed properly. It is impossible to do good work on wheels that are grooved or rounded.

3. Move the work across the face of the wheel while grinding. This prevents putting a groove in the wheel.

4. When sharpening small chisels, scribers, or punches, always hold the points up on the wheel away from the tool rest, never near it.

5. An offhand tool grinder is used mainly for sharpening hardened steel cutting tools. It is not good practice to grind soft metals on these grinders. Soft metals will quickly clog a wheel. Soft metals can be filed or machined. Some shops may be equipped with a grinder which is used only for soft metals.

DRESSING AND TRUING A WHEEL

As an abrasive wheel is used, several things happen to it.

1. The wheel becomes clogged (loaded) with small bits of metal.

2. The abrasive grains on the wheel face are worn smooth (glazed). The wheel loses its grinding or cutting action (Fig. 24-3).

3. The wheel becomes worn irregularly, with grooves or high spots and rounded edges.

When any of these things happen, the wheel must be dressed and trued. *Dressing* refers to sharpening the face of the wheel by removing the dull abrasive grains and exposing new ones which are sharp. *Truing* is the process of making the wheel run true by removing high spots and squaring the face so that balance and shape are both correct. Both processes can be done at the same time with one of the several types of wheel dressers available.

1. A *disk-type dresser*, usually called a *star dresser*, has several pointed disks loosely mounted on a pin with solid disks as separators. The disks are made from hardened steel and mounted on a handle (Fig. 24-4A).

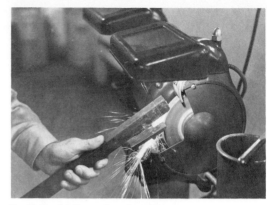

Fig. 24-6. Grinding a piece of metal.

WRONG

RIGHT

Fig. 24-5. Dressing a grinding wheel with a wheel dresser.

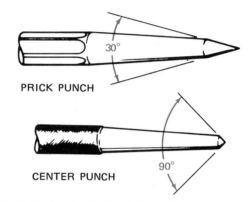

PRICK PUNCH 30°

CENTER PUNCH 90°

Fig. 24-7. Correct angles for grinding punches.

2. An *abrasive wheel* or *stick* uses an abrasive which is held against the wheel (Fig. 24-4B).

3. A *diamond dresser* has a small industrial diamond mounted on its end. This diamond is held against the wheel.

Use a star dresser to dress and true an off-hand grinding wheel. Hold the tool against the wheel in one location until the wheel is sufficiently dressed. Then move the tool about three-fourths of its width to a new location. Repeat until the width of the wheel has been dressed. Be sure to hold the tool firmly against the tool rest and firmly against the wheel. A finish cut may be taken by moving the dresser across the wheel face once or twice to even it (Fig. 24-5).

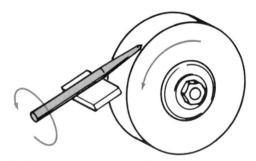

Fig. 24-8. The punch is rotated while grinding.

GRINDING METAL

1. Check the safety rules before starting.

2. Hold the workpiece firmly on the tool rest, and guide it back and forth across the wheel

face (Fig. 24-6). Cool the metal by dipping it in the waterpot.

3. To grind a curved surface, swing the workpiece in an arc.

4. Always remove the burrs after grinding (on soft metals use a file or hold the work at an angle against the wheel).

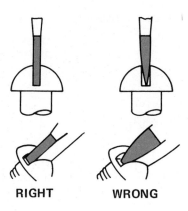

RIGHT **WRONG**

Fig. 24-9. Grinding the tip of a screwdriver.

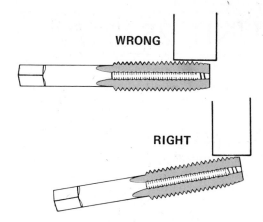

Fig. 24-10. Note how the tap is held at a slight angle.

SHARPENING HAND TOOLS

The correct methods of sharpening cold chisels and drills are covered in Units 21 and 35. Other hand tools should be sharpened as follows.

Cone-pointed Punches. Center punches and prick punches are ground to cone points. The correct point angle for center punches is about 90 degrees (°) and for prick punches, approximately 30 degrees. These angles may be altered for special work (Fig. 24-7). Adjust the rest so the punch meets the face of the wheel at the desired angle. Rotate the punch during grinding to make the point symmetrical (Fig. 24-8). Dip the punch in water at frequent intervals to avoid *burning*. Do not grind away more material than necessary to secure a satisfactory point. Repair a mushroomed head by grinding to original shape. Always temper the punch after repairing a mushroomed head or it will quickly mushroom again.

Standard-type Screwdriver. Screwdriver tips should be ground with sides parallel to keep the tool from lifting from the screw slot when in use (Fig. 24-9).

CAUTION

Dip the screwdriver in water frequently during grinding to prevent loss of temper due to overheating.
First, adjust the rest to hold the screwdriver at right angles to the grinding surface of the wheel. Grind the end of the screwdriver square. Do not grind away more material than is necessary to remove "nicks" and "square up" the end. Next, adjust the rest to hold the screwdriver against the wheel to give the desired parallel or concave shape. Grind both sides until the tip is of the required thickness.

Taps. Dull leading or chamfered threads cause much tap breakage. To prevent breakage, taps should be sharpened periodically. The proper procedure for grinding a tap is shown in Fig. 24-10.

UNIT 25.
Screw Threads and Thread Measuring

A *screw thread* is a spiral (helical) groove of uniform shape and size formed on the inside of a hole or on the outside of a rod or pipe (Fig. 25-1). Screw threads have many uses. They *hold* or *fasten* parts together. They *transmit motion,* as on a lathe lead screw. They are used in *measuring* instruments, such as a micrometer. They can be used to increase *torque,* such as raising a heavy building with a screw jack.

There are seven common methods used for making threads.

1. Cutting threads by hand with a tap and die.

2. Tapping threads (internal) on a machine using rotary cutters (Fig. 25-2).

3. Cutting external threads with a single-point tool on a lathe or similar machine (Fig. 25-3).

4. Cutting external threads on a machine with a threading or die head (Fig. 25-4).

5. Milling threads on a milling machine (Fig. 25-5).

6. Grinding a thread on a cylindrical grinder (Fig. 25-6).

7. Rolling threads, the latest and fastest method of cutting a thread (Fig. 25-7).

Years ago, rolling was considered satisfactory only for parts requiring a minimum degree of accuracy. Today, however, many qualities of threads can be formed by rolling.

The great majority of screw threads conform to certain established standards. The more common of these are described in this unit. There are, however, many special and unusual thread forms that are designed for specific purposes. Information about these can be found in *Machinery's Handbook* or *The New American Machinist's Handbook.*

HISTORY OF THE SCREW THREAD

No one knows exactly when the first thread was used. It was first suggested by Archimedes about 2,200 years ago. During the first century, B.C., the

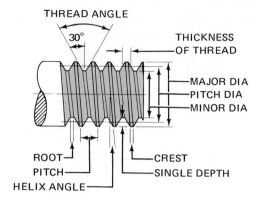

Fig. 25-1. Parts of a screw thread.

Fig. 25-2. Tapping a large hole on a turret lathe.

Fig. 25-3. Cutting external threads on a lathe with a single-point cutting tool.

Fig. 25-4. Using an adjustable die head to cut threads.

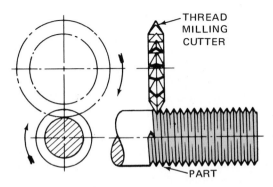

THREAD
MILLING
CUTTER

PART

Fig. 25-5. A screw thread can be produced by a rapidly revolving single milling cutter. The cutter is fed into the workpiece to the desired depth. The part is then moved at a rate which will produce the proper lead.

Fig. 25-6. The grinding process is similar to that of milling a thread by the single-cutter method. The principal difference is that in grinding, a large grinding wheel replaces the cutter and one or more light cuts are taken. The grinding process is used wherever it is necessary to eliminate distortion from a part after it has been heat-treated.

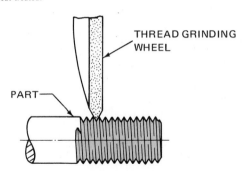

THREAD GRINDING
WHEEL

PART

Romans used hand-carved wood screws in wine presses. The thread outline was scratched on a cylindrical blank and filed by hand. After Rome fell, the use and development of the screw thread vanished from Europe. However, the Arabs and the Greeks continued to use hand-made screws. With the Renaissance in Europe in the fifteenth century, knowledge of the screw thread was renewed, possibly by the Near Eastern artisans who had fled the Turks. A suit of armor made for a French warrior about 1457 employed a handmade screw and nut to hold the plume onto the helmet (Fig. 25-8). King Louis XV of France slept in a bed held together

Fig. 25-7. A closeup of a thread being produced on a thread rolling or forming machine. Rolling is essentially a forging process producing the finished part by displacing metal to conform to the dies used. Very precise threads can be produced by this method.

Fig. 25-8. In the Middle Ages, nuts and bolts were used to hold the parts of armor suits together.

by strong, large, hand-fashioned metal screws. Gutenberg used screws in his original printing press.

About 1500, Leonardo da Vinci sketched designs for a screw-cutting machine, but there is no record of it ever having been built or used. In 1519, a Frenchman named Besson made the first actual machine for cutting threads. It consisted of a crude foot-operated lathe spindle and a thread "combing" tool. The tool was traversed along the work by means of a large handmade screw. News of his invention traveled very slowly, however, and for another 150 years screws continued to be manufactured by hand.

By the middle of the eighteenth century, two English brothers named Wyatt improved upon Besson's screw-cutting machine and started the first mechanized factory for producing about 100,000 wood screws per week.

With the industrial revolution of 1800 in England, steam power made heavier machinery possible and Henry Maudslay designed and built the first all-metal screw-cutting lathe. He spent 10 years trying to make an accurate *master* or *lead screw*. Finally he made one that was 7 feet long and with a total lead error of only $\frac{1}{16}$ in. Using this lead screw, Maudslay was able to produce others and thus to build screw-cutting engine lathes.

During these early years, all screw threads were produced by cutting either with single-point chasing tools in engine lathes or with thread combing tools and thread cutting dies. In 1887, A. B. Landis of the United States produced the first workable self-opening, thread-cutting die head employing many tangential-type thread-cutting chasers.

SCREW-THREAD TERMINOLOGY

There are several terms used in describing screw threads and screw-thread systems with which you should be familiar (Fig. 25-9).

● *Helix*—the curve formed on any cylinder by a straight line in a plane that is wrapped round the cylinder with a forward progression.

● *Screw thread*—a ridge of uniform section in the form of a helix on the external or internal surface of a cylinder. It is a spiral groove produced on the outside of a bolt or rod or machined on the inside of a nut or cylinder.

● *External thread*—a thread on the external surface of a cylinder.

● *Internal thread*—a thread on the internal surface of a hollow cylinder.

● *Major diameter*—the diameter of a cylinder that bounds the crest of an external thread or the root of an internal thread.

● *Minor diameter*—the diameter of a cylinder that bounds the root of an external thread or the crest of an internal thread.

● *Pitch diameter*—the diameter of an imaginary cylinder. The surface of this cylinder is of such size that it would pass through the threads, making the width of the thread and the width of the spaces between the threads equal. This definition holds true for straight threads.

● *Crest*—the top of the thread (bounded by the major diameter on external threads and by the minor diameter on internal threads). The crest is the top surface joining the two sides of the thread.

● *Root*—the bottom of the thread (bounded by the minor diameter on external threads and by the major diameter on internal threads).

● *Thread angle*—the angle formed by adjacent flanks of a thread.

● *Flank*—the side of the thread.

● *Height of thread*—the distance from the crest to the root of a thread measured perpen-

Fig. 25-9.   Common terms for describing screw threads.

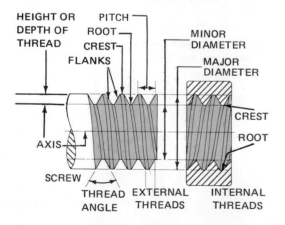

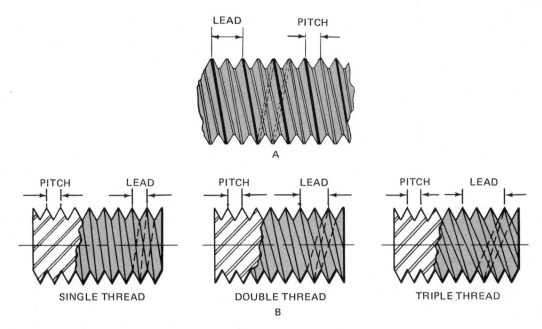

Fig. 25-10. (A) The difference between pitch and lead. The thread shown here is a double thread. (B) Single and multiple threads.

dicular to the axis of the threaded piece (also called *depth of thread*).

● *Slant depth*—the distance from the crest to the root of a thread measured along the angle forming the side of the thread.

● *Axis*—line running lengthwise through the center.

● *Angle of thread*—the angle included between the sides of the thread.

● *Pitch*—the distance from a point on one thread to the same or corresponding point on the next thread. The pitch in inches is equal to 1 divided by the number of threads per inch. For example, a screw with 10 threads per inch has a pitch of $\frac{1}{10}$ in. (Fig. 25-10).

● *Lead*—the distance a screw will advance or move into a nut in one complete turn. On a single-thread screw the *lead and pitch are equal.* On a double-thread screw the *lead is twice the pitch.*

● *Single thread*—a thread made by cutting one groove around a rod or inside a hole. Most bolts, nuts, and machine screws are single threaded. A *double thread* has two grooves cut

around the cylinder. There may be two, three, or four threads cut at equally spaced intervals around a cylinder. These are called *multiple threads.*

● *Right-hand thread*—a thread in which a bolt or nut must be turned clockwise or to the right to tighten it.

● *Left-hand thread*—a thread in which the bolt or nut must be turned counterclockwise or to the left to tighten it.

● *Thread fit*—the way the bolt and nut fit together as to looseness or tightness.

● *Thread series*—groups of diameter pitch combinations which differ in the number of threads per inch to a specific diameter. The common thread series are the coarse series and the fine series.

● *Thread form*—the axial plane profile of a thread for a length of one pitch.

● *Allowance*—an intentional difference in correlated dimensions of mating parts. It is the minimum clearance (positive allowance) or maximum interference (negative allowance) between such parts.

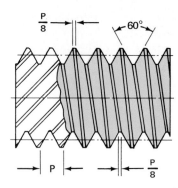

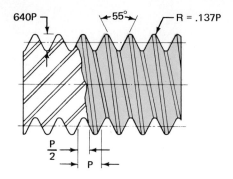

Fig. 25-12. British Standard Whitworth thread.

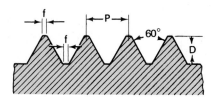

Fig. 25-11. American National thread form. "P" is pitch, "D" is the depth, and "f" is the root and crest flat.

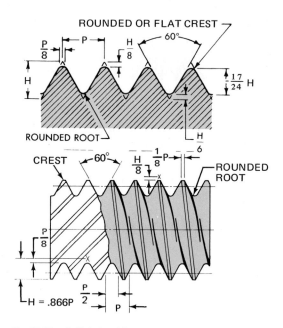

Fig. 25-13. Unified thread form.

UNIFIED NATIONAL THREAD

In the past, the United States has used a wide number of thread forms, many of which were not standard. The American National thread form was previously known as the United States Standard and was used for many years (Fig. 25-11). This thread form has an included angle of 60 degrees (°) and a crest and root that are flat. In England and Canada, the standard thread form was the Whitworth thread (Fig. 25-12). This thread form has a 55° angle with a crest and root rounded. The American National and the Whitworth thread could not be interchanged because of the differences in forms and angles. This caused a great deal of waste in both time and cost during World War II, when replacement parts were badly needed overseas.

In 1948, Great Britain, Canada, and the United States agreed on a thread form known as the Unified form (Fig. 25-13). This thread form has a 60° angle. The crest of the external thread may be either flat or rounded. The rounded or flat root of the external thread may be made intentionally or be the result of a worn tool. The internal thread has a flat crest and a rounded or flat root. This makes it possible to interchange the Unified thread form with the American National thread form. Since the American National thread form and the Unified thread form are interchangeable, they can be thought of as one system, the Unified National. There are minor differences between the two systems, but these differences are so technical that they do not need to concern the average machinist. Most threaded fasteners made by industry use one of the Unified National thread forms.

Classes of thread fit are distinguished from each other by the amount of tolerance or allowance specified. Classes 1A, 2A, and 3A apply to external threads, and classes 1B, 2B, and 3B apply to internal threads. Classes 1A and 1B are seldom used. Most standard industrial fasteners are produced with class 2A fit for bolts and a class 2B fit for nuts. The class 2A allowance assures easy assembly for mating parts and can be used with all electroplated fasteners. Classes 3A and 3B afford no allowance for clearance for mating parts and are used chiefly where close tolerance fit is important. Class 5 is a special fit, which actually results in overlapping of material when the threaded parts are fitted together.

There are 11 standard series of threads available in the American National and Unified National thread system. However, only the coarse and fine series find wide use in general machine-shop work. (The coarse series comprises the vast majority of bolts and nuts. The fine series is used when greater accuracy is required.)

Threads are identified by: (1) the number of threads per inch applied to a specific diameter, (2) the initial letters of the thread standards (UN or N), (3) the letters C or F to identify coarse or fine series, and (4) the thread fit.

Example.

$$\tfrac{1}{2} \text{ in.} - 13\text{UNC-2A}$$

where $\tfrac{1}{2}$ in. = nominal diameter of thread
13 = number of threads per inch
UN = thread form standard (Unified National)
C = coarse-thread series
2A = class of thread fit

It is necessary to understand the *number sizes* of screw threads as used in the coarse and fine series. The diameter is always stated first, then the number of threads per inch. For example, a 10-32 screw means that the diameter is a No. 10 and the screw has 32 threads per inch. In order to make a 10-32 screw, a machinist needs to know the diameter of a No. 10 screw in thousandths of an inch. You can figure the diameters of all the number-size screws quickly and easily since the smallest number size (No. 0) has a diameter of 0.060 in. and each number size increases by 0.013 in. Therefore, to find the diameter of any number-size screw thread, multiply the number of the screw by 0.013 and add

0.060. For example, to find the major diameter of a 5-40 screw, you would multiply 5 × 0.013, which equals 0.065. Then add 0.060, which equals 0.125 in. or

$$5 \times 0.013 = 0.065$$

$$0.065 + 0.060 = 0.125$$

There are only 10 number sizes used in the National coarse and fine series of screw threads. These are Nos. 0, 1, 2, 3, 4, 5, 6, 8, 10, and 12. Occasionally, you may find a No. 14 (0.242 diameter) size, but this number is so close in diameter to a $\tfrac{1}{4}$ in. (0.250) diameter that it is rarely used.

Specific standards for dimensions and tolerances of screw threads are issued by the American National Standards Institute (ANSI) in cooperation with the American Society of Mechanical Engineers (ASME) and the Industrial Fastening Institute (IFI).

OTHER THREAD FORMS

There are 108 external thread forms used throughout the world. However, only a few of these are in common use. The major ones are:

1. *The international metric thread.* Established by the International Organization for Standardization (ISO), this is the standard thread used in Europe and most of the world. It is similar to the American National except that the depth is greater. This thread has a 60° included angle with a crest and root that is flattened one-eighth the depth, although a rounded root is recommended (Fig. 25–14). This system forms the basis for the metric series. Complete information on this thread is given in *Machinery's Handbook.*

2. *IFI metric threads.* One of the problems with both metric and inch size threads is that there are far too many diameters and pitches. In the typical UNF- and UNC-inch thread series, there are 59 standard diameter-pitch combinations, 33 in the coarse thread series (UNC) and 26 in the fine thread series (UNF). The ISO metric threads contain 66 diameter-pitch combinations, with 43 in the coarse thread series and 23 in the fine thread series. The Industrial Fasteners Institute (IFI), has researched and developed 25 sizes of metric threads in a single-pitch series. This recommended metric diame-

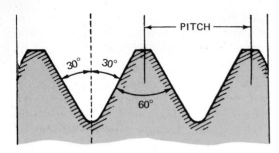

Fig. 25-14. Metric thread form.

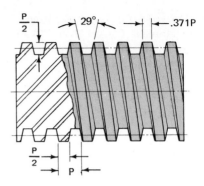

Fig. 25-15. Acme thread form.

ter-pitch series, if adopted, would replace the 125 different inch and metric sizes presently used by American industry. This would greatly reduce the number of different threaded fasteners needed.

3. *The acme screw thread.* This is a heavy-duty thread having a thread angle of 29°. It is used for feed screws on machine tools and for many other purposes where a precision, long-wearing screw is necessary. There are old and new standards for acme threads. Both use a 29° angle thread, but they are not interchangeable (Fig. 25-15). Before you cut this kind of thread on the

lathe, check the dimensions in *The New American Machinist's Handbook.*

4. *American pipe threads.* These threads come in three series, the most common of which is the National pipe thread series (NPT). The threads are tapered ($\frac{3}{4}$ inch per foot), but are always cut at right angles to the axis of the pipe (Fig. 25-16). It is necessary to find the pipe diameter and number of threads per inch by looking up this information in a handbook.

Fig. 25-16. Taper pipe thread.

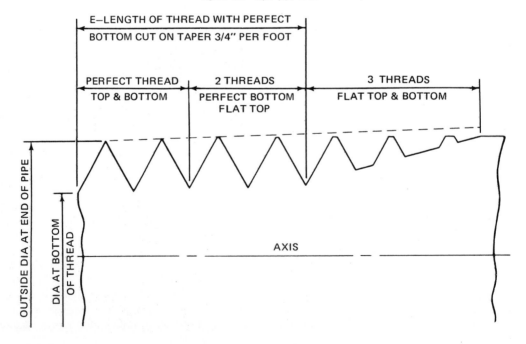

MEASURING NUMBER OF THREADS PER INCH

It is often necessary to determine the number of threads per inch on various types of work in a machine shop. You can do this in two ways:

1. Use a steel rule and hold it lengthwise on the threaded portion of the screw. If the thread is 1 in. or longer, you can count the number of threads in a whole inch of length. The first thread is always counted as zero. If the threaded portion is less than 1 in. long, count the number of threads in a fractional part of the inch, such as $\frac{1}{8}$ in., and multiply by 8 to get the threads per inch (Fig. 25-17).

2. A *screw-pitch* gage can be used. This gage is made up of a number of thin blades. Each blade has V-shaped teeth cut along one edge that equal standard thread shapes. Try several

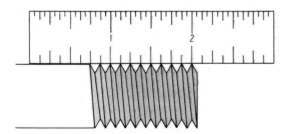

Fig. 25-17. A simple method of finding the number of threads per inch with a steel rule. Notice that there are eight threads per inch.

Fig. 25-18. Using a screw pitch gage to find the number of threads per inch. The sawlike teeth are cut to correspond to a standard thread section. Place the teeth of each blade against the screw thread being measured until one fits exactly.

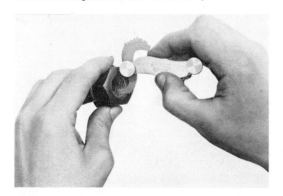

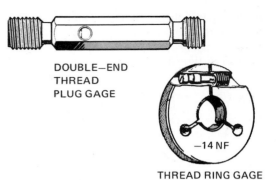

DOUBLE—END THREAD PLUG GAGE

—14 NF

THREAD RING GAGE

Fig. 25-19. Thread plug and ring gages.

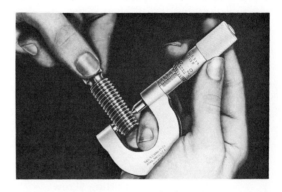

Fig. 25-20. Using a thread micrometer.

Fig. 25-21. Using an indicator-type gage to measure threads.

blades against the screw thread until you find the one that fits exactly in the grooves. The number stamped on the blade tells you the number of threads per inch (Fig. 25-18).

MEASURING SCREW THREADS

Screw threads can be measured for size and accuracy using thread gages, the thread micrometer, or the indicating thread gage.

1. Thread plug and ring gages are similar to plain plug and ring gages, except they are threaded. The ring gages are usually split and are provided with an adjusting and locking screw. Adjustable thread snap gages are also similar to plain snap gages, except that a thread form is ground in the face of the gaging members. They are faster to use than a ring gage and can be used to check work in process (Fig. 25-19).

2. A thread micrometer is used to measure the pitch diameter of V-shaped threads such as the American National and Unified National (Fig. 25-20). V-shaped interchangeable anvils and spindles are available to measure threads from 2.5 to 64 threads per inch. Be sure to use the correct set for the threads to be measured. The end of the spindle point and the bottom of the V in the anvil have allowance for clearance so they will not rest on the top or bottom of the threads.

3. The indicating thread gage gives an accurate reading of pitch diameter and is also capable of computing the eccentricity of the blank body of a screw (Fig. 25-21). These are set to standard, usually by gage blocks, and the indicator needle adjusted to zero. When the part is applied, the needle shows the amount by which the part differs from standard.

UNIT 26. Cutting Screw Threads with Taps and Dies

No other method of holding things together offers the flexibility of threaded parts. Threads can be cut by hand using taps and dies. Taps are used to cut inside, or internal, threads. Dies cut outside, or external, threads. Just as a drill cuts material away to make a hole, taps and dies cut material away to make a thread. A set of taps and dies, together with the tap wrenches and die stocks for cutting a range of common thread sizes, is called a *screw plate* (Fig. 26-1).

TAPS

A *tap* is a hardened steel tool used for cutting threads (Fig. 26-2). It has a threaded portion with flutes running lengthwise along the thread. The flutes provide the cutting-edges for each of the threads. They also provide a passage for oil to reach the cutting-edges and for chips to flow out of the workpiece.

The *four-flute hand tap* is the most com-

monly used tap in industry today. Though originally designed for hand use, it is now used also with machines. Two other types of taps are the *spiral-fluted tap* and the *spiral-pointed tap*. Both are designed for maximum chip relief and are especially useful for tapping the softer and non-free-machining alloys. The spiral-fluted tap tends to lift the chip out of the hole. It is highly recommended for blind-hole tapping (Fig. 26-3). The spiral-pointed tap cuts the thread with a shearing action and pushes the chips formed

Fig. 26-1. A screw-plate set includes all the common sizes of taps and dies.

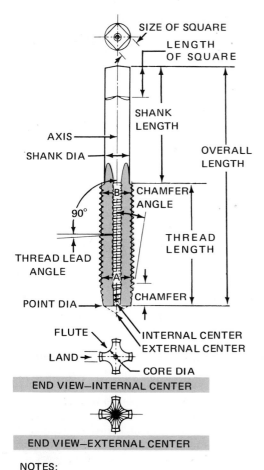

SIZE OF SQUARE

LENGTH OF SQUARE

SHANK LENGTH

AXIS

SHANK DIA

OVERALL LENGTH

CHAMFER ANGLE

90°

THREAD LENGTH

THREAD LEAD ANGLE

POINT DIA

CHAMFER

INTERNAL CENTER
EXTERNAL CENTER

FLUTE

LAND

CORE DIA

END VIEW—INTERNAL CENTER

END VIEW—EXTERNAL CENTER

NOTES;
"A"— PITCH DIAMETER AT FIRST FULL THREAD. THIS IS THE CORRECT POINT FOR MEASURING PITCH DIAMETER.

BACK TAPER—THE PITCH DIAMETER AT "A" IS GREATER THAN THE PITCH DIAMETER AT "B."

Fig. 26-2. Parts of a tap. This is a four-flute tap.

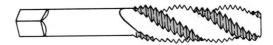

Fig. 26-3. A spiral-fluted tap.

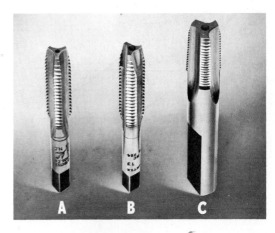

Fig. 26-4. A comparison of three types of taps: (A) standard, (B) spiral-point, and (C) pipe-thread.

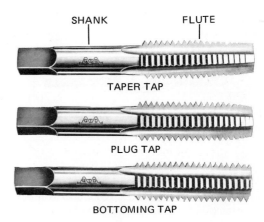

SHANK   FLUTE

TAPER TAP

PLUG TAP

BOTTOMING TAP

Fig. 26-5. Three basic types of taps.

ahead of the tap. It can be used for through-hole tapping in almost any type of material (Fig. 26-4).

A square at the end of the tap shank fits into the tap wrench which is used to turn the tap. Taps are hard and brittle and break quite easily if improperly used. They will stand considerable twisting, however, if the pressure at each end of the tap wrench is equal. They can-

not be bent from side to side without breaking.

There are three basic types of taps (Fig. 26-5). *Plug taps* are used for ordinary threading and have a 3- to 5-thread chamfer, or relief, at the point. *Taper taps* have 8 to 10 threads chamfered for easy starting. They are used for tough threading jobs. *Bottoming taps,* with their short chamfer (1 to 1½ threads), are used where the thread must go to the bottom of a hole. In

161

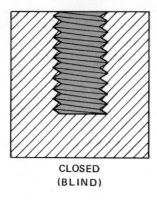

CLOSED
(BLIND)

Fig. 26-6. Use a bottoming tap to finish cutting the thread to the bottom of a blind hole.

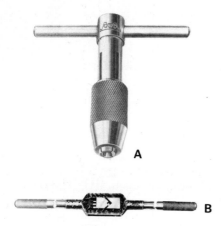

Fig. 26-7. Two types of tap wrenches: (A) T-handle tap wrench and (B) adjustable tap wrench.

addition, special kinds of taps are also available; for example, *left-hand taps* are made for cutting left-hand threads.

When tapping threads completely through a short hole, the tapered tap is all that is needed. However, if the hole is longer than the distance of the full-depth threads on the taper tap, a plug tap would be required. The plug tap is generally used for most of the ordinary work in a machine shop. When threads must be cut to the bottom of a blind hole (a hole that does not go through), a bottoming tap is used. Bottoming taps are only used to finish-cut the thread to the bottom of the hole. A plug tap is always used first (Fig. 26-6).

All taps have the thread diameter and the number of threads stamped on the shank. For example, if the tap is stamped $\frac{1}{2}$-13NC (or UNC), the thread is $\frac{1}{2}$ in. in diameter and has 13 threads per inch. The C of UNC means coarse.

Taps are held and turned with either an *adjustable tap wrench* or a *T-handle tap wrench* (Fig. 26-7). The T-handle tap wrench is used for small-size taps, and the adjustable tap wrench for larger taps. Both types of wrenches are made in several sizes. Taps can be easily broken if the wrench used is too large. Your sense of feel is greatly reduced or lost when you use a large wrench on a small tap.

DIES

A die is used to cut threads on a bolt or rod. The type of thread die used most is called an *adjustable* or *split die* (Fig. 26-8A). This die can be adjusted to cut a thread to the kind of fit desired, such as loose, snug, or tight. Some split dies have a setscrew in the die itself, and others contain no setscrew. In either case, the die may be spread open or expanded by (1) tightening one of the three screws of the die stock into the split part of the die or (2) by tightening the setscrew in the die itself. The correct procedure for obtaining a good fit is first to expand the die, then run it over the rod to be threaded. Check the fit with a gage, a nut, or the part it is to fit into. It should be a tight fit after this first cut. Back off the setscrew, which expanded the die, about one turn, and run over the work again. After two or three tries, the desired fit should be obtained.

The *two-piece die* is made in two parts that fit into a die stock especially designed for this type of die (Fig. 26-8B). A *solid square die* is sometimes used (Fig. 26-8C). Two other kinds of dies are the *precision die* (Fig. 26-8D) and the *rethreading die* (Fig. 26-8E).

Dies are held in a *die stock* (Fig. 26-9). Some die stocks are equipped with a guide to help get the die started straight on the workpiece. Where there is no guide, good judgment and skill are required to start the die straight. A short chamfer or angle filed on the end of the rod helps start the die easily. If you examine the threads on each side of a die, you will see that on one side the threads are tapered or chamfered back a distance of three or four threads.

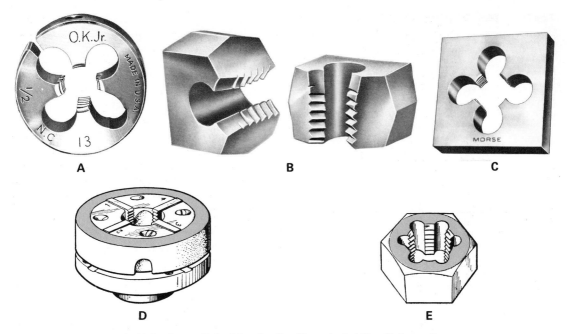

Fig. 26-8. Common kinds of threading dies: (A) round adjustable split die, sometimes called button die, (B) two-piece threading die, (C) solid square die, (D) precision die, and (E) rethreading die.

The opposite side has only one thread chamfered. Always start the chamfered side of the die on the work first. If you wish to thread as close to a shoulder as possible, turn the die over.

TAPPING HOLES

1. Always determine the size of the thread to be cut and select the tap before you drill the hole. Then determine the correct size of drill to be used. There is a correct size tap drill for each size of tap. You may find the correct drill size to use by looking in a table of tap-drill sizes, as shown in Table 26-1. For example, if the tap is stamped $\frac{1}{2}$-20NF (or UNF), the table shows that a $\frac{29}{64}$-in. drill should be used.

Most machinists like to calculate the tap-drill size. This can be done by *subtracting the pitch from the tap diameter*. For example, to find the tap-drill size for a $\frac{3}{8}$-16 tap, subtract $\frac{1}{16}$, which is the pitch, from $\frac{3}{8}$, the diameter of the tap. Thus, $\frac{3}{8} - \frac{1}{16} = \frac{5}{16}$, which is the correct drill to use. This drill produces a hole that, after tapping, will give 70 to 75 percent depth of thread. This thread is only 5 percent weaker than a full depth of thread. Nearly all tap-drill sizes are

calculated to give about 70 to 75 percent depth of thread. The holes are easier to tap and the thread is strong enough for all practical purposes. In fact, it has been found that a bolt will break before the thread is stripped.

2. Drill the hole with the correct size drill. Hold the work in a drill vise, and use oil on the drill.

3. Set the workpiece in the bench vise so the hole is in a vertical position.

4. Select the correct size and type of tap wrench, and tighten the tap in the wrench.

5. Grasp the tap and wrench in your right hand, with your hand cupped over the center of the wrench. Place the tap in the hole. Applying pressure downward, turn the tap to the right to get it started.

Fig. 26-9. Diestock.

Table 26-1.   Thread hole element chart.

For American National Coarse Threads

Screw Thread	Major Diameter	Body Drill	Tap Drill	Pitch Diameter	Thread Depth	% Thread Depth
5-40	.1250	29- .1360	39-.0995	.1088	.0612	71
6-32	.1380	27- .1440	36-.1065	.1177	.0203	71
8-32	.1640	18- .1695	29-.1360	.1437	.0203	69
10-24	.1900	9- .1960	25-.1495	.1629	.0270	69
$\frac{1}{4}$-20	.2500	$\frac{17}{64}$-.2656	7-.2010	.2175	.0325	70
$\frac{5}{16}$-18	.3125	$\frac{21}{64}$-.3281	F-.2570	.2764	.0361	72
$\frac{3}{8}$-16	.3750	$\frac{25}{64}$-.3906	$\frac{5}{16}$-.3125	.3344	.0406	72
$\frac{7}{16}$-14	.4375	$\frac{29}{64}$-.4531	U-.3680	.3911	.0464	70
$\frac{1}{2}$-13	.5000	$\frac{33}{64}$-.5156	$\frac{27}{64}$-.4219	.4500	.0499	73
$\frac{5}{8}$-11	.6250	$\frac{41}{64}$-.6406	$\frac{17}{32}$-.5312	.5660	.0590	75
$\frac{3}{4}$-10	.7500	$\frac{49}{64}$-.7656	$\frac{21}{32}$-.6563	.6850	.0649	68
$\frac{7}{8}$- 9	.8750	$\frac{57}{64}$-.8906	$\frac{49}{64}$-.7656	.8028	.0721	72
1- 8	1.0000	$1\frac{1}{64}$-1.0156	$\frac{7}{8}$-.8750	.9188	.0812	73

For American National Fine Threads

Screw Thread	Major Diameter	Body Drill	Tap Drill	Pitch Diameter	Thread Depth	% Thread Depth
5-44	.1380	29- .1360	37-.1040	.1102	.0147	63
6-40	.1380	27- .1440	33-.1130	.1218	.0162	69
8-36	.1640	18- .1695	29-.1360	.1460	.0180	70
10-32	.1900	9- .1960	21-.1590	.1697	.0203	68
$\frac{1}{4}$-28	.2500	$\frac{17}{64}$-.2656	3-.2130	.2268	.0232	72
$\frac{5}{16}$-24	.3125	$\frac{21}{64}$-.3281	1-.2720	.2854	.0220	67
$\frac{3}{8}$-24	.3750	$\frac{25}{64}$-.3906	Q-.3322	.3479	.0220	71
$\frac{7}{16}$-20	.4375	$\frac{29}{64}$-.4531	$\frac{25}{64}$-.3906	.4050	.0325	65
$\frac{1}{2}$-20	.5000	$\frac{33}{64}$-.5156	$\frac{29}{64}$-.4531	.4975	.0325	65
$\frac{5}{8}$-18	.6250	$\frac{41}{64}$-.6406	$\frac{37}{64}$-.5781	.5889	.0361	58
$\frac{3}{4}$-16	.7500	$\frac{49}{64}$-.7656	$\frac{11}{16}$-.6875	.7094	.0406	71
$\frac{7}{8}$-14	.8750	$\frac{57}{64}$-.8906	$\frac{13}{16}$-.8125	.8286	.0464	62
1-14	1.0000	$1\frac{1}{64}$-1.0156	$\frac{15}{16}$-.9063	.9459	.0464	67

6. After two or three turns, check to make certain the tap is starting straight. A tap must always be checked at two points about 90 degrees (°) apart. Loosen the wrench without disturbing the tap, and use a small square (Fig. 26-10A). If a tap is not started straight and the hole is quite deep, the tap will eventually cut more stock from one side of the hole than the other. The tap may also bind and break, ruining both the tap and your work. Also, the part that fits into the tapped hole would be out of square, which may also spoil the job.

7. Always use cutting oil when tapping holes, except on cast iron.

8. When tapping by hand, it is good practice to back up the tap after two or three turns, especially on tough steel parts. This breaks the chips, helps to avoid clogging the flutes, and prevents breaking the tap.

9. Turn the tap forward and backward alternately, until the thread is cut (Fig. 26-10B).

10. When tapping to the bottom of a blind

A

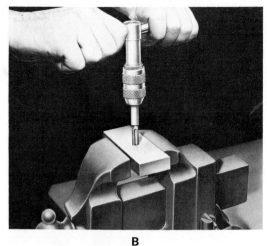

B

Fig. 26-10. (A) Checking the tap to make sure that it is square. (B) Cutting the thread.

Fig. 26-11. Hand-tapping fixture.

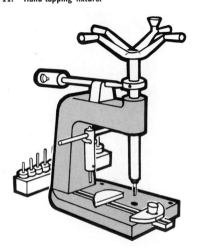

hole, it may be necessary to remove the tap several times to clean the chips from the hole. Use the plug tap first, then finish to the bottom with a bottoming tap. Be very careful when the tap reaches the bottom. To force it at this point may break it.

Threads produced by conventional hand tapping are satisfactory for maintenance purposes but, if more accuracy is required, it may be obtained by using a fixture known as a hand tapper, such as shown in Fig. 26-11.

CUTTING EXTERNAL THREADS

1. Grind or file a chamfer or bevel on the end of the rod to help the die to start more easily (Fig. 26-12).

2. Fasten the die in the die stock with the stamped size on the top. The threads on the opposite side are tapered to help start the die.

Fig. 26-12. A bevel on the end of a rod to be threaded.

Fig. 26-13. Cutting a thread with a die and a diestock.

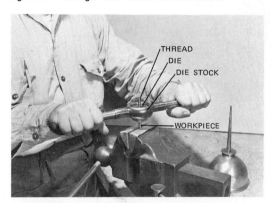

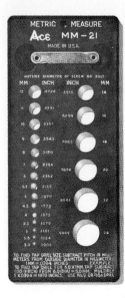

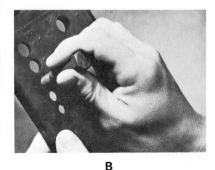

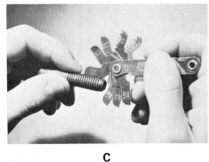

B   C

A

Fig. 26-14. (A) Gage for measuring metric threads. (B) Checking the outside diameter of the threads in millimeters. (C) Checking the metric pitch of the thread.

3. If the die stock has a guide, adjust it for a free fit on the rod.

4. Clamp the workpiece in the bench vise. If the rod is short, set it in a vertical position. If it is long, hold it in a horizontal position.

5. Place the die over the end of the rod.

6. Cup your hand over the die, apply pressure, and turn it to get the first threads started.

7. Apply cutting oil with a brush or oilcan so the oil gets down into the threads.

8. Check to make sure the die sets on the rod squarely. This is important when the die stock has no guide. If a die starts out of square, it will continue to cut a crooked thread. We call this a *drunken thread*. After two or three forward turns, back the die up for at least half a turn to break the chips (Fig. 26-13).

9. After the thread is cut to the correct length, back the die off the work by turning counter-clockwise.

10. Check the thread by using a gage, a nut, or the part it is to fit. If the thread is too tight, close the die slightly by backing up the setscrew in the die slot and tightening the opposite set-screws in the die stock. Then run the die over the thread again. Doing this once or twice should size the thread correctly.

METRIC THREADS

Metric taps and dies are used when metric threads are required (Fig. 26-14). Working with metric threaded screws and bolts need not pose a problem. The ISO (International Standards Organization) metric threads come in two series; the coarse series and the fine series (see Table 26-1). However, for all practical purposes, only the coarse series is used in threading and assembling. The fine thread series is employed only

Fig. 26-15. A set of tap extractors for standard size taps.

for precision work such as the manufacture of microscopes and other fine instruments.

In the coarse series, the 12 common sizes range in diameter from 2 to 24 millimeters, (mm) with a pitch range from 0.4 to 3.0 millimeters. You can quickly find the size of metric bolts by either using the metric measure gage or a metric micrometer. If the metric measure is used, the

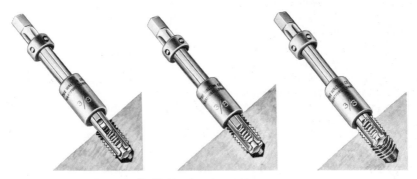

Fig. 26-16. Steps in removing a tap.

Table 26-2. Metric thread series.

ISO METRIC THREAD—COARSE SERIES

Diameter	2	2.5	3	4	5	6	8	10
Pitch	0.4	0.45	0.5	0.7	0.8	1.0	1.25	1.5
Basic effective diameter	1.740	2.208	2.675	3.545	4.480	5.350	7.188	9.026
Depth of thread in screw	0.25	0.28	0.31	0.43	0.49	0.61	0.77	0.92
Area of root diameter (mm^2)	1.79	2.98	4.47	7.75	12.7	17.9	32.8	52.3
Diameter of tapping drill	1.6	2.05	2.5	3.3	4.2	5.0	6.8	8.5
Diameter	12	16	20	24	30	36	42	48
Pitch	1.75	2.0	2.5	3.0	3.5	4.0	4.5	5.0
Basic effective diameter	10.863	14.701	18.376	22.051	27.727	33.402	39.077	44.752
Depth of thread in screw	1.07	1.23	1.53	1.84	2.15	2.45	2.76	3.07
Area of root diameter (mm^2)	76.2	144	225	324	519	759	1,050	1,380
Diameter of tapping drill	10.2	14.0	17.5	21.0	26.5	32.0	37.5	43.0

ISO METRIC THREAD—FINE SERIES

Diameter	8	10	12	14	16	18	20
Pitch	1.0	1.25	1.25	1.5	1.5	1.5	1.5
Basic effective diameter	7.350	9.188	11.188	13.026	15.026	17.026	19.026
Depth of thread in screw	0.61	0.77	0.77	0.92	0.92	0.92	0.92
Area of root diameter (mm^2)	36.0	56.3	86.0	116	157	205	259
Diameter of tapping drill	7.0	8.8	10.8	12.5	14.5	16.5	18.5
Diameter	22	24	30	36	42	48	
Pitch	1.5	2.0	2.0	3.0	3.0	3.0	
Basic effective diameter	21.026	22.701	28.701	34.051	40.051	46.051	
Depth of thread in screw	0.92	1.23	1.23	1.84	1.84	1.84	
Area of root diameter (mm^2)	319	365	586	820	1,210	1,540	
Diameter of tapping drill	20.5	22.0	28.0	33.0	39.0	45.0	

outside diameter of the bolt or screw is found by simply inserting it into the correct size hole. The correct pitch of the thread is then measured with the metric measurer's screw pitch gage. The pitch of metric threads is measured from one thread to the next. For example, an M6×1.0 thread is 6 mm in diameter and has a distance of 1.0 mm between threads. The tap drill is always equal to the outside diameter minus the pitch. For example, for the above size thread, the diameter of the tap drill would be 5.0 mm. Specific details on metric threads are found in the latest edition of *Machinery's Handbook*.

TAP EXTRACTORS

No matter how carefully tapping is done, there is always the danger that the tap will break. Removal of a tap that has broken off in a hole is difficult because a tap is extremely hard and can not be drilled. If a piece of the tap extends above the hole, take hold of it with a pair of pliers and work it back and forth to loosen it. If a tap is broken off below the surface, the best method is to use a tap extractor as follows (Fig. 26-15).

1. Thoroughly remove all chips of the broken tap. Insert the extractor fingers into the flutes of the broken tap, pushing them gently but firmly into position (Fig. 26-16).

2. Push the holder down until it touches the broken tap. Slide the sleeve down until it touches the work. Both of these steps are very important.

3. Apply a tap wrench to the square end of the holder. Twist forward and backward a few times to loosen, then back out the broken tap.

UNIT 27. Reaming at the Bench

Reaming is the operation of finishing a hole so that it is very smooth and accurate in size. A drill will not produce a hole to the exact size of the drill. The hole may not be smooth enough for a precision job. Therefore, when a very accurate, smooth hole is required, the hole is first drilled a little undersize. Then it is reamed to the correct size. Hand reamers, when properly used, produce very accurate holes. A hand reamer can be identified by the square end for attaching a wrench.

KINDS OF HAND REAMERS

1. *Hand reamers* are solid straight reamers with either straight or helical flutes. They may be made of carbon steel or high-speed steel. These reamers are used only for sizing holes. A tap wrench is used on the square of the shank to turn the reamer. Hand reamers are available in sizes from $\frac{1}{8}$ to $1\frac{1}{2}$ in. The ends of the teeth are tapered slightly for a short distance so the reamer can be started square in the hole (Fig. 27-1).

2. *Expansion hand reamers* are used to enlarge a hole a few thousandths of an inch to obtain the necessary fit. The reamer is made hollow through the center and has a tapered piece with threads that fits into the end of the reamer. When the screw is tightened, the cutting-edges expand in diameter. These reamers are ground with a starting taper on the teeth so that the reamer can be started easily in the hole. If expanded too much, they are easily broken. This type of reamer can be expanded or adjusted to cut 0.006 in. oversize in sizes from $\frac{1}{4}$ to $\frac{15}{32}$ in., and 0.015 in. oversize in the larger sizes (Fig. 27-2).

3. *Adjustable hand reamers* have blades inserted in tapered slots cut along a threaded body. They are used for reaming odd-sized holes for repair parts and are widely used by auto mechanics. These reamers can be increased in size from $\frac{1}{32}$ in. to as much as $\frac{5}{16}$ in. About 20 reamers in a set will take care of all sizes from $\frac{1}{4}$ to 3 in. (Fig. 27-3).

4. *Taper reamers* are made for finishing taper holes accurately and smoothly. Taper reamers are made with either straight or spiral flutes. The spiral flute is generally preferred because it has

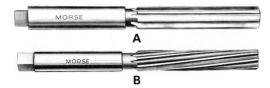

Fig. 27-1. (A) Hand reamers are used for final sizing of holes. The cutting end is ground with a starting taper for easy entrance. (B) Hand reamers with helical flutes are recommended for use in operations where there is an interruption to the cut, such as a keyway.

Fig. 27-2. Expansion hand reamers.

Fig. 27-3. Adjustable hand reamer.

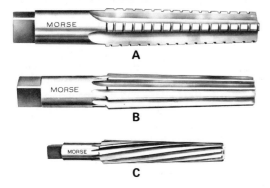

Fig. 27-4. Taper reamers: (A) roughing, (B) finishing and (C) helical.

a shearing action and eliminates chatter. Larger sizes of taper reamers are made in roughing and finishing types. A *roughing reamer* has small nicks or spaces ground into the teeth which prevent overloading the entire length of each cutting tooth. These nicks are staggered on the various teeth to help distribute the stock removal. When considerable stock must be removed, the roughing reamer is used. The *finishing reamer* is used to smooth and size the hole.

Taper reamers are made for all standard tapers such as Morse, Brown and Sharpe, and taper pins (Fig. 27-4).

5. *Burring reamers* are used for removing burrs from pipe or conduit. They can also be used to enlarge holes in thin material or for countersinking holes (Fig. 27-5).

SUGGESTIONS FOR USING REAMERS

1. Always select the correct size and type of reamer for the job.

2. Always start a reamer square with the hole.

3. Always turn the reamer in a clockwise direction.

4. Always continue to turn the reamer in the same direction when removing it.

5. Apply only slight, even pressure to the reamer.

6. Apply a small amount of oil when reaming steel.

7. No oil is needed when reaming cast iron.

8. Special reamers should be used when reaming copper, brass, or other nonferrous metals.

9. When reaming closed holes, remove the reamer frequently to clean out the chips from the flutes.

10. When using a roughing reamer, always leave from 0.005 to 0.010 in. to be removed by the finishing reamer.

REAMING

1. Holes to be reamed must always be drilled undersize first. For hand reaming, not more than 0.005 to 0.010 in. of stock should be left in the hole. Shops in industry usually grind or buy drills that will produce holes just the right size for reaming. In the average shop, the general prac-

Fig. 27-5. Burring reamer.

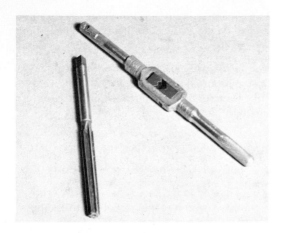

Fig. 27-6. A reamer with an adjustable tap wrench.

Fig. 27-7. Using a T-handle tap wrench on a small reamer. Wrenches should be just large enough to permit a steady torque, which will help to control vibration and chatter. The feed should be steady. A feed up to one-quarter of the reamer diameter per revolution is satisfactory.

tice is to use a drill $\frac{1}{64}$ in. smaller than the reamer size. This is often referred to as a *reamer drill size.*

2. Clamp the workpiece in the bench vise with the hole vertical. If the workpiece is irregular in shape, the square end of the hand reamer can be clamped in the vise and the work turned over the reamer.

3. Attach an adjustable tap wrench to the square end of the reamer (Fig. 27-6).

4. Set the end of the reamer into the hole. Brush cutting oil over all the reamer teeth. Rotate the reamer clockwise, making certain to hold it at right angles to the hole. If the hole is the correct size, the reamer will soon align itself (Fig. 27-7).

5. In the beginning, a slight downward pressure may be needed. A hand reamer will practically feed itself once it is started. It may advance into the hole as much as one-fourth the reamer diameter for each revolution. If forced too much, a hand reamer becomes jammed into the hole. If this happens, the reamer must be pressed out carefully from the opposite side.

CAUTION

Never turn a reamer backward. To do so ruins the delicate cutting-edges.

6. Unless a hand reamer is kept cutting, chatter develops. *Chatter* is a series of rough lines or marks in the surface and is most undesirable. Once started, the chatter marks get worse, unless the downward pressure is increased just enough to keep the reamer cutting.

7. Continue to turn the reamer clockwise until the hole is reamed. Don't forget to run the reamer far enough through the work to take care of the tapered end on the reamer.

8. If possible, the reamer should be passed on through the hole and removed from the far side without stopping the rotation. If this is not possible, it should be withdrawn without stopping the *forward* rotation.

UNIT 28.
Metal Fasteners and Tools for Assembling

Machines and instruments of all kinds are made up of many separate parts. These parts, when assembled, are held together by various types of *metal fasteners*. Some of the common metal fasteners are bolts, screws, nuts, rivets, washers, and pins. There are several types and many sizes of each. Also they are made of many kinds of metals to serve a specific purpose.

THREADED METAL FASTENERS

Some of the most commonly used bolts, nuts, and screws are listed below.

1. A *machine bolt* has a head on one end of the shank and a thread on the other. It is designed for insertion through holes in assembled parts to mate with a nut. Bolts have various styles of heads (Figs. 28–1A and 28–1B). Tension is induced in the shank by rotating or torquing the nut (Fig. 28–1C). A bolt used without a nut is called a *screw*.

The diameter of all bolts is equal to the outside, or major diameter, of the thread. The length of a headed bolt is measured from the largest diameter of the bearing surface of the head to the extreme end of the point in a plane parallel to the axis of the bolt. For example, square or hexagon head bolts are measured from under the head to the end of the bolt; a bolt with a countersunk head is measured overall. The point on a bolt is always included in the measured length. Headless fasteners such as studs are measured overall.

Bolts are available in diameters from $\frac{1}{4}$ to 4 in. and in lengths from $\frac{1}{2}$ to 30 in. They may be obtained with either fine or coarse threads. When special threads are required, they are made to order. Bolts are made in semifinished and finished quality. A *semifinished bolt* is made with a flat bearing surface under the head hav-

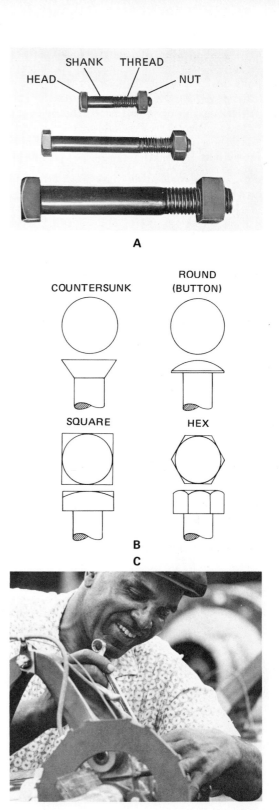

Fig. 28-1. (A) Machine bolts and nuts. (B) Common styles of heads for machine bolts and nuts. (C) A good machinist must know how to use wrenches and other assembly tools.

171

ing a washer face. A *finished bolt* is the same in appearance, but is made more accurately. Bolts may be either regular or heavy. The *heavy-type bolt* is a little larger across the flats of the hexagon or square head. The height of its head is slightly greater than the regular head. Bolts generally require the use of hexagon or square nuts.

2. *Cap screws* are made to a standard of accuracy like finished machine bolts. In addition to the hexagon head, they are made with round, flat, and fillister heads (Fig. 28-2). The heads may be slotted for a screwdriver or have a socket head. The socket-type screw may be either hexagonal or fluted. These types require special keys for turning the screws. A cap screw is considered a more finished product than a bolt. Another difference between the two is that a cap screw is tightened by turning the head, and a bolt is secured by tightening a nut. Cap-screw sizes vary from $\frac{1}{4}$ to $1\frac{1}{2}$ in. in diameter and from $\frac{1}{2}$ to 6 in. in length.

3. *Machine screws* are made with round, flat, oval, fillister, binding, pan, truss, and hexagon

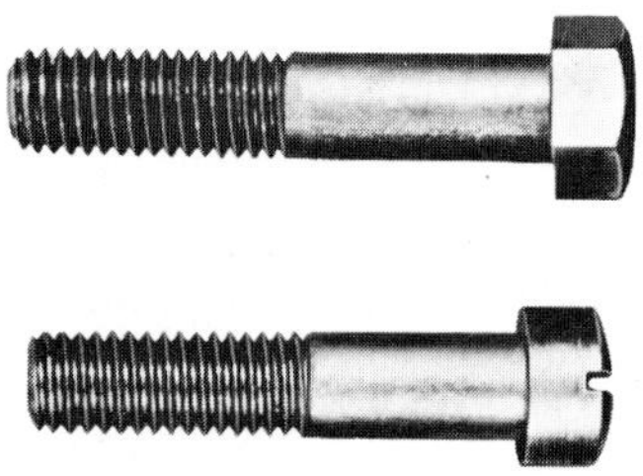

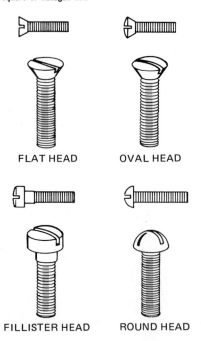

Fig. 28-2. Hexagon and fillister-head cap screws.

Fig. 28-3. Common shapes of machine screws. All types use either a square or hexagon nut.

FLAT HEAD   OVAL HEAD

FILLISTER HEAD   ROUND HEAD

CUP POINT   CONE POINT   FLAT POINT

HEADLESS SETSCREW   SOCKET-TYPE SETSCREW

Fig. 28-4. Types of setscrews.

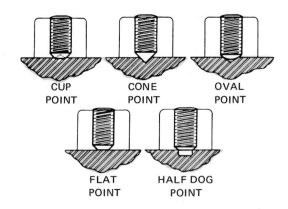

CUP POINT   CONE POINT   OVAL POINT

FLAT POINT   HALF DOG POINT

Fig. 28-5. Types of setscrew points.

Fig. 28-6. Stud.

heads (Fig. 28–3). They may be purchased with either fine or coarse threads. Below $\frac{1}{4}$ in. diameter the sizes are stated by numbers instead of fractions. For example, a 6-32 screw has a No. 6 (0.138) diameter and 32 threads per inch. These screws are commonly made from brass and steel, but can be obtained in other metals. Lengths vary from $\frac{1}{8}$ to 3 in. Machine screws are used to hold parts together when one part has a tapped hole and the other part has a clearance or body-size hole. A *clearance* or *body-size hole* is one that permits the screw to slip through freely and has no threads. Square or hexagon machine-screw nuts are often used with these screws. The heads of machine screws may be either slotted for a plain screwdriver or recessed for a Phillips-type screwdriver.

4. *Setscrews* are made with or without heads. They have a cup, cone, or other shaped point which is designed to prevent or restrict the movement of two assembled parts, such as a pulley on a shaft. The head-type setscrew has a square head. Headless types have either a slot for a screwdriver or a socket which requires a hexagonal or fluted-type of key (Allen hex key) (Fig. 28–4). Different types of points are shown in Fig. 28–5.

5. *Studs* are short shafts having a threaded portion at each end or a continuous thread that runs the entire length. The unthreaded portion may be of any shape or size. Studs seldom exceed 12 in. in length. In use, one end of the stud is screwed into a tapped hole. The part to be clamped is slipped over the stud or studs. A nut is used at the top of the stud to clamp the parts together. The cylinder head on an automobile engine is held in place by studs (Fig. 28–6).

6. *Thread-forming screws* form or cut a thread in one or both parts of an assembly when driven or turned into a hole of proper size. Use of these *self-tapping* screws eliminates tapping, riveting, and soldering. This saves much of the cost of machining and assembly. These screws are made in all the commonly used head types, as well as several special types (Fig. 28–7).

7. *Thread-cutting screws* have threads very similar to machine screws with a blunt point. They also have tapered entering threads having one or more cutting-edges and chip-clearance space. These screws can be used in materials such as aluminum, zinc, lead, steel sheets, cast iron, brass, and plastics. The flutes at the ends of the screws provide cutting action in brittle

Fig. 28–7. Thread-forming screws.

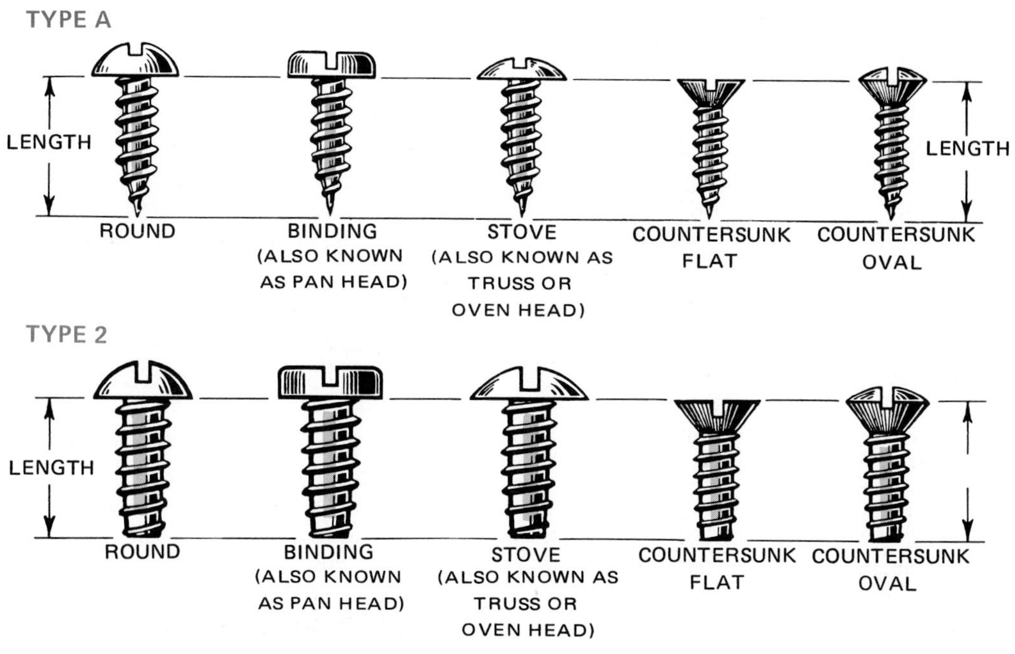

TYPE A

LENGTH LENGTH

ROUND BINDING (ALSO KNOWN AS PAN HEAD) STOVE (ALSO KNOWN AS TRUSS OR OVEN HEAD) COUNTERSUNK FLAT COUNTERSUNK OVAL

TYPE 2

LENGTH

ROUND BINDING (ALSO KNOWN AS PAN HEAD) STOVE (ALSO KNOWN AS TRUSS OR OVEN HEAD) COUNTERSUNK FLAT COUNTERSUNK OVAL

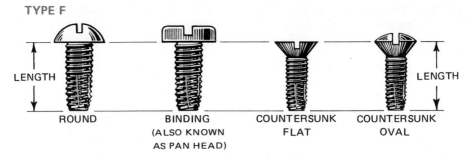

TYPE F

LENGTH | ROUND | BINDING (ALSO KNOWN AS PAN HEAD) | COUNTERSUNK FLAT | COUNTERSUNK OVAL | LENGTH

Fig. 28-8. Thread-cutting screws.

material like plastics which will not give or move (Fig. 28-8).

8. *Nuts* of various types are used with bolts, machine screws, and studs. The most common types are the hexagon and square nuts. These are graded as *regular* and *heavy*. A heavy nut is thicker and slightly larger across the flats than a regular nut. In addition, these nuts are classified as *finished* or *semifinished*. The only difference between them is in the quality of manufacture and the closeness of tolerance. Regular square nuts are not finished on any surface. Finished and semifinished nuts are machined on the bearing surface and have a washerlike face (Fig. 28-9).

a. *Jam nuts* are hexagonal and much thinner than regular nuts. They are tightened against regular nuts to lock them in position or are used in narrow spaces. They have a washer face and are fully machined (Fig. 28-10).

b. *Machine-screw nuts* may be either square or hexagonal. Finished and semifinished hexagonal nuts have one end chamfered, but can be obtained with both ends chamfered if required. Square nuts are flat at top and bottom and have no chamfer.

c. *Slotted nuts* and *castle nuts* are slotted across the flats of the hexagon so that a cotter pin can be placed through a hole in the bolt after the nut has been tightened. The cotter pin keeps the nut from working loose (Fig. 28-11).

d. *Self-locking nuts* provide positive locking action under shock or vibration. The nut is fitted with a special locking pin which travels between the bolt threads. The pin

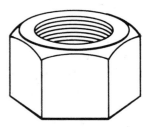

Fig. 28-9. Hexagon nut.

Fig. 28-10. Jam nut.

end acts as a ratchet, sliding along the thread as the nut is tightened, but holding the nut tight and preventing any tendency to back off under vibration. They can be easily disassembled and reused (Fig. 28-12).

e. The *cap* or *acorn nut* is generally used for work that requires a decorative touch or neat appearance. They are usually made of brass and can be chrome- or nickel-plated for appearance (Fig. 28-13).

f. A *wing nut* is used on various types of threaded fasteners where frequent adjustment or removal is necessary. They are made from various metals in both fine and coarse threads. The nut can be tightened and loosened by hand and does not require a wrench (Fig. 28-14).

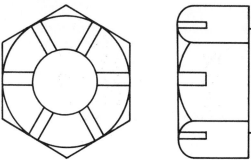
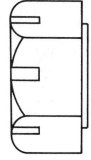

Fig. 28-11. Slotted nut.

Fig. 28-14. Wing nut.

Fig. 28-12. Self-locking nut.

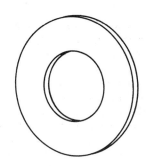

Fig. 28-15. Plain washer.

Fig. 28-13. Cap or acorn nut.

Fig. 28-16. Lock washer.

Fig. 28-17. Three types of tooth lock washers.

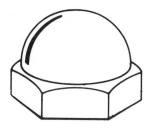
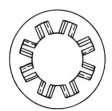

9. *Washers* are used with threaded metal fasteners. The three basic types of washers are *plain, spring lock,* and *tooth lock.* All three types are available in standard sizes to fit standard bolts and screws.

a. *Plain washers* are used under the head of a screw or bolt, or under a nut to spread a load over a greater area. They are also used to prevent the marring of parts during assembly. (Fig. 28-15).

b. *Spring lock washers* are made of steel, bronze, or aluminum alloys. They serve as spring take-up devices to compensate for developed looseness and the loss of tension. They are also used to facilitate assembly and disassembly (Fig. 28-16).

c. External, internal, and internal-external types of *tooth lock washers* are shown in Fig. 28-17. The hardened teeth of these washers are twisted so as to bite or grip both the bolt head (or nut) and the work surface. This helps to prevent the loosening of an assembly due to vibration.

RIVETS

Rivets are used to hold parts together when it is not necessary to take them apart. Rivets are made of soft iron, copper, or aluminum, so the ends can be peened over easily. Figure 28-18 shows the common head shapes of rivets.

PINS

A *cotter pin* is a split pin having a loop or eyelet at one end. It is used to hold parts on a shaft or to keep a slotted nut from working loose. It is placed through a hole in a shaft. Then the split ends are bent outward, one in each direction, to keep the pin in place (Fig. 28-19).

Taper pins are widely used on many machines and instruments to hold two parts in alignment. The pins are easy to remove when necessary. The parts can be realigned to the original position when the taper pin is replaced. Taper pins have a taper of $\frac{1}{4}$ in. to the foot and are made in many sizes and lengths. The holes for a taper pin must first be drilled with an ordinary twist drill. Then the hole is reamed with a *taper-pin reamer* of the correct size for the pin

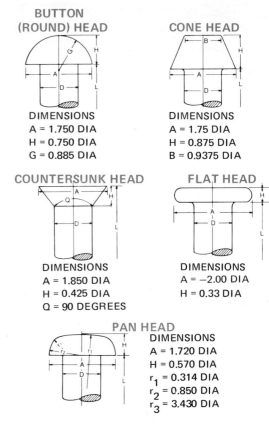

BUTTON (ROUND) HEAD

DIMENSIONS
A = 1.750 DIA
H = 0.750 DIA
G = 0.885 DIA

CONE HEAD

DIMENSIONS
A = 1.75 DIA
H = 0.875 DIA
B = 0.9375 DIA

COUNTERSUNK HEAD

DIMENSIONS
A = 1.850 DIA
H = 0.425 DIA
Q = 90 DEGREES

FLAT HEAD

DIMENSIONS
A = −2.00 DIA
H = 0.33 DIA

PAN HEAD

DIMENSIONS
A = 1.720 DIA
H = 0.570 DIA
r_1 = 0.314 DIA
r_2 = 0.850 DIA
r_3 = 3.430 DIA

THE LENGTH (L) IS MEASURED FROM UNDER THE HEAD TO THE END OF THE RIVET FOR ALL SHOWN EXECPT COUNTERSUNK, FOR WHICH (L) IS THE OVERALL LENGTH.

Fig. 28-18.   Standard rivet heads.

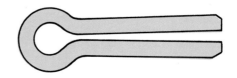

Fig. 28-19.   Cotter pin.

Fig. 28-20.   Taper pin.

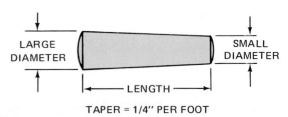

LARGE DIAMETER

SMALL DIAMETER

LENGTH

TAPER = 1/4″ PER FOOT

Fig. 28-21. Dowel pin.

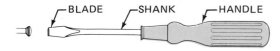

Fig. 28-22. Two common types of screwdrivers for slotted-head and recessed Phillips-head screws.

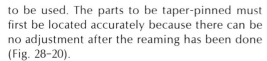

Fig. 28-23. Offset screwdriver.

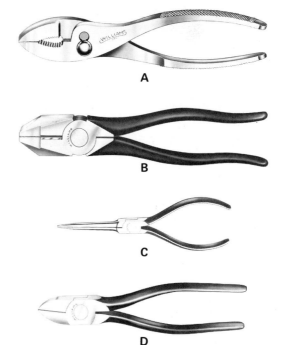

Fig. 28-24. Four types of pliers: (A) combination or slip-joint; (B) side-cutting, (C) needle-nose, and (D) diagonal.

to be used. The parts to be taper-pinned must first be located accurately because there can be no adjustment after the reaming has been done (Fig. 28-20).

Dowel pins are used to align two units of an assembly so they can be taken apart and put together again in the same exact position. A dowel pin is a straight round pin that is made oversize from 0.0005 to 0.002 in. so it can be press-fitted into one hole. The hole in the mating part slips snugly over the dowel pin for easy removal and replacement. One end of the pin is chamfered to aid in starting it straight in the hole (Fig. 28-21).

TOOLS FOR ASSEMBLING BOLTS, NUTS, AND SCREWS

1. The screwdriver is made in many sizes, lengths, and styles. The larger sizes have a square shank so a wrench can be used to get extra leverage. Blades are made for slotted heads or recessed heads (Fig. 28-22). When selecting a screwdriver, make sure that the blade fits the slot in the screw correctly. There is a correct type and size of screwdriver for the many sizes of screws. The offset screwdriver is used to get at screws in out-of-the-way places (Fig. 28-23).

2. Pliers are used to hold and grip small parts and to make adjustments (Fig. 28-24). They are not a substitute for a wrench and should never be used to turn bolts or nuts. To do so would soon round the corners and make the bolt or nut useless. The four common types are:

a. Slip-joint or combination pliers are for holding or turning round bars and pipes. They are also used for light work that may require some bending or twisting.

b. Side-cutting pliers are for cutting wire and gripping it while doing electrical work.

c. Needle-nose or long-nose pliers are useful for getting into difficult places and for holding small work.

d. Diagonal pliers are used for cutting wire and small pieces of soft metal.

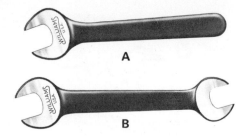

Fig. 28-25. Open-end wrenches: (A) single and (B) double.

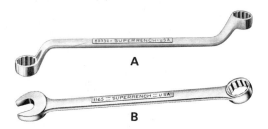

Fig. 28-26. Box wrenches: (A) double offset and (B) combination box and open-end.

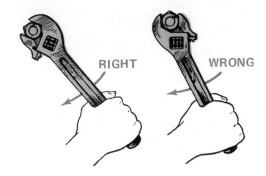

RIGHT   WRONG

Fig. 28-27. Proper method of using an adjustable wrench.

Fig. 28-28. Monkey wrench.

3. *Open-end wrenches* are made to fit standard bolt heads and nuts. A simple open-end wrench has an opening at one end. A double open-end wrench has an opening at each end for two sizes of bolts or nuts (Fig. 28-25). The head and opening are usually made at an angle of 15 degrees (°) or $22\frac{1}{2}$ degrees to the body so a nut or bolt can be tightened where the space is limited. Merely by turning the wrench over, you can get a new grip on the nut or bolt to turn it. Some of these wrenches are made in an S shape, and they are called S-handle wrenches.

4. *Box wrenches* have closed ends and are popular because there is less danger of the wrench's slipping (Fig. 28-26). They can be used in places difficult to see and reach with other wrenches. The modern box wrench has 12 points or notches around the circle which fit over the bolt head or nut. This permits the nut to be moved a short distance in difficult places before changing it for a new grip. Box wrenches are made either straight or with the ends offset at an angle with the handle. A *combination box and open-end wrench* has a box wrench on one end and an open-end wrench on the opposite end. There are many special shapes of these wrenches for special kinds of work.

5. The *adjustable wrench* is both handy and useful since one or two sizes can take care of a wide range of bolts and nuts (Fig. 28-27). However, good machinists are careful never to use an adjustable wrench when other, safer types are available. There is a right and a wrong way to use this type of wrench. Figure 28-27 shows the proper way. The force must always be against the solid jaw. The adjustable jaw should always be tightened against the nut or bolt head.

6. The *monkey wrench* is an adjustable wrench for general work (Fig. 28-28). It has many uses in the shop, such as bending and twisting metal, loosening large, heavy nuts and bolts, and making adjustments.

7. The *pipe wrench* is designed for turning pipes, pipe fittings, and round parts that cannot be gripped or turned otherwise (Fig. 28-29). The sharp teeth bite into the metal when pressure is applied to the handle. It must never be used on finished machine parts without protecting the surface or teeth marks will be left in the surface.

8. There are several kinds of *socket wrenches*. The simplest is the T socket or L socket (Fig.

PIPE WRENCH

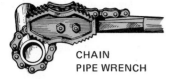

CHAIN
PIPE WRENCH

Fig. 28-29. Pipe wrenches.

Fig. 28-30. T-socket and L-socket wrenches.

Fig. 28-31. A set of socket wrenches.

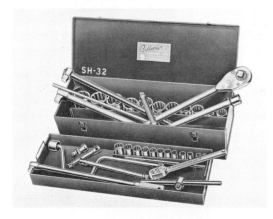

SOCKET END   DRIVE END

SLIDING OFFSET HANDLE

SPEED
HANDLE

UNIVERSAL JOINT

HINGED OFFSET HANDLE

Fig. 28-32. Several types of handles used with the socket wrench.

28-30). These can be used in hard-to-reach places. Most socket wrenches come in sets, with each socket made in a hexagon or 12-point shape (Fig. 28-31). With the set is an extension bar, a ratchet handle, and a swivel-joint connector (Fig. 28-32). Such a set is widely used by auto mechanics and airplane mechanics who assemble and disassemble parts.

9. The *spanner wrench* is used to adjust, tighten, or loosen round nuts or threaded collars that have notches or pinholes around the outside (Fig. 28-33). When a round nut has notches or slots, a *hook-spanner wrench* is used. When it has holes, a *pin-spanner wrench* is used.

10. *Socket-head screws* require their own wrenches, supplied by the screw manufacturers. One type has a hex hole and uses an L-shaped bar of hex tool steel. Other types have holes of

HOOK SPANNER

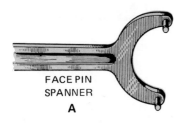

FACE PIN
SPANNER

A

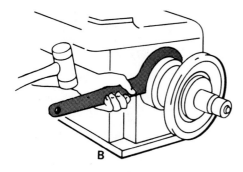

B

THE "SUPERRENCH"

C

Fig. 28-33. (A) Hook and face pin spanner wrenches. (B) A spanner wrench is needed for attaching and releasing lathe chucks and faceplates for certain types of lathes. (C) Adjustable hook spanner wrench.

Fig. 28-34. Hollowhead screw wrench. This is sometimes called an Allen wrench.

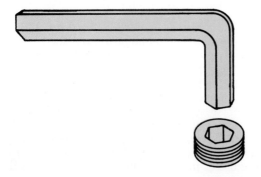

different shapes with matching wrenches. Keep the end of the wrench free from burrs, and resist the impulse to obtain added leverage by a piece of pipe slipped on the end, or by hammering (Fig. 28-34).

11. *Torque wrenches* are a type of wrench that is also a measuring tool. The tool can be set to measure resistance to turning or torque (Fig. 28-35). *Torque* is a twisting or turning force measured in inch-ounces, inch-pounds, foot-pounds, or in metric form. It is distinctly different from *tension,* which is a force usually measured in pounds per square inch (psi) (Fig. 28-36). Torque measurement is calculated in terms of distance and force. *Distance* is the length of the lever. *Force* is the amount of pull or push applied to the end of the lever (Fig. 28-37).

12. All types of wrenches described in this unit are available with size openings indicated in millimeters. *Metric wrenches* are needed to service foreign machine tools and other products. Tools are clearly marked as to the metric sizes. Do not attempt to use English measurement wrenches on metric bolts and screws.

HINTS FOR USING WRENCHES

1. Always select a wrench that fits the nut or bolt correctly. A loose-fitting wrench may cause serious injury if it slips. It will also round off the corners of the bolt or nut.

2. Always pull on a wrench, never push on it. You can't control a wrench when you are pushing on it.

3. Never use a piece of pipe for added leverage. It is safer to use a heavier wrench.

4. Never strike a wrench with a hard hammer. In some cases it may be necessary to loosen a tight bolt or nut by tapping the wrench with a soft-faced hammer.

5. When using large wrenches, always be sure of your footing or balance in case the wrench slips or the bolt breaks.

REMOVING BROKEN STUDS
AND SCREWS

Bolts or screws sometimes break off in a threaded hole when you apply too much pres-

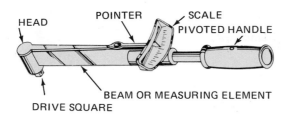

HEAD   POINTER   SCALE
                     PIVOTED HANDLE

BEAM OR MEASURING ELEMENT
DRIVE SQUARE

Fig. 28-35.   Torque wrench.

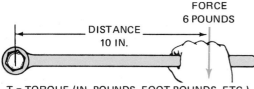

FORCE
6 POUNDS

DISTANCE
10 IN.

T = TORQUE (IN. POUNDS, FOOT POUNDS, ETC.)
D = DISTANCE OR LENGTH OF LEVER (IN., FEET)
F = FORCE (OUNCES OR POUNDS)
D TIMES F = T 6 POUNDS TIMES 10 IN. = 60 IN.
POUNDS

Fig. 28-36.   The torque on this wrench is 60 in. pounds.

Fig. 28-38.   A simple method of removing a broken stud.

Fig. 28-37.   Using a torque wrench to make an accurate
adjustment on a crankshaft.

THREADED
EXTRACTOR

Fig. 28-39.   Another method of removing a broken stud with a
screw extractor or threaded extractor.

sure in tightening or when you try to remove a jammed or badly corroded part. If enough of the stud projects above the surface of the workpiece, it may be possible to remove it with a pair of pliers. Another method is to use a hacksaw to cut a slot, after which a screwdriver is used to remove the broken screw or bolt (Fig. 28-38). A broken bolt may also be removed with a screw extractor (Fig. 28-39). Drill a hole in the broken bolt (the correct size is shown on the extractor). Put the correct size screw extractor

in the hole and, with a tap or adjustable wrench, turn it counterclockwise. The screw extractor acts like a corkscrew. It grips into the sides of the hole and removes the broken part on its own threads without damaging the threaded hole. A diamond-point chisel may also be used to remove a stud. A small hole is first drilled into the stud. Then, the tapered end of the chisel is driven into the screw. By turning the chisel counterclockwise with a crescent wrench, the stud is removed from the hole.

UNIT 29. Safe Use of Hand Tools

Incorrect use of hand tools is responsible for the majority of accidents which occur in the machine shop (Fig. 29-1). Common misuses include putting a pipe over a wrench handle to gain added leverage, using a pair of pliers when a wrench is required, and using a screwdriver as a prybar. Suggestions for the safe use of common hand tools follow.

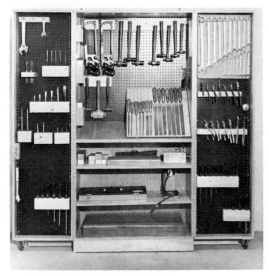

Fig. 29-1.　Correct Storage

VISES

1. Never put a handle extension on a vise. The leverage available is sufficient to hold work securely in place (Fig. 29-2).

Fig. 29-2.

2. Never hammer the handle. Too much pressure may damage the work or the vise (Fig. 29-3).

Fig. 29-3.

3. When using jaw caps, make sure there are no sharp points or edges that can cut your hand (Fig. 29-4).

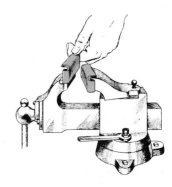

Fig. 29-4.

4. Remove all chips and dust with a wire brush or file card (Fig. 29-5).

Fig. 29-5.

LAYOUT TOOLS

1. Pointed tools such as scribers, dividers, and screwdrivers should not be carried in your pocket.

2. When walking with a pointed hand tool, hold the tool by the handle, and the point down. Be extra careful in areas where there is danger of slipping or tripping. Never point with a sharp tool.

3. Always keep pointed tools well sharpened. They will work better, and there is less danger of an accident.

4. When not in use, pointed tools should be kept in a cabinet or case so they will not touch one another.

HAMMERS

1. Check all hammers before using. The handle should fit tight in the head of the hammer. The face should be flat and not too smooth.

2. Inspect a soft-face hammer to make sure it is in safe condition. If necessary, replace the tip.

3. Never use a machinist's hammer where there is danger of damaging the surface being struck (such as on a surface plate).

4. Do not strike with more force than is necessary.

5. Grip the handle properly when hammering (Fig. 29-6).

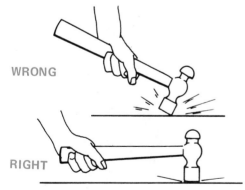

WRONG

RIGHT

Fig. 29-6.

HACKSAWS

1. Always select a saw blade that is suitable for the material to be cut. If the blade should break while cutting, replace it with the same kind of blade.

2. Never bend or twist a hacksaw, because the blade will break.

3. Always cut away from yourself and saw with straight, steady strokes. Use almost the entire length of the blade. To avoid dulling the teeth, ease up on the backward stroke.

4. When sawing in a vise, make sure that the work is held tight. A loose vise is dangerous and inefficient (Fig. 29-7).

Fig. 29-7.

5. When work is held in a vise, be sure the blade will not cut the vise.

CHISELS

1. Use a chisel that is large enough for the job and a hammer that is heavy enough for the chisel.

2. Always wear goggles when chipping. If there are other workers close by, see that they also wear goggles or protective glasses.

3. Make sure that the cutting-edge is sharp and that the head is not mushroomed. Re-dress the chisel before using it (Fig. 29-8).

BEFORE AND AFTER DRESSING

Fig. 29-8.

4. Do not chisel a small workpiece without first fastening it in a vise.

PUNCHES

1. Use a punch that is suitable for the work. Do not use a punch that is bent or dull.

2. Keep the points of the center punch and prick punch properly ground.

3. Be sure the work is held in a firm position before striking with a punch.

4. Do not jam a punch into an opening.

5. Do not use a punch on work that is hard enough to shatter the point.

FILES

1. It is very dangerous to use a file without a handle (Fig. 29–9). The tang is quite sharp and can cut the hand.

FIRST AID

Fig. 29-9.

2. Always put on a tight-fitting handle before starting to work (Fig. 29–10).

Fig. 29-10.

3. Never drive a file into its handle with a hammer or other object. It may chip or break the file or split the handle. Never twist files in work that is slotted because they may break.

4. Avoid using a file as a prybar, chisel, or wrench.

5. Always store files in boxes or on a rack so that each file is kept separate.

6. Files are very brittle. They will break in many pieces if struck with a hammer.

7. Do not use a file on materials that are too hard or soft. Hard objects wear the teeth smooth and soft objects clog the teeth.

SCREWDRIVERS

1. Always use the right size and type of screwdriver for the job. Never attempt to turn a recessed-head screw with a plain screwdriver or vice versa.

2. Dull or improperly ground screwdrivers can be dangerous. Make sure that the screwdriver fits the slot properly.

3. Never use a screwdriver as a pry, chisel, or scribing tool.

4. Never hammer on the end of a screwdriver. This will mushroom or split the handle.

5. Never attempt to use a screwdriver on a workpiece held in the hand.

6. Never use a screwdriver to check high amperage.

Fig. 29-11.

7. Never use pliers on a screwdriver (Fig. 29-11).

WRENCHES

1. There are many sizes and types of wrenches. Always select the one that is best suited to the job.

2. Make sure that the wrench fits the bolt or screw properly. Never use a worn or damaged wrench (an open-end wrench with the jaws spread, or a wrench that has teeth that are rounded or worn smooth on socket walls).

3. Always pull but never push on a wrench to loosen or tighten a nut or bolt.

4. Never choose an adjustable wrench if a fixed wrench is available that will fit.

5. Always stop machinery before making adjustments or repairs with wrenches.

6. Never put a pipe or another wrench over the handle of a wrench to increase leverage.

7. Develop the proper "feel" in using a wrench so that you do not strip the threads of the screw or bolt.

8. Use adjustable wrenches with great care. They are not designed for heavy-duty work.

9. Always place an adjustable wrench on a bolt or nut so that the pull will be on the stationary jaw (Fig. 29-12).

10. Never strike a wrench with a hammer except for those designed for striking (Fig. 29-13).

STRIKING WRENCH

THIS WRENCH IS DESIGNED TO STRIKE WITH A HAMMER

Fig. 29-13.

11. When using a wrench, guard against slipping or falling. Brace yourself so you will not be thrown off balance.

PLIERS

1. Select the correct type and size of pliers required for the job. Never use a pliers when a fixed wrench will do the work. Do not use pliers on nuts (Fig. 29-14).

Fig. 29-14.

2. When applying pressure on the handles of the pliers, keep your fingers away from the jaws. Do not place them in between the handles.

3. Never force long-nose pliers, since this will split the ends of the jaws.

4. Never try to cut hardened metals with cutting pliers.

5. Be sure electric current is turned off before using pliers around wiring. Wear rubber gloves and stand on dry insulated flooring.

6. Be careful not to pinch your hands or knuckles.

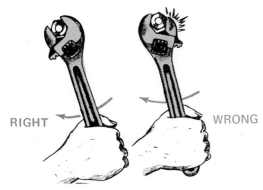

RIGHT   WRONG

Fig. 29-12.

UNIT 30. Discussion Topics and Problems

1. What kind of blade should be used for cutting pipe, tubing, and conduit?

2. What is the best kind of hacksaw blade to use for sawing aluminum?

3. What is the best method of starting a cut in hard materials?

4. How should the teeth of a hacksaw blade be installed in the frame?

5. Name the four types of chisels.

6. At about what angle should a chisel be held for shearing?

7. How are files classified?

8. To what does coarseness of a file refer?

9. Why should a file always have a handle?

10. What is the difference between straight filing and drawfiling?

11. Describe a precision file.

12. What is broaching?

13. Why is a surface scraped?

14. Name two kinds of artificial abrasives.

15. How are abrasives graded?

16. List five safety precautions for using a bench or pedestal grinder.

17. What is meant by dressing and truing a grinding wheel?

18. Sketch a screw thread and name the principal parts.

19. When are pitch and lead the same on a screw thread?

20. What is a Unified thread form?

21. How does a metric thread form differ from a Unified thread form?

22. Name the three taps in a set of hand taps. Tell for what purpose each is used.

23. What are threading dies?

24. What is the procedure for cutting external threads?

25. What is the procedure for cutting a metric thread?

26. Name several kinds of reamers.

27. Why should a hole be drilled undersize before reaming? How much undersize should it be?

28. Name five kinds of metal fasteners.

29. What are some of the hand tools used for assembling threaded fasteners?

30. Why is safety so important when using hand tools?

SECTION 4

BAND MACHINING

UNIT 31. Band Machining Equipment

Band machining provides a fast, efficient, and accurate method for cutting both ferrous and nonferrous metals (Fig. 31-1). With speed and precision, the band machine makes straight, contour, internal, and external cuts. The cutting tool used is an endless band of single-point cutting tools in the form of teeth. A *vertical contour band saw* is used for most band machining operations, while the *horizontal band saw* and *power hacksaw* are designed primarily for cutting stock to length (Fig. 31-2). Sometimes a *vertical band saw* is reserved for straight cut-off work (Fig. 31-3).

The advantages of band machining are illustrated in Fig. 31-4. Note that the band saw can cut material of any type to any shape with the least amount of material waste. Material is removed in sections instead of chips as in many other kinds of machining. The band saw cuts continuously and, as a result, chip removal is fast and accurate. Since the thin band saw makes it possible to cut directly to a finish line, material is saved. It cuts all shapes and designs with no limitation on angle, direction, or length of cut.

The band saw can be used to make internal cuts because its blade can be easily cut and re-welded. It requires simple fixtures, but many of

Fig. 31-1. Parts of a contour band machine showing the operation controls.

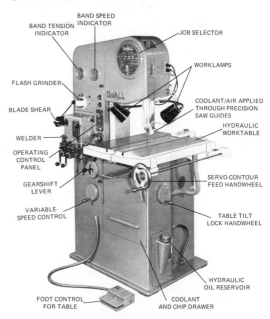

BAND SPEED INDICATOR
BAND TENSION INDICATOR
JOB SELECTOR
WORKLAMPS
FLASH GRINDER
BLADE SHEAR
COOLANT/AIR APPLIED THROUGH PRECISION SAW GUIDES
HYDRAULIC WORKTABLE
WELDER
OPERATING CONTROL PANEL
SERVO-CONTOUR FEED HANDWHEEL
GEARSHIFT LEVER
TABLE TILT LOCK HANDWHEEL
VARIABLE-SPEED CONTROL
HYDRAULIC OIL RESERVOIR
FOOT CONTROL FOR TABLE
COOLANT AND CHIP DRAWER

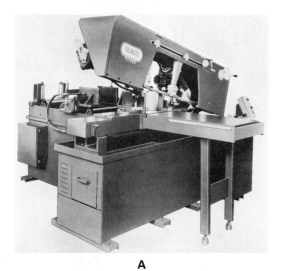

A

Fig. 31-3. **Some types of vertical bandsaws are designed largely for cutting to length. Note the wide blade.**

B

Fig. 31-2. **(A) The horizontal bandsaw is used primarily for cutting stock to length. (B) The power hacksaw is also used for cutting to length.**

the operations can be done with the work held freehand on the table.

Band machining requires less horsepower than other kinds of machine tools due to its narrow-tooth kerf. Each tooth of a band saw is a precision cutting tool. The cutting tool holds sharpness longer than many other tools since wear is evenly distributed over a large number of teeth.

SIZE AND PARTS

The size of the band saw is indicated by the diameter of its wheels and/or its throat capacity (the distance from the blade to the inside of the frame). Whereas most band saws have only an upper and lower wheel, some of the larger machines have a three-wheel arrangement. Many smaller machines are designed for both wood and metal cutting, while most of the larger ones are used exclusively for metal cutting.

In the *two-wheel band saw*, the upper-head assembly has a wheel that is free running. It has two adjustments. One moves the wheel up and down to adjust for blade length and tension. The other tilts the wheel forward or backward to make the blade stay on the wheel (*tracking*). The lower wheel is powered by belts and step pulleys or by a combination of a variable-speed drive and a transmission system.

Most saws have tables fitted with trunnions so they can be tilted 45 degrees (°) to the right and from 5 to 10° to the left. On some models the table can be moved forward or backward with hydraulic action by means of a foot pedal.

The *saw* or *blade guides* consist of two sets of slide guide blocks or rollers. One set is located above the table and the other below the table. These guides hold the blade in line. Both have a small back-up guide wheel behind the guide blocks or rollers. This guide wheel should

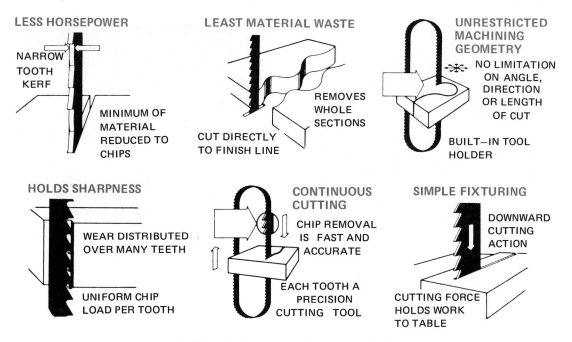

LESS HORSEPOWER

NARROW TOOTH KERF

MINIMUM OF MATERIAL REDUCED TO CHIPS

LEAST MATERIAL WASTE

REMOVES WHOLE SECTIONS

CUT DIRECTLY TO FINISH LINE

UNRESTRICTED MACHINING GEOMETRY

NO LIMITATION ON ANGLE, DIRECTION OR LENGTH OF CUT

BUILT—IN TOOL HOLDER

HOLDS SHARPNESS

WEAR DISTRIBUTED OVER MANY TEETH

UNIFORM CHIP LOAD PER TOOTH

CONTINUOUS CUTTING

CHIP REMOVAL IS FAST AND ACCURATE

EACH TOOTH A PRECISION CUTTING TOOL

SIMPLE FIXTURING

DOWNWARD CUTTING ACTION

CUTTING FORCE HOLDS WORK TO TABLE

Fig. 31-4. Advantages of using a bandsaw for machining.

not turn unless it absorbs pressure against its face. The upper guides are attached to a guide-post that can be raised and lowered when cutting different thicknesses of material. The large steel upper and lower wheels are covered with a rubber tire, or band facing, so that the blade runs on this soft material rather than the hard steel wheels. Both the upper and lower wheels and the blade are covered by guards.

Variable-speed drive machines are equipped with a job selector chart built into the machine itself. This circular chart gives a variety of information in selecting the correct size of blade, cutting speed, feed, and other important information. By dialing the correct material on the chart, all other information is immediately visible. Some band machines are equipped with a *tachometer* or speed selector that tells the speed the blade is traveling in feet per minute. Many are also equipped with a *butt welder* for making butt welds under automatically controlled conditions. A *contour feed,* which is a hydraulically driven device for feeding the work into the saw at a regulated rate, is standard equipment on larger models of contour band saws (Fig. 31-5).

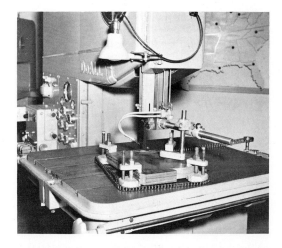

Fig. 31-5. A contour sawing attachment is a device for making contour cuts more easily and accurately.

BAND SAW BLADES

There are hundreds of different sizes and kinds of band saw blades available. Only a few, however, are commonly used for band machining. Many of the others are designed for special operations where a band machine is used constantly for a specialized manufacturing process.

Band saw blades are available in specific sizes, or in 100-foot coils. They are made from several different metals. These include:

1. *Carbon steel blades,* which are widely used because of their general adaptability for all types of work and their low cost. They are excellent for cutting nonferrous metals and plastics.

2. *High-speed steel blades,* which resist heat generated in cutting to a far greater extent than carbon steel blades. They are best suited for cutting ferrous metals.

3. *Alloy-steel blades,* which are tougher and more wear resistant than either of the above. They will cut faster and last longer than blades of carbon or high-speed steel.

4. *Carbide-tipped blades,* which are best used for cutting unusual materials such as uranium, titanium, and beryllium. These metals are difficult to cut with other types of blades.

TOOTH SHAPES

The *regular* or *standard tooth* is preferred for all ferrous metals and general-purpose cutting (Fig. 31–6A). The *skip-tooth blade* has widely spaced teeth to provide the added chip clearance needed for cutting softer nonferrous materials. The *hook-* or *sabre-tooth saw* or blade has a 10° undercut which permits better feed and chip removal. It is best for the harder, nonferrous alloys.

TYPES OF SET

Regular or *raker* set is generally furnished on saws which have 2 to 24 teeth per inch (Fig. 31–6B). These blades have one tooth set to the left, one tooth to the right, and one unset tooth called a *raker*. This set is used when material is to be contour cut. *Wavy set* is furnished on saws which have 8 to 32 teeth per inch. This set has groups of teeth bent alternately to the left and right, which greatly reduces the strain on individual teeth. Saws with wavy set are used where tooth breakage is a problem, such as in cutting thin stock or where a variety of work is cut without changing blades.

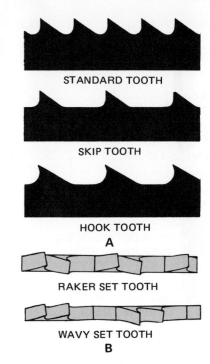

STANDARD TOOTH

SKIP TOOTH

HOOK TOOTH
A

RAKER SET TOOTH

WAVY SET TOOTH
B

Fig. 31-6. (A) Kinds of teeth. (B) Types of set.

SELECTING THE PROPER BLADE

To get the most satisfactory results, it is important to choose a blade that is correct for the work. Blade life, straightness of cut, quality of finish, and cutting efficiency are all directly related to the choice of blade. Blade breakage, stripping of teeth, crooked cuts, and other common complaints are, in most instances, caused by using the wrong blade. There are three factors governing the choice of the proper blade for the job.

1. *Type of material to be cut.* Hard material requires a blade with finer teeth because of the greater number of teeth needed to absorb the wear caused by the material. Coarse teeth are used on soft materials because these teeth afford more space for larger chips to form.

2. *Thickness of material.* Fine teeth are designed for use on thin sheet stock. Fine teeth used on large sections become loaded with chips, causing teeth to break or the saw to cut crooked. Coarse teeth are used for large sections. The use of coarse teeth on thin sections puts undue strain on individual teeth.

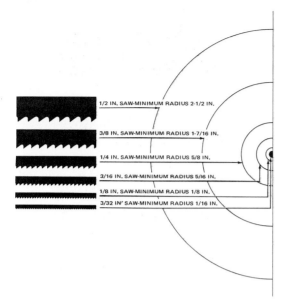

1/2 IN. SAW-MINIMUM RADIUS 2-1/2 IN.

3/8 IN. SAW-MINIMUM RADIUS 1-7/16 IN.

1/4 IN. SAW-MINIMUM RADIUS 5/8 IN.

3/16 IN. SAW-MINIMUM RADIUS 5/16 IN.

1/8 IN. SAW-MINIMUM RADIUS 1/8 IN.

3/32 IN' SAW-MINIMUM RADIUS 1/16 IN.

Fig. 31-7.   Minimum radius that can be cut with various widths of blades.

3. *Size of radius to be cut.* When selecting a saw for contour work, the size of the radius to be cut should be considered. Figure 31-7 illustrates the minimum radii that can be cut with various widths of blades.

WELDING A BAND MACHINE BLADE

Although a band saw blade can be purchased already made up to the desired length, it is usually purchased in 100-foot rolls. The proper procedure for preparing a blade from roll stock is as follows.

1.   Handle the blade with gloves. Use cut-off shears to cut the blade to correct length (Fig. 31-8A). Square the ends of the blade.

2.   Place the blade in the welder. Most vertical band saw machines have a built-in resistance-type butt welder.

Fig. 31-8.   (A) Determining the length of a bandsaw blade. (B) Welding a bandsaw blade. Note that the self-contained unit includes a shear for cutting the blade to length, a welder for welding and annealing the blade, and the flash grinder that is used to grind the excess material from the weld.

A

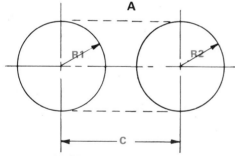

B

1. ADJUST WHEELS TO CORRECT POSITION, BUT NOT AT THE OUTER EXTREME, AS SOME TAKE—UP WILL BE NEEDED TO TENSION THE BAND. ALSO, DO NOT POSITION AT THE SHORTEST POINT, AS SOME ALLOWANCE MUST BE MADE FOR REWELDING WHERE NECESSARY.

2. HAVING ADJUSTED THE WHEELS AT ABOUT HALFWAY IN THE TAKE—UP RANGE, MEASURE THE DISTANCE FROM THE CENTERS OF THE HOLES BETWEEN THE TWO WHEELS ("C" IN IN.).

3. FIND THE RADIUS OF EACH WHEEL ("R1" AND "R2" IN IN.)

4. USE THE FORMULA:
   $$(R1 \times 3.1416) + (R2 \times 3.1416) + 2 \times C = \text{BAND LENGTH}$$

Fig. 31-9. (A) Keeping the blade "hewing to the line" when it engages the workpiece is the most important part of good band sawing. These are block-type side guides. (B) These are roller-type side and back-up guides. One set of three adjustable rollers (sides and thrust or back-up) operates above the workpiece and table and the other set below. In each set, the grooved thrust roller holds the blade firmly against the feed pressure of the work being cut. The two rollers on the side serve to keep the blade running straight and true, free from twist and vibration.

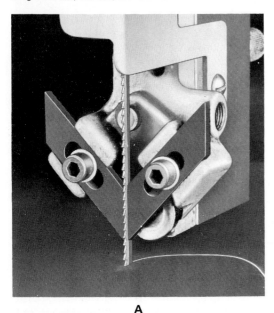

A

B

3. Position the blade correctly in the welder's jaw. Make sure the jaws are clean both before and after making the weld. Also make sure that the blade ends are touching. The amount of tension adjustment should conform to the width of the blade.

4. Turn on the switch to complete the weld (Fig. 31-8B).

5. After the weld is complete, reset the jaws for annealing. Remember the weld is brittle and must be annealed before it can be used.

6. Grind the weld on the flash grinder until the sides are smooth and are the same thickness as the blade itself.

INSTALLING A NEW BLADE

1. Turn off the power to the machine.

2. Release the tension on the upper wheel.

3. Loosen the locking screws on all guides of the upper- and lower-guide assemblies and back off all the guides so they are out of the path of the new blade.

4. Remove the alignment pin or screw from the table slot and remove the table insert.

5. Open the wheel guards to expose the upper and lower wheels.

6. Uncoil the new blade. Be sure the teeth are pointed in the proper direction. Hold the blade with the teeth facing your body. If the teeth in your right hand point downward, the teeth are pointed in the proper direction. If they do not, try turning the blade inside out; they should then be in the proper position.

7. Still holding the blade in proper position, carefully work it through the table slot and slip it onto the upper and lower wheels.

8. Replace the table alignment pin in the slot.

TRACKING A NEW BLADE

1. Tighten the tension on the upper wheel. Proper tension may be indicated by a blade width table or by a dial indicator located on the tensioning mechanism. Often, however, proper tension is largely a matter of experience.

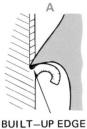

BUILT—UP EDGE FORMING

FULLY FORMED BUILT—UP EDGE

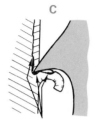

SLOUGHING AWAY ON CHIP AND WORKPIECE

Fig. 31-10. These three illustrations show the formation of, and damage caused by, a "built-up" edge.

2. Turn the upper wheel slowly by hand; at the same time, adjust the tracking control until the blade runs on the center of the rubber tire. Rotate the upper wheel by hand several more times to make sure the blade stays on the wheels.

3. Check the tracking by clicking the power switch on and off. Use longer bursts of power-on until you are sure the blade runs true.

CAUTION

Stand to one side while doing power-on testing, since the wheel guards must be open to see what is going on. There is always the possibility of the blade's coming off the wheels or breaking.

ADJUSTING THE BLADE GUIDES

1. Loosen the locking screws of the upper guide (Fig. 31-9). Bring the guide assembly forward until the front edges of the side supports are about $\frac{1}{64}$ in. behind the tooth gullets. Then place slips of thin paper on either side between

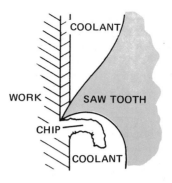

Fig. 31-11. The coolant must get between the saw tooth and the work to be effective.

the guide and the blade. Push the guides against the paper and tighten the locking screws. The paper should provide a clearance of 0.003 or 0.004 in. on each side.

2. Repeat the above procedure on the lower-guide assembly located below the table.

3. Move the backup guide wheel to a point $\frac{1}{64}$ in. behind the back edge of the blade. The wheel should not touch the blade until a cutting load is applied. A simple way to set the backup wheel is to turn on the power and bring the wheel up until it begins to move with the blade. Then back the wheel off until it stops moving. Repeat on the lower guide.

4. Inspect the machine to make sure that none of the guide parts touch the running blade until a cutting load is applied.

COOLANTS AND CUTTING FLUIDS

Coolants of air or cutting fluids are used for the following reasons.

1. They help spread out and reduce heat.

2. They reduce the rubbing action of the chip against the cutting-edges of the saw blade (Fig. 31-10).

3. They help to control *built-up edge* on saw teeth (Fig. 31-11).

4. They wash away and clean the chips from the cutting-edge.

5. They lubricate, making cutting easier.

UNIT 32. Band Machining

Contour sawing, or band machining, enables the machinist to cut away unwanted metal by merely chipping away that part of the metal contained in a narrow saw kerf. In all other forms of machining, all unwanted metal must be removed in the form of chips. This enables the contour saw to produce a piece of the desired shape in considerably shorter time than required for other forms of machining.

Contour sawing also saves metal. In many instances the scrap pieces may be used again.

SAFETY

1. Check the material to be cut to be sure that it is free of imperfections.

2. Wear gloves when handling and repairing band saw blades.

3. Wear safety glasses or a shield (Fig. 32–1).

4. Make sure that the saw blade has proper tension. Follow the manufacturer's instructions; too much tension can cause the blade to break.

5. Avoid backing out of a cut, as this will pull the blade off the wheels.

Fig. 32–1. Always wear safety glasses or goggles when cutting. For rough work, gloves will protect the hands. Notice that here the saw guidepost is set too high.

6. Never attempt to cut round or irregular stock without a holding fixture.

7. Never cut a curve of small radius with a wide blade.

8. If you hear a rhythmic click as the material is being cut, this usually indicates a cracked blade or an improperly welded joint. Stop the machine and inspect.

9. If the blade breaks, shut off the power and stay away from the machine until it comes to a complete stop.

10. Never try to free the blade while the wheels are still turning.

11. Never have your fingers or arms in direct line with the blade.

12. Make sure that all guards are in place before starting the machine.

13. Never try to remove small pieces of material from the table while the saw is operating.

BASIC OPERATING TECHNIQUES

1. Unless some type of machine guide is used, draw guidelines on the workpiece to indicate the shape to be cut.

2. Check for proper size and kind of blade, speed, and feed. Most large machines have a built-in job selector chart on the cover of the upper wheel. This circular chart can be set for the kind of material to be cut. It indicates the kind of blade to use, speed, feed, and other information.

Blade speed is an important factor in successful band saw use. If the speed is too fast for the material being cut, the teeth will not dig into the material. They will just ride over the surface of the work, create friction, rapidly dull the cutting-edge, and wear out the blade. Table 32–1 gives recommended saw speed ranges for efficient cutting of different metallic materials.

It is not practical to provide feed data in table form. Under general conditions, however, an even pressure without forcing the work gives best results. A free-cut curl indicates ideal feed pressure. Burned or discolored chips indicate excessive feed pressure which can cause premature wear and tooth breakage.

Table 32-1. Recommended speeds for band sawing common metals.

AISI Type	Description	Average Recommended Saw Speeds in FPM	
Easily machinable			
		Carbon-Steel Blades	High-Speed Steel Blades
1010–1035	Straight-Carbon Steels	150–175	300
1040–1050	Medium-Carbon Steels	100–150	200
1108–1130	Free cutting Low-Carbon Steels	150–175	300
1137–1150	Free cutting Medium-Carbon Steels	100–150	250
Moderately difficult to machine			
1065–1095	High-Carbon Steels	80–125	150
1320–1345	Manganese Steels	70–125	200
2317–2517	Nickel Steels	75–100	175
3115–3315	Nickel-Chrome Steels	50–100	200
4017–4068	Moly Steels	75–135	200
4130–4150	Chrome-Moly Steels	50–100	225
4317–4340	Nickel-Chrome Moly Steels	50–100	200
4608–4820	Nickel-Moly Steels	50–100	200
Nonferrous			
	Aluminum Bronze	700	
	Beryllium Copper	800–2,000	
	Manganese Bronze	200–900	
	Phosphor Bronze	300–700	
	Silicon Bronze	200–900	
	Aluminum Castings & Forgings	300–1,500	
	Aluminum Extrusions	2,000–3,000	
	Aluminum Sheet, Plate, Rod & Tubing	3,000–5,000	
	Copper, Brass	1,500	
	Babbitt, Lead	1,500–3,000	

3. Lower the saw guidepost so that it is about $\frac{1}{4}$ in. above the stock. Feed the waste stock into the blade and come up to the layout line. Then follow the layout line, keeping the blade just to the outside of this line. In cutting, guide the stock with your left hand and apply forward pressure with your right. Move the stock into the work as rapidly as it will cut; moving too slowly will tend to dull the blade. Do not feed the work into the blade until the machine is at full operating speed. In all cutting, accuracy is important and can only be obtained by carefully following the layout line. A correct stance and position will help you to control the work more accurately.

Straight Sawing. For straight sawing, a fence or miter fixture can be used (Fig. 32-2). A *miter gage* is used for cutting short lengths, and a *fence* is used for ripping (Fig. 32-3).

Contour Cutting. Cutting curves and other irregular shapes can easily be done on the band saw (Fig. 32-4). When sawing, come directly up to the layout line leaving only the small amount of material that might be necessary for finishing.

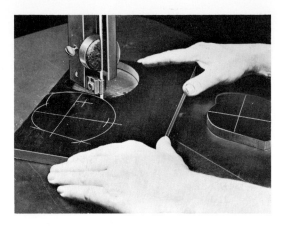

Fig. 32-2. This combination work fixture can be used on the T-slotted table to hold work square with the saw blade. It can also be used for angle cutting up to 45°. It eliminates the need for laying out the work and enables the operator to work directly and accurately to the required dimensions.

Fig. 32-4. For contour sawing, make a careful layout and cut directly up to the line.

Fig. 32-5. Dimensional cuts are part of the geometry of band machining.

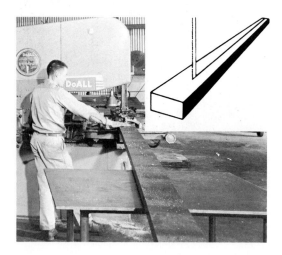

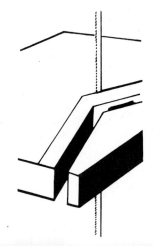

Fig. 32-3. Ripping a strip 4 in. wide is best done by guiding the stock with a fence.

Dimensional Cuts. These cuts are made in a manner similar to contour cutting (Fig. 32–5).

Angle Cuts. When making angle cuts, the table must be tilted to the correct degree. Use a fixture to hold the material (Fig. 32–6).

Internal Cuts. Internal cuts can be made on the band saw if the machine has a self-contained unit that can cut, weld, and grind the blade. To do internal cutting, first drill a hole in the waste

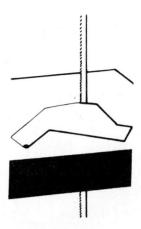

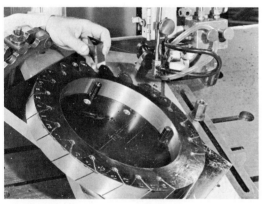

Fig. 32-6. Angle cuts are made with the table tilted and the work held in a fixture.

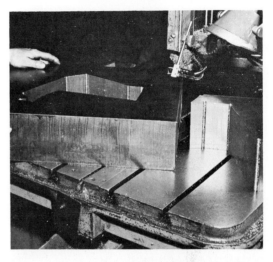

Fig. 32-7. Internal cuts are easily done using a band machine. Cut the blade; thread it through a drilled starting hole; and reweld it on the built-in welder.

Fig. 32-8. Precision slotting is easy when a simple fixture is used to hold the workpiece.

stock (Fig. 32-7). Then remove the blade from the machine and cut it apart. Place the workpiece on the table and thread the blade through the hole. Weld the blade together, anneal, and grind it. Move the workpiece and the endless blade into position and then install, track, and adjust the blade. Now make the internal cut. After the cut is completed, the blade must again be cut apart to remove the finished work from the machine.

Other Cutting. Other kinds of straight cutting include precision slotting and splitting stock. *Precision slotting* can be done using a fixture to hold the parts (Fig. 32-8). *Splitting round* or *flat stock* also requires the use of a fixture to hold the material (Fig. 32-9).

Fig. 32-9. Splitting a metal cylinder. Note how the round cylinder is firmly held to the table.

Fig. 32-10. (A) A fixture for cutting circles. (B) This power-feed control is operated by a hand-feed wheel and foot control. It maintains constant feed force between the work and the bandsaw.

A

B

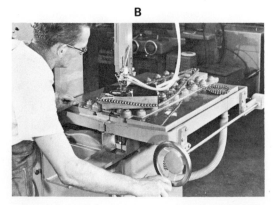

USING ACCESSORIES

In many band machining operations, accessories are used to move the work into the saw blade (Fig. 32–10). These accessories may be controlled either manually or hydraulically. The operator should follow the manufacturer's directions for using these accessories.

FRICTION SAWING

Friction cutting is economical when cutting stock up to $\frac{1}{2}$ in. in thickness, especially when cutting some of the hard alloy steels (Fig. 32–11). Equipment must be able to operate at speeds from 5,000 to 15,000 surface feet per minute (sfpm). The speed required is determined by the material to be cut and its cross-sectional area. Many band saws are not equipped to do friction sawing. Normally, a raker set blade with 10 to 14 teeth per inch is used. Friction sawing is usually not done on nonferrous metals such as brass, bronze, aluminum, or copper.

In friction cutting, an intense heat is generated which softens the material. The blade teeth do not actually cut but, rather, scoop out the soft material.

Fig. 32-11. Friction sawing is done by bringing the work in contact with a rapidly moving saw blade.

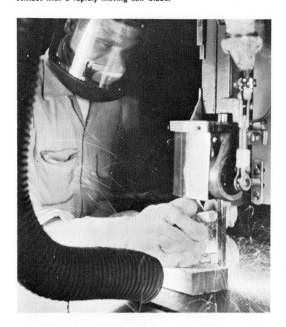

The process can be explained as follows: A momentary contact of the fast-moving saw tooth against the material being cut produces enough friction to heat the material to its softening point. This heating is largely confined to a very small area of contact immediately ahead of the saw blade (though some is spread toward the sides of the cut). As the material is fed into the saw, this narrow line of softened material is removed by the rapid motion of the blade.

BAND FILING

The band saw is also used for band filing (Fig. 32-12). To accomplish this, a series of small files is attached to a band saw blade that fits in the machine. A variety of filing operations can be done using such a blade.

Fig. 32-12. Filing a die part on a vertical bandsaw.

UNIT 33. Discussion Topics and Problems

1. Name the three types of band saws.

2. Describe the advantages of the contour band saw for machining metal parts.

3. List the steps in installing and tracking a band saw blade.

4. Describe the types of band saw blades used in contour band sawing.

5. Why are cutting fluids sometimes used?

6. Name the three basic types of cutting fluids.

7. What advantage does contour sawing by band machining have over other types of metal machining?

8. List five safety rules to be followed when using a contour band saw.

9. What should the speed in feet per minute be when cutting medium-carbon steel with a high-speed steel blade?

10. How can you tell when you are using the proper amount of feed?

11. What is the key to successful band machining?

12. What kind of an accessory is necessary in making angle cuts?

13. Describe how to make an internal cut on a band saw.

14. What is friction sawing?

15. Can filing be done on the band saw? Explain.

SECTION 5

DRILLING MACHINES

UNIT 34. Types of Drilling Machines

Cutting round holes in metal stock is one of the most common operations performed in the machine shop. Very few metal pieces go through a factory without having holes drilled in them. Later operations are often located by referring to these holes. *Drilling machines* are used to produce most of these holes (Fig. 34-1). They are also used in operations such as reaming, boring, countersinking, counterboring, and tapping (Fig. 34-2).

In your school shop, you will probably use a bench-type or medium-sized floor-type drill press. The latter is the one described here in detail. Other drilling machines are described in Unit 40.

SIZE

The size of a drilling machine is expressed in one or more of the following four ways:

1. By the diameter of the largest disk that can be center drilled. An 18-in. drill press, for exam-

ple, can drill a hole through the center of an 18-in.-diameter disk.

2. By the distance the spindle moves up and down.

3. By the maximum distance between the spindle and the table.

4. By the distance from the column to the center of the spindle.

PARTS

The principal parts of the drill press are the base (or lower table), column, table, and head. The heavy metal base and upright column have the table and drill head attached. The drill head consists of the main operating parts, including the speed and feed mechanisms, the motor, the spindle, and the quill.

There are several types of mechanisms used to control the speed of a drilling machine. The simplest arrangement utilizes a belt for transferring power from a four-, five-, or six-step V pulley located on the motor to a similar pulley attached to the drill press spindle (Fig. 34-3A). To increase power on some belt and pulley ma-

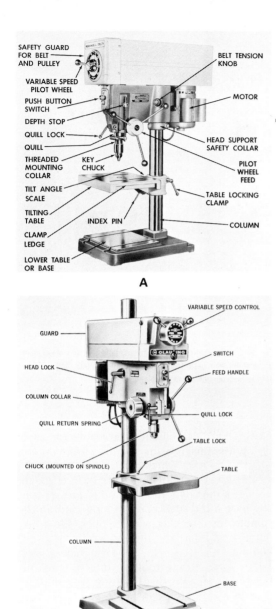

A

SAFETY GUARD FOR BELT AND PULLEY
VARIABLE SPEED PILOT WHEEL
PUSH BUTTON SWITCH
DEPTH STOP
QUILL LOCK
QUILL
THREADED MOUNTING COLLAR
KEY CHUCK
TILT ANGLE SCALE
TILTING TABLE
INDEX PIN
CLAMP LEDGE
LOWER TABLE OR BASE

BELT TENSION KNOB
MOTOR
HEAD SUPPORT SAFETY COLLAR
PILOT WHEEL FEED
TABLE LOCKING CLAMP
COLUMN

B

GUARD
HEAD LOCK
COLUMN COLLAR
QUILL RETURN SPRING
CHUCK (MOUNTED ON SPINDLE)
COLUMN

VARIABLE SPEED CONTROL
SWITCH
FEED HANDLE
QUILL LOCK
TABLE LOCK
TABLE
BASE

Fig. 34-1. (A) A bench model sensitive drilling machine with the parts named. **(B)** A floor model drilling machine. Note that the nomenclature (names given to parts) varies slightly from one manufacturer to another. Major parts are given the same names, however.

chines, a *countershaft drive* is sometimes added (Fig. 34-3B). Another mechanism used is the *variable-speed pulley*, which makes it possible

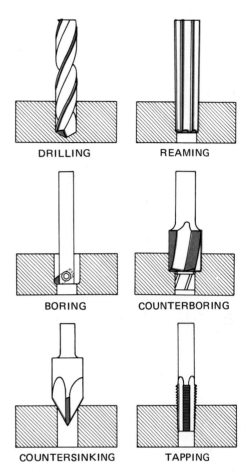

DRILLING   REAMING

BORING   COUNTERBORING

COUNTERSINKING   TAPPING

Fig. 34-2. The six common operations that can be done on drilling machines.

to change the machine's speed without stopping it (Fig. 34-4). *In fact, the speed must only be changed while the machine is running.* Pulleys of a variable-speed drive are made of two parts having V-shaped sides. By means of an adjusting screw attached to a crank wheel, one side of the driver pulley may be opened or spread apart. As it spreads, the belt moves inward toward the smaller diameter, producing slower speed in the driven pulley that has closed to make a larger pulley. As the sides of the driver pulley are brought together, the belt is forced outward toward the larger diameter; this increases the speed of the driven pulley that opens to make the smaller pulley.

The *feed* on most drill presses is hand controlled with a hand-feed lever. An automatic

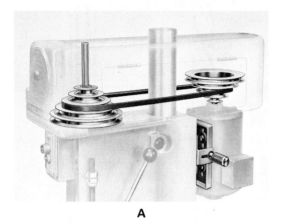

A

B

Fig. 34-3. (A) A drill press with five-step pulleys and belt. (B) A drill press with a step pulley countershaft drive.

Fig. 34-4. Variable-speed drive. The spindle speed can be changed from a low of 500 rpm to a high of 4,500 rpm.

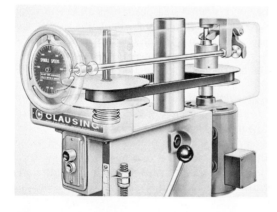

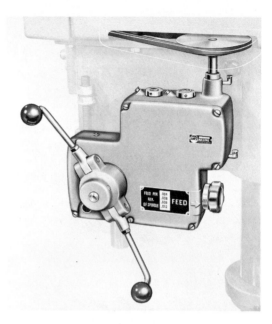

Fig. 34-5. Automatic feed attachment. Note that this attachment provides for four basic feeds of 0.004, 0.006, 0.009, and 0.012. This is feed per revolution of spindle.

power feed attachment is available for some drill presses (Fig. 34-5).

The *spindle,* which rotates and moves the cutting tool up or down, may have either a taper hole or a threaded end. Small drill presses usually have a threaded or short taper end on the spindle for attaching a *drill chuck.* Most medium-sized floor-type drill presses have a self-holding (No. 1 or No. 2 Morse taper) hole. Taper-shank cutting tools fit directly into this taper hole. Straight-shank cutting tools must be held in a drill chuck. A *depth gage and stop,* mounted on the *quill,* can be set when drilling holes to a certain depth.

Drill presses are normally equipped with a table that can be tilted to the right and left (Fig. 34-6). Some heavier duty machines, however, have a table with an oil ring around its edge and often a T slot for clamping work (Fig. 34-7). This type of table cannot be tilted.

COMMON ADJUSTMENTS

1. *To raise or lower the table,* grasp one side with your left hand. Loosen the clamp on the

Fig. 34-6. The standard table can be tilted to the right or left. An index pin drops into a hole at 30, 45, and 90° for easy setting to these angles.

Fig. 34-7. A bench-type drill press with a production base having T slots and an oil ring.

Fig. 34-8. This locking attachment allows the head to be moved up and down with a mechanical device. Sometimes this same kind of attachment is used to move the table up and down.

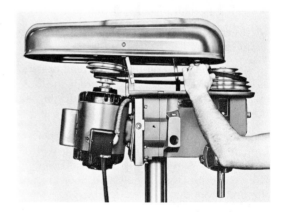

Fig. 34-9. Note how the electric motor can be tilted for ease in changing belts.

table. Then use both hands to lift the table up or slide it down. Center the hole in the table under the chuck or spindle. On some floor-type drill presses, a screw is provided for raising and lowering the table (Fig. 34-8).

2. *To tilt the table,* loosen the nut underneath. Turn the table to the correct angle and tighten the screw. Most drill presses have a pin that locates the table at 45- or 90-degree (°) positions.

3. *To change* spindle *speeds* on a belt and pulley drill press, turn off the power and open or remove the belt guard. Loosen the thumb-screw that holds the motor bracket to the head. Move the belt to the new position. On some machines the motor bracket is hinged. To move the belt, just lift up the motor to release the belt tension (Fig. 34–9).

SAFETY

1. Never leave the chuck key in the chuck.

2. Keep the floor around the machine clean.

3. Clamp the workpiece securely. Never hold thin or small work with your hands. Use a drill vise.

4. Always use a brush to remove chips, never your hands.

5. Don't try to stop the spindle after the power is shut off by grasping it with your hands.

6. Never touch or try to handle long spiral chips with your hands.

7. Apply oil to cutting tools with a small brush. Do not spill oil on the machine or floor. A few drops in the right place is all that is needed.

8. Keep your head away from the machine to avoid catching hair in the spindle.

9. Always ease up on the down-feed pressure as the drill begins to break through the hole. Heavy feed will cause the drill to dig in, and the drill may break or pull the work loose.

10. Never attempt to drill brass, copper, or bronze with a drill ground for steel. It will dig in and break, ruin the work, or cause an injury. Ask your instructor to show you how to grind the drill properly.

CUTTING SPEEDS

Cutting speed is the rate, expressed in feet per minute (fpm), that a point on the drill travels in one minute. You might say it is the distance in feet that a drill would travel in one minute if it were rolled on its side along the floor. Cutting speed is also called *surface feet per minute* (sfpm) or *circumferential speed*. It is *not* the same as revolutions per minute (rpm).

All metals have average cutting speeds at which the metal may be machined efficiently, that is, without ruining the cutting tool. When the cutting speed is too great, a cutting tool may burn up, get dull rapidly, or even break. When the cutting speed is too slow, the cutting tool may chip or break, and the time required for the operation will be much greater. A small drill must rotate faster than a large drill to maintain the same cutting speed.

The cutting speeds for drills depend upon:

1. The kind of material being drilled. A general rule to follow is *the softer the material, the higher the speed* (Table 34–1).

2. The cutting-tool material. High-speed steel drills can be operated at about twice the speed of carbon-steel drills.

3. The quality of hole desired.

4. The efficient use of cutting fluid.

5. The way in which the work is set up or held.

6. The size and type of drilling machine.

A machinist generally knows the average cutting speeds for different materials. He needs

Table 34-1. Suggested cutting speeds for drill press.

Material	Cutting Speed for High-Speed Steel Drills,* Surface Feet per Minute
Aluminum and alloys	200–300
Brass and bronze, soft	100–300
Bronze, high tensile	70–90
Cast iron:	
Soft	100–150
Medium	70–100
Hard	40–60
Copper	60–80
Malleable iron	80–90
Steel:	
Low-carbon	80–150
Medium-carbon	60–100
High-carbon	50–60
Tool-and-die	40–80
Alloy	50–70

*Carbon steel drills should operate at from 40 to 50 percent of the speed for high-speed steel drills.

this information in order to calculate the rpm at which to run his machine. To find the rpm at which to run the drilling machine for a given cutting speed, it is first necessary to find the circumference of the drill in inches (circumference = diameter × 3.1416). Then the cutting speed in feet per minute must be changed to inches per minute by multiplying by 12. The rpm would then be cutting speed in inches per minute divided by the circumference of the drill in inches. The complete formula is:

$$rpm = \frac{cutting\ speed \times 12}{diameter \times 3.1416}$$

For example, suppose you wish to drill bronze with a $\frac{1}{2}$-in. high-speed drill. First, you would look at Table 34-1 to find the cutting speed for bronze when using a high-speed steel drill. The range is 70 to 90 fpm. The average would be 80 fpm. Then,

$$rpm = \frac{80 \times 12}{\frac{1}{2} \times 3.1416} = \frac{960}{1.5708} = 611\ rpm$$

However, it is not necessary to calculate rpm this accurately. To make the calculations simpler, we multiply the diameter by 3 instead of 3.1416. Then the simple formula becomes

$$rpm = \frac{CS \times 12}{d \times 3} \quad or \quad \frac{CS \times 4}{d}$$

where CS = cutting speed

d = diameter

Solving the same problem above with this simpler formula,

$$rpm = \frac{80 \times 4}{\frac{1}{2}} = \frac{320}{\frac{1}{2}} = 640\ rpm$$

The difference between 611 rpm when using the long formula and 640 rpm when using the short formula is not important for practical purposes. When using a drill press with step pulleys, it is seldom possible to set the machine at the exact rpm calculated.

The average drill press has only four to six speeds. These are often indicated on the front of the machine (Fig. 34-10). Choose the speed that comes closest to the rpm calculated when using the short formula. Note that the slowest speed is obtained with the belt on the smallest step of the motor pulley (Fig. 34-11). With a

variable-speed drill press, the exact rpm can be set by turning the control handle while the machine is running.

FEED

Feed refers to the distance a drill moves into the work with each complete turn of the drill. Table 34-2 suggests the correct feed for different sizes

Fig. 34-10. This belt-driven drill press has a simple chart mounted on the front to show spindle speed with an 1,800 rpm motor. Which belting arrangement would you choose for the example shown?

Fig. 34-11. This drill-press has a five-step pulley on the motor and spindle. The speed at each position depends on the size of the pulley and the speed of the motor.

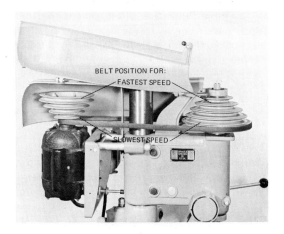

BELT POSITION FOR:
FASTEST SPEED
SLOWEST SPEED

Table 34-2. Correct feeds for different sizes of drills.

Drill Size, Inches	Feed per Revolution
$\frac{1}{8}$ and less	0.001–0.002
$\frac{1}{8}$ to $\frac{1}{4}$	0.002–0.004
$\frac{1}{4}$ to $\frac{1}{2}$	0.004–0.007
$\frac{1}{2}$ to 1	0.007–0.015
1 and larger	0.015–0.025

of drills. However, with a hand-feed drill press, it isn't possible to follow definite rules. The best way to determine correct feed is to watch the chips and be aware of the feed pressure. The correct pressure makes a uniform spiral chip. You have to feel the drill cutting. With experience, your hand becomes skilled at feeding the drill just the right amount. Too heavy a feed may chip the cutting-edge, heat it up, or even break the drill. Too light a feed causes a noisy scraping or chattering action and dulls the cutting-edge. A drill must be kept cutting properly while in contact with the metal.

CUTTING FLUIDS

Cutting fluids consist of oils, compounds, or emulsions made from animal, vegetable, or mineral oils. They are used to:

1. Cool the point of the cutting tools by carrying away the heat generated

2. Improve the cutting action and finish

3. Aid in clearing away the chips from the hole

Cutting fluids are often called *coolants*. Apply cutting fluids to the drill point or other cutting tools with a small brush. On production-type drilling machines, the coolant is piped right to the machine from a central system. The correct cutting fluids to use for various materials are shown in Table 34–3.

WORK-HOLDING METHODS

Workpieces must be set up correctly and held securely for drilling. If the workpiece springs or moves, the drill usually breaks. There is always danger of a serious accident if the workpiece becomes loose and spins around.

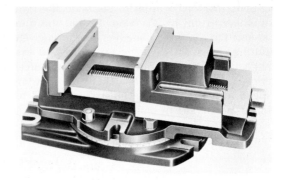

Fig. 34-12. A common type of drill press vise.

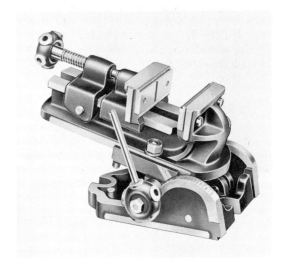

Fig. 34-13. An angle vise. The scale from 0 to 90° mounted on the semicircular part of the vise allows setting it to any angle.

Holding Devices. Some of the holding devices are listed below.

1. A *drill vise* is widely used for holding small work of regular shape, such as flat, square, and round pieces. Drill vises are used by machinists and toolmakers when drilling work that has been laid out and center-punched (Fig. 34–12). Some machine vises have a base that can be fixed to the table while the upper portion of the vise can be turned in a 360° angle.

2. An *angle vise* provides a means of drilling holes at an angle without tilting the table of the drill press (Fig. 34–13).

Table 34-3. Selection of cutting fluids.

MATERIAL	ORDER OF DECREASING EFFECTIVENESS		ORDER OF INCREASING EXPENSE	
ALUMINUM AND ALLOYS		Kerosene Kerosene and Lard Oil Soluble Oil		Soluble Oil Kerosene Kerosene and Lard Oil
BRASS AND BRONZE	Deep Holes	Dry Kerosene and Mineral Oil Lard Oil Soluble Oil	Deep Holes	Dry Soluble Oil Kerosene and Mineral Oil Lard Oil
MAGNESIUM AND ALLOYS		Mineral-Lard Oil Kerosene Dry		Dry Kerosene Mineral-Lard Oil
COPPER		Mineral-Lard Oil and Kerosene Soluble Oil Dry		Dry Soluble Oil Mineral-Lard Oil and Kerosene
MONEL METAL		Mineral-Lard Oil		Soluble Oil
MILD STEELS		Mineral-Lard Oil		Soluble Oil
TOUGH ALLOY STEELS		Sulfurized Oil		Mineral-Lard Oil
STEEL FORGINGS		Sulfurized Oil		Mineral-Lard Oil
CAST STEEL		Soluble Oil		Sulfurized Oil
WROUGHT IRON		Soluble Oil		Sulfurized Oil
HIGH TENSILE STEELS		Soluble Oil		Sulfurized Oil
MANGANESE STEEL		Dry		Dry
CAST IRON		Dry		Dry
MALLEABLE IRON		Soluble Oil Dry		Dry Soluble Oil
STAINLESS STEEL		Soluble Oil		Sulfurized Oil
TITANIUM ALLOYS		Soluble Oil		Sulfurized Oil
TOOL STEEL		Mineral-Lard Oil and Kerosene Kerosene Mineral-Lard Oil		Kerosene Mineral Oil and Kerosene Mineral-Lard Oil

Fig. 34-14. Universal machine vise with three separate angular adjustments. The base rotates 360°. The lower cradle rotates 45° to the right and left for a total of 90°. The upper cradle rotates from a horizontal to a vertical position for a total of 90°. With these three adjustments, a hole can be drilled at any compound angle.

Fig. 34-15. Using the safety work holder on an odd-shaped piece. A quarter of a turn on the handles locks the arms in place.

Fig. 34-16. A universal compound vise can be used for clamping work securely for many drilling operations. Note that the vise is bolted to the drill press table.

3. For more precise work, the *universal compound angle vise* is best. On this one, the base rotates 360°. The lower cradle can move 45° to the right or left, and the upper cradle can move 0 to 90° (Fig. 34-14).

4. A *safety work-holder* fits around the column of the drill press and has instantly adjustable arms that will give a firm, true grip on odd shapes. It is easily swung out of the way when not in use (Fig. 34-15).

5. A *universal compound vise* can be moved in two directions for more accurate drilling (Fig. 34-16).

6. *V blocks* hold round workpieces. On some types, a U-shaped clamp holds the work in place (Fig. 34-17).

7. *Strap clamps* and *T bolts* are used to clamp large or odd-shaped workpieces directly to the

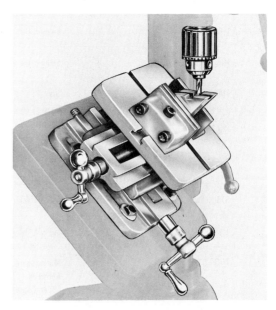

table (Fig. 34–18). The workpiece is first located on the table. The T bolts of correct size and length are inserted in the T slots of the table. Strap clamps are placed in position and blocked up at the outer end with step blocks or pieces of scrap metal. This makes the clamp level or parallel with the top of the workpiece. A washer must always be placed between the nut and the strap clamp. The correct clamping of large workpieces requires great skill. If not correctly done, the workpiece may be forced out of shape. The T bolts must always be as close to the work as possible. The step blocks or scrap pieces that support the end of the clamp must be as far from the T bolt as possible. Some of the common types of clamps are listed below.

a. *Straight strap clamps* made of flat stock have an elongated slot for positioning the clamp conveniently. They are used for many types of work (Fig. 34–17).

b. *Bent-tail* or *gooseneck clamps* are sometimes more convenient. A shorter T bolt can be used. These clamps are usually made of forged steel and are very strong (Fig. 34–17).

c. *U-strap clamps* are used like straight clamp straps. One end is open so they can be removed or placed in position by loosening the nut on the T bolt (Fig. 34–17).

d. *Finger clamps* have a small round or flat finger that extends from the clamp body. This makes it possible to use a hole or slot on a workpiece for clamping purposes (Fig. 34–17).

8. An *angle plate* is a precision tool which has been machined very square and parallel. Most are made with one or more V slots and T slots, and numerous tapped holes. Workpieces can be clamped directly to one of the faces for layout, drilling, reaming, and other operations (Fig. 34–19).

9. A *drill jig* is a production tool used to drill holes at an exact location in duplicate parts. The drill or drills are guided by *drill bushings*. Workpieces are clamped in the jig. The hole or holes drilled will always be in the same location on each of the different parts (Fig. 34–20).

Accessories. In addition to the various types of work-holding devices, there are a number of tools or accessories used in connection with clamps and vises. Some of the more important ones are listed below.

1. *Parallels* or *parallel bars* are used to seat work parallel on the drill-press table or in a vise. They are made in pairs and may be either square or rectangular. They come in many sizes and lengths. Usually they are hardened, then ground very square and parallel to size. Besides seating

Fig. 34-17. Common drilling tools and accessories for holding work in place.

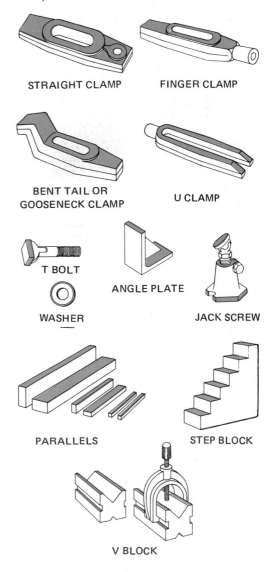

STRAIGHT CLAMP   FINGER CLAMP

BENT TAIL OR GOOSENECK CLAMP   U CLAMP

T BOLT

ANGLE PLATE

WASHER

JACK SCREW

PARALLELS   STEP BLOCK

V BLOCK

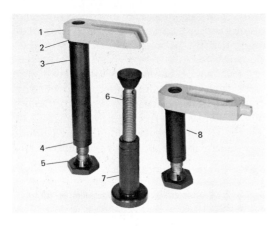

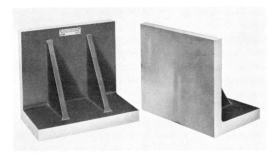

Fig. 34-18. A clamp-and-jack system used for holding large pieces on a drill press table. The basic parts include: (1) clamp, (2) tube coupling, (3) spacer tube, (4) ball screw, (5) swivel base, (6) jack screw, (7) jack base, and (8) finger clamp.

Fig. 34-20. A drill jig for drilling three holes at the same time.

Fig. 34-19. Angle plates are made with or without holes.

Fig. 34-21. Note this setup for drilling holes in a large piece of angle iron. An angle plate is bolted to the table. The part is clamped to the angle plate with a C clamp, and the outer edge is supported with a jack screw. If this outer edge is not supported, the drill may chatter and break.

the work parallel and square, they are used to raise the work held in a vise or on the table so the drill can pass through the work without touching vise or table (Fig. 34-17).

2. *Jack screws* are used to level and support workpieces which overhang beyond the vise or clamps. Sometimes they are placed directly under a part of the workpiece on which the clamp is located. This prevents the part from springing (Fig. 34-21).

3. *Step blocks* are used with strap clamps to provide a support for the end of the clamp. The steps of the block are made at different heights so the clamp can be located as level as possible. Some step blocks have a series of steps of different dimensions for convenience (Fig. 34-17).

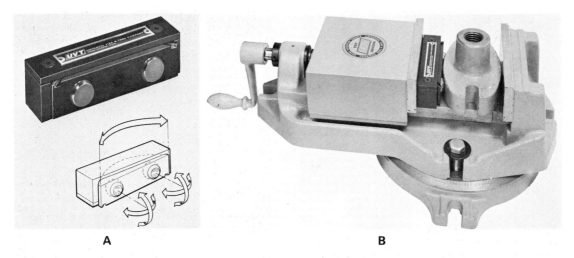

Fig. 34-22. (A) A universal swivel block may be used when clamping irregular surfaces. (B) Clamping an oval piece in a vise using a universal swivel block.

4. *Shims* are thin pieces of metal used to block up or level up work of irregular shape before clamping. Paper may also be used for this purpose.

5. *Swivel blocks* are placed between any irregular work and the vise jaw. They swivel to compensate for the shape of the work and allow for clamping the work securely (Fig. 34-22).

UNIT 35. Twist Drills

The cutting tools used most often in the drill press are the *twist drills* (Fig. 35-1). These tools are made by machining spiral flutes or grooves that run lengthwise around the body of the drill. The flutes provide for the cutting-edges and permit chips to escape as the drill cuts. The twist drill is one of the most efficient cutting tools in the shop. It is most important to know all the parts of a drill and how to grind and sharpen them for all kinds of materials.

DRILL SHANKS

Twist drills are made with either straight or taper shanks (Fig. 35-2). Straight-shank drills are held in a drill chuck. There are several types of straight shanks. The average mechanic working with metal need concern himself with only two,

full- and reduced-size shanks. *Straight-shank drills* up to $\frac{1}{4}$ in. fit easily into small power drills and drill presses and are the most common type. However, to drill holes over $\frac{1}{4}$ in. with most power drills ($\frac{1}{4}$ in. chuck capacity), you must use a drill with a reduced shank. Reduced shanks greatly extend the range of portable power drills and small drill presses.

CARBON- AND HIGH-SPEED-STEEL DRILLS

Twist drills are made from both carbon steel and high-speed steel. *Carbon-steel drills* are cheaper, but are not satisfactory for most machine-shop work. They have a low cutting speed. Once the cutting-edge becomes overheated from drilling or sharpening, the temper or hardness is lost, making the drill useless. High-speed-steel drills have largely replaced carbon-steel drills. They have doubled the cutting speed of carbon drills.

Fig. 35-1. Production drilling of metal in a multispindle machine.

STRAIGHT SHANK⌐   TAPER SHANK⌐

Fig. 35-2. Straight-shank and taper-shank twist drills.

Also the temper is not easily removed, even when the drill becomes hot. You can tell a high-speed-steel drill by the HS or HSS stamped on the shank. Also, when grinding a drill, a high-speed-steel drill gives off orange-colored sparks and a carbon-steel drill gives off white sparks.

Drills marked chrome steel, speed steel, or similar names are usually made of carbon steel and are not suitable for use with electric drills.

PARTS OF A TWIST DRILL

The main parts of a twist drill are illustrated in Fig. 35-3.

1. The *shank* fits into the chuck or spindle. The taper-shank drill always has a *tang* at the end, which fits into a slot in the spindle. The tang helps to drive the drill, prevents it from slipping, and provides a means of removing it from the taper spindle (Fig. 35-4).

2. The *body* is that part between the shank and the point. It consists of:

  a. The *flutes,* which are two spiral grooves cut around the body. These flutes form the cutting-edges on the point, allow the chips to escape, cause the chips to curl, and permit cutting oil to reach the cutting-edges.

  b. The *web,* which is the thickness between the flutes. The web becomes increasingly thicker from the point to the shank (Fig. 35-5).

  c. The *margin,* which is the narrow strip along the body. The drill is full size only across the margins. Back of the margin the body is smaller in diameter. This reduces friction between the drill body and the hole.

3. The *point* of the drill is the entire cone-shaped surface at the cutting end (Fig. 35-6). It includes the *cutting lips* formed by the flutes. Other parts of the point are:

  a. The *dead center,* or *chisel edge,* which is the end of the web. This surface does no cutting.

  b. The area back of the cutting lip, called the *surface of the point*.

  c. The *lip relief* (clearance angle), which is the amount the surface of the point slopes back from the cutting-edge. A drill could not cut without this lip clearance. With proper lip clearance, only the cutting-edges touch the metal as it is drilled.

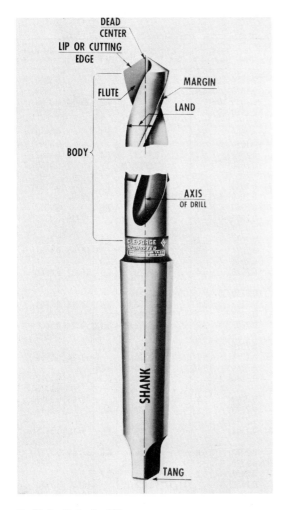

Fig. 35-3. Parts of a drill.

Fig. 35-4. (A) A drill sleeve is used when the taper on the drill is smaller than the taper hole on the spindle. (B) A drill socket is used when the taper shank of the drill is larger than the taper hole in the spindle.

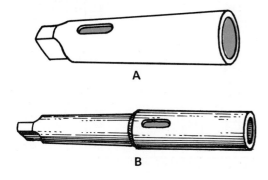

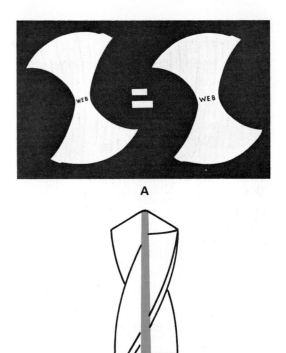

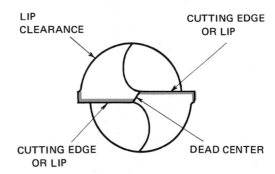

Fig. 35-5. (A) Note how the web increases from the point to the shank. Left: web near the point. Right: web near the shank. (B) The web is thicker near the shank.

Fig. 35-6. The point of the drill.

SIZES OF DRILLS

There are four ways of designating the sizes of twist drills (Table 35-1).

1. By *wire gage* (numbers) from No. 80, the smallest, to No. 1, the largest. All are smaller than $\frac{1}{4}$ in. and range in diameter from 0.0135 in.

Table 35-1. Drill sizes: metric and decimal equivalents.

Inch	Decimal	Wire	M/M	Inch	Decimal	Wire	M/M	Inch	Decimal	Wire	M/M	Inch	Decimal	Wire & Letter	M/M	Inch	Decimal	Letter	M/M	Inch	Decimal	Letter	M/M	Inch	Decimal	Letter	M/M
1/64	0.0156				0.0550	54			0.1110	34			0.1910	11			0.2810	K			0.3860	W					
	0.0157		0.4		0.0551		1.4		0.1130	33			0.1929		4.9	9/32	0.2812				0.3898		9.9				
	0.0160	78			0.0571		1.45		0.1142		2.9		0.1935	10			0.2835		7.2					25/64	0.3906		
	0.0165		0.42		0.0591		1.5		0.1160	32			0.1960	9			0.2854		7.25						0.3937		10.0
	0.0173		0.44		0.0595	53			0.1181		3.0		0.1969		5.0		0.2874		7.3		0.3970	X					
	0.0177		0.45		0.0610		1.55		0.1200	31			0.1990	8			0.2900	L			0.4040	Y					
	0.0180	77		1/16	0.0625				0.1220		3.1		0.2008		5.1		0.2913		7.4					13/32	0.4062		
	0.0181		0.46		0.0630		1.6	1/8	0.1250				0.2010	7			0.2950	M			0.4130	Z					
	0.0189		0.48		0.0635	52			0.1260		3.2	13/64	0.2031				0.2953		7.5		0.4134		10.5				
	0.0197		0.5		0.0650		1.65		0.1280		3.25		0.2040	6		19/64	0.2969							27/64	0.4219		
	0.0200	76			0.0669		1.7		0.1285	30			0.2047		5.2		0.2992		7.6		0.4331		11.0				
	0.0210	75			0.0670	51			0.1299		3.3		0.2055	5			0.3020	N						7/16	0.4375		
	0.0217		0.55		0.0689		1.75		0.1339		3.4		0.2067		5.25		0.3031		7.7		0.4528		11.5				
	0.0225	74			0.0700	50			0.1360	29			0.2087		5.3		0.3051		7.75					29/64	0.4531		
	0.0236		0.6		0.0709		1.8		0.1378		3.5		0.2090	4			0.3071		7.8					15/32	0.4688		
	0.0240	73			0.0728		1.85		0.1405	28			0.2126		5.4		0.3110		7.9		0.4724		12.0				
	0.0250	72			0.0730	49		9/64	0.1406				0.2130	3		5/16	0.3125							31/64	0.4844		
	0.0256		0.65		0.0748		1.9		0.1417		3.6		0.2165		5.5		0.3150		8.0		0.4921		12.5				
	0.0260	71			0.0760	48			0.1440	27		7/32	0.2188				0.3160	O						1/2	0.5000		
	0.0276		0.7		0.0768		1.95		0.1457		3.7		0.2205		5.6		0.3189		8.1		0.5118		13.0				
	0.0280	70		5/64	0.0781				0.1470	26			0.2210	2			0.3228		8.2					33/64	0.5156		
	0.0292	69			0.0785	47			0.1476		3.75		0.2244		5.7		0.3230	P						17/32	0.5312		
	0.0295		0.75		0.0787		2.0		0.1495	25			0.2264		5.75		0.3248		8.25		0.5315		13.5				
	0.0310	68			0.0807		2.05		0.1496		3.8		0.2280	1			0.3268		8.3					35/64	0.5469		
1/32	0.0312				0.0810	46			0.1520	24			0.2283		5.8	21/64	0.3281				0.5512		14.0				
	0.0315		0.8		0.0820	45			0.1535		3.9		0.2323		5.9		0.3307		8.4					9/16	0.5625		
	0.0320	67			0.0827		2.1		0.1540	23			0.2340	A			0.3320	Q			0.5709		14.5				
	0.0330	66			0.0846		2.15	5/32	0.1562			15/64	0.2344				0.3346		8.5					37/64	0.5781		
	0.0335		0.85		0.0860	44			0.1570	22			0.2362		6.0		0.3386		8.6		0.5906		15.0				
	0.0350	65			0.0866		2.2		0.1575		4.0		0.2380	B			0.3390	R						19/32	0.5938		
	0.0354		0.9		0.0886		2.25		0.1590	21			0.2402		6.1		0.3425		8.7					39/64	0.6094		
	0.0360	64			0.0890	43			0.1610	20			0.2420	C		11/32	0.3438				0.6102		15.5				
	0.0370	63			0.0906		2.3		0.1614		4.1		0.2441		6.2		0.3445		8.75					5/8	0.6250		
	0.0374		0.95		0.0925		2.35		0.1654		4.2		0.2460	D			0.3465		8.8		0.6299		16.0				
	0.0380	62			0.0935	42			0.1660	19			0.2461		6.25		0.3480	S						41/64	0.6406		
	0.0390	61		3/32	0.0938				0.1673		4.25		0.2480		6.3		0.3504		8.9		0.6496		16.5				
	0.0394		1.0		0.0945		2.4		0.1693		4.3	1/4	0.2500	E			0.3543		9.0					21/32	0.6562		
	0.0400	60			0.0960	41			0.1695	18			0.2520		6.4		0.3580	T			0.6693		17.0				
	0.0410	59			0.0965		2.45	11/64	0.1719				0.2559		6.5		0.3583		9.1					43/64	0.6719		
	0.0413		1.05		0.0980	40			0.1730	17			0.2570	F		23/64	0.3594							11/16	0.6875		
	0.0420	58			0.0981		2.5		0.1732		4.4		0.2598		6.6		0.3622		9.2		0.6890		17.5				
	0.0430	57			0.0995	39			0.1770	16			0.2610	G			0.3642		9.25					45/64	0.7031		
	0.0433		1.1		0.1015	38			0.1772		4.5		0.2638		6.7		0.3661		9.3		0.7087		18.0				
	0.0453		1.15		0.1024		2.6		0.1800	15		17/64	0.2656				0.3680	U						23/32	0.7188		
	0.0465	56			0.1040	37			0.1811		4.6		0.2657		6.75		0.3701		9.4		0.7283		18.5				
3/64	0.0469				0.1063		2.7		0.1820	14			0.2660	H			0.3740		9.5					47/64	0.7344		
	0.0472		1.2		0.1065	36			0.1850	13			0.2677		6.8	3/8	0.3750				0.7480		19.0				
	0.0492		1.25		0.1083		2.75		0.1850		4.7		0.2717		6.9		0.3770	V						3/4	0.7500		
	0.0512		1.3	7/64	0.1094				0.1870		4.75		0.2720	I			0.3780		9.6								
	0.0520	55			0.1100	35		3/16	0.1875				0.2756		7.0		0.3819		9.7								
	0.0531		1.35		0.1102		2.8		0.1890		4.8		0.2770	J			0.3839		9.75								
									0.1890	12			0.2795		7.1		0.3858		9.8								

214

(No. 80) to 0.228 in. (No. 1). Wire gage sizes are used where exact sizing is required below $\frac{1}{4}$ in. A standard set of number drills consists of Nos. 1 to 60. The No. 61 to 80 drills are not so widely used.

2. By *letters* from A, the smallest, to Z, the largest (see Table 35–1). All letter-sized drills are larger than number-sized drills.

3. By *fractional sizes* that vary in diameter by $\frac{1}{64}$ in., from $\frac{1}{64}$ to $3\frac{1}{2}$ in. Larger drills are generally specially ordered. A standard set of fractional-sized drills from $\frac{1}{16}$ to $\frac{1}{2}$ in. by sixty-fourths is called a *jobber's set* of drills. They are stored in a drill stand when not in use.

4. By standard *metric sizes* measured in millimeters (mm). The range in jobber's twist drills with parallel (straight) shanks is from 0.20 mm to 16.00 mm.

Note that the first three groups of drill sizes are made so that each larger drill is only a few thousandths of an inch different in diameter (Table 35–1). No two drills are exactly the same size, except the $\frac{1}{4}$-in. drill and the E drill, which are both 0.250 in.

Drill-size gages, made for number, letter, and fractional sizes up to $\frac{1}{2}$ in., may be used to check the correct size of a drill. Most machinists, however, prefer to check the drill size with a micrometer. The drill must be measured directly across the margins. Form the habit of always checking or measuring the drill size before using it. Do this yourself and never rely upon another person's word that the size is correct. You are the only person responsible for the accuracy of the work (Fig. 35–7).

TYPES OF DRILLS

General-purpose. General-purpose high-speed drills are designed to perform satisfactorily under a variety of conditions. They are by far the most commonly used of all straight-shank drills and are suited for high production jobs on most types of materials and setups. They are not a good choice for jobs which present a particu-

Fig. 35–7. (A) This is a drill gage for checking letter-sized drills. (B) This is a drill-size gage for fractional-size drills. (C) This is a number-size drill gage.

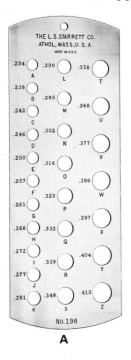

A

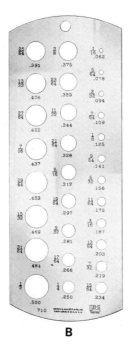

B

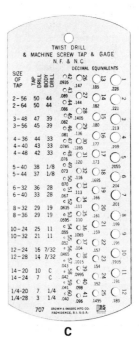

C

larly difficult problem because of materials, setup conditions, or both.

Two-flute Drill. This drill is the basic cutting tool for producing a cylindrical cavity. It has two cutting lips and two flutes, spiral or straight, for the passage of chips and the admission of a cutting fluid (Fig. 35–8).

Heavy-duty. Heavy-duty or heavy-web high-speed drills are designed primarily for jobs where maximum strength and rigidity are required. These drills are made with a heavier cross section and therefore should be thinned at the web after being repointed.

Fast Spiral. These drills, made with wide polished flutes and narrow lands, are recommended mainly for nonferrous metals and drilling in fiber and plastic. They have also been used with some success in drilling stainless steels and in deep-hole drilling.

Slow Spiral. Slow spiral high-speed drills have been developed primarily for use in molded plastic materials, brass, fiber, hard rubber, and for some horizontal drilling. They have a low spiral angle, wide polished flutes, and comparatively thin webs for easy penetration and maximum chip space.

Super Cobalt. Manufactured of special 8 percent cobalt high-speed steels, these drills are designed for tougher drilling applications beyond the scope of conventional high-speed drills. They are used when drilling work-hardened stainless steels, silicon chrome and certain chrome-nickel alloy steels, armor plate, acid-resisting castings and forgings, and similar materials. To ensure the best performance, these drills should be used in a rigid setup with steady feed and constant speed. They can often be run at higher speeds than recommended for high-speed drills, except in the high-manganese steels.

Carbide-tipped. Tungsten carbide-tipped drills are designed with a spiral that provides maximum strength and proper rake for the carbide tip. These drills are manufactured with hardened high-speed steel bodies. Carbide drills are particularly advantageous when used in extremely

Fig. 35-8. Two-flute drill for general-purpose drilling.

Fig. 35-9. The carbide-tipped, two-flute drill for removing large amounts of material economically.

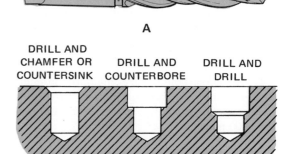

A

DRILL AND CHAMFER OR COUNTERSINK   DRILL AND COUNTERBORE   DRILL AND DRILL

B

Fig. 35-10. (A) A subland drill. (B) The different kinds of cuts which can be made with such a drill.

Fig. 35-11. A core drill.

abrasive materials such as urea; phenolic, glass-bonded and laminated plastics; cast iron; and most nonferrous metals such as aluminum, brass, bronze, and magnesium (Fig. 35–9).

Subland Drill (2-2). A subland drill (2-2) is basically a two-flute drill having two different diameters on one tool. The individual characteristics and proper geometry of each are retained (Fig. 35–10A). The subland drill (2-2) eliminates steps by performing two operations at one time (Fig. 35–10B). Its built-in concentricity assures accuracy.

Core Drill. Core drills are basically twist drills having either three or four flutes used for enlarging previously drilled, punched, cast, or cored holes. They give better tolerance control and surface finish than two-flute drills (Fig. 35–11).

Fig. 35-12. A coolant feeding or oil hole drill.

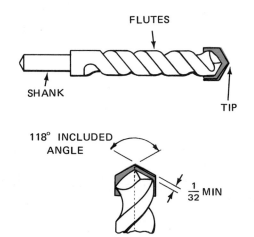

Fig. 35-13. A masonry drill.

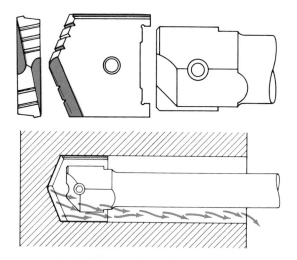

Fig. 35-14. A spade drill. Note how this drill allows chips to escape.

Coolant Feeding Drills (Oil Hole). Coolant feeding drills are basic two-flute drills that have either oil tubes imbedded in the clearance area between margins or oil holes drilled in the core of the drill. In this way, coolant emerges under

pressure at the point of the tool. Taper-shank tools are usually side coolant feeding, with an optional plug for top feeding. Straight-shank tools feed coolant at the top of the shank (Fig. 35-12). Coolant feeding drills are used primarily in deep-hole, heavy-duty drilling. Though more expensive than conventional drills, high speeds and feeds are possible. These can result in productivity increases of 300 percent or more. Coolant feeding drills also provide better size control, longer tool life, and an improved finish.

Masonry Drills. Masonry drills are tipped with a special ultrahard metal (cemented carbide) for drilling in concrete or masonry materials. Any portable rotary electric drill or drill press can be used. Normal speeds of portable electric drills are satisfactory for drilling usual masonry materials. Use lower speeds when drilling extremely hard or very abrasive materials. The drill is kept sharp by grinding with a silicon-carbide wheel. The drill should be sharpened as shown in Fig. 35-13.

Spade Drills. Spade drills are available in a wide range of sizes above one inch. They are readily adaptable to many types of machines and most provide through-the-drill cutting fluid feed capabilities. The basic spade drill is an assembly consisting of three basic parts: a cutting blade; a blade holder or shank; and a retaining device such as a screw, which fastens the blade to the holder (Fig. 35-14).

CHATTER AND OTHER DRILLING PROBLEMS

Chatter, or vibration in the drilling operation, generally is caused by a lack of rigidity in the drill, the work, the machine, or a combination of all three. These vibrations cause a hammering action of the cutting-edges against the work which may result in chipped cutting-edges, a body fracture of the tool, or even failure of the machine due to fatigue.

One common cause of chatter is a looseness in the moving parts of the machine due to wear or careless adjustment. Worn parts that cannot be adjusted should be replaced when necessary. The machine itself should be fastened as rigidly as possible. Drill spindles and other driving parts should be sufficiently strong

COMMON DRILLING PROBLEMS
THEIR PROBABLE CAUSE AND CORRECTION

OUTER CORNERS BREAK DOWN
CUTTING SPEED TOO HIGH • HARD SPOTS IN MATERIAL • NO CUTTING COMPOUND AT DRILL POINTS • FLUTES CLOGGED WITH CHIPS

CUTTING LIPS CHIP
TOO MUCH FEED • LIP RELIEF TOO GREAT

CHECKS OR CRACKS IN CUTTING LIPS
OVERHEATED OR TOO QUICKLY COOLED WHILE SHARPENING OR DRILLING

MARGIN CHIPS
OVERSIZE JIG BUSHING

DRILL BREAKS
POINT IMPROPERLY GROUND • FEED TOO HEAVY • SPRING OR BACKLASH IN DRILL PRESS, FIXTURE OR WORK • DRILL IS DULL • FLUTES CLOGGED WITH CHIPS

TANG BREAKS
IMPERFECT FIT BETWEEN TAPER SHANK AND SOCKET CAUSED BY DIRT OR CHIPS, OR BURRED OR BADLY WORN SOCKETS

DRILL BREAKS WHEN DRILLING BRASS OR WOOD
FLUTES CLOGGED WITH CHIPS • IMPROPER TYPE DRILL

DRILL SPLITS UP CENTER
LIP RELIEF TOO SMALL • TOO MUCH FEED

DRILL WILL NOT ENTER WORK
DRILL IS DULL • LIP RELIEF TOO SMALL • TOO HEAVY A WEB

HOLE ROUGH
POINT IMPROPERLY GROUND OR DULL • NO CUTTING COMPOUNDS AT DRILL POINT • IMPROPER CUTTING COMPOUND • FEED TOO GREAT • FIXTURE NOT RIGID

HOLE OVERSIZE
UNEQUAL ANGLE OF THE CUTTING—EDGES • UNEQUAL LENGTH OF THE CUTTING—EDGES • LOOSE SPINDLE

CHIP SHAPE CHANGES WHILE DRILLING
DRILL BECOMES DULL OR CUTTING LIPS CHIPPED

LARGE CHIP COMING OUT OF ONE FLUTE, SMALL CHIP OUT OF OTHER FLUTE
POINT IMPROPERLY GROUND, ONE LIP DOING ALL THE CUTTING

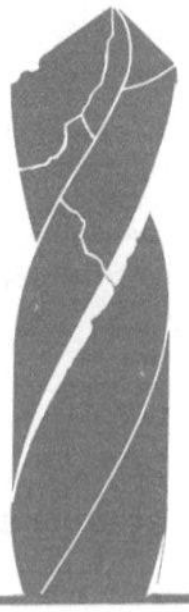

Fig. 35-15. Common drilling problems.

to avoid deflection during drilling. Holding fixtures and supports should be adequate for the work being done. Also, all unnecessary overhang should be eliminated wherever possible. All these precautions should be taken periodically to ensure chatterfree operation and eliminate possible drill failure. Other common kinds of drilling problems are described in Fig. 35-15.

DRILL POINT

The shape of the drill point is most important. To ensure that the drill will cut properly, check it for these things.

1. The included angle must be correct. For most work, this angle is 118 degrees (°), or 59 degrees from either side of the axis or center line of the drill point (Fig. 35–16). At this angle the cutting-edges form a straighter line due to the shape of the flutes.

2. The length of the cutting lips should be equal. A longer lip on one side and a shorter

Fig. 35–16. (A) The included angle of a drill point should be 118° or 59° on either side of its center. (B) Drill points recommended for various other kinds of drilling.

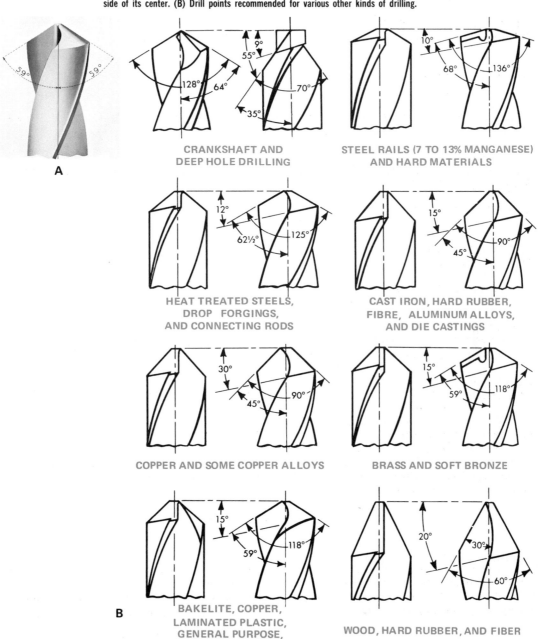

A

CRANKSHAFT AND
DEEP HOLE DRILLING

STEEL RAILS (7 TO 13% MANGANESE)
AND HARD MATERIALS

HEAT TREATED STEELS,
DROP FORGINGS,
AND CONNECTING RODS

CAST IRON, HARD RUBBER,
FIBRE, ALUMINUM ALLOYS,
AND DIE CASTINGS

COPPER AND SOME COPPER ALLOYS

BRASS AND SOFT BRONZE

B

BAKELITE, COPPER,
LAMINATED PLASTIC,
GENERAL PURPOSE,
MILD STEELS, ETC.

WOOD, HARD RUBBER, AND FIBER

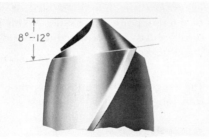

Fig. 35-17. The clearance or relief angle back of the cutting-edge should be 8 to 12° for the average drill. For special-purpose drilling, see Fig. 35-16B.

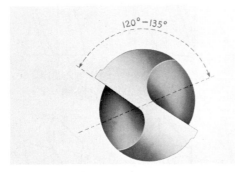

Fig. 35-18. The line across the dead center or chisel edge should be at an angle of 120 to 135° from the cutting-edge.

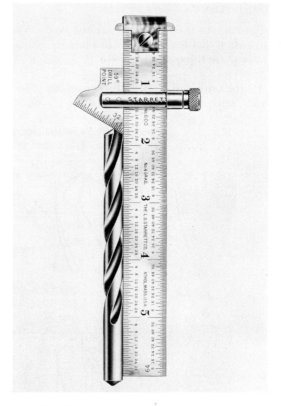

Fig. 35-19. Checking a drill point with a drill-point gage.

lip on the other will cause a drill to cut oversize. In fact, a drill may be ground with a longer lip on one side when an oversize hole is desired. It must be used in solid metal and not in a hole previously drilled.

3. There must be proper relief or clearance back of the cutting-edge (Fig. 35-17). The lip relief or clearance angle is usually 8 to 12° for steel and cast iron. If there is not enough clearance angle, the point merely rubs and cannot cut (Fig. 35-18). If there is too much clearance angle, the cutting-edges dull rapidly or the outer corners break off.

GRINDING A DRILL BY HAND

One of the traits of a good machinist is his ability to recognize a dull tool and be able to resharpen it accurately and quickly. Good work-

manship depends upon the sharpness of your cutting tools. To grind a drill by hand:

1. Examine the drill to check its condition. If it is dull or the margins near the point are worn or burned off, it will be necessary to grind off the entire point and regrind a new one.

2. Use the coarse grinding wheel first if much metal is to be ground away. Finish on the smooth wheel. Grinding wheels should be dressed and trued before you start.

3. Use a drill-point gage to check the drill-point angle (Fig. 35-19).

4. To hold a drill correctly for grinding, place the forefinger of one hand on the tool rest of the grinder (either the right or the left hand may be used). Place the drill on the forefinger. With the thumb, grasp the drill just snug enough to

hold it steady against the wheel. Hold the drill by the shank with the other hand.

5. Place the lip against the grinding wheel while holding the drill at an angle of approximately 59° from the face of the wheel. With a little experience, you will soon be able to judge this angle quite accurately. It is seldom, if ever, necessary to have this angle exact. To help you position the drill angle, aim the drill straight at the wheel face. Then move the drill shank to the left about 30°. This leaves a difference of 60° for the cutting-lip angle. It is quite easy to judge 30 and 60° angles after some practice (Fig. 35-20).

6. The movement of your hand holding the drill shank is most important. Move the hand downward naturally, and try not to twist the drill as you do so. As your hand goes down, it will follow a slight natural arc without any effort on your part. This puts the correct curve on the surface of the drill back of the cutting-edge. When moving the drill back to the starting point for successive grinds, *never* raise the shank end above the level of the cutting lip. To do so will give you a negative angle, and the drill will not

cut. If you twist the drill as you feed the shank downward, you will grind the cutting-edge off the opposite lip.

7. Grind a little at a time off each lip, working toward the center point.

8. Use a drill gage to check as you grind, to make sure that:

   a. The cutting-edges are the same length

   b. The cutting-edges make an equal angle with the axis, 59°.

   c. The clearance behind the cutting-edges is about 12°.

9. Do not apply so much pressure as to overheat the drill point. Carbon drills must be cooled often in water as they are being ground. High-speed-steel drills may be cooled frequently, but it is not good practice to cool a hot drill point in cold water. This sudden cooling may cause cracks in the metal. Let it cool in the air.

10. Avoid these common mistakes in grinding drills:

   a. Not enough lip clearance. The point will rub and heat up rapidly, and the drill will be broken.

   b. Too much lip clearance. This causes the cutting-edge to wear or break down rapidly.

   c. One lip longer than the other. This makes the dead center, on which the drill pivots, off-center from the axis, causing the drill to wobble and cut an oversize hole (Fig. 35-21).

   d. Lips at different angles. One lip does all the cutting. The drill will wobble and cut oversize (Fig. 35-22).

11. After the drill has been ground many times, the web becomes thicker and drilling becomes difficult. This is true even though the drill has been ground properly. It requires more pressure to force the drill into the metal. To overcome this, *thin the web*. To thin the web, use the sharp corner of the regular grinding wheel, or use a very narrow wheel with a rounded face, if available. Hold the cutting-edge parallel with the side of the wheel. Grind back into the flutes on either side until the web is about as thick as that of a new drill of the same size.

Fig. 35-20.   The correct position for grinding a drill.

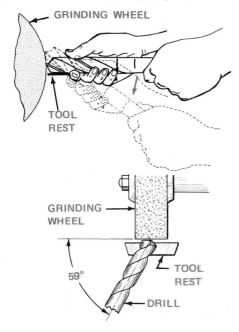

GRINDING WHEEL

TOOL REST

GRINDING WHEEL

59°

TOOL REST

DRILL

Fig. 35-21. Here is what happens when the lips are unequal in length.

Fig. 35-22. The hole is oversized when the cutting-edges are at different angles.

Fig. 35-23. A drill-grinding attachment can be used on an offhand grinder. Note how the unit is set to grind an included angle of 118°.

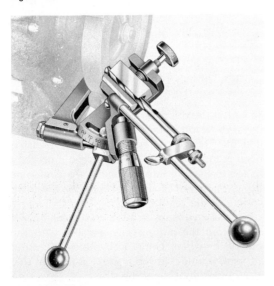

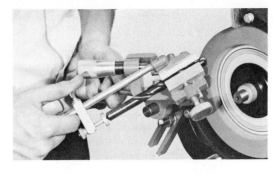

Fig. 35-24. Using a drill-grinding attachment.

Fig. 35-25. A regrinding fixture that can be used on a tool grinder.

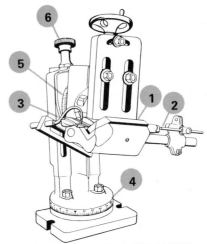

PRINCIPLE OF OPERATION

1. TOOLS ARE CLAMPED IN V—BLOCK (1) WITH ENOUGH OVERHANG TO PREVENT WHEEL CONTACTING V—BLOCK.

2. LENGTH IS ESTABLISHED AND MAINTAINED BY SETTING OF TAILSTOCK CENTER (2).

3. CORRECT ALIGNMENT OF FLUTES IS ACHIEVED BY SETTING FINGER (3) SO THAT IT CONTACTS THE FLUTE BEING GROUND AT THE CLOSEST POINT TO THE WHEEL. THIS ALSO ASSURES THE NEXT OPERATION WILL BE GROUND IDENTICALLY.

4. STEP ANGLE IS DETERMINED BY THE BASE SCALE (4).

5. CLEARANCE ANGLE IS DETERMINED BY THE BODY SCALE (5).

6. TOOL TO WHEEL RELATIONSHIP IS ACHIEVED BY VERTICAL MOVEMENT OF CUTTER GRINDER HEAD OR VERTICAL MOVEMENT OF HANDSCREW (6).

USING A DRILL-GRINDING ATTACHMENT

The drill-grinding attachment is very helpful when accurately ground drills are required (Fig. 35-23). To use:

1. Lay the drill in the V of the attachment. Adjust the angle setting to the correct location. Note that the standard 59° angle is indicated.

2. Move the lower support until the drill point is very close to the grinding wheel. Tighten the support.

3. Now turn the micrometer adjustment until one lip just touches the grinding wheel.

4. Move the end of the attachment back and forth to sharpen one cutting-edge.

5. Then turn the drill halfway around and sharpen the other cutting-edge (Fig. 35-24).

6. There are many types of precision regrinding attachments that can be used on tool grinders (Fig. 35-25). In industry, precision drill-grinding units designed specifically for sharpening drills are employed. You should follow the manufacturer's directions for using these machines (Fig. 35-26).

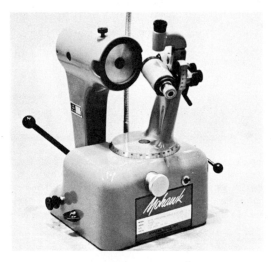

Fig. 35-26. A precision drill grinder for small drills. Once the proper settings have been made, drill grinding is almost an automatic operation.

UNIT 36. Drilling Holes in Flat Workpieces

Drilling looks simple, but there is really a lot to learn about it (Fig. 36-1). The "feel" of the feed handle tells you if the tool is cutting correctly. The sound of the drill tells you if the cutting is being done freely, or if the tool is laboring. The appearance of the chips shows if the drill is grinding correctly and whether it is sharp or dull (Fig. 36-2).

DRILLING SMALLER HOLES

Holes $\frac{1}{2}$ in. or smaller are usually drilled with straight-shank twist drills held in a drill chuck.

1. First lay out two lines at right angles that intersect at the center location of the hole. Mark this point with a prick punch.

2. Enlarge the prick punch mark with a center punch so the drill will start easily. Remember that the chisel edge or dead center of a drill will not cut. The punch mark permits the drill to enter and the cutting-edges to begin cutting.

3. Select the correct size of drill as shown on the drawing or print. Look at the size stamped on the shank. If the size is worn off, check the drill with a drill-size gage, or measure across the margins with a micrometer (Fig. 36-3).

4. Insert the drill in the chuck, and tighten it with a chuck key (Fig. 36-4).

CAUTION

Always remove the key immediately.

5. Start the drill press, and check to make sure the drill is running straight. If it wobbles, the

Fig. 36-1. The correct way to dress when operating a drill press. Note that the work has been securely fastened in the vise. Parallels are placed below the workpiece to keep the drill from striking the vise. The operator is using power feed and, therefore, must be alert to release the feed when the drilling is complete.

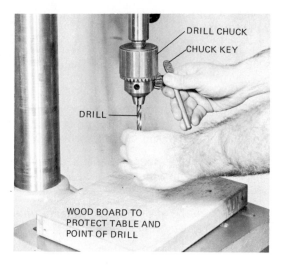

Fig. 36-4. Fastening a straight-shank drill in a drill chuck. The wood block is used to protect the drill point and table in case the drill is dropped.

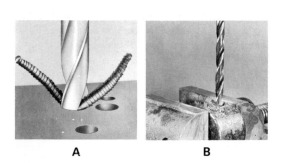

A   **B**

Fig. 36-2. (A) A correctly ground drill produces continuous steel chips like this. (B) Chips from cast iron are different.

Fig. 36-3. Checking the size of a drill with a drill gage.

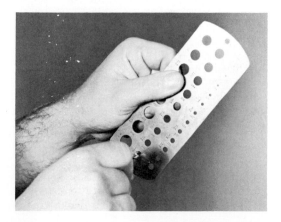

drill may be bent, the shank may be badly worn, or it may have been placed in the chuck off-center.

6. Adjust the drill press for the correct speed.

7. Fasten the workpiece in the drill vise or directly to the table, using T bolts, clamps, and step blocks (Fig. 36-5).

8. Move the drill down with the feed handle to see if the point lines up with the punch mark. If necessary, move the workpiece or the table to correct any error. Check also to make certain the drill can go all the way through the workpiece. Raise the table if necessary.

9. Turn on the power, and bring the point of the drill down to the surface of the workpiece. Apply pressure to start the drill. Raise the drill, and examine the work to see if the drill is starting correctly. If not, use a diamond-point or small roundnose chisel to cut a groove on the side toward which the drill should move (see Fig. 36-13). Beginners make the mistake of thinking that if the workpiece is moved, the drill can be brought back on center. This is not possible. The drill is merely forced out of alignment and still follows the original hole.

10. Apply a little cutting fluid, and continue the drilling. Apply even pressure to keep the drill

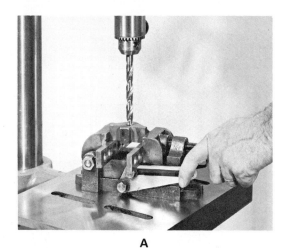
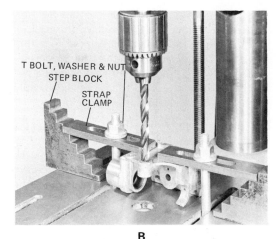

T BOLT, WASHER & NUT
STEP BLOCK
STRAP CLAMP

A   B

Fig. 36-5. (A) Work properly clamped in a vise can be held freehand on the table if the twist drill is not a large one. Note also that there is plenty of clearance between the workpiece and the vise. (B) This irregular-shaped casting is fastened to the table with step blocks, strap clamps, bolts, and nuts.

cutting freely. Don't try to force the drill. Watch for these signs of poor drilling:

a. Squeaking indicates a dull drill or one that is not ground properly.

b. Groaning of the machine indicates overloading. You may be using a dull drill or one that is incorrectly ground. You may also be applying too much pressure. Sometimes a chip gets under the cutting-edge or dead center of the drill and revolves with the drill. This makes it impossible for the drill to start cutting again. When this happens, raise and lower the drill several times to clear the chip.

11. As you drill a hole of any depth, raise the drill frequently. Break the continuous chip and brush some oil on the point of the drill.

12. As the drill begins to break through the hole, ease up on the feed handle. Let the drill cut its way through. If forced too much, it may bind in the hole and break the drill or damage the work. Also, the work may be pulled loose and start whirling around. Remember, this is the time accidents usually happen. Your sense of feel when the drill breaks through is most important.

13. After the hole is drilled, back the drill out of the hole steadily, then shut off the power.

CAUTION

Never try to stop a turning chuck with your hand.

DRILLING LARGER HOLES

1. Holes larger than $\frac{1}{2}$ in. may be drilled with taper-shank drills held in the spindle hole. Remember, the shanks of these drills have self-holding tapers (from No. 1 to No. 6 Morse taper). After using taper-shank drills for a while, you should be able to look at the shank and know the number of the taper.

2. The lower end of a drill-press spindle has a self-holding (Morse) taper hole. The number or size of the taper hole varies according to the size of the drill press. If the spindle taper-hole and the taper-drill shank are the same size, the drill can be inserted directly in the spindle. For example, a No. 3 taper-shank drill will fit directly into a No. 3 taper-spindle hole.

3. If the drill shank is smaller than the spindle hole, a *taper sleeve* is used. This sleeve is tapered outside to fit a spindle hole or another hole. The inside has a taper hole to receive a drill shank or another smaller sleeve. An elongated hole through the diameter provides a means of sepa-

225

rating the sleeves from the drill. A tapered *drift* is used to remove the sleeve from the drill, or the drill from the drill-press spindle. If a drill has a No. 2 taper shank and the drill-press spindle has a No. 3 taper hole, a sleeve having a No. 2 taper inside and a No. 3 taper outside would be used. This is called a *No. 2 to 3 sleeve*.

4. When the taper-drill shank is larger than the spindle taper hole, a *drill socket* is used. A drill socket is much longer than a taper sleeve. The end with the taper hole may be much larger in diameter than the taper shank that fits into the spindle. Drill sockets are usually used on larger drilling machines.

5. When drilling holes larger than $\frac{1}{2}$ in., it is good practice to drill a smaller hole first. This is called a *pilot hole* (Fig. 36-6). You remember that the chisel edge or dead center does no cutting. On large drills the chisel edge is quite wide, which requires a lot of power to get it started. It may also run off the punch mark. Drilling a pilot hole assures better accuracy and makes the job easier. Choose a small drill for the pilot hole with a diameter slightly larger than the web thickness of the large drill. The large drill will always follow in the small hole.

6. After the pilot hole has been drilled, remove the chuck so you can insert the larger taper-shank drill.

7. Be sure the inside of the taper spindle, the drill shank, and the sleeve are clean and free of chips, oil, or dirt. If dirty or dented, these parts will not fit together tightly and will not run true.

CAUTION

Never attempt to clean a taper hole in the spindle while it is turning, and never place your finger in a taper hole while it is turning. If you do, you may leave your finger in the hole!

8. Mount the sleeve or socket on the drill first, then place the drill in the spindle. Tap the end of the drill with a soft-faced hammer to seat it securely (Fig. 36-7). Be sure to align the tang with the slot in the spindle.

9. Adjust the belt for correct speed.

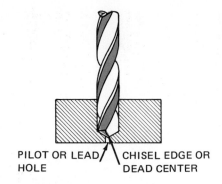

PILOT OR LEAD HOLE \ CHISEL EDGE OR DEAD CENTER

Fig. 36-6.   Drilling a pilot or lead hole first helps the larger drill to cut more easily.

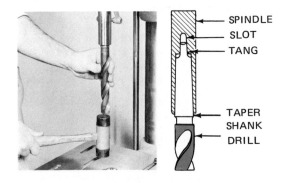

SPINDLE
SLOT
TANG

TAPER
SHANK
DRILL

Fig. 36-7.   Inserting a taper-shank drill in the spindle. A soft-faced hammer is used to seat the drill firmly in place. Note how the tang fits into the spindle slot.

10. Clamp the workpiece in place (Fig. 36-8).

11. Drill the hole (Fig. 36-9).

12. Place a block of wood under the drill. Use a *drill drift* to remove the drill from the spindle (Fig. 36-10). The wood block prevents damage to the table if the drill should drop.

PRECISION DRILLING

1. Apply a thin coat of layout fluid to the workpiece.

2. Scribe two intersecting lines to locate the center of the hole. Prick-punch the location.

3. Set a divider equal to the radius of the hole, and scribe the circle.

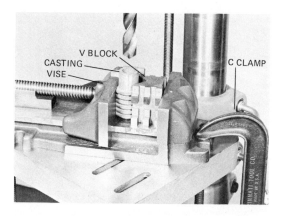

Fig. 36-8. Holding a casting in a drill vise with a V-block. Two C-clamps hold the vise to the table. This workpiece is held very securely and safely.

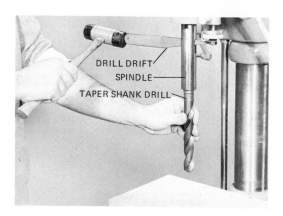

Fig. 36-10. Removing a taper-shank drill with a drill drift. A board has been placed on the table to prevent damage to the table in case the drill drops.

Fig. 36-9. Drilling the hole. Cutting oil should be applied to the drill point when drilling steel.

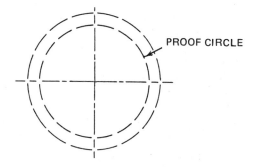

Fig. 36-11. Layout for precision drilling.

4. Set the divider slightly smaller, and scribe another circle inside the first one. This is called the *proof circle.*

5. Make a number of prick punch marks around the proof circle (Fig. 36-11).

6. Center-punch the hole to be drilled.

7. Fasten the workpiece securely, and start the drill. As the point of the drill reaches the proof circle, stop and raise the drill. Check to see if the circle cut by the drill is concentric or true with the proof circle.

8. If it is not, cut a groove in the side toward which the drill should be moved. Use a round-nose or diamond-point chisel. The groove should be cut directly opposite the point where the drill touches the layout circle. It should extend to the layout circle in depth (Fig. 36-12).

9. When the hole has been started accurately, complete the drilling.

10. In industry, precision drilling is often done with the workpiece held in a fixture. This eliminates the need to lay out the hole location on each piece (Fig. 36-13).

DRILLING BLIND HOLES

A *blind hole* is one that is drilled only part way through the workpiece. To get the correct depth,

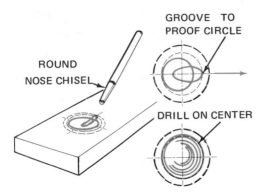

Fig. 36-12. Chipping a groove to draw the drill back when it has started inaccurately.

use the *depth stop* or *gage* on the drill press. To set the depth stop, place a line on the workpiece at the depth desired. Feed the drill down until the point is even with the line. Tighten the nut on the depth stop. Another way is to use the *depth scale* on the drill press. Note the reading when the drill touches the work. Then add the depth of hole desired, and drill until the combined dimension is obtained on the scale. Always make certain the drills are set in the chuck as far as possible, so they won't slip upward and change the setting.

Fig. 36-13. A precision drill press is used for drilling and reaming a small accurate hole in these fuel-injection valves.

UNIT 37. Drilling Holes in Round Workpieces

Holes through the diameter of rods, pipes, shafts, and other round workpieces are difficult to set up and drill accurately. A good job requires care in layout and clamping.

1. Mark the location of the hole with a prick punch. Then enlarge it with a center punch.

2. Place the work in one or two V blocks. If the hole is to go through the workpiece, make sure the drill will clear the V block (Fig. 37–1).

3. Check to make certain the hole will be drilled through the center by using one of the following methods.

a. Locate and fasten the V block to the table so that the bottom of the V slot is lined up exactly with the drill.

b. Place the workpiece in a V block. Place work and V block on the flat surface of the drill-press or a surface plate. Place the beam of a square on the flat surface with the upright blade against the round workpiece. Hold a steel rule against the blade and at right angles to the square at the top of the workpiece. Rotate the workpiece until the prick-punch mark is located one-half of the diameter from the square blade. Place the square on the opposite side and check to see if the distance is the same. If not, rotate the workpiece and recheck until the measurements are equal (Fig. 37-2).

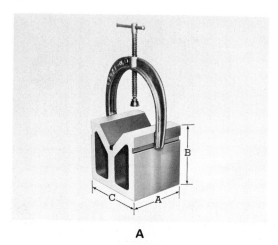

A

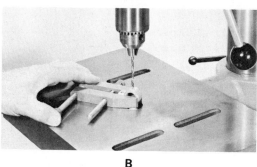

B

Fig. 37-1. (A) V-block with clamp used when drilling holes in round stock. (B) A clamp can be used to hold small parts.

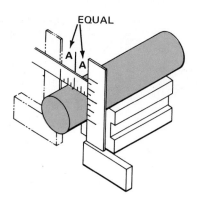

Fig. 37-2. Measuring from each side of the V-block. Make sure the work is centered.

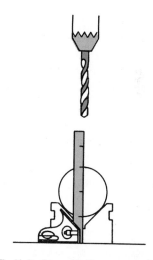

Fig. 37-3. The blade of a combination square can be used to line up the drill with the workpiece.

c. Draw a center line across the end of the cylinder directly in line with the hole to be drilled. Then use the blade of a combination square to align the drill with the work (Fig. 37-3).

4. A V block can be clamped in a vise or to the table with strap clamps, bolts, and step blocks (Fig. 37-4). A pair of V blocks may be used as shown in Fig. 37-5.

5. A drill jig can be used when there are a large number of parts to be drilled. The *drill jig* is a device for holding the workpiece and guiding the drill. Drills of different diameters can be used by changing the *drill bushings* in the jig. The drill jig eliminates the need of making a layout on each piece. It saves a lot of time on any production job (Fig. 37-6). Simple drill jigs can be quickly made for drilling holes in several duplicate pieces. Use any piece of square or flat

stock somewhat thicker than the diameter of the workpiece. Scribe a line across one end, and continue the line along one side. Center-punch and drill a hole in the end to permit the workpiece to fit in freely. Locate, center-punch, and drill a hole on the line scribed along the side. A thumbscrew or setscrew can be located conveniently to hold the workpiece. The round workpiece can then be inserted in the end hole, the setscrew tightened, and a hole drilled through the center.

6. When necessary to drill the same size of hole through the diameter of several identical workpieces, turn a disk with the same diameter

A

B

Fig. 37-4. (A) Drilling a blind hole. Note that there is no clearance under the workpiece. It cannot be drilled all the way through. (B) Using a V-block, strap clamp, and step block for drilling a hole completely through a round piece.

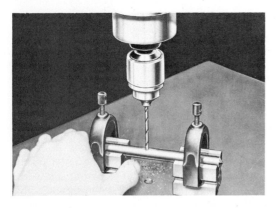

Fig. 37-5. Drilling a small hole through a workpiece using a pair of V-blocks. The setup is held with the hand. This can be done only when small holes are drilled.

JIG BUSHING

DRILL JIG

WORKPIECE

A

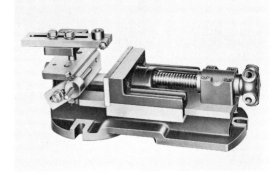

B

Fig. 37-6. (A) Using a drill jig to hold the workpiece. Notice the jig bushing used to guide the drill. Bushings may be changed for different size drills. (B) This standard machine vise is equipped with an attachment for drilling holes in round stock. The stop controls the distance from the end of the work to the hole. A drill bushing is used to guide the drill.

as the workpiece in the lathe; drill a hole through the center, which will be the same size as the hole to be drilled in the workpiece; cut the turned disk off at a convenient length for use as a drill bushing; and clamp the work in a drill vise with the disk on top of the work. The disk will locate the drill centrally on the work.

230

UNIT 38. Reaming in a Drill Press

Reamers are precision cutting tools used to enlarge existing holes smoothly and accurately by removing a small amount of metal. Reamers vary widely in style and design. They may have four or more flutes with spiral (helical) or straight cutting-edges and are made for either a left- or right-hand cut (Fig. 38-1). Reamers are used in predrilled, bored, punched, or cast holes to improve size, roundness, straightness, and surface finish.

Reaming can be done at the bench, in a drill press, a lathe, or milling machine. The drill press can be used for both hand and machine reaming. Hand reamers have been described in Unit 27.

MACHINE REAMERS

Good machine reamers are made of high-speed steel. Production-type reamers are often made with carbide-tipped cutting-edges (Fig. 38-2). Several types of reamers are listed below:

1. *Jobber's reamers* are solid with straight or spiral (helical) flutes and taper shanks. They are similar to hand reamers except they are designed for machine use (Fig. 38-3).

2. *Shell reamers* are made in two separate parts, the arbor and the reamer. The *arbor* is provided with driving lugs and has the end tapered slightly to fit into the reamer hole. The *reamer* may have either straight or spiral flutes. Shell reamers are designed as sizing or finishing reamers. This style of reamer is more economical because only the reamer end needs to be re-

Fig. 38-1. Parts of a machine reamer.

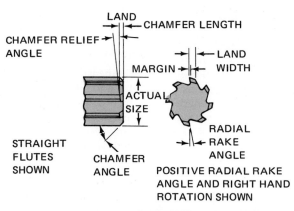

CHUCKING REAMER, STRAIGHT AND TAPER SHANK

MACHINE REAMER

231

Fig. 38-2. Carbide-tipped reamers usually have four or more straight or spiral flutes. Their ability to hold their size longer makes them particularly useful in manufacturing. Carbide reamers will outlast high-speed steel reamers many times over on castings which contain sand or hard steel.

Fig. 38-3. A tapered-shank, straight-flute jobber's reamer.

Fig. 38-4. A straight-flute shell reamer.

Fig. 38-5. Straight- and taper-shank fluted chucking reamers.

Fig. 38-6. Rose chucking reamer.

Fig. 38-7. Expansion chucking reamer.

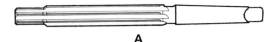

A

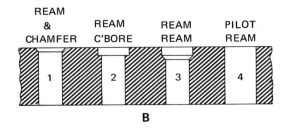

REAM & CHAMFER	REAM C'BORE	REAM REAM	PILOT REAM
1	2	3	4

B

Fig. 38-8. (A) A step reamer is used largely in production work. (B) Types of reaming that can be done with step reamers.

Fig. 38-9. Morse taper reamer.

placed when worn out or damaged. Several sizes of reamers fit the same arbor (Fig. 38-4).

3. *Fluted chucking reamers* are made with straight or taper shanks and with straight or spiral (helical) flutes. These are considered precision machine reamers. Each tooth has a clearance angle ground on it for the entire length of the tooth. The ends of the teeth are ground on a slight chamfer for end cutting (Fig. 38-5).

4. *Rose chucking reamers* are made with straight or taper shanks and with straight or spiral flutes. The actual cutting is done at the ends of the teeth only. The flutes allow the chips to escape and the cutting fluid to reach the cutting end. Rose reamers have fewer teeth than fluted machine reamers (Fig. 38-6). They will remove considerably more material, but will not produce a smooth hole.

5. *Expansion chucking reamers* have straight flutes and either straight or taper shanks. There is an expansion screw at the end of the reamer which increases the diameter slightly. As the reamer wears or is resharpened, it can be adjusted back to its original size. Also, if a slightly larger hole than standard size is required, this reamer can be enlarged (Fig. 38-7).

6. *Step reamers* are conventional reamers which have had a second diameter created by

grinding down a portion of the larger diameter, creating a step (Fig. 38-8A). They are used to enlarge existing holes smoothly and accurately by removing a small amount of metal. Two diameters allow multiple operations in one production step (Fig. 38-8B).

7. *Morse taper reamers* with taper shanks can be used in the drill press the same as taper hand reamers (Fig. 38-9).

HINTS ON REAMING

1. Select the best style of reamer. Generally a spiral-fluted reamer gives better results.

2. Always use a slower speed for reaming than for drilling. A speed that is about two-thirds that for a drill of equal size is usually correct.

3. Be sure the reamer is sharp on the ends of the teeth. There should be no burrs or nicks on the long teeth. Run your thumbnail along each tooth to find burrs or nicks. Use a smooth oilstone to remove them.

4. To make sure a reamer will cut the size and quality of hole you want in your workpiece, drill and ream a hole in a piece of scrap metal of the same kind as your workpiece. The same reamer produces different results in different metals.

5. Feed the reamer into the hole slowly and steadily. If you force a fluted machine reamer, both the reamer and the hole may be damaged. Feed can usually be judged by the feel on the drill-press handle. A reamer can be fed faster than a drill of the same size.

6. *A reamer must never be turned backward, even for part of a turn. To do so ruins the cutting-edges.*

7. Always use a cutting oil or coolant when reaming all metals except cast iron.

8. Cutting fluids for reaming should be selected on the basis of the finish they will produce rather than for their cooling properties. In general, the cutting fluids suggested for drilling will be found to perform satisfactorily.

9. Storage and handling of reamers should be given particular attention. They are delicate tools that are easily damaged. They should be

Fig. 38-10. Reamers are expensive and should be handled with a great deal of care.

transported and stored in containers that have a separate compartment for each reamer. They should also be covered with a good rust preventative compound when not in use (Fig. 38-10).

10. The quality of finish and the accuracy of reamed holes depend upon such factors as the rigidity of the machine tool and fixture, the speed and feed, the use of suitable cutting fluids, and the proper resharpening of dulled reamers. Conditions such as poor finish, chatter, bellmouth, or oversize holes can usually be traced back to a lack of rigidity and alignment in the setup or oversize bushings.

USING A HAND REAMER IN THE DRILL PRESS

1. Drill the hole $\frac{1}{64}$ in. undersize. Hand reamers are intended to remove only 0.001 to 0.003 in. of material. However, it is quite impossible to drill holes this amount undersize in the average shop without the use of special drills. When a hole is drilled $\frac{1}{64}$ in. undersize, the drill cuts the hole somewhat oversize anyway. The hand reamer can then be used satisfactorily.

2. Leave the workpiece clamped to the table or in the vise. The alignment after drilling should not be disturbed.

3. Remove the drill, and insert a 60-degree (°) pointed center in the drill chuck. Such a center point can be quickly turned in the lathe if necessary.

4. Select the correct hand reamer, and attach an adjustable tap wrench to the square end (Fig. 38-11).

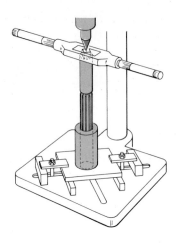

Fig. 38-11. Using a drill press to do hand reaming.

5. Place the end of the reamer lightly in the hole. Feed the center down and into the center hole of the reamer.

6. Turn the tap wrench clockwise as you apply light pressure to the feed handle. Too much pressure will jam the reamer in the hole so tightly that you will not be able to turn it.

7. Apply plenty of cutting oil to the reamer.

8. After the hole is reamed through, hold the reamer against the center point. Turn it slowly clockwise as you raise the feed handle to withdraw it.

USING MACHINE REAMERS

1. Drill the hole $\frac{1}{64}$ in. undersize for holes with diameters up to $\frac{1}{2}$ in. Drill the hole $\frac{1}{32}$ in. undersize for holes with diameters up to $1\frac{1}{2}$ in.

2. Choose the correct machine reamer. Clean the shank and insert it in the spindle hole. Use a drill chuck for straight-shank reamers.

Fig. 38-12. In reaming, the work should be firmly clamped to the table. In this setup parallels and a strap clamp are used to provide space for the reamer to go completely through the hole.

3. Adjust the belt for reduced speed.

4. Line up the drilled hole with the reamer. Apply cutting fluid to the reamer, and feed it into the hole (Fig. 38-12).

5. Sometimes the reamer *chatters*. Chatter is caused by vibrations that are set up between the work and the reamer. It leaves rough, uneven ridges in the metal which are most undesirable. Once started, chatter is difficult to overcome. It may be caused by a dull reamer, or the workpiece or reamer may not be held rigidly enough. Check back to see if any of these causes need correcting. If not, try reducing the speed.

UNIT 39. Using Other Cutters in a Drill Press

The drill press is a very versatile machine tool. It can do many things besides drilling holes. Here are some of the other operations that can be done.

COUNTERSINKING

Countersinking is the operation of machining a cone-shaped opening or recess at the outer end of a hole. This recess is cut so that a flathead screw or rivet can be inserted with its head flush with the metal surface. A *countersink* is the cutting tool used for this operation (Fig. 39–1). Countersinks are made with an included angle of either 60 or 82 degrees (°). All flathead screws have an angle of 82°. Here is how to countersink a hole for a flathead screw:

1. Insert an 82° countersink in the drill chuck.

2. Adjust the speed to about half that used when drilling the hole. A slow speed must be used, or the countersink will chatter. To eliminate chatter and get a smooth, clean countersunk recess, try putting a small piece of abrasive cloth or cotton waste over the hole. Then feed the countersink into the metal.

Fig. 39–1.   Countersink.

Fig. 39–2.   Countersinking a hole with the work held in a vise.

82° COUNTERSINK

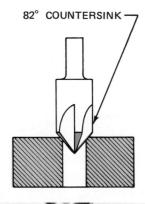

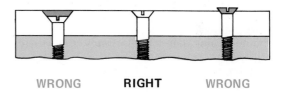

WRONG   **RIGHT**   WRONG

Fig. 39–3.   Correct and incorrect way to countersink. The hole is countersunk correctly when the opening at the top is the same as the largest diameter of the screw head.

Fig. 39–4.   Countersinking a series of holes using the stop gage to control depth of cut.

3. Feed the countersink by hand until the required diameter is reached (Fig. 39-2). Check the diameter of the recess by using the screwhead. Place the screw in the hole. The top of the head should be flush with (not above or below) the metal surface (Fig. 39-3).

4. When countersinking several holes, set the stop gage so all the holes will be the same (Fig. 39-4). After you drill the first hole correctly, stop the drill press. Hold the hand-feed lever down to keep the countersink at the bottom of the recess, and set the stop nut.

COUNTERBORING

Counterboring is the operation of enlarging a hole for part of its length (Fig. 39-5). The large hole forms a square shoulder with the smaller hole (Fig. 39-6). A hole is counterbored to receive fillister-head screws, bolt heads, and shoulder pins (Fig. 39-7). Counterbores are made with straight or taper shanks and with straight or spiral teeth. They differ from other cutting tools in that they require a *pilot* that extends beyond the end of the cutting teeth. The pilot fits freely into the hole to be counterbored. It guides the cutting end and keeps it in line with the hole. Some counterbores have interchangeable pilots, so they can be used in various sizes of holes. Counterbores and pilots for machine screws are made solid for only one size of hole or screwhead (Fig. 39-8).

TAPPING

Taps may be started straight in a hole by using the drill press by hand. First drill the hole to the correct size. Leave the workpiece clamped to the table. Insert the tap in the drill chuck if it is small enough to fit. If a tap is too large to fit the chuck, use a 60° pointed center in the chuck. Place the point in the center hole of the tap. Use a tap wrench to turn the tap while

Fig. 39-5. Parts of a counterbore.

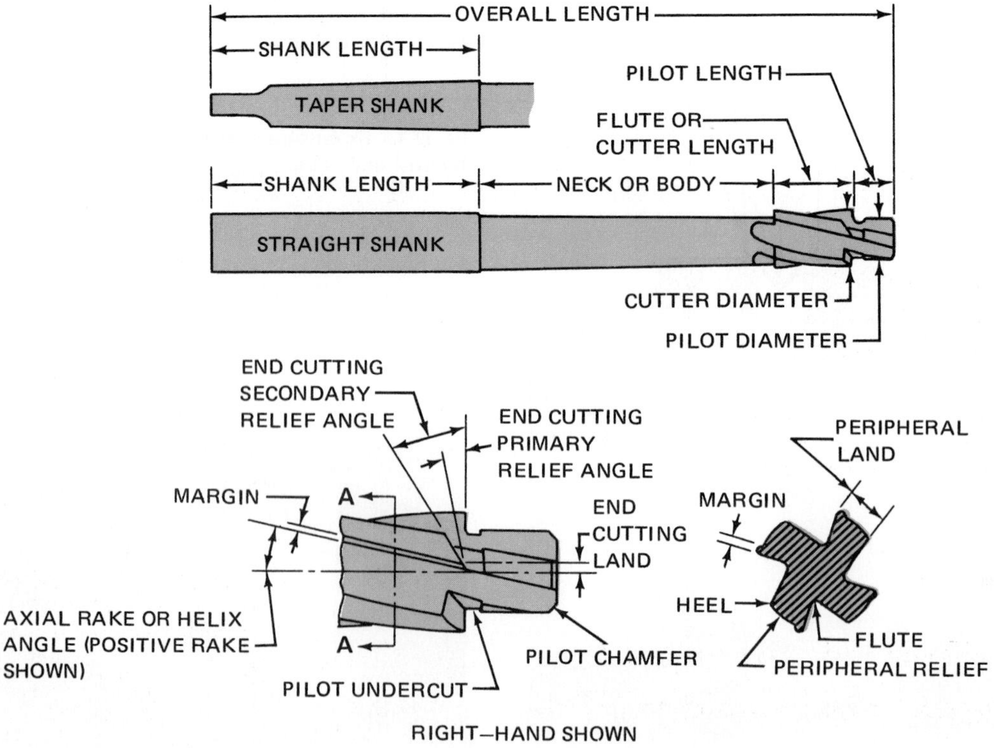

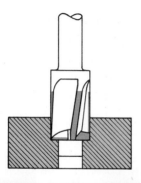

Fig. 39-6. Counterboring; using a counterbore with an interchangeable pilot.

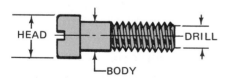

HEAD — BODY — DRILL

Fig. 39-7. The counterbore must match the dimensions of the screw or bolt to be installed. (*A* equals the diameter of the body; *D* equals the diameter of the head.)

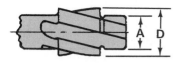

Fig. 39-8. A counterbore with a fixed pilot. This can also be used for spot facing.

MORSE

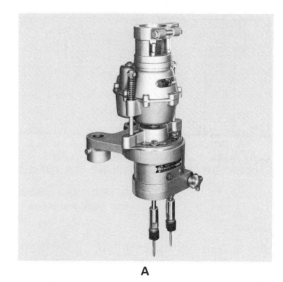

A

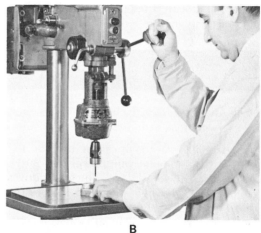

B

Fig. 39-9. (A) A two-spindle adjustable drill head with friction-chuck tapping attachment. (B) Using a single-head tapping attachment.

Fig. 39-10. Spot facing a casting. This is especially important when a hole is near a radius section of the casting.

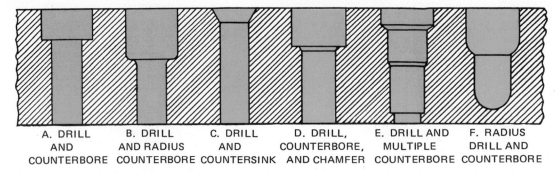

A. DRILL AND COUNTERBORE B. DRILL AND RADIUS COUNTERBORE C. DRILL AND COUNTERSINK D. DRILL, COUNTERBORE, AND CHAMFER E. DRILL AND MULTIPLE COUNTERBORE F. RADIUS DRILL AND COUNTERBORE

Fig. 39-11. Some combination cuts that can be made with step drills and/or step reamers.

holding the hand-feed lever down. If the tap is held in the chuck, feed the tap into the hole. Turn the chuck by hand until the tap is started for several threads. Then loosen the drill chuck and finish tapping the hole with a tap wrench.

CAUTION

Never use power to tap a hole in this manner. The tap will break and perhaps ruin your work.

A *tapping attachment* can be used on the drill press to tap holes with power (Fig. 39–9). This attachment has a friction clutch that drives the tap forward when you feed the handle down. It reverses the tap when you raise the handle. You can feed the tap into the work, stop the tap, or back it out by controlling the feed lever properly.

SPOT FACING

Spot facing is similar to counterboring (Fig. 39–10). The operation removes a small amount of metal around the top surface of a hole. A washer or bolt head can then be seated square with the hole. A counterbore is often used for this operation or a special spot-facing tool may be made to do the job.

COMBINATION CUTTING

Step drills and reamers are used in production machining when it is desirable to form a hole of two or more diameters, a hole with a chamfer, a counterbore, or a counterbore and chamfer in one operation. These and other combination cuts involving angles or radii are shown in Fig. 39–11.

OTHER OPERATIONS

Boring is most often done in the lathe (see Unit 47). However, it can also be performed in the drill press. The drill press can also be used for surface grinding, buffing, polishing, and filing. Although these are rather special operations for a drill press, they represent a type of work that is possible when other machines are not available.

UNIT 40. Drilling Machines in Industry

Drilling machines are made in a wide range from the simple manually controlled drill press to the highly complex numerically controlled machines for high-speed production work (Fig. 40-1). Regardless of their size or design, drilling machines operate more or less in the same way. Their major purpose is to drill holes in metal. In addition, such tools as reamers, countersinks, counterbores, taps, and special-purpose tools add to the versatility of this machine tool.

Standard bench and floor-type sensitive drill presses are the simplest types used in industry. These machines are similar in design to the type used in your shop or laboratory. They are called *sensitive drill presses* because their feed lever is operated by hand. This allows the operator to "feel" how the drill is cutting.

The plain, *vertical spindle drilling machine,* sometimes called the *standard upright drilling machine,* is very similar to the sensitive drill press except it is larger and heavier (Fig. 40-2). It is made in a wide variety of sizes, and usually has gear-driven mechanisms for obtaining different spindle speeds. It is usually equipped with an automatic or power-feed device as well. In power feeding, the depth to which the drill cuts is controlled by a feed stop which can be set to any depth of feed within the travel range of the quill. Often, the worktable is made with straight and T slots for bolting work into position. Frequently the worktable can be rotated to different positions and locked in place. The base of the machine also may be used as a working surface for extra large pieces. This too may contain T slots for holding work in place.

The *gang drilling machine* consists of a large base which supports a very long table onto which a number of individual drilling heads are fastened (Fig. 40-3). The table has a deep groove around the edge to collect excess cutting lubricant. These machines are used in mass production for doing a series of operations, one after another. For example, one drilling head may hold a small drill, the next a larger drill, and the last a counterbore (Fig. 40-4). The workpiece is moved along the table from one spindle to the next, each doing a different operation. Gang drills may have from two to as many as eight or ten spindles.

The *multiple drill head machine* has a number of spindles contained in a single head. It is designed so the position of these spindles can be varied to fit almost any shape within the area enclosed by the head. Multiple-spindle units are

Fig. 40-1. (A) The simplest type of drilling machine used in industry is the hand-operated sensitive drill press. (B) Engine blocks stream down past this semiautomatic drilling machine. The blocks are rigidly held in precision jigs as the drilling is done.

A

B

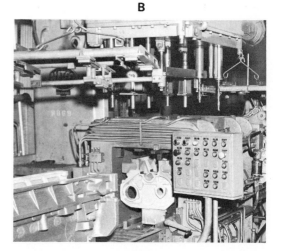

Fig. 40-4.   Drilling and tapping on a gang drilling machine.

Fig. 40-2.   A heavy-duty, sliding head upright drilling machine with automatic speed and feed controls.

Fig. 40-5.   Seventeen-spindle, U-joint adjustable drill head.

Fig. 40-3.   A gang drilling machine with eight drilling heads.

Fig. 40-6.   Drilling bolt holes using a multiple spindle machine.

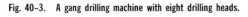

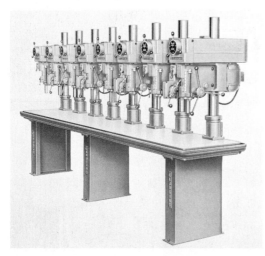

available as accessories that fit standard upright machines and as complete pieces of equipment (Fig. 40-5). Twenty or more spindles may be used in the head of a single large machine (Fig. 40-6). In some industries, combinations of two or more heads are used to enable one operator to drill more than 100 holes in one operation.

The *radial drilling machine* is designed for use with large workpieces that cannot be easily moved (Fig. 40-7). The drilling machine head is mounted on a heavy radial arm which may be from three to twelve or more feet long. This arm can be raised or lowered with power and can be turned in a complete circle around the column. The drilling head moves back and forth along this arm. On most radial drilling machines, movement of the arm, drill head, and spindle is controlled by power feed. Since the drilling head contains the spindle, cutting tools can be located in any position by moving the head back and forth and swinging the arm (Fig. 40-8). This makes it possible to drill holes in many different locations without moving the workpiece. Spindle feeds and speeds are controlled by selector levers which engage the proper gears in the drill head. Depth of feed is also controlled directly in the drill head by a suitable mechanism. In addition to drills, other tools such as reamers, countersinks, counterbores, and boring heads add a great deal of versatility to this machine (Fig. 40-9).

Fig. 40-7. Parts of a radial arm drill.

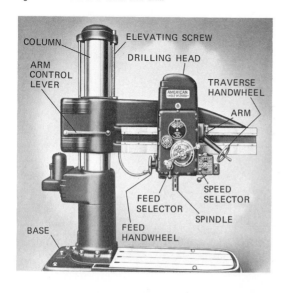

Fig. 40-8. Using a 2 in. drill to drill a part. This piece is made of cast iron; therefore, no coolant is used.

Fig. 40-9. Here a 10-in. diameter tapping is done on a radial drill.

THE TURRET DRILLING MACHINE

The *turret drilling machine* utilizes a head on which six or more spindles work on a single axis. As the turret is indexed from one spindle to the next, the tool is locked in place and accurately aligned with the main machine spindle. The

241

turret head can be set up with six or more tools in any desired series of operations for such work as drilling, counterboring, reaming, boring, tapping, and spot facing. The machine may be manually operated or numerically controlled. The numerically controlled machine is applied to large volume manufacturing. Because of the rigid nature of the turret and the spindle, a drill jig isn't necessary. A universal parts fixture can be used to hold workpieces. The machine can be programmed to move the drilling head into position and to move the table back and forth or in and out (Fig. 40-10). A numerically controlled machine is operated by a master tape which provides necessary information on sequence of operation, spindle rotation, movement of the table, speeds and feeds, and miscellaneous controls.

TAPPING AND THREADING MACHINES

Cutting internal threads on holes drilled in metal is a common manufacturing operation. Much of this type of work can be performed on a drilling machine which has a tapping attachment. However, industry often uses an adaptation of a drilling machine designed specifically for tapping, called a *tapping machine* (Fig. 40-11). The tapping machine has automatic controls for both speed and feed. There is also an automatic backout device for removing the tap. With the exception of the lead screw used for feeding the spindle, a tapping machine is almost identical to a drilling machine.

WORK-HOLDING ACCESSORIES

Industry makes use of many of the same types of work-holding accessories that you utilize in the shop or laboratory. Some, however, are designed specifically for high production work. They include:

1. A *pneumatic or hydraulic operated drilling vise* for quick, positive clamping and unclamping of workpieces (Fig. 40-12).

2. A *precision rotary table* that can be used in either a horizontal or vertical position. Work can be clamped to this table and rotated in a 360-degree (°) circle (Fig. 40-13). This is particularly valuable in drilling a series of holes in a circular layout. It also provides a means of drilling holes at specific angles.

Fig. 40-10. A numerically controlled turret drilling machine.

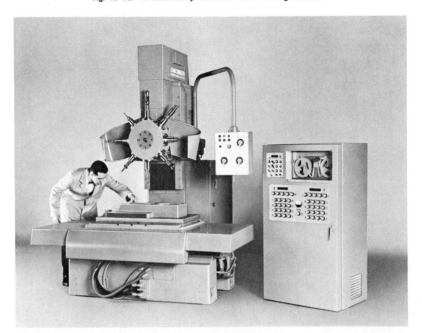

Fig. 40-11. The tapping machine resembles the drilling machine. The major difference is the lead-screw control.

Fig. 40-12. An air-operated vise.

Fig. 40-13. A precision rotary table.

Fig. 40-14. A heavy-duty drill fixture used with a precision rotary table. The drill bushing can be moved up or down and in or out to position it directly over the location where the drilling is to be done.

3. A *heavy-duty drill fixture* used to clamp a part in place for precision drilling. It has an adjustable drill bushing arm which can be moved up and down or in and out with great accuracy (Fig. 40-14).

4. A *drill jig* used for holding the workpiece and guiding the drill. This is the most common drilling accessory used in industry. The design of such jigs varies widely (Fig. 40-15). The drill and other cutting tools are guided by hardened steel drill bushings. Drill jigs are essential production accessories and are used wherever parts are produced in large quantity.

THE JIG BORER AND JIG GRINDER

The *jig borer* resembles both the drill press and the vertical milling machine (Fig. 40-16). The head of this unit is similar to a drill press, and the table is very much like that of a vertical milling machine. The jig borer is used in the manufacture of *jigs, fixtures,* and *dies* which require extremely accurate dimensions. Since the work can be clamped securely to a table that moves back and forth and in and out and since the drilling head is made with great precision, it is possible to locate and drill holes more accurately on this machine than on any other

Fig. 40-15.   (A) A relatively simple drilling jig used to drill six holes in a casting. (B) A complicated drilling jig.

Fig. 40-16.   The jig borer resembles a drilling machine and a vertical milling machine. This is an extremely precise and accurate machine used largely for jig, fixture, and die manufacturing. The machine may be either manually or numerically controlled.

Fig. 40-17.   A precision jig grinder.

machine tool. This machine is designed to provide accuracy of positioning to thirty-millionths of an inch.

The *jig grinder* is designed specifically for grinding holes to accurate locations after hardening (Fig. 40-17). It will also grind a tapered hole. Industry uses jig grinders to produce fixtures, jigs, and dies where high standards of accuracy are essential.

A specially designed *measuring machine* is used in conjunction with the jig borer and grinder to inspect hole locations to less than one ten-thousandth of an inch (Fig. 40-18). It is an accurate instrument used in the inspection of jigs, fixtures, and dies.

SPECIAL DRILLING APPLICATIONS

Industry uses a variety of combinations of drilling heads, installed in vertical, horizontal, and angular positions, to do special drilling operations. Frequently, several drilling heads will be arranged in both vertical and horizontal positions so that all the drilling on a workpiece can be done in a single operation (Figs. 40-19A and 40-19B). More complex machines are built to do drilling, boring, and tapping with the workpiece mounted on a rotating worktable. Special fixtures are used to hold the parts (Fig. 40-19C).

Fig. 40-18.   A universal, three-dimensional measuring machine.

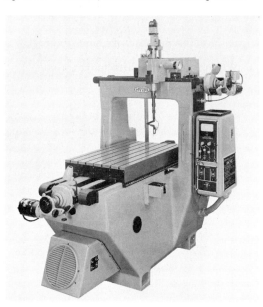

Fig. 40-19.   (A) This special drilling machine consists of one vertical and two horizontal drilling heads. (B) A three-way drilling and tapping machine. (C) This special machine drills, bores, and taps 315 different connecting rods per hour.

A

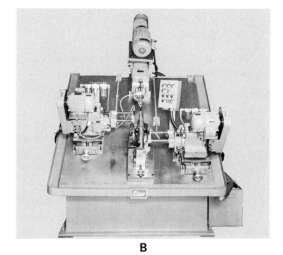

B

C

UNIT 41. Discussion Topics and Problems

1. What is the major use of a drill press?

2. How is the size or capacity of a drill press determined?

3. Name the four major parts of a drill press.

4. List five safety rules to follow in using a drill press.

5. What factors affect the speed for drilling?

6. What is the simple formula for figuring the speed (rpm) of a drill?

7. What should the rpm be for drilling a piece of mild steel with a $\frac{3}{4}$-in. high-speed steel drill?

8. How is the feed controlled on most bench and small floor-type drill presses?

9. Name five devices or methods for holding work to be drilled.

10. Name the principal parts of a twist drill.

11. What are the four systems of drill sizes?

12. Which is larger, a letter A drill or a $\frac{3}{8}$-in. drill?

13. What are the three things you must watch for when grinding a drill?

14. What happens if there is too much lip relief?

15. What will happen if one lip is longer than the other?

16. What advantage is there in using a drill-grinding attachment?

17. How are drills $\frac{1}{2}$ in. or smaller usually held in a drill press?

18. What is the procedure in drilling a small hole?

19. When is it necessary to clamp a workpiece securely to the table?

20. At what time during the drilling of a through hole should you use great care to avoid injury or accident?

21. What kind of drills are generally used for holes larger than $\frac{1}{2}$ inch?

22. What is meant by a pilot hole? Why is it used?

23. What special steps must be followed for precision drilling?

24. What is a blind hole?

25. How should round workpieces be held for drilling a hole through the center?

26. Name three methods that are used to make certain that a hole will be drilled through the exact center of a round workpiece.

27. Name five kinds of machine reamers.

28. Why is reaming done?

29. How much undersize should a hole be drilled for a fluted machine reamer?

30. What is countersinking? When must it be done?

31. Discuss the purpose of counterboring.

32. When is a tapping attachment used?

33. What is a radial drill?

34. What is the difference between a gang-type and a multiple-spindle-type drilling machine?

SECTION

ENGINE LATHE

UNIT 42. The Engine Lathe

The *engine lathe* is a power-driven machine tool used to turn and cut metal (Fig. 42-1). It is one of the oldest and perhaps most important machine tools ever developed (Fig. 42-2).

HISTORY

An unknown Frenchman is credited with developing the first useful lathe in about 1700. The man most responsible for the lathe as we know it today, however, was the English inventor Henry Maudslay. Starting out as an instrument maker, Maudslay developed into one of the first great tool engineers. He devoted his entire career mainly to the improvement of screw-cutting machinery. Maudslay's first important invention was a bar lathe made entirely of iron (no wooden frame) and equipped with a highly original slide rest (Fig. 42-3). This device laid the groundwork for his series of increasingly more accurate, self-acting screw-cutting lathes. He perfected his first model in 1800, the same year Eli Whitney initiated the American system of mass production.

Maudslay combined a lead screw, a slide rest, and change gears in one all-iron lathe. The slide rest, mounted like a small platform to the lead screw, held the cutting tool firmly against the turning metal workpiece. As the lead screw was turned, the tool advanced along the length of the metal. The various combinations of change gears allowed the operator to vary the rotational speed of the lead screw in relation to the speed of the work. The all-iron construction, being heavier and sturdier than that of wood, increased the accuracy and power of the machine as well as the speed. Maudslay's accomplishments with screw production machinery formed the basis of the machine tool industry, and led to the development of complex lathes, milling machines, and other heavy machinery.

The need for fasteners used in assembling metal parts prompted the development of the most basic of all machine tools, the lathe. The turret lathe was designed and built by Stephen Fitch of Middlefield, Connecticut, in 1845 (Fig. 42-4). It carried eight tools in a horizontally mounted turret and was invented specifically to produce the large number of screws required for the locks of 30,000 pistols ordered by the U.S. government.

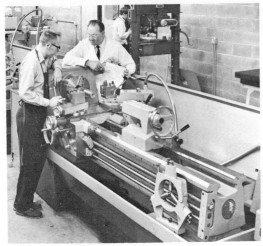

A

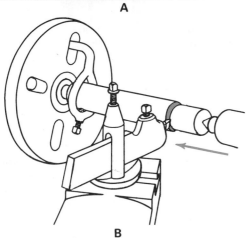

B

Fig. 42-1. (A) The lathe is a basic machine tool. (B) Turning is one of the five basic ways of machining metal.

Fig. 42-2. Examples of parts that can be machined.

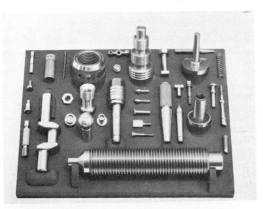

Fig. 42-3. Maudsley's first all-metal lathe.

Fig. 42-4. Fitch's screw-cutting turret lathe, 1845.

Fig. 42-5. Spencer's automatic turret lathe, 1869.

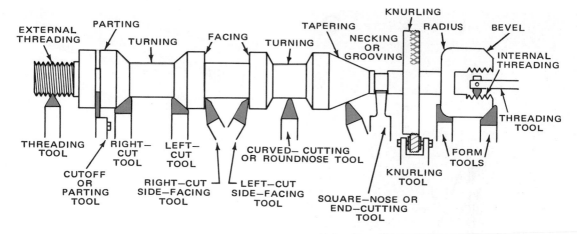

Fig. 42-6. Common cuts made by different cutting tools.

The completely automatic turret lathe was invented by Christopher Spencer shortly after the Civil War. Spencer, the inventor of a repeating rifle used by the Union Army, built his lathe expressly for turning metal machine screws automatically (Fig. 42-5). Its key feature was a "brain wheel," as Spencer called it. Actually, the wheel was a series of cams that fed a tool into the work, withdrew it after the cut was finished, and then turned the turret to present the next tool to the work. Spencer is also credited with the development of the first multiple-spindle lathe. His three-spindled automatic screw machine produced small screws from coiled wire fed continuously into the machine.

PARTS OF AN ENGINE LATHE

You should be familiar with the names of the principal parts of a lathe as well as its construction. This will help you to understand how the lathe works and the type of work that can be done on it. You will also better understand the instructions you will receive from your teacher or employer.

A lathe can perform many different operations. A few of the more common operations are facing, straight turning, taper turning, parting, necking, knurling, thread cutting, and forming (Fig. 42-6).

SIZE

Lathe size is determined by swing and length of the bed (Fig. 42-7). The *swing* is twice the distance from the live center point of the spindle to the top of the bed, or the largest diameter that can be turned over the ways of a lathe. For example, a 10-in. lathe will turn a 10-in.-diameter workpiece over the ways, but not over the carriage cross-feed slide. Sometimes two numbers are used to indicate swing, such as 17-12. The 17-in. swing would be over the bed and the 12-in. swing over the cross slide.

The *length of the bed* includes the part the headstock rests on. It determines also the distance between centers. A typical size might be a 3-foot bed with a distance of 23 in. between centers. Lathe beds are offered in many different lengths for each available swing size.

Fig. 42-7. Size is indicated by swing and the length of the bed.

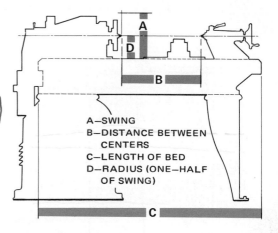

A—SWING
B—DISTANCE BETWEEN CENTERS
C—LENGTH OF BED
D—RADIUS (ONE—HALF OF SWING)

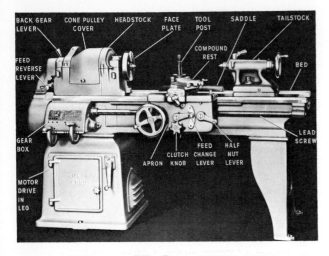

BACK GEAR LEVER · CONE PULLEY COVER · HEADSTOCK · FACE PLATE · TOOL POST · SADDLE · TAILSTOCK · COMPOUND REST · BED · FEED REVERSE LEVER · LEAD SCREW · GEAR BOX · MOTOR DRIVE IN LEG · APRON · CLUTCH KNOB · FEED CHANGE LEVER · HALF NUT LEVER

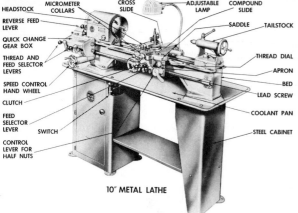

HEADSTOCK · MICROMETER COLLARS · CROSS SLIDE · ADJUSTABLE LAMP · COMPOUND SLIDE · REVERSE FEED LEVER · SADDLE · TAILSTOCK · QUICK CHANGE GEAR BOX · THREAD DIAL · THREAD AND FEED SELECTOR LEVERS · APRON · BED · SPEED CONTROL HAND WHEEL · LEAD SCREW · CLUTCH · COOLANT PAN · FEED SELECTOR LEVER · SWITCH · CONTROL LEVER FOR HALF NUTS · STEEL CABINET

10" METAL LATHE

Fig. 42-9. Note that the bed of this lathe has both flat and V-ways.

A lathe should have a swing capacity and distance between centers that is at least 10 percent greater than needed to do any job that may be required. Standard lathes come in a variety of designs and styles and may have a swing ranging from about 9 to 53 in. They are generally classified as small, medium swing, and heavy duty (Fig. 42-8).

BED

The *bed* is the base or foundation of the lathe (Fig. 42-9). It is a heavy, rigid casting made in one piece. It is the "backbone" of the lathe and holds or supports all the other parts. Located on the top of the bed are the *ways*. More expensive lathes have a combination of V ways and flat ways. Less expensive lathes have flat ways only. Construction of ways varies according to make. Some builders use ways made of hardened steel that can be replaced if necessary. Others use flame-hardened ways that are an integral part of the bed section.

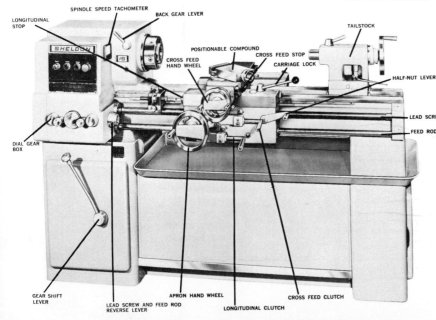

LONGITUDINAL STOP · SPINDLE SPEED TACHOMETER · BACK GEAR LEVER · POSITIONABLE COMPOUND · CROSS FEED STOP · TAILSTOCK · CROSS FEED HAND WHEEL · CARRIAGE LOCK · HALF-NUT LEVER · LEAD SCREW · FEED ROD · DIAL GEAR BOX · GEAR SHIFT LEVER · APRON HAND WHEEL · CROSS FEED CLUTCH · LEAD SCREW AND FEED ROD REVERSE LEVER · LONGITUDINAL CLUTCH

Fig. 42-8. Several popular models of lathes.

The accuracy of the ways determines the performance that can be expected from a lathe. Ways must be true and accurate so that the headstock, tailstock, and carriage are always in true alignment.

Located directly under the front ways on the bed is a *rack*. A *pinion gear* meshes into the rack for moving the carriage when the handwheel is turned.

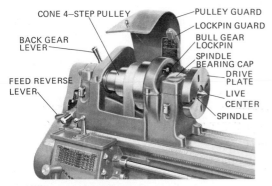

CONE 4–STEP PULLEY

PULLEY GUARD

LOCKPIN GUARD

BACK GEAR LEVER

BULL GEAR LOCKPIN

SPINDLE BEARING CAP

DRIVE PLATE

FEED REVERSE LEVER

LIVE CENTER

SPINDLE

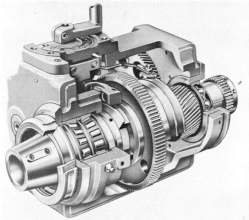

DELTA

Fig. 42-10.   Three types of headstock assemblies.

HEADSTOCK ASSEMBLY

The headstock assembly is permanently fastened to the left end of the lathe (Fig. 42-10). It contains the headstock spindle, which is rotated by gears or by a combination of gears and pulleys. The *spindle* holds the attachments which, in turn, hold and turn the workpiece. Spindles come in several quality ratings and are supported in headstocks by three to five bearings. Since the accuracy of the work done on a lathe depends on the axis of rotation of the spindle holding the workpiece, the spindle and all its accessories must be built and assembled with the greatest possible care.

A hole extends through the spindle itself. The front end of this hole is tapered for holding tools having a tapered shank. A *taper sleeve* (a hollow-round part) fits into the taper spindle hole (Fig. 42-11), when holding a headstock, or live center (Fig. 42-12). The headstock center is called a *live center* because it turns with the work. The center is a tapered metal part with a pointed end. It is used to support the end of a workpiece as it is being turned. All lathe center points have a 60-degree (°) included angle.

Three common types of spindle noses are used to hold attachments on the spindle.

1. The *threaded spindle nose* has been used on lathes longer than any of the other types (Fig. 42-13A). Attachments to be mounted are screwed onto the spindle until they fit firmly against the spindle flange. The major disadvantage of the threaded spindle nose is that turning cannot be done in the reverse position

Fig. 42-11.   A taper spindle sleeve.

Fig. 42-12.   A lathe center.

MORSE

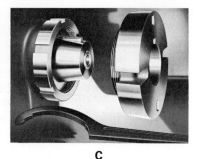

A   B   C

Fig. 42-13. Three types of spindle noses: (A) threaded spindle nose, (B) cam-lock spindle nose, and (C) long-taper, key-drive spindle nose.

(with the spindle turning clockwise). This is because certain attachments, a chuck for example, would come loose.

2. The *cam lock spindle nose* has a very short taper which fits into a tapered recess in the back of a faceplate or chuck (Fig. 42-13B). A series of cam lock studs projects from the back of the faceplate or chuck. These cam lock studs fit into the holes in the spindle nose. They are locked into position by turning a series of cams.

3. The *long* (*steep*) *taper key drive spindle nose* has a long taper with a key attached and an internal threaded collar. The faceplate or chuck must have an equal taper and keyway plus an external thread. This positive lock-type of spindle is most popular on medium-size lathes. It permits cutting with the spindle turning in either direction (Fig. 42-13C).

Power for driving the spindle is provided by an electric motor. There are four common ways of transmitting the power from the electric motor to the spindle. These include:

1. *Flat belt drive.* On most belt-driven lathes, direct drive power is delivered through belts to a step pulley attached to the spindle. The spindle speed is changed by moving the belt to different positions on the step pulley. To obtain slower speeds and more power, back gears are used (Fig. 42-14).

To understand how the back gears operate, study Fig. 42-14. Notice that gear F is fastened securely to the spindle. This gear is often called

a *bull gear. The small end of the step pulley has a small gear attached to it called the *pinion gear*. This gear (E) always turns when the pulley turns. The step pulley and pinion gear are connected with the bull gear by a sliding pin called the *bull-gear lock-pin*. At the back of the headstock are two gears mounted on the same shaft. They are spaced to line up or mesh with the bull gear (F) and pinion gear (E). These are called *back gears*. To engage the back gears, the pin in the bull gear is pulled out (when the pin is out, the pulley and pinion gear will turn, but the spindle will not turn). Pull the back-gear handle forward to mesh the back gears with bull gear F and pinion gear E. Do this by turning the step pulley *by hand—never* while the power is on. When

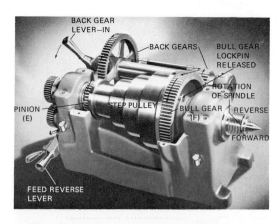

Fig. 42-14. A flat belt-driven lathe. The use of the back gears reduces the speed and increases the power.

engaged, power is delivered directly to the bull gear (F) and spindle by the back gears.

At the left end of the headstock assembly is a *feed reverse lever.* It is used for reversing the direction or movement of the lead screw. This lever can be moved to three positions. When it is in the upper position with the automatic feed engaged, the carriage will move toward the headstock (to the left) and the cross-feed will move in. When in the center position, the gears are out of mesh and the lead screw will not move. When in the lower position with the automatic feed engaged, the carriage will move toward the tailstock (to the right) and the cross-feed will move out.

2. *V-belt drive.* A V-shaped groove is cut around the circumference of each pulley, and a V belt fits accurately into this groove. The V belt does not touch the bottom of the pulley. This type of drive has a back gear arrangement similar to that used on flat belt machines (Fig. 42–15).

3. *Variable-speed drive.* In this arrangement it is possible to change the speed between the driver and driven pulleys without stopping the lathe (Fig. 42–16). In fact, the speed must be changed *only when the machine is running.* The driving pulley of a variable-speed drive is made with two parts having V-shaped sides. One side of the pulley may be opened or spread apart from the other side. As it spreads apart, the belt moves inward toward the smaller diameter, producing a slower speed on the driven pulley. As the sides of the pulley are brought together, the belt is forced outward toward the large diameter which increases the speed of the driven pulley. The speed change may be done either manually or hydraulically. On the hydraulic type, a control dial located on the top of the headstock accurately activates the hydraulic system. Do not turn the control dial unless *the motor is running.* Speeds are from 300 to 1,600 revolutions per minute (rpm) in direct drive. For slower speeds, the lathe must be stopped and the back gear knob moved. This will provide slower speeds of 43 to 230 rpm.

4. *Geared head.* This headstock contains gears and changing mechanisms for obtaining many different spindle speeds (Fig. 42–17). The speed index plate attached to the headstock will help

Fig. 42–15. A V-belt drive. This type has a back gear arrangement very similar to the one shown in Fig. 42–14.

Fig. 42–16. A variable-speed drive operated by a handle located at the front of the machine. Variable-speed pulleys are the two in the middle between the upper and lower belt drives.

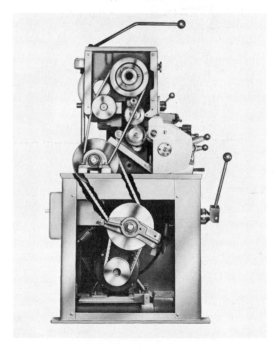

the operator select the required speed. Two or three levers or knobs must be moved to adjust the speed.

TAILSTOCK ASSEMBLY

The tailstock can be moved along the bed ways and clamped in position (Fig. 42-18). It consists of two castings or main parts. The lower part rests directly on the ways, and the upper part rests on the lower part. Adjusting screws hold the parts together. The upper casting can be moved toward or away from the operator to offset the tailstock for taper turning and to realign the tailstock center for straight turning. The *tailstock spindle* or *ram* moves in and out of the upper casting when the *tailstock handwheel* is turned. This spindle has a taper hole into which the dead center or other tools such as drills and reamers fit. Only tools having the same taper as the tailstock spindle should be placed in the spindle hole. To remove tools from the spindle,

Fig. 42-17. A heavy-duty belt is used to transmit the power from the electric motor counter drive to the headstock assembly on this gear-head lathe.

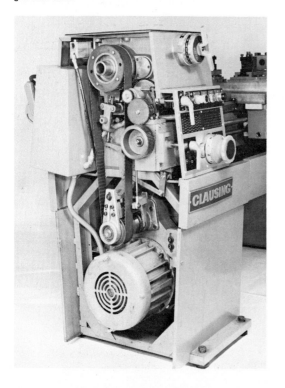

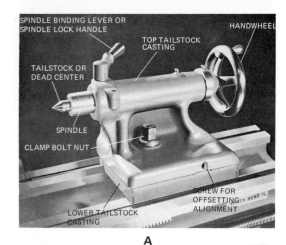

A

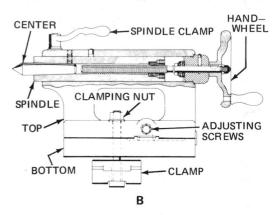

B

Fig. 42-18. (A) Tailstock assembly with parts named. (B) A cutaway showing construction of the tailstock.

Fig. 42-19. Revolving dead center installed in the tailstock. This is extremely valuable for heavy-duty work.

it is only necessary to back up on the handwheel until the spindle end is nearly inside the casting. The end of the screw that moves the spindle loosens the taper shank so it can be removed.

Fig. 42-20. Carriages from four different types of lathes. Note the slight difference in controls. *A*, *B*, and *C* use a lead screw for both power feed and thread cutting. *D* has a separate feed rod and a lead screw for thread cutting only.

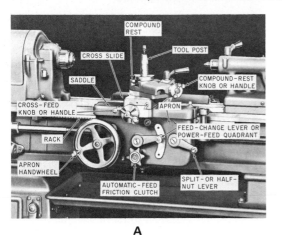

A

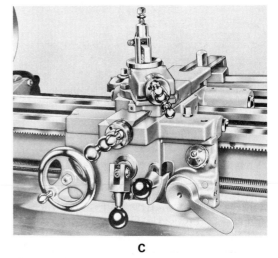

C

B

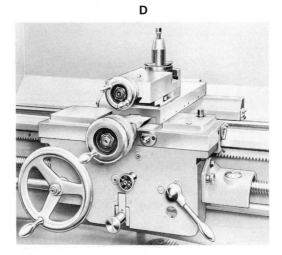

D

CARRIAGE

TOOL POST

TOOL–POST SLIDE HANDWHEEL

CROSS FEED HANDWHEEL

LOCK SCREW

CLUTCH KICKOUT

THREADING DIAL

CARRIAGE HANDWHEEL

HALF NUT LEVER

CLUTCH LEVER

POWER FEED LEVER

Care must be taken to avoid using a taper which does not fit properly. When this happens, it is not possible to use the handwheel screw to remove the taper. Such a taper may be removed without damaging the tailstock spindle using either of two methods:

1. Run the tailstock spindle or ram out a short distance. Open the chuck jaws on the three-jaw

chuck. Slide the tailstock forward until the stuck taper can be clamped in the chuck jaws. Tighten the tailstock clamp, and back up the handwheel to remove the part from the spindle.

2. Fasten a lathe dog on the end of the part that is stuck in the spindle. Use a mallet to tap the dog and remove the part.

Care must be used when backing up the tailstock handwheel. If backed to the end of the screw with any great force, it will jam. This strains, or may even damage, the threads inside. Also, when the screw is jammed, it is usually impossible to move the handwheel forward by hand. When this happens, good judgment on your part prevents further damage. Place a large monkey wrench on the rim of the handwheel, and move it forward. Never attempt to hammer on the handle of the handwheel to free it.

The *dead center* or *tailstock center* is a hardened taper part that fits the spindle hole. The outer end has a 60° point. This supports the end of the workpiece when turning between centers, or when turning long work that extends from a chuck. It is called a dead center because it does not revolve.

A *revolving dead center,* sometimes called a *live dead center,* is also available. This type of center has ball or tapered roller bearings that permit the center to rotate with the workpiece. No lubrication is required between the center and the workpiece (Fig. 42–19).

CARRIAGE

The carriage controls and supports the cutting tool. It has five major parts (Fig. 42–20):

1. The *saddle* is an H-shaped casting that fits over the bed and slides along the ways. The carriage *lock screw* in the saddle locks the carriage to the bed for facing and cutoff operations.

CAUTION

Be sure to release the lock before moving the carriage.

2. The *apron* is fastened to the saddle and hangs over the front of the bed (Fig. 42–21). It contains the gears, clutches, and levers for operating the carriage by hand and power feeds. The apron handwheel can be turned to move the carriage longitudinally (back and forth) by hand. It is attached to a pinion gear that meshes with the *rack* under the front of the bed. The apron also contains friction clutches for the automatic feeds and a *splitnut*. The splitnut can be closed over the lead screw threads and is used only when cutting screw threads.

3. The *cross slide* is mounted on the saddle. The crosspiece of the saddle is machined with a dovetail way or bearing. The dovetail is exactly at a right angle to the center line of the lathe itself. The cross slide also has a dovetail that fits over the saddle dovetail. The cross-slide handle is turned to move the slide *transversely* (in or out from the operator).

4. The *compound rest* is mounted on top of the cross slide (Fig. 42–22). It can be turned in a 360° circle and clamped in any position. The bottom of the compound slide is graduated in degrees for a distance of half a circle, or 180°. This part, too, has a dovetail slide that permits the upper part to be moved by means of a precision screw. Both the cross slide and the compound-rest screws are equipped with micrometer collars (graduated dials) divided into thousandths of an inch. These are used in making accurate adjustments when turning workpieces to close measurements and when cutting screw threads.

5. The *tool post* with *ring collar* and *rocker* slides in a T slot on top of the compound rest. The tool post clamps and holds the toolholder securely in position.

FEEDING AND THREADING MECHANISM

The feeding and threading mechanism consists of a quick-change gearbox, a lead screw, a feed rod, and the gears and clutches in the apron (Fig. 42–23A). The *quick-change gearbox* is located directly below the headstock assembly (Fig. 42–23B). Power from the left end of the spindle is transmitted through gears to the quick-change gearbox. This gearbox contains a number of different-sized gears, which provides a means to change (1) the rate of feed and (2) the ratio between revolutions of the headstock spindle and the movement of the carriage for thread cutting.

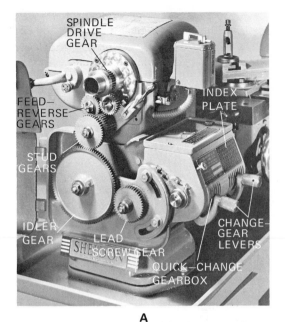

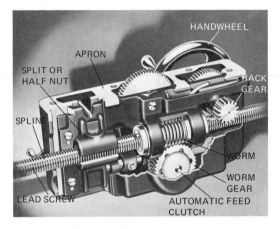

Fig. 42-21. Parts of an apron.

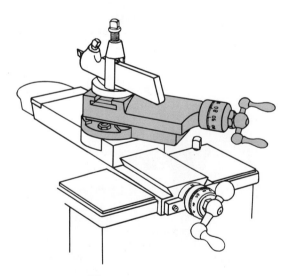

Fig. 42-22. Compound rest.

Fig. 42-23. (A) The gear train and quick-change gearbox are found in all lathes. (B) Two types of quick-change gearboxes. Note that two or three levers must be changed for feeds and threads per inch.

Usually two or three levers must be moved to obtain the correct feed or the correct number of threads per inch. An *index chart* or *plate* is attached to the front of the gearbox and indicates the position of the levers for obtaining the desired feed or threads per inch. The *lead screw* and *feed rod* transmit the power to the carriage for operating the automatic feed and for thread cutting. On smaller lathes, one feed rod is used, but on larger lathes, there are two separate rods.

You can get power feed of the carriage for either longitudinal movement or cross-feed movement. The direction of longitudinal feed is controlled by the position of the *reverse lever* on the headstock. Power feed is obtained in various ways using different control levers.

Fig. 42–24. Attachments for the lathe: (A) three-jaw chuck, (B) four-jaw chuck, (C) collet attachment, (D) follower rest, (E) steady rest, and (F) faceplate.

A   B

C

D

E

F

1. On older machines, the *feed-change lever* on the apron is moved to the *up* position for longitudinal feed (*down* on some lathes). Then the automatic feed knob is turned to the right to start the carriage moving.

To operate the cross-feed automatic, move the feed-change gear to the *down* position. Turn the same automatic feed knob to the right. The direction of cross-feed (in or out) depends upon the position of the reverse lever on the headstock.

2. A second type of lathe has a feed-selector lever that is moved up for longitudinal feed and down for cross-feed. Then a clutch is moved to operate the power feed.

3. A third type has a power longitudinal feed lever or clutch and a separate cross-feed lever or clutch.

4. Manufacturers of large lathes use other types of controls. All lathes have a reverse lever for the lead screw and/or feed rod located near the headstock spindle.

For thread cutting, the feed-change lever on the apron is placed in the center or neutral position (or the power-feed levers and clutches are released). Only in this position will the *halfnut* (splitnut) operate. This is a nut split lengthwise that closes over the Acme threads of the lead screw when the *halfnut lever* on the apron is moved. Closing the halfnut causes the carriage to move a fixed distance for each revolution of the spindle. The direction it moves (right or left) depends upon the position of the feed-reverse lever on the headstock. To cut a right-hand thread, the carriage must move from right to left, or toward the headstock. To cut a left-hand thread, the carriage must move from left to right, or toward the tailstock. The splitnut is used only for thread cutting and never for any other operation.

WORK-HOLDING ATTACHMENTS FOR THE LATHE

The range and variety of work that can be done on a lathe are greatly increased through the use of various work-holding attachments. Some of the common attachments are three-jaw universal chuck, four-jaw independent chuck, collet

Fig. 42-25. The headstock end of the lathe setup for turning a workpiece between centers.

chuck, faceplates, follower rest, and steady rest (Fig. 42-24). Most of these work-holding tools are described in later units.

For turning work between centers, a *reducing sleeve* and *live center* are inserted in the headstock spindle. A drive plate is mounted on the threaded nose of the spindle. It has slots into which the tail of a lathe dog fits and is used for driving the lathe dog which is attached to the workpiece (Fig. 42-25). A workpiece can also be clamped or bolted to a faceplate. A faceplate is much larger in diameter than a drive plate and has more slots.

Lathe dogs are considered accessories rather than work-holding tools. They are clamped on workpieces to drive them when turning between centers. There are three common types (Fig. 42-26). The *bent-tail standard-type* has an exposed setscrew. The *bent-tail safety-type* has a headless setscrew to prevent catching in the sleeve or otherwise injuring the operator. The *clamp-type* lathe dog is used on rectangular or square-shaped work. It may be used on round work when the driving force required is not too great. These lathe dogs are available in sizes that range from $\frac{1}{4}$ to 8 in. You should always select the smallest size that will fit over your work.

Large, heavy dogs cause the lathe to vibrate and will eventually damage the spindle bearings. Avoid using a dog with an exposed setscrew. There is always the danger of an accident. If possible, replace such a screw with a headless-type.

OTHER LATHE ACCESSORIES

There are many accessories available to make the lathe more versatile. These include the *tool post grinder* used for internal and external grinding, the *precision bed turret* for accurate machining of duplicate parts on a production

Fig. 42-27. (A) A tool post grinder for internal and external precision grinding. (B) A six-tool station bed turret. (C) A tracer or duplicating attachment.

A

Fig. 42-26. Lathe dogs.

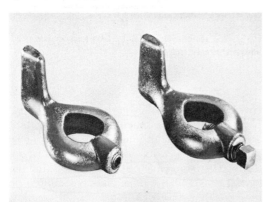

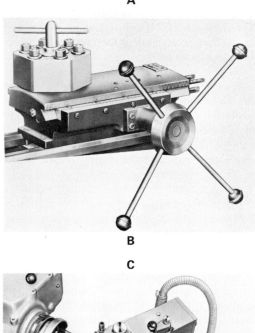

B

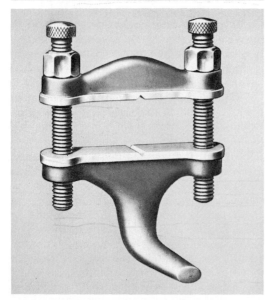

C

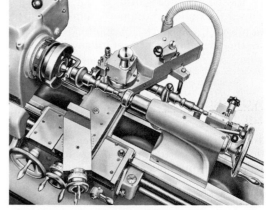

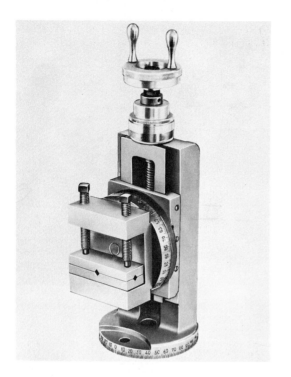

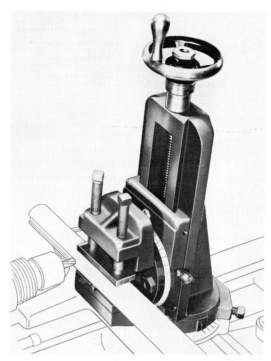

Fig. 42-28. (A) A milling attachment. (B) Using an end mill to cut a keyway.

basis, and the *tracer* or *duplicating attachment* for duplicating parts (Fig. 42-27). A *milling attachment* is an accessory that can be used on the lathe for face milling, milling dovetails, cutting keyways and slots, squaring shafts, and other machining operations (Fig. 42-28). This attachment is fastened to the carriage (on some lathes it replaces the compound rest) and can hold work at any angle. Its face is graduated 90° to the right and left of center. The position of the vise is controlled by a feed screw with micrometer collar that moves up and down. The vise can be swiveled to any angle. The cutters are mounted on an adaptor or toolholder that fits into the headstock spindle. A *mica undercutter* is another accessory used on the lathe. It is used for reconditioning armatures and consists of a small saw attached to the electric motor which is fed through mica by turning the lathe carriage handwheel. The height of the cutter arbor is adjusted by an elevating screw (Fig. 42-29).

Fig. 42-29. A mica undercutter for reconditioning armatures.

UNIT 43.
Getting Acquainted with the Lathe: Checking and Adjusting

Do not attempt to operate a lathe until you are thoroughly familiar with all its controls and functions (Fig. 43-1). Although every lathe has the same basic parts, the operating levers, buttons, and handles may be at slightly different positions on different machines and may require somewhat different adjustments. Therefore, it is important that you read all manufacturer's instructions carefully before using a machine with which you are not familiar (Fig. 43-2).

LEVELING THE LATHE

If a lathe is not mounted properly, its bed may become twisted. Even a slight amount of twist will move centers out of alignment and result in inaccurate work and excessive wear. A correctly mounted lathe is one which is level. Make it a habit to check the levelness of the lathe bed regularly. Use a precision level that is at least 6 in. long for this job (Fig. 43-3). Be sure to compensate for variations in level readings by turning the leveling screw located on the lathe base. This will help to avoid such problems as chatter, taper turning, boring a taper, and concave or convex facing which often result when an improperly leveled lathe is used (Table 43-1).

MOVEMENTS AND ADJUSTMENTS TO TRY WITH THE POWER OFF

1. Move the carriage back and forth by turning the *apron handwheel* (longitudinal feed). Feeding a cutting tool requires a very steady, even movement of the handwheel. It is difficult to control this movement with only one hand. Therefore, two hands are used to turn the wheel whenever possible.

2. Move the cross-feed in and out by turning the *cross-feed handle*. Learn to do this by using both hands in order to obtain a steady, even movement. Then practice using the right hand alone, and finally the left hand alone.

3. Move the compound-rest slide in and out by turning the *compound-rest handle*. Here

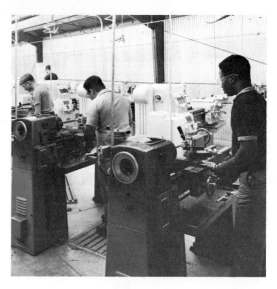

Fig. 43-1. The first step in operating a lathe is to get acquainted with the various controls.

Fig. 43-2. Using the power feed clutch to make a longitudinal cut.

again, it is necessary to turn the handle with both hands to obtain a steady, even movement. Usually the thumb and forefinger of each hand are used to keep the handle moving. There are times when only one hand may be used, so practice turning the handle using only one hand. When adjusting the compound rest, remember

262

Table 43-1. Trouble shooting chart.

TROUBLE	PROBABLE CAUSE	CORRECTION
VIBRATION	Loose leveling screws	Set all screws so they bear evenly on leveling plates.
	Torn or mismatched belts	Renew belts with matched set.
	Work or chuck out of balance operating at high spindle speeds	Balance chuck or reduce spindle speed.
	Loose motor pulley	Tighten pulley.
CHATTER	Cutter bit improperly ground or too wide for area of contact	Regrind cutter bit or adjust toolholder so that area of contact between tool bit and work is decreased.
	Tool overhang too great	Keep point of cutter bit as close as possible to toolholder.
	Using improper surface feet	Reduce or increase spindle speed.
	Feed rate too high	Reduce feed.
	Gibs of cross slide or compound rest loose	Adjust gibs.
	Work improperly supported	Adjust tailstock center. Use steady rest on long slender shafts.
	Spindle bearing loose	Adjust spindle bearings.
WORK NOT TURNED STRAIGHT	Headstock and tailstock centers not aligned	Align tailstock center.
	Work improperly supported	Use steady rest or follow rest. Reduce overhang from chuck.
	Bed not level	Relevel bed, using precision level.
	Tool not on center when using taper attachment	Put tool on center.
WORK OUT OF ROUND	Work loose between centers or centers are excessively worn—work centers out of round	Adjust tailstock center. Regrind centers. Lap work centers.
CROSS-SLIDE OR COMPOUND-REST MOVEMENT DOES NOT COINCIDE WITH DIAL MOVEMENT OR RESPECTIVE ADJUSTING SCREW.	Gib setting too tight or loose	Adjust gibs.
	Work is too long and slender	Use steady rest or follow rest.

that the upper slide must not overhang the lower one, especially when heavy cuts are being made (Fig. 43-4). The cutting tool must be held rigid. It cannot be rigid if the overhang is too great.

④ Check the cross-feed and compound-rest slides for looseness. Between the dovetails on each of the slides is a thin piece of metal called a gib. Gibs provide a means of taking up wear and adjusting slides for correct fit. They are held in place by several setscrews. Taper gibs have adjusting screws at their outer ends. Vibration may loosen these screws, causing play or loose movement between the parts. This makes good workmanship impossible. Check for looseness by gripping the tool post with one hand to see if it can be moved back and forth. If so, the gib screws require adjusting. Adjust each of the setscrews until a smooth, snug movement is obtained while turning the feed handle (Fig. 43-5).

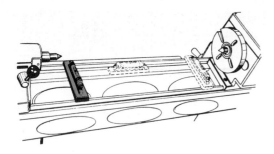

Fig. 43-3. Note the various positions in which the level is placed to check the bed.

5. Loosen the *tailstock-clamp nut or bed-clamp lever* and slide the tailstock back and forth along the bed ways (Fig. 43-6). The ways should be oiled before you do this. Try clamping the tailstock in several positions. It is not necessary to remove the wrench or make several turns of the nut. To do so wastes time. Set the wrench in a position so the nut can be loosened or tightened without removing the wrench.

6. Loosen the *binding* or *ram lock lever* on the top or side of the tailstock. Move the spindle or ram in and out by turning the *tailstock handwheel.* Clean the tailstock center and spindle hole. Place the center firmly in the spindle hole. Now, back up the handwheel until the center is loosened so you can remove it.

7. Change the speed of the lathe. To change spindle speed on a flat or V-belt lathe, loosen the tension on the belt by lifting up or pulling in on the belt tension release lever. Move the belt to the new position, and check the lower pulley to be certain the belt is on the right step. Make sure you can turn the belt and pulley by hand before resetting the belt tension lever.

The speed on a lathe having a variable-speed pulley can only be changed while the motor is running. Many lathes of this type have a variable-speed pulley arrangement in which the speeds are changed hydraulically by means of a control lever located on the headstock (Fig. 43-7). *Remember, do not turn the control dial on a lathe having a variable-speed pulley unless the motor is running.*

A back gear arrangement is included on all types of belt-driven lathes to provide slower speeds than are possible when the lathe is run-

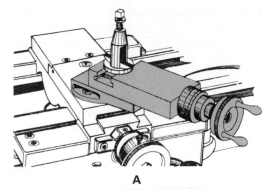

A

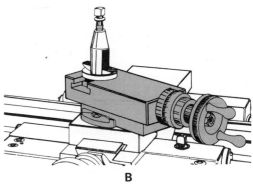

B

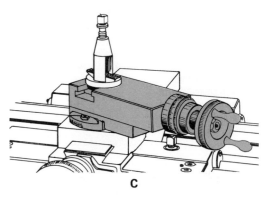

C

Fig. 43-4. (A) This is wrong. The slide is back too far and requires excessive tool overhang. (B) This is wrong. Slide overhangs too far forward. This puts unnecessary strain on the middle of the T slot. (C) This is right. Top slide should be flush with bottom slide to give greatest tool support.

ning by direct drive. Remember, the back gear must be changed with the *power off.* First, locate the pin or handle that releases or changes the back gear. On some lathes this pin is located next to the bull gear (Fig. 43-8A). On others a handle, located on the front of the machine, is

Fig. 43-5. Gib adjustment on a carriage produced by one lathe manufacturer. (A) Compound gib with two adjusting screws. Loosen rear adjusting screw (1) approximately $\frac{1}{2}$ turn and then tighten the front screw $\frac{1}{2}$ turn. (B) Cross-slide gib and cross feed compensating nut. The cross-slide gib is adjusted from the rear. Loosen the jam nuts (1) on the gib adjusting plate and turn the gib adjusting screw (2) until the proper tension is obtained. There should be sufficient tension to take up any excess play, while still allowing the slide to travel smoothly and freely. Be sure to tighten the jam nuts when all adjustments have been made.

A

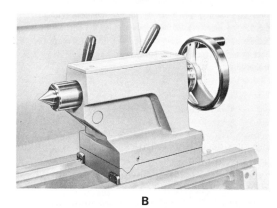

B

Fig. 43-6. (A) Loosening the tailstock-clamp nut. (B) The lever on the right is pulled to the left to tighten the tailstock to the bed.

Fig. 43-7. Spindle speeds on this lathe are changed hydraulically. The control dial located on the top of the headstock starts a hydraulic system. Speeds between 43 and 230 rpm are available in back gear drive, and from 300 to 1,650 rpm in direct drive.

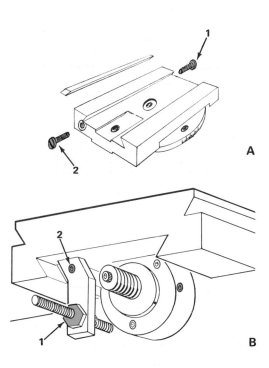

A

B

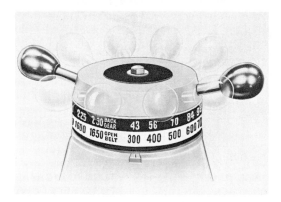

used to move the gears to the back gear position before a back gear pin is disengaged (Fig. 43–8B). Always rotate the machine spindle by hand after changing the back gear to make certain that the gears mesh properly. The number of available back gear speeds depends on the kind of belt arrangement used on the lathe. There are usually four speeds in direct drive and four speeds in back gear on a lathe driven by a flat or V belt. With a variable-speed drive, there is a wide range of speeds possible in both direct and back gear drive.

Speeds are changed on a lathe having a geared head arrangement by moving selected gears in the headstock assembly. For example, a typical geared head lathe may have 16 available speeds. These can be obtained by changing two or three levers on the headstock assembly.

CAUTION

Do not move speed selector controls while the spindle is rotating.

8. Adjust for feed or threads using the quick-change gear box. A variety of feeds is available from the gear box of a standard lathe by simply moving two, three, or four levers. A chart is usually mounted on the front of the gear box to tell you which of the levers to move to obtain a specific feed or screw thread (Fig. 43–9).

9. Change the feed-reversing gear lever. Find the feed-reversing lever located near the left end of the headstock assembly. Move the lever to the *up* position. Turn the chuck forward by hand, and note the direction the lead screw turns. Now place the lever in the *down* position, and check the direction of the lead screw.

MOVEMENTS TO BE CHECKED USING POWER

1. Turn on the switch that starts the motor. On belt-driven lathes a switch lever is used to start the spindle turning. On other lathes a clutch lever is used.

2. If the lathe has a reversing switch, try reversing the direction of spindle rotation.

CAUTION

Never push the reverse switch while a chuck is moving forward. If the chuck is not securely fastened to the spindle and the switch is reversed, the chuck will unscrew and drop off, damaging the ways, and may cause serious injury to you or someone nearby.

For most machining, the spindle must turn in a counterclockwise direction or downward as you stand in front of the lathe. The reverse direction is used mainly when threading with taps

Fig. 43–8. (A) To use the back gears with the flat belt lathe, pull out the bull gear lock and then pull on the back gear lever. (B) To engage the back gear drive on this machine, stop the lathe spindle and then turn the back gear knob to the left. Rotate the spindle by hand if the gears do not mesh. Then disengage the back gear pin from the drive pulley by pulling the pin away from the headstock.

Cone Pulley

Back Gear Lever

Bull Gear Lock

Feed Reverse Lever

1 2 3 4

A

B

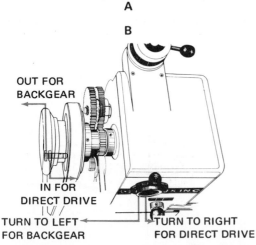

OUT FOR BACKGEAR

IN FOR DIRECT DRIVE

TURN TO LEFT FOR BACKGEAR

TURN TO RIGHT FOR DIRECT DRIVE

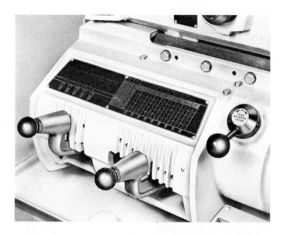

Fig. 43-9. For most feeds, only two levers need to be changed on this machine.

and dies, for loosening chucks and drive plates, and for some special operations.

3. Set the *feed-change* or *selector lever* located on the apron to the correct position for carriage power feed. This is usually the *up* position on belt-driven lathes. Turn the *automatic feed knob* or move the *feed lever*. Observe the direction in which the carriage is moving. For most operations, the carriage should move toward the headstock. To change direction, use the *feed-reverse lever*.

4. Set the *feed-change lever* to the correct position for automatic cross-feed. Use the *automatic feed knob* or *cross-feed lever* to operate the power cross-feed. Cross-feed direction (in or out) may be changed by moving the *feed-reverse lever*.

5. To operate the splitnut lever for cutting threads, move the *feed-change lever* to the neutral or center position. This will permit the splitnut lever to be moved. Never engage the splitnut lever with the lead screw turning at high speed. To do so may seriously damage the lathe. Use the *feed-reverse lever* to change the direction of the lead screw.

CHECKING THE ALIGNMENT OF CENTERS

1. Before machining a workpiece held between centers, it is important to check alignment between the live center and the dead center. The two centers must be in a straight line and true with the center line of the lathe.

2. Check alignment using one of the following five methods. Note that methods *a* and *b* are only approximate and are not accurate enough for precision work.

a. Move the tailstock center close to the headstock center, and see if the points meet (Fig. 43-10).

b. A *witness* mark or line is usually scribed into the tailstock. This line indicates the relative position of the tailstock parts (top and bottom). Make sure that the marks on the top and bottom parts of the tailstock lines line up (Fig. 43-11).

c. Use a steel test bar and dial indicator gage (Fig. 43-12). Mount the test bar between the centers. Fasten the dial indicator and holder in the tool post. Set the indicator contact point against the test bar at or near a right-angle position. Move the cross-feed in slightly to obtain an indicator reading. Set the dial of the indicator to zero if you wish. Then move the carriage to feed the indicator across the test bar. If the centers are out of alignment, you will get a different reading on the indicator from one end of the bar to the other. If the indicator hand does not change or move, the centers are in true alignment.

Fig. 43-10. Checking the alignment of the centers by observing if the point of the dead center touches the point of the live center.

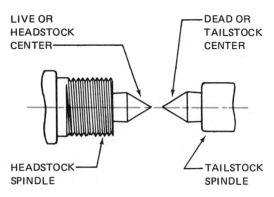

LIVE OR HEADSTOCK CENTER

DEAD OR TAILSTOCK CENTER

HEADSTOCK SPINDLE

TAILSTOCK SPINDLE

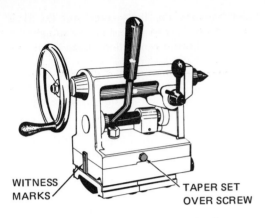

WITNESS MARKS

TAPER SET OVER SCREW

Fig. 43-11. Checking alignment by making sure the witness marks on the two parts of the tailstock assembly are lined up.

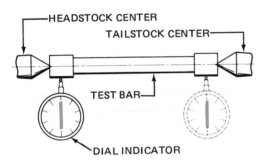

HEADSTOCK CENTER

TAILSTOCK CENTER

TEST BAR

DIAL INDICATOR

Fig. 43-12. Checking the alignment with a steel test bar and dial indicator. The dial indicator must stay at zero as the carriage is moved back and forth.

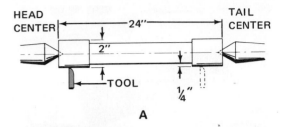

HEAD CENTER

TAIL CENTER

24"

2"

TOOL

1/4"

A

B

Fig. 43-13. (A) By taking a light cut at both ends of a piece of scrap stock and measuring with a micrometer, you can determine if the cut is straight or tapered. (B) Checking the alignment after machining the test bar.

d. Select a piece of round scrap stock of suitable length, with center holes already in the ends if possible. Mount this stock between centers in the usual manner. Take a light cut for a short distance near the headstock end. Do not disturb the setting of the cutting tool or cross-feed once the cut has been made. Back up the tailstock center, and swing the workpiece to clear the cutting tool. Move the carriage toward the tailstock until the cutting tool clears the end of the workpiece. Place the workpiece back between the centers, and take a short cut on the workpiece at the tailstock end. Check both diameters with a micrometer. If both are the same, the centers are in alignment (Fig. 43-13). If the diameter at the

tailstock end is smaller, adjust the tailstock away from you. If larger, move it toward you slightly. Always recheck after adjusting the tailstock by repeating the process.

e. A quicker method of checking alignment is to place your work between centers and take a light cut across the work for a distance of 2 or 3 in., if the length of the work permits. After you have done this, use a micrometer to check the diameter at each end of the cut.

3. If the centers are not in alignment, the upper casting of the tailstock must be adjusted or moved, either toward you or away from you. The direction to move the tailstock depends upon whether the diameter of the work at the

tailstock end is greater or less than the diameter at the headstock end. Before adjusting the tailstock, loosen the clamp nut. Then loosen the setscrew on one side, and tighten the setscrew on the opposite side.

On some lathes, the tailstock adjusting screws *pull* the tailstock casting, and on others, the adjusting screws *push* the tailstock casting. You should try the screws before making the alignment so you will know whether the screws pull or push the top part of the tailstock.

When correcting errors in center alignment, the amount to move the setscrews is usually very small. Most beginners make the mistake of turning the screws too much. It is easier to keep the adjustment in one direction, rather than to overshoot the mark and have to use the opposite setscrew to move the tailstock back.

UNIT 44. Care of Lathes and Personal Safety

Keep the lathe clean and well lubricated at all times. Like any precision machine, the lathe requires careful treatment. It will operate better and do accurate work as long as you care for it properly. Don't make the mistake of relying upon others to keep the lathe oiled and in good repair. Your own personal safety depends upon your ability to keep the lathe in a safe operating condition. The proper care of a lathe includes such things as cleaning, oiling, adjusting, and making minor repairs.

CLEANING THE LATHE

Clean the lathe thoroughly after each work period (Fig. 44-1). When chips and dirt are left on ways, gears, and other moving parts, the surfaces become roughened and dented. This causes fast wear and makes it difficult to operate the parts.

Fig. 44-1. Keep the area around your machine clean and neat.

The following procedure is recommended for cleaning a lathe:

1. Use a brush first to remove all chips (Fig. 44-2).

CAUTION

Most chips are razor sharp, so never use your hands.

A 2-in. paintbrush or a small bench brush is convenient for this purpose. Move the tailstock to the right end of the bed.

2. Wipe off all painted surfaces with a clean cloth or cotton waste. Oil left on the painted surfaces becomes hardened and stains the paint.

3. Using the same cloth or cotton waste, remove oil and grease from all machined surfaces.

4. Brush all chips from the chip pan, then wipe it clean.

5. Before mounting a chuck, clean its inside threads with a wire thread cleaner (Fig. 44-3). Wipe off the spindle threads, and place a drop or two of oil on them.

6. Clean the spindle holes and taper shanks of centers before mounting them in place (Fig. 44-4). If centers have burrs or rough spots on

Fig. 44-2. Always clean away chips with a brush; never with your fingers. Long chips are especially dangerous. Never attempt to pick them up with your hands. Use a pair of pliers to remove these chips.

Fig. 44-3. Clean the threads in the chuck before mounting it.

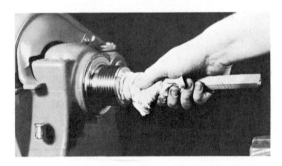

Fig. 44-4. Use a rag wrapped around a small dowel rod to clean the spindle hole.

them, use a file or an oilstone to remove them before placing the centers in the spindle holes.

7. Occasionally, clean the thread grooves of the lead screw with a piece of cord (Fig. 44-5). Place the cord around the lead screw. Adjust the gears to turn the lead screw at a medium speed. Start the lathe, and with the lead screw turning, move the cord back and forth as it feeds along the screw.

8. When oiling a lathe, wipe off any oil that may spill or drip on the painted surfaces.

9. Always make certain there is a light film of oil on the ways before you start to work.

Fig. 44-5. Use a piece of cord to clean the lead-screw threads.

Fig. 44-6. When using a tool post grinder, cover machine parts so that they will not be damaged by abrasive dust.

10. Adjust the cross-feed and compound-slide gib screws to remove looseness or play between the parts. When you can move the cross-feed by grasping the tool post with your hand and move it back and forth, it means the gib screws are too loose. Adjust each of the gib screws until a smooth movement is obtained on the cross-feed handle. When they are properly adjusted, it will not be possible to move the cross-feed by pulling or pushing on the tool post.

11. Never lay tools or workpieces on the ways of a lathe. To do so destroys the accuracy of these precision handscraped surfaces. Place your tools on a lathe board.

12. When using a tool-post grinder, always protect the machined surfaces of the lathe by covering them (Fig. 44-6). Abrasive particles from the grinding wheel can become imbedded in the surface bearings and soon destroy the accuracy of the lathe if surfaces are not covered during the grinding operation.

13. Once a week wipe down the entire lathe with a clean cloth dampened with kerosene. Do the painted surfaces first, then the machined surfaces. Wipe dry, and place a thin film of clean oil over all machined surfaces.

OILING AND GREASING THE LATHE

It is important that the lathe be properly lubricated. An oiling or lubrication chart comes with each machine. Be sure to use the grades and kinds of oil and grease called for in the chart. Form the habit of oiling your lathe each day before you start work. Certain parts require daily oiling. Other parts should be oiled weekly or monthly as the chart says. Too often, when several persons use the same lathe, each one depends on the other, and the result is that no one does the oiling or maintenance.

SAFETY PRECAUTIONS

To prevent injury to yourself or others and damage to the lathe and work, it is necessary to understand and obey certain safety rules and precautions. The following rules should be carefully studied and remembered.

1. You must not attempt to operate a lathe until you have received instructions from your instructor and have passed a written safety test.

2. Correct dress is important. Remove rings and wrist watches. Roll up your sleeves. Wear an apron. Put on your safety glasses. Do not wear sweaters or neckties (Fig. 44-7).

3. It is both dangerous and foolish to try to lift heavy chucks and attachments alone. Always get help.

4. Always make certain your work is set up securely and tightly when using chucks and collets.

5. When holding work between centers, make sure you use the correct size of centers with

271

Fig. 44-7. A well-run machine shop is neat and everyone is properly dressed.

good points. Never use a soft center in the tailstock. Soft centers may be used in the headstock spindle only. Apply oil or white lead to the tailstock center, and adjust it properly. If too tight, the point will heat up and burn off.

6. Tool bits must be sharp and ground to the correct shape. Be sure they are set at the proper height and angle to the work.

7. Guards over belts and gears must never be removed unless you first get permission from your instructor. The power must be shut off at the switchboard before removing guards for any reason.

8. After setting up the lathe, remove all wrenches, oilcans, and other tools from the work area. When work is held on a faceplate, turn the faceplate by hand for a complete revolution to make certain the work will not strike any part of the lathe.

9. Always stop the lathe before making adjustments of any kind.

10. Do not change spindle speeds until the lathe comes to a dead stop.

11. Never attempt to measure work while it is turning.

12. Never file lathework unless the file has a handle.

13. It is dangerous practice to leave a chuck wrench in the chuck—even for a moment.

14. Keep rags, cotton waste, and brushes away from knurling tools while knurling the work.

15. It is unsafe to have small-diameter work extend more than an inch or two from a chuck or collet unless it is supported by the tailstock center.

16. You should always know in what direction and how fast the carriage or cross-feed will move before you turn on the automatic feeds.

17. Be very careful not to run the carriage or compound slide into the turning chuck.

18. When you hear unusual noises from your machine, stop it and find out what is causing them. If you don't know, see your instructor.
19. You must always start and stop your own machine—never let other students do this for you. Do not allow others to fool with or loaf around your machine. Accidents happen when your mind is distracted.

20. When adjusting the work or removing it from the lathe, always remove the tool bit, or turn the holder, so your hand will not slip against it. When gaging a bored hole with a plug gage, be sure to wrap a rag around the cutting tool or move it a good safe distance away from the hole. If the gage lets go suddenly, you might puncture your hand against the cutting tool.

UNIT 45. Cutting Tools and Toolholders

To machine a workpiece successfully you must have:

1. The correct kind of *cutting tool* or *tool bit*

2. The right type of toolholder

3. A tool with a sharp cutting-edge

4. The cutting tool set or adjusted to the correct height and position (Fig. 45-1)

CUTTING-TOOL MATERIALS

Tool bits used on the lathe are made from one of six basic materials: water-hardening steels, high-speed steels, hard-cast nonferrous alloys, sintered (cemented) carbides, ceramics, and diamonds. The selection of the material used depends upon many factors including: tool cost, resharpening cost, size and design of tool, metal-removal rate, length of run, finish and tolerance of part, and condition and capability of the machine tool. Because of these factors, material selection is more often based on general experience than on precise evaluation. There are, however, certain general characteristics of the different cutting-tool materials you should understand.

Water-hardening Steels. These include the high-carbon tool steels (either plain carbon or those with minor additions of chromium, vanadium, or tungsten). The different grades of water-

hardening tool steels are classed as *W steels* in the American Iron and Steel Institute's system of classification. Tools made from these materials have very sharp, smooth cutting-edges when properly heat-treated. They are adequate for limited turning at a relatively low cutting speed or when old, low-speed equipment, such as a flat-belt lathe, is used.

The main limitation of tools made from water-hardening steels is that they soften if the cutting-edge temperature exceeds approximately 300–400°F during sharpening or cutting. A second disadvantage is low resistance to edge wear.

High-speed Steels. High-speed steels offer great improvement in cutting efficiency over water-

Fig. 45-1. All conditions must be correct in order to do good cutting on the lathe.

273

hardening tool steels. Tools made from high-speed steel retain enough hardness to machine at rapid rates even when the tool temperature reaches 1050°F. They can be used even though they become dull red with heat. Upon cooling to room temperature, the original hardness of these steels does not change.

Wear resistance of high-speed steels is much better than that of the carbon or alloy steels. This is due to the high carbide content, especially in the higher-alloy types of high-speed steel. Fully hardened, high-speed steels have greater resistance to shock than carbides or hard-cast alloys.

There are two main types of high-speed steels designated in the American Iron and Steel Institute system, *M steels* (molybdenum base) and *T steels* (tungsten base). Tool bits made from these materials can be purchased already ground to various shapes. Unground tool bits called *tool-bit blanks* can also be purchased. These tool-bit blanks are made in standard sizes to fit the commonly used lathes. The common sizes are $\frac{3}{16}$ in. square by 1 in. long, $\frac{1}{4}$ in. square by 2 in. long, $\frac{5}{16}$ in. square by $2\frac{1}{2}$ in. long, and $\frac{3}{8}$ in. square by 3 in. long. High-speed steel tool bits are the type most used in the school machine shop.

Hard-cast (nonferrous) Alloys. These materials do not contain sufficient iron to be classed as steels. Rather, they are mainly alloys of cobalt, chromium, and tungsten with other elements added for special purposes. They reach full hardness in the as-cast condition, without heat treatment. They must be ground to size after casting. In terms of resistance to heat, wear, shock, and initial cost, cast alloys rank between high-speed steels and carbides.

Hard-cast alloys are weaker in tension and more brittle than high-speed steels and thus are not suitable for severe shock loads. They are

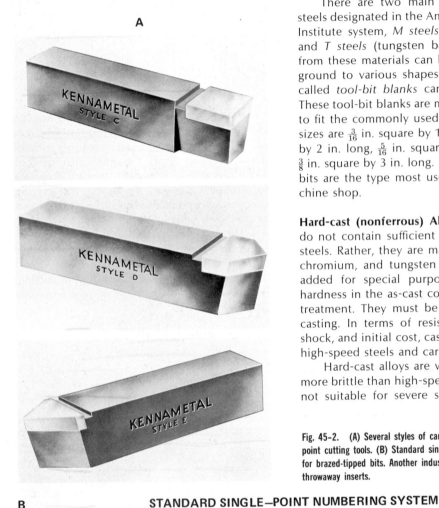

A

B

Fig. 45-2. (A) Several styles of carbide, brazed-tipped single-point cutting tools. (B) Standard single-point numbering system for brazed-tipped bits. Another industry standard is used for throwaway inserts.

STANDARD SINGLE—POINT NUMBERING SYSTEM
AR—10

TOOL SHAPE	GENERAL APPLICATION	HAND	SHANK SIZE
A — 0° LEAD B — 15° LEAD C — SQUARE NOSE D — 30° LEAD E — 45° LEAD	SHOULDERING FORMING TO LEAD ANGLE GROOVING AND FACING UNDERCUTTING AND CHAMFER THREADING	R — RIGHT L — LEFT	SHANKS ARE SQUARE EXPRESSED IN 1/16." NO. AR-10, 10/16" OR 5/8" SQUARE.

known by such commercial names as stellite, Rex alloy, and tantung.

Sintered (cemented) Carbides. For efficient and high-speed machining, best results can be obtained with sintered carbide tools. Carbide tools are available in solid form and as inserts which are either brazed or clamped in toolholders (Fig. 45-2). Clamped inserts are usually round, square, or triangular in shape and have all edges preground. These inserts can be rotated so that a sharp edge is always available (Fig. 45-3). With modern machine tools and the proper grade of cemented carbide, it is possible to use cutting speeds 10 to 30 times faster than those feasible with high-speed steels.

Carbides are suitable for most machining operations such as single-point turning, drilling, milling, thread cutting, and reaming. Carbides should be used only when they can be supported rigidly and when the machine tool has adequate power and speed to enable their efficient use.

Ceramic. With the exception of industrial diamonds, ceramic inserts are the hardest and strongest inserts available. They resist abrasive wear, chipping, and breakage. These inserts work best on very rigid machine tools and on well-supported workpieces. For most operations, cutting fluids are not needed.

Diamonds. Industrial diamonds that have either circular or faceted cutting-edges are used for light finishing cuts when an extremely high-quality surface finish is required. Although a very smooth finish can be achieved using other cutting-tool materials, diamond turning can provide even smoother finishes with very small tolerances.

TOOLHOLDERS

The toolholder holds the cutting tool rigid during cutting operations. Four types of toolholders are in general use.

1. *The tool post with standard toolholders.* The tool post is comprised of the post, screw, washer, collar, and rocker (Fig. 45-4A). The washer fits the top slide piece slot. The collar and the rocker elevate or lower the point of the

A

B

Fig. 45-3. (A) Throwaway carbide tips. (B) The carbide-tipped tool will take a heavy, clean cut.

tool. The screw clamps the toolholder in place (Fig. 45-4B).

The standard toolholder for *high-speed steel cutter bits* comes in three common shapes:

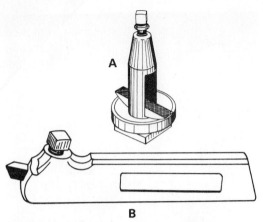

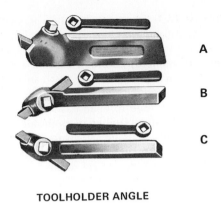

A

B

TOOLHOLDER ANGLE

Fig. 45-4. (A) The tool post. (B) Universal tool-bit holders.

Fig. 45-5. Three kinds of toolholders: (A) straight, (B) right-hand, and (C) left-hand.

Fig. 45-6. Applications of the various types of holders.

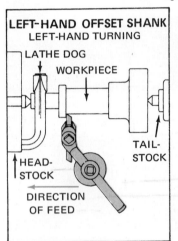

LEFT-HAND OFFSET SHANK
LEFT-HAND TURNING

LATHE DOG

WORKPIECE

HEAD-STOCK

TAIL-STOCK

DIRECTION OF FEED

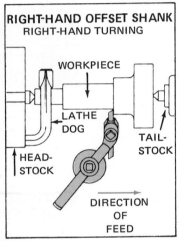

RIGHT-HAND OFFSET SHANK
RIGHT-HAND TURNING

WORKPIECE

LATHE DOG

HEAD-STOCK

TAIL-STOCK

DIRECTION OF FEED

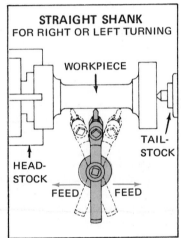

STRAIGHT SHANK
FOR RIGHT OR LEFT TURNING

WORKPIECE

HEAD-STOCK

TAIL-STOCK

FEED   FEED

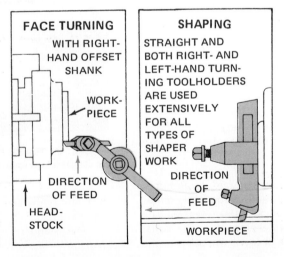

FACE TURNING

WITH RIGHT-HAND OFFSET SHANK

WORK-PIECE

DIRECTION OF FEED

HEAD-STOCK

SHAPING

STRAIGHT AND BOTH RIGHT- AND LEFT-HAND TURNING TOOLHOLDERS ARE USED EXTENSIVELY FOR ALL TYPES OF SHAPER WORK

DIRECTION OF FEED

WORKPIECE

straight, right-hand offset or shank, and left-hand offset or shank (Fig. 45–5). You can identify right-hand and left-hand offset holders by holding the setscrew end in your hand. If the shank bends to the right, it is a right-hand offset holder. If the shank bends to the left, it is a left-hand offset holder.

The straight toolholder is used for most work. The left-hand toolholder is used when you need to cut close to the chuck or lathe dog. The right-hand (shank) holder is used when feeding toward the tailstock of the lathe (Fig. 45–6). The cutting-tool bit is held in each of these toolholders at an angle of 14 to $16\frac{1}{2}$ degrees (°) (15° is most common). This is called the *toolholder angle* (Fig. 45–7).

Carbide toolholders also come in three styles and are similar in appearance to those mentioned above (Fig. 45–8). The hole for the cutter bit, however, is parallel to the bottom edge of the holder (Fig. 45–9).

2. The *open-side* or *heavy-duty tool block* holds one tool at a time and consists of a T-slot clamp, a C-shaped block, and two or more tool clamping screws. Because this unit is very rigid, it is especially useful for heavy cuts. A tool bit can be mounted directly in the tool block or some type of carbide toolholder can be used (Fig. 45–10).

3. The *turret tool block* or *four-way toolholder* consists of a swiveling block in which the tools

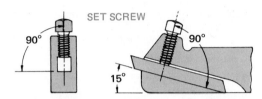

Fig. 45-7. The tool angle on most common types of toolholders is 15°, although it might vary from 14 to $16\frac{1}{2}$°.

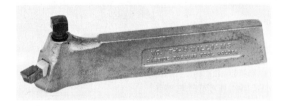

Fig. 45-8. Carbide tool-bit holders are similar in appearance to those used for high-speed steel.

Fig. 45-9. The carbide toolholder has a tool angle of zero degrees.

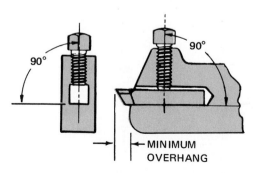

Fig. 45-10. Using an open-side or heavy-duty tool block.

Fig. 45-11. The turret or four-way toolholder.

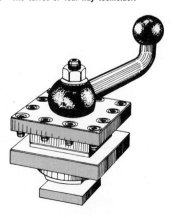

are clamped (Fig. 45-11). Common turret blocks hold four tools (Fig. 45-12). Each can be quickly swiveled into cutting position and clamped in place. Some turret blocks have eight tool stations (Fig. 45-13). Frequently, an open-side-type tool block is also mounted on the rear of the cross slide to add one additional cutting operation (Fig. 45-14). With this arrangement, anywhere from five to nine different kinds of tools can be mounted and operated in sequence for turning, forming, facing, knurling, and cutting off of duplicate parts.

4. The *quick-change-type tool system* holds only one tool at a time, but three different sides can be used to position the tool. It consists of a quick-change tool post with a clamping lever and a series of toolholders for turning, facing, boring, cutting off, threading, knurling, and thread cutting (Figs. 45-15 and 45-16).

SINGLE-POINT CUTTING TOOLS (TOOL BITS)

Tool Parts. Before you can grind a tool bit, you must become acquainted with some of the terms used to describe the various parts of the cutting tool (Fig. 45-17).

1. The *face* is the top of the tool bit. It is the surface on which a part of the chip (built-up edge) attaches as it is cut away from the workpiece.

2. The *cutting-edge* is that part of the cutter bit which actually does the cutting.

3. The *nose* is the corner or arc formed by the side and end cutting-edge.

4. The *flank* is the surface below the cutting-edge.

5. The *point* is the part of the tool bit which is shaped to form the cutting-edge and face.

Tool Angles. The following are important tool angles used for all single-point cutting tools.

1. The *side relief angle* is the angle between the ground surface (flank) and the vertical side of the tool bit before it is ground (Fig. 45-17). This angle was formerly called *side clearance*, and many machinists still use this term. The side

Fig. 45-12. The four-way toolholder with the tools in position.

Fig. 45-13. This eight-station turret toolholder is excellent for many types of production work.

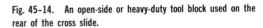

Fig. 45-14. An open-side or heavy-duty tool block used on the rear of the cross slide.

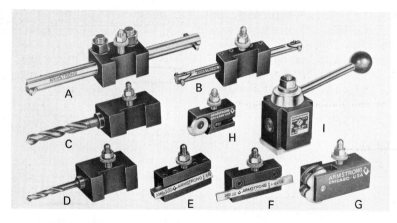

Fig. 45-15. Quick-change tool system: (A) heavy-duty boring toolholder, (B) light-duty boring toolholder, (C) a No. 3 Morse taper drill toolholder, (D) a No. 2 Morse taper drill toolholder, (E) turning toolholder, (F) cutoff toolholder, (G) knurling toolholder, (H) threading toolholder, and (I) quick-change tool post.

relief angle provides clearance between the cut surface of the work and the flank of the tool. Tool wear reduces the effective side clearance angle. If the angle is too small, the cutter will rub and heat. If the angle is too large, the cutting-edge will be weak and the tool will have a tendency to dig into the workpiece.

2. The *end relief angle* is the angle formed between the end of the cutting-edge and a vertical line (Fig. 45-17). It was formerly called *front clearance*. The end relief angle provides clearance between the finished surface of the work and the tool. If this angle is too small, the tool will rub on the finished surface and produce a

Fig. 45-16. This quick-change toolholder is used in a facing operation.

Fig. 45-17. Terms used in describing the parts and tool angles of a cutting tool. Typical tool angles for a roughing tool for steel would be as follows: end-relief angle, 8°; side-relief angle, 6°; back-rake angle, 8°; side-rake angle, 14°; end cutting-edge angle, 6°; side cutting-edge angle, 15°; and nose radius, $\frac{1}{8}$ in.

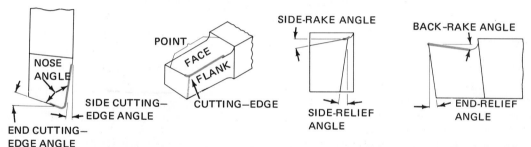

poor finish. Wear tends to reduce this angle. If the angle is too large, the tool may dig into the work, chatter, and fail through chipping. An angle of 8 to 15° is recommended for steel tools and 6 to 8° for carbide tools. If the tool is set above the center of rotation, the effective clearance angle is reduced. This must be considered in choosing the proper angle.

3. The *end cutting-edge* angle provides clearance between the cutter and the finished surface of the work (Fig. 45–17). If this angle is too small, it may cause chatter. A small angle of about 6° is desirable on light finishing cuts, however, in order to produce a smooth finish.

4. The *side cutting-edge angle* turns the chip away from the finished surface (Fig. 45–17). Recommended angles are between 5 and 15°.

5. The *nose radius* removes the fragile corner of the tool, prolongs tool life, and improves finish (Fig. 45–17). The radius may be large for maximum-strength rough-cutting tools and may be reduced for light feeds. The larger the nose radius, the better the finish as long as chatter does not occur. Recommended nose radii are 0.010 to 0.030 in. or more for finishing cuts, and $\frac{1}{32}$ to $\frac{1}{2}$ in. for roughing cuts.

6. To help shape the cutting-edge and face, it is necessary to grind *rake angles* on a tool bit (Fig. 45–17). *Rake is an inclination from the vertical or horizontal*. A tool bit has no rake angles when the top is flat and horizontal. The two rake angles are *back rake* and *side rake*.

Back rake, in a single-point feeding to the side, turns the chip away from the finished work and gives the tool a slicing action. A zero back rake tends to make a spiral chip, and a back rake angle greater than zero (positive) tends to stretch the spiral chip out into a helix. A back-rake angle of from 5 to 15° is used to keep chips from scratching the workpiece. High-speed steel tool bits are always ground with a positive rake (one sloping down from the cutting-edge). However, cemented carbide tools may have either a positive or negative rake. Negative rake increases the shear angle at which the chip is formed, providing for a good chip and a good surface finish. Negative rake tools are generally used on a heavy-duty lathe that is operated at high speed with a heavy feed.

Side rake refers to the angle between the face of the tool and a line that would represent the top of the unground tool bit as viewed from the end. Side rake controls the type of chip produced during machining as well as the direction in which the chip will travel. A tool with a small side-rake angle will produce shorter chips than one with a large rake angle.

7. The *nose angle* is the angle between the side-cutting edge and the end-cutting edge.

CLASSES OF SINGLE-POINT TOOLS

Different shapes of tool bits are needed to do certain machining operations. Most tool bits are ground to cut in one direction only. The two common types are referred to as *right cut* and

Fig. 45–18. This will help you identify a right-cut and a left-cut tool.

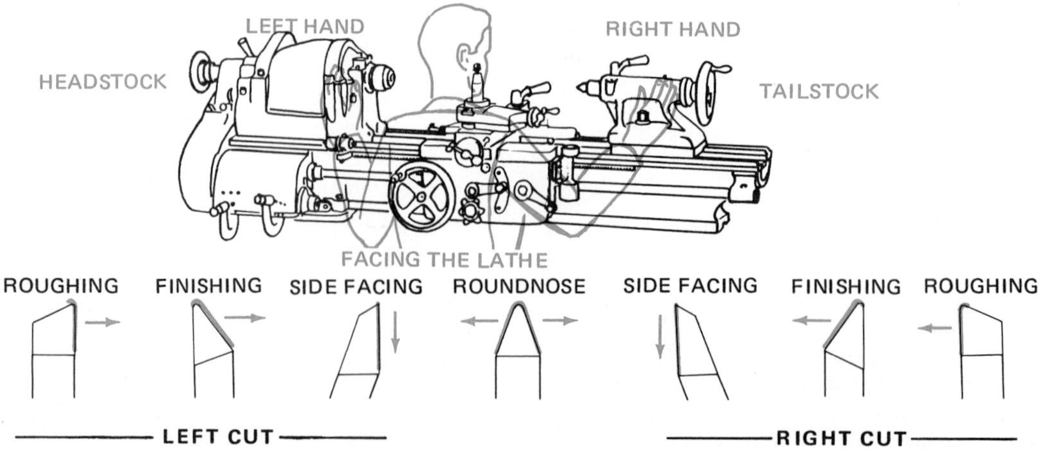

LEFT HAND   RIGHT HAND

HEADSTOCK   TAILSTOCK

FACING THE LATHE

ROUGHING FINISHING SIDE FACING ROUNDNOSE SIDE FACING FINISHING ROUGHING

——— LEFT CUT ———   ———RIGHT CUT———

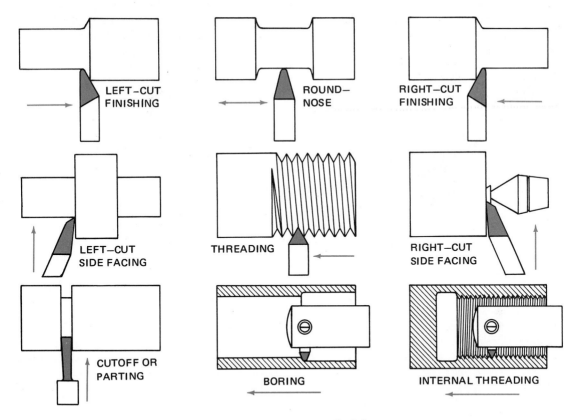

Fig. 45-19.   Some common cutting tools.

left cut. These were formerly called right-hand and left-hand tool bits.

A *right-cut single-point tool* is one that, when viewed from the point end with the face up, has its cutting-edge on the right side (Fig. 45-18). When the tool bit is placed in the lathe, the cutting-edge is on the left side. This tool bit cuts from the right to the left, or from the tail-stock end toward the headstock of the lathe.

A *left-cut tool bit* has the cutting-edge on the left when viewed from the point end with the face up. This tool bit is ground to cut from the left to the right or toward the tail-stock of the lathe.

Commonly used types of tool bits include the following (Fig. 45-19):

1. A *roughing tool* is a tool bit designed to take heavy roughing cuts to reduce the diameter of a workpiece to approximate size. Because finish is not important when roughing work, such a tool bit may be ground to almost a sharp point. However, the point is usually rounded very slightly to prevent its breaking down.

2. A *finishing tool* is one that has a keenly ground cutting-edge which may be honed with an oilstone to produce a very smooth finish. A finish tool generally has a larger rounded nose than a roughing tool.

3. A *roundnose cutting tool* is a general-purpose tool used for many types of work. When ground flat on the top, it can be used for both right and left cuts and for turning brass. It may also be used to form a radius at the corner of a shoulder. Roundnose tool bits are used as finishing tools.

4. The *square-nose tool* cuts on the end only. It is used for chamfering and for roughing cuts to square a shoulder.

5. A *cutoff or parting tool* cuts on the end only and is used for cutting off stock or workpieces held in a chuck.

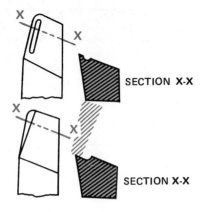

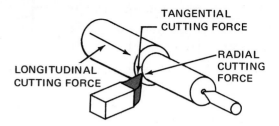

Fig. 45–22. The three major cutting forces in turning.

Fig. 45–20. Common types of chip breakers used for high-speed steel tools.

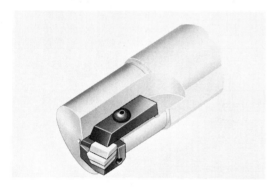

Fig. 45–21. Note that a separate chip breaker is clamped over the insert for this throwaway carbide-tipped unit.

6. *Side-facing tools* or *side tools*, as they are often called, are used for finishing the ends of work square and smooth. A right-cut side-facing tool is always used to finish the end of a shaft. A left-cut side-facing tool may be used to finish the left side of a shoulder.

CHIP BREAKERS

To eliminate the problem of a continuous chip, a chip breaker is often ground on a high-speed steel tool bit. Common types of chip breakers are shown in Fig. 45–20. These can either be ground on an off-hand grinding wheel, or in the case of the grooved chip breaker, it can be done with a thin grinding wheel on a surface grinder. A separate chip breaker is often used with insert-type carbide tools (Fig. 45–21).

CUTTING ACTION

In lathe turning, there are three basic cutting forces, the *longitudinal force* of the workpiece against the side of the tool, the *radial force* of the workpiece against the front of the tool, and the *tangential force* of the workpiece against the top of the tool (Fig. 45–22). The tangential cutting force is by far the greatest and has the most influence on the cutting action. This tremendous force (downward pressure) is exerted against the cutting-edge. Pressures as great as a quarter-million pounds per square foot have been measured on large metal-cutting lathes. If the tool is shaped incorrectly or set at an incorrect angle, it will dull rapidly.

Here is what actually happens when cutting on the lathe. As the workpiece meets the cutting-edge of the tool bit, chips or a continuous ribbon of metal are wedged away from the material being machined. On soft, ductile material, this wedging is continuous. On harder materials, the wedging force causes the metal to compress. Compression continues until a shearing point is reached, and the compressed metal is separated from the workpiece. This is repeated throughout the cutting operation.

The shape is much more important than the actual sharpness of a cutting-edge. Lack of clearances permits the tool to drag on the workpiece, greatly increasing the pressure on the cutting-edge and interfering with tool performance. Too-large clearance angles make the tool weak and do not provide a good enough support for the cutting-edge. Such an edge breaks off or wears out rapidly.

GRINDING A HIGH-SPEED STEEL TOOL BIT

A tool bit is ground:

1. To provide a sharp cutting-edge

2. To obtain the correct or best shape for a particular operation

3. To provide clearance away from the end of the tool bit (end relief)

4. To provide clearance away from the side of the tool bit (side relief)

5. To provide good chip movement over the face of the tool bit and away from the cutting-edge (side and back rake)

Here is the correct procedure for grinding a right-cut roundnose tool bit:

1. Check the grinding wheels to make certain the faces of the wheels are dressed properly. It is difficult to grind good cutting tools on wheels that are uneven or have grooves in them. Use a bench or floor grinder that is used only for grinding cutting tools. Such a grinder should have a coarse-grit aluminum-oxide wheel on one side and a fine-grit wheel on the other side. Use the coarse-grit wheel for roughing the tool bit to shape. Then use the fine-grit wheel for finishing the tool bit.

2. The tool grinder should be equipped with tool rests. Rest your hands on them to control the movement of the tool bit. Hold the tool bit firmly to keep it from bouncing around on the wheel. Do not grip it so tightly, however, that you have difficulty moving it (Fig. 45–23).

3. Grind the *side-relief angle* to form the *side-cutting-edge angle* by holding the tool bit against the wheel, as shown in Fig. 45–24. This angle should be about 6° for mild steel. Hold the tool bit against the wheel, and tilt the bottom inward to get this angle. As you grind, move the tool bit back and forth across the face of

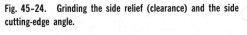

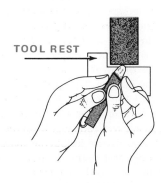

Fig. 45-23. The correct way to hold a tool bit when grinding.

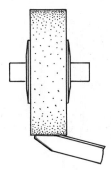

Fig. 45-25. Grinding the other side-relief angle on the opposite side.

Fig. 45-24. Grinding the side relief (clearance) and the side cutting-edge angle.

Fig. 45-26. Grinding the end-relief angle. Note that if the end relief (front-clearance angle) is to be 8°, then the actual angle ground on the end must be 23° since the tool will be held at an angle of 15° in the toolholder.

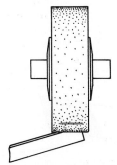

the wheel without changing its position. This helps to grind the tool faster and prevents grooving the wheel. As the tool bit heats up, dip it in water to cool it. A beginner often makes the mistake of moving the tool bit up and down. This forms many different angles on the flank, and it becomes very irregular. To avoid this, hold the tool bit in a fixed position on the wheel. Move it back and forth, but never up or down.

4. Grind the side-relief angle on the opposite side to form the shape of the tool bit, as shown in Fig. 45-25.

5. To grind the end-relief angle, hold the tool with the end up. Swing the shank of the tool bit in a semicircle. Try to blend the end radius to meet the sides neatly and cleanly (Figs. 45-26 and 45-27). Always ease up on the pressure when grinding the roundnose of the tool bit. If you fail to do this, you will grind a larger roundnose tool than desired.

Table 45-1. Rake angles for common materials.

Material	Back Rake, Degrees	Side Rake, Degrees
Aluminum and alloys	8	18
Brass and bronze, soft	2	2
Bronze, high tensile	6	5
Cast iron:		
Soft	5	5
Medium	4	4
Hard	3	3
Copper	$16\frac{1}{4}$	20
Malleable iron	4	5
Steel:		
Low-carbon	8	14
Medium-carbon	10	12
High-carbon	5	10
Tool-and-die	8	12
Alloy	8	12

6. Grind the *side-* and *back-rake angles*. The correct angle for each can be found in Table 45-1. To grind side rake for a right-cut tool bit, hold the tool bit, face or top, at right angles to the *right* side of the grinding wheel. Tilt the tool inward at the bottom (Fig. 45-28). Hold it in this position until the wheel cleans up the entire face to the cutting-edge. To grind the side-rake angle for a left-cut tool bit, hold the tool bit at the left side of the grinding wheel. Tilt the bottom inward, and let the grinding wheel clean up the entire face to the cutting-edge. There is no reason to grind the face of the tool bit below the shank at the front end. To do so wastes the expensive tool bit and results in a poorly shaped cutting tool.

7. It is good practice to hone tool bits used for finishing work. Select a medium-fine oil-

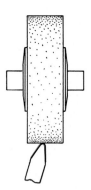

Fig. 45-27. Rounding off the nose of the cutting tool.

Fig. 45-28. Grinding the side and back rake of a right-cut tool bit.

Fig. 45-29. Honing the cutting-edge.

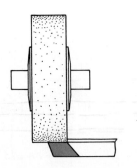

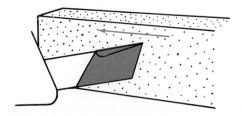

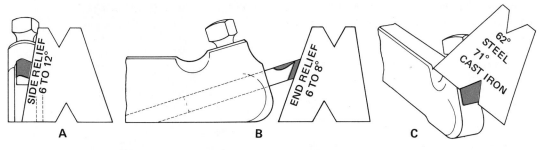

Fig. 45-30. (A) Checking the side-relief angle. (B) Checking end relief. The actual angle at the end of the tool bit will be 21 to 23° if the bit is to be held in a 15° toolholder. (C) Checking the tool angle for cast iron.

stone. Apply a little kerosene or lard cutting oil to the oilstone (Fig. 45-29). Move the cutting-edge back and forth against the oilstone. Be sure to hold the bit flat so as not to change any angles.

With a little practice, you will be able to grind a tool bit correctly. Remember, a well-ground bit is one that has proper tool angles together with flat, evenly ground surfaces (Fig. 45-30).

UNIT 46. Speed, Feed, and Depth of Cut

For a most efficient production, the lathe should be run at the highest speed and coarsest feed which will give the desired results. Knowing how to pick the best speeds and feeds is a part of what makes a man a first-class lathe operator (Fig. 46-1). The experienced machinist can say, "It's turning at about the right speed; this is about the correct feed, and the depth of cut is just about right."

CUTTING SPEED

Cutting speed is the distance in feet a workpiece moves past a cutting point in one minute. Measurement is on the circumference of the workpiece, and the result is expressed in surface feet per minute (sfpm). In other words, cutting speed is equal to the length of a chip, measured in feet, that can be removed in one minute's time.

There are many things that should be considered in determining cutting speed, including:

1. Kind of material in the cutter bit (high-speed steel, carbide, ceramic, etc.)

2. Kind of material being machined (its hardness, how it is heat-treated, if it is a casting or bar stock)

3. Size and condition of the lathe

Fig. 46-1. Being able to select the correct speed, feed, and depth of cut is essential when using a lathe.

Table 46-1. Suggested cutting speeds and feeds for lathe.

Material	Cutting speed for high-speed steel tools, sfpm	Feed
Aluminum and alloys	200–400	0.003–0.020
Brass and bronze, soft	100–300	0.003–0.020
Bronze, high-tensile	70–90	0.003–0.020
Cast iron:		
Soft	100–150	0.003–0.020
Medium	70–100	0.003–0.020
Hard	40–60	0.003–0.020
Copper	60–150	0.003–0.020
Malleable iron	80–90	0.003–0.020
Steel:		
Low-carbon	80–150	0.012–0.025
Medium-carbon	60–100	0.012–0.015
High-carbon	50–60	0.005–0.012
Tool-and-die	40–80	0.003–0.010
Alloy	50–70	0.003–0.010

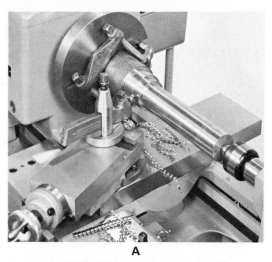

A

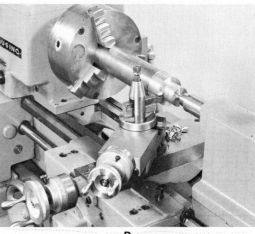

B

4. Amount of feed

5. Depth of cut

6. Kind of machining (whether it is roughing or finishing)

7. Size and shape of the workpiece

8. Shape of cutter bit

9. Use of cutting fluids and how applied

Table 46-1 contains suggested speeds for machining various materials using high-speed steel tool bits. With cemented carbide bits, cutting speeds can be approximately three times as fast (Fig. 46-2). Note that the table gives a range for each material. You must decide on whether to use the lower or higher speed. Table 46-2 is provided to help you in this regard.

SPINDLE SPEEDS

Remember, cutting speeds are given in surface feet per minute (sfpm). The spindle of the lathe operates in revolutions per minute (rpm). To convert cutting speed to spindle speed, use this simple formula:

Fig. 46-2. (A) This lathe is equipped with a standard toolholder and a high-speed steel bit. A slow speed and a small depth of cut are being utilized. (B) The same lathe equipped with a carbide-tipped tool bit can take a much heavier cut at a higher speed.

Table 46-2. Speed ranges.

Use Lower Speed Ranges for	Use Higher Speed Ranges for
Hard materials	Softer materials
Tough materials	Better finishes
Abrasive materials	Smaller diameter cutters
Heavy cuts	Light cuts
Minimum tool wear	Frail workpieces or setups
Maximum cutter life	Hand-feed operations
	Maximum production rates
	Nonmetallics

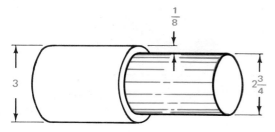

Fig. 46-3. Note that the diameter is reduced twice the amount of the depth of cut.

Approximate rpm

$$= \frac{\text{surface speed in feet per minute (sfpm)} \times 4}{\text{diameter in inches}}$$

Suppose you wish to make a roughing cut on a 2-in. diameter workpiece that is made of low-carbon steel which has a cutting speed of 100. The correct rpm is found as follows:

$$\text{rpm} = \frac{100 \times 4}{2} = 200 \text{ rpm}$$

You would therefore choose a speed on the lathe that is closest to 200 rpm. To be on the safe side, always use the spindle speed that is just below the number you found to be correct.

FEED

Feed is the distance the point of the tool moves longitudinally along the bed with each revolution of the lathe. There are no rules for determining correct feed. Feed varies with depth of cut, speed, kind of material, and condition of the lathe. Generally, coarser feeds are used for rough turning, and finer feeds for finish turning. Approximate feeds to use for various metals are listed in Table 46-1.

Fig. 46-4. Note the depth of cut being taken as this huge roll lathe turns a forged steel mill roll.

DEPTH OF CUT

Depth of cut is the distance from the bottom of the cut to the uncut surface of the workpiece measured at right angles to the machined surface. It is actually the difference between the *machined surface* (the surface left by the cutting tool) and the *work surface* (the surface to be machined). For example, if the workpiece is 3 in. at the start of the cut and $2\frac{3}{4}$ in. after the cut is made, the depth of cut is one-half the amount that the workpiece was reduced in diameter (Fig. 46-3). Notice that half the metal is cut off either side when turning a workpiece.

The depth of cut may be in the range of $\frac{1}{16}$ to $\frac{1}{4}$ in. for small work or $\frac{1}{2}$ to $1\frac{1}{2}$ in. for medium to large work (Fig. 46-4). A lighter depth of cut is used for finish turning than for rough turning.

UNIT 47. Locating and Drilling Center Holes

There are two principal methods for holding work to be turned in the lathe. Work may be held in chucks or collets, or it may be held between *centers*. Much of the lathework done in the average shop is held between centers.

Before you can turn between centers, you must lay out and drill a *center hole* in each end of the workpiece. These center holes provide bearing surfaces for the lathe center points.

LOCATING CENTER HOLES

Several methods are used to locate the center of a round workpiece. The method used depends upon the size of the round stock, the degree of accuracy required, and the amount of stock to be turned off. For example, if the diameter of a workpiece is to be reduced by $\frac{1}{4}$ in., it would be unnecessary to locate its exact center. On the other hand, if there is very little stock to be removed, great care and accuracy will be required to locate the center.

1. File the *burrs* from the ends of the stock.

2. Chalk or color each end with layout fluid so you can see the layout lines.

3. Select one of the following methods to locate the center:

   a. Use a center-head attachment and steel rule from a combination set. After scribing one line, move the center head about 90 degrees (°) and scribe a second line. The center of the workpiece is the point where the two lines intersect (Fig. 47–1).

   b. Set a hermaphrodite caliper to approximately half the diameter of the workpiece. Scribe four arcs by holding the caliper leg at different locations (about 90° apart). The center of the arcs will be the center of the workpiece (Fig. 47–2).

   c. Place the workpiece on a surface plate. Open a divider to approximately half the diameter, and scribe four lines. Rotate the workpiece about 90° for each line (Fig. 47–3).

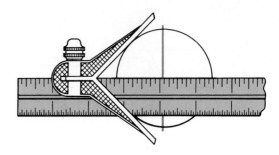

Fig. 47-1. Using the center head to locate the center of a piece of round stock.

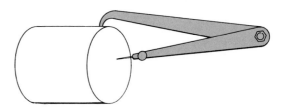

Fig. 47-2. Using the hermaphrodite caliper to locate the center on the end of a round workpiece. Four lines are scribed to mark the approximate center.

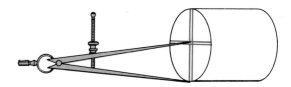

Fig. 47-3. Using a divider to locate the center.

Fig. 47-4. Locating the center of round stock by using a surface height gage. Note how the workpiece is placed on a V-block, using a surface plate as a base for both the workpiece and the layout tool.

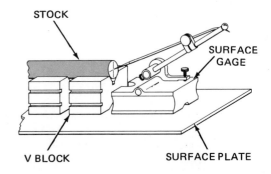

STOCK

SURFACE GAGE

V BLOCK

SURFACE PLATE

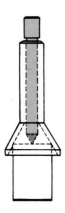

Fig. 47-5. Using a bell center punch.

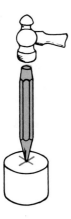

Fig. 47-6. Prick-punching the center-hole location.

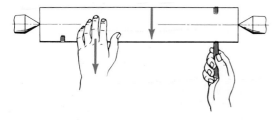

Fig. 47-7. Checking the workpiece to make sure the center-hole locations are correctly placed. Place the workpiece between centers. Hold a piece of chalk near the workpiece as you rotate it to mark the high side.

d. Place the workpiece in a V block. Set the scriber point of a surface-height gage to the approximate center of the workpiece. Scribe four lines across the end by rotating the workpiece about 90° for each line (Fig. 47-4).

e. Another method of finding the center is to use a bell-type center punch (Fig. 47-5). To obtain accuracy with this tool, the ends of the shaft should be faced square and all burrs removed. Hold the punch straight up and down, and tap it with a hammer.

4. Mark the center of the workpiece with a prickpunch (Fig. 47-6).

5. It is always a good idea to check the accuracy of your layout at this point. Place the work in the lathe with the points of the centers in the prick-punch marks (Fig. 47-7). Hold a piece of chalk close to the work, and spin the work by hand. The chalk will mark high spots. Use a center punch if the location of the center holes needs correcting. Tilt the punch at an angle away from the direction of the high spot, and strike it with a hammer. Then recheck for accuracy.

DRILLING CENTER HOLES

1. A *center hole* is actually two holes in one, a short straight hole and a conical-shaped hole having an included angle of 60°. The 60° hole provides a bearing surface for the 60° points of the lathe centers. A center hole is made in this manner for two reasons:

a. The straight-drilled hole provides a clearance space for the sharp point of the center.

b. The straight hole will hold a small quantity of lubricant for the dead center.

2. Drill the center holes deep enough to provide a good bearing surface for the center point. Figure 47-8 shows what happens when the holes are too deep or too shallow. Good judgment is necessary, as there is no hard and fast rule for the size of a center hole.

3. The most common tool used for drilling center holes is the *combination drill and countersink* (Fig. 47-9). Sometimes a separate *center drill* and *center reamer* are used in a two-step procedure. The *bell-type combination center drill* is best to use when center holes remain in the workpiece and the ends must be faced with the workpiece held between centers.

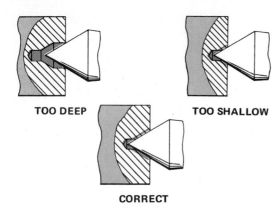

TOO DEEP   **TOO SHALLOW**

CORRECT

Fig. 47-8. Correct and incorrect center holes.

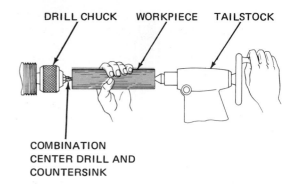

DRILL CHUCK   WORKPIECE   TAILSTOCK

COMBINATION
CENTER DRILL AND
COUNTERSINK

Fig. 47-11. Hold the workpiece firmly against the dead center as you turn the handwheel to drill the center hole.

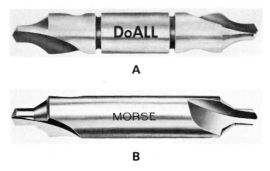

A

B

Fig. 47-9. (A) Plain-type combination center drill and countersink. (B) Bell-type combination center drill and countersink.

Fig. 47-10. Drilling center holes on a drill press.

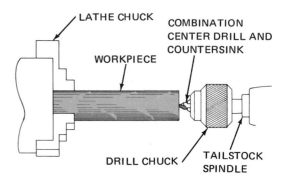

LATHE CHUCK

COMBINATION
CENTER DRILL AND
COUNTERSINK

WORKPIECE

DRILL CHUCK

TAILSTOCK
SPINDLE

Fig. 47-12. Drilling center holes with the workpiece held in a three-jaw chuck.

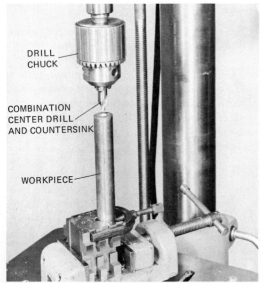

DRILL
CHUCK

COMBINATION
CENTER DRILL
AND COUNTERSINK

WORKPIECE

4. There are three ways of drilling the holes.

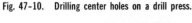 *a. On the drill press.* Fasten the combination center drill in the chuck. Clamp the work in a vertical position in the vise. Lower the table so the end of the workpiece clears the center drill. Adjust the drill press to a medium speed. *Too great a speed or too fast a feed may break the tool.* Apply a little cutting oil to the center-punch mark. Drill the hole to the correct depth by applying light pressure to the feeding handle (Fig. 47-10).

b. In the lathe with the workpiece held against the dead center. Install a drill-press chuck in the headstock spindle. Insert the combination center drill. Move the tailstock until the workpiece just clears between the center drill and the dead center. Lock the tailstock. Tighten the handle slightly so the spindle moves under slight pressure. Use a medium spindle speed. Hold the workpiece firmly in the left hand with the center-punch mark against the dead center. Turn on the lathe. Apply a little cutting fluid to the punch mark near the center drill. Turn the tailstock handwheel with your right hand, slowly forcing the workpiece into the revolving center drill (Fig. 47-11). Reverse and repeat.

c. *On the lathe with the workpiece held in a chuck.* Install a universal- or independent-jaw chuck on the headstock spindle. Fasten the stock in the chuck. Remove the dead center and install a drill chuck in its place. Drill the center holes as shown in Fig. 47-12. This method works best when

Fig. 47-13. Using a steady rest to support long workpieces when drilling center holes.

the diameter of the workpiece is small enough to go through the spindle or when the workpieces are comparatively short. On long workpieces, use a steady rest to support the outer edge of the stock (Fig. 47-13).

UNIT 48. Facing the Ends with the Workpiece Held between Centers

Facing is the operation of machining the ends of the workpiece square with the axis. A faced end should also be finished smooth and flat. Facing is necessary to machine work to correct length. If quite a lot of material is to be removed from a workpiece, it is better to face to exact length after rough turning. The reason for this is that pressure on the centers during the roughing operation may cause a burr to develop around the center holes. Figure 48-1 shows the correct setup for facing between centers.

TOOLS AND EQUIPMENT NEEDED

1. *Right-cut facing tool.* Grind the tool bit with a nose angle of 58 degrees (°). This will provide sufficient clearance between the tool bit and the center point.

2. A straight or left-hand *offset toolholder.*

3. The smallest-size *lathe dog* that will fit your workpiece.

4. A steel rule, scriber, hermaphrodite caliper, or outside caliper. These tools will be used to mark off the amount to be faced from each end and the overall length.

5. A *half center.* This tailstock center is very convenient when facing work between centers.

Fig. 48-1. Correct setup for facing between centers.

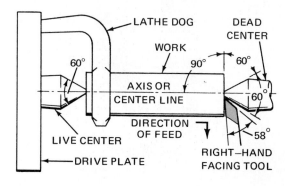

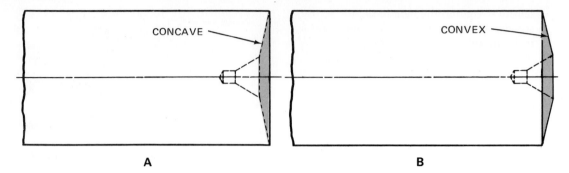

Fig. 48-2. Facing the ends with the tailstock out of alignment: (A) offset toward you (concave) and (B) offset away from you (convex).

It has about one-half of the point ground away so you can feed the tool bit right up to the center hole.

Fig. 48-3. (A) There is plenty of clearance between the tail of the lathe dog and the faceplate. (B) This lathe dog is too small for turning work between centers. It binds on the faceplate and pulls the workpiece off the live center.

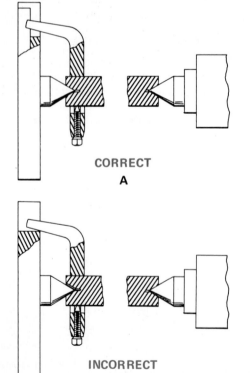

CORRECT
A

INCORRECT
B

PREPARING THE LATHE AND THE WORKPIECE

1. Make sure the centers are aligned accurately. Figure 48-2A shows what happens when the dead center is offset toward you. Figure 48-2B shows the kind of end that is machined if the center is offset the other way.

2. Adjust the lathe for the same speed as for turning.

FACING THE END

1. Fasten a lathe dog to one end of the workpiece. Place the workpiece on the live center first, and then swing the workpiece in line with the dead center. Bring the tailstock up to about 1 in. of the other end, and lock it in place. Apply a little lubricant (white lead and oil) to the center hole. Then turn the dead center into the center hole.

2. Adjust the dead center until the workpiece

Fig. 48-4. A right-cut side-facing tool.

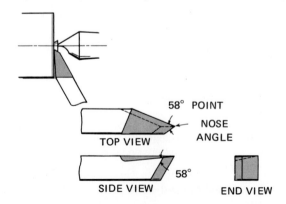

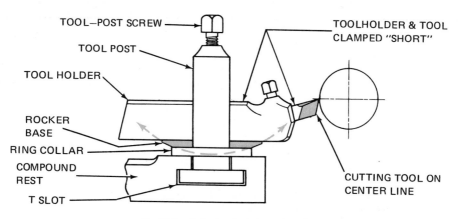

Fig. 48-5. Tool setup for facing and turning.

TOOL–POST SCREW

TOOL POST

TOOL HOLDER

ROCKER BASE

RING COLLAR

COMPOUND REST

T SLOT

TOOLHOLDER & TOOL CLAMPED "SHORT"

CUTTING TOOL ON CENTER LINE

is held snugly between centers. The workpiece should not be so loose that the lathe dog clatters, nor so tight that the dead center becomes scored or burned. Check to be sure that the tail of the lathe dog has plenty of clearance between the sides and bottom of the faceplate slot (Fig. 48-3).

3. Place the right-cut facing tool in the holder with the point well extended (Fig. 48-4). Place the toolholder in the tool post, and adjust it so the cutting-edge of the tool bit is at right angles to the center line. Adjust this by eye.

4. Turn on the power. Place your left hand on the carriage handwheel and your right hand on the cross-feed handle. For a roughing cut, the tool is fed from the outside toward the center. For a finishing cut, the tool is always fed from the center hole toward the outside of the workpiece.

5. If there is a great deal of material to be removed, try to make sure that half is machined from each end. Feed the tool from the outside toward the center for rough cuts. Make several cuts, feeding the tool sideways after each cut.

6. For a finishing cut, turn the cutting-edge of the tool slightly toward the live center. Turn the cross-feed in until the point of the tool just clears the dead center. Do not bump the point of the hardened center (Fig. 48-5).

7. Move the carriage to the left until a light cut is taken. Hold the carriage firmly, or tighten the carriage clamp screw.

Fig. 48-6. Note the position of the cutting tool for facing the end of the workpiece.

Fig. 48-7. A reference line marked 1 in. from the end line makes it easy for you to check for exact length.

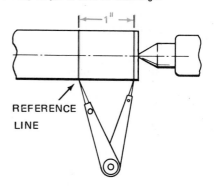

REFERENCE LINE

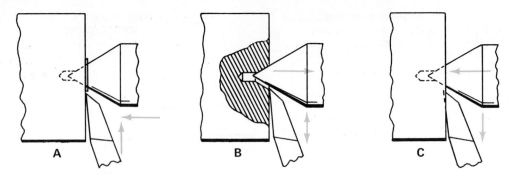

Fig. 48-8. Correct method of removing the burr from around the center hole: (A) facing tool against the workpiece and next to the burr; (B) dead center moved back slightly, burr removed, cutting tool moved out, cut completed; (C) dead center retightened.

8. Now slowly feed from the center hole out. A thin chip should form. On small diameters of 1 in. or less, use the hand feed. On larger diameters, the power cross-feed can be used. Remember to release the carriage clamp screw after each cut (Fig. 48-6).

9. Remove the workpiece from the lathe, and take off the lathe dog. Carefully lay off the length, using a hook rule and scriber or a caliper. Now measure back from this length exactly 1 in. and mark another line around the stock (Fig. 48-7). This will serve as a *reference line* since the exact length line will be covered by chips during the cutting operation.

10. Place the lathe dog on the faced end. Replace the workpiece in the lathe. Rough cut very close to the layout line. Then make a finish cut exactly 1 in. from the reference line. You can use a hermaphrodite caliper to check the distance from the reference line to the end of the stock.

11. In facing, a slight burr will develop along the edge of the center hole. This should be removed during the final facing operation (Fig. 48-8). Place the cutting tool near the tailstock center and against the workpiece that is revolving. Release the tailstock spindle slightly. This will allow the tailstock center to move away from the workpiece. Feed the facing tool manu-

ally against the burr to cut it off. As soon as the burr is removed, back off the facing tool and tighten up the tailstock. Complete the finish facing by slowly moving the cutting tool out or away from the dead center.

12. A *half center* may be used in place of the dead center (Fig. 48-9). This eliminates the problem of removing the burr since the cutter bit can start at the center hole. Use the half center only for facing, never for turning. The half center does not have enough bearing surface and will not hold lubricant.

Fig. 48-9. Using a half center to face the ends of the workpiece. This eliminates the problem of cutting off the burr around the hole.

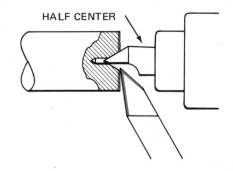

HALF CENTER

UNIT 49. Rough Turning between Centers

Rough turning is the operation of removing excess stock (material) from the workpiece as quickly and efficiently as possible. The workpiece should be rough-machined to about $\frac{1}{32}$ in. over the finished size or dimension given on the print.

TOOLS NEEDED

1. A *lathe dog* with an opening that is a little larger than the diameter of the workpiece.

2. A *right-cut roughing tool* for making heavy roughing cuts toward the live center (Fig. 49-1). This tool will cut easily but will not produce a very smooth finish. The cutting-edge of the tool is straight and the nose only slightly rounded. This small nose radius helps to prevent the point from breaking off. The exact shape of the tool will vary with the machining to be done.

3. A *straight toolholder*.

4. An outside caliper and rule to measure the diameter.

PREPARING THE LATHE

1. Make sure that the live and dead centers are aligned and that the live center runs true (Fig. 49-2). To check if the center runs true, reverse the toolholder in the tool post. Adjust it finger tight to the same angle as the center. Bring the end of the holder close to the center. Then revolve the spindle by hand, and watch for the space between the center and the end of the holder. If necessary, true up the center point by setting the compound slide to one-half the included angle of the center point and taking a light cut with the tool bit.

2. Check to see that the driving plate is tight. Adjust the compound rest at about 30 degrees (°) to the right so that the compound-feed handle will not be in the way of the cross-feed handle.

3. Adjust the speed and feed (see Unit 46). Generally, fast speeds are needed for soft metals and smaller diameters, and slow speeds for large diameters and hard metals.

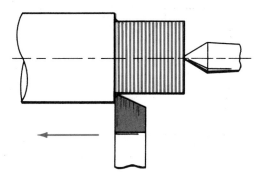

Fig. 49-1. A good type of roughing tool to use for removing a lot of material quickly.

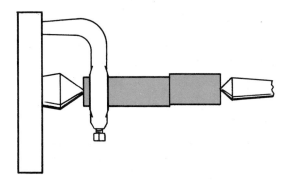

Fig. 49-2. This shows what happens when the center does not run true. Note that the machined diameters are out of alignment.

4. Check to see that the carriage is free (not locked) and that the feed-change lever is in the correct position so you can use the power feed.

ROUGH TURNING

1. Attach the lathe dog to the workpiece. Clamp the dog near one end with the tail turned out. When the workpiece is in position between centers, the tail of the dog should be in the slot of the driving plate (Fig. 49-3).

Make sure that the tail of the lathe dog does not bind in the faceplate slot. If this happens, the workpiece will be pulled off center and the

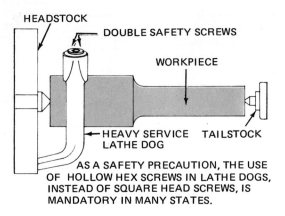

HEADSTOCK

DOUBLE SAFETY SCREWS

WORKPIECE

HEAVY SERVICE LATHE DOG   TAILSTOCK

AS A SAFETY PRECAUTION, THE USE OF HOLLOW HEX SCREWS IN LATHE DOGS, INSTEAD OF SQUARE HEAD SCREWS, IS MANDATORY IN MANY STATES.

Fig. 49-3. A good setup for turning between centers.

turning will be inaccurate. If necessary, change the size of the lathe dog or use a different face-plate.

2. Put the workpiece in the lathe. Make sure the spindle of the tailstock is in as far as it will go. Move the tailstock assembly until the distance between centers is about 2 in. more than the length of the workpiece. Clamp the tailstock to the bed.

3. Place the dog end of the workpiece over

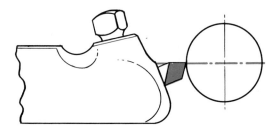

Fig. 49-4. Note that the cutting-edge is set exactly on center.

Fig. 49-5. (A) The cutting-edge of the tool should be set exactly on center to obtain proper front clearance and back rake. (B) This tool is set too high. Note that the front of the tool may actually be rubbing the workpiece rather than cutting. (C) This tool is set too low. Here there is danger that the workpiece may climb over the top of the tool. If a long, thin piece is being turned, the workpiece may actually bend.

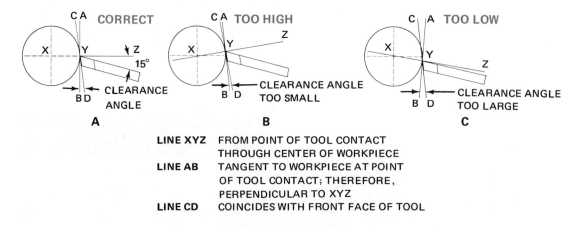

LINE XYZ   FROM POINT OF TOOL CONTACT THROUGH CENTER OF WORKPIECE
LINE AB   TANGENT TO WORKPIECE AT POINT OF TOOL CONTACT; THEREFORE, PERPENDICULAR TO XYZ
LINE CD   COINCIDES WITH FRONT FACE OF TOOL

the live center. Apply some lubricant (white lead and oil) to the tailstock center hole.

4. Turn the tailstock handwheel until the dead center fits firmly into the center hole. Do not tighten enough to cause it to bind, or have it so loose that the dog rattles when the workpiece turns. Move the dog tail back and forth as you adjust the tailstock center to get the proper feel.

5. Insert the cutting tool in the toolholder with only the cutting-edge showing. Clamp it securely.

6. Place the toolholder in the tool post and check for the following.

a. The toolholder must not extend too far out from the tool post (too much overhang).

b. The tool post should be at the left-hand end of the T slot of the compound.

c. The face of the tool bit should be set at center height (on the true axis between the live and dead centers) (Fig. 49–4). Figure 49–5A shows a tool bit with an 8° end relief (23° total angle including the 15° toolholder angle) set exactly on the center line of a workpiece. The clearance angle is measured between the front of the tool (CD) and the line AB, which is tangent to the work at the point of tool contact. The back rake is measured between the top of the tool and the line XYZ, which is a center line through the workpiece at the point of contact and is at a right angle to line AB. If the same tool is set above the center, an entirely different condition exists (Fig. 49–5B). The front clearance is still measured between the front of the tool (CD) and the tangent line AB. However, AB is no longer vertical and the angle of clearance has been greatly reduced. The center line XYZ has also moved so the back rake is now much larger. A tool set in this position would have to be ground entirely different in order to cut properly. If the point of the tool is dropped below the center of the work, the clearance angle increases and the back rake decreases (Fig. 49–5C).

There are some machinists who make a practice of setting the tool slightly above center line; however, they must grind their tools differently. For the average operator, it is recommended that the tool bit be ground to the given angles and *set exactly on center*. For turning some materials such as soft aluminum, the tool can be set slightly above center, if it is ground properly. There are several ways to make sure that the top of the tool is on the center line: (1) line up the point with the live center (Fig. 49–6A); (2) measure the distance from the ways to the headstock center and transfer this measurement to the point of the tool; (3) scribe a light center line on the tailstock spindle or ram, to serve as a guide when setting the tool (Fig. 49–6B).

7. Turn the toolholder until the cutting-edge turns slightly toward the tailstock end (Fig. 49–7A). Figure 49–7B shows what will happen if the tool slips when it is set up in the wrong position.

Fig. 49-6. (A) Setting the cutting tool on center using the live center as a guide. (B) A center line on the ram of the tailstock aids tool setting.

A

B

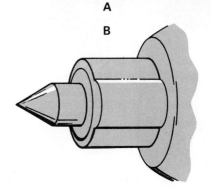

8. Check to see that the carriage can move the required distance without the lathe dog striking the compound rest. It should be able to move slightly more than half the length of the workpiece.

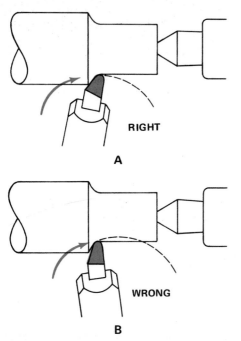

RIGHT

A

WRONG

B

Fig. 49-7. (A) The tool should be set so that it will not dig into the workpiece if anything occurs during machining to change its direction. (B) If set incorrectly, the cutting tool will dig into the workpiece.

Fig. 49-8. Checking diameter with a caliper.

9. Turn on the power and pull in the clutch.

10. Place your left hand on the carriage handwheel and your right hand on the cross-feed handle. Move the carriage to the tailstock end of the workpiece. Turn in the cross-feed until a chip starts to form.

11. Make a trial cut about $\frac{1}{4}$ in. wide and deep enough to true up the workpiece.

12. Stop the lathe and check the diameter with a caliper (Fig. 49-8). If the workpiece is a good deal oversize, it may be necessary to make two or three roughing cuts.

13. Turn on the power and throw in the power longitudinal feed. Check the cutting action. The chip should roll off in small sections (Fig. 49-9). Long chips are dangerous. They get wound around the work, and their razor-sharp edges may cause a bad cut if you try to remove them with your fingers.

CAUTION

When a heavy roughing cut is under way, watch carefully so that the dead center does not become overheated. Excess heat can score the center. Remember, as the workpiece becomes hot from friction it expands. Therefore, you may have to loosen the tailstock a little and also replace the tailstock lubricant several times. A revolving dead center can reduce the problem. A good machinist can smell when the dead center is becoming overheated.

14. There should be no *chattering*. Chattering is a vibration caused by a slight jumping of the workpiece away from the cutting tool. Such vibration results in the formation of small ridges on the surface of the workpiece. Chattering is usually caused by:

   a. A cutting tool that is dull or ground incorrectly

   b. A lack of rigidity in the workpiece or tool

   c. Too much overhang on the cutting tool or holder

   d. A loose part on the lathe

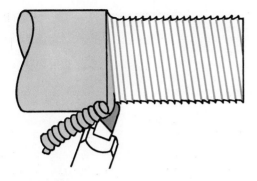

Fig. 49-9.   Rough turning.

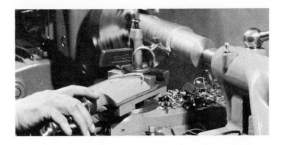

Fig. 49-10.   Machining the first half of the workpiece. In this setup, one end of the workpiece is held in a chuck.

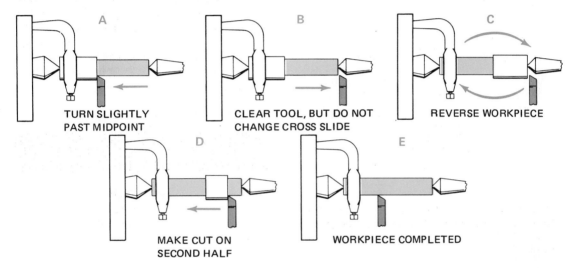

A   TURN SLIGHTLY PAST MIDPOINT

B   CLEAR TOOL, BUT DO NOT CHANGE CROSS SLIDE

C   REVERSE WORKPIECE

D   MAKE CUT ON SECOND HALF

E   WORKPIECE COMPLETED

Fig. 49-11.   Turning between centers without resetting the cross slide.

15. Make a cut that is somewhat longer than half the length of the workpiece. Watch the cutting action, and look at the dead (tailstock) center at intervals. Don't allow the dead (tailstock) center to become dry and to smoke. You can easily ruin a center this way. When the cutting has reached past the halfway point, release the longitudinal power feed and back out the cross-feed (Fig. 49-10).

16. Return the carriage to the starting position.

17. If necessary, make a second and third cut until the caliper size is correct. Always stop the machine before measuring the workpiece.

18. Remove the stock from the lathe. Place the lathe dog on the machined end. Lubricate the dead-center hole and replace the work in the lathe.

19. Turn the other half to rough size.

20. Some machinists prefer not to back out the cross-feed after releasing the longitudinal power feed. Instead, they stop the machine. The workpiece is then removed, the carriage returned to the starting position, the lathe dog reversed, and the second end machined without changing the setting of the cross-feed (Fig. 49-11). If this method is used and a heavy cut is made, reduce the feed to avoid overloading the tool.

UNIT 50. Finish Turning between Centers

The second step in machining between centers is finish turning. *Finish turning* involves machining a surface to an accurate size and, at the same time, getting a very smooth finish.

TOOLS AND EQUIPMENT NEEDED

1. A *lathe dog*. This may be somewhat smaller than the one used for rough turning. Always use the smallest size dog available.

2. A small piece of soft copper or aluminum to protect the finished surface of the metal from the setscrew in the dog.

3. A *right-cut finishing tool*. This is similar in shape to the roughing tool, except that the nose radius is larger. Also, this tool should be honed to a very keen cutting-edge (Fig. 50-1). A round-nose tool bit may also be used for this operation because it can cut in both directions.

4. A *straight toolholder*.

5. A *micrometer caliper*.

PREPARING THE LATHE

Check the operation of the micrometer collars on the cross- and compound-rest feeds. These collars are usually divided into 100 or 125 equal parts (Fig. 50-2). Therefore, one complete turn of the cross-feed handle will equal 0.100 or 0.125 in.

Fig. 50-2. This micrometer collar is divided into 125 parts (0.125 in.). Eight complete turns of the handle will move the tool bit 1 in.

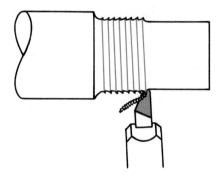

Fig. 50-3. Note how the finishing cut removes a smaller chip and results in a much smoother surface than does the roughing cut.

There is a set- or thumbscrew that locks each collar to its shaft. Loosening these screws allows the collars to move freely. Therefore, they can be readily set at zero. Before setting the collars to zero, be sure to turn the feed handles at least a half turn in the direction in which the feed screw is rotated. This is necessary because there is always some play (backlash) between a thread and nut. Play must be taken up before adjusting the collars.

To obtain a fine finish on the workpiece, adjust the speed faster than that for rough turning. Also use a finer feed (Fig. 50-3).

Fig. 50-1. A right-hand finishing tool is designed to take a light cut.

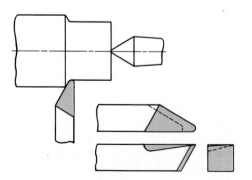

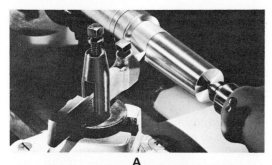

A

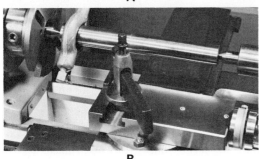

B

Fig. 50-4. (A) Making a finishing cut with the compound rest set at 90°. (B) Some machinists like to adjust the compound rest at right angles to the cross slide when making the finishing cut. This helps to eliminate errors due to backlash.

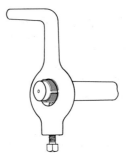

Fig. 50-5. Protecting the finished surface of a workpiece with a soft metal collar.

Fig. 50-6. Checking diameter with a micrometer.

FINISH TURNING

1. Insert the finishing tool bit in a toolholder, and adjust it as described in the previous unit.

2. Place the workpiece between centers, and lubricate the dead-center end. Make a *light* trial cut about $\frac{1}{2}$ in. long. Do not move the cross-feed after taking the trial cut.

3. Mike the machined surface to see how much stock is to be removed. Let us suppose that the machined surface is 0.004 in. oversize.

4. Set the micrometer collar to zero without disturbing the cross-feed screw. Move the tool to the right of the workpiece. Now turn in the cross-feed 0.002 in.

5. Make a trial cut about $\frac{1}{2}$ in. long by moving the carriage with the handwheel.

6. Stop the machine and mike the surface. If necessary, change the setting on the micrometer collar to obtain the correct diameter.

7. Metal shrinks when it is cooled. Therefore, when close limits are to be held, be sure the workpiece is cool before the finish cut is taken.

8. Finish turn the first half of the workpiece (Fig. 50-4). Then remove it from the lathe.

9. Place a piece of soft sheet copper or aluminum around the finished end of the workpiece, and replace the lathe dog (Fig. 50-5).

10. Turn the second half to size, using the same micrometer collar. Always check the size of the workpiece with a micrometer (Fig. 50-6).

11. Sometimes two- to three-thousandths of an inch may be left for filing, grinding, and polishing operations.

Perhaps the most difficult operation for a beginner in machine work is to make accurate measurements. So much depends on the accuracy of the work that every effort should be made to become proficient in the use of measuring instruments. A certain "feel" in the application of micrometers is developed through experience alone; do not be discouraged if your first efforts give imperfect results.

UNIT 51. Turning Work to Two Diameters

On many jobs the workpiece must be turned to several different diameters. The part that connects two diameters is called a *shoulder*. There are four kinds of shoulders (Fig. 51-1):

1. The *square* shoulder

2. The *angular, beveled,* or *chamfered* shoulder

3. The *filleted* shoulder (a concave surface), which gives the most strength between the diameters

4. The *undercut* shoulder

TOOLS AND EQUIPMENT NEEDED

1. A lathe dog, rule, scriber, outside caliper, and hermaphrodite caliper.

2. A right-cut roughing and finishing tool bit, a right-cut side-facing tool bit, a straight-shank cutting-off tool bit, and a roundnose (radius) turning tool bit.

3. A *radius gage* is needed if a filleted shoulder is to be cut. A radius gage consists of a number of thin blades, each of which has a very accurate concave or convex end cut to a specific radius. This gage is used to grind the tool and check the workpiece (Fig. 51-2).

SETTING UP THE JOB

1. Study the drawing or print, and select rough stock of the right size.

2. Face the ends to rough length.

3. Rough-turn the workpiece to about $\frac{1}{32}$ in. over the largest diameter.

ROUGH-TURNING THE RIGHT-HAND END

1. Face the right end of the stock with a right-cut side-facing tool. This becomes the reference point for all other measurements on the workpiece.

2. Choose a right-cut roughing tool, and adjust it for straight turning.

3. Mark the first length with a rule and scriber or a hermaphrodite caliper (Fig. 51-3). Then cut a small recess at this layout line.

4. Rough-turn the first diameter to $\frac{1}{32}$ in. oversize.

5. Remeasure the length of the first diameter from the faced end. At this point make a nick around the workpiece with a sharp cutter bit, or lay off the distance with the hermaphrodite caliper.

FINISH-TURNING THE RIGHT-HAND END OF THE WORKPIECE

1. Turn the first diameter to finished size with a right-cut finishing tool.

2. If a filleted shoulder is to be turned, a roundnose tool can be used for turning and facing. Using the power feed, turn to within $\frac{1}{32}$ in. of the shoulder mark. Then, with the hand feed, turn up to the shoulder.

3. Turn the cross slide out by hand to do the facing. If an exact radius is shown on the print, use a radius gage to grind the nose of the tool

Fig. 51-1. Four kinds of shoulders.

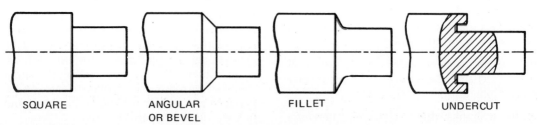

SQUARE   ANGULAR OR BEVEL   FILLET   UNDERCUT

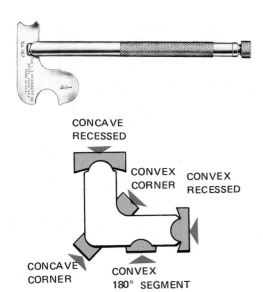

Fig. 51-2. A radius gage with handle. These gages are available in sizes from $\frac{1}{32}$ to $\frac{1}{2}$ in. Each size has five different gaging edges of the same radius.

CONCAVE RECESSED

CONVEX CORNER

CONVEX RECESSED

CONCAVE CORNER

CONVEX 180° SEGMENT

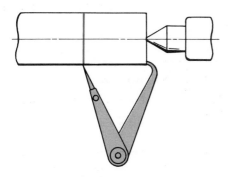

Fig. 51-3. Marking the location of a shoulder from the end using a hermaphrodite caliper.

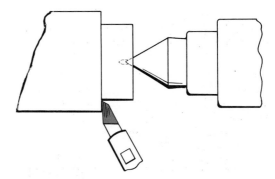

Fig. 51-4. Machining a square shoulder.

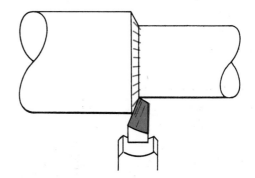

Fig. 51-5. Machining an angular or beveled shoulder.

parting tool is inserted about $\frac{1}{32}$ in. back of the shoulder line, and enters the work within $\frac{1}{32}$ in. of the smaller diameter. Stock may then be machined away by taking heavy cuts (Fig. 51-8). This eliminates detailed measuring and speeds up production.

CAUTION

Never attempt to cut off stock that is held between centers.

and to check the shoulder. Check the length from the faced end with a rule.

4. If a square or beveled shoulder is required, use a right-cut side-facing tool (Figs. 51-4, 51-5, and 51-6).

5. If there are more than three different diameters on the same workpiece, turn the other diameters as described above.

6. A parting tool can also be used when machining a straight shoulder (Fig. 51-7). The

ROUGH- AND FINISH-TURNING THE LEFT-HAND END

1. Reverse the workpiece in the lathe. Cover the finished end with a piece of soft metal, and then install a smaller dog.

Fig. 51-6. Machining a shoulder on a piece held in a collet.

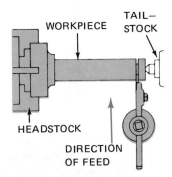

Fig. 51-7. Using a straight-shank cutting-off tool to locate the position and depth of a shoulder.

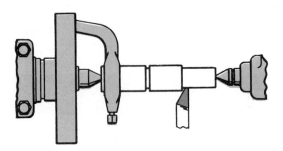

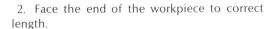

Fig. 51-8. Note that the cutting tool can easily cut up to the shoulder.

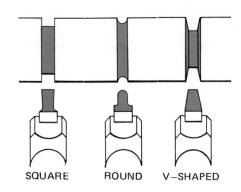

SQUARE   ROUND   V-SHAPED

Fig. 51-9. Types of grooves.

Fig. 51-10. Cutting a groove in work held in a chuck.

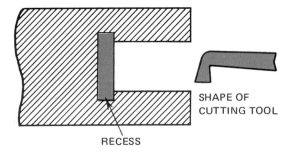

SHAPE OF CUTTING TOOL

RECESS

Fig. 51-11. Cutting a recess with a boring tool.

2. Face the end of the workpiece to correct length.

3. Mark the width of the largest diameter. Cut a nick with the sharp point of a cutting tool.

4. Rough-turn the small diameter up to this nick.

5. Finish-turn the small diameter up to this nick.

6. Face the shoulder at the largest diameter until the length is correct.

7. Turn the outside of the cylinder to the finish diameter.

CUTTING A GROOVE (NECK) OR RECESS

1. The process of cutting a groove in a workpiece is sometimes referred to as *undercutting,* or *necking.* The groove can be square, rounded, or V shaped (Fig. 51-9). Often, in left-hand thread cutting, a groove is machined at the end of the threads to start the cutting tool.

2. A square-nose tool bit or a cutoff tool is used for a square groove. A roundnose tool bit is used if the groove is rounded.

3. Set up the tool at right angles to the workpiece (Fig. 51-10).

4. Feed the tool in slowly by hand. If chatter develops, reduce the spindle speed.

5. *Recessing* refers to cutting a groove on the inside of a hole. This must be done with a square-nose boring tool (Fig. 51-10).

UNIT 52. Installing a Chuck and Mounting the Workpiece

Workpieces too short to be held between centers are clamped in a chuck. A *lathe chuck* is a device for holding and rotating workpieces. It is used for such operations as drilling, boring, reaming, and sometimes for turning. When used for turning, the chuck holds one end of the workpiece while a dead center supports the other.

TYPES OF CHUCKS

The *three-jaw universal chuck* is the simplest to use because all three of its jaws move in and out together (Fig. 52-1). It is very accurate when new and will center work to within 0.003 in. It loses its accuracy as the jaws become worn.

The three-jaw universal chuck comes equipped with two sets of jaws. One set has the high ends toward the center and these are called *inside jaws.* The other set has the high ends toward the outside of the chuck. These are called *outside jaws* (see Fig. 52-1). For short workpieces of small diameter, use the inside jaws since they provide the greatest tool clearance. These jaws can also be used to clamp the inside of pipe or tubing by gripping internally. For large-diameter workpieces, the jaws with the high ends toward the outside are used (Fig. 52-2).

To change jaws on the universal chuck, open them with a chuck key as far as they will go. Remove the jaws one by one. On most chucks the jaws and the slot into which they fit are stamped with Nos. 1, 2, and 3. When installing the new jaws, turn the chuck key until the end of the thread just clears the No. 1 slot, then put the No. 1 jaw in position. Tap it lightly with a mallet or soft-faced hammer. Turn the chuck key until the thread catches the No. 1 jaw, then proceed to Nos. 2 and 3. Completely close the jaws to see if they center properly.

The *four-jaw independent chuck* is more accurate than the three-jaw universal and can

Fig. 52-1. A three-jaw universal chuck set including two sets of jaws and a chuck key or wrench.

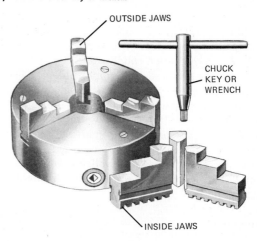

OUTSIDE JAWS

CHUCK KEY OR WRENCH

INSIDE JAWS

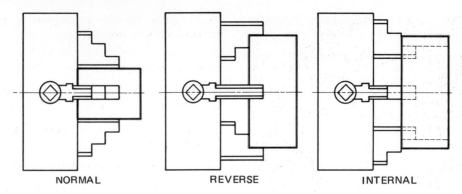

NORMAL   REVERSE   INTERNAL

Fig. 52-2. Ways of holding a workpiece in a three-jaw chuck.

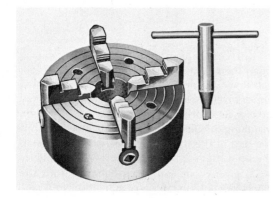

Fig. 52-3. Four-jaw independent chuck.

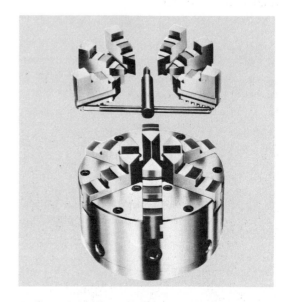

Fig. 52-4. This six-jaw combination (universal) chuck has a micrometer adjusting mechanism that permits accuracy.

hold most shapes of workpieces including irregular shapes, such as brackets, castings, or forgings (Fig. 52-3). Each jaw can be adjusted independently, and the chuck's accuracy is not affected by wear. The jaws can be reversed to grip either the inside or the outside of the work. Adjusting a four-jaw independent chuck requires more skill than does a three-jaw chuck.

The *combination chuck* is one in which the jaws can be adjusted either independently, like a four-jaw independent chuck, or all together as in the three-jaw universal chuck. The combination chuck is often used when turning duplicate parts that are irregular in shape. The first workpiece is carefully positioned, moving the jaws independently. Then duplicate workpieces are fastened in position using the self-centering socket (Fig. 52-4).

The *drill chuck* is a small universal chuck used mostly for holding drills, reamers, and taps

(Fig. 52-5). It is the same kind of chuck used on a drill press. Attached to the chuck is a taper shank that fits into the headstock or tailstock spindle.

The *headstock chuck* is a small universal chuck (Fig. 52-6A). It is hollow on one end and threaded to fit the spindle nose of the lathe. It can be used for holding small-diameter workpieces for turning. This chuck is also used for holding long bars and rods that slide through the spindle.

A *center-rest chuck* is used in the tailstock of a lathe to support a workpiece that doesn't

306

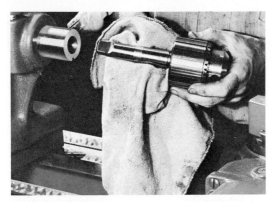

Fig. 52-5. A drill chuck. The shank should be wiped clean before putting it into the spindle hole.

Fig. 52-6. (A) A headstock chuck that screws onto a threaded spindle nose. (B) Mounting work between a drill chuck and a center-rest chuck. The center-rest chuck has bronze jaws for supporting centerless shafts.

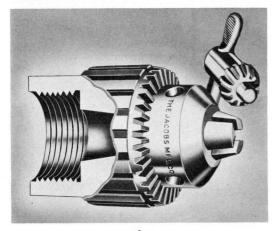

A

B

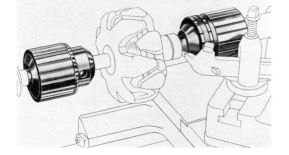

have a center. Bronze jaws are used to hold the workpiece (Fig. 52-6B).

CARE OF CHUCKS

1. Always use the correct chuck key for each kind and size of chuck.

2. When not in use, keep the chuck on a rack or an individual holder.

3. Keep the chuck surface lightly oiled.

4. Clean the moving parts, and keep them free of chips and dirt. Apply a little graphite to the scroll threads and jaw slots. Do not use oil as it will fly out and ruin your clothing when the lathe is started.

TYPES OF SPINDLE NOSES

Lathes come equipped with three types of spindle noses: the threaded spindle nose, the long taper key-drive spindle nose, and the cam-lock drive spindle nose. The method of installing chucks and faceplates varies with the kind of spindle nose used on the lathe.

INSTALLING A CHUCK ON A THREADED SPINDLE NOSE

Many chucks are mounted on a plate that has an internal thread. This thread matches the external thread of a threaded spindle nose.

1. Remove the faceplate by turning it counter-clockwise.

2. Force out the live center and reducing sleeve with a knock-out bar. Grasp the live center in your right hand as you tap lightly with the bar (Fig. 52-7). Do not let the center drop.

3. With a rag wipe the threads and the shoulder of the spindle to remove any chips or dirt. Apply a few drops of oil.

4. If a short workpiece is to be machined, place a rag or piece of cotton waste in the spindle hole to keep out the chips. Of course, this can't be done when long bar stock is to be fed through the spindle.

5. Place a scrap piece of wood or a wooden cradle over the ways of the bed. Lift the chuck onto it.

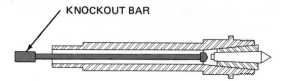

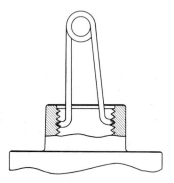

Fig. 52-7. Removing the live center with a knock-out bar.

Fig. 52-8. Cleaning the threads of a chuck with a wire cleaner.

Fig. 52-9. Installing a chuck on a threaded spindle. Notice how the wooden cradle on which the chuck rests protects the bed of the lathe.

6. Clean out the threads of the chuck with a bent wire cleaner (Fig. 52-8).

7. Open the jaws until you can get your finger into the center.

8. Move the cradle and chuck directly up to the spindle.

9. Lift the chuck and turn it clockwise onto the spindle (Fig. 52–9).

10. After it is started, hold the chuck firmly and rotate the spindle by hand.

When the chuck is about $\frac{1}{32}$ in. from the shoulder, rotate the chuck itself with a sharp turning motion. A soft thud indicates a good, firm seating. Do not tighten the chuck too much or it will be difficult to remove later on.

Removing a Chuck from a Threaded Spindle Nose. There are many ways to remove lathe chucks. Each machinist has his favorite way. Some of the methods are as follows.

1. Turn the chuck until the wrench hole is at a top position. Pull in the back gears that lock the spindle. Place the wrench in the chuck, and pull toward you sharply.

2. Engage the back gears so the spindle will move under pressure. Place a short stick between the bed and one of the jaws, as shown in Fig. 52-10. Turn the pulley by hand in a clockwise direction.

3. On a really tight chuck, engage the back gears. Get a soft metal bar (brass or copper) several feet long. Place one end between the jaws of the chuck. Slowly lift up on the end of the bar and then, with a quick jerk, draw it toward you. This will usually loosen the chuck. If necessary, strike the bar near the chuck with a soft lead or brass hammer while pulling down on the bar.

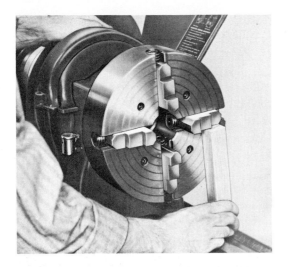

Fig. 52-10. Removing a chuck. A short stick is used to keep the chuck from turning. Note that the machinist is turning the belt clockwise to loosen the chuck.

When the chuck is loose, open the jaws until you can get your finger into its center. Place the board or cradle under the chuck. Slowly turn the chuck until it comes off. Then lower the chuck onto the cradle, and return it to its storage place.

MOUNTING A CHUCK ON A LONG-TAPER KEY DRIVE NOSE

1. Before mounting the chuck on the lathe, carefully clean the taper on the spindle nose and the threads of the spindle nose collar. Also clean the taper and threads of the chuck or faceplate.

CAUTION

Chips and dirt may score mating surfaces, causing an inaccurate fit.

2. Rotate the lathe spindle until its key is in the up position. Lock the spindle by engaging the back gear and push the handwheel pin in. Next, lock the chuck or faceplate on the spindle nose (Fig. 52–11). Then tighten the collar by turning it with a spanner wrench in a counter-clockwise direction (Fig. 52–12). Be sure to unlock the spindle before turning the power on.

Removing a Chuck on a Long-taper Key Drive Nose.

To remove the chuck:

1. Lock the spindle by placing the back gear knob in the engaged position and pushing the handwheel pin in.

Fig. 52-11. Installing a chuck on a long-taper key-drive nose.

Fig. 52-12. Tightening the collar with a spanner wrench.

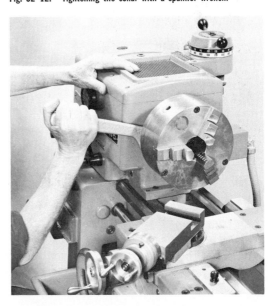

2. Place a heavy board or wooden cradle across the bed ways to protect them if the chuck is dropped.

3. Loosen the collar by turning the spanner wrench clockwise.

4. *Carefully* remove chuck or faceplate.

5. Be sure to unlock the spindle before turning the power on.

CHUCK MOUNTING ON A CAM-LOCK DRIVE SPINDLE

When fitting chucks and faceplates with a cam-lock drive, make sure that the spindle and the chuck tapers are completely clean. Use a wrench to make sure that all the cam-locks are in the released position. Place the chuck on a wooden cradle and slide it against the spindle. Then use the chuck wrench to tighten each cam-lock to the correct position (Fig. 52-13). Once a chuck or faceplate is in position, it is a good idea to mark a reference line on the spindle nose and the chuck. This will help in remounting the chuck. Reverse the above procedure to remove the chuck. It is a good idea to have someone help if it is a fairly heavy chuck.

MOUNTING A WORKPIECE IN A UNIVERSAL CHUCK

1. With the correct chuck key, open the jaws slightly more than the diameter of the work-piece. You must decide on how the workpiece is to be held and which set of jaws to use (Fig. 52-14).

2. Slip the workpiece into the jaws. Rotate the workpiece, and move it up and down as the jaws are tightened. This will help center it accurately.

3. A workpiece of small diameter should not project more than four or five times its diameter.

4. Do not apply too much pressure when holding a workpiece near the outer ends of the jaws. This may spring the jaws and cause them to become inaccurate.

5. Never try to clamp irregular shapes in a universal chuck.

6. Always remove the chuck key before turning on the power.

MOUNTING A WORKPIECE IN AN INDEPENDENT JAW CHUCK

1. Open each of the four jaws until the work-piece will slide in approximately on center. Use the circles on the chuck face as a guide. Match the nearest circle on the chuck face to the corresponding marks on the jaws.

2. Tighten each opposing jaw a little at a time until the workpiece is held firmly, but not too tightly.

3. Follow one of the following methods to center the workpiece accurately.

Fig. 52-13. The chuck installed on a cam-lock drive spindle.

Fig. 52-14. A workpiece correctly mounted in the universal chuck.

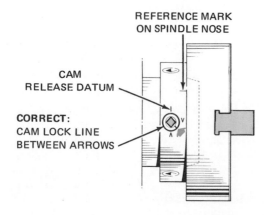

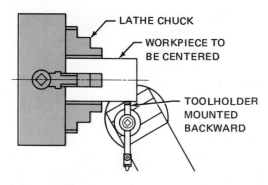

Fig. 52-15. Aligning the workpiece with the butt end of the toolholder.

Fig. 52-17. Aligning the workpiece with a dial indicator.

Fig. 52-16. Aligning the workpiece using a piece of chalk to determine the high or low side.

Fig. 52-18. Note how the four-jaw chuck can be used to hold rectangular-shaped work.

a. Turn the butt end of a toolholder inward, and tighten it finger-tight only in the tool post (Fig. 52-15). Move the carriage and cross slide until the end of the toolholder just clears the outside of the workpiece. Now slowly rotate the chuck by hand. The workpiece is centered if the space between it and the toolholder is uniform. If the toolholder touches the workpiece on one side (the high side) and there is clearance on the other side (low side), the workpiece is not centered. Turn the low side near you and loosen the jaw. Tighten the opposite jaw. You may need to do this several times to get the workpiece true. The beginner often has difficulty because he opens one jaw too much. Remember, the amount to move the jaw is always one-half the amount of the error. Also, do not tighten the jaws too

tightly while centering the work. When the work is centered accurately, tighten each jaw in turn to hold the work securely. A hollow workpiece will spring out of shape if jaws are tightened too much.

b. Hold a piece of chalk near the workpiece, and revolve the chuck slowly with your left hand (Fig. 52-16). The chalk will mark the high side of the workpiece. Loosen the jaw across from this chalk mark and tighten the opposite jaw slightly.

c. For more accurate centering use a dial indicator gage (Fig. 52-17). Clamp the gage holder in the tool post, and fasten the gage to it. Move the carriage until the plunger of the indicator is in contact with the workpiece. Set the indicator at zero. Now rotate the chuck slowly by hand. This will

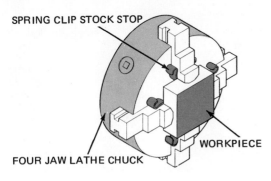

SPRING CLIP STOCK STOP

WORKPIECE

FOUR JAW LATHE CHUCK

Fig. 52-19. Using spring-clip stops to hold the workpiece away from the chuck. Spring-clips are used when drilling, boring, and reaming to keep the cutting tool from striking the chuck.

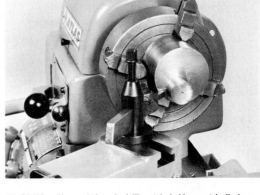

Fig. 52-20. The workpiece is deliberately held eccentrically in a four-jaw independent chuck in order to make this cut.

show the high and low sides. Adjust the jaws one-half the amount of the error until the indicator hand does not move during one revolution of the chuck.

4. If you are machining several identical workpieces, loosen only two adjoining jaws to remove the workpiece. Then mount the next workpiece by tightening these same two jaws. The work should be quite accurately centered, but be sure to check it with the indicator before machining.

5. The four-jaw chuck can be used to hold square, rectangular, or irregular shaped workpieces as well as round stock (Fig. 52–18).

6. If several identical pieces are to be turned, drilled, or bored, a good way to hold the pieces away from the chuck is to use sets of brass spring clips. (Fig. 52–19).

7. Sometimes the workpiece is mounted eccentrically in the four-jaw chuck to turn a cylinder that is eccentric with the larger diameter (Fig. 52–20).

UNIT 53.

Facing, Turning, and Cutting Off a Workpiece Mounted in a Chuck

On workpieces that are short in length, all machining can be done with the workpiece mounted in a chuck. This includes such operations as facing, turning, and cutting off (Fig. 53–1).

FACING IN A CHUCK

Facing is the process of machining the end of the workpiece so that it is square with the center line. Generally, for rough cutting, the tool

is fed from the outside of the workpiece toward its center. For finish cutting, the tool is fed from the center of the workpiece to the circumference.

1. For roughing cuts use a left-cut roughing tool. Clamp the cutting tool in the holder. Fasten the holder in the tool post near the left side of the T slot of the compound rest. The holder should be at an angle of somewhat less than 90 degrees (°) to the workpiece face (Fig. 53–2). Make sure the face of the cutting tool is on center. Adjust to the approximate cutting speed used to turn the outside of the workpiece. Start at the outside of the workpiece, and move the carriage until the chip begins to form. Lock the

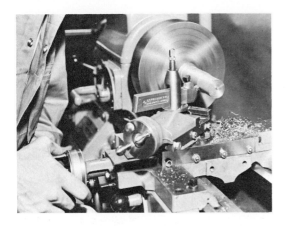

Fig. 53-1. Turning the outside of a workpiece that is held in a chuck. Although a straight-shank toolholder is used here, it would have been better if a left-hand (offset) holder had been used.

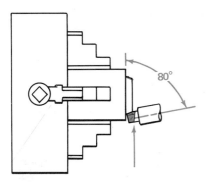

TOOL FEED FROM OUTSIDE

Fig. 53-2. When rough facing with a cutting tool like that shown, the tool should be set at an angle of approximately 80° to the workpiece.

Fig. 53-3. For finish turning, the tool is held at an angle of about 80° and fed toward the outside of the workpiece.

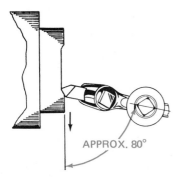

APPROX. 80°

carriage to the bed with the carriage lock screw. Use the power cross-feed to make the cut to the center of the face.

2. For finishing cuts use a right-cut side-facing tool. Clamp the tool in a left-hand offset holder. Adjust the holder until the cutting edge makes an angle of about 8 to 10° with the workpiece face. Turn in the cross-feed until the point is at the center of the workpiece. Apply slight pressure to the carriage until the chip begins to form (Fig. 53-3). Lock the carriage. If the diameter is small, turn the cross-feed out by hand. For larger diameters use the power cross-feed. Always make the finishing cut from the center out.

3. If the cutting tool isn't exactly on center, a small projection (nub) will form. A rounded nub will form if the tool is above center. A square nub will form if the tool is below center.

4. There are two ways to remove a very accurate amount of material during the facing operation. The compound rest can be adjusted parallel to the bed of the lathe so that feed can be controlled with the micrometer collar. The compound rest can be adjusted so that it is 60° to the left of the center line or 30° to the right of the cross slide. With this setting, a movement of 0.002 in. on the compound rest will move the cutting tool in 0.001 in.

5. If a large amount of material must be removed by facing, it may be best to rough machine to length by making a number of deep cuts longitudinally instead of across the face. This is known as *step facing* (Fig. 53-4).

Fig. 53-4. Step facing.

TURNING THE OUTSIDE OF A WORKPIECE HELD IN A CHUCK

1. Fasten a right-cut tool in a left-hand (offset) toolholder.

2. Clamp the toolholder in a tool post near the left side of the T slot of the compound rest.

3. Check to see that the cutting tool can machine the finished length of the workpiece without allowing the chuck to strike the carriage or the compound slide (Fig. 53-5).

4. Adjust for the correct speed and feed.

5. Follow the same procedure for rough and finish turning as for turning between centers.

CUTTING OFF STOCK

1. Cutting off can be done with the workpiece held in a chuck or collet. *Never try to cut off the workpiece when turning between centers. It can't be done.*

2. Two types of cutting-off toolholders are available: rigid-pattern and spring- (gooseneck) pattern. A rigid-pattern toolholder may have a straight, right-hand, or left-hand shank. The spring pattern toolholder is available with straight and right-hand shanks only (Fig. 53-6). The advantage of the spring or gooseneck toolholder is that it provides automatic relief from any sudden or excessive pressure on the cutter

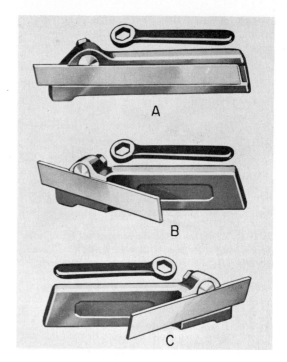

Fig. 53-6. Cutting-off tools and holders: (A) straight, (B) right-hand offset, and (C) left-hand offset.

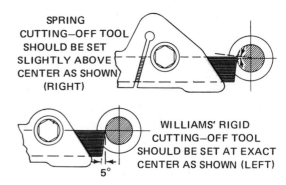

SPRING CUTTING—OFF TOOL SHOULD BE SET SLIGHTLY ABOVE CENTER AS SHOWN (RIGHT)

WILLIAMS' RIGID CUTTING—OFF TOOL SHOULD BE SET AT EXACT CENTER AS SHOWN (LEFT)

5°

Fig. 53-7. Note the difference in settings when using a spring cutting-off toolholder and a rigid toolholder.

Fig. 53-5. Turning with the workpiece held in a chuck.

blade (Fig. 53-7). A cutting-off tool blade that fits a quick-change toolholder can also be used for cutting off stock (Fig. 53-8).

Tools used for cutting off stock have a side clearance of about 5°, a square cutting-edge, and no back rake. Their end relief should be about 5 to 10° (Fig. 53-9). Cutoff blades are sharpened by grinding their ends only.

Fig. 53-8. Cutting off stock using the quick-change toolholder unit.

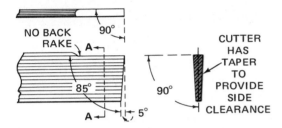

Fig. 53-9. Proper clearance angles for the cutting-off blade.

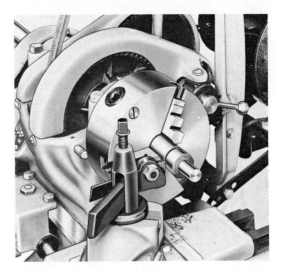

Fig. 53-10. Cutting off a workpiece held in a chuck.

3. There are two common problems associated with cutting off stock to length: chattering and hogging in.

a. *Chattering* occurs when the tool is not held rigidly enough. Any looseness in the tool, holder, or any part of the lathe itself can result in chattering.

b. *Hogging in* occurs when a tool digs into the metal or when the workpiece climbs over the top of the tool's cutting-edge. This usually stops the spindle rotation or breaks off the blade. There are several reasons why a workpiece might climb the tool bit. The reason may be that the tool is set too low, the spindle is loose in its bearings, or the tool is deflected by the force of the cut so that it swings below center and into the work. Spring toolholders are available that will permit the tool to swing away from the workpiece.

4. Fasten the tool in the toolholder. The blade should extend from the holder a distance equal to a little more than half the diameter of the workpiece.

5. When using a rigid holder, adjust the cutting-edge of the tool so that it is on center and at right angles to the workpiece. If the cutting-edge is too high, the tool will rub. If it is too low, the tool will dig in. When using a spring-type holder, set the cutting-edge of the tool slightly above center.

6. Lock the toolholder in the tool post near the left side of the slot of the compound.

7. Adjust the speed to about two-thirds the speed required for turning.

8. Mark the location of the cut. Try to cut off as close to the chuck as possible.

9. Slowly feed the cutting tool into the workpiece (Fig. 53-10). Grip the cross-feed handle with both hands in order to feed it steadily and uniformly.

10. Apply plenty of cutting lubricant with a brush or oilcan. No lubricant is needed for cast iron or nonferrous metals.

11. If the tool hogs in, turn off the power and reverse the spindle by hand. Then back out the cutting tool with the cross-feed.

UNIT 54. Drilling

To make a hole of the right size and finish, one or more of the following operations must be performed.

1. *Drilling* is cutting a hole in solid stock. Most drilling is done on a drill press.

2. *Boring* is enlarging a hole already drilled or made when it was cast in the foundry.

3. *Reaming* finishes a drilled or bored hole so that it is smooth and accurate in size.

When great accuracy is not required, drilling a hole with the correct-size drill is satisfactory. For greater accuracy, the hole may be drilled $\frac{1}{64}$ in. undersize and then machine-reamed to size. For greatest accuracy, the hole is first drilled $\frac{1}{32}$ in. too small, then bored 0.007 to $\frac{1}{64}$ in. undersize, and finally machine-reamed to finish size. Boring after drilling trues up the hole and makes it straight, thus removing any errors caused by the drill running out from end to end (Fig. 54-1).

Drilling in the lathe can be done in three ways.

1. With the workpiece revolving in a chuck and the drill held in the tailstock drill holder or a drill chuck.

2. With the workpiece revolving in a chuck and the drill held in a quick-change toolholder mounted on the carriage (Fig. 54-2).

3. With the drill revolving in a drill chuck and the workpiece held against a *tailstock pad* or *crotch*.

DRILLING WITH WORK REVOLVING IN A CHUCK

1. Center the workpiece accurately in a three- or four-jaw chuck.

CAUTION

Make sure there is clearance behind the workpiece so the drill will not strike the chuck or the spindle as it comes through the workpiece.

2. Face the workpiece.

3. Center drill the location of the hole with a combination center drill and countersink (Fig. 54-3).

4. Check the size of the hole. If it is $\frac{1}{2}$ in. or smaller, use a straight-shank drill held in a drill chuck. If it is over $\frac{1}{2}$ in., use a taper-shank drill held in a *drill holder,* or directly in the tailstock spindle hole (Fig. 54-4).

Fig. 54-1.   Steps in drilling, boring, and reaming.

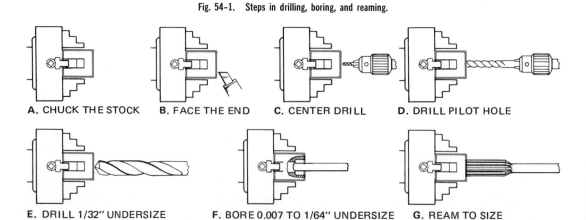

A. CHUCK THE STOCK   B. FACE THE END   C. CENTER DRILL   D. DRILL PILOT HOLE

E. DRILL 1/32" UNDERSIZE   F. BORE 0.007 TO 1/64" UNDERSIZE   G. REAM TO SIZE

Fig. 54-2. Drilling with the tool held in a quick-change toolholder.

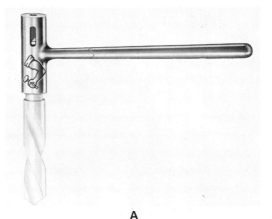

A

Fig. 54-3. Drilling a center hole.

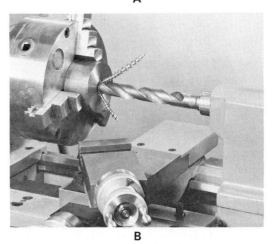

B

Fig. 54-4. (A) A drill holder for taper-shank drills. (B) Sometimes the drill is placed directly in the tailstock spindle or ram. Make sure there is clearance behind the workpiece before starting to drill.

5. Drilling holes $\frac{1}{2}$ in. or smaller:

   a. Remove the dead (tailstock) center, and replace it with a drill chuck. Fasten the drill securely in the chuck.

   b. Adjust the speed for the size of drill.

   c. Turn back the tailstock spindle as far as it will go.

   d. Bring the tailstock assembly up until the point of the drill just clears the workpiece. Lock it tight.

   e. Apply slight tension to the tailstock spindle with the clamp screw.

   f. Turn on the power. Turn the tailstock handwheel to feed the drill into the workpiece. Apply the correct fluid (Fig. 54-5).

   g. If the hole is quite deep, back out the drill several times to clean out the chips.

   h. Reduce the feed as the drill breaks through the back of the workpiece.

   i. Release the tailstock assembly and pull it back to remove the drill.

6. Drilling holes over $\frac{1}{2}$ in.:

   a. Drill a pilot hole with a drill about equal to the web of the larger drill (see step 5).

Fig. 54-5. Drilling with a straight-shank drill held in a drill chuck.

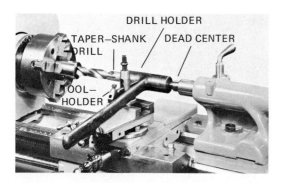

DRILL HOLDER

TAPER–SHANK
DRILL

DEAD CENTER

TOOL–
HOLDER

Fig. 54-6. Drilling with the drill held in a drill holder. Note how the tool post and holder are used to control the depth of drilling.

Fig. 54-7. A four-flute carbide-tipped core drill. Note the flat point.

Fig. 54-8. Drilling with the workpiece held in a chuck and supported by a steady rest.

A

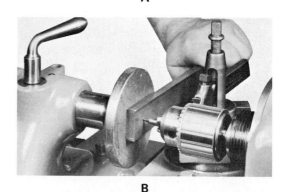

B

Fig. 54-9. (A) Drill pad. (B) Using a center drill to start a hole in flat stock. If a hole is to be drilled completely through the work, then a backup piece of scrap metal or wood should be used.

b. Select a drill holder that fits the taper shank of the drill. If the drill is mounted directly in the tailstock spindle, tap the end of the drill lightly with a lead- or plastic-headed hammer to make sure it is held securely.

c. Fasten a toolholder backward in the tool post. This is done for safety reasons. As a drill breaks through the back or inner end of a workpiece, it may be pulled into the workpiece. If this should happen, the drill holder will be pulled away from the dead center and will swing around with great force. There is a temptation to try to steady the drill and holder with your hand. This is extremely dangerous and can cause serious injury to your hand. The toolholder clamped in the tool post helps to prevent this kind of accident.

d. Place the end of the drill holder against the dead center. Arrange the tool post against the handle so that it cannot be pulled away from the dead center (Fig. 54-6).

e. Adjust the lathe for correct speed.

f. Turn on the power. Feed the drill into the hole by turning the tailstock handwheel. This will force the carriage to move along slowly. The resistance offered by the lathe toolholder will help keep the end of the drill holder against the dead center.

g. After the hole is drilled, turn off the power. Loosen the tailstock. Hold the drill and holder against the dead center as you pull to remove the drill.

7. Drilling a cored hole:

a. When drilling a hole already formed in a casting, it is best to use a three- or four-flute core drill. A standard two-flute drill tends to follow the hole which might be slightly off-center.

b. Make sure the hole is beveled slightly to make sure the drill starts true (Fig. 54-7).

8. Drilling a hole in the end of long stock: If a hole must be drilled in the end of a long workpiece, fasten one of its ends in the chuck and support the other end with a steady rest (Fig. 54-8).

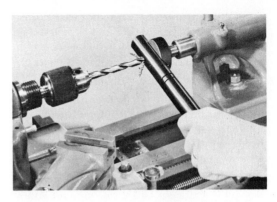

Fig. 54-10.   Drilling a hole with the workpiece held against a crotch center.

DRILLING WITH WORK HELD ON A CROTCH CENTER OR DRILL PAD

1. Fasten a drill chuck in the headstock spindle.

2. Insert a drill of the correct size in the chuck.

3. For a flat or square workpiece, replace the dead center with a *drill pad* (Fig. 54-9).

4. For round stock use the *crotch center* (Fig. 54-10).

5. Adjust the speed.

6. Hold the workpiece in the left hand. Advance the workpiece by turning the tailstock handwheel. A wooden block on the lathe bed can act as a rest for your hand and the workpiece.

UNIT 55. Boring

Boring is a method of rounding and straightening a hole with a single-point cutting tool. This method is also used to cut odd-size or very large holes.

The original hole may have been made with a drill, or it may be a cored hole produced by casting.

If the hole is to be machine-reamed, it should first be bored about $\frac{1}{64}$ in. undersize

(0.007 for $\frac{1}{4}$-in. hole, 0.020 for 1-in. hole, and 0.045 for 3-in. hole). For hand reaming, about 0.005 to 0.008 in. is allowed.

BORING TOOLS, BARS, AND HOLDERS

There are five basic types of boring toolholders in common use.

1. *Light boring toolholder.* This is very often used when boring small diameters. Each tool will hold a number of sizes of bars, varying from

$\frac{1}{8}$ to $\frac{7}{16}$ in. in diameter. The holder has an offset shank that is reversible for right- or left-hand work. By swinging the yoke 180 degrees (°), the holder becomes a right-hand or left-hand tool (Fig. 55-1).

2. *Toolholder and bar with interchangeable ends.* This holder comes equipped with three interchangeable heads for the boring bar. One head holds the cutting tool at an angle of 45°, another at 60°, and the third at 90° (Fig. 55-2).

3. *Clamp-type with plain or sleeve bar.* A plain bar holds a straight cutter on one end and an angular cutter at the other. A sleeve bar provides for rapid adjustment of straight or angular cutters (Figs. 55-3A and 55-3B). Boring bars of this type are also used in conjunction with throwaway carbide-tipped tool bits (Fig. 55-3C).

4. *Three-bar boring tool.* The holder accommodates three sizes of bars. Each bar comes equipped with three heads for 45, 60, and 90° cutting. Speedy changes can be made by a slight turn of the toolholder nut (Fig. 55-4).

5. *Boring bar with quick-change toolholder.* This unit slips on the quick-change tool post. The bar has three ends for 45, 60, and 90° cutting (Fig. 55-5).

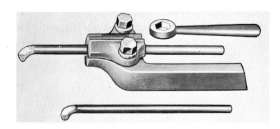

Fig. 55-1. Light boring toolholder. This type should be used only for very small holes.

Fig. 55-2. Toolholder and bar with interchangeable ends.

GRINDING BORING TOOLS

The boring tool is ground like a left-cut turning tool. The boring tool must have more end relief, however, to keep its heel from rubbing. The amount of end relief depends on the size of the

Fig. 55-3. (A) Clamp-type toolholder with plain sleeve. (B) Clamp-type toolholder with adjustable head. A single head holds the cutter at either 45 or 90°. Use the 90° slot for threading. (C) Using a boring tool with a throwaway carbide blade.

A

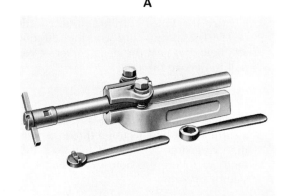

B

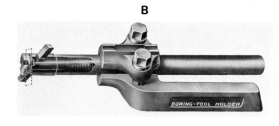

C

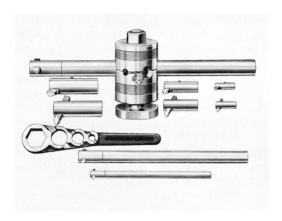

Fig. 55-4. Three-bar boring tool.

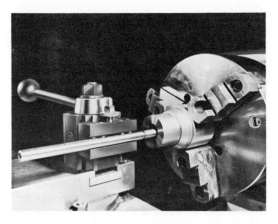

Fig. 55-5. Boring toolholder for quick-change tool post.

Fig. 55-6. (A) The correct angles on a forged boring tool. (B) Boring tools used with a boring tool post holder or a three-bar boring tool.

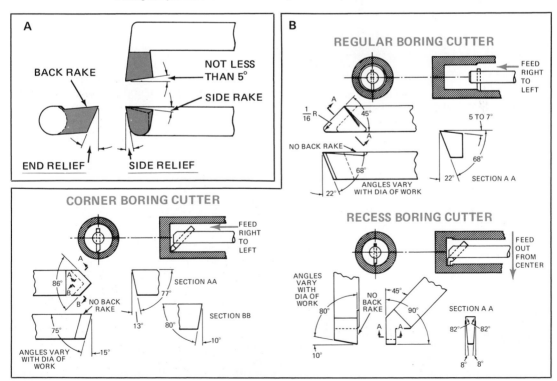

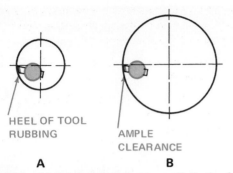

HEEL OF TOOL
RUBBING

AMPLE
CLEARANCE

A   **B**

Fig. 55-7. Note how the end relief must vary with the size of the hole. (A) The heel of the tool is rubbing. (B) Here there is ample clearance between the workpiece and the cutting tool. Note that both cutting tools have the same end relief.

Fig. 55-8. Note, in this setup, that the cut could not be done completely through the workpiece because the end of the boring bar would strike the chuck.

hole. It is never less than 10°, and may be as much as 20° (Fig. 55-6). Figure 55-7 shows one boring tool being used on two holes of different diameter. At the left, the heel of the cutting tool rubs on the workpiece, while in the other hole, it does not. Too large an end-relief angle weakens the cutting-edges and quickly dulls the tool. The side-cutting angle should be about 20° to cause the chip to curl away from the finished cut. The boring tool should also have 12 to 14° side-relief angle and about half the back and side rake as for turning.

Cutting tools come in different shapes. Usually, a roundnose shape is used to bore completely through a hole. For boring up to a shoulder, the tool is ground with a larger *side-cutting angle*. The tool bit in a boring bar is held at right angles to bore all the way through the metal. It is held at an angle of 30, 45, or 60° for boring up to a shoulder.

SETTING UP THE LATHE TO BORE A STRAIGHT HOLE

1. Center the workpiece in the chuck. Make sure there is enough clearance behind the workpiece to keep the tool bit from cutting into the chuck (Fig. 55-8).

2. Fasten the boring toolholder in the tool post or on the compound rest. The tool or bar should be as large in diameter as possible. Its cutting-edge must extend out only far enough to clear through the workpiece. The tool should be as rigid as possible. If it is not, chattering will

Fig. 55-9. Cutting can be done completely through the workpiece with this setup.

THREE—BAR BORING TOOL

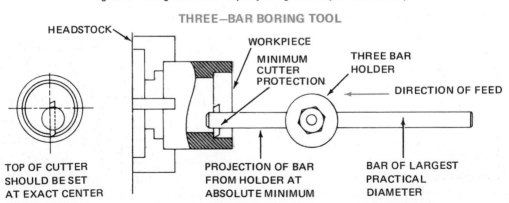

HEADSTOCK

WORKPIECE

MINIMUM
CUTTER
PROTECTION

THREE BAR
HOLDER

DIRECTION OF FEED

TOP OF CUTTER
SHOULD BE SET
AT EXACT CENTER

PROJECTION OF BAR
FROM HOLDER AT
ABSOLUTE MINIMUM

BAR OF LARGEST
PRACTICAL
DIAMETER

develop. Adjust the tool so that its face is directly on center when using a solid bar, or slightly above center when using a forged bar. The forged bar is adjusted in this way because the tool tends to spring down during the machining operation. See that the toolholder is parallel to the center line of the lathe (Fig. 55-9).

3. Move the carriage back and forth. Check to see that the tool will not strike the chuck and that the tool clears the hole all the way through.

4. Use the same speed and feed as for turning. If chatter develops, reduce the speed or try a smaller depth of cut. Sometimes increasing the feed helps.

BORING THE HOLE

1. Turn on the power, and bring the point of the cutting tool up to the inside of the hole (Figs. 55-10 and 55-11). Keep in mind that boring increases an inside diameter. Therefore, you must turn the cross-feed handle in the direction opposite that for turning. Be sure a chip is removed all the way around the hole.

2. Move the carriage by hand until the hole is bored about $\frac{1}{8}$ in. deep.

3. Stop the lathe, and move the carriage out of the way.

4. Check the diameter of the hole. This can be done in several ways.

a. Measure the hole with an inside caliper.

b. Use a telescope gage to find the diameter. Then measure this with an outside micrometer.

c. Use an inside micrometer.

d. Use a vernier caliper (Fig. 55-12).

e. Many special types of gages are used in industry when great accuracy is required (Fig. 55-13).

Fig. 55-10. Using a forged boring tool for boring a small hole. Never use this kind of tool in a large hole. It has a tendency to spring, especially when used to cut a long hole.

Fig. 55-11. Use a boring bar when boring large holes.

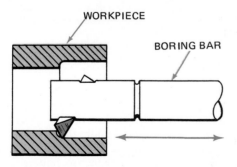

WORKPIECE

BORING BAR

Fig. 55-12. Using a vernier caliper to check the inside measurement on a bored hole.

Fig. 55-13. This operator is using an air gage to check the bore of an aluminum part.

5. If there is a good deal of material to remove, take several light cuts. Depth of cut depends largely on how rigidly the tool is held.

6. When the hole is within a few thousandths of finished size, take a light cut for about $\frac{1}{8}$ in.

7. Stop the lathe. Back out the tool, but do not move the cross-feed.

8. Check the diameter. If there are only a few thousandths to go, say 0.006 in., turn out the cross slide 0.003 in. as shown on the micrometer collar.

9. Make the finish cut, using a very fine feed. Sometimes a *bell-shaped hole* develops. This happens when you take several light cuts at the edge of the hole to reach the correct diameter and then bore all the way through. As the heavier cut is taken, the tool springs away, making the hole larger in front than in back. If this happens, adjust the tool to the same setting as the finish cut, and run it through again.

10. A tapered hole is bored in the same way as a straight hole except that the taper attachment is used. A short tapered hole can be turned using the compound-rest feed.

11. *Counterboring* or cutting a large hole only part way through an existing hole is done as follows.

> a. Place a cutter of the correct shape at an angle in the boring bar. The tool is normally mounted at 45° to the holder so that it clears the end of the bar.
>
> b. Bore the hole to the correct depth.
>
> c. Turn in the cross-feed to form the shoulder.

12. In boring thin shell stock, the workpiece must be held in a collet attachment. A very light cut is used on such material (Fig. 55-14).

13. If you must rebore a hole to change the size slightly, use a dial indicator gage to position the workpiece (Fig. 55-15).

BORING WITH THE TOOL HELD IN THE HEADSTOCK SPINDLE

A piece difficult to hold in a chuck or on a faceplate may be bored by substituting a stand-

Fig. 55-14. Boring thick shell stock held in a collet attachment. A very light cut must be made on this kind of job. Care must be taken not to strike the collet holder.

Fig. 55-15. Using a dial indicator gage to reset a hole that has already been bored.

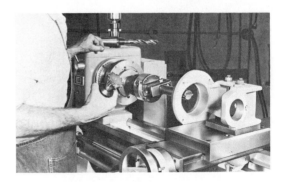

Fig. 55-16. Note how the boring is done with the workpiece held on a work-holding fixture. The cutting tools are held in the headstock spindle.

ard work-holding fixture in place of the lathe compound (Fig. 55-16). The boring tool is held in the headstock spindle during such an operation. After completing the job, the fixture base is removed and replaced by the standard lathe compound for normal turning operations.

UNIT 56. Reaming

Reaming is done to improve the accuracy and finish of a hole. Reaming will not straighten out a hole that has been incorrectly drilled.

HAND REAMING

1. Drill or bore the hole to within 0.005 to 0.008 in. of finished size.

2. Remove the toolholder and tool post.

3. Choose the correct type and size of reamer.

4. Fasten a tap wrench to the square end. The tap wrench must be short enough to clear the lathe bed. An adjustable wrench can also be used to turn the reamer.

5. Move the tailstock until there is enough space for the reamer between the dead center and the workpiece. Place the reamer in this space with the shank supported on the dead center.

6. Apply cutting fluid to the reamer. *Don't turn on the power.* Rotate the reamer with the wrench as you turn the tailstock handwheel (Fig. 56-1). When the hole is reamed, continue to rotate it clockwise as you pull it out of the hole.

CAUTION

Never turn a reamer backward.

MACHINE REAMING

1. Drill or bore the hole to allow stock for reaming as follows.

> 0.007 in. for $\frac{1}{4}$-in. hole
> 0.015 in. for $\frac{1}{2}$-in. hole
> 0.020 in. for 1-in. hole
> Up to 0.025 in. for 1$\frac{1}{2}$-in. hole
> Up to 0.030 in. for 2-in. hole
> Up to 0.045 in. for 3-in. hole

2. If the reamer has a tapered shank, insert it directly in the tailstock spindle or in a drill holder. Use a drill chuck to hold a straight-shank reamer (Fig. 56-2).

Fig. 56-1. Using a hand reamer in the lathe. Notice that an adjustable wrench is used to turn the reamer. The spindle of the lathe does not rotate.

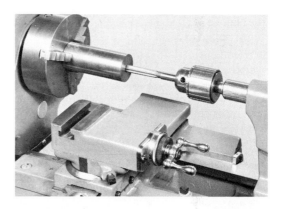

Fig. 56-2. Reaming with the reamer held in a drill chuck.

Fig. 56-3. Reaming a steel workpiece with a spiral-fluted reamer. Use cutting lubricant for this kind of job.

3. Adjust the lathe to a very slow speed (about half that required for drilling).

4. Apply some cutting fluid to the reamer. (No lubricant is necessary when reaming cast iron or brass.)

5. Turn the tailstock handwheel slowly so the reamer advances into the workpiece at a slow, steady feed (Fig. 56-3).

6. Back out the reamer occasionally to clear chips from the hole.

7. Continue to feed the reamer until it has cleared the back of the workpiece.

8. Stop the lathe, and back the reamer out of the hole.

CAUTION

Never reverse spindle direction or turn the reamer backwards for any reason. This will dull and damage the cutting-edges.

UNIT 57.   Turning with the Workpiece on a Mandrel

After a hole has been drilled, bored, or reamed in a workpiece, further machining is often completed while the work is held on a mandrel. This procedure is followed when making such parts as gear blanks, pulleys, candlestick holders, and any other parts that have an accurate hole through the center.

KINDS OF MANDRELS

A *mandrel* is a shaft, bar, or tube used for holding a workpiece to be machined. Mandrels are sometimes confused with arbors. Remember, a *mandrel* is used to hold *workpieces,* and an *arbor* is used to hold *cutting tools.*

1. A *solid mandrel* is a hardened shaft tapered 0.006 inch per foot (Fig. 57-1A). The small end is usually about 0.001 in. undersize, and the large end about 0.004 in. oversize. Mandrels are made in standard sizes. The size of each is stamped on its large end. Mandrels are precision tools. Be very careful not to nick or cut the surface or ruin the center holes.

2. An *expansion mandrel* consists of a shaft and a slotted sleeve. A taper pin fits through the sleeve to expand it for holding workpieces with odd-sized holes. These mandrels expand up to about $\frac{1}{16}$ in. in the smaller sizes and up to $\frac{1}{2}$ in. in the larger ones (Fig. 57-1B).

3. A *gang* or *nut mandrel* is used to hold two or more parts so that all pieces can be machined alike (Fig. 57-1C).

4. A *chucked* or *threaded mandrel* is used for turning the face and exterior of threaded workpieces. This kind of mandrel is frequently made by chucking a piece of scrap stock, turning it to the required size, and cutting threads on it for holding the workpiece (Fig. 57-1D).

ARBOR PRESS

An *arbor press* (sometimes called a *mandrel press*) is used for pressing a shaft, mandrel, or other part either into or out of a hole or recess (Fig. 57-2).

INSTALLING A MANDREL

1. Select a mandrel of the correct size.

2. Wipe it clean. Apply a thin coat of oil. If not oiled, the workpiece may "freeze" to the mandrel.

3. Slip the small end (the large end has the size stamped on it) into the hole in the workpiece as far as it will go.

4. Use an arbor press to secure the workpiece.

5. If an arbor press is unavailable, install the mandrel by striking it with a soft-faced lead or brass hammer.

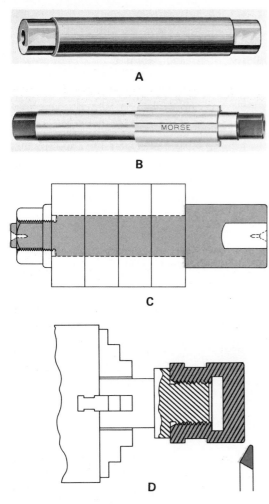

Fig. 57-1. (A) A solid mandrel. (B) Expansion mandrel. (C) A gang mandrel is useful when turning duplicate parts. (D) A threaded mandrel.

Fig. 57-2. Arbor presses vary in size. Larger ones are used for many purposes, including assembling parts that have a press fit.

Fig. 57-3. Turning with the workpiece held on a mandrel.

TURNING ON A MANDREL

1. Fasten a dog to the large end of the mandrel, and lubricate the dead center (opposite end).

2. Mount the workpiece in the lathe.

3. Use a right- and left-cut side-facing tool to machine the sides of the workpiece.

4. Cut from the center toward the outside for finishing cuts. Start the point of the tool about paper thickness away from the mandrel. Be careful not to score or cut the mandrel surface with the tool point.

5. Sometimes the workpiece is reversed so that both sides can be faced with the same side-facing tool.

6. If a large workpiece must be held on a small-diameter mandrel, the cut must be light to keep the mandrel from springing (Fig. 57-3).

7. When turning the outside of a workpiece, always feed toward the large end of the mandrel.

UNIT 58.

Mounting a Workpiece in a Lathe Collet Chuck or on a Faceplate

Lathe collet chucks and faceplates are both work-holding devices. Lathe collet chucks are used to hold small-sized workpieces. Faceplates are used to hold large or irregularly shaped workpieces.

LATHE COLLET CHUCKS

There are several types of lathe collet chucks.

1. *Draw-in collet chuck.* This type consists of a four-part assembly as follows (Fig. 58-1):

  a. A set of spring *collets.* These collets are made to hold round, square, or hexagon-shaped workpieces. The collet can be used only on workpieces that are within ±0.001 in. of the size stamped on the collet.

  b. A *spindle-nose cap* that fits over the threaded end of the spindle nose to protect the screw threads.

  c. A *collet sleeve* that fits into the end of the spindle to receive the spring collet.

  d. A *draw bar* that extends through the headstock spindle to tighten the spring collet on the workpiece.

2. *Multisize collets and chucks.* These collets have full-grip steel blades that move in and out with a spring arrangement, permitting machining right up to the collet face (Fig. 58-2). Each collet does the work of 20 spring collets and can handle hex, decimal, metric, or special sizes. There are 12 collets to a set. Each has a range of $\frac{1}{8}$ in. For example, one collet will fit workpieces with diameters from $\frac{1}{8}$ to $\frac{1}{4}$ in. Each collet will also hold stock 0.020 in. above and below the range indicated. These collets fit into several different types of spindle noses. One type is operated with a key (Fig. 58-3). A second has a large handwheel that can be turned to open and close the collet. A third type is lever-operated and is used in high production. It can be opened and closed without stopping the lathe spindle (Fig. 58-4).

3. *Flexible rubber collet chuck.* This type of lathe collet chuck is similar to the multisize unit. However, the collets used are made from molded rubber and steel (Fig. 58-5). Eleven collets are needed to cover the range from $\frac{1}{16}$ to $1\frac{3}{8}$ in.

ADVANTAGES OF A COLLET CHUCK

1. It has a much faster releasing and gripping action than does a chuck.

2. It provides automatic and accurate centering of the workpiece.

Fig. 58-1. (A) A draw-in collet chuck assembly. (B) A complete set of collets properly stored in a rack.

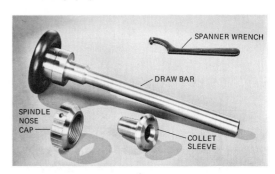

SPANNER WRENCH

DRAW BAR

SPINDLE NOSE CAP

COLLET SLEEVE

A

B

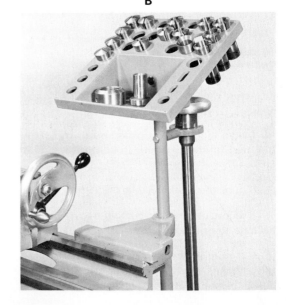

Fig. 58-2. Multisize collet.

Fig. 58-3. Collet that operates with a key.

Fig. 58-4. This collet operates with a lever attachment and is used in production.

Fig. 58-5. Turning stock held in a flexible rubber collet.

Fig. 58-6. Thread cutting can be done with the work held in a collet.

3. It grips firmly, even on small pieces on which only a short hold is possible.

4. It provides maximum tool clearance. Machining can be done right up to the collet nose.

5. Long bars of stock can be fed through the assembly for machining many identical workpieces.

USING A DRAW-IN COLLET CHUCK ATTACHMENT

1. Fasten the spindle-nose cap over the end of the spindle.

2. Insert a collet sleeve in the tapered hole of the spindle.

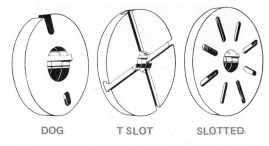

DOG   T SLOT   SLOTTED

Fig. 58-7. Three types of faceplates.

Fig. 58-9. A casting clamped to an angle plate which in turn is fastened to a faceplate.

Fig. 58-8. A large-slotted faceplate. When turning using this faceplate, the maximum rpm is 625.

STRAP CLAMPS
FACEPLATE
WORKPIECE
DIAL INDICATOR

Fig. 58-10. A workpiece clamped to a faceplate. Note that machinist's buttons have been installed in three places.

3. Select a spring collet of the correct size and shape. Slip it into the sleeve.

4. Insert the draw bar from the back of the headstock spindle. Turn the handle so the threaded end of the draw bar engages the threaded end of the collet.

5. Slip the workpiece into the collet, letting it extend just far enough for machining the length required. Tighten the collet by turning the handwheel on the draw bar (Fig. 58-6).

FACEPLATES

There are three basic kinds of faceplates (Fig. 58-7).

1. The *drive* or *dog plate* is made with a slot into which the tail of the lathe dog fits.

2. The *T-slot faceplate* is designed to hold stock by use of T bolts.

3. The *slotted faceplate* is used in conjunction with a variety of clamps to hold work for turning (Fig. 58-8).

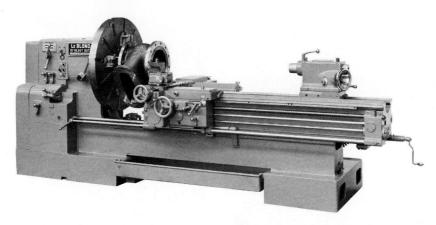

Fig. 58-11. A large casting clamped on the faceplate of a "gap bed" lathe. Note the extra space between the headstock assembly and the bed.

Faceplates are used to hold unusually shaped workpieces that cannot be held in the standard chuck or between centers (Fig. 58-9). A major part of faceplate work involves clamping the stock in proper position so that machining can be done (Fig. 58-10). Every job requires a different setup, and you must determine just how the work can best be held. For most jobs, the workpiece must be away from the faceplate so boring and reaming can be done without striking the faceplate with the cutting tool (Fig. 58-11).

UNIT 59. Knurling

Knurling is a process of pressing a diamond-shaped or straight-line pattern onto the surface of a workpiece. It is not a *cutting operation,* but rather an *embossing* or *extruding* one. Knurling is done for practical as well as ornamental purposes. For example, handles of tools are often knurled to keep them from slipping out of the hand. Knurling is also done to increase slightly the diameter of a workpiece used in a press-fit assembly.

KNURLING TOOLS

There are two basic types of knurling tools, the single self-centering head with one pair of knurls and the revolving head with three pairs of knurls (Fig. 59-1). A *knurling tool* is a holder in which hardened steel wheels are fastened.

These wheels have teeth or ridges on their faces that form the impression on the workpiece. Patterns produced by several commonly used knurling tools are shown in Fig. 59-2.

PROCEDURE

1. Work to be knurled should be held between centers or with one end in a chuck and the other in a revolving dead center (Fig. 59-3). Long and extremely light pieces should be supported with a *steady rest*. In other words, the work must be prevented from springing away when pressure is applied with the knurling rolls (Fig. 59-4).

2. Hold a rule against the workpiece surface and scribe lines showing the beginning and end of the knurl.

3. Adjust the lathe to a fairly slow speed by using the back gears. Also adjust the lathe for medium feed.

A

B

Fig. 59-1. (A) A self-centering knurling toolholder. (B) A revolving head with three pairs of knurls. This toolholder is also self-centering. Revolving heads allow change of knurling without altering the setup.

STRAIGHT—LINE KNURLS

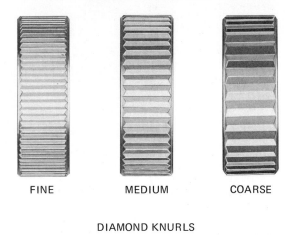

FINE   MEDIUM   COARSE

DIAMOND KNURLS

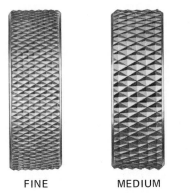

FINE   MEDIUM   COARSE

Fig. 59-2. All knurls are made from high-speed steel. They are available in diamond or straight-line patterns having fine, medium, or coarse pitch.

4. Set the knurling toolholder well back in the tool post and position it so that the top and bottom rolls are equidistant above and below the center of the work. The tool post screw should be securely tightened (Fig. 59-5).

5. Move the carriage to the starting point near the tailstock (Fig. 59-6).

6. Start the tool so that only half the width of the roll face contacts the work. Begin feeding toward the headstock. Abruptly force the knurling tool into the work to approximately the full depth of the knurl. This should be accomplished before the rolls can make one complete revolution (Fig. 59-7). Apply a little cutting fluid to the wheels.

CAUTION

Do not let the brush get caught between the work and knurls.

7. Stop the lathe to see if the tool is working properly. A diamond-pattern knurling tool should produce a diamond-shape pattern. If one wheel is not tracking correctly, the impression will be incomplete (Fig. 59-8). If this happens, release the cross-feed pressure, move the tool a little to the left, and begin again.

8. If the knurl is correct, increase the pressure slightly. Apply cutting fluid to the surface to be

Fig. 59-3. Knurling with one end of the workpiece held in a chuck and the other in a revolving dead center. This is a good setup.

Fig. 59-7. Note that the first knurl has been made. In this setup, the knurling tool fits in a quick-change toolholder.

LONG AND EXTREMELY LIGHT PIECES SHOULD BE SUPPORTED WITH A STEADY REST TO PREVENT WORK FROM SPRING-ING AWAY FROM THE CROSS PRESSURE OF THE KNURLS.

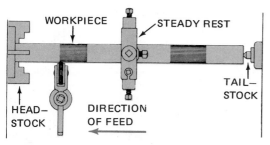

Fig. 59-4. Use a steady rest when knurling a long piece of work.

TOP AND BOTTOM KNURLS SHOULD BE EQUI-DISTANT ABOVE AND BELOW CENTER OF WORK. SELF-CENTERING FEATURE COMPENSATES FOR ANY SLIGHT VARIATION.

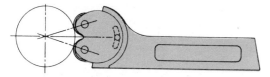

Fig. 59-5. Note that the knurls are set on center.

Fig. 59-6. Starting the knurling.

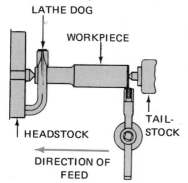

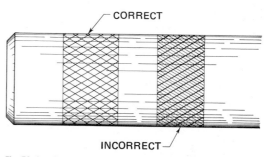

Fig. 59-8. Correct and incorrect impressions for knurling.

Fig. 59-9. The first pass of the knurling is complete. Now reverse the carriage and recut.

knurled. Engage the longitudinal power feed and let the tool travel across the face of the work the desired distance. Clean the wheels of the knurling tool by brushing frequently with a wire brush.

9. As the tool reaches the end of the area to be knurled, turn off the power, but do not release the automatic power feed (Fig. 59-9).

10. Reverse the direction of the carriage. Apply a little more pressure to the wheels with the cross feed.

11. Now run the tool back toward the tailstock. Usually two times across the surface is enough to produce a good knurl.

UNIT 60. Filing and Polishing

Filing and polishing are finishing operations. *Filing* is done to fit one part into another, to remove tool marks, to obtain a fine finish, to round off sharp corners, to remove burrs, or to correct a slight error on a taper. *Polishing* is done to produce a high, mirrorlike finish on the workpiece. Filing and polishing are not usually done in production work because it is very difficult to do accurate work by these methods.

FILING

1. Select a 10- or 12-in. *mill file* (a single-cut file) or a *long-angle lathe file* (a single-cut file with teeth cut at a longer angle) to give a true shearing cut without producing ridges or scores (Fig. 60-1). The angle of the teeth helps to prevent clogging or pinning.

2. Adjust the lathe for a fast speed. The speed of the lathe should be about 50 percent higher than that used when turning work of the same diameter. Be sure the work will revolve toward the operator.

3. Loosen the dead center slightly, and lubricate well.

4. Move the carriage to the extreme right, and remove the tool-post holder.

5. There are two methods of holding the file, the *right-handed method* (the same as in bench filing) and the *left-handed method*. Safety experts and many manufacturers recommend the left-handed method. However, other machinists think it is too awkward for the beginner.

6. To use the right-handed method, hold the handle of the file in your right hand and the point in your left (Fig. 60-2).

CAUTION

Always use a lathe dog with a safety screw when filing with this method.

Hold the file at a slight angle. Start near the headstock (Fig. 60-3). Note how you must arc

Fig. 60-1. Long angle lathe file.

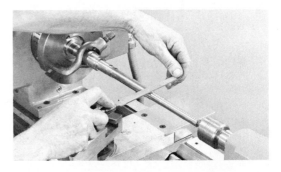

Fig. 60-2. *Danger.* Notice that the setscrew of the lathe dog could strike the left arm of the operator. An incorrect movement might result in a deep gash in the operator's arm.

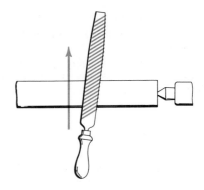

Fig. 60-3. Hold the file at an angle of about 10° to the workpiece.

your left hand to avoid the revolving dog. File using long forward strokes. Release the pressure on the return stroke. Move across the piece about half the width of the file after each stroke. Don't press too hard on the file. This would cause the workpiece to become "out of round." It is a good idea to apply chalk on the file to prevent pinning and clogging. Clean the file after every few strokes. Work from the headstock end toward the tailstock end.

Fig. 60-4. The left-hand method of filing. You should learn to use this technique since it is safer than the right-hand method.

Fig. 60-5. Polishing with abrasive cloth. Notice that the left-hand method is used.

7. To use the left-handed method, hold the handle of the file in your left hand and the point in your right (Fig. 60-4). Start near the tailstock, and file toward the headstock. There is no danger of your left arm's coming near the dog when filing in this manner.

POLISHING

Polishing is usually done on small tools and decorative objects to obtain a very high mirror-like finish. Use an aluminum oxide abrasive cloth for steels and other hard metals and silicon carbide cloth for copper and brass.

1. Select the correct grade of abrasive cloth, and cut off a strip about 6 to 8 in. long.

2. Set the lathe to high speed, or one step faster than for filing. Be sure to lubricate the dead center well.

3. Place a few drops of cutting oil on the workpiece.

4. There are several methods you can use to hold the abrasive.

a. Place the abrasive cloth over a file or stick, and move it across the workpiece as for filing.

b. Wrap the cloth once around the workpiece, and hold the ends. Move the cloth back and forth. Be sure to keep your arms clear of the revolving lathe dog (Fig. 60-5).

c. Wrap the cloth once around the workpiece. Turn the toolholder backward in the tool post. Fasten the ends of the cloth between the toolholder and wedge. Now use the power feed to move the cloth back and forth along the workpiece.

5. For a superfine finish, allow the abrasive grains in oil to remain on the workpiece. Turn the cloth around with the grains out, and move the cloth back and forth several times.

CAUTION

Clean the carriage and ways of the lathe thoroughly after polishing to remove all abrasive particles. Otherwise, they may cause excessive wear on the moving parts of the machine.

UNIT 61. Taper Turning with Tailstock Set Over

The term *taper* may be defined as the gradual lessening of the diameter or thickness of a piece of work toward one end. The amount of taper in any given length of work is found by subtracting the size of the small end from the size of the large end. Taper is usually expressed as the amount of taper per foot of length, or as an angle.

Example 1. Find the taper per foot (tpf) of a piece of work that is 2 in. long. The diameter of the small end is 1 in. and the diameter of the large end is 2 in.

Solution. The amount of the taper is 2 in. minus 1 in., which equals 1 in. The length of the taper is given as 2 in. Therefore, the taper in 2 in. of length is 1 in. In 12 in. of length, the taper would be 6 in.

Example 2. Find the tpf of a piece 6 in. long. The diameter of the small end is 1 in., and the diameter of the large end is 2 in.

Solution. The amount of taper is the same as in Example 1, that is, 1 in. However, the length of this taper is 6 in. The tpf, therefore, is equal to 1 in. $\times \frac{12}{6}$ or 2 in. per foot.

There are four ways to turn a taper. These include setting over the tailstock, using a taper attachment, using the compound rest, and using a forming tool.

Setting over the tailstock is the simplest method of turning a taper. It is probably the method used most in school shops. Remember, the lathe tailstock consists of two parts, a lower part that fits the ways of the bed and an upper part that is movable. To turn tapers, the upper part is set over the amount needed to cut the taper.

There are two disadvantages associated with the setover method of turning a taper.

1. The *dead center* must be moved out of line with the *live center* (Fig. 61-1). If other operations follow on the same workpiece, it is necessary to realign the centers. This requires time and skill.

2. The center holes in the ends of the workpiece are out of alignment with the lathe centers. Therefore, contact between bearing surfaces is reduced (Fig. 61-2). Sometimes a bell-type center drill is used for drilling the center hole. This helps to provide additional support for the workpiece (Fig. 61-3).

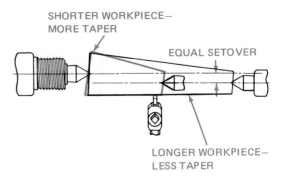

Fig. 61-1. A taper can be turned by offsetting the dead center. The amount of taper depends on the length of the workpiece. When the length of the workpiece varies, different tapers will be cut with the same offset.

Fig. 61-2. Note that the holes in the end of a workpiece do not align with the lathe centers when the tailstock is offset for tapering.

Fig. 61-3. A bell-type center hole provides more support area for the workpiece.

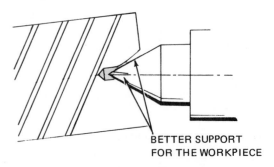

BETTER SUPPORT FOR THE WORKPIECE

CALCULATING SETOVER

Setover is figured in four ways (Fig. 61-4). The method selected is dependent upon the kind and location of the tapered surface.

1. *When the tpf is known,* the setover equals the tpf (in inches) times the total length of the workpiece divided by 24.

$$\text{Setover} = \frac{\text{tpf} \times L}{24}$$

where tpf = taper per foot in inches
L = total length in inches

2. *When the taper is to be cut on only part of the workpiece* (a prick or center punch, for example) *and the drawing does not show the tpf,* the setover equals the total length divided by the length to be tapered times the large diameter minus the small diameter divided by 2.

$$\text{Setover} = \frac{L}{l} \times \frac{D - d}{2}$$

where L = the total length of the workpiece in inches
l = the length to be tapered in inches
D = the large diameter in inches
d = the small diameter in inches

When using this formula, remember that the total length is the actual length of the workpiece as it is, *not the finished length.* For example, calculate the setover for turning a taper on part of the workpiece shown in Fig. 61-5.

Answer.

$$\frac{12}{4} \times \frac{(1\frac{1}{2} - 1)}{2} = 3 \times \frac{\frac{1}{2}}{2}$$

$$= 3 \times \frac{1}{2} \times \frac{1}{2} = \frac{3}{4} \text{ in.}$$

3. *When taper per inch (tpi) is known,* setover can be found by dividing the taper per foot by 12, or by subtracting the small diameter from the large diameter and dividing this by the length of the taper.

$$\text{Setover} = \frac{L \times \text{tpi}}{2}$$

4. *When the workpiece is tapered for its entire length,* setover should equal one-half the differ-

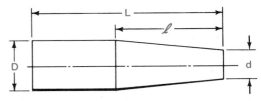

L = TOTAL LENGTH   **d** = SMALL DIAMETER
l = LENGTH OF TAPER **tpi** = TAPER PER IN.
D = LARGE DIAMETER **tpf** = TAPER PER FOOT

Fig. 61-4. Terms used in figuring offset.

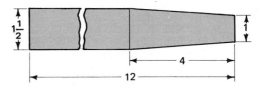

Fig. 61-5. In this drawing, the taper per inch or foot is not given. However, the dimensions needed to turn a taper are provided.

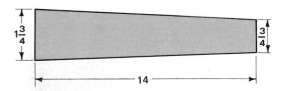

Fig. 61-6. This workpiece is tapered along its entire length.

ence between the large diameter and the small diameter. Then,

$$\text{Setover} = \frac{D - d}{2}$$

For example, calculate the setover for turning a taper on the workpiece shown in Fig. 61-6.

Answer.

$$\frac{1\frac{3}{4} - \frac{3}{4}}{2} = \frac{1}{2} \text{ in.}$$

PREPARING THE LATHE

1. Loosen the clamp-bolt nut that holds the tailstock to the bed.

2. Adjust the setscrews to move the upper part of the tailstock. Generally the upper part is moved toward you so that the small end of the taper is on the tailstock end. To move the upper part, loosen the setscrew on the side toward which the tailstock is to be moved (Fig. 61-7). Then tighten the other setscrew an equal amount. There are four ways of measuring the amount of setover.

a. Two witness or index lines are machined on the handwheel end of the tailstock. Measure the distance between these lines with a rule (Fig. 61-8).

b. Measure the amount of setover by holding a rule between live and dead centers (Fig. 61-9). This does not provide an accurate reading, however.

c. To measure the amount of setover with the cross-feed micrometer collar, fasten a toolholder sideways in the tool post. Turn the tailstock spindle out far enough to expose a surface for measuring. Turn in the cross-feed screw until the tool post is close to the tailstock spindle. Take out all backlash in the *cross-feed screw* by backing it out a turn. Then set the micrometer collar at zero. Place a thin piece of paper between the tailstock spindle and the tool post. Turn in the *compound-rest feed screw* until the paper touches the tailstock spindle (Fig. 61-10A). Next turn out the cross-feed screw an amount equal to the setover. Move the upper part of the tailstock out until the spindle just touches the paper again when held between tailstock spindle and tool post (Fig. 61-10B).

d. Use a dial indicator to offset the tailstock accurately. First, turn out the tailstock spindle or ram and lock in position. Move the carriage so that the plunger on the dial indicator touches the spindle. Turn the cross-feed in until the dial registers at least 0.020 in., then back out about 0.010 in. to remove all the backlash in the cross slide (Fig. 61-11A). Next, set the collar on the cross slide and the dial indicator to zero, and move the cross slide out until the graduated collar shows the correct offset. Finally, move the upper part of the tailstock

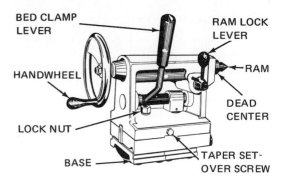

Fig. 61-7. The tailstock assembly is made in two parts. Taper setover screws are used to move the top part off center from the base.

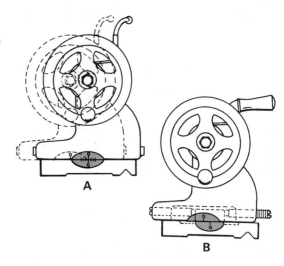

Fig. 61-8. (A) Note how the tailstock can be moved. (B) A rule can be used to measure the distance between the witness marks.

Fig. 61-9. Measuring the amount of setover using a steel rule held between centers. This method is not very accurate.

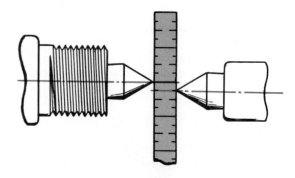

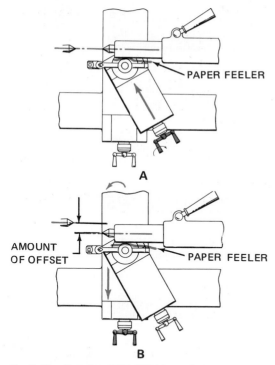

A

AMOUNT
OF OFFSET

PAPER FEELER

B

Fig. 61-10. Measuring setover with the cross-feed micrometer collar: (A) turn the compound rest in until the tool post touches the tailstock spindle and (B) turn the cross-feed to the correct setover and reposition the spindle.

Fig. 61-11. A dial indicator may be used to offset the tailstock accurately. (A) Set the dial indicator and the collar to zero. (B) To offset the tailstock $\frac{1}{4}$ in., turn the cross-feed to 0.125 in. and reposition the spindle. The dial indicator should again read zero.

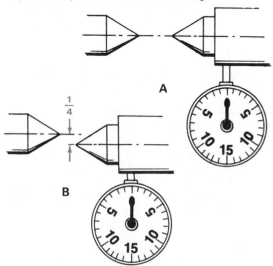

until the dial indicator again reads zero (Fig. 61-11B).

3. If a taper is to be duplicated, place the original piece between centers. Place a dial indicator exactly on center in the tool post holder (Fig. 61-12). Set over the tailstock until the dial indicator stays at zero when the carriage is moved back and forth. This method is accurate only if the length and centers of the new piece are identical with the original piece.

CAUTION

Before machining the workpiece, make sure that the setscrews are tight so that the top part of the tailstock will not move.

TOOLS AND EQUIPMENT NEEDED

1. A rule and outside caliper or micrometer for measuring

2. A lathe dog

3. A roundnose cutting tool

4. A straight toolholder

TAPER TURNING

1. Place the workpiece between centers as for straight turning. Keep the dead center well lubricated.

2. Adjust the cutting tool so that it is exactly on center.

3. Start at the tailstock end and take a light cut. If the workpiece is small in diameter, be especially careful that it doesn't climb over the cutting-edge. This would ruin the workpiece (Fig. 61-13).

4. Make several cuts until the taper is at least an inch long. With a rule, carefully measure a unit of length such as 1 or 2 in. Now measure the large and small ends at each point with a micrometer or outside calipers. Figure the amount of taper in the unit of length. Compare this with the required tpf or tpi.

5. If necessary, readjust the offset. It is always necessary to test the amount of taper in this way before machining to the correct size.

Fig. 61-12. Using a dial indicator to check the taper.

Fig. 61-13. Machining the taper.

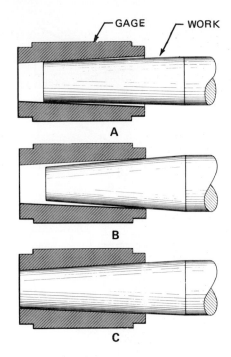

Fig. 61-14. Checking a taper plug with a taper ring gage. (A) Small end too large. (B) Small end undersized. (C) Correct fit.

6. If a taper does not have to fit into a mating part (such as the taper on a center punch), you can measure the small and large diameters with an outside caliper or micrometer.

7. If the taper is to fit into an existing tapered hole, the taper should be checked with a *taper ring gage*, or by inserting it into the taper spindle or sleeve with which it will be used. The taper must be checked both for amount and for size (Fig. 61-14). To do this, draw several light chalk marks lengthwise along the taper. Insert it into the spindle or sleeve lightly, and turn it slightly to the left. If the chalk rubs off unevenly, further machining is required. For example, if the chalk rubs off near the small end of the taper, the offset must be increased.

8. Sometimes, if the taper is only slightly incorrect, a little filing may make it fit satisfactorily.

9. After taper turning, be sure to realign the centers.

10. You can turn only external tapers using the tailstock offset method.

UNIT 62. Taper Turning with a Taper Attachment

The most accurate way to turn and bore tapers is with a *taper attachment* (Fig. 62-1). The use of this device provides certain advantages.

1. The lathe centers are kept in alignment since the tailstock doesn't have to be set over. Therefore, it is easy to change from straight to taper turning.

2. The taper attachment can be permanently set to a standard taper and used whenever necessary.

3. Once the correct taper per foot (tpf) is set, the taper can be cut on any piece, regardless of length (Fig. 62-2).

4. Long tapers (as long as the taper attachment) and sharp tapers (as much as $5\frac{1}{2}$ inches per foot on some machines) can be turned.

5. Boring a taper can be easily done. A taper can be turned on a shaft and the taper hole bored on its mating part using the same setup. Only the swivel bar must be reversed.

6. The tapering attachment permits machining of tapers to be followed by other operations, such as straight turning and threading without changing the setup.

7. Greater degrees of taper can be obtained by offsetting the tailstock.

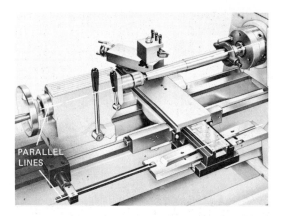

Fig. 62-2. The cutting tool will always follow a line parallel to the guide bar.

KINDS OF TAPER ATTACHMENTS

The taper attachment is fitted to the back of the lathe bed. There are two types.

1. To use the *plain taper attachment,* it is necessary to remove the binding nut or bolt which holds the cross-feed screw to the saddle (Fig. 62-3).

2. The *telescope taper attachment* works without loosening or removing the binding nut or bolt which holds the cross-feed screw to the saddle. It has a slide block that allows the cross-feed to follow the guide bar (Fig. 62-4).

SETTING THE TAPER

1. Tapers are shown on most drawings in taper per foot, taper per inch (tpi), or in degrees (°). On most attachments the graduations at the end of the swivel bar are divided into inches per foot on one end and in degrees (included angle) on the other (Fig. 62-5). Graduations may differ from one model attachment to another. On one type, for example, each small division on the end showing inches per foot represents $\frac{1}{16}$ in. On another, each small division represents $\frac{1}{8}$ in. If a taper of $\frac{5}{8}$ inch per foot must be cut, set the scale at 10 small divisions if each represents $\frac{1}{16}$ in., or 5 divisions if each represents $\frac{1}{8}$ in. If the tpf on the drawing is given in decimal fractions, convert it to the closest common fraction indi-

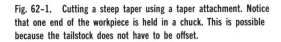

Fig. 62-1. Cutting a steep taper using a taper attachment. Notice that one end of the workpiece is held in a chuck. This is possible because the tailstock does not have to be offset.

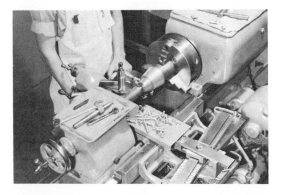

341

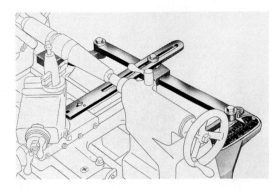

Fig. 62-3. A plain taper attachment. This kind is less convenient to use.

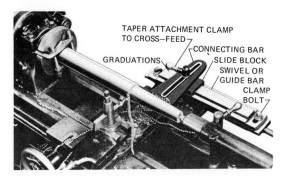

TAPER ATTACHMENT CLAMP
TO CROSS–FEED
CONNECTING BAR
GRADUATIONS
SLIDE BLOCK
SWIVEL OR
GUIDE BAR
CLAMP
BOLT

Fig. 62-4. Parts of a telescopic taper attachment.

Fig. 62-5. The left end of this taper attachment is marked in inches per foot and the right end in degrees.

cated on a decimal equivalent table. You must remember that the graduations on the swivel bar are there for convenience only. They do not represent a high degree of accuracy. You should always check the taper before finishing it to exact size.

2. If the included angle of the taper is given (an angle of 10°, for example), set the swivel bar to the 10° mark on the scale. The lathe will then cut a total included angle of 10° (5° on either side of the center line).

TOOLS AND EQUIPMENT NEEDED

1. Straight toolholder and roundnose cutting tool

2. Rule and outside caliper or micrometer for measuring the taper

3. Plug or ring gage for accurate checking of the taper

CUTTING THE TAPER WITH A TELESCOPIC TAPER ATTACHMENT

1. Make sure the taper attachment is installed properly (Fig. 62-6). Position the attachment so it is about in the center of the workpiece. Lock the clamp bracket to the lathe bed.

2. Fasten a roundnose cutting tool in the toolholder. See that the cutting-edge is exactly on center. If the tool is above or below center, the angle of the cut will not be the same as the setting of the taper attachment.

3. Mount the work in the lathe. Whenever possible, the taper cut should be made from the small diameter of the workpiece to its large diameter.

4. The lathe cross slide and taper slide should move freely, but without up-or-down play. If necessary, adjust the tension by turning the gib screws located on the cross slide and support bracket.

5. Move the carriage by hand to make sure there is sufficient travel to complete the taper cut. If there is not, adjust the compound rest and move the carriage or the taper attachment to a different position.

6. Set the taper bar to the taper desired. Graduations on the right end of the bar are in inches per foot. On the left end of the bar, graduations are marked in degrees (Fig. 62-7).

    a. Loosen the two lock screws (A) on each end of taper bar.

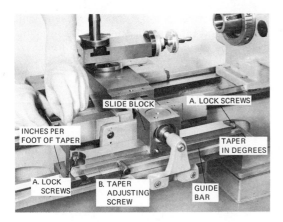

Fig. 62-6. When installing the taper attachment, make sure it is parallel to the bed of the lathe. The slide block allows you to adjust the cross slide.

Fig. 62-8. Cutting the taper using power feed.

Fig. 62-7. The three adjustments that must be made in setting the taper.

b. Turn taper adjusting screw (B) to taper desired.

c. Tighten the two taper bar lock screws (A).

d. Be sure clamp bracket (C) is locked to the lathe bed.

7. Move the carriage to the small end of the taper until the cutting tool is about 1 in. past the end of the workpiece.

8. Turn the cross-feed until the cutting tool will take a light cut. Remember to remove all backlash from the cross-feed screw and taper attachment. If this is not done, part of the cut will be straight.

9. Run the carriage in the direction of the taper by hand until the tool just starts to cut. Then change to power feed (Fig. 62-8).

10. Continue turning until about one-third of the taper length is cut.

11. Stop the machine and check the taper with a micrometer or caliper. For more accuracy, use a taper ring gage. Adjust the taper attachment if necessary.

12. Rough turn the tapered section to within $\frac{3}{4}$ in. of the large end.

13. Finish turn the taper until the desired size is reached. If the taper is to be ground, finish cut the workpiece 0.008 to 0.015 in. oversize.

CAUTION

When the taper attachment is not in use, loosen clamp (C) so it will slide freely along the lathe bed. Lock the taper bar at zero degrees.

CUTTING A TAPER WITH A PLAIN TAPER ATTACHMENT

The *plain taper attachment* operates in much the same manner as does the *telescopic taper attachment*. When using the plain taper attachment for taper turning, however, the cross-feed screw must be disengaged from the cross-feed nut.

Fig. 62-9. The setup for using a plain taper attachment. The attachment will not function unless the cross-feed unit is disengaged.

The procedure for cutting a taper using the plain taper attachment follows (Fig. 62-9).

1. Disengage the cross-feed nut (X).

2. Position and clamp the guide bar (A) at the desired angle.

3. Clamp the draw bar (B) to the guide bar slide by tightening screw (C). Be sure the clamp brackets (D) are locked to the lathe bed.

4. After mounting the work in the lathe, set the compound rest at right angles to the bed ways. The point of the tool bit should align with the lathe's center line. For most operations, the small diameter of taper should be toward the tailstock, and the cut should be taken toward the headstock.

5. Engage the feed with the tool approximately 1 in. away from the beginning of the cut to be sure backlash is removed before the tool commences to cut.

CAUTION

Do not allow the guide bar slide to strike the cap screws at either end of the guide bar, especially when using the power feed.

6. Be sure to loosen the upper slide and clamp bracket, and replace the cross-feed bolt or nut when the plain taper attachment is not being used.

BORING A TAPER

A taper attachment is used when boring a tapered hole. The actual procedure is similar to that used when boring a straight hole. Use a taper plug gage to check the hole. Taper holes may be rough bored on the lathe and finished to size by using a taper reamer.

MEASURING TAPERS

There are six basic ways of measuring the accuracy of a taper.

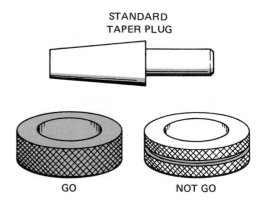

Fig. 62-10. Plug-and-ring taper gage.

Fig. 62-11. Measuring a taper with drill rod, gage blocks, and a micrometer.

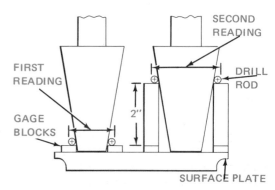

1. *Comparing a new taper to an existing taper.* The tapered part is fitted into an existing taper holder and checked for size. This method was described in the previous unit.

2. *Using a plug or ring gage.* A taper plug or ring gage can be used to check the basic dimensions of the workpiece as well as the angle of taper (Fig. 62-10).

3. *Using a taper-test gage.* This device consists of a base with two adjustable straight edges. The taper is set to the correct tpf and the workpiece to be checked is placed in the taper test gage.

4. *Using gage blocks, drill rod, and micrometer.* Stand the workpiece on a surface plate, with its small end down. Place gage blocks of equal size on either side of the taper (Fig. 62-11).

Place two pieces of drill rod on the gage blocks. Measure the distance across the drill rods with a micrometer. Now increase the height of the gage blocks by 2 in. Replace the drill rod and take a second reading with the micrometer. Subtract the first reading from the second reading and multiply by 6 to find the taper in inches per foot.

5. *Using a sine bar.* A very accurate method of measuring a taper is with a sine bar and gage blocks (See Unit 17).

6. *Using a micrometer.* Scribe two lines exactly 1 in. apart on the taper. With a micrometer, measure the diameter of the taper at these two points. The difference in readings will indicate the tpi. Multiply by 12 to find the tpf.

UNIT 63.
Taper Turning and Cutting Angles with the Compound Rest

Short tapers and steep angles can be cut using the compound rest. This is possible because the base of the compound rest is graduated in degrees and can be set at any angle to the center line or axis of the workpiece.

Truing a lathe center is one example of the use of the compound rest for taper work. Other examples include the refacing of an angle-type valve disk and the machining of the face of a bevel gear. Such jobs are often referred to as working to an angle rather than as taper work.

TURNING STEEP TAPERS AND ANGLES

Before you attempt to adjust the compound rest for turning a steep taper or angle, you should know these common terms.

1. An *angle* is the space between two lines that meet at a point or *vertex* (Fig. 63-1A).

2. Angles are measured in degrees (°), minutes ('), and seconds ("). There are 360° in a complete circle. Each degree can be divided into 60 equal parts called *minutes*. Each minute can be divided into 60 equal parts called *seconds*.

3. A *right* angle is formed when two lines perpendicular to each other intersect (Fig. 63-1B).

4. An *acute angle* is one which is less than 90° (Fig. 63-1C).

5. An *obtuse angle* is one which is more than 90° (Fig. 63-1D).

6. If two angles added together equal 90°, they are called *complementary angles*. For example, a 60° angle is the complement of a 30° angle (Fig. 63-1E).

7. If two angles total 180°, they are called *supplementary angles*. For example, a 60° angle is the supplement of a 120° angle (Fig. 63-1F).

8. Workpieces with an included angle of 8° or less are called *tapers*. If the included angle is more than 8°, it is called an *angle*.

9. Methods used by draftsmen to show an angle follow:

   a. The included angle of the taper. For example, the point of a center punch has an included angle of 90° (Fig. 63-2A).

   b. The angle made with the center line or axis of the workpiece. For example, the point of the lathe center makes an angle of 30° with the center line or axis (Fig. 63-2B).

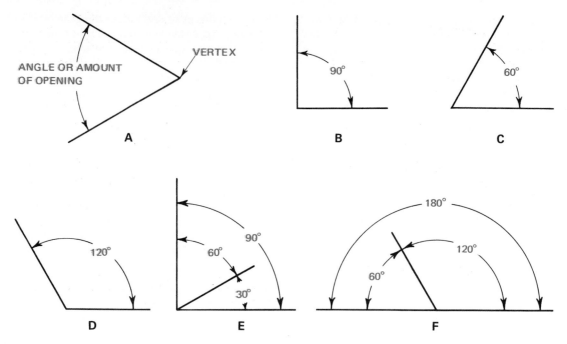

Fig. 63-1. Kinds of angles: (A) an angle, (B) a right angle, (C) an acute angle, (D) an obtuse angle, (E) complementary angles, and (F) supplementary angles.

c. The angle made with a line that is perpendicular (at right angles) to the center line or axis (Fig. 63-2C).

ADJUSTING THE COMPOUND REST

1. The graduations on the base of the compound rest are not the same on all machines. This is often confusing for the beginner. The zero mark may be on the front or on the side when the compound rest is at right angles to the center line. In either case, when set at zero, the compound rest is perpendicular to the lathe axis. When set at 90°, the compound rest is parallel to the lathe axis.

2. To adjust the compound rest:

a. Determine the angle formed between the outside of the workpiece and its center line or axis. (For example, the angle on the point of a lathe center would be one-half the included angle or 30°.)

b. Rotate the compound rest in a clockwise direction an amount in degrees equal to the *complement* of the angle made with the center line. (For example, to machine the angle shown in Fig. 63-3, the compound slide would have to be set at 70°. This is the complement of 20°.)

c. Rotate the compound rest in a counter-clockwise direction an amount equal to 90° plus the angle made with the center line (axis).

3. The compound-rest swivel can be locked in three different positions for cutting the same angle.

a. With the compound-rest handle turned toward the headstock (Fig. 63-4)

b. With the compound-rest handle turned toward the tailstock (Fig. 63-5)

c. With the compound-rest handle turned toward the tailstock but away from the operator (Fig. 63-6)

Remember that cutting must be done with the workpiece turning toward the cutting tool.

4. A vernier bevel protractor can be used to adjust the compound rest when a very accurate

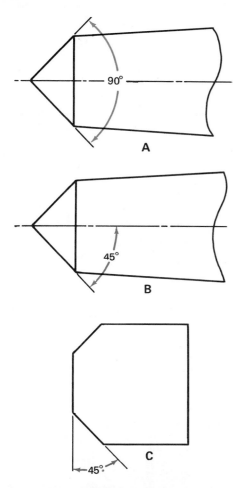

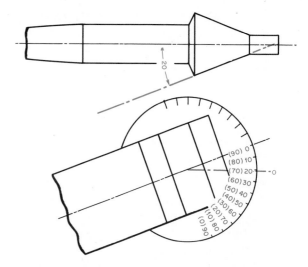

Fig. 63-3. Adjusting the compound rest to an angle of 20° with the center line or axis. Note the compound rest is rotated 70° clockwise from its right angle position.

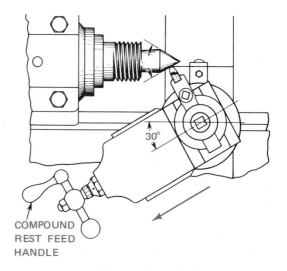

COMPOUND
REST FEED
HANDLE

Fig. 63-4. The compound rest has been rotated 60° clockwise from the original position with the handle turned toward the headstock. Cutting is done in the direction of the arrow.

Fig. 63-2. Methods of showing an angle on a drawing: (A) included angle, (B) angle with the axis or center line, and (C) angle with a line drawn perpendicular to the axis.

setting is required. To do this run the carriage up to the faceplate. Set the vernier bevel protractor to the required angle. Hold the bevel of the protractor on the flat surface of the faceplate, and align the compound rest with the opposite side of the protractor.

TURNING THE TAPER

1. Use a straight toolholder and a roundnose cutting tool.

2. Adjust the cutting tool as shown in Fig. 63-7 with the tool on center.

3. Feed the compound rest back and forth to see if the total taper can be cut with the length of the feed screw.

4. Turn on the power. Turn the cross slide to bring the tool into contact with the workpiece. Lock the carriage by tightening the carriage lock

Fig. 63-5. Here a compound rest has been turned counterclockwise with the handle turned toward the tailstock. In this position, cutting would have to be done on the backside of the workpiece with the spindle rotating opposite the normal direction.

Fig. 63-6. Setting the compound rest to turn a 60° point on the lathe center. Note that the compound rest has been rotated counterclockwise 120°.

Fig. 63-7. Cutting the center. Note that this is a view from the back of the lathe. The arrow indicates the direction in which the feed is to take place.

screw. Always start the cut at the highest point of the workpiece, which will be the small-diameter end of the workpiece.

5. Feed the compound rest by hand to cut the taper.

BORING TAPERED HOLES

Use a boring tool or boring bar for this operation. The procedure is the same as for turning a taper, except that the compound rest is swiveled to the opposite side to feed the tool parallel to the taper. A tapered hole is usually finished by reaming.

UNIT 64.

Turning and Boring with a Steady or Follower Rest

When turning or boring long small-diameter workpieces, it is often necessary to use extra support to prevent the piece from springing or bending. This extra support will also eliminate chattering. There are two attachments used: the *steady rest* (center rest) and the *follower rest*.

THE STEADY REST

The steady rest supports long work during turning, boring, or threading operations (Fig. 64-1). Work that is less than $\frac{3}{4}$-in. in diameter and machined more than 5 or 6 in. away from the headstock should be supported by a steady rest (Fig. 64-2).

The base of the steady rest is clamped to the lathe bed ways. Adjustable jaws are used to hold the workpiece in exact position. The simplest steady rest employs a set of bronze jaws for this purpose (Fig. 64-3). The telescopic-type steady rest has either bronze-tipped jaws or wheels (Fig. 64-4).

USING A STEADY, OR CENTER, REST WITH THE WORKPIECE HELD BETWEEN CENTERS

1. Place the workpiece between centers. Carefully turn a short section near the center, but somewhat closer to the headstock.

2. Remove the workpiece from the lathe. Move the carriage to the tailstock end. Clamp the steady rest to the bed at about the center of the workpiece. Open the top of the steady rest, and swing it out of the way.

3. Replace the workpiece.

4. Adjust the steady rest. Accurate positioning of the steady rest jaws to the work is important. The jaws must form a true bearing for the work, allowing it to turn freely but without play.

Adjust the bottom jaws first, then the top jaw. (Cellophane paper is sometimes placed between the jaws and the work to obtain proper clearance.) After all three jaws have been properly adjusted, tighten the adjusting screw lock nuts and the jaw clamp screws.

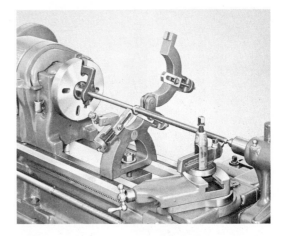

Fig. 64-1. Using a steady or center rest to support a long, small-diameter workpiece.

Fig. 64-2. Facing the end of a workpiece using a steady rest for support.

5. Turn half the workpiece to the desired size. Be sure to apply lubricant to the bearing surfaces. Scoring will result if the top jaw is too tight. Chatter results when the top jaw is too loose.

6. Reverse the stock, readjust the jaws, and turn the other half of the workpiece.

349

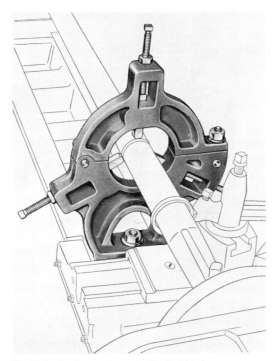

Fig. 64-5. A type of follower rest.

Fig. 64-3. Steady or center rest with adjustable jaws.

Fig. 64-4. A telescopic-type steady rest with small wheels that come in contact with the workpiece.

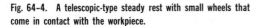

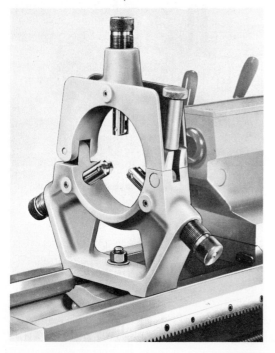

Fig. 64-6. In this setup, both the follower rest and the steady rest are used.

USING THE STEADY, OR CENTER, REST FOR BORING OPERATIONS

1. Fasten one end of the workpiece in a three- or four-jaw chuck.

2. Position the steady rest at the other end of the workpiece. It is often a good idea to adjust the rest to the workpiece near the chuck and then move it to the outer end. This will help to assure its being on center.

3. Face the end of the workpiece before drilling, boring, or reaming straight or tapered holes.

350

THE FOLLOWER REST

The follower rest clamps to the saddle of the carriage and moves along with it (Fig. 64-5). It is used to prevent a workpiece from springing away from the point of the cutting tool during a turning operation. It can also be used when cutting threads on a long thin piece of stock.

The follower rest has two jaws or a two-point support that follows the cutting tool. These jaws bear on the finished work surface. On some follower rests, smaller rolls replace the jaws. This helps to prevent marring the surface.

USING THE STEADY AND FOLLOWER REST

To machine thin shafts, it may be necessary to use both the steady rest and follower rest at the same time. Both types of rests are used in the setup shown in Fig. 64-6. Remember, the jaws of the two rests must be accurately positioned to form a true bearing for the workpiece, allowing it to turn freely but without play.

UNIT 65. Cutting External Threads

The ratio between the rotation of the headstock spindle and carriage movement on an engine lathe can be controlled by means of gears. Therefore, it is possible to use the lathe for cutting threads on both internal and external surfaces. For example, to cut 8 threads per inch on a workpiece, the lathe's gears are adjusted so the spindle rotates eight times for every 1 in. of carriage movement.

TOOLS AND EQUIPMENT NEEDED

1. A *screw-thread tool gage* is a circular disk having 60-degree (°) openings of different sizes around its circumference (Fig. 65-1). This gage is used to check the thread-cutting tool when accurate American National or Unified threads must be cut. It gives the correct width of flat (or point) on the threading tool.

2. A *center gage* is used to grind the cutting tool and adjust it when an all-purpose 60° threading tool is used (Fig. 65-2). All angles of the center gage are 60°. Note that the center gage does not provide a means for gaging the flat at the end of the threading tool.

3. A *threading tool* is a single-point cutting tool ground to cut American National or Unified screw threads. The point of the tool is ground to an included angle of 60°. It has 3 to 5° *side clearance* (relief) and about 8° *front clearance* (relief) (Figs. 65-3A and 65-3B).

Clean, accurate threads are impossible unless the side and the front of the tool are given enough clearance to permit the tool to advance as the work revolves. A tool which is satisfactory for cutting a fine thread may not have enough clearance to cut a coarse thread (Fig. 65-4). *Hogging* and rough threads are usually the result of insufficient clearance.

Fig. 65-1. A screw-thread gage.

Fig. 65-2. A center gage.

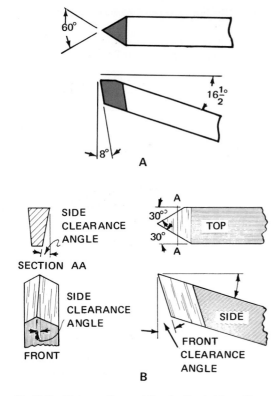

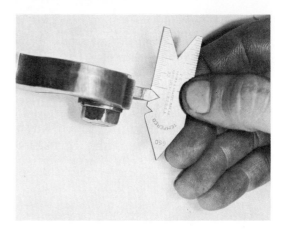

Fig. 65-5. Checking a thread-cutting tool with a center gage.

Fig. 65-3. (A) A correctly ground thread-cutting tool for cutting toward the headstock. (B) The side clearance angle should be reversed for left-hand threading.

Fig. 65-6. A formed threading tool and holder is an excellent device for cutting threads.

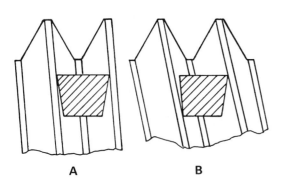

Fig. 65-4. (A) Tool with sufficient clearance. (B) When the thread pitch is increased, the same tool has inadequate clearance.

For most threading, the point of the cutting tool is left sharp or is rounded slightly. The *center gage* is used to check its included angle (Fig. 65-5). For greater strength and accuracy, the *screw-thread tool gage* is used to check the width of flat located at the end of the cutting tool. For example, if 10 threads per inch are to be cut, the cutting-edge must fit the opening marked 10. When a threading tool is ground to the No. 10 opening, *it can be used only for cutting 10 threads per inch.*

4. A *straight toolholder* is used to hold the thread-cutting tool.

5. A *formed threading tool* is designed specifically for cutting threads. It comes already ground and may be resharpened if necessary (Fig. 65–6). To resharpen it, all you have to do is grind the top face slightly and adjust the tool so that its top is horizontal (Fig. 65–7). The formed threading tool can replace the thread-cutting tool bit and regular toolholder (Fig. 65–8).

6. A *spring-head threading toolholder* may be used for both fine or coarse threading. Its spring head is equipped with a special locking nut

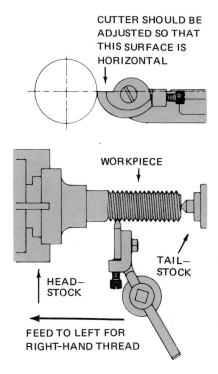

CUTTER SHOULD BE ADJUSTED SO THAT THIS SURFACE IS HORIZONTAL

WORKPIECE

HEAD-STOCK

TAIL-STOCK

FEED TO LEFT FOR RIGHT-HAND THREAD

Fig. 65-8. How the formed threading tool is used in cutting external threads.

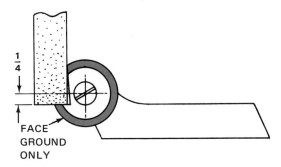

$\frac{1}{4}$

FACE GROUND ONLY

Fig. 65-7. Grinding a formed threading tool.

Fig. 65-9. This spring-head threading toolholder is particularly good for very accurate threading. The tool is ground so that a 60° angle is on one side of the bit only.

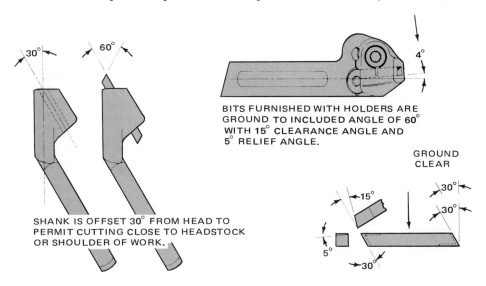

30°   60°

SHANK IS OFFSET 30° FROM HEAD TO PERMIT CUTTING CLOSE TO HEADSTOCK OR SHOULDER OF WORK.

4°

BITS FURNISHED WITH HOLDERS ARE GROUND TO INCLUDED ANGLE OF 60° WITH 15° CLEARANCE ANGLE AND 5° RELIEF ANGLE.

GROUND CLEAR

15°   30°

30°

5°

30°

which provides the rigid backing required for heavy cuts; when loosened, the holder becomes a spring tool for finishing work. High-speed steel square bits are furnished with each holder. Each end is ground to an included angle of 60° for cutting coarse and fine 60° sharp V threads. The size of the bit used determines the pitch of the thread that the tool is capable of cutting (Fig. 65-9).

7. A *screw-pitch gage* is used to measure the number of threads per inch on a workpiece. Most gages have 30 separate blades with pitches from 4 to 42 per inch (Fig. 65-10).

8. A *dog* or *chuck* is used to hold one end of the workpiece.

9. A *rule* is needed to measure length and number of threads per inch.

GETTING THE WORKPIECE READY FOR THREAD CUTTING

1. Machine the workpiece until its diameter is equal to the major diameter of the screw thread. For example, if the drawing calls for a $\frac{1}{2}$-13NC or UNC screw thread, the workpiece should be machined to a diameter of 0.500 in. For extremely accurate threads, the workpiece must be machined within a few thousandths of an inch tolerance. A listing of allowances for external

threads can be found in *The New American Machinist's Handbook* or *Machinery's Handbook*.

2. Measure the length to be threaded with a rule. Chalk the surface, and mark the distance with a pencil or a scriber.

3. Some threads are *undercut* at the end of the thread. This undercut makes thread cutting much easier for the beginner (Fig. 65-11). If an undercut is used, machine it to the exact minor diameter of the thread. Make the undercut with a cutoff tool or square-nose cutting tool.

ADJUSTING THE GEARBOX

When you know the correct number of threads per inch to be cut, locate this number on the index chart or plate over the quick-change gearbox. For example, if the thread to be cut is $\frac{1}{2}$-13NC or UNC, first find 13 on the index chart or plate. This plate tells how to move the levers to obtain the correct ratio between the spindle and carriage.

Usually there are two or three levers to move.

1. A sliding gear at the left end of the gearbox that moves in or out.

2. A lever that can be moved to the left, to the center, or to the right.

Fig. 65-10. A screw-pitch gage.

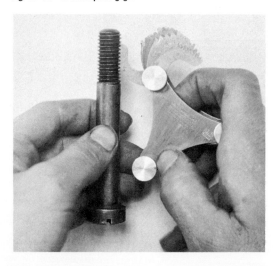

Fig. 65-11. Preparing the work for cutting an external thread.

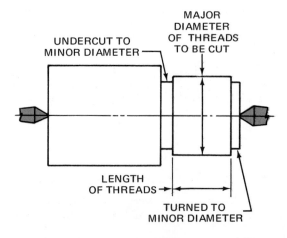

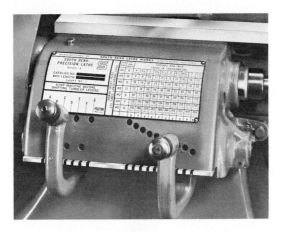

Fig. 65-12. Setting the quick-change gearbox to cut the correct number of threads per inch. This one is set to cut 26 threads per inch.

Fig. 65-13. A thread-chasing dial.

3. A lever that can be moved directly under the numbers stamped on the index plate.

Although the exact arrangement varies with each kind of lathe, all are quite similar (Fig. 65-12). If you study the gearbox and index chart or plate, you will soon learn how to adjust it.

CHECKING THE THREADING MECHANISM

1. For threading, the *splitnut, or halfnut,* must close over the lead screw to move the carriage with positive motion.

2. Move the *feed-change lever* to a neutral position (usually in the center). This will allow the split- or halfnut to close. Move the halfnut lever (up or down) to see if it will close over the lead screw. Move the carriage slightly by the hand feed while engaging the halfnut lever.

Never use the splitnut, or halfnut, for turning work. It is used only for thread cutting.

CHECKING THE THREAD-CHASING DIAL

1. Most lathes are equipped with a *thread-chasing dial* which is attached to the carriage

(Fig. 65-13). This dial tells when to close the splitnut or halfnut.

2. If there is no thread-chasing dial, the split-nut or halfnut must be kept closed over the lead screw at all times during the thread-cutting operation. Therefore, at the end of each cut, the direction of rotation of the lathe must be reversed to bring the cutting tool back to the starting position. Few lathes are without this dial, however.

3. On the top of the thread-chasing device is a revolving dial marked with lines and numbers. This dial revolves when the lathe is running and the carriage is not moving. When the splitnut is closed, the carriage moves but the dial does not rotate.

4. Use the thread-chasing dial as follows.

   a. For cutting *even* numbers of threads per inch (2, 4, 6, etc.), close the splitnut *at any line.*

   b. For cutting *odd* numbers of threads per inch (1, 3, 5, etc.), close the splitnut *at any numbered line.*

   c. For cutting *half* threads (such as $11\frac{1}{2}$), close the splitnut *at any odd-numbered line.*

ADJUSTING THE SPEED

Spindle speed should be about one-third to one-fourth that used for turning. You will probably have to use the back gears to obtain this slow speed. The correct speed to use is one that permits you to control the movements of the cutting tool at all times. Beginners should use slower speeds until skill and good judgment have been developed. Fine-pitch threads may be cut at a faster speed than coarse threads. Also, faster speeds may be used to cut threads in soft metals such as brass. Slower speeds are necessary for hard metals like tool steel.

SETTING THE THREADING TOOL AND MOUNTING THE WORKPIECE

1. To cut a right-hand thread, turn the compound rest to the right (counterclockwise). Clamp it at an angle of 30° to the cross-feed (Fig. 65-14A). (Some machinists recommend an angle of 29°.) The compound rest is moved for several reasons.

   a. It frees the cross-feed handle for moving the threading tool in and out at the start and finish of each cut.

   b. The depth of cut is controlled with the compound-rest screw.

   c. It allows the left side of the cutting tool to do most of the cutting. The right side only shaves the thread smooth. Figure 65-14B shows how the tool cuts when fed straight in. Figure 65-14C shows how the tool cuts when fed at a 30° angle.

2. Allow only the point of the threading tool to project beyond the holder.

3. Mount the workpiece in the lathe. When mounting work between centers, be sure the lathe dog is securely attached before starting to cut the thread. If the dog should slip, the thread will be ruined. Do not remove the lathe dog from the workpiece until after the thread has been completed. Always be sure that the lathe dog is replaced in the same slot of the driving plate should it become necessary to remove the workpiece from the lathe.

When threading work in the lathe chuck, be sure the chuck jaws are tight and the work is well supported (Fig. 65-15). The chuck must be tight enough on the spindle to prevent unscrewing when the lathe is reversed. Do not remove the work from the chuck until after the

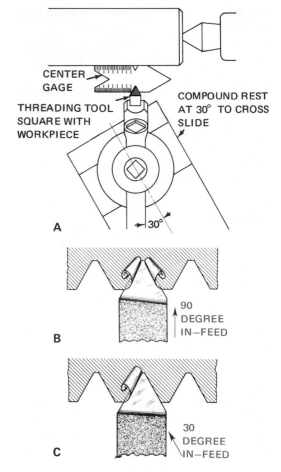

Fig. 65-14. (A) Setting the threading tool square. (B) Tool fed straight in. (C) Tool fed at 30°.

Fig. 65-15. In this threading setup, one end of the workpiece is held in a chuck. Make sure the workpiece does not slip, since this will ruin the threads.

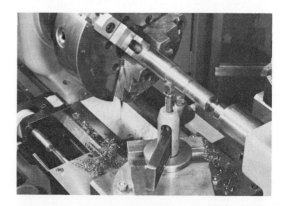

thread has been completed. When threading long, slender shafts, use a follower rest (Fig. 65-16).

4. Mount the toolholder, and use a center gage to adjust the cutting tool square with the workpiece. Hold the center gage square on the tool bit, and feed it in close to the work. Have a slight space between the center gage and work. Tap the toolholder until the length of the center gage is parallel to the work. Be sure the point or face of the cutting tool is set to the exact center height.

MAKING A TRIAL CUT

1. Turn the cross-feed in until the point of the tool almost touches the workpiece. Now rotate the micrometer collar until it is set at zero. Tighten the setscrew.

2. Turn in the compound-rest feed until the point of the tool just touches the workpiece. Rotate the micrometer collar on the compound-rest slide until it is set at zero. Tighten the setscrew. You can now use this graduated collar to determine when you have obtained the correct depth of thread. Table 65-1 shows the depth setting for cutting threads with the compound rest at 30°. Notice, for example, that if you are cutting 13 threads to the inch, the micrometer collar of the compound rest must show 0.0577 when the thread is completed. You

Table 65-1. Depth setting for cutting threads on engine lathe with compound rest at 30 degrees.

Threads per Inch	Depth to Feed Compound Slide in Thousandths of an Inch
64	0.0117
56	0.0134
48	0.0156
44	0.0170
40	0.0187
36	0.0208
32	0.0234
28	0.0270
24	0.0312
20	0.0375
18	0.0417
16	0.0468
14	0.0537
13	0.0577
12	0.0629
11	0.0681
10	0.0751
9	0.0831
8	0.0935
7	0.1074
6	0.1247

can calculate the depth by dividing 0.750 by the number of threads. Stated as a formula,

$$\text{Depth to feed tool} = \frac{0.750}{N}$$

Turn out the cross-feed one complete counterclockwise turn after each pass of the tool.

3. Move the carriage to the extreme right so that the point of the tool clears the workpiece. Turn in the cross-feed one complete turn until it reaches zero on the micrometer collar. Go slowly as you approach the zero line. If you go beyond zero, turn out the cross-feed one turn and try again. You must always get the backlash out of the cross-feed screw.

4. Now turn in the compound-rest feed about 0.001 in.

5. Turn on the power, and watch the thread-chasing dial as it rotates.

6. Place your left hand on the cross-feed handle and your right hand on the splitnut, or half-nut, lever.

Fig. 65-16. Use a follower rest when cutting threads on a long, thin rod. If this is not done, the rod will spring away and the thread will not be full depth in the middle of the workpiece.

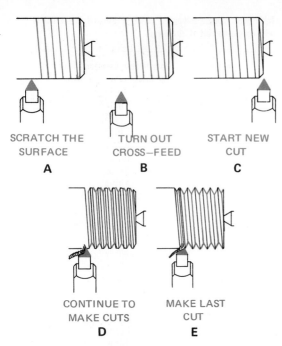

SCRATCH THE SURFACE
A

TURN OUT CROSS—FEED
B

START NEW CUT
C

CONTINUE TO MAKE CUTS
D

MAKE LAST CUT
E

Fig. 65-17. Steps in cutting a thread. (A) Make a trial cut. (B) Release the cutting tool. (C) Return to the starting position. (D) Most of the thread is completed. (E) Feeding the last cut.

7. Close the splitnut, or halfnut, at the correct point on the dial. Watch the tool move across the workpiece. The point of the tool should just scratch the surface (Fig. 65-17A).

8. As the point of the tool nears the end of the threaded section, prepare to do two things quickly and at the same time.

    a. Turn the cross-feed out (counterclockwise) one turn (Fig. 65-17B).

    b. Open the splitnut lever.

9. Stop the machine and check the threads. Hold a rule over the threaded section, and check the number of spaces in 1 in. For example, if 6 threads per inch are being cut, there should be six spaces within the inch. If the thread length is less than 1 in., count the threads in $\frac{1}{2}$ or $\frac{1}{4}$ in. and multiply by 2 or 4, as the case may be (Fig. 65-18).

10. A screw-pitch gage can also be used to check the number of threads.

CUTTING THE THREADS

1. Return the carriage to the starting position.

2. Turn in the cross-feed handle one turn (clockwise) until zero is reached on the micrometer collar. Some lathes have a *stop* on the cross-feed which can be set so you cannot feed in too far.

3. Turn in the compound-rest feed 0.002 or 0.003 in.

4. Apply cutting fluid to the workpiece (Fig. 65-19). This is not necessary when threading cast iron.

5. Make a second cut (see Fig. 65-17C). Do not make the following mistakes.

    a. Closing the splitnut on the wrong line of the dial.

    b. Turning the cross-feed in instead of out at the end of the cut. This usually ruins the workpiece.

Fig. 65-18. To check the number of threads per inch, place a rule against the workpiece so that it rests on the point of the thread or at one end of the scribed line. Count the scribed lines between the end of the rule and the first inch mark. This will give you the number of threads per inch.

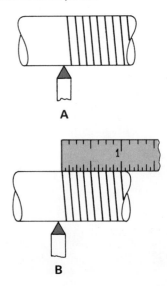

A

B

Fig. 65-19. Applying cutting fluid with a brush.

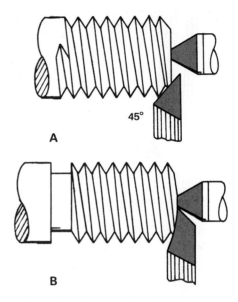

Fig. 65-20. Finishing the end of a threaded piece. (A) Cutting a chamfer. (B) A formed tool is used to round off the end of the thread.

c. Opening the splitnut without turning out the cross-feed. *This can only be done if there is an undercut at the end of the threads.*

d. Forgetting to reset the cross-feed at zero before adjusting the compound-rest feed for the next cut.

6. Continue to cut the thread a little at a time. It may require as many as 10 or more cuts to complete the thread (see Fig. 65–17D).

7. A narrow crest will appear on each thread as it nears its finished shape (see Fig. 65–17E).

8. It may be necessary to file the tops of the threads lightly in order to remove any burrs which may have formed.

9. Finish the end of the threaded piece. A 45° chamfer cut on the end of a thread is commonly used to finish bolts and cap screws. The ends of machined parts and special screws are often finished by rounding them with a forming tool (Fig. 65–20).

10. Remove the workpiece from the lathe. Leave the dog in place.

CHECKING THE THREADS

1. The simplest method of checking the threads is to try the workpiece in a threaded hole or nut. For most jobs this is enough. If it won't go in, the thread must be cut a little deeper.

2. *Thread-ring gages* are used when greater accuracy is necessary.

3. A *thread micrometer caliper* can be used to measure the *pitch diameter* of the thread. This diameter is then compared to the required pitch diameter as indicated in *The New American Machinist's Handbook,* the *Machinery's Handbook,* or in any thread chart. For example, the pitch diameter of a $\frac{1}{2}$-13NC or UNC thread would be 0.4500.

RESETTING THE TOOL

If the workpiece is removed from the lathe dog, or if the thread tool must be reground before threading is complete, the tool bit must be readjusted before doing any further cutting.

1. Close the splitnut at the correct dial position with the cutting tool away from the workpiece.

2. Allow the carriage to move a short distance.

3. Turn off the power. Do not disturb the carriage position. Move the cross-feed and compound-rest feed alternately until the point of

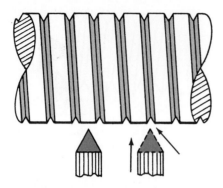

Fig. 65-21. Resetting a tool in the original groove.

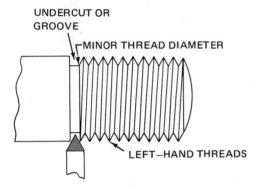

Fig. 65-22. An undercut or groove is absolutely necessary when cutting left-hand threads. This undercut or groove provides a place for the cutting tool to start.

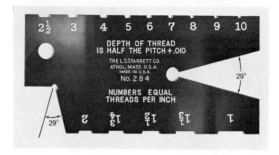

A

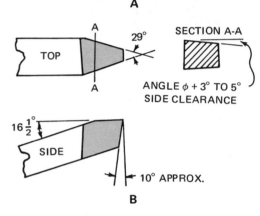

B

Fig. 65-23. (A) A 29° Acme thread gage. (B) Proper method of grinding a cutter for an Acme thread.

the tool matches the partially cut threads (Fig. 65–21).

4. Reset the micrometer collar on the cross-feed to zero. Then proceed as before.

CUTTING LEFT-HAND THREADS

To cut a left-hand thread:

1. Make an undercut at the end of the length to be threaded (Fig. 65–22).

2. Set the compound rest to 30° to the left of the cross-feed.

3. Reverse the direction of the lead screw so that the carriage moves toward the tailstock.

4. Start the thread at the left end of the threaded section and cut toward the right end.

CUTTING ACME THREADS

Acme threads are cut on machinery parts such as lead screws. They have a 29° included angle.

1. Grind a cutting tool to the proper shape. Be sure to provide enough end and side relief. Check the point and angle of the tool with an *Acme thread gage* (Fig. 65–23).

2. Turn the compound rest to the right of the cross-feed at an angle of $14\frac{1}{2}°$. Adjust the cutting-edge of the tool to line it up exactly with the beveled edge of the gage (Fig. 65–24). Note that a 29° Acme thread gage is used in the same manner as the center gage.

3. In cutting an Acme thread, there should be a clearance of 0.010 in. between the top of the thread of the screw and the bottom of the thread of the nut in which it fits.

4. Cut the threads in the same way as described for other threads.

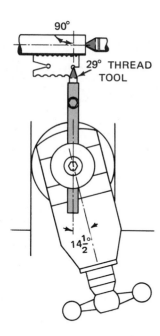

Fig. 65-24. Adjusting the compound rest and the cutting tool for cutting an Acme thread.

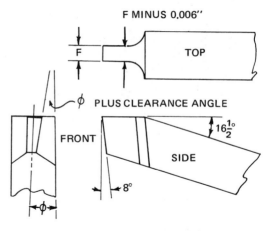

Fig. 65-25. Proper method of grinding a cutting tool to cut square threads.

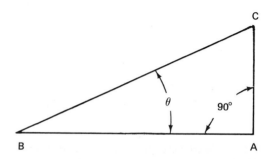

Fig. 65-26. Determining the angle θ. Draw line AB equal to the circumference of the thread (3.1416 × major diameter). Then draw line AC at right angles to AB and equal in length to the thread pitch (or lead, if a multiple thread). Draw line BC. The angle θ is equal to the angle made by lines BA and BC.

CUTTING SQUARE THREADS

The square thread is stronger than the Acme thread. It is used on certain vise and clamp screws, and on other worm-screw forms.

In cutting a square thread with a large lead, the tool angles must be absolutely correct. Clearance should be allowed on two sides, tapering from both the top and front of the tool (Fig. 65-25). Figure 65-26 explains how angle θ is determined.

External square threads should be cut to the minor diameter plus about 0.005 in. Internal square threads should be cut to the major diameter plus about 0.005 in. The additional 0.005 in. allows a small clearance at the bottom of the thread. This helps to compensate for small inaccuracies in the tool bit or cutting operation.

The tool is fed directly into the work with the cross-feed, or compound-rest feed. The simplest method is to set the compound rest at zero degrees, feed in with the compound, and back out and return the tool with the cross-feed. Care must be taken to avoid chatter and hogging-in. Take very light cuts when turning or boring a square thread.

CUTTING METRIC THREADS

Many of the newer lathes come equipped with a quick-change gearbox designed for cutting both Unified National (English) and metric threads (Fig. 65-27). On other lathes, metric threads may be obtained with the use of a metric transposing attachment.

The metric thread angle and form is identical to that of the Unified National thread. The cutting operation is the same, with one important exception, the motor must be reversed after each cut to return the carriage to the starting position. This procedure is necessary because metric threads have no definite relation to the threading dial. After the halfnut lever on the

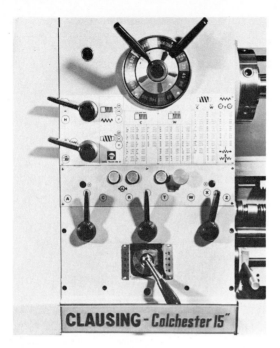

Fig. 65-27. This lathe is equipped to cut both Unifed National and metric threads.

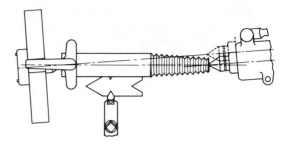

Fig. 65-28. Cutting a thread on a tapered surface.

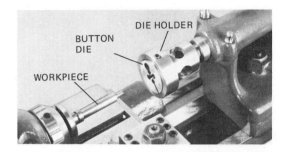

DIE HOLDER
BUTTON DIE
WORKPIECE

Fig. 65-29. Using a button die held in the tailstock.

Fig. 65-30. Using a button die held in a diestock.

carriage is engaged for the first cut, it *must not* be released until the thread has been completed. As the tool reaches the end of each cut, back out the cross-feed, stop the lathe, and reverse the motor until the tool has been returned to the starting position. Then advance the cross-feed to its original zero position, turn in the compound-rest feed for the next cut, start the motor, and repeat the cutting operation.

CUTTING A THREAD ON A TAPER

Thread cutting on a taper is done in the same way as on a straight shaft. However, the threading tool must be set at right angles to the axis of the taper (Fig. 65-28). A common mistake is to set the tool at right angles to the tapered surface.

CUTTING EXTERNAL THREADS WITH BUTTON DIES AND A DIE HOLDER

Adjustable round split (button) dies held in a die holder may be used to cut threads on small diameter workpieces.

1. Select a button die of the correct size.

2. Select a lathe die holder to match. Most die holders are made to hold 1- or $1\frac{1}{2}$-in. diameter dies.

3. Insert the die in the die holder (Fig. 65-29).

4. Place the die holder in the tailstock spindle.

5. Use a very slow speed (back gears).

6. Turn in the tailstock handwheel as the die cuts the threads. Use plenty of cutting fluid. Be

careful to stop the machine as soon as the correct length of thread is machined. Some die holders are made in two parts, arbor and die holder. The die holder is slipped over the shank of the arbor. In using this type, hold on to the die holder itself until the correct length of thread is machined. Then release your grip. The die holder will turn freely on the shank. This type of holder is especially useful when cutting threads up to a shoulder. Figure 65-30 shows a method of cutting threads with a *button die* in a die stock.

UNIT 66. Cutting Internal Threads

Internal threads are cut in the same general way as external threads. However, the threading operation itself is more difficult. This is because you can't see the threading operation. Also, it isn't possible to hold the tool as rigidly as when cutting external threads.

TOOLS AND EQUIPMENT NEEDED

1. A *forged boring tool* can be used for cutting internal threads. Its end should be ground similar to that of an external thread-cutting tool. The cutting-edge may need a little more end relief to keep its bottom from rubbing on the work.

2. A *standard tool bit* ground as a threading tool can be used with a boring bar if the hole is large enough. Always use the largest boring bar possible to provide maximum rigidity (Fig. 66-1).

3. A *center gage* is needed for grinding the tool and for setting it.

4. A *steady rest* should be used to support the outer end of long workpieces.

SETTING UP THE LATHE FOR INTERNAL THREAD CUTTING

1. Drill or bore a hole of the correct size for the thread. The hole size must be no smaller than the minor diameter of the thread. This would give a full depth of thread. Usually the hole is made slightly larger to give clearance between the mating parts. The *tap-drill size* will produce a hole that will give a 75 percent depth of thread, which is preferred in most work.

2. If the thread is cut only part way through the hole, it is a good idea to cut a groove or *recess* at the beginning and end of the thread (Fig. 66-2). Groove A serves as a guide for measuring depth. When the tool point has cut to the

Fig. 66-1. The correct method of grinding a cutter bit for thread cutting. That the amount of end relief or front clearance varies with the diameter of the workpiece.

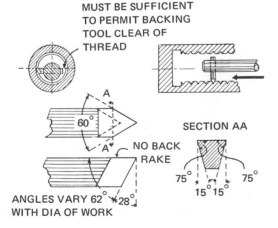

CLEARANCE HERE
MUST BE SUFFICIENT
TO PERMIT BACKING
TOOL CLEAR OF
THREAD

SECTION AA

ANGLES VARY 62° ↦ 28°
WITH DIA OF WORK

Fig. 66-2. Machining the opening for cutting internal threads. With this setup, either right-hand or left-hand threads can be cut.

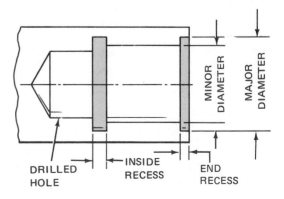

DRILLED HOLE   ← INSIDE RECESS   END RECESS

depth of groove A, the thread has been finished. This outer groove is not necessary if the thread is being cut to fit a certain screw; the proper depth is then reached when the screw fits the thread correctly. Groove B should be about twice as wide as the thread pitch and a few thousandths of an inch larger than the major diameter. This groove provides a brief interval at the end of each cut during which the work can revolve freely while the halfnut lever is disengaged. Grooves A and B can be omitted after the operator has learned internal thread-cutting operations.

3. Set the compound rest to 29 or 30 degrees (°) to the left of the cross-feed. This is just the opposite of the setting for external threading.

4. If threads are to be cut through the work-piece, make sure there is enough clearance between the workpiece and the chuck.

5. Fasten the threading tool in a holder or boring bar.

6. Hold the center gage against the face surface of the workpiece as shown in Fig. 66-3. This can be done by holding the center gage against the side of the workpiece. Adjust the tool on center and at right angles to the workpiece. To set the tool at center height, use a surface gage. Set the scriber point to the point of dead center. Then set the tool bit to the surface-gage scriber point.

7. If the thread is cut only partially through the hole, move the carriage by hand to the point where the thread will end. Mark a line on the lathe bed with a piece of chalk or a pencil. This will tell you when the tool bit has reached the end of the thread length so you can open the splitnut lever and stop the carriage.

8. With the work chucked or held on a face-plate, right-hand threading is done from the outer edge of the bore toward the headstock. Left-hand threading is done from left to right, with the lead screw direction reversed.

CUTTING THE THREADS

1. Set the micrometer collar of the cross-feed at zero.

2. Turn the compound-rest feed out until the point of the tool just touches the workpiece. Set

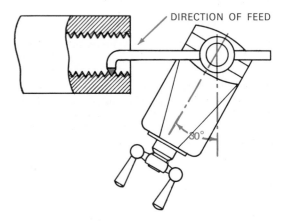

Fig. 66-4. Cutting the internal thread.

Fig. 66-5. Using a tap to cut the internal thread. Note how the tap is supported with the dead center.

Fig. 66-3. Adjusting the cutting tool for internal cutting. The center gage can also be held against the side of the workpiece to make this adjustment.

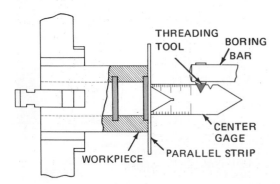

its micrometer collar at zero. Using the *compound-rest screw* (not the carriage cross-feed), feed into the work 0.002 to 0.004 in. Repeat until the desired thread depth is attained. The finishing cut should be only about 0.001 in. deep. Due to the spring of an internal tool, cuts should be much lighter than when cutting external threads (Fig. 66-4).

3. Remember these two points:

a. The cross-feed *must be turned in* rather than *out* when opening the splitnut at the end of each cut.

b. If a recess was already machined at the end of the threaded area, you can open the splitnut without turning in the cross slide to stop the carriage. You must, however, turn the cross-feed in before you move the carriage back for the next cut.

CUTTING INTERNAL THREADS ON A LATHE WITH A TAP

The best and simplest way to cut internal threads is with a tap. Figure 66-5 shows one method of using a hand tap in a metal lathe. Remember, hand taps are designed for turning back and forth (to clear out the chips). Machine taps are designed for continuous tapping.

UNIT 67. Turret (Indexing) Lathes

When machining a complex workpiece on a general-purpose lathe, a great deal of time is spent changing and adjusting the several tools that are needed to complete the work. One of the first adaptations of the engine lathe which made it more suitable to mass production was the addition of a multitool turret in place of the tailstock. Although most turrets have six stations, some have as many as eight (Fig. 67-1).

High-production turret lathes are very complicated machines with a wide variety of power accessories. The principal feature of all turret lathes, however, is that the tools can perform a consecutive series of operations in proper sequence. Once the tools have been set and adjusted, little skill is required to turn out duplicate parts.

FEATURES OF TURRET INDEXING LATHES

The principal features of all turret, or indexing, lathes are: (1) Cutting can be done rapidly using a succession of tools. These tools are indexed one after the other into proper cutting position. (2) The turret moves longitudinally (back and forth) to feed the cutting tools into the end of the workpiece. (3) Cross-feeding tools are mounted on tool blocks located on the front and back of the cross slide. Often, the front tool

block is a four-sided turret tool post. The result is that eleven different tools can be mounted on one lathe (six on the turret, four on the front turret tool post, and one on the back toolholder). (4) The workpiece can be either bar stock, which is held in collets, or individual workpieces held in chucks or fixtures.

HAND-FED TURRET INDEXING LATHES

The simplest turret lathe is one that has been converted from a standard engine lathe (Fig. 67-2). A turret attachment replaces the tailstock

Fig. 67-1. Although most turrets have six stations, some are designed with as many as eight.

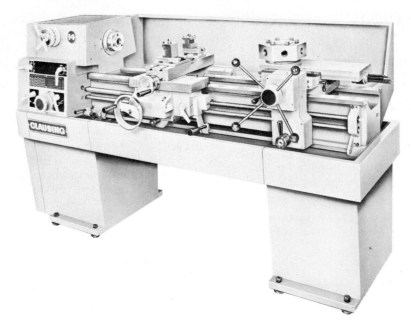

Fig. 67-2.   A conventional, 14-in. lathe that has been converted to a turret lathe.

Fig. 67-3.   This lathe is tooled up to turn out small, externally threaded parts. Note that all tooling is on the turret except for the cutoff tool, which is mounted on the cross slide.

Fig. 67-4.   Another tooling setup.

and a double tool cross slide is mounted in place of the carriage cross slide. Adjustable turret stops are used to limit the amount of movement that the ram can make. This type of turret lathe is ideal for limited production runs of from 100 to 5,000 pieces (Fig. 67-3). The major tool-handling unit is the turret which moves back and forth (Fig. 67-4).

Tools mounted on the turret attachment may be used for both interior and exterior cutting. Normally, additional exterior cutting tools are mounted on the double tool cross slide. A good example of this kind of arrangement is shown in Fig. 67-5. The production part to be made is the base of a cigarette lighter (Fig. 67-5A). The tooling for interior cutting includes a

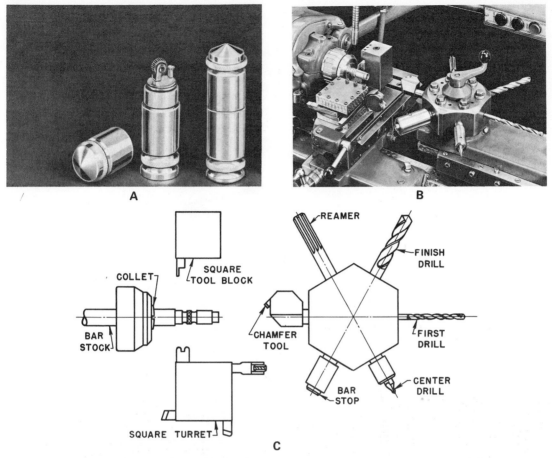

Fig. 67-5. (A) The base of this lighter is the part to be turned on the lathe. (B) Here the lathe is set up with the correct tooling. Note that all stations are fitted with tools. Eleven operations are to be performed. (C) A diagram showing the tooling. The first station on the turret is the bar stop, and the last is the chamfer tool.

bar stop to limit the distance the stock can move out from the collet, a center drill, a pilot drill, a finish drill, a reamer, and an interior chamfer tool (Fig. 67–5B). Note that these tools will rotate clockwise, starting with the bar stop. Exterior cutting tools are all mounted on the turret tool post except for the cutoff tool, which is mounted on the back tool block. The tools mounted on the turret tool post include a forming tool, a cutting tool, a chamfer tool, and a knurling tool. Cutting off is done by the cutoff tool mounted in the back tool block (Fig. 67–5C). Note that the cutoff tool is mounted upside down since the workpiece is always rotating counterclockwise.

All hand-fed turret lathes are of the ram type; that is, the turret is mounted on a ram and the ram, in turn, is mounted on a base that is clamped to the ways of the bed. Only the ram moves back and forth as the cutting tools are fed into the work. As the operator moves the ram all the way to the right, it indexes to the proper position. Adjustable turret stops can be used to stop the feed motion of each tool at the correct point.

POWER-FEED HORIZONTAL TURRET LATHES

There are two major types of power-feed horizontal turret lathes, the ram-type and the saddle-type (Fig. 67–6). Either type can be equipped

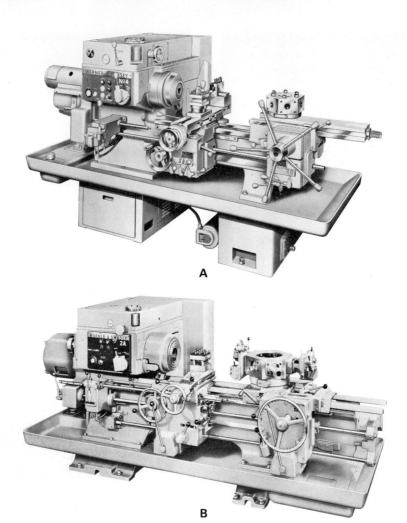

A

B

Fig. 67-6. (A) Ram-type turret lathe. (B) Saddle-type turret lathe.

Fig. 67-7. (A) These are the kinds of small parts that can be turned out on a bar turret lathe. (B) This casting is machined on a chucking lathe.

A

B

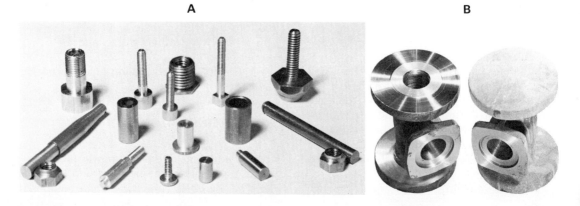

as a *bar* or *chucking* lathe. Bar turret lathes are used to machine parts from bar stock, and chucking turret lathes are used to hold individual parts (Fig. 67-7).

The *ram-type turret lathe* is similar to the converted-turret engine lathe just described, except that it has power longitudinal and cross-feed, and it is a larger machine. Normally, these machines also have automatic controls for speeds and feeds. This type of turret lathe is primarily used for relatively light cutting jobs because extending the ram diminishes the machine's ability to support the cutting tool rigidly.

The *saddle-type turret lathe* is heavier and larger than the ram-type lathe. Its entire turret assembly, including the ram and saddle, moves back and forth on the lathe ways. Saddle-type machines are used for heavy cuts.

Fig. 67-8. Tools commonly used on the turret lathe.

Fig. 67-9. Note that cutting tools mounted on the front of the cross slide have their cutting-edges up, and those mounted on the back of the lathe have their cutting-edges down.

Fig. 67-10. A multiple turning head that will do internal boring and external turning at the same time.

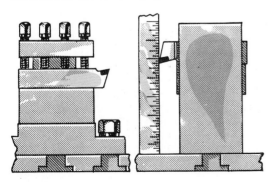

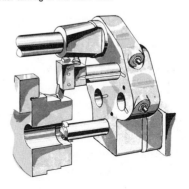

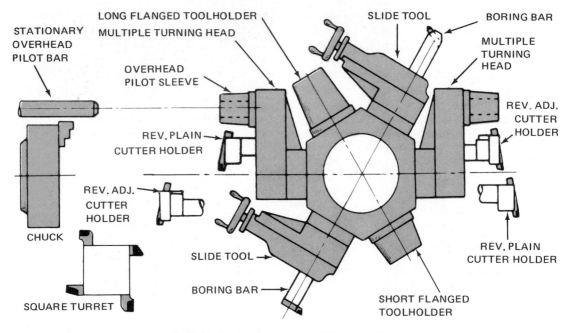

Fig. 67-11. Permanent setup on a saddle-type turret lathe.

Labels on figure:
STATIONARY OVERHEAD PILOT BAR
LONG FLANGED TOOLHOLDER
MULTIPLE TURNING HEAD
SLIDE TOOL
BORING BAR
MULTIPLE TURNING HEAD
OVERHEAD PILOT SLEEVE
REV. ADJ. CUTTER HOLDER
REV. PLAIN CUTTER HOLDER
REV. ADJ. CUTTER HOLDER
CHUCK
SLIDE TOOL
BORING BAR
REV. PLAIN CUTTER HOLDER
SQUARE TURRET
SHORT FLANGED TOOLHOLDER

TURRET LATHE TOOLING

A wide variety of cutting tools have been designed specifically for use on the turret lathe. These include all kinds of drilling, boring, and reaming tools, holding devices, and a variety of taps and dies. In addition, many kinds of combination cutting tools are used for both interior and exterior turning (Fig. 67-8). Many of these cutting tools appear quite different from those used on the engine lathe. However, both types provide the same basic kinds of cutting action (Fig. 67-9). All tools designed for the turret lathe are made so they can be quickly mounted in the turret and adjusted for use. Some can perform more than one cutting operation at a time (Fig. 67-10).

On a chucking lathe that must do a variety of small jobs, a permanent setup of universal adjustable tools is kept on the turret. With this permanent tooling, setup time can be limited to setting cutters in adjustable holders and setting machine stops. Flanged toolholders remain in position on the turret and shank tools are mounted as needed for the job (Fig. 67-11).

UNIT 68. Lathes in Industry

Lathes are widely used in industry to produce all kinds of machined parts. Some are general-purpose machines, and others are used to perform highly specialized operations.

ENGINE LATHES

Engine lathes, of course, are general-purpose machines used in production and maintenance shops all over the world. Sizes range from small bench models to huge heavy-duty pieces of equipment. Many of the larger lathes come equipped with attachments not commonly

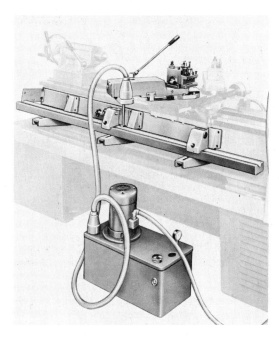

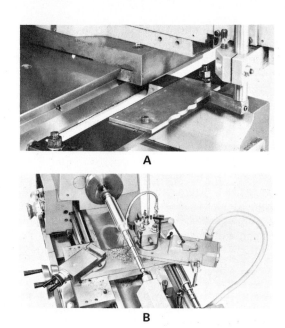

A

B

Fig. 68-1. A tracer attachment on a standard 14-in. engine lathe. Note the hydraulic control unit.

Fig. 68-2. (A) On this tracer lathe, the pattern or template is a flat piece of metal. (B) Note that the pattern or template used on this lathe is a cylindrical part.

Fig. 68-3. This tracer lathe has multiple tooling for machining both ends of automobile axle shafts.

found in the ordinary shop, such as automatic stops for the carriage and cross-feed. Huge engine lathes are often equipped with a gap bed in order to increase their capacity to handle large castings.

TRACER OR DUPLICATING LATHES

The tracer or duplicating lathe is designed to produce irregularly shaped parts automatically (Fig. 68-1). The basic operation of this lathe is as follows. A template of either a flat or three-dimensional shape is placed in a holder (Fig. 68-2). A guide or pointer then moves along this shape and its movement controls that of the cutting tool. The duplication may include a square or tapered shoulder, radii, grooves, tapers, and contours. Work such as motor shafts, spindles, valve stems, pistons, rods, car axles, turbine shafts, and a variety of other objects can be turned using this type of lathe (Fig. 68-3).

TURRET LATHES

The *turret lathe* is a production lathe used to make any number of identical pieces. Refer to Unit 67.

AUTOMATIC SCREW MACHINES

Screw machines are similar in construction to turret lathes, except that their heads are designed to hold and feed long bars of stock. Otherwise, there is little difference between them (Fig. 68-4). Both are designed for multiple tooling, and both have adaptations for identical work. Originally, the turret lathe was designed as a chucking lathe for machining small castings, forgings, and irregularly shaped workpieces. The first screw machines were designed to feed bar stock and wire used in making small screw parts. Today, however, the turret lathe is frequently used with a collet attachment, and the automatic screw machine can be equipped with a chuck to hold castings (Fig. 68-5).

The *single-spindle automatic screw machine,* as its name implies, machines work on only one bar of stock at a time. A bar 16 to 20 feet long is fed through the headstock spindle and is held firmly by a collet. The machining operations are done by cutting tools mounted on the turret and on the cross slide. When the

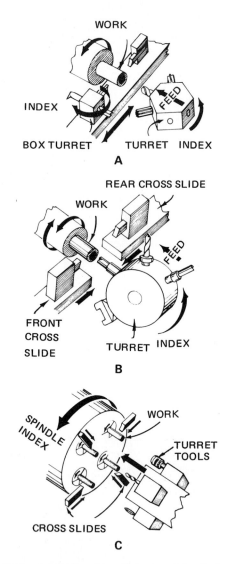

Fig. 68-4. A description of how (A) the turret lathe, (B) the single-spindle automatic screw machine, and (C) the multiple-spindle automatic screw machine operate in comparison with each other.

machine is in operation, the spindle and the stock are rotated at selected speeds for different operations. If required, rapid reversal of spindle direction is also possible.

In the single-spindle machine, a specific length of stock is automatically fed through the spindle to a machining area. At this point, the turret and cross slide move into position and automatically perform whatever operations are required (Fig. 68-6). After the machined piece

Fig. 68–5. (A) A single-spindle automatic bar screw machine. Note that it is designed to hold long bars of stock in a collet. (B) An automatic single-spindle chucking machine. Note that this machine can hold castings and forgings.

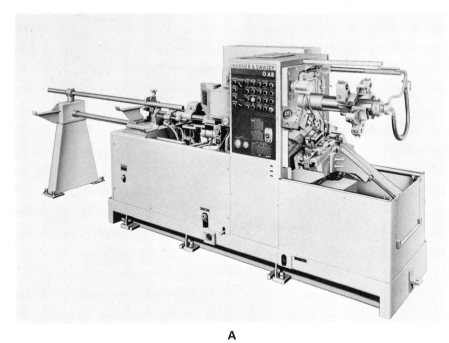

A

B

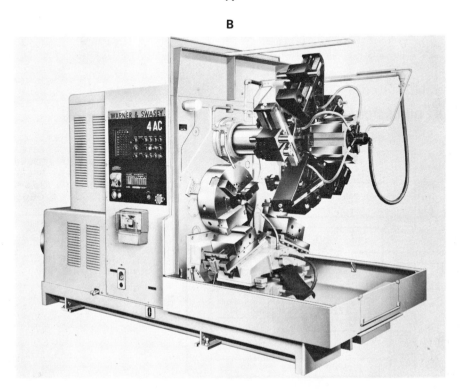

Fig. 68-6. Steps in machining a simple part on a single-spindle chucking automatic.

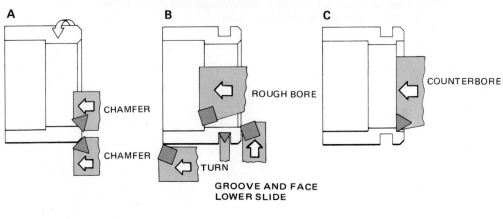

A   CHAMFER   CHAMFER

B   ROUGH BORE   TURN   GROOVE AND FACE LOWER SLIDE

C   COUNTERBORE

A

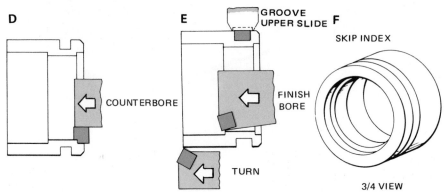

D   COUNTERBORE

E   GROOVE UPPER SLIDE   FINISH BORE   TURN

F   SKIP INDEX   3/4 VIEW

PIECE PART DIMENSIONAL DRAWING

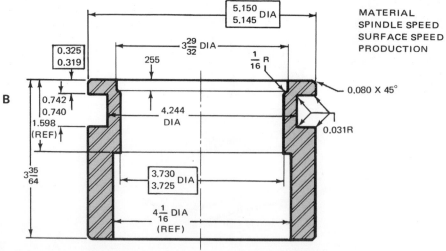

B

5.150 / 5.145 DIA

$3\frac{29}{32}$ DIA

255

$\frac{1}{16}$ R

0.080 X 45°

0.031R

0.325 / 0.319

0.742 / 0.740

1.598 (REF)

4.244 DIA

3.730 / 3.725 DIA

$4\frac{1}{16}$ DIA (REF)

$3\frac{35}{64}$

PRODUCTION

MATERIAL   8617–C
SPINDLE SPEED   350 RPM
SURFACE SPEED   358 SFM MAX
PRODUCTION   19.5 PER HOUR, GROSS

is cut off, stock is again fed into the machining area and the entire cycle is repeated.

Multiple-spindle automatic screw machines have from four to eight spindles located around a spindle carrier (Fig. 68-7). Long bars of stock, supported at the rear of the machine, pass through these hollow spindles and are gripped by collets. With the single-spindle machine, the turret indexes around the spindle. When one tool on the turret is working, the others are not. With a multiple-spindle machine, however, the spindle itself indexes. Thus the bars of stock are carried to the various end-working and side-working tools. Each tool operates in only one position, but all tools operate simultaneously. Therefore, four to eight workpieces can be machined at the same time.

VERTICAL TURRET LATHES

A *vertical turret lathe* is basically a turret lathe that has been stood on its headstock end (Fig. 68-8). It is designed to perform a variety of

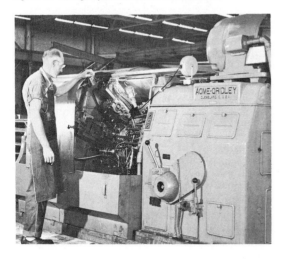

Fig. 68-7. An eight-spindle automatic screw machine.

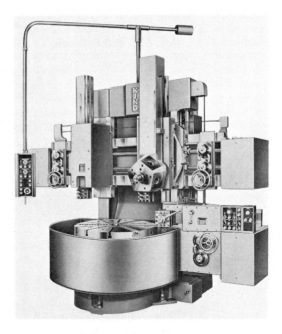

Fig. 68-8. A vertical turret lathe.

turning operations. It consists of a turret, a revolving table, and a side head with a square turret for holding additional tools. Operations performed by any of the tools mounted on the turret or side head can be controlled through the use of stops.

MACHINING CENTERS

Many of today's more sophisticated lathes are called *machining centers* since they are capable of performing, in addition to the normal turning operations, certain milling and drilling operations. Basically, a machining center can be thought of as being a combination turret lathe and milling machine. Additional features are sometimes included by manufacturers to increase the versatility of their machines.

UNIT 69. Discussion Topics and Problems

1. List some of the operations that can be done on the engine lathe.

2. Name the five main parts of the lathe.

3. Describe how the back gears operate.

4. What are the four major parts of the carriage?

5. What is the purpose of the quick-change gearbox?

6. When is the splitnut, or halfnut, used?

7. Name and describe three kinds of lathe dogs.

8. What is the difference between the live and dead center?

9. How do you obtain power cross-feed?

10. What part must be turned to move the carriage back and forth by hand?

11. How can the movement of the carriage be reversed?

12. Why should the lathe centers be checked for alignment before turning a workpiece?

13. Describe three methods of checking the alignment of lathe centers.

14. Tell the proper way of cleaning a lathe at the end of each work period.

15. Why is the oiling of a lathe often neglected?

16. What is a cutting tool?

17. How can you identify a right- or left-hand toolholder?

18. Name the tool angles found on all lathe cutting tools.

19. What is the tool angle?

20. How can you tell the difference between a right- and left-cut tool?

21. Describe how to grind a cutting tool.

22. What is cutting speed on a lathe?

23. What should be the rpm for turning a piece of mild steel that is $1\frac{1}{2}$ in. in diameter?

24. What is feed on a lathe?

25. What should be the feed for rough-turning low-carbon steel?

26. If the depth of cut is $\frac{1}{8}$ in. and the diameter of the rough stock is 3 in., what will be the diameter after the cut?

27. How much extra stock should be included if the center holes must be removed from the workpiece?

28. Name four ways of finding the center of rough workpieces.

29. Describe three ways of drilling center holes.

30. What is the purpose of rough turning?

31. Why do you use the micrometer for finish turning?

32. Why do you use a soft copper or aluminum collar on the finished end of the workpiece?

33. What is a shoulder?

34. Name four kinds of shoulders.

35. What is a groove or neck? How is it cut?

36. What is a recess?

37. When should a half center be used?

38. Name four common kinds of chucks.

39. Which chuck is the most accurate?

40. Name three ways of loosening a chuck from the spindle.

41. Describe one method of centering a workpiece in an independent jaw chuck.

42. What is a crotch center and a drill pad?

43. Define boring.

44. What is the difference in end relief and tool angle between a boring cutting tool and a turning cutting tool?

45. What is the advantage of a boring bar over a forged boring tool?

46. What is a bell-shaped hole? What causes it?

47. What is reaming?

48. How much stock is allowed for hand reaming?

49. What is the difference between a mandrel and an arbor?

50. What is an arbor press used for?

51. Why can't a workpiece be cut off when turning between centers?

52. What is hogging in?

53. What are the advantages of using a collet chuck?

54. What is the difference between a drive plate and a faceplate?

55. What is meant by knurling?

56. Name the two types of knurl patterns.

57. When is knurling used?

58. How much material should be removed in filing and polishing?

59. Why are filing and polishing not done in production work?

60. What kinds of files are used for lathe filing?

61. Why is the left-hand filing method often recommended?

62. What is a taper?

63. Name three ways of turning a taper.

64. What is the formula for offsetting the tailstock when the taper per foot is known?

65. If a taper on a prick punch is to be cut, what is the correct setover? The punch is 6 in. long. The length of taper is $2\frac{1}{2}$ in. The large diameter is $\frac{1}{2}$ in. The small diameter is $\frac{1}{8}$ in.

66. Describe three ways of measuring the amount of setover.

67. Name some of the advantages of using a taper attachment.

68. What is the difference between a plain taper attachment and a telescopic taper attachment?

69. At what angle to the axis should the compound rest be set for turning the point on a lathe center?

70. What is the difference between a steady rest and a follower rest?

71. Describe how to use a steady rest for boring.

72. What is a center gage used for in threading?

73. Name the parts of a screw thread.

74. If an accurate American National thread must be cut, what kind of gage is used to check the cutting tool?

75. What is a screw-pitch gage used for?

76. Describe how to cut an external thread.

77. When cutting odd numbers of threads per inch, when is the splitnut, or halfnut, closed?

78. Why is the compound rest set at an angle of 30° for most threading?

79. Name three ways of checking the thread.

80. How can a left-hand thread be cut?

81. What is an Acme thread?

82. What kind of gage must be used to check the cutting tool for an Acme thread?

83. Describe how to cut internal threads.

84. Name four kinds of lathes commonly used in industry.

85. What is the difference between a turret lathe and an automatic screw machine?

SECTION 7

THE SHAPER

UNIT 70. The Shaper

The shaper is used to surface and shape metal parts (Fig. 70-1). The cutting tool is similar to that used on a lathe. It is clamped in the tool post attached to a *ram* (a heavy metal arm). The

Fig. 70-1. A shaper uses a single-point cutting tool to remove a chip from a metal surface.

ram pushes the cutting tool across the workpiece on the *power* or cutting stroke and withdraws it on the return stroke. The workpiece is clamped to the table, usually in a vise. The cutting tool and the table can move vertically (up or down). The table also moves longitudinally (back and forth) under the cutting tool.

The shaper is a relatively slow machine with a limited capacity for metal removal. For this reason, it is rapidly being replaced in job shops by the more versatile vertical milling machine. Many machinery manufacturers have already discontinued production of the shaper. However, many of these machine tools are still used in school laboratories and small job shops. Therefore, you should learn how to operate them. Another reason for learning to use this machine is that it works on the same basic principle as the *vertical shaper* (slotting machine or slotter) and the *planer*. Although these are not commonly found in school laboratories, they are basic machines used in industry. You can, therefore, easily adapt much of what you will learn on the shaper to these machines.

Shapers are used mostly for machining horizontal (flat), vertical (up and down), or angular surfaces. They can be used to machine *concave* (curved in) or convex (curved out) surfaces also. As with other machines, there are some differences in the controls provided on different shaper models. However, all operate in the same basic way.

SIZE

The size of a shaper is determined by its maximum stroke in inches. This is about the same as the largest cube it will machine. Common sizes range from 7 to 36 in. In the school shop the 7-, 8-, 10-, 14-, or 16-in. size shapers are most common.

PARTS OF A CRANK-TYPE SHAPER

The main parts of a shaper are shown in Fig. 70-2. Learn these so you will understand what your teacher or future employer is talking about when he gives you instructions.

1. The *base* is the heavy casting that supports the machine.

2. The *column* or *frame* is a hollow casting in which the driving parts operate. The upper surface has two *ways* on which the ram moves. The front of the column has *column rail bearings* on which the *crossrail* fits. The left side has an inspection plate for oiling and checking. The right side (operator's side) contains most of the controls (levers and handles) for making adjustments and operating the machine.

3. The *ram* is a heavy steel casting which moves back and forth on the ways of the column.

4. The *toolhead* is fastened to the front of the ram and can be swiveled in either direction for machining angular cuts (Fig. 70-3). The *tool slide* moves up and down for adjusting the depth of the cut. The *feed screw* has a micrometer collar on it for making accurate adjustments. The *clapper box* attached to the slide can be offset (top moved to right or left) so that the tool will clear the work on the return stroke when making angular cuts. The *clapper block* is hinged at the top of the clapper box. On the forward stroke,

Fig. 70-2. The principal parts of a 14-in. crank-type shaper.

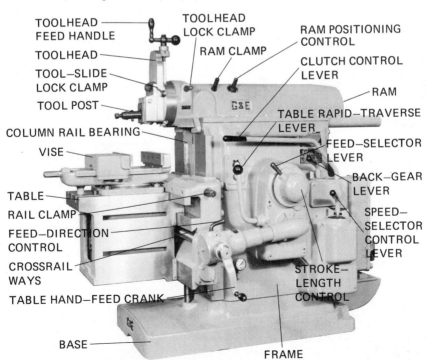

TOOLHEAD FEED HANDLE
TOOLHEAD LOCK CLAMP
RAM CLAMP
RAM POSITIONING CONTROL
CLUTCH CONTROL LEVER
TOOLHEAD
TOOL–SLIDE LOCK CLAMP
TOOL POST
RAM
COLUMN RAIL BEARING
TABLE RAPID–TRAVERSE LEVER
FEED–SELECTOR LEVER
VISE
BACK–GEAR LEVER
TABLE
RAIL CLAMP
SPEED–SELECTOR CONTROL LEVER
FEED–DIRECTION CONTROL
CROSSRAIL WAYS
STROKE–LENGTH CONTROL
TABLE HAND–FEED CRANK
BASE
FRAME

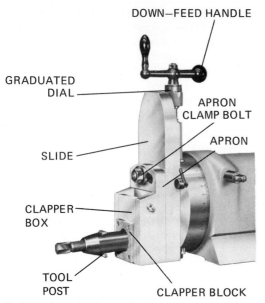

DOWN—FEED HANDLE

GRADUATED
DIAL

APRON
CLAMP BOLT

APRON

SLIDE

CLAPPER
BOX

TOOL
POST

CLAPPER BLOCK

Fig. 70-3. Parts of a shaper toolhead.

Fig. 70-4. Pulley and gear-drive mechanisms for a crank-type shaper.

Fig. 70-5. The shaper changes rotating motion to back-and-forth motion.

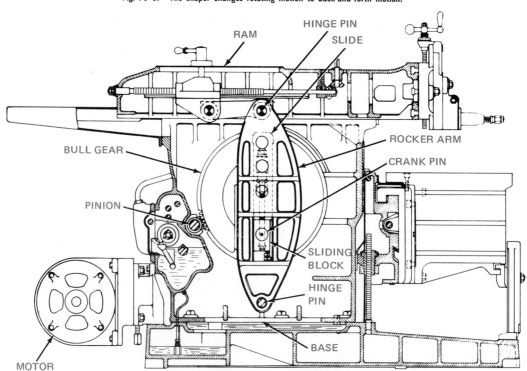

RAM

HINGE PIN

SLIDE

BULL GEAR

ROCKER ARM

CRANK PIN

PINION

SLIDING
BLOCK

HINGE
PIN

MOTOR

BASE

SHAPER CROSS SECTION

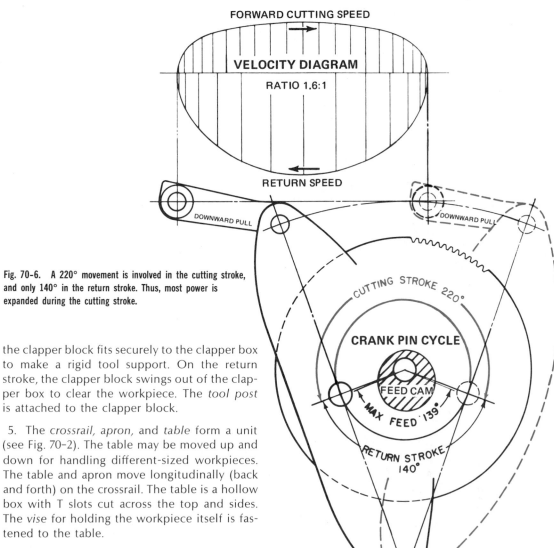

Fig. 70-6. A 220° movement is involved in the cutting stroke, and only 140° in the return stroke. Thus, most power is expanded during the cutting stroke.

the clapper block fits securely to the clapper box to make a rigid tool support. On the return stroke, the clapper block swings out of the clapper box to clear the workpiece. The *tool post* is attached to the clapper block.

5. The *crossrail, apron,* and *table* form a unit (see Fig. 70-2). The table may be moved up and down for handling different-sized workpieces. The table and apron move longitudinally (back and forth) on the crossrail. The table is a hollow box with T slots cut across the top and sides. The *vise* for holding the workpiece itself is fastened to the table.

6. A *motor, pulleys,* and a *countershaft* supply power to the gears for operating the machine (Fig. 70-4).

HOW A CRANK-TYPE SHAPER WORKS

The shaper changes the rotary motion of the motor to a back-and-forth, or reciprocating, motion at the ram (Fig. 70-5). The motor delivers power to a pulley which is attached to a small gear called a *pinion* or *driving gear*. This pinion turns a large bull gear. Attached to the bull gear is a crank pin that fits into a hole in the sliding block. The sliding block, in turn, fits into a slide in the rocker arm. The long rocker arm is connected to the base and ram with two hinge pins. As the crank pin on the bull gear revolves, the sliding block is forced to move up and down in the slide. This forces the rocker arm to swing back and forth on the hinge pins in an arc, forcing the ram to move back and forth. It takes about $1\frac{1}{2}$ times as long for the ram to move out (power stroke) as it does to move in (return stroke). The position of the sliding block in the

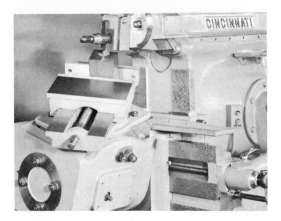

Fig. 70-7. Note how the table has been rotated and the work surface tilted to cut a compound angle.

slide determines the length of stroke (Fig. 70-6). The *crank pin,* which fits into the *sliding block,* is fastened to a second block which operates in a radial slide on the bull gear. The position of this block is adjusted by turning the stroke-

length control. As the crank pin is moved toward the center of the bull gear, the distance the rocker arm moves is shortened. This, in turn, shortens the stroke of the ram.

THE HYDRAULIC SHAPER

Many of the larger shapers are hydraulically driven. The ram on such a shaper is moved by oil pressure developed by a pump that is driven by the electric motor. A reversing valve is used to change the direction of the oil pressure, thereby changing the direction in which the ram will move. Table feed is also operated by an oil pressure. Speed and feed changes are made by control valves.

Many hydraulic shapers have a universal table which has two working surfaces, a solid surface for shaping flat, or plain, angular work and a tilting surface used for compound angle work (Fig. 70-7). Another feature that is often found on larger shapers is an automatic tool lifter. This unit automatically lifts the cutting tool.

UNIT 71.
Getting Acquainted with the Shaper: Checking and Adjusting

Before using a shaper, it is important that you familiarize yourself with the parts of the machine and the controls necessary to operate it (Fig. 71-1). Generally, smaller shapers are controlled manually, and the larger models are provided with automatic or power controls. Since you will probably be using a small shaper, its operation is described here. If you have the larger type in your shop, your instructor will explain its operation.

ADJUSTMENTS TO TRY WITH THE POWER OFF

1. Move the slide of the *toolhead* up or down (Fig. 71-2). Turn the handle of the feed screw to move the slide. Do this with your right hand. The *depth of cut* or *down feed* is adjusted with

the tool slide. Keep the amount of overhang between the tool slide and the toolhead to a minimum (Fig. 71-3).

2. Move the table back and forth. Place the crank handle on the *longitudinal* or *cross-feed screw,* and turn it to move the table. In starting a cut, the right hand is usually placed on the handle of the tool-slide feed screw. At the same time the left hand operates the crank on the cross-feed.

3. Raise or lower the table. The position of the table is changed only when very large work-pieces must be machined. For most jobs, the table is left in about the same position. Move the table until it is centered with the column. Loosen the *crossrail clamping nuts* directly back of the *column-rail bearing.* Also, loosen the *table support.* Place the crank handle on the *vertical screw* or *table elevating control,* and move the table up or down. When moving the table down, always lower it a little more than necessary and then raise the table to the correct position. This takes out any backlash in the adjust-

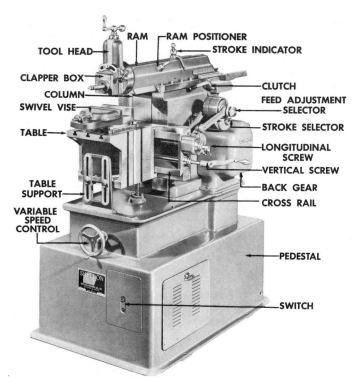

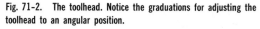

Fig. 71-1. The controls and principal parts of a 12-in. back-geared shaper. This type of machine is commonly found in the school shop.

Fig. 71-2. The toolhead. Notice the graduations for adjusting the toolhead to an angular position.

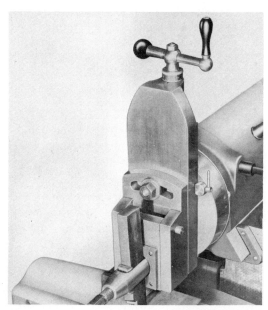

ment screw. Be sure to tighten the clamp nuts on the crossrail and table support.

4. Change the length of stroke. The *length of stroke* should be from $\frac{3}{4}$ to 1 in. longer than the surface to be machined. To adjust the stroke, loosen the locknut if the shaper is equipped with one. Place the crank handle on the *stroke selector* or *adjusting shaft*. Rotate the countershaft or handwheel until the ram is as far back as it will go (return stroke). A scale on the top of the column and a pointer on the ram is used to indicate the length of stroke. Turn the crank in either direction until the length desired is shown on the scale. Then tighten the locknut. On larger machines the length of stroke is shown on a small dial (Fig. 71-4). On this type of shaper the stroke may be adjusted with the ram in any position.

5. Adjust the position of stroke. The position of the stroke is adjusted only after the workpiece and the cutting tool are mounted. Move the ram out as far as it will go. Loosen the *ram*

383

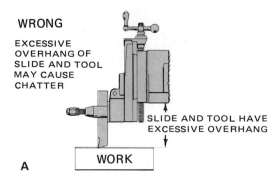

WRONG

EXCESSIVE
OVERHANG OF
SLIDE AND TOOL
MAY CAUSE
CHATTER

SLIDE AND TOOL HAVE
EXCESSIVE OVERHANG

WORK

A

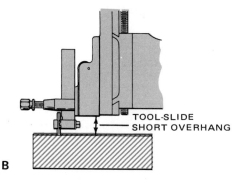

TOOL-SLIDE
SHORT OVERHANG

B

Fig. 71-3. (A) Avoid excessive overhang. Raise the table if necessary. (B) Keep the tool slide up and the toolholder high in the tool post for greater rigidity.

Fig. 71-4. This dial shows the length of stroke.

hand clamp, and place the crank on the *ram positioner.* Turn the crank until the point of the tool clears the front of the workpiece by about $\frac{1}{4}$ in. (Fig. 71-5). Tighten the ram clamp.

6. Adjust the speed. The *speed* at which the shaper should operate depends on the following.

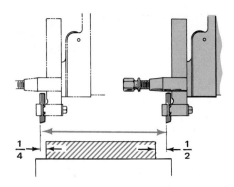

Fig. 71-5. The cutting tool should clear the back of the workpiece by about $\frac{1}{2}$ in. This allows the clapper to seat firmly in the box before the next stroke. The tool must also clear the front of the workpiece by about $\frac{1}{4}$ in.

a. The material in the cutting tool

b. The kind of metal being machined

c. The depth of cut

d. The condition of the machine

e. The rigidity of the machine

Suggested cutting speeds are shown in Table 71-1. The cutting speed is determined by the number of strokes per minute at which the shaper is operating and the length of the stroke. With the same number of strokes per minute, a longer stroke will increase the cutting speed; a shorter stroke will decrease it. To find the number of strokes at which the shaper should operate, use this simple formula:

$$N = \frac{CS \times 7.5}{L}$$

where N = the number of strokes per minute
CS = the cutting speed in surface feet per minute (sfpm)
L = the length of stroke in inches

For example, if a medium-carbon steel block that requires a 5-in. stroke is to be machined, then (using 60 for the cutting speed as shown in Table 71-1):

$$N = \frac{60 \times 7.5}{5} = 90 \text{ strokes per minute}$$

Most belt-driven shapers have only four to

Table 71-1. Suggested cutting speeds for shaper.

Material	Cutting speed for high-speed steel tools, surface feet per minute
Aluminum and alloys	200–400
Brass and bronze, soft	100–300
Bronze, high-tensile	70–90
Cast iron:	
Soft	100–150
Medium	70–100
Hard	40–60
Copper	60–150
Malleable iron	80–90
Steel:	
Low-carbon	80–150
Medium-carbon	60–100
High-carbon	50–60
Tool-and-die	40–80
Alloy	50–70

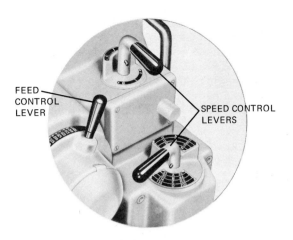

Fig. 71-6. Speed and feed control levers.

eight possible machine speeds (number of strokes the machine makes per minute). Change the belt to give the closest speed. On shapers equipped with a variable-speed control and on large machines, check the speed indicator and adjust accordingly (Fig. 71-6).

7. Adjust the feed. *Feed* is the distance the table moves after each cutting stroke. The amount of feed depends on the same factors as the cutting speed. Generally, a slower feed is used with a heavy depth of cut (roughing cut), and a faster feed with a lighter cut (finishing cut). On most shapers, the feed is changed by moving one end of the *connecting* (feed) *rod* that operates the feed screw shaft. To increase the feed, loosen the nut or screw on the *feed-adjustment selector* or *slotted crank disk*. Slide the end toward the outer edge, and then tighten. The feed must be set so that the table advances on the backward, or return, stroke. If it is adjusted incorrectly, the table will advance

Fig. 71-7. One feed-selector lever can be moved to obtain 18 feed changes.

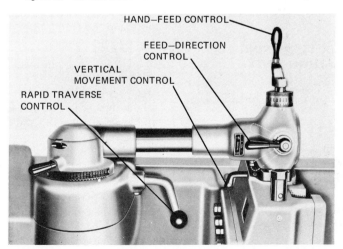

on the forward stroke. If this happens, move the end of the connecting rod to the opposite side of the slot. *Never machine a workpiece with the table moving sideways on the forward stroke of the ram.* This will ruin the cutting tool. On larger models, the feed is changed by moving a lever located near the feed-indicator plate (Fig. 71-7).

CHECKING THE ACCURACY OF THE SHAPER VISE

Most jobs can be done with the workpiece fastened in a vise. The top part of the vise can be rotated in a complete circle. Its jaws may be set either parallel or at right angles to the ram stroke. The base of the vise is marked in degrees with a witness mark on the upper casting. For most jobs the vise is set using the scale and the witness mark. If greater accuracy is required, check as follows.

1. Set the solid (fixed) jaw parallel to the ram stroke. Open the vise jaws. Adjust the length and position of stroke slightly shorter than the length of the jaws. Place a dial-indicator gage in the tool post. Place the plunger of the gage against the fixed jaw, and turn the dial face until the pointer is at zero. Move the ram back and forth with the handwheel, and check the readings (Fig. 71-8). Adjust the vise until the pointer stays at zero throughout the stroke (Fig. 71-9).

2. A similar procedure is followed when checking a vise jaw placed at right angles to the ram stroke. Note, however, that the longitudinal hand feed must be used to feed the table back and forth under the indicator's plunger.

ADJUSTMENTS MADE BY TURNING THE POWER ON AND OFF AFTER EACH STEP

1. Start the motor. Engage the clutch lever to operate the ram.

CAUTION

Always use the handwheel to move the ram through a complete stroke before turning the power on.

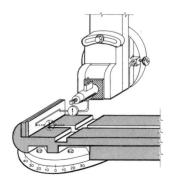

Fig. 71-8. Using the dial indicator to make sure the solid jaw of the vise is parallel to the ram stroke.

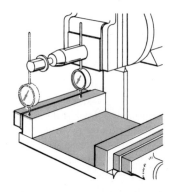

Fig. 71-9. Checking to see if the table is level with the ram stroke. A parallel has been placed against the solid vise jaw. Sometimes it is necessary to adjust the table support or to tighten the crossrail.

Newer shapers have no handwheel for this purpose and the clutch lever must be used to control ram movement.

2. Engage the automatic cross-feed lever to start the table moving on the crossrails. When the lever is turned to the right, the table moves to the right when viewed from the front. When the lever is shifted to the left, the table moves to the left.

SAFETY AND CARE OF THE SHAPER

The safe operation of the shaper requires that you be aware of certain hazards. When you know the hazards to avoid, you are less likely to have an accident or be injured. A safe machine is one that is kept in good operating condition at all times. Study and practice the following rules of safety.

1. Do not attempt to operate a shaper until you have received instructions from your instructor.

2. Clamp all work tightly. When shaping work to a line, make sure that the line is at least $\frac{1}{8}$ in. above the vise jaw.

3. Set the *length of stroke* and the *position of the ram* correctly before starting the machine to cut the work.

4. Always check the speed-control levers before starting the machine.

5. Make certain that the tool bit is tight in the toolholder. The toolholder must also be tight in the tool post. A loose tool bit or holder can cause serious damage when the shaper is started.

6. Be sure the tool bit is clear of the work before starting the machine. If not, it will be broken off when it strikes the workpiece.

7. Keep your fingers and hands at a safe distance from the cutting tool at all times. It is never necessary to place your hands near a moving cutting tool.

8. Always wear safety glasses.

9. Be sure to lock the tool-slide clamp screw after setting the depth of cut. This prevents the tool slide from moving downward during the cut.

10. Make no adjustments until the machine is shut off and comes to a dead stop.

11. Never feed the cutter down into the work abruptly. The tool must be fed into the work gradually. Feeding must be done on the return stroke only.

12. Place a piece of cardboard or a chip guard in front of the vise to shield against flying chips. This prevents the chips from injuring you or others.

13. Be sure to feed the workpiece in a direction which will cause it to contact only the cutting-edge of the tool bit.

14. After shaping angular work, be sure to reset the toolhead at its zero position. If you have been using a long stroke, shorten it before leaving the machine. The next operator may be injured if this is not done.

15. Remove all tools, such as wrenches and oilcans, from the danger zone before starting the machine.

16. All working parts of a shaper must operate freely. You should never force parts to work. If something seems wrong, stop and find out what it is. If you don't know, it is always best to ask your instructor.

17. Keep the machine well oiled at all times. Never oil a machine while it is running. Place oilcans in a safe place after using.

18. When shaping a casting in the vise, place a cardboard strip between the casting and the jaws. This improves the grip and prevents the smooth vise jaws from becoming damaged.

19. When you finish working on a machine, shut off the motor. Remove all chips with a brush: never use your hands for this purpose.

UNIT 72. Cutting Tools and Toolholders

To machine a workpiece on the shaper you must have:

1. The correct kind of cutting tool

2. The right kind of toolholder

3. A cutting tool with a correctly ground cutting-edge

Although some forged shaper tools are still used, most machining is done with a cutting tool bit mounted in a toolholder.

TOOLHOLDERS

There are several kinds of toolholders.

1. Regular *lathe turning toolholders* can be used for most operations. Remember, however, that the cutting tool is held in this holder at a 15-degree (°) incline. Therefore, the end relief angle (front clearance) of the tool bit must be modified (unless front clearance is required).

2. A *parallel toolholder* holds the cutting tool parallel to the edges of the holder. This type requires that more of an end relief angle (front clearance) be ground on the cutter bit.

3. The *swivel-head or universal toolholder* will hold the cutting tool rigidly in five different positions (Fig. 72-1). It is very convenient to use for all shaper work. The cutting tool is held parallel to the edges of the holder.

4. The *extension toolholder* is needed for inside shaping, for cutting internal keyways, and for other special jobs (Fig. 72-2).

CUTTING TOOLS

Cutting tools used on the shaper are similar to those used on the lathe. However, because the shaper cuts on the forward stroke only, side relief (side clearance) and end relief (front clearance) angles are smaller. The *side relief angle* needs to be only about 3 or 4°. The end relief angle (front clearance) should also be

Fig. 72-2. Using the extension toolholder to machine the interior surface of a workpiece.

Fig. 72-1. A swivel-head or universal toolholder is commonly used on small shapers. It can be positioned for vertical cuts (A and E), angular cuts (B and D), and horizontal cuts (C).

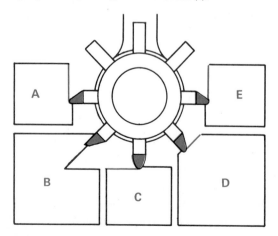

about 3 or 4°. If the cutting tool is held in a lathe toolholder at an incline of 15°, the end relief angle must be increased to 19° so as to provide the necessary 4° of front clearance. The *side-* and *back-rake* angles vary with the kind of material being machined. The side rake for steel should be about 10 to 20°, and the back rake should be from 2 to 8°. For cast iron, the side rake should be 3 to 10° and the back rake from 0 to 3°.

Right-cut and *left-cut* shaper tools are identified in the same way as lathe tools. When viewed from the point with the face up, the cutting-edge of a left-cut tool is on the left side. Mounted in the shaper, the cutting-edge would still be on the left side. The workpiece would have to move under the cutter from left to right.

Fig. 72-3. A square-nose tool used for finishing cast iron.

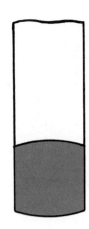

Fig. 72-4. A shear tool for finishing steel with a coarse feed.

The left-cut tool is the one most often used on the shaper.

Some of the commonly used cutting tools include:

1. A left-cut roughing tool

2. A left-cut finishing tool

3. A left-cut side-facing tool for vertical shaping and for shaping to sharp corners

4. A curved cutting-edge tool (roundnose) for general-purpose work such as rough cutting steel or cast iron

5. A parting tool used to cut grooves, keyways, etc.

6. A square-nose (end cutting) tool for finishing flat surfaces on cast iron (Fig. 72-3)

7. A shear tool for finishing steel with a coarse feed (Fig. 72-4)

UNIT 73. Work-holding Devices

It is important that the workpiece be held securely while it is machined. There are several ways of doing this.

SHAPER VISE

Most jobs can be machined with the workpiece held in a vise. A keyway may be provided on the bottom of the vise and in the table top to keep the vise in alignment. The vise is held firmly in position with two to four T-slot bolts. Before the vise is clamped to the table, make sure the table top is free of burrs or nicks (Fig. 73-1). Always clean the bottom of the vise before placing it on the table.

PARALLELS

Parallels are used to seat the workpiece so that it will be above the vise jaw and parallel with the vise bottom (Fig. 73-2). Hardened steel parallels are made in pairs and come in a variety of sizes. They must be kept free of burrs or dents.

HOLD-DOWNS

Hold-downs are hardened, wedge-shaped pieces of steel having a back edge tapered to an angle of 2 or 3 degrees (°) (Fig. 73-3). The thick edge is usually ground to an angle of 92°. Pressure applied by the vise screw tends to force the thin edge downward to hold the work tight on the parallel bars. Hold-downs may be used to keep thin workpieces in position.

Fig. 73-1. The vise is the most common holding device used on the shaper.

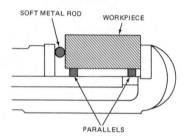

SOFT METAL ROD   WORKPIECE

PARALLELS

Fig. 73-2. Supporting the workpiece in a vise with parallels.

HINTS ON CLAMPING A WORKPIECE IN A VISE

1. If the surface of the workpiece is rough, place a piece of brass, cardboard, or abrasive cloth on either side to hold it firmly (Fig. 73–4).

2. If the workpiece has one true surface, always place this surface against the solid jaw of the vise. Put a soft copper or aluminum rod between the workpiece and the adjustable jaw to hold the workpiece squarely in place (see Fig. 73–2).

3. Always select parallels small enough to seat the workpiece well inside the vise jaws.

4. If thin stock must be machined, use parallels that are about two-thirds the height of the vise jaws. Lay the workpiece on these parallels. Then hold it in place with hold-downs.

5. Always machine a narrow workpiece in the center of the vise jaws. If you must clamp it to one side, place a scrap piece of equal thickness

or width on the other side of the jaws. This prevents forcing the movable jaw out of alignment as the vise is tightened.

6. After you tighten a workpiece in the vise, tap its surface with a soft-faced (lead or brass) hammer to seat it on the parallels. If you are able to move the parallels with your fingers, the work is not seated correctly.

7. A piece of brass placed between the workpiece and the movable jaw will prevent the workpiece from raising or from slipping during machining.

OTHER CLAMPING DEVICES

The workpiece may be clamped directly to the table using angle plates, clamps, T-slot bolts,

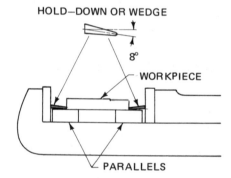

HOLD—DOWN OR WEDGE

8°

WORKPIECE

PARALLELS

Fig. 73-3. Hold-downs force the workpiece firmly against the parallels.

Fig. 73-4. If rough casting is to be held, the first cut should be made with abrasive cloth between the vise jaws and the casting to protect the vise jaws and to hold the workpiece firmly in the vise.

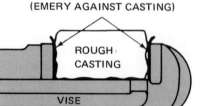

EMERY CLOTH
(EMERY AGAINST CASTING)

ROUGH CASTING

VISE

SHAPING ROUGH CASTINGS

390

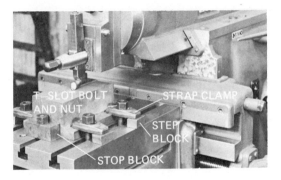

Fig. 73-5. This casting is clamped directly to the top of the table. The stop block in front of the casting keeps it from moving forward.

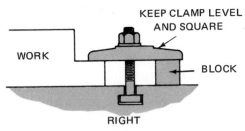

KEEP CLAMP LEVEL AND SQUARE

WORK

BLOCK

RIGHT

CLAMPING EFFECT IS ON WORK

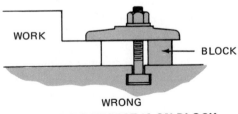

WORK

BLOCK

WRONG

CLAMPING EFFECT IS ON BLOCK

Fig. 73-6. Clamping work to the table using strap clamps and T bolts.

Fig. 73-7. Using a dial indicator for setting work level and parallel.

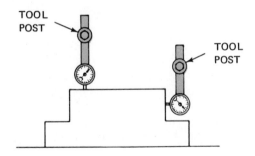

TOOL POST

TOOL POST

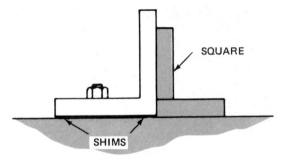

SQUARE

SHIMS

Fig. 73-8. A precision square is helpful in making sure the angle plate is at right angles to the table.

Fig. 73-9. Cutting a spline with the workpiece held between the indexing head and the tailstock.

Fig. 73-10. Cutting grooves around a hollow workpiece.

step blocks, and other clamping devices (Fig. 73-5). Always clean the table thoroughly before placing the workpiece on it. If the workpiece is held with clamps and T bolts, make sure that the height of the clamp-block is equal to or slightly less than the height of the location where the workpiece is to be clamped (Fig. 73-6). Before clamping the workpiece tightly, be certain it is level (Fig. 73-7). If the workpiece is to be clamped to an angle plate, make sure that the plate is square with the table (Fig. 73-8).

After fastening the workpiece to the table, tap it with a soft-face hammer to make certain it is properly seated.

INDEXING HEAD

An indexing head and tailstock is used when cutting splines with a shaper. With this attachment, an equal number of splines or grooves can be cut on cylindrical workpieces (Fig. 73-9).

ROTARY TABLE

A rotary table can be mounted on the shaper when it is necessary to cut grooves around a hollow, cylindrical workpiece (Fig. 73-10).

UNIT 74. Machining a Horizontal Surface

The shaper is used to machine flat, true surfaces on workpieces held in a vise. This is the first step in squaring up a block.

TOOLS AND EQUIPMENT NEEDED

1. Vise, parallels, hold-downs, and soft metal rod to clamp the workpiece.

2. A roundnose or left-cut roughing or shear tool, a left-cut finishing tool (for steel) or a square-nose tool (for cast iron).

3. A straight lathe toolholder or a shaper toolholder.

4. A soft-faced (lead or brass) hammer.

PREPARING THE SHAPER

All directions are given as if you were facing the front of the shaper.

1. Turn the vise with the solid jaw parallel to the ram stroke and the vise screw to the right. Check to see that the vise and the table are free of burrs. Burrs would keep the workpiece from being clamped securely.

2. Mark a line across the end of the workpiece to show how much material is to be removed. If the piece is to be machined to thickness, remove about half the amount from either side.

3. Place the workpiece in the vise with the long side parallel to the jaws. For example, place a 2- by 3- by 6-in. block with the 6-in. length parallel to the ram stroke. Shaping a workpiece lengthwise is efficient because there is less "cutting of the air."

4. Use parallels to raise the workpiece, if necessary. Place a soft metal rod (copper or aluminum) between the movable jaw and the workpiece. The metal rod is necessary only if the workpiece is irregular in shape or out of square. Tighten the vise. Tap the workpiece with a soft-faced hammer to make sure it is properly seated. Some machinists place thin strips of paper under the four corners of the workpiece before tightening the vise (Figs. 74-1 and 74-2). Then, if one or more of the paper pieces are loose, they know that the workpiece is not seated properly.

5. Use chalk to mark the location of the workpiece on the vise jaws. This will help you to relocate the workpiece should it become necessary to remove it from the vise before all machining is completed.

Fig. 74-1. Lay four small strips of paper near each corner of the vise. Place the workpiece carefully in position. Tighten the vise and tap the work down. If one piece of paper is loose, the corner of the workpiece directly above it is high and should be tapped down again.

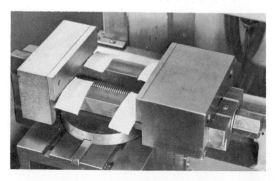

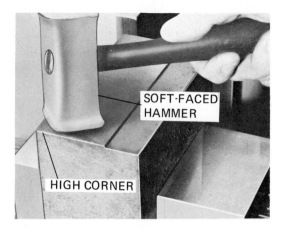

SOFT-FACED HAMMER

HIGH CORNER

Fig. 74-2. Tap the corner sharply with a soft-faced hammer or mallet.

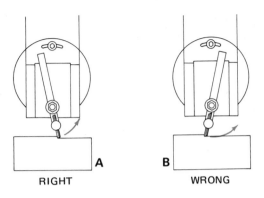

RIGHT A   B WRONG

Fig. 74-4. Correct and incorrect way to adjust the toolholder in the tool post. (A) If right, the tool swings out of the way. (B) If wrong, the tool digs into the workpiece.

Fig. 74-3. Fastening the toolholder in the tool post.

6. Certain workpieces can be mounted directly on the table when machining a flat surface.

7. Make sure the toolhead is set vertically at zero and that the clapper box is centered.

8. Insert the cutting tool in the toolholder. Fasten the holder in the tool post (Fig. 74-3). The toolholder should be turned slightly to the right so that the cutting tool will swing away from the workpiece if for some reason it slips (Fig. 74-4). The toolholder should not extend any farther than necessary. The shorter it is held, the more rigid it is.

9. Turn the slide up so it does not extend below the dovetail with an excessive overhang.

10. If necessary, move the table up or down. There should be at least 2 in. of clearance between the underside of the ram and the top of the workpiece.

11. Check the length and position of stroke. Adjust the length $\frac{3}{4}$ to 1 in. more than the length of the workpiece. Adjust the position of stroke so that the point of the tool clears the front of the workpiece by about $\frac{1}{4}$ in. There must be more clearance at the end of the backstroke than at the front.

12. Adjust for correct speed. Maintain a slower speed for long workpieces or harder materials and a higher speed for shorter workpieces and softer materials.

13. Adjust for correct feed. Make sure the table moves on the return stroke.

MAKING THE ROUGH CUT

1. Stand or sit (on a metal stool) to the front and right of the shaper. Your eyes should be a little above the top of the workpiece. You should be able to watch the depth of cut, the feed, and the cutting action.

CAUTION

Wear goggles or an eyeshield.

2. With the cross-feed crank, move the workpiece to the left (away from you) just enough to clear the tool from the work.

3. Turn on the power.

4. Place your right hand on the down-feed (tool-slide) handle and your left hand on the cross-feed crank.

5. Turn the cutting tool down, and move the workpiece toward you until the cutting tool takes off a chip about $\frac{1}{16}$ to $\frac{1}{8}$ in. deep. When machining cast iron, you should use a slightly heavier depth of cut to get below its hard outer scale.

6. Turn the cross-feed crank about one-eighth to one-fourth turn during each return stroke until three or four strokes are complete.

7. Stop the machine. Inspect the surface of the workpiece and adjust the machine as required. If the tool chatters, you should check the following.

   a. Is the cutting tool ground correctly? Is there too much or too little clearance?

   b. Is the workpiece clamped securely? Has it shifted or moved?

   c. Are you using the correct kind of tool-holder?

   d. Is the cutting tool clamped and adjusted properly?

   e. Is the speed too fast or the feed too great?

   f. Is there a loose part on the machine itself?

8. If the tool is cutting properly, the chip should curl when the workpiece is steel. If it is cast iron, the stock removed crumbles away into small chips.

9. Turn on the power, and engage the automatic feed.

10. When the first cut is complete, return the workpiece to the starting position. Never cut back and forth in both directions.

11. Take additional cuts to within 0.010 or 0.015 in. of the layout line on steel, or 0.005 to 0.010 in. on cast iron.

MAKING THE FINISHING CUT

1. Use a finishing or shear tool for finishing steel. Use a square-nose tool to finish cast iron.

2. If the workpiece is cast iron, file a chamfer (a 45-degree (°) bevel edge) on its front and right side to prevent metal from chipping off below the finished surface.

3. Increase the speed, use a finer feed, and take a lighter cut.

4. Apply cutting fluid (on steel) to improve the finished surface.

5. Make one or two light cuts (0.003 to 0.008 in.) across the workpiece until you reach, or split, the layout line.

6. Check the thickness with a caliper or micrometer.

MACHINING SERRATIONS

Serrating is the process of notching or corrugating a surface. It is similar to knurling except that it is done on a flat surface. It often involves cutting two sets of grooves or notches that crisscross each other to form sharp points. Serrating is used for a variety of reasons. For example, surfaces may be serrated to resist relative motion between parts. Countersunk holes are often serrated so that the screws or rivets won't turn after they are set in place. To cut serrations with a shaper, pivot the vise 30° in one direction. Use a sharp-pointed tool set to the correct depth. Sometimes two or more cuts must be made at the same location. After each cut, move the workpiece a precise distance for the next cut. Complete one series of cuts, rotate the vise 30° in the other direction, and repeat.

UNIT 75. Making a Vertical Cut

A vertical (up and down) cut is made when machining the end of a long workpiece, squaring up a block, or cutting a shoulder.

TOOLS AND EQUIPMENT NEEDED

1. A vise, parallels, and hold-downs to clamp the workpiece. If the workpiece must be mounted directly on the table, use clamps, step blocks, and T-slot bolts.

2. A straight or universal toolholder.

3. A left-cut side-facing tool.

PREPARING THE SHAPER

1. Turn the vise with the solid jaw at right angles to the ram stroke.

2. Mark the layout line on the workpiece.

3. Clamp the workpiece so the end to be machined clears the right side of the vise jaws.

Fig. 75-1. Notice how the clapper box is turned for making a vertical cut.

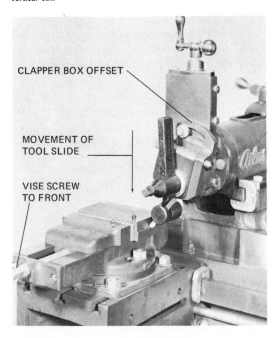

CLAPPER BOX OFFSET

MOVEMENT OF TOOL SLIDE

VISE SCREW TO FRONT

Fasten the workpiece so the down feed will move the shortest distance. For example, if the workpiece is 3 by 4 by 6 in., mount it with the 4-in. side down.

4. Turn the top of the clapper box away from the direction in which the cut is to be made (Fig. 75-1). This is done so the cutting tool will clear the workpiece on the return stroke without digging in.

5. Mount the tool in the holder and the holder in the tool post.

6. Turn the tool slide up so it does not overhang too much at the completion of the cut.

7. Move the table to the left until the cutting tool clears the right end of workpiece.

8. Turn the slide down to see if the cutting tool can reach the bottom of the workpiece without excessive overhang of the slide. If necessary, raise the table. Turn the tool slide up to the starting position.

9. Adjust for correct length and position of stroke.

10. Adjust for correct speed.

MAKING THE ROUGH CUT

1. Turn on the power.

2. Place your left hand on the cross-feed crank and your right hand on the down-feed handle.

Fig. 75-2. Machining the horizontal surface.

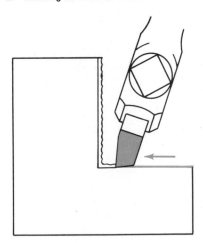

Move the workpiece toward you and the cutting tool down until the cutting tool touches the work.

3. Release your hand from the cross-feed crank. Move the cutting tool down about 0.004 or 0.005 in. at the end of each cutting stroke. After the first cuts, stop the machine and check the cut with the layout line. About 0.010 to 0.015 in. should remain for finishing to the layout line. Check the workpiece with a square after the first cut has been completed.

4. Continue to machine the entire vertical surface.

MAKING THE FINISHING CUT

1. Grind or hone the cutting tool, and then machine up to the layout line.

2. A sharp tool and a slow feed will improve the finish on the workpiece.

MAKING A COMBINATION VERTICAL AND HORIZONTAL CUT TO SQUARE A SHOULDER

1. Turn the vise jaws parallel to the ram stroke.

2. Lay out the location of the shoulder cut.

3. Fasten the workpiece in the vise with the area to be removed above or to the right of the vise jaws.

4. Use a left-cut roughing tool to remove most

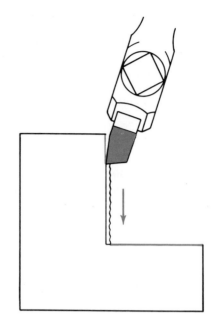

Fig. 75-3. Machining the vertical surface.

of the material to within about $\frac{1}{32}$ in. of the layout line.

5. Fasten a left-cut side tool in the toolholder.

6. Machine the horizontal surface of the workpiece from the outside to the corner (Fig. 75-2).

7. Set the clapper box to the right. Machine the vertical surface of the workpiece from the top to the finished horizontal surface (Fig. 75-3).

UNIT 76. Other Shaping Processes

SHAPING A BLOCK SQUARE AND PARALLEL

Shaping a rectangular block square and parallel to a certain size is a typical shaper job. Always select material that is between $\frac{1}{8}$ and $\frac{1}{4}$ in. larger than the finished size required. Metal should be shaped from all four surfaces and the two ends. The steps in machining the block shown in Fig. 76-1 are:

1. Machine the first (No. 1) surface.

2. Machine the second (No. 2) surface.

3. Machine the third (No. 3) surface.

4. Machine the fourth (No. 4) surface.

5. Machine the ends.

MACHINING AN ANGLE OR BEVEL

There are two methods of machining an angle or bevel. The simplest is to hold the workpiece

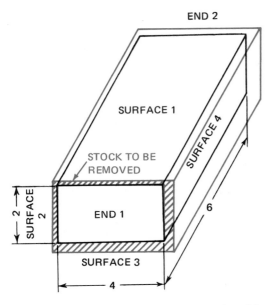

Fig. 76-1. A rectangular block to be shaped square and parallel.

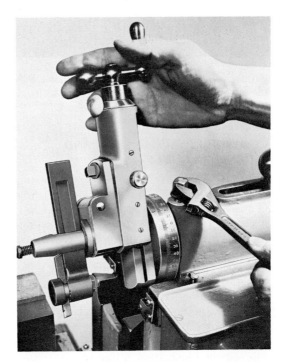

Fig. 76-3. Adjusting the toolhead for an angle cut.

Fig. 76-2. Machining an angle or bevel by clamping the workpiece in the vise with the layout line parallel to the top or side of the vise jaws.

Fig. 76-4. Cutting a keyway in a large gear.

in the vise with the layout line parallel to the top of the vise jaws. The angle or bevel is then machined in the same way as is a horizontal surface (Fig. 76-2). The second method is to machine the workpiece as you would a vertical surface using the tool slide set at an angle (Fig. 76-3).

CAUTION

Do not run the ram back into the column with the tool slide at an angle. The slide would strike the column and be badly damaged.

CUTTING KEYWAYS, KEYSEATS, AND INTERNAL OPENINGS

A *slot* or *groove* is a rectangular shaped opening. A *keyway* is a groove cut on the inside of a hole in a wheel, pulley, or gear (Fig. 76-4). A *keyseat* is cut on a shaft. It may be cut on the end or located any distance from the end (Fig. 76-5). When the keyway and keyseat line up for the key, they form a square opening.

A keyway or other internal opening is made with the cutting tool held in an extension toolholder. The cutting tool should be kept as close to the toolhead as possible. Note also that in internal cutting it is usually necessary to keep the clapper block from lifting on the return stroke (Fig. 76-6). A piece of wood or metal is generally inserted behind the upper end of the toolholder to accomplish this.

Fig. 76-5. Note how holes must be drilled for a keyseat that has two blind ends.

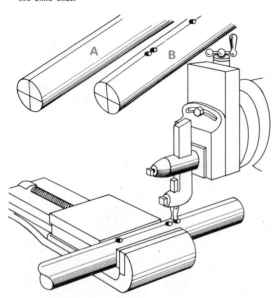

SHAPING AN IRREGULAR SURFACE

The shaper is capable of machining both concave and convex contours. For narrow, irregular surfaces, use a forming tool ground to the exact shape needed (Fig. 76-7).

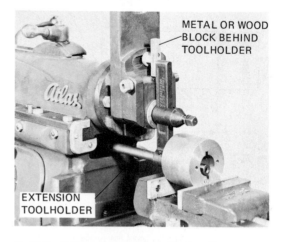

Fig. 76-6. Cutting a keyway on the inside of a pulley.

Fig. 76-7. The steps in machining a contour or irregular surface.

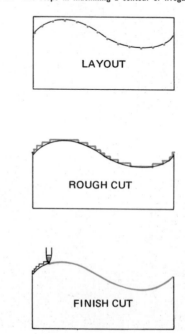

LAYOUT

ROUGH CUT

FINISH CUT

UNIT 77. Shapers and Planers in Industry

Industry uses several types of reciprocating machine tools to produce flat, straight surfaces. These include vertical shapers, planers, and broaching machines.

VERTICAL SHAPERS (SLOTTERS)

The *vertical shaper,* sometimes called a *slotting machine* or *slotter,* is similar to the horizontal shaper except that its ram moves vertically (Fig. 77-1). The machine can be used for cutting slots and keyways and for many other types of internal-external machining. The cutting head of the vertical shaper can be tilted from the vertical position to make angular cuts. The horizontal worktable is attached to a fixed knee. The table can be moved in and out and to the right or left either by hand or by power. The worktable is usually equipped with a power-driven rotary table for indexing gear teeth and similar forms. Setup on the vertical shaper is simplified because it is easy to see and align the workpiece

Fig. 77-1. A hydraulic slotter.

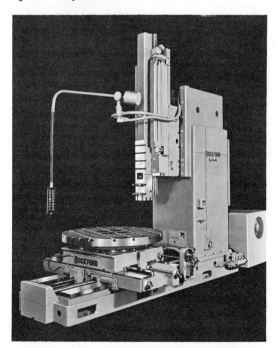

with the cutting tool. The vertical shaper also provides better support for the workpiece than does the horizontal shaper.

PLANERS

The *planer* is used to machine flat surfaces that are too large for the shaper. It differs from the

Fig. 77-2. (A) On a planer the worktable moves back and forth while the cutting tool remains stationary. Cutting tools can be moved up or down and to the right or left after each cut. (B) Parts of a planer.

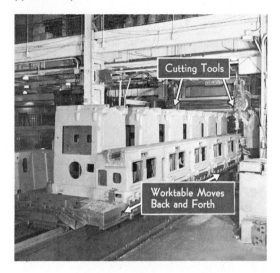

A

B

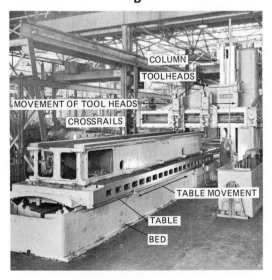

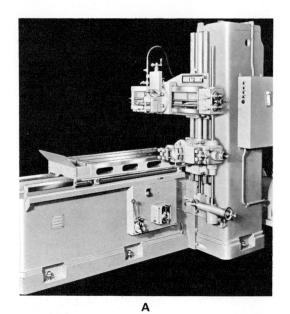

| A | B |

Fig. 77-3. (A) A small, open-side planer with one cutter head. (B) A larger, double-housing-type planer with two cutter heads.

Fig. 77-4. This planer is equipped with a direct hydraulic duplicator attachment. The original pattern is on the left. Four cutter heads are used to reproduce the pattern automatically.

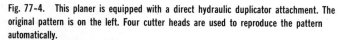

shaper in that the table holding the workpiece moves back and forth under a stationary cutting tool. In planing, the cutting tool is fed across the workpiece on a crossrail which straddles the table (Fig. 77-2A). The main parts of the planer include the bed, the table that moves back and forth, the column on which the crossrails move up and down, and the *toolheads* that are fastened to the crossrails (Fig. 77-2B). The planer is capable of handling very large pieces of work and producing very smooth, true surfaces.

There are two basic classes of planers, *open side* and *double housing* (Figs. 77-3A and 77-3B). Size is indicated by the largest piece of work that can be surfaced. Work-holding devices and cutting tools used are similar to those for the shaper except that they are larger. Some types of planers are equipped with a duplicating attachment which operates hydraulically (Fig. 77-4).

The planer, like the shaper, is a relatively slow machine tool. It is possible to improve efficiency by replacing the toolhead or heads that hold single-point cutting tools with a milling head. This results in an increase in the speed of chip removal.

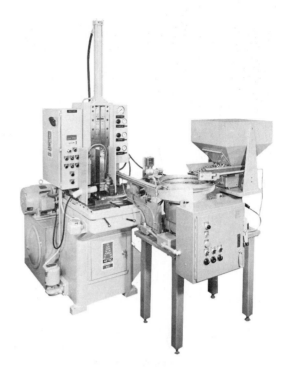

Fig. 77-5. A small vertical broaching machine being used to shape parts shown in Fig. 77-6.

Fig. 77-6. Typical jobs that can be done on the broaching machine.

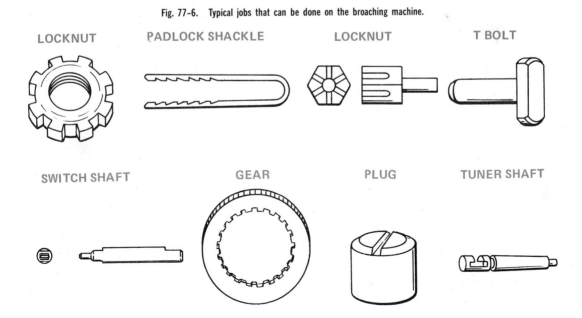

LOCKNUT PADLOCK SHACKLE LOCKNUT T BOLT

SWITCH SHAFT GEAR PLUG TUNER SHAFT

BROACHING MACHINES

Broaching is a one-pass operation combining both roughing and finishing cuts. Broaching machines consist essentially of a device for holding the work firmly, a long, straight tool with multiple cutting-edges, and a means of pushing or pulling the tool along the surface of the work. Broaching machines may be either horizontal or vertical (Fig. 77–5).

The broaching machine utilizes a precision cutting tool having a series of regularly spaced cutting-edges or teeth. These teeth vary in height, and each is capable of removing a specific amount of material. Unlike conventional milling operations, the broach machine's ram, which normally carries the broach, is the only moving part. Thus, the machine has far greater rigidity during the machining cycle. It is possible to surface broach anything that a broach can pass. Typical operations include slotting, straddling, and contouring. Internal broaching of serrations, splines, keyways, and round, square, hex- and odd-shaped holes is also quite common (Fig. 77–6). Broaches are made of high-speed steel. Many have carbide teeth. Nearly all broaches are designed and manufactured specifically for the metal and broaching method used.

UNIT 78. Discussion Topics and Problems

1. What is a shaper used for?

2. Name the important parts of a shaper.

3. How does a shaper change rotary motion into back-and-forth motion?

4. Why is the length of stroke set for $\frac{3}{4}$ in. longer than the surface that is to be machined?

5. What factors affect shaper speed?

6. What should be the number of strokes per minute when machining a piece of copper 6 in. long?

7. How is the feed controlled on most small shapers?

8. When should the feed take place? On the forward or return stroke?

9. How can a vise be checked for accuracy?

10. Why shouldn't a lathe toolholder be used on a shaper?

11. How does a shaper tool differ from a lathe tool?

12. How can you identify a right-hand (or right-cut) tool?

13. What is a hold-down? Describe how it is used.

14. List five suggestions for clamping a workpiece in a shaper.

15. What should be the depth of cut for roughing on a horizontal surface?

16. List five things that might cause the tool to chatter.

17. What can you do to prevent the edge on cast iron from cracking out as the finishing cut is made?

18. Why must the clapper be moved when making a vertical cut?

19. Sketch a block, and number the order in which its surfaces should be machined for squaring.

20. Name two common methods of machining an angle or bevel.

21. What precaution must be taken when the toolhead is at an angle?

22. What is another name for the vertical shaper?

23. Describe the difference in operation between a planer and a shaper.

24. What is a broaching machine and how does it cut?

SECTION 8

MILLING MACHINE

UNIT 79. The Milling Machine and Its Parts

The *milling machine* is basically a machine tool that has one or more multiedged, rotating, cutting tools. The milling cutter is attached to a spindle and rotates against the workpiece (Fig. 79-1). The workpiece is attached to a table that can be moved to bring it in contact with the cutting tool. The path of movement of the workpiece and the shape of the cutting-edges of the tool determine the final contour of the

Fig. 79-1. Milling is done with a rotating cutter.

workpiece. The milling machine can perform so many different operations that it ranks next to the lathe in importance.

Milling operations can be classified into two general categories.

1. *Plain milling* produces a machined surface that is flat or formed. The surface is parallel to the periphery (outside) of the cutter. When the cutter is quite wide, the operation is called *slab milling*. When the cutter used is irregular in shape, it is called *form milling* (Fig. 79-2).

2. *Face milling* involves the machining of a face that is held at right angles to the axis of the cutter (Fig. 79-3).

TYPES OF MILLING MACHINES

There are many types of milling machines. Most, however, are very similar. The *column-and-knee type* is most commonly found in schools and industrial shops. It is called by this name because the spindle (the part that rotates) is fixed in the column. The table can be adjusted longitudinally (back and forth), transversely (in and out or across), and vertically (up and down).

The three most common column-and-knee machines are the plain, universal, and vertical. The hand miller is a smaller version of the column-and-knee-type. Usually, but not always, the table feed on these machines is hand controlled (Fig. 79-4).

SIZES OF MILLING MACHINES

The sizes of the column-and-knee machines are determined by four things.

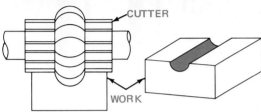

FORM MILLING

Fig. 79-2. Peripheral milling. Note the sawlike cutter that machines the metal. This is also called plain or slab milling. Insert shows example of form milling.

Fig. 79-3. Face milling.

Fig. 79-4. A small bench-type milling machine with power table feed.

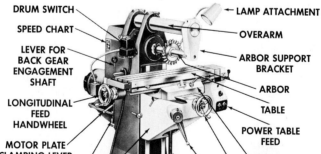

DRUM SWITCH
SPEED CHART
LEVER FOR BACK GEAR ENGAGEMENT SHAFT
LONGITUDINAL FEED HANDWHEEL
MOTOR PLATE CLAMPING LEVER
BELT TENSION SPRING
KNEE
CABINET BASE

LAMP ATTACHMENT
OVERARM
ARBOR SUPPORT BRACKET
ARBOR
TABLE
POWER TABLE FEED
SADDLE
CROSS FEED HANDWHEEL
TABLE RAISING CRANK
RAISING SCREW

Fig. 79-5. (A) The parts of a plain horizontal knee-type milling machine. It gets its name from the fact that the table does not rotate (it is plain). The spindle is in a horizontal position, and the machine has an adjustable knee. (B) An exploded view of a plain horizontal knee-type machine.

A

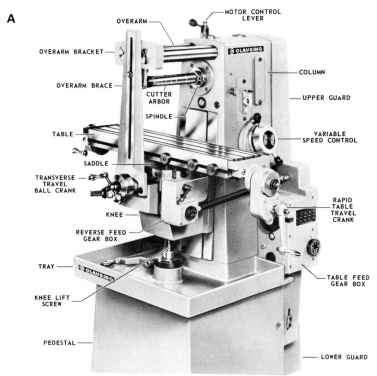

B

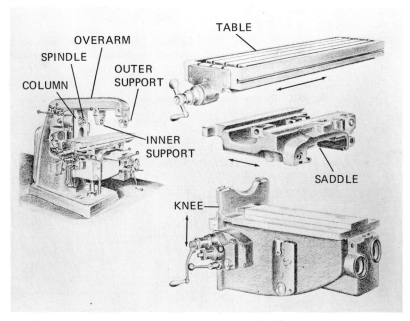

1. The *size of the table*. The size of the working surface may range from 7 × 26 in. for a smaller machine to 14 × 60 in. for a medium-size machine.

2. The *amount of table travel*. This indicates the distance the table will move longitudinally. Other movements of the table are closely related to this as far as size is concerned. Common sizes range from 15 to 34 in. of table travel.

3. The *amount of horsepower*. Milling-machine sizes are also expressed in rated horsepower of the spindle-drive motor. The really small hand millers use a $\frac{1}{3}$-horsepower (hp) motor. The smaller floor hand millers use a 1- to $1\frac{1}{2}$-hp motor. Medium-size machines use a 5- to 7.5-hp motor. Large milling machines may have a rated horsepower of 50. If a separate motor is used for feed drive, its horsepower is also indicated.

4. The *model and type*. Milling machines are also classified according to model and type. The *model* is the number given the machine by its manufacturer. The *type* is the classification of the machine such as plain, universal, or vertical.

PARTS OF THE PLAIN HORIZONTAL KNEE-TYPE MILLING MACHINE

Every shop that does milling has need for at least one column-and-knee milling machine. These general-purpose machines are especially suitable for use in job shops, toolrooms, repair shops, experimental laboratories, and schools.

Plain machines are suited chiefly to reciprocal milling, straddle milling, milling keyways and keyseats, gang milling, or any straight-line milling job (Fig. 79–5). The plain machine consists of a column, which is a heavy boxlike structure. The column houses the motor and the gears or belt mechanism for operating the spindle and table. The base projects out from the front of the column. The face (ways) of the column forms a very accurate slide. The knee slides vertically on the column face (Fig. 79–6). A feed, or elevating, screw extends from the base to the knee. On top of this knee is a saddle. The saddle can move transversely (cross movement toward and away from the column). On top of the saddle

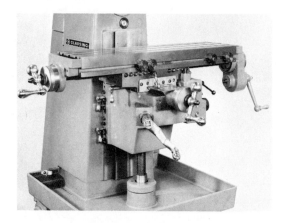

Fig. 79–6. Close-up of the knee, saddle, and table. Note the handles for longitudinal, cross, and vertical adjustments.

Fig. 79–7. The three movements on a plain milling machine.

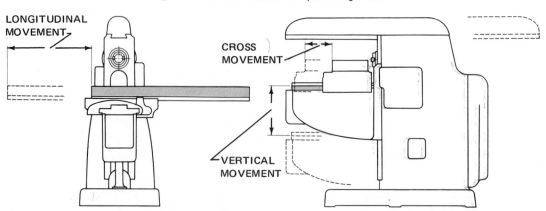

LONGITUDINAL MOVEMENT

CROSS MOVEMENT

VERTICAL MOVEMENT

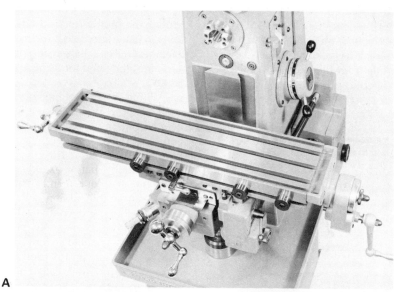

A

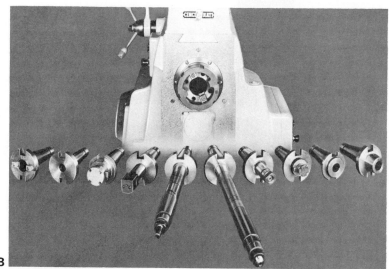

B

Fig. 79-8. (A) Note the spindle on this machine. This type requires the use of a draw-in bar. (B) An arbor lock spindle nose eliminates the need for a draw-in bar. The operator can change the cutting tools from the front of the machine. A partial turn is all that is necessary to secure adaptors, collets, and even long arbors in the spindle nose.

is the table. The table moves longitudinally (back and forth) in front of the column. The surface of the table is cut with T slots to which work-holding devices such as the vise can be clamped.

The machine provides for three movements of the workpiece (Fig. 79-7):

1. Vertical (up and down) movement of the knee

2. Transverse, or cross (in-and-out), movement of the saddle

3. Longitudinal (back-and-forth) movement of the table

Driving power for the cutting tool comes from the rotation of the spindle, which is a hollow shaft that rotates in bearings. Its front (end near the table) has a tapered hole. Two set-in lugs protrude from the front of the spin- dle (Fig. 79-8A). A draw-in bar is inserted through the spindle and is used to pull the arbor firmly in place and hold it securely. Some milling machines have a lock-type spindle nose that eliminates the need for using a draw-in bar (Fig. 79-8B).

Milling cutters can be mounted on an arbor or an adaptor, or the cutter may be fastened directly into the spindle nose. An overarm ex- tends out from the top of the column above the spindle (Fig. 79-9A). This overarm may be a single or double bar or a solid ram. The overarm can be moved in or out and clamped at different distances from the column. An arbor or overarm support fits on this overarm to support the outer end of the arbor. There are two types of overarm supports. One is called an *inner support* because it has a large hole and is used near the middle of an arbor. The other, called an *outer support,* is made to hold the very end of the arbor. For added rigidity, braces are sometimes fastened from the overarm to the knee (Fig. 79-9B).

The universal horizontal knee-type milling machine is the same as the plain horizontal machine with one added feature. The saddle is in two parts so the table can be horizontally rotated (Fig. 79-10).

Universal machines do many of the same machining jobs that plain machines do. The chief difference is that its table can be swiveled horizontally 45 degrees (°) to either the left or right. This makes the universal machine well suited for milling spur and helical gears, as well as worms and cams. All universal machines in- clude a standard 10-in. universal dividing head and an enclosed standard lead driving mecha- nism (Fig. 79-11).

The *vertical milling machine* is very similar to the plain horizontal milling machine except that the spindle is held in a vertical instead of horizontal position (Fig. 79-12). Vertical ma- chines are used with end mills and face mills for profiling interior and exterior surfaces, for locating and drilling holes in jigs and fixtures, and for precision step milling. More detailed information on the vertical milling machine can be found in Units 88 and 89.

MACHINE CONTROLS

Controls on most machines are operated either by hand or by power. Some machines are

Fig. 79-9. (A) Here you see the overarm and the arbor support holding the arbor in place. Many larger milling machines use a ram-type overarm. (B) Note how the overarm brace adds stability to the arbor.

A

B

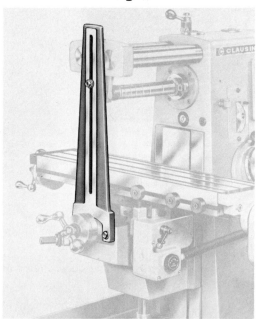

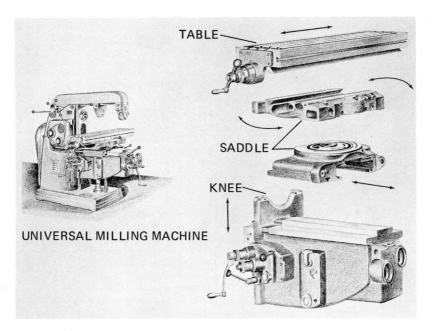

TABLE

SADDLE

KNEE

UNIVERSAL MILLING MACHINE

Fig. 79-10. Parts of a universal milling machine. Note how the saddle is made in two parts so that the upper part can swivel.

Fig. 79-11. Using a universal milling machine to cut the flute in a drill.

equipped with hydraulic controls. The exact location of the controls varies with each different machine model. All are similar, however, and once you have learned to operate one machine, it is relatively easy to handle another.

1. *Changing the spindle speed.* Spindle speed is determined by the kind and size of milling cutters used, the depth of cut, the rate of feed, the kind of metal in the workpiece, and numerous other factors. The spindle speed, in revolutions per minute (rpm), is controlled by belts or gears. To change the speed on the smaller machines, belts are generally shifted. On small milling machines equipped with variable-speed drives, speeds are changed hydraulically (Fig. 79-13). Larger machines generally have gears housed in a *speed box* located on the upper part of the column. Speeds are regulated by a speed-selector lever, which engages the proper gears for a given speed. When one or more levers are moved, the dial shows the exact spindle speed (Fig. 79-14).

2. *Adjusting table feed.* Most milling machines have a power feed for operating the table longitudinally. Larger machines are generally equipped with power vertical and power cross-feeds, as well. The power-feed box is most often located in the knee or on the right side of the machine. Usually 12 to 16 different feeds in inches per minute (ipm) are available by moving one or two levers. The feed per minute on smaller machines may range from a low of 0.250

Fig. 79-12. A double spindle N/C vertical milling machine.

Fig. 79-13. Note how this variable-speed drive operates. Speeds are changed hydraulically.

Fig. 79-14. In larger machines such as this, the movement of one handle determines spindle speed. The lever that is just above and to the right of the speed dial changes the direction of rotation. The feed at the front of the machine also requires the rotation of a handwheel. Speeds and feeds operate by separate motors and are not related.

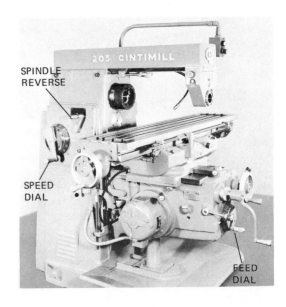

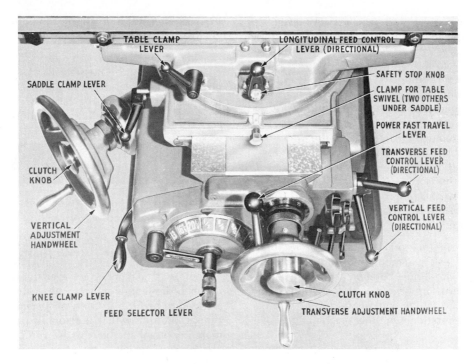

TABLE CLAMP LEVER

LONGITUDINAL FEED CONTROL LEVER (DIRECTIONAL)

SADDLE CLAMP LEVER

SAFETY STOP KNOB

CLAMP FOR TABLE SWIVEL (TWO OTHERS UNDER SADDLE)

POWER FAST TRAVEL LEVER

TRANSVERSE FEED CONTROL LEVER (DIRECTIONAL)

VERTICAL FEED CONTROL LEVER (DIRECTIONAL)

CLUTCH KNOB

VERTICAL ADJUSTMENT HANDWHEEL

KNEE CLAMP LEVER

FEED SELECTOR LEVER

CLUTCH KNOB

TRANSVERSE ADJUSTMENT HANDWHEEL

Fig. 79-15. The feed-selector lever on the front of this milling machine allows for feeds ranging from $\frac{1}{2}$ to $20\frac{1}{4}$ ipm.

Fig. 79-16. These feed screws are fitted with collars that are graduated in thousandths of an inch. The collars are free to revolve on a sleeve, but can be locked in position for making adjustments.

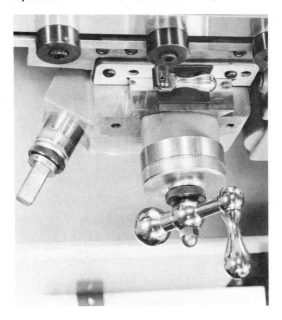

ipm to a high of 9 ipm. On larger machines, feed may go as high as 30 ipm (Fig. 79-15).

3. *Raising or lowering the knee.* For peripheral milling, the workpiece is positioned and the depth of cut controlled by raising or lowering the knee. Loosen the *knee clamp lever* that holds the knee firmly to the column. Find the *vertical-feed handwheel.* Turn it to the left to lower the knee. Turn it to the right to raise it. Note that there is a micrometer collar on this control and also on the cross-feed handwheel and the table handwheel (Fig. 79-16).

4. *Moving the saddle toward or away from the column* (cross movement). Find the *cross-feed* or *traverse handwheel.* Turn it to the right to move the table toward the column. Turn it to the left to move the table away from the column. This adjustment is made to position the workpiece under the cutter. Some machines are equipped with a power cross-feed (cross-feed engaging lever).

5. *Moving the table longitudinally (side to side) in front of the column.* Find the *table*

411

handwheel. Most machines have one on either end of the table. Turn the wheel to the right to move the table to the right. Turn the wheel to the left to move the table to the left. Many machines are equipped with a table power feed. If a machine has power feed, there will also be an *engaging lever* near the front and center of the table. Moving the lever to the right will move the table to the right. Along the front edge of the table are *adjustable stops* or *trip dogs,* used to set or limit the distance of table travel. These can be adjusted and locked in any position. When the power feed is engaged, these dogs, or stops, disengage the power feed at a certain point.

6. *Reversing the direction of spindle rotation.* There are two common ways of reversing the direction of spindle rotation. Some machines have a reversing switch with one button for clockwise rotation and another for counterclockwise rotation. On other machines, a single lever on the left side of the column can be changed to reverse spindle direction.

7. *Using the rapid-traverse lever.* Many machines have a rapid-traverse lever that gives fast power travel in any direction of feed engaged. It is used to position the table quickly or to return the table to its starting position.

CAUTION

Be extremely careful when engaging this lever because the parts move with such great speed.

HORIZONTAL SPINDLE ATTACHMENTS

Numerous attachments are available for most makes of horizontal millers. These attachments are used to perform a variety of special jobs that cannot be done with a horizontal spindle. The most important of these is the vertical milling attachment, which converts the horizontal miller into a vertical-spindle type of machine (Fig. 79–17).

Fig. 79-17. This horizontal milling machine is equipped with a vertical milling head that is independent of the horizontal spindle.

Fig. 79-18. Good and poor housekeeping.

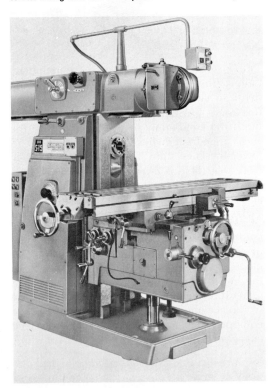

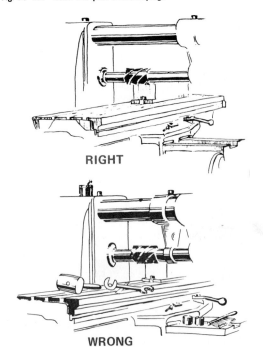

RIGHT

WRONG

GIBS

DO NOT OPERATE THE MACHINE WITH GIBS OUT OF ADJUSTMENT. THIS RESULTS IN INACCURATE WORK. CHECK ALL GIB ADJUST—MENTS PERIODICALLY.

CLAMPS

CLAMPS ARE PROVIDED FOR TABLE, KNEE, AND SADDLE UNITS TO IN—CREASE THEIR RIGIDITY WHEN NOT USED TO FEED THE WORK.

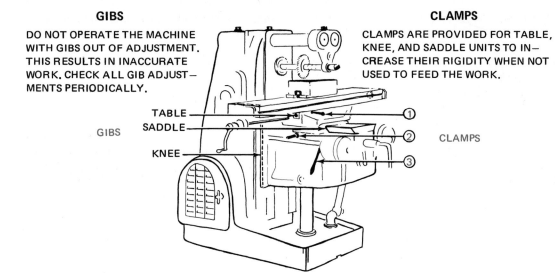

GIBS

TABLE
SADDLE
KNEE

CLAMPS

①
②
③

Fig. 79–19. Make sure that all gibs have been adjusted properly and that the only clamp that is free (loose) is the one necessary for correct movement of the table, saddle, or knee.

CARE OF THE MILLING MACHINE

1. Keep the machine clean. Brush chips away, and wipe the table clean with a cloth.

2. Always wipe the spindle nose before installing an arbor, adaptor, or cutter.

3. Never blow away chips with an air blower. This may cause chips to lodge in the moving parts of the machine.

4. Keep the machine well lubricated. Oil or grease the machine as indicated in the lubrication chart supplied with each machine.

5. Never leave tools on the table. The table must be kept in perfect condition, free of burrs. Never drop a tool on the table. The milling machine is a piece of precision equipment (Fig. 79–18).

6. Handle the arbors and cutters very carefully.

7. Make sure that the gibs are in proper adjustment. Keep all clamps tight except when the part (table, knee, or saddle) must be moved or is operating (Fig. 79–19).

8. Adjust the *trip dogs* to a distance slightly more than the length of the cut.

SAFETY

The milling machine can cause serious injuries unless certain precautions are carefully observed. Some important safety rules are listed below. Study and remember them.

1. You must not attempt to operate a milling machine until you have received instructions from your instructor.

2. Before operating the milling machine, be sure you know how to stop it quickly. It is just as important to know how to stop a machine as to start it.

3. Do not lean against or rest your hands on the moving table. This careless habit may cost you your fingers some day.

4. Keep your fingers and hands away from all moving cutters. There is never any reason to place your fingers near a turning cutter. Stop the machine first (Fig. 79–20).

5. Never wear long sleeves or a sweater while working on a machine tool. Always wear safety glasses to protect your eyes.

6. It is dangerous to use cutters, wrenches, and

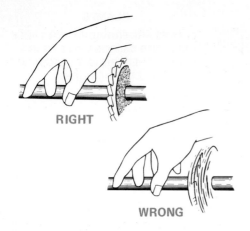

Fig. 79-20. Reaching over a turning center can be very dangerous.

Fig. 79-21. Always use a brush to remove chips; never use your fingers.

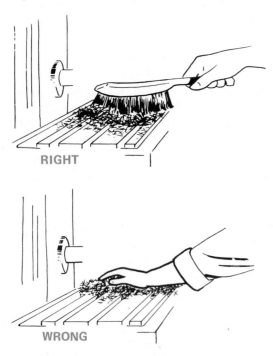

other tools which do not fit the machine properly.

7. When using large wrenches, be sure to brace yourself. If the wrench slips or the nut loosens suddenly, you can be injured.

8. When using thin saws, be sure there is no spring in the work. Make sure the vise and the work are securely fastened. The pieces of a broken saw will fly like a bullet.

9. It is very dangerous to use rags, cotton waste, or a cleaning brush near a moving cutter (Fig. 79-21).

10. Never attempt to set up work, make adjustments, or try to measure work while the cutter is turning. Stop the machine first (Fig. 79-22).

11. When removing cutters, always hold a rag or cloth over the cutter to prevent being cut (Fig. 79-23).

12. Do not attempt to lift heavy attachments alone. Get help. When placing heavy attachments on the table, first lower the table as far as it will go.

13. Never permit another person to start or stop a machine for you.

14. When mounting the arbor support, keep your fingers away from the bearing hole.

Fig. 79-22. Never make any adjustments with the machine operating.

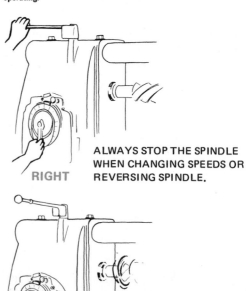

RIGHT **ALWAYS STOP THE SPINDLE WHEN CHANGING SPEEDS OR REVERSING SPINDLE.**

WRONG **NEVER CHANGE SPEEDS OR REVERSE THE SPINDLE WHILE IT IS ROTATING. CLASHING OR STRIPPING OF GEARS MAY RESULT.**

STEPS IN USING A MILLING MACHINE

Although each operation requires a different cutter and setup, all milling operations are similar. Follow these steps:

1. Select the correct kind and size of cutter to be used.

2. Choose the correct arbor or adaptor to hold the cutter.

3. Select the correct kind or kinds of work-holding devices.

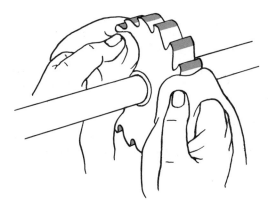

Fig. 79-23.   Handle all cutters carefully.

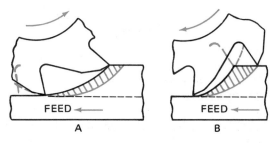

Fig. 79-24.   Two methods of milling: (A) conventional or up milling, and (B) climb or down milling.

Fig. 79-25.   Up milling. Each tooth of the cutter must slide along the already cut surface before it begins to cut into the metal. In conventional milling, the portion of the finished surface that is produced by a tooth is formed at the beginning of its contact with the workpiece. At this point the chip thickness is very small.

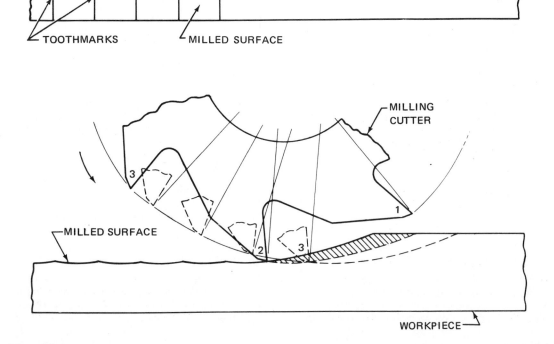

TOOTHMARKS   MILLED SURFACE

MILLED SURFACE

MILLING CUTTER

WORKPIECE

415

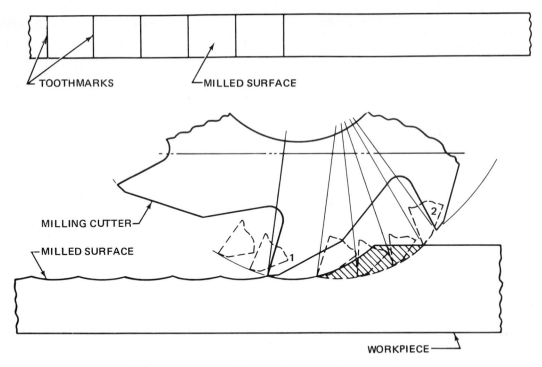

TOOTHMARKS   MILLED SURFACE

MILLING CUTTER

MILLED SURFACE

WORKPIECE

Fig. 79-26. In climb or down milling, the finished surface is produced at the end of the tooth engagement with the workpiece.

4. Mount the work-holding devices and the workpiece on the table.

5. Mount the cutter holder to the spindle and then put the cutter on it.

6. Select and adjust the correct speed and feed.

7. Adjust the table for the correct position and location of cut.

8. Adjust the depth of cut.

9. Take the cut.

METHODS OF CUTTING

Conventional or *up milling* involves rotating the cutter against the direction of feed. This has long been considered the only practical way to use milling cutters. It has only been in the past few years that *climb,* or *down, milling* (rotating the cutter in the direction of the feed) has become recognized as an acceptable procedure.

Climb milling results in a better surface finish, greater feeds per tooth, and longer cutter life per grinds than does conventional milling. It is not applicable to every milling job, however, and should be attempted only when the machine is of a heavy-duty type and is in excellent repair. Also, the workpiece and cutter must be held rigidly, and the nature of the job must be appropriate for climb milling.

Figure 79-24A illustrates conventional, or up, milling. Because great pressure is required to break through the surface being milled, the tooth has a tendency to slide along the surface for a short distance. This sliding under pressure tends to dull the cutter. The alternating sliding and sudden breaking through the metal causes revolution marks so familiar on milled surfaces (Fig. 79-25). In conventional milling, the chips are formed by the cutter entering the already machined surface at a very shallow angle. There is a burnishing action on the tooth clearance and cutting forces tend to push the workpiece up off the table.

Figure 79–26B illustrates climb, or down, milling. Here, full engagement of the tooth with the metal is practically instantaneous. This prevents gradual build up of peripheral pressures and the resulting sliding and dulling of the cutter as mentioned above. It further permits a more gradual disengagement of the teeth from the work, so that feed marks are largely eliminated. Because climb milling chips are formed by the cutter entering virgin metal at a steep angle, forces are directed down into the table, and this tends to hold the workpiece down.

Machine backlash must be eliminated before utilizing the climb-milling method. This is because the variable cutting forces are in the same direction as the feed. Any backlash will cause excessive feed at the instant when the cutter engages the workpiece. This, of course will result in a poor finish on the workpiece.

Advantages of climb milling are:

1. Feed can frequently be doubled over conventional milling.

2. Metal can be removed twice as fast without vibration or chatter.

3. Finish can be considerably improved.

4. Tool life is improved 25 to 50 percent if work-hardened metals are involved (Fig. 79–26).

Before attempting climb milling, the following factors should be considered:

1. The milling machine must be of a fairly heavy type (compared to the cut). All gibs, slides, feed screws, nuts, and gear trains should be free from play and backlash. Many newer machines have an antibacklash eliminator built into the table mechanism.

2. The cutter arbor must be as large as possible and the cutter properly keyed and tightened on the arbor.

3. Climb milling is not recommended on frail pieces unless the cut is light and the piece well supported.

4. The holding fixture should be rigid.

5. On older and smaller machines, climb-cut milling will pull the work into the cutter. This may result in a broken cutter or damaged work.

UNIT 80. Milling Cutters and Cutter Holders

A *milling cutter* is a rotary cutting tool that comes in contact with the workpiece and removes metal in the form of chips (Fig. 80–1). There must be movement between the workpiece and the cutter. Usually the cutter is held in a fixed (but rotating) position, and the workpiece moves. Milling cutters are made in many sizes, shapes, and kinds to perform the necessary operations (Fig. 80–2). Cutters are usually made of high-speed steel or cemented carbide. Sometimes carbon-steel cutters are used on hand millers. If cemented carbide is used, the cutting tool may have brazed tipped blades or inserted blade cutters with replaceable blades. The replaceable blades are most commonly used in industry since it is normally less expensive to replace them than to resharpen them (Fig. 80–3).

There are many different kinds of milling cutters. Many of these are for operations that are done only in the more advanced machine shop. Some of the more common kinds of cutters are described below.

1. *Plain milling cutters.* Often called *slab cutters,* these are cylindrical in shape with teeth on the periphery (around the outside) only. They are used for milling plain or flat surfaces.

a. *Light-duty plain milling cutters* with faces less than $\frac{3}{4}$ in. wide are made with straight teeth (parallel to the axis) (Fig. 80–4). Cutters more than $\frac{3}{4}$ in. wide have helix-angle teeth that are fairly close together (Fig. 80–5).

b. *Heavy-duty plain milling cutters* have a sharper spiral and fewer teeth. Wider spacing of teeth gives more chip space (Fig. 80–6).

c. *Helical plain milling cutters* have still coarser teeth, and the helix angle is greater. They cut with a shearing action that produces a very fine finish (Fig. 80–7).

2. *Side-milling cutters.* These cutters have teeth around their periphery and also on one or both sides.

a. *Plain side-milling cutters* have straight teeth around the outside and side teeth on both sides. The side teeth extend part of the distance from the outside toward the center (Figs. 80-8 and 80-9). These cutters are made in widths from $\frac{3}{16}$ to 1 in. and in diameters from 2 to 8 in.

b. *Staggered-tooth side-milling cutters* have teeth arranged in an alternating helix pat-

Fig. 80-1. High-speed milling using a cemented carbide face miller with inserted blades. Since carbide is a dense, brittle, and extremely hard material, it shatters easily. Consequently, the cutter must be rigidly supported and the workpiece must be solidly and firmly held.

Fig. 80-2. Some typical milling cutters.

Fig. 80-3. Parts of a milling cutter.

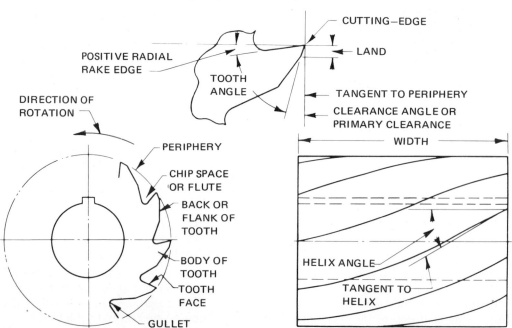

POSITIVE RADIAL RAKE EDGE

CUTTING—EDGE

LAND

TOOTH ANGLE

TANGENT TO PERIPHERY

CLEARANCE ANGLE OR PRIMARY CLEARANCE

DIRECTION OF ROTATION

PERIPHERY

CHIP SPACE OR FLUTE

BACK OR FLANK OF TOOTH

BODY OF TOOTH

TOOTH FACE

GULLET

WIDTH

HELIX ANGLE

TANGENT TO HELIX

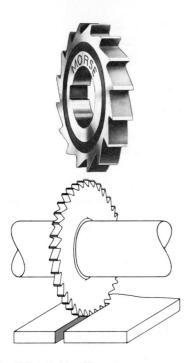

Fig. 80-4. Light-duty plain milling cutters.

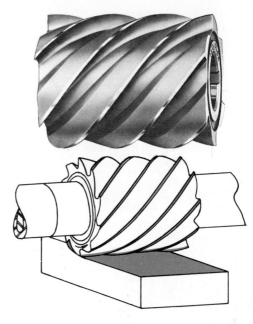

Fig. 80-6. Heavy-duty plain milling cutters are used when it is necessary to take heavy cuts. Heavy-duty cutters have fewer teeth than light-duty cutters.

Fig. 80-5. This cutter is designed for moderate cuts on plain surfaces and is used on ordinary types of horizontal milling machines.

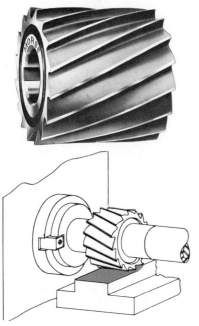

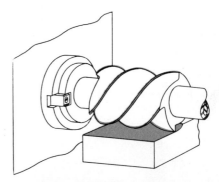

Fig. 80-7. The helical plain milling cutter can be run at high speeds and will produce exceptionally smooth finishes. A large helical angle causes the cutter to absorb most of the load in end thrust; therefore, it does not force the cutter away from the workpiece. This condition prevents the cutter from "hogging in" when entering or leaving the cut.

tern (Figs. 80-10 and 80-11). This type is better for milling deep slots because the teeth provide more chip clearance. The only limit to the depth of cut is the distance from the circumference to the hub.

419

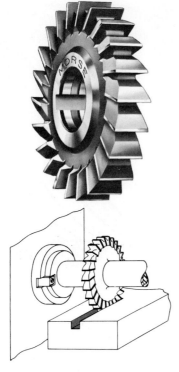

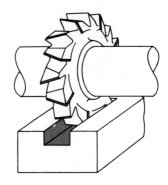

Fig. 80-10. Staggered-tooth side milling cutters are designed for deep slotting operations. The alternate right- and left-hand helical teeth reduce chatter and give ample chip space for higher speeds and feeds than is possible with the regular side milling cutter.

Fig. 80-8. Side milling cutters are perhaps the most useful of all milling cutters. They are recommended for side milling, straddle milling, and slotting. For heavy-duty side milling, half-side milling cutters are recommended.

Fig. 80-9. A carbide side milling cutter with inserted blades.

Fig. 80-11. A cemented carbide, staggered tooth milling cutter with inserted cutter blades.

c. *Half side-milling cutters* have teeth on only one side and around the circumference. They are made as right- and left-hand cutters (Fig. 80-12).

d. *Interlocking side-milling cutters* are made in two parts. Two cutters interlock to make one cut. By placing thin spacers or shims between the cutters, a slot or groove of an exact width can be milled in one cut (Fig. 80-13).

3. *Metal-slitting saws.* These resemble small circular-saw blades. They have teeth around the circumference, and some also have side teeth. They are used for cutting-off operations and for

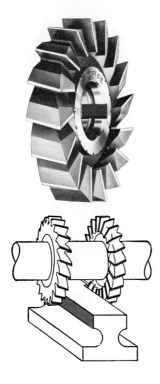

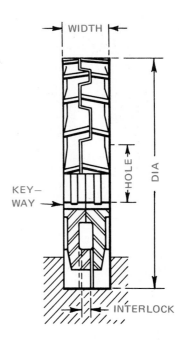

Fig. 80-13.   Interlocking side milling cutter.

Fig. 80-12.   Half-side milling cutters have many advantages over ordinary types of side milling cutters. This is particularly true for side operations where only one side of the cutter is used, as in straddle milling. Helical gashes give positive side rake to the teeth and promote smooth cutting action and long tool life. This also tends to lessen the power consumption for a given cut. The side teeth have considerably deeper gashes than the ordinary side milling cutters. They provide larger chip space and increased sharpening life.

slotting. They come in sizes from $2\frac{1}{2}$ to 8 in. in diameter.

a. *Plain metal-slitting saws* have the sides slightly dished (concave) on both sides for clearance. They are limited in width to a maximum of $\frac{3}{16}$ in. (Fig. 80-14).

b. *Staggered-tooth metal-slitting saws* are very similar to staggered-tooth side-milling cutters. They are limited in width to $\frac{1}{4}$ in.

c. *Metal-slitting saws* with side teeth are similar to side-milling cutters. They are used for cutting off heavier material (over $\frac{3}{4}$ in.) and for deep slotting (Fig. 80-15).

4. *End mills*. These are designed for milling slots, keyways, keyseats, and pockets where the ordinary arbor type of milling cutter cannot be used. A depth of cut equal to one-half the diameter of the cutter can generally be taken from solid stock (Fig. 80-16). The helix angle of the cutting-edges and the free cutting construction of end mills promote smooth, efficient operation even at high feeds and speeds. Operating them at comparatively high speeds is recommended because this avoids feed overloads and breakage. This is especially true when using cutters of small diameters.

Successful operation of end mills is dependent on proper mounting in the holder and in the machine. Holders should be carefully checked for rigidity, fit, and runout. The milling machine, the work-holding fixture, and the work itself should be examined for rigidity. Springing, looseness, or backlash is often fatal to this type of cutter.

End mills vary as to diameter of cut, diameter of shank, length of cut, length, overall single or double end, and style (Fig. 80-17). End mills vary the most in style. For example, they may have two, three, four, or six flutes (Fig. 80-18). Their teeth may be shaped for center cutting or

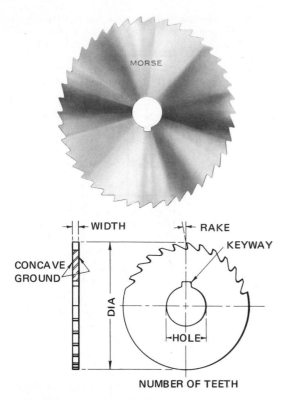

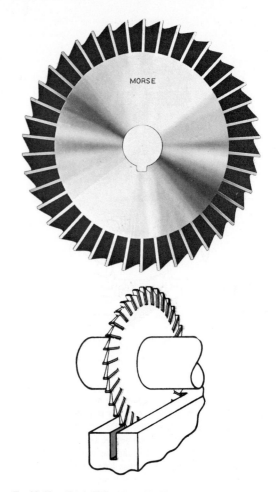

Fig. 80-14. Metal slitting saws are concave ground on both sides for clearance. This clearance extends from the periphery to the hub around the hole. The hub is flat and of the same width as the cutting-edges. Plain, metal slitting saws are designed for ordinary slotting and cutting-off operations. For deep cuts, saws having side chip clearance are desirable.

Fig. 80-15. Metal slitting saws with side teeth are similar to side milling cutters. Side chip clearance makes these saws suitable for deep slotting and sinking in cuts.

may have a gashed end (Fig. 80-19A). Some have a ball-end shape. They may have a straight shank or one with a Brown and Sharpe or Morse taper. Their length may be short (stub), standard, or long. End mills are normally made of high-speed steel but are also available with brazed carbide cutting-edges or with replaceable carbide blade cutters (Fig. 80-19B).

5. *Shell end mills.* These have a center hole for mounting the cutter on a short (stub) arbor. They are made in larger sizes than the solid end mills. There are cutting-edges on the end and around the periphery of the shell. The center of the face of the shell is recessed so a screw or nut will fit into it to hold the shell to the stub arbor (Fig. 80-20).

Fig. 80-16. End mills are commonly used for all types of cutting.

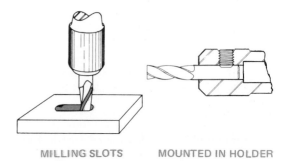

MILLING SLOTS   MOUNTED IN HOLDER

422

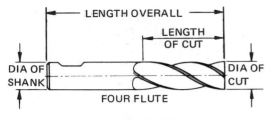

LENGTH OVERALL
LENGTH OF CUT
DIA OF SHANK
DIA OF CUT
FOUR FLUTE

SINGLE-END END MILLS

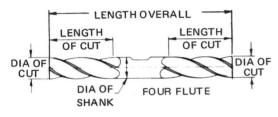

LENGTH OVERALL
LENGTH OF CUT
LENGTH OF CUT
DIA OF CUT
DIA OF CUT
DIA OF SHANK
FOUR FLUTE

DOUBLE-END END MILLS

Fig. 80-17. Standard dimensions for single-end and double-end mills. Note the flat surface on each. A setscrew in the toolholder is tightened against this flat surface to prevent the end mill from twisting in the holder.

6. Some of the other kinds of solid cutters in common use are as follows.

a. *Angular milling cutters* are made as single- or double-angle cutters and are used to machine angles other than 90 degrees (°) (Figs. 80-21 and 80-22).

b. *T-slot milling cutters* are used for milling T slots (Fig. 80-23).

c. *Woodruff keyseat milling cutters* are used for milling keyseats (Figure 80-24).

d. *Dovetail milling cutters* are used for milling dovetails (Fig. 80-25).

7. *Form-relieved cutters.* These are made in various shapes to mill irregular-shaped surfaces. Some of the common shapes are concave, convex, and corner-rounding cutters (Figs. 80-26 to 80-28).

Gear-milling cutters are a kind of form-relieved cutter used to machine any standard gear tooth (Fig. 80-29). These cutters are described in greater detail in Unit 87.

8. *Face-milling cutters.* These cutters are of the solid-type and have brazed carbide teeth or

Fig. 80-18. Common types of end mills: (A) single-end mills, (B) double-end mill, (C) two-flute and multiflute taper-shank end mills with Morse taper shanks, (D) end mill with ball end, and (E) two-flute and multiflute short or stub end mills.

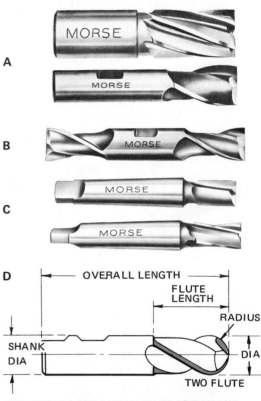

A
B
C

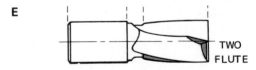

D

OVERALL LENGTH
FLUTE LENGTH
RADIUS
SHANK DIA
DIA
TWO FLUTE

SPECIFY DEGREE AND HAND OF SPIRAL AND ROTATION (RIGHT—HAND SPIRAL, RIGHT—HAND CUT SHOWN)

E

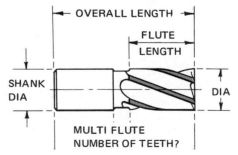

TWO FLUTE

SPECIFY DEGREE AND HAND OF SPIRAL AND ROTATION (RIGHT-HAND SPIRAL—RIGHT HAND CUT SHOWN)

OVERALL LENGTH
FLUTE LENGTH
SHANK DIA
DIA
MULTI FLUTE
NUMBER OF TEETH?

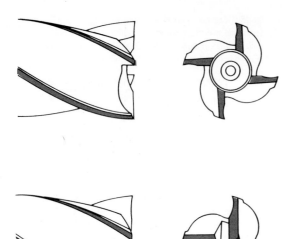

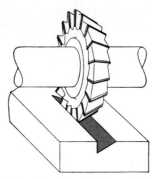

Fig. 80-21. Single-angle milling cutters are available either with right-hand or left-hand included angles of 45 and 60°. They have teeth on the angular face and on the side adjacent to the largest diameter. Single-angle cutters are suitable for cutting dovetails, ratchet wheels, and similar items.

Fig. 80-19. Types of end teeth on end mills.

Fig. 80-20. Shell mills are designed for both end- and face-milling operations. They fit standard shell and mill arbors.

Fig. 80-22. Double-angle milling cutters are furnished with included angles of 45, 60, and 90°.

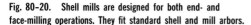

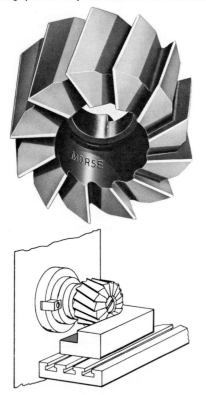

replaceable carbide blade inserts. They are used for machining large, flat surfaces (Fig. 80-30). The teeth cut on the face and periphery. The cutter may be mounted on an arbor which passes completely through the cutter or it may be mounted on the nose of the spindle, with its face completely free. The teeth on the periphery remove most of the metal. Those on the face serve just to clean up the surface.

HOW MILLING CUTTERS ARE CLASSIFIED

To identify milling cutters, check the following.

1. *Method of holding the cutter.* Cutters are mounted in the following ways.

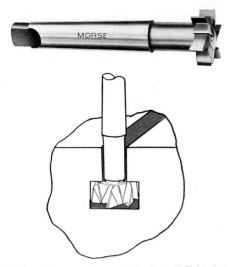

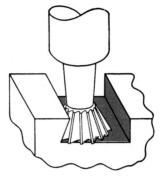

Fig. 80-25. A dovetail cutter is used to cut a standard dovetail.

Fig. 80-23. T-slot milling cutters are used to mill T slots in table tops.

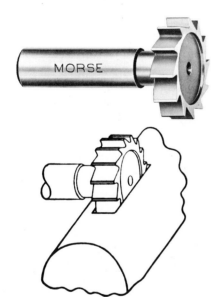

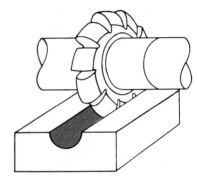

Fig. 80-26. Convex milling cutters are used to mill concave half circles.

Fig. 80-24. Woodruff keyseat cutters are used to cut the keyseat for a standard Woodruff key.

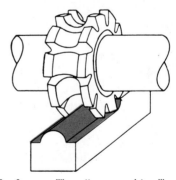

Fig. 80-27. Concave milling cutters are used to mill convex half circles.

a. Arbor-type milling cutters are made to be mounted on a machine arbor.

b. Shank-type cutters have a shank on the cutter that is used to mount and drive the cutter. The shank may be straight or tapered.

c. Facing-type cutters may be mounted directly on the spindle nose or they can also be mounted on an arbor or an adaptor.

2. *How the teeth are sharpened.* Most cutters are sharpened by grinding the surface back of

the cutting-edge. On form-relieved cutters, the face of each tooth is ground to sharpen it without changing the shape.

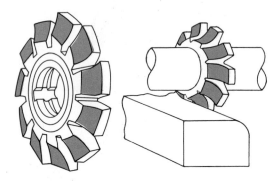

Fig. 80-28. Corner rounding cutters are available for both right-hand and left-hand operations.

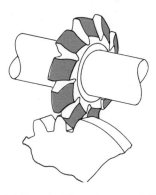

Fig. 80-29. Finishing gear milling cutters are available in a wide range of pitches.

Fig. 80-30. Face milling cutters are designed for milling plain areas of workpieces.

3. *Use of the cutter.* Many cutters are named for the kind of cut they make. For example, a T-slot cutter is used to cut a T slot. A Woodruff keyseat cutter is used to cut a semicircular depression to fit a Woodruff key.

4. *Construction of the cutter.* Most of the cutters you will use are solid. However, there are also cutters with inserted teeth.

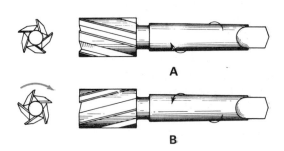

Fig. 80-31. The difference between right- and left-hand cutters: (A) right-hand cutting with right-hand helix and (B) left-hand cutting with left-hand helix.

Fig. 80-32. Arbor.

Fig. 80-33. (A) Style A arbor. (B) Style B arbor. (C) Style C arbor.

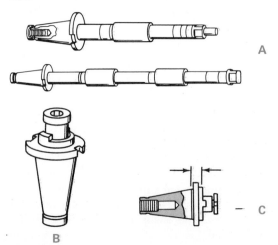

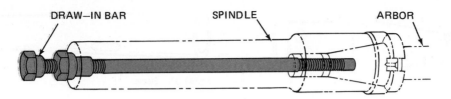

Fig. 80-34. The draw-in bar or bolt holds the arbor firmly in place.

HAND OF MILLING CUTTERS

The term *hand* is used to describe both the direction of rotation of the cutter and the helix of the teeth.

1. *Hand of cut* (rotation). This term refers to how the cutter is rotating. When viewed toward the spindle, the cutter is operating with a right-hand motion when it is moving counterclockwise. If it is moving clockwise, it is operating with left-hand rotation (Fig. 80-31).

2. *Hand of helix* (spiral). Many cutters have straight teeth. Others have teeth cut in a *helix* (a line or form that winds around a cylinder like a thread). When viewed from one end, it is a right-hand helix when the flutes twist away in a clockwise direction. It is a left-hand helix if the flutes twist in a counterclockwise direction (see Fig. 80-31).

CUTTER-HOLDING DEVICES

The larger, older milling machines used arbors with self-holding (Brown and Sharpe) tapers. All new horizontal milling machines use the American Standard steep machine taper ($3\frac{1}{2}$ inches per foot). Vertical milling machines are available with a wide variety of tapers on their spindles. Some manufacturers give the customer the choice of two, and others provide as many as four or more choices. The important point to remember is that the spindle taper determines the kind of arbors, adaptors, toolholders and collets that will be needed. In other words, the outside taper on the end of the arbor adaptor or toolholder must always be the same taper as on the spindle of the machine.

There are several types of cutter-holding devices with which the machinist must be acquainted.

1. An *arbor* is a shaft on which a cutter is mounted (Fig. 80-32). Arbors fit either the machine spindle, an adaptor, or toolholder. They hold cutting tools concentric or square with the spindle axis. Arbors are made in three styles (Fig. 80-33). Style A has a pilot at the outer end that fits into a bearing in the arbor support. Style B is very similar in appearance but does not have a pilot. It is supported by using a bearing sleeve which fits over the arbor. Style C is a shorter arbor on which a cutter is mounted on one end and held in place with a nut.

a. *Spacing collars* are used on either side of the cutter. These collars come in various widths so that the cutter can be expertly spaced.

b. A *bearing sleeve* is used on a style B arbor to provide a rigid support as close to the cutter as possible.

c. A *draw-in bolt* or *bar* is used on many types of machines. It fits the back of the spindle and its threaded end is screwed into the threaded end of the arbor or adaptor (Fig. 80-34). Some types of milling machines do not require the draw-in bolt since the arbor or adaptor can be locked into the spindle.

2. *Adaptors* are units that hold or accommodate tools, holders, and/or arbors. They fit the machine or attachment spindle directly and provide the means for changing from one holder-arbor to another (Fig. 80-35). Adaptors are used whenever the spindle taper is incompatible (doesn't match) with the tool or arbor.

3. A *toolholder* is a unit that holds or accommodates cutting tools, arbors, or other holders (Fig. 80-36). It may fit either a machine spindle or adaptor. It is used to hold tools either parallel or concentric with the spindle axis. For example,

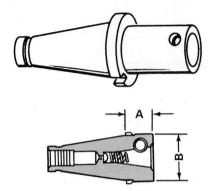

Fig. 80-35. Adaptor.

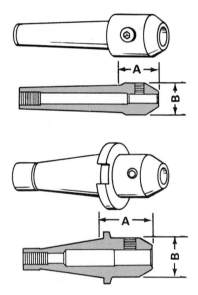

Fig. 80-36. Toolholders.

Fig. 80-37. Sleeve.

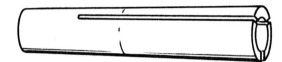

Fig. 80-38. Collet.

CUTTER SIZE AND TYPE OF DRIVE

1. *Arbor-type cutters* should be as small in diameter as is practical for a given arbor size. This makes for stronger tools with less torque placed on the cutter arbor. Consequently, there will be less chance of vibration.

2. *Shank-type tools* have a straight or tapered shank. They are mounted in an adaptor or toolholder, or directly in the machine spindle. These tools should be as large and rugged as shank and overall size will permit.

3. *Face-milling cutters* will give better results when their diameter is considerably greater than the width of the cut, provided they are well supported by the spindle nose. In general, the outside diameter of a face mill should be less than twice the bearing diameter of the spindle nose or adaptor. Cutters working at the end of an extended bar or spindle should be kept small and compact to provide rigidity.

CARE OF MILLING CUTTERS AND CUTTER-HOLDING DEVICES

1. An arbor is a precision-made piece of equipment that must be handled with care. Always wipe the arbor with a clean cloth before using. Keep the arbor in a rack, and protect it at all times from nicks (Fig. 80-39).

2. Milling cutters are delicate cutting tools that are difficult to sharpen. Protect the cutter when you are not using it by placing it on a rack (Fig. 80-40).

3. A cutter must slide freely on the arbor.

it is necessary to use a toolholder to fasten a straight-shank end mill to a spindle. Adaptors and toolholders are very similar in appearance and purpose.

4. A *sleeve* is a tapered, hollowed holding device used to take up space between the tapered hole of the adaptor and the smaller, tapered shank of the cutter tool (Fig. 80-37).

5. A *collet* is very similar to a sleeve or adaptor. This device is split lengthwise to give some flexibility to its holding power (Fig. 80-38).

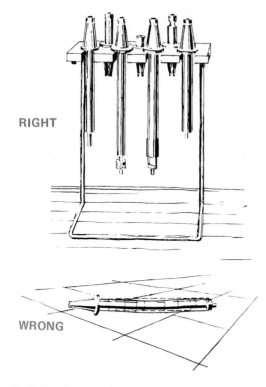

RIGHT

WRONG

Fig. 80-39. The right and wrong way to take care of arbors.

RIGHT

WRONG

Fig. 80-40. Take proper care of cutters.

Never force it on. To do so will damage the arbor and may break the cutter. Getting it off will also be a difficult job (Fig. 80-41).

4. Never bump the cutter against the machine or a metal part. This may cause the cutter to be nicked.

5. To remove an arbor or adaptor:

   a. Loosen the nut on the arbor (Fig. 80-42).

   b. Loosen the nut on the draw-in bolt a turn or two.

   c. Rap the draw-in bolt with a soft hammer.

   d. Take hold of the arbor with your left hand.

   e. Unscrew the draw-in bolt. Remove the arbor (Fig. 80-43).

6. Milling cutters should be protected against damage immediately after sharpening or removal from the milling machine. The cutter may

be stored in a strong wooden box or coated with plastic.

SHARPENING

It is suggested that milling cutters be sharpened on a regular basis. Several suggested schedules follow.

1. *At a predetermined wear land.* Sharpen cutters as soon as the wear land reaches a predetermined width (Fig. 80-44). This width should permit sharpening without excessive loss of tool life. It may vary from a few thousandths of an inch to $\frac{1}{16}$ in., depending on the type of cutter and finish required. This method is followed on production runs where uneven amounts of stock are removed, where material in stock varies in machinability, or when the quantity of products is small.

2. *After a predetermined period of use.* The time period is the length of time it takes a sharp cutter to develop a width of wear land indicating that it should be sharpened.

3. *When product quality indicates.* Sharpen cutters when product finish is unsatisfactory or

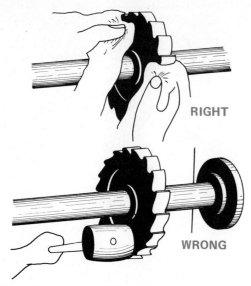

RIGHT

WRONG

Fig. 80-41. Cutters must slide freely on the arbor. Never force them.

Fig. 80-42. Correct and incorrect way to loosen the arbor nut.

RIGHT

LEAVE ARBOR SUPPORT IN PLACE WHEN LOOSENING ARBOR NUT.

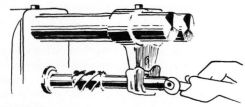

WRONG

DO NOT REMOVE ARBOR SUPPORT BEFORE END NUT ON ARBOR IS LOOSENED. WITHOUT THE SUPPORT THE ARBOR CAN BE SPRUNG.

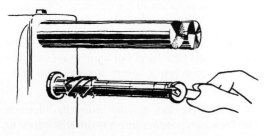

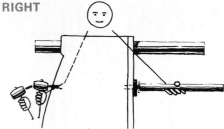

RIGHT

TO REMOVE THE ARBOR, LOOSEN THE NUT ON THE DRAW-IN ROD A FEW TURNS, THEN TAP THE ROD LIGHTLY TO LOOSEN THE ARBOR FROM THE SPINDLE NOSE BEFORE REMOVING.

WRONG

STRIKING THE DRAW-IN ROD SHARPLY AFTER THE REMOVAL OF THE NUT IS BAD PRACTICE. THE ARBOR CAN BE KNOCKED OUT OF THE SPINDLE DAMAGING THE TABLE SURFACE AND KNEE WAYS.

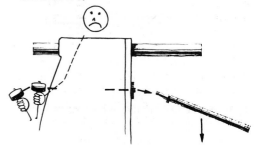

Fig. 80-43. The right and wrong way to remove an arbor.

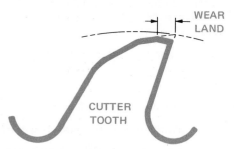

Fig. 80-44. Check the width of the land to determine whether the cutter teeth have excessive wear.

when product size is not within dimensional tolerances. As a cutter dulls, it cuts less freely and has a tendency to produce rough surfaces which affect finish and size.

4. *When power increases.* If the amount of stock to be removed and product machinability are reasonably uniform, an increase in power required to perform a particular operation indicates when a cutter needs sharpening.

UNIT 81.
Cutting Speeds, Feeds, and Coolants

Speeds and feeds are very important factors in milling. Improper speeds and feeds often result in low production, poor work quality, and unnecessary damage to the cutter (Fig. 81-1). It is important that a machinist know how to figure cutting speeds and feeds. Although there are formulas to help, judgment must be used in the final adjustment of the machine. The experienced machinist merely uses the result of the formula as a guide.

Milling as a production process is primarily concerned with the rapid removal of metal. The amount of metal removed in a given length of time is the important thing in figuring correct cutting speed and feed. As a beginner, it is usually best to start with slower speeds and feeds and then to increase them to the maximum limits. Suppose you want to machine a piece of mild steel (AISI 1020) with a high-speed steel cutter that is 6 in. in diameter. The cutting-speed range for a high-speed steel cutter used on mild steel is between 60 and 80 (see Table 81-1). Then, using the lowest cutting speed:

$$\text{rpm} = \frac{4 \times 60}{6} = \frac{240}{6} = 40$$

Machine speed (rpm) is adjusted in one of the following ways.

1. Most small bench and floor hand millers are belt driven, just like a drill press. To change the spindle speed, you must change the position of the belt on the pulleys. A plate fastened to the side of the machine will tell you the machine speed when the belt is in different positions.

Sometimes there is a back gear that can be engaged to give about eight possible machine speeds.

2. On larger milling machines, several methods can be followed for adjusting speed.

    a. Some machines have two or three levers on the left side of the machine that can be moved to obtain the desired cutting speed.

    b. Other machines have one lever or knob and a speed-selector dial. When the lever or knob is turned, the machine speed will be indicated on the dial.

FEED

Feed is the rate at which the workpiece advances under the cutter. It is really the most important single factor in determining how fast metal can be removed from the workpiece. Actually, feed, plus depth of cut, plus width of cut, determines how many cubic inches of metal are removed from the workpiece in any given length of time. There are three ways feed is controlled.

1. *Manual feed.* On many small hand millers there is no power feed. Therefore you must depend on your own judgment about how fast to move the workpiece under the cutter. In general, a slower feed is best for heavy roughing cuts and a faster feed for light, finishing cuts. Usually the tendency is to go too slow rather than too fast. A slow feed causes excessive wear on the cutter because a slow speed produces more rubbing than cutting action.

2. *Inches per revolution of the spindle or cutter.* On some machines, the feed is directly related to speed. As the machine's speed in-

Fig. 81-1. Care in the selection of spindle speeds and table feeds is of extreme importance in producing a good finish and extending cutter life.

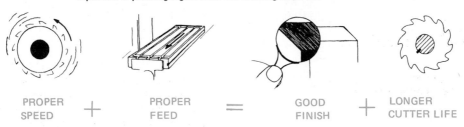

PROPER SPEED + PROPER FEED = GOOD FINISH + LONGER CUTTER LIFE

431

Table 81-1. Cutting speeds*.

MATERIAL TO BE MILLED	MATERIAL IN CUTTER					
	Carbon tool steel	High-speed steel	Super high-speed steel	Stellite	Tantalum carbide	Tungsten carbide
	CUTTER SPEED IN FEET PER MINUTE					
Aluminum	250–500	500–1000	. . . .	800–1500	. . . .	1000–2000
Brass, soft	40–80	70–175	. . . .	150–200	. . . .	350–600
Bronze:						
Hard	30–60	65–130	. . . .	100–160	. . . .	200–425
Very hard		30–50	. . . .	50–70	. . . .	125–200
Cast iron:						
Soft	30–40	50–80	60–115	90–130	. . . .	250–325
Hard		30–50	40–70	60–90	. . . .	150–200
Chilled			30–50	40–60	. . . .	100–200
Malleable iron	35–50	70–100	80–125	115–150	. . . .	250–370
Steel:						
Soft	30–45	60–90	70–100	. . . .	150–250	
Medium	30–40	50–80	60–90	. . . .	125–200	
Hard		30–50	40–70	. . . .	100–150	

*Learn what cutters will stand. Start with slow speeds and step up. For hand millers it is a good idea to use the lowest cutting speed shown in the table.

creases, the feed also increases. This feed arrangement is found on cone-driven machines. Some of the smaller hand millers have this arrangement, as well.

3. *Inches per minute* (ipm). Most larger milling machines use a feed rate shown in inches per minute. The feed rate is independent of the speed. In other words, the feed is set at the desired amount in inches per minute.

CUTTING SPEED

Cutting speed is the distance one tooth of the cutter moves in one minute as measured in feet on its circumference. It is expressed in surface feet per minute (sfpm). Cutting speed is also called *peripheral speed* and *surface speed*.

Cutting speed is not the same as machine speed (rpm). The spindle of the milling machine operates at certain given revolutions per minute. If you place a 4-in.-diameter cutter on the spindle, a tooth will travel about 12 in. (4 × 3.1416) in one complete revolution. If a 1-in.-diameter cutter is employed, it will travel only about 3 in. (1 × 3.1416).

Cutting speed is affected by many things.

The two most important are the kind of material being machined and the kind of material in the milling cutter. The cutting speeds shown in Table 81-1 represent averages that will provide fast removal of metal without damaging the cutter. Of course, they should be tempered to suit specific job conditions. For example, use higher speed ranges for softer materials, better finishes, smaller diameter cutters, light cuts, nonmetallics, frail workpieces or setups, hand-feed operations, and maximum production rates. Use lower speed ranges for hard materials, tough or abrasive materials, heavy cuts, minimum tool wear, and maximum cutter life. Too fast a speed will dull or burn the cutter. The cutting speed for finishing cuts can be as much as 40 to 80 percent higher than for roughing cuts.

To find the machine speed to use or the rpm at which the spindle must rotate, the following formula can be used.

$$rpm = \frac{4 \times sfpm}{d}$$

where sfpm = surface feet per minute

d = diameter of cutter in inches

The feed rate is independent of the speed. In other words, the feed is set at the desired amount in inches per minute. A change in the machine speed does not affect this feed.

The actual feed to use is determined by the following:

A. The kind of material in the workpiece

B. The kind of cutter

C. The kind of material in the cutter

D. The power available at the spindle (horse-power)

E. The way the workpiece is held (how rigid the setup is)

F. The shape and kind of workpiece (how rigid it is)

As a general rule, feeds should be as coarse as possible to obtain the desired finish. At the same time, they must be fine enough to secure a long cutter life. Feed is generally reduced a little for the finish cut. A formula commonly used to find the feed rate in inches per minute is as follows.

$$F = f \times T \times N$$

where F = feed rate
f = feed per tooth
T = number of teeth
N = rpm of cutter

Table 81-2 gives the average value for f when using a variety of high-speed steel cutters on various materials. This formula takes into consideration only the first three factors to be considered in feed selection. The following should be kept in mind when using this table. Use higher feeds for heavy roughing cuts, rigid setups, easy-to-machine work, rugged cutters, slab milling cuts, high tensile strength materials, coarse-toothed cutters, and abrasive materials. Use lower feeds for light and finishing cuts, frail setups, small cutters, deep slots, materials of low tensile strength, and fine-toothed cutters.

In production milling, feed rate is an important factor in getting the maximum amount of milling completed in a minimum length of time. To select maximum feed, production machinists make use of a chart developed by manufacturers of milling machines. This chart shows the maximum rate at which metal can be removed in cubic inches per minute (ipm^3). This rate is determined by the rated horsepower (hp) of the machine and the kind of metal being machined. For example a 15-hp machine removes soft steel at a rate of 7 ipm^3. If the depth of cut and the width of cut are known, the feed (F) in inches per minute can be found as follows:

$$F = \frac{\text{maximum metal removal in cubic inches per minute}}{\text{depth of cut} \times \text{width of cut}}$$

When the feed rate (F) in inches per minute has been found, then the feed per tooth (f) can be found as follows:

$$f = \frac{\text{feed in inches per minute}}{\text{cutter rpm} \times \text{number of teeth on cutter}}$$

Table 81-2. Recommended feed per tooth (*f*) for high-speed steel cutters.

Material	Face mills	Spiral mills	Slotting and side mills	End mills	Form cutters	Saws
Aluminum. Soft bronze	0.022	0.017	0.013	0.011	0.006	0.005
Medium bronze. Cast iron, soft	0.018	0.014	0.011	0.009	0.005	0.004
Malleable iron. Cast iron, medium	0.015	0.012	0.009	0.008	0.005	0.004
AISI X-1112 steel. Cast iron, hard	0.013	0.010	0.008	0.006	0.004	0.003
AISI 1020 steel. AISI X-1335 steel	0.011	0.009	0.007	0.005	0.004	0.003
AISI 1045 steel. Cast steel	0.009	0.007	0.006	0.005	0.003	0.003
Alloy steel:	0.008	0.006	0.005	0.004	0.003	0.002
Medium	0.007	0.005	0.004	0.004	0.002	0.002
Tough	0.005	0.004	0.003	0.003	0.002	0.0015
Hard	0.006	0.005	0.004	0.003	0.002	0.0015

This feed per tooth (*f*) can then be compared with the suggested feed per tooth for milling different materials to discover if the feed is too fast or too slow (Table 81–2).

COOLANTS

A cutting fluid or coolant is required when using high-speed steel cutters for milling steel. The coolant dissipates heat from the cut and minimizes possible damage to the cutter or workpiece due to friction. On equipment which can provide a copious supply of cutting fluid under pressure, the fluid helps to clear the chips from the cuts as well as to cool the cutter and workpiece.

Soluble oil and water is a common coolant fluid, but various mineral- and sulfur-base oils are also quite popular. Water-base solutions have good cooling qualities. Oil-base solutions tend to give a good finish on the milled surface.

Should chips accumulate around the cutter, such as when milling T slots, a blast of compressed air can be used to disperse the chips. Be sure, however, to place safety guards around the operation to prevent chips and dust from causing accidents.

Cast iron, brass, and plastics are generally cut dry. A cutting fluid is seldom used when machining steel with carbide cutting tools, due to the tendency of the carbide to chip from intermittent cooling.

UNIT 82. Work-holding Devices and Their Uses

In order to do precision work on a milling machine, the workpiece must be rigidly held on the table so as to preserve the accuracy of motion. Several factors govern the method of holding the workpiece. These include the type of machine, the nature of the cut (roughing or finishing), the direction of the cut, the type of cutter, the shape and rigidity of the work, and the quantity of pieces to be produced.

Many different devices are available for holding the workpiece to be machined.

1. The *plain vise* is the most common work-holding device used on the milling machine. This vise can be fastened to the table with its jaws either parallel or at right angles to the T slots (Fig. 82–1). The plain vise has hardened and ground steel jaws which are very accurately assembled. Fixture keys or tongues are fastened to the bottom of the vise to locate its jaws parallel with or at right angles to the table center line.

2. The *swivel vise* is similar to the plain vise except that its top part can be turned in a complete circle. Its base is divided into 360 degrees (°) (Fig. 82–2). The jaws of the swivel vise can be set to any angle in a horizontal plane, per-

mitting a precise angular relationship between cutter and workpiece.

3. The *adjustable* or *angle vise* is a very useful work-holding device. The simplest kind has a fixed base and a body which is adjustable from 0 to 90° on a vertical plane (Fig. 82–3). A second type has a swivel base with an adjustable body.

Fig. 82-1. Two plain vises used to hold a long piece of work.

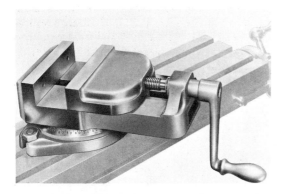

Fig. 82-2. The swivel vise has a base which is graduated in degrees. The vise body can be swiveled to any angle.

Fig. 82-4. This complex universal angle (toolmaker's) vise has a body that can be adjusted in two planes for machining a compound angle.

Fig. 82-3. The adjustable angle vise is very useful, particularly in toolroom work. The body of this type vise can be adjusted in one plane.

Fig. 82-5. A vise rack used to hold an arbor for cutting a long keyseat.

The *complex universal-angle vise* (sometimes called a *toolmaker's vise*) has a 360° swivel base and a body that can be adjusted in two planes for machining compound angles (Fig. 82-4).

4. The *rack vise* is an accurately made holding device used to clamp long workpieces lengthwise on the table of the milling machine (Fig. 82-5). This vise is also used to hold several small, regularly shaped workpieces at one time. The rack vise is similar to the plain vise in construction. However, it is equipped with several equally spaced clamping screws rather than one.

This arrangement produces an equalized clamping pressure over the full length of the vise jaws.

5. The *universal chuck* is a precision holding device frequently used in milling operations to

Fig. 82-6. A universal chuck mounted on a rotary table. It is used to hold round stock.

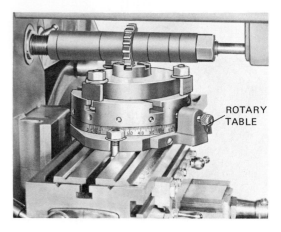

Fig. 82-7. This rotary table has the workpiece clamped directly to it.

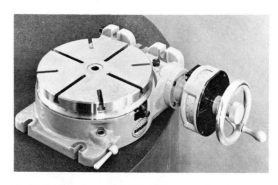

Fig. 82-8. A precision rotary table that can be adjusted to degrees, minutes, and seconds.

Fig. 82-9. The cross-slide table provides lateral movement without disturbing the milling-machine table.

hold cylindrical workpieces (Fig. 82-6). Its principal elements include a chuck body, scroll, and jaws. All working parts of the chuck body are made of heat-treated alloy steel. The jaws are reversible, enabling them to grip internally or externally. All three jaws are adjusted through a single pinion in mesh with the scroll. The universal chuck may be employed in several ways in the milling process. For example, it may be mounted on the machine spindle, the dividing head spindle, or the table itself.

6. The *rotary table* is used to hold workpieces for accurate spacing, dividing, and radius milling operations (Fig. 82-7). Its base is divided into 360°, allowing the workpiece to be rotated in a complete circle (Fig. 82-8). The simplest type is mounted directly on the table for indexing. Another type is mounted on a cross-slide table that can be moved in and out and to the right or left. Rotary tables may also be mounted on a tilting cross-slide table. Both hand-operated and power-driven models are available.

7. The *cross-slide table* is a precision device that can provide lateral feed in one or two directions (Fig. 82-9).

8. The *dividing head* (index head or index center) is a device for holding and turning the workpiece so that a number of equally spaced divisions or cuts can be made around it. It con-

Fig. 82-10. Plain index center.

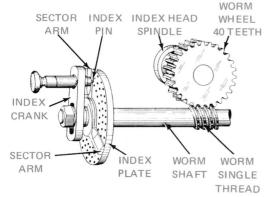

Fig. 82-11. The construction and parts of an indexing mechanism.

Fig. 82-12. Dividing head.

sists of a headstock (index head) and a footstock (tailstock). The workpiece may be held between centers (using the footstock), or it may be held in a chuck mounted on the headstock spindle. With this attachment, you can mill a square or hexagonal head on the end of a bolt or rod. In advanced machine shops, the dividing head is used for milling flutes on reamers or taps. It is also used for milling the teeth on all kinds of gears.

An *index center* is a simple type of dividing head. It can be used for dividing operations in splining, fluting, and simple gear cutting. A plate with holes or notches around its circumference is fastened to the outer end of the index center. One plate has 30 and 36 holes or notches, another has 28 and 48 holes (Fig. 82-10). If, for example, the 30- and 36-index-hole plate is used, a circle can be divided into 2, 3, 5, 6, 10, and 15 equal parts (using the 30-hole circle).

The universal dividing head has a crank which is geared to a spindle. One revolution of the crank will turn the spindle part of one revolution. On most dividing heads, 40 turns of the crank rotate the spindle one complete turn.

The construction of a simple indexing mechanism is shown in Fig. 82-11. Note that the

Fig. 82-13. A simple fixture such as a V-block can be used to hold several different sizes of round stock.

index plate does not turn when the crank is turned. Note also that each circle contains a different number of holes. A pin on the crank drops into these holes to hold the crank in place. By using different circles of holes and index plates, any fractional part of a turn of the index crank can be obtained. The dividing head can be used for direct indexing. It can also be used to divide a circle into equal or unequal parts (Fig. 82-12). When operated by power, the dividing head is driven from the machine's table lead screw by means of either a low or conventional lead attachment.

FIXTURES

It is often impossible to accommodate workpieces in a conventional work-holding attachment; hence, it becomes necessary to use a special device known as a *milling fixture*. The

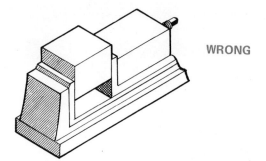

MOUNTING A WORKPIECE ON PARALLELS BEFORE TIGHTENING IT IN A VISE PROVIDES A RIGID BASE FOR CHATTER FREE MACHINING.

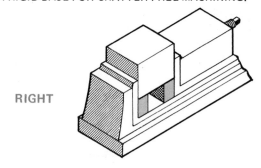

Fig. 82-16. Be sure that the workpiece is properly supported in the vise.

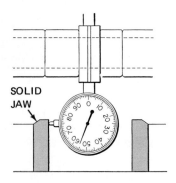

Fig. 82-14. Aligning a vise with an indicator.

Fig. 82-15. Aligning the vise with a square. This method is satisfactory for many ordinary machining jobs.

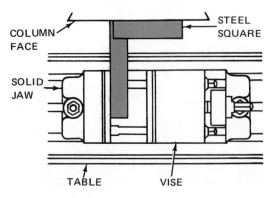

primary purpose of the fixture is to hold the workpiece securely in a fixed location (Fig. 82-13). Most fixtures are specially made for a particular job.

Always clean the base of a fixture before installing the fixture on the milling machine. Be sure to clean all work-support points after every cut. Even a tiny chip can throw the fixture or work out of line and cause inaccurate work.

CLAMPING WORKPIECES IN A VISE

1. Clean the base of the vise carefully before installing it on the table. Check to make sure it is accurately aligned. For precise work, use a dial indicator. Clamp the indicator on the arbor and then move the table so that the indicator tip rests on the fixed jaw. Set the dial to zero and use the manual cross-feed to move the jaw past the indicator. Adjust the vise until there is no variation between the ends (Fig. 82-14). A simpler, but less accurate method of aligning the vise is illustrated in Fig. 82-15.

438

2. If necessary, place the workpiece on parallels before tightening the vise (Fig. 82-16).

3. Make sure that the workpiece is centered in the vise so that it will be held securely (Fig. 82-17).

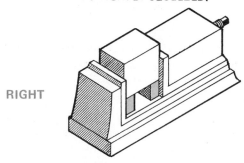

WRONG

UNLESS THE PIECE IS HELD IN THE CENTER OF THE VISE THERE IS A CHANCE THAT IT WILL MOVE DURING THE CUT, OR THAT ONE SIDE WILL BE TOO TIGHTLY SQUEEZED.

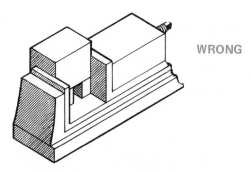

RIGHT

Fig. 82-17. Grip the workpiece in the center of the vise jaws to equalize clamping pressure.

Fig. 82-19. Parallels are used to align an angle plate parallel to the column of the milling machine.

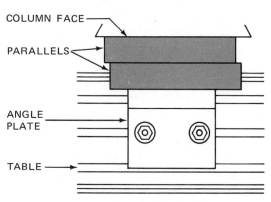

COLUMN FACE

PARALLELS

ANGLE PLATE

TABLE

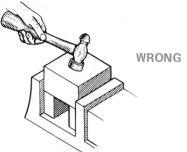

WRONG

IT IS GOOD PRACTICE TO TAP THE WORK—PIECE BEFORE AND AFTER CLAMPING, BUT USE LEAD, BRASS, LEATHER, OR WOOD TO PROTECT STEEL, CAST IRON, BRASS, OR PLASTIC MATERIAL, RESPECTIVELY.

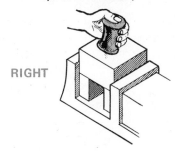

RIGHT

Fig. 82-18. Use a soft-face mallet to strike the workpiece.

Fig. 82-20. A sub-base placed under rough castings will ensure the long life and accuracy of the machine's table.

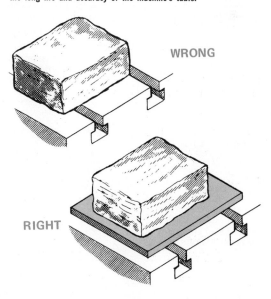

WRONG

RIGHT

4. Tighten the vise until snug and then tap the workpiece with a soft-face mallet (Fig. 82-18).

5. After tightening the vise as much as possible by hand, strike the handle a single blow with a lead or babbitt hammer in order to securely grip the workpiece.

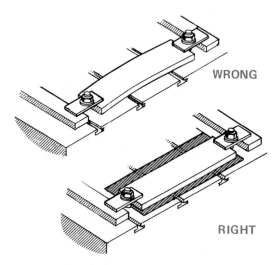

Fig. 82-21. Care must be taken in clamping thin material to prevent bowing as the clamps are tightened.

HOLDING WORKPIECES WITH CLAMPS

Often clamps can be used when the workpiece cannot be held in a vise. Although each job requires a special setup, the following principles generally will apply.

1. Make sure the workpiece will not shift under the cutting load.

2. Don't let the workpiece be distorted by the clamps.

3. Make sure the workpiece is adequately supported so that a good cut can be taken.

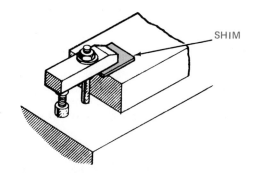

Fig. 82-22. Note how a thin shim of brass, copper, or aluminum is used to protect a finished surface.

Fig. 82-23. Setups using various shapes of strap clamps.

A. TYPICAL USE OF PLAIN SLOT STRAP CLAMP

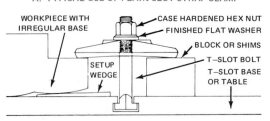

C. TYPICAL USE OF GOOSE NECK STRAP CLAMP

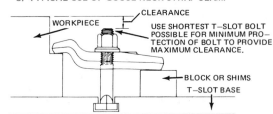

B. TYPICAL USE OF ADJUSTABLE STEP STRAP CLAMP

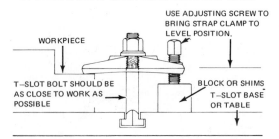

D. TYPICAL USE OF U PATTERN STRAP CLAMP

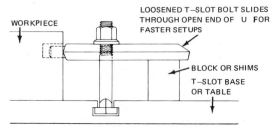

4. Remember that the clamps must not interfere with the arbor, cutter, or table support.

5. If a workpiece must be attached to an angle plate, align the angle plate with parallels as shown in Fig. 82-19.

6. For simple shapes, clamp the workpiece directly to the table. When machining rough castings, use a sub-base in order to protect the table top (Fig. 82-20).

7. Use extreme care in clamping thin stock. Make sure it doesn't spring out of shape (Fig. 82-21).

8. Place V blocks under round workpieces.

9. Protect the top of machined workpieces by putting a shim under the clamps (Fig. 82-22).

10. Always make sure the tail of the clamp is as high as, or slightly higher than, the clamping surface (Fig. 82-23). A clamp that is tipped away from the workpiece will probably slip. Arrange the clamp so that the bolt is near the workpiece (Fig. 82-24).

11. Support all parts of the workpiece. When necessary, put jack screws under a thin section of the workpiece (Fig. 82-25).

12. A step block can be used to support the clamp heel at the desired height (Fig. 82-26).

13. During many cutting operations, the cutter tends to move the workpiece along the table. To prevent this, put a stop block or pin at the end of the workpiece.

14. Always make the setup as close to the column as possible.

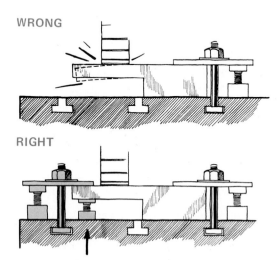

WRONG

RIGHT

Fig. 82-25. All parts of the workpiece must be rigidly supported before making a cut.

Fig. 82-24. Locating the T bolt close to the workpiece permits the clamp to exert maximum holding power on the work.

Fig. 82-26. Using step blocks and strap clamps to hold a casting.

WRONG

IT IS WRONG TO PLACE THE CLAMP STUD CLOSE TO THE JACK BECAUSE THEN THE JACK IS CLAMPED, NOT THE WORKPIECE

RIGHT

PLACE CLAMP STUD CLOSE TO WORK PIECE FOR CORRECT EFFECTIVE HOLDING.

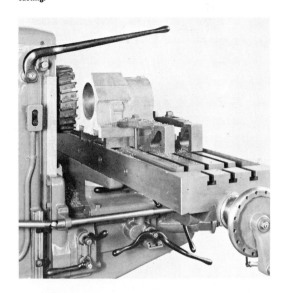

UNIT 83.

Milling a Flat Surface (Plain or Slab Milling)

There are two common methods of milling a flat surface, peripheral milling and face milling (Fig. 83-1). Face milling is described in the next unit. Peripheral milling is also called *plain* or *slab* milling. Once you have learned to do this operation, other similar operations which use a cutter mounted on an arbor can be done also.

SETTING UP THE MACHINE

1. Clean off the table. Clear it of chips, dirt, and burrs.

2. The workpiece can be mounted directly to the table or can be clamped in a vise (Fig. 83-2).

3. If a vise is used, mount it about center along the table. The jaws should be parallel to the T slots. For extremely accurate work, align the vise with a precision square or a dial indicator.

4. Open the vise jaws wide enough to receive the workpiece. Place the workpiece on two parallels so that the part to be machined is above the top of the jaws. A scrap of paper placed under each corner will help you to tell when the work is properly seated. We will assume that the workpiece is a block of mild steel. Its dimensions are 3 by 4 by 6 in. Be sure the workpiece is centered in the vise.

5. Tighten the vise with hand pressure. Now tap the workpiece lightly with a soft-faced hammer to seat it against the parallels. Check to see if any of the papers are loose.

6. Move the saddle toward the column with the cross-feed handwheel. The workpiece should be positioned as close as possible to the column.

7. Select a plain milling cutter wide enough to cover the total width of the workpiece. The cutter diameter should be as small as possible, but still large enough to prevent any interference when the cut is made (Fig. 83-3). Figure 83-4 illustrates the advantage of using a small cutter. Note that it takes less time to make the cut when using a small cutter.

8. Select an arbor that is the same diameter as the hole in the cutter.

9. Place a clean cloth on the table. Carefully lay the cutter and the arbor on it.

10. Wipe the tapered end of the arbor and insert it in the spindle (Fig. 83-5). Use the draw-in bar to hold the arbor firmly in place (Fig. 83-6).

11. Remove the nut from the outer end of the arbor. Remove spacing collars and position the cutter directly over the workpiece.

12. Hold the cutter with a cloth, and then slip it on the arbor. If a plain cutter with helix-angle

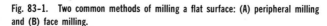

Fig. 83-1. Two common methods of milling a flat surface: (A) peripheral milling and (B) face milling.

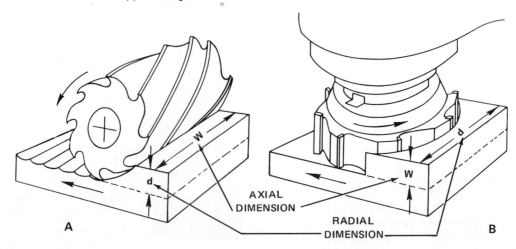

AXIAL DIMENSION

RADIAL DIMENSION

A

B

Fig. 83-2. For most slab milling, the workpiece can be held in a vise.

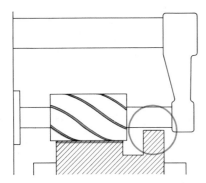

Fig. 83-3. The cutter must be large enough to allow the arbor to clear the workpiece.

Fig. 83-4. A small cutter is more efficient because it travels less distance.

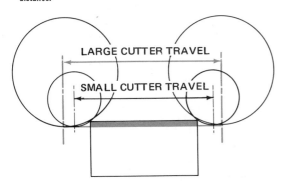

Fig. 83-5. Inserting the arbor in the spindle. Make sure spindle and taper are perfectly clean.

Fig. 83-6. Spindle-drive keys or lugs provide a positive drive for the arbor by preventing slippage. The draw-in bar or bolt holds the arbor firmly in the spindle.

teeth is used, mount it so that cutting forces will cause it to work toward the spindle (Fig. 83-7). The cutter should be mounted to turn clockwise (left-hand rotation) as viewed from the spindle end.

13. Line up the keyseat in the arbor with the keyway in the cutter. Insert a key to hold the cutter firmly to the arbor (Fig. 83-8).

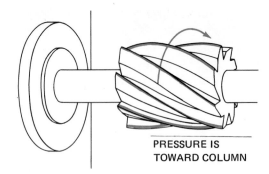

Fig. 83-7. The plain helical cutter should be mounted so that cutting forces will direct the cutter toward the spindle.

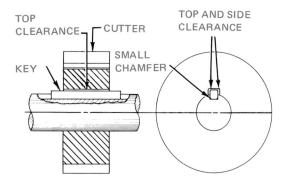

Fig. 83-8. The key helps to drive the cutter and prevents it from slipping on the arbor.

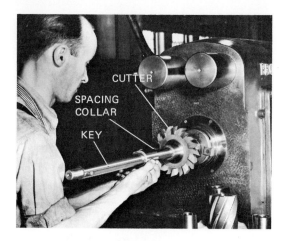

Fig. 83-9. Mounting the spacing collar.

14. Replace the spacing collars, then the bearing collar (if necessary), and finally the arbor nut (Fig. 83-9). If the bearing collar is used, it should be placed as close to the cutter as possible. Tighten the arbor nut by hand only. Do not use a wrench as yet.

15. Loosen the clamp that holds the overarm (or overarms), and pull it out slightly beyond the end of the arbor. Then tighten it.

16. Slip the *arbor* or *overarm support* over the overarm. Move it in until it is over the bearing sleeve or over the end of the arbor pilot. Tighten the overarm.

17. Lock or hold the spindle firmly, and then tighten the arbor nut with a wrench.

18. Center the workpiece directly under the cutter.

19. If the cutter is of high-speed steel and 4 in. in diameter, adjust the machine to a speed of 80 revolutions per minute (rpm):

$$\text{rpm} = \frac{4 \times 80 \text{ (suggested cutting speed)}}{4 \text{ (diameter of cutter in inches)}} = 80$$

20. Adjust for a suitable feed.

21. Adjust the stop or trip dogs on the table to about $\frac{3}{4}$ in. beyond the ends of the workpiece.

22. Check the spindle rotation. The cutter should turn clockwise so *conventional milling,* or *upcutting,* will be done.

23. Check to see that the workpiece and vise will clear the underside of the cutter and the arbor support as the machining is done.

24. Check the setup before turning on the power (Fig. 83-10).

MAKING THE CUT

1. Turn on the power and start the cutter rotating. Move the workpiece directly under and below the cutter.

2. Loosen the clamp that locks the knee. Carefully turn the crank and raise the knee until the rotating cutter just touches the workpiece surface. Set the micrometer collar at zero. There is always a certain amount of backlash in any screw. If you are adjusting the depth of cut,

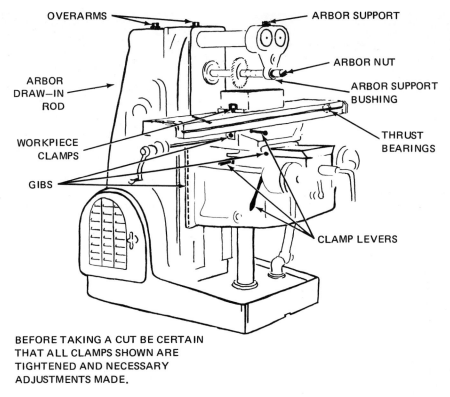

OVERARMS

ARBOR SUPPORT

ARBOR NUT

ARBOR SUPPORT BUSHING

ARBOR DRAW—IN ROD

THRUST BEARINGS

WORKPIECE CLAMPS

GIBS

CLAMP LEVERS

BEFORE TAKING A CUT BE CERTAIN THAT ALL CLAMPS SHOWN ARE TIGHTENED AND NECESSARY ADJUSTMENTS MADE.

Fig. 83-10.   Points to check before taking a cut on a new setup.

always start with the knee in a lower position. Raise it by turning the crank slowly to the right to the exact position desired. If you turn the crank too far, never turn it back only a few thousandths. Always turn it counterclockwise at least a full turn, and then turn it back up to the exact location. This is true of all screw adjustments on the milling machine.

3. Move the workpiece to the left of the cutter. The right end of the workpiece should touch the cutter first.

4. Turn the crank handle to raise the knee for the correct depth of cut. Generally, two cuts are made, a roughing and a finishing cut. If material must be removed from both sides of the workpiece, about half should be removed from each. The roughing cut should be at least 0.015 in.

An accurate way of setting the depth of cut involves the use of a long, thin piece of paper as a feeler. Turn on the machine so that the cutter is rotating. Locate the workpiece directly

Fig. 83-11.   Put a long, thin piece of paper between the cutter and the workpiece to establish the contact point. A long piece of paper is far safer to use than a short one.

under the cutter. Hold the long sliver of paper over the surface of the workpiece with one hand and slowly raise the table with the other. Continue until the cutter just grips the paper (Fig. 83-11).

Next, stop the machine and move the workpiece clear of the cutter. Set the micrometer collar to zero and raise the table the required distance plus 0.002 in. for the thickness of the paper.

5. Feed the workpiece into the revolving cutter by hand for about $\frac{1}{4}$ in., and then back it away from the cutter.

Table 83-1. Trouble shooting chart for milling.

TROUBLE	CAUSE	CORRECTION
CHATTER	1. Lack of rigidity in the machine, fixtures, arbor or workpiece.	1. Improve rigidity.
	2. Cutting load too great.	2. Decrease number of teeth in contact with workpiece.
	3. Dull cutter.	3. Resharpen.
	4. Poor lubrication.	4. Improve lubrication.
	5. Straight tooth cutter.	5. Use helical tooth cutter.
	6. Peripheral relief angle too great.	6. Decrease relief angle.
CANNOT HOLD SIZE	1. Cutting load too great causing deflection.	1. Decrease number of teeth in contact with the workpiece.
	2. May be due to chip packing.	2. Increase oil pressure or redirect flow so as to wash chips out of teeth.
	3. Chips causing misalignment of work.	3. Brush or blow all chips away before mounting new piece of work.
PREMATURE CUTTER DULLING	1. Cutting load too great.	1. Decrease number of teeth in contact with the workpiece.
	2. Insufficient coolant.	2. Add blending oil to lubricant.
POOR SURFACE FINISH	1. Feed too high.	1. Decrease feed and increase speed.
	2. Dull tool.	2. Resharpen.
	3. Speed too low.	3. Increase sfpm.
	4. Insufficient number of cutter teeth.	4. Use cutter with more closely spaced teeth.
CUTTER "HOGS IN"	1. Peripheral relief too great.	1. Use recommended angles.
	2. Rake angle too large.	2. Decrease rake angle.
	3. Improper speed.	3. Check and adjust.
VIBRATION	1. Insufficient clearance causing rubbing.	1. Use recommended clearance angles.
	2. Machine at fault.	2. Check machine, be sure arbor is at least $\frac{1}{3}$ diameter of cutter.
WORK BURNISHING	1. Cut is too light.	1. Increase depth of cut.
	2. Insufficient peripheral relief.	2. Increase peripheral relief angle.
	3. Land too wide.	3. Decrease width of land.
CUTTER BURNS	1. Insufficient lubricant.	1. Add more sulfur base oil.
	2. Speed too fast.	2. Decrease speed.
TEETH BREAKING	1. Feed too high.	1. Decrease feed per tooth. May be possible to maintain rate by increasing the number of teeth.

If it is necessary to reach over the cutter, first stop the machine. Do not reach over a revolving cutter.

6. Stop the machine and back the workpiece away from the cutter. Check the cutting. Also check the depth of cut. Table 83–1 lists troubles, their causes, and how they are corrected.

7. If the cutting is satisfactory, start the machine again and engage the *power table feed.* Always use cutting fluid on milling cutters, except when milling cast iron.

8. Do not stop feeding the workpiece while the machine is cutting. If you do, the cutter will undercut at the point where you stopped the feed. This is important when making a finish cut.

9. After the first cut is complete, stop the machine and check the surface.

Never try to feel the finished surface while the cut is being taken.

10. Never back the workpiece under the revolving cutter. Stop the machine.

11. If additional cuts must be made, move the workpiece back to the starting position. Then raise the knee for the finishing cut.

12. Check the thickness of the workpiece with a steel rule or micrometer while it is in the vise.

SQUARING A BLOCK

1. Place the first machined surface against the fixed jaw of the vise. Insert a soft rod between the adjustable jaw and the workpiece.

2. Machine the second surface.

3. Lay out the correct width on the ends of the workpiece.

4. Place the workpiece in the vise with one finished surface against the solid jaw, and the other against the bottom of the vise. Put the soft rod again between the adjustable jaw and the workpiece.

5. Machine to correct width.

6. Lay out the correct thickness on the ends of the workpiece.

7. Place the first finished surface on clean parallels. Do not use the soft rod. Tighten the workpiece in the vise. Tap it lightly to seat it properly.

8. Machine to correct thickness.

9. Machine the ends as described in either of the next two units.

DISASSEMBLING THE SETUP

1. Turn off the power.

2. Remove the workpiece from the vise. Brush away all chips.

3. Loosen the arbor nut with a wrench.

4. When a milling machine has two overarms, do not remove the arbor support. Loosen the nut on the right side and the two top clamping nuts. Leave the overarm support clamped to the left overarm. Pull out and swing the overarm up and out of the way.

5. Remove the cutter, clean it, and place it back on the rack.

6. Remove the arbor and place it in the rack. Replace all spacing collars and the nut. Place them in the rack or holder.

7. Remove the vise and clean up the machine.

UNIT 84. Face Milling

Face milling is a process of machining a surface that is parallel to the face of the cutter or at right angles to the axis of the cutter. To machine large flat surfaces, a face mill is most often used. Face mills are usually made with *inserted teeth* (blade cutters) held in a cutter body (Fig. 84–1). The cutter is mounted to a driving collar. To face smaller surfaces, a shell end mill mounted on an arbor can be used (Fig. 84–2). Very small surfaces can be face milled with a solid end mill (Fig. 84–3).

SETTING UP THE MACHINE

1. Select the correct facing cutter, and mount it on or in the spindle. Generally, the cutter should be about 1 in. larger in diameter than the maximum width of the workpiece. This extra diameter provides a way for the chips to escape.

2. Fasten the workpiece in a vise, directly to the table, or to an angle plate (Fig. 84–4). The workpiece should be mounted so that it extends about 1 in. beyond the inside of the table. This

Fig. 84-2. Face milling by use of a shell end mill.

Fig. 84-3. Using a solid end mill for face milling. Note how a compound angle vise is used to hold the workpiece.

Fig. 84-4. Face milling.

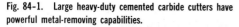

Fig. 84-1. Large heavy-duty cemented carbide cutters have powerful metal-removing capabilities.

provides plenty of clearance for machining. If the workpiece is mounted on an angle plate, check the alignment of the angle plate before clamping the workpiece to it. Check to make sure the workpiece extends uniformly beyond the edge of the table and that it is about centered lengthwise along the table.

3. Adjust for the correct speed and feed. Use the periphery diameter in figuring the correct speed.

MAKING THE CUT

1. Move the knee until the workpiece is centered on the cutter. Move the saddle in until the workpiece just clears the cutter face. Then move the table so the workpiece is clear of the cutter. Adjust the cross-feed micrometer collar or dial to zero (Fig. 84–5).

2. Turn on the power, and check the rotation of the cutter.

3. Turn the cross-feed in the correct amount for a roughing cut (from $\frac{1}{8}$ to $\frac{1}{4}$ in.).

4. Feed the workpiece against the cutter by hand, and check the cutting action. If the cutting action is correct, use the power table feed. Be sure to use plenty of cutting fluid (except when machining cast iron).

5. Make sure the workpiece completely clears the cutter before turning off the automatic feed. If this is neglected, the surface will not be completely flat. Although most of the material is removed by the principal cut taken by the peripheral teeth, there is also a secondary cut taken by the back side of the cutter which removes a smaller amount of material.

6. When the cut is completed, return to the starting position. Measure the length. Take additional cuts if needed.

7. Figure 84–6 shows how a shell end mill is used for milling a flat surface. Figure 84–7 illustrates how two right angle surfaces are milled using a shell end mill.

8. After the finishing cut has been made, disassemble the setup and return all cutters and clamping equipment to their proper places.

Fig. 84-5. Adjusting the micrometer dial or collar to zero before adjusting for depth of cut.

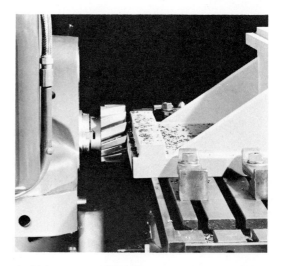

Fig. 84-6. Using a shell end mill for face milling a flat surface.

Fig. 84-7. A shell end mill can be used to mill surfaces at right angles.

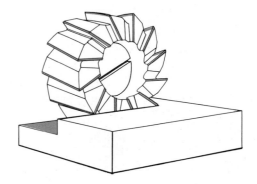

UNIT 85.

Side Milling, Straddle Milling, and Milling a Slot or Keyseat

Side and straddle milling are similar milling procedures. In side milling, a side-milling cutter is used to machine one vertical surface. In straddle milling, two cutters are used at the same time to machine two parallel vertical surfaces (Fig. 85-1). Straddle milling is done to mill parallel surfaces to a specific width or length and to mill squares and hexagons. A pair of right- and left-hand side-milling cutters is best for straddle milling, although any side-milling cutters can be used. Side-milling cutters are also used to cut slots, grooves, and keyseats.

SIDE MILLING

Side milling is done when it is necessary to machine a vertical surface on the side of a workpiece. To do side milling, proceed as follows.

1. Fasten the vise to the table with the jaws at right angles to the T slots. The workpiece can also be mounted in a fixture as shown in Fig. 85-2. Fasten the workpiece so that the surface to be machined will clear the vise.

2. Select the correct kind and size of cutter. Remember that the top of the workpiece must clear the underside of the arbor.

3. Place the cutter as close to the column face as is possible in the setup.

4. Adjust the saddle or cross-feed until the side of the cutter is in line with the layout line on the workpiece (Fig. 85-3).

MILLING PARALLEL SURFACES TO A SPECIFIC WIDTH

1. Place the left-hand half-side cutter on the arbor first. Position it as close to the column as possible to get the job done.

2. Select one or more collars equal to the width or length of the workpiece. It may be necessary to use thin metal shims shaped like collars to get the exact distance between cutters (Fig. 85-4).

3. Place the right-hand half-side cutter on the arbor. Carefully measure the distance between the cutters. Add or remove thin spacing collars if necessary.

4. Support the arbor as close to the second cutter as possible.

5. Center the workpiece under the cutters.

6. Turn on the power.

7. Move the table to the left, and raise it to proper height. Feed the workpiece into the cutter by hand. Check the cutting action.

Fig. 85-2. Milling the vertical surface of a bracket with a side milling cutter. In this setup, the cutter rotates counterclockwise and the table moves from right to left.

Fig. 85-1. Straddle milling using half-side milling cutters.

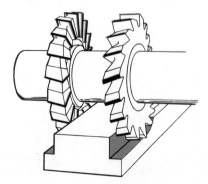

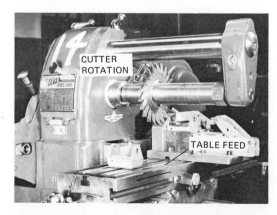

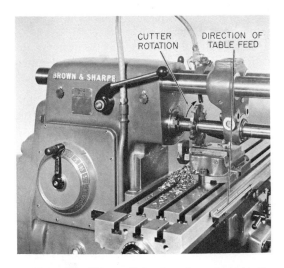

Fig. 85-3. Side milling a vertical surface using a staggered-tooth side milling cutter. The cutter rotates clockwise, and the table moves from left to right.

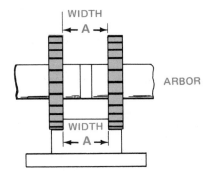

Fig. 85-4. Arbor spacers are needed to set the distance between the cutters. These spacers are available in a large selection of sizes. If a correct combination cannot be obtained, a standard size can be ground to the size needed; it is also possible to use thin shim stock to build up spaces to the width needed.

8. Turn on the power feed, and do the straddle milling in a single cut (Fig. 85-5).

MILLING A SQUARE OR HEXAGON ON THE END OF A BOLT

1. Determine the width across the flats of the bolt or nut. For example, on a regular $\frac{1}{2}$-in. bolt head, this distance is $\frac{3}{4}$ in. The dimensions for all bolts and nuts can be found in *The New American Machinist's Handbook* and *Machinery's Handbook*.

2. Place two half-side-milling cutters on the arbor. The distance between them should equal the width across flats. Use a spacing collar of the correct width.

3. Fasten the dividing head to the table, and turn the spindle to a vertical position. Mount the universal chuck on its spindle (Fig. 85-6).

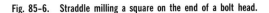

Fig. 85-5. Straddle milling using a pair of half-side milling cutters.

Fig. 85-6. Straddle milling a square on the end of a bolt head.

4. Tighten the workpiece in the chuck.

5. Center the workpiece under the cutters.

6. Move the table to the left, and raise the knee until the outside of the cutter is below the surface to be machined.

7. Make the first cut.

8. Use the rapid indexing feature of the dividing head to rotate the workpiece one-fourth turn for a square-head bolt. Make the second cut.

9. The operation can be done as shown in Fig. 85-7 by mounting the chuck on a rotary index table.

10. The same procedure is followed to mill a hexagon, except that indexing must be set for six divisions.

MILLING A SLOT IN A RECTANGULAR WORKPIECE

1. Use a staggered-tooth side-milling cutter or a pair of interlocking cutters of the correct width (Fig. 85-8).

2. Clamp the workpiece in the vise.

Fig. 85-7. Straddle milling a square on the end of a shaft. Note how the chuck is fastened to the rotary index table.

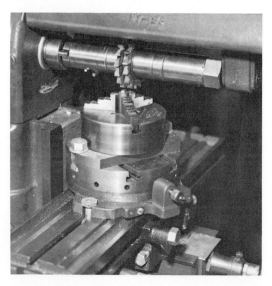

3. Bring the workpiece up until the cutter is fairly close to the surface. Move the saddle in or out until the cutter is directly over the location of the slot. Measure the correct distance from the side, as shown in Fig. 85-9.

4. Hold a long thin piece of paper over the workpiece surface and under the cutter. This

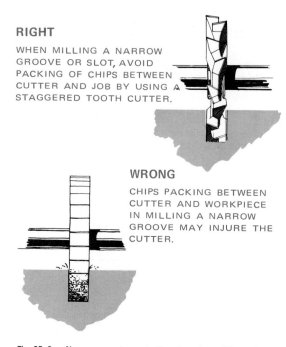

RIGHT

WHEN MILLING A NARROW GROOVE OR SLOT, AVOID PACKING OF CHIPS BETWEEN CUTTER AND JOB BY USING A STAGGERED TOOTH CUTTER.

WRONG

CHIPS PACKING BETWEEN CUTTER AND WORKPIECE IN MILLING A NARROW GROOVE MAY INJURE THE CUTTER.

Fig. 85-8. Always use a stagger-tooth cutter when milling a deep slot.

Fig. 85-9. Measuring the location of a slot or groove in a rectangular workpiece.

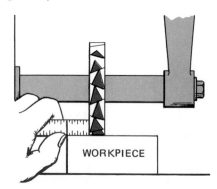

WORKPIECE

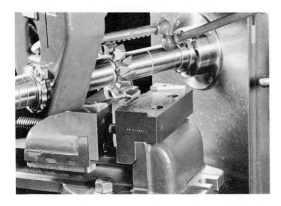

Fig. 85-10. Milling a slot at an angle using a staggered-tooth milling cutter.

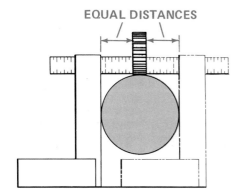

Fig. 85-11. Locating the cutter directly over the center of the workpiece. A steel square and rule are used for this purpose.

will be used as a feeler so you can tell when the cutter just touches the work. Keep your fingers away from the cutter.

5. Turn on the power and raise the knee until the cutter just tears the paper.

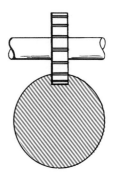

Fig. 85-12. Milling a keyseat in an arbor.

6. Set the micrometer collar on the knee at zero.

7. Move the workpiece to the left of the cutter. Raise the knee the correct depth of the slot or groove. Lock the knee.

8. Turn on the power, and cut the slot or groove (Fig. 85-10).

MILLING A SLOT OR KEYSEAT IN THE CENTER OF A ROUND WORKPIECE

1. Use a staggered-tooth side-milling cutter.

2. Fasten the workpiece in a vise or vises, in a V block, between centers, or in a fixture.

3. Center the cutter over the workpiece. One method is shown in Fig. 85-11.

4. Move the table to the left of the cutter.

5. Raise the table an amount equal to the depth of the keyseat or slot (Fig. 85-12). The correct depth can be found in *The New American Machinist's Handbook*, or *Machinery's Handbook*.

UNIT 86.

Sawing, Slotting, and Other Milling Operations

Sawing can be done in the milling machine by using metal-cutting saws of various diameters and thicknesses. A *slitting saw* is used when the accuracy required is greater than can be obtained with the power saw. Slotting includes a variety of cuts in which a narrow slot is cut part way through metal (Fig. 86-1). The slot in the head of a machine screw is an example.

CUTTING OFF

1. Select a saw of the proper width and diameter.

2. Fasten the workpiece securely to the table. The cutoff line should be directly over one of the T slots (Fig. 86-2). This slot will provide clearance for the saw. Hold the workpiece with strap clamps to keep it from slipping (Fig. 86-3).

3. Mount the saw on the arbor as close to the column as possible. Always use a key to hold the saw; never drive a saw by friction alone.

Slippage can damage the saw and the workpiece. When using very thin or large-diameter saws, place large-diameter collars on either side to help support the blade (Fig. 86-4).

4. Locate the cutoff line directly under the saw.

5. Move the table to the right, and then raise the knee until the saw is below the lower surface of the workpiece.

6. Make the cut.

7. Sawing can also be done with the workpiece held in a vise. The part to be cutoff must extend outside the vise jaw (Fig. 86-5).

SLOTTING

1. Slotting is done in the same general way as cutting off except that the cut is made only part way through the workpiece (Fig. 86-6).

2. If the slots are to be cut in the heads of machine screws, the screws are often held in special vise jaws or in a fixture (Fig. 86-7).

3. Since screw-slotting cutters have little side clearance, the feed must be rather slow.

Fig. 86-1. Cutting slots on an impellar blade. Large collars are used to support the saw.

Fig. 86-2. The cutoff line is located directly over a T slot so there will be clearance below the workpiece.

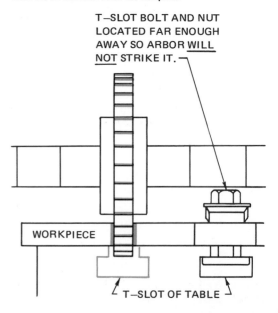

T—SLOT BOLT AND NUT LOCATED FAR ENOUGH AWAY SO ARBOR WILL NOT STRIKE IT.

WORKPIECE

T—SLOT OF TABLE

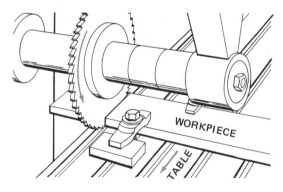

Fig. 86-3. Cutting off stock clamped to the table. Machining is done with the saw rotating counterclockwise.

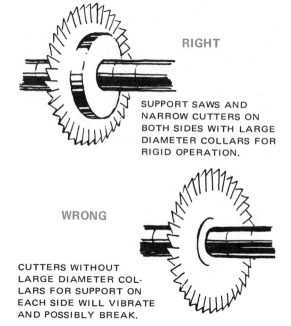

RIGHT

SUPPORT SAWS AND NARROW CUTTERS ON BOTH SIDES WITH LARGE DIAMETER COLLARS FOR RIGID OPERATION.

WRONG

CUTTERS WITHOUT LARGE DIAMETER COLLARS FOR SUPPORT ON EACH SIDE WILL VIBRATE AND POSSIBLY BREAK.

Fig. 86-4. Support the saw with large diameter collars. Never use a large diameter saw without such support.

CUTTING A KEYSLOT FOR A WOODRUFF KEY

A Woodruff key is used to keep a gear or wheel from turning on a shaft. The key is in the shape of a half disk. A Woodruff keyslot cutter is used to cut the slot in the shaft.

1. Fasten the workpiece to the table, in a vise, or in the dividing head.

Fig. 86-5. Cutting work held in a vise. The material is supported on parallels.

Fig. 86-6. Cutting a slot on a workpiece held in a vise.

2. Insert a keyslot cutter in the spindle.

3. To center the cutter, first place a thin sheet of tissue paper around the workpiece. Carefully move the saddle until the end of the cutter touches the paper. Adjust the micrometer collar or dial on the cross-slide saddle to zero (Fig. 86-8). Lower the table. Then move the saddle in an amount D which is equal to half the width of the cutter (t), plus half the diameter of the workpiece (r), plus 0.001 in. (thickness of tissue paper). If, for example, the keyslot cutter is $\frac{1}{4}$ in. wide and the workpiece is 1 in. in diameter, then the saddle must be moved 0.626 in. ($D = \frac{1}{2}$ of $0.250 + \frac{1}{2}$ of 1.000 plus 0.001).

Fig. 86-7. Cutting slots in the top of screwheads with the screws held in a fixture.

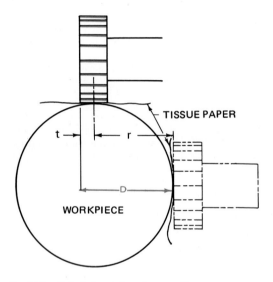

TISSUE PAPER

WORKPIECE

Fig. 86-8. Method of centering a keyway cutter.

to mill several slots or dimensions at the same time. With this method several surfaces of a workpiece can be machined to the desired shape with one movement of the table (Fig. 86-9). Gang milling is widely used in production work. When gang milling, the spindle speed is always determined by the diameter of the largest cutter. The cutters should be as alike in size and number of teeth as possible to allow for maximum speed and feed.

Fig. 86-9. Gang milling using both form and plain cutters.

Fig. 86-10. Adjustable boring heads and tools.

4. Turn on the power. Place a piece of tissue paper over the workpiece. Then raise the knee until the cutter just tears the paper.

5. Adjust the micrometer collar to zero. Slowly raise the knee the correct distance to cut the slot. The correct depth to feed the cutter can be found in *The New American Machinist's Handbook*.

GANG MILLING

In gang milling, a number of cutters of the same or different diameters are fastened to the arbor

DRILLING AND BORING

The milling machine is often used for very accurate drilling and boring. Small drills are held in a standard Jacobs chuck which fits in the spindle. Large taper-shank drills are held in an adaptor or collet. Spade drills are also frequently used.

Industry makes use of many types of adjustable boring heads. The boring head may have a straight shank that is held in a collet or adaptor, or a taper shank that fits directly into the spindle. Many adjustable boring heads have a micrometer vernier adjustment for precision boring of small diameter holes (Fig. 86–10). A variety of boring tools fit the boring head and are used for spot facing, counterboring, and boring.

END MILLING

End milling is often done on a plain horizontal milling machine. The vertical milling machine, however, is better suited for end-milling operations.

UNIT 87. Cutting A Spur Gear

Gears are cut on the milling machine primarily for purposes of repair and replacement. Industry uses other types of machines to produce gears on the production line (Fig. 87–1). Spur and straight-toothed bevel gears are the most common types made in the machine shop.

GEAR TEETH

For many years there were two recognized forms of teeth in spur gearing, the *involute* (single curve) and the *cycloidal* (double curve). These forms permit gears to run together smoothly and with constant relative velocity. At present, the involute form of gear tooth is used almost exclusively since it presents fewer difficulties when cutting. Also, slight variations in center distances will have little effect on the way in which the gear transmits uniform motion.

THE INVOLUTE PRINCIPLE

An *involute* is a curve traced by any point of a flexible thread, kept taut as it is unwound from another curve (Fig. 87–2A). Curve *af* (Fig. 87–2A) is an involute curve. Note that all tangents to the circle meet the involute curve at right angles. In Fig. 87–2B, the thread is shown hanging vertically. As the circle rotates from point *A* to point *B*, the thread unwinds a distance *ab*. As rotation continues, the thread drops to position *c*, *d*, *e*, and finally to position *f*. Note that several involute curves are formed as the circle rotates.

TERMINOLOGY

The parts of a spur gear are illustrated in Fig. 87–3. Letter symbols for each are also shown. Table 87–1 lists rules and formulas for calculating the various spur-gear dimensions.

GEAR-MAKING PROCESSES

Gears can be machined by milling, hobbing, or shaping (Fig. 87–4). Gears can also be stamped, drawn, or cast.

Milling. The gear tooth is cut by a *formed milling cutter* that revolves in a plane perpendicular to

Fig. 87-1. These spur gears are typical of the type that can be produced in great quantity on production machines.

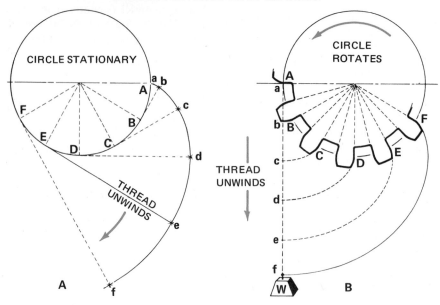

Fig. 87-2. The involute principle.

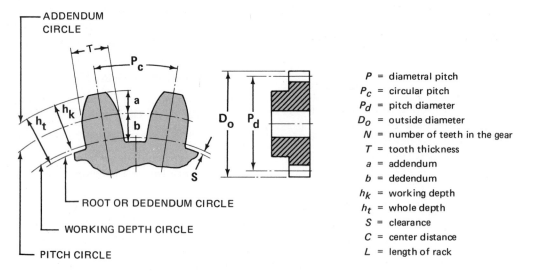

P = diametral pitch
P_c = circular pitch
P_d = pitch diameter
D_o = outside diameter
N = number of teeth in the gear
T = tooth thickness
a = addendum
b = dedendum
h_k = working depth
h_t = whole depth
S = clearance
C = center distance
L = length of rack

Fig. 87-3. Common terms used to define a spur gear. See Table 81-1.

the gear blank. After each tooth is cut, the work is indexed into a new position. Teeth cannot be undercut, since the shape of each tooth is an exact reproduction of the cutter form.

Hobbing. A hob is similar to an oversize screw whose thread has been gashed to produce a large number of cutting teeth. As the hob revolves on its own axis, its "screw" action cuts

Table 87-1. Rules and formulas for spur gear calculations.

TO FIND	RULE	FORMULA
Diametral pitch P	Divide 3.1416 by the circular pitch.	$P = \dfrac{3.1416}{P^c}$
Circular pitch P^c	Divide 3.1416 by the diametral pitch.	$P^c = \dfrac{3.1416}{P}$
Pitch diameter P^d	Divide the number of teeth by the diametral pitch.	$P^d = \dfrac{N}{P}$
Outside diameter D^o	Add 2 to the number of teeth and divide the sum by the diametral pitch.	$D^o = \dfrac{N + 2}{P}$
Number of teeth N	Multiply the pitch diameter by the diametral pitch.	$N = P^d P$
Tooth thickness T	Divide 1.5708 by the diametral pitch.	$T = \dfrac{1.5708}{P}$
Addendum a	Divide 1.0 by the diametral pitch.	$a = \dfrac{1.0}{P}$
Dedendum b	Divide 1.157 by the diametral pitch.	$b = \dfrac{1.157}{P}$
Working depth h^k	Divide 2 by the diametral pitch.	$h^k = \dfrac{2}{P}$
Whole depth h^t	Divide 2.157 by the diametral pitch.	$h^t = \dfrac{2.157}{P}$
Clearance S	Divide 0.157 by the diametral pitch.	$S = \dfrac{0.157}{P}$
Center distance C	Add the number of teeth in both gears and divide the sum by two times the diametral pitch.	$C = \dfrac{N_1 + N_2}{2P}$
Length of rack L	Multiply the number of teeth in the rack by the circular pitch.	$L = N P^c$

teeth in the workpiece. The hob keeps pace with the rotary feed of the gear blank and in doing so progressively generates a true involute (Fig. 87-5).

Shaping. The cutter used resembles a spur gear. Cutting is accomplished by the reciprocating motion of the cutter, which is held perpendicular to the side of the gear blank. Work and

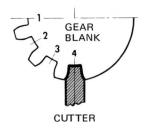
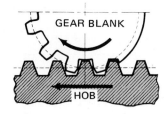
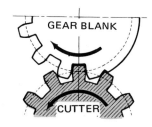

A. MILLING—
   CUTTER FORMING

B. HOBBING—
   HOB GENERATING

C. SHAPING—
   CUTTER GENERATING

SHAPED MILLING
CUTTER

HOB

SHAPING CUTTER

Fig. 87-4. Machining processes used in gear making.

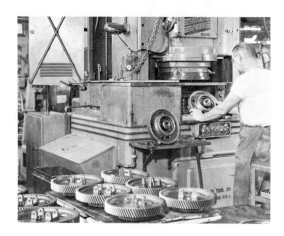

Fig. 87-5. Gears being produced with a hobbing machine.

Fig. 87-6. This machine is used for shaping gears. The cutter moves up and down to shape the gear.

cutter are fed by rotation after each pass, thereby generating true involute teeth on the gear blank (Fig. 87-6).

GEAR MILLING CUTTERS

These cutters are capable of cutting gears from 12 teeth up to a rack. There are eight cutters in

a set for each diametral pitch (Fig. 87-7). Although called *involute gear cutters*, these cutters do not produce true involute shapes.

SPUR GEARS

Spur gears are used to transmit or manipulate power and movement between parallel shafts.

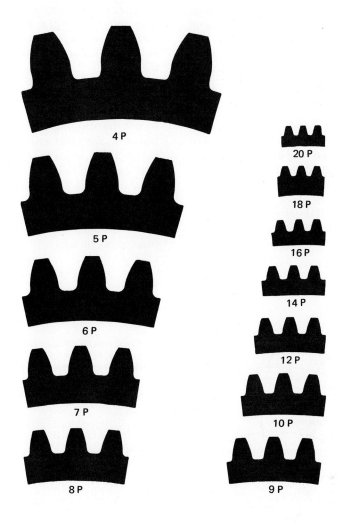

FINISHING GEAR MILLING CUTTERS ARE MADE WITH EIGHT CUTTERS FOR EACH PITCH AND ARE ADAPTED TO CUT FROM A PINION OF TWELVE TEETH TO A RACK. THE INDIVIDUAL CUTTERS FOR EACH PITCH HAVE A RANGE AS FOLLOWS:

# 1 WILL CUT GEARS FROM	135 TEETH TO A RACK
# 2 WILL CUT GEARS FROM	55 TO 134 TEETH
# 3 WILL CUT GEARS FROM	35 TO 54 TEETH
# 4 WILL CUT GEARS FROM	26 TO 34 TEETH
# 5 WILL CUT GEARS FROM	21 TO 25 TEETH
# 6 WILL CUT GEARS FROM	17 TO 20 TEETH
# 7 WILL CUT GEARS FROM	14 TO 16 TEETH
# 8 WILL CUT GEARS FROM	12 TO 13 TEETH

Fig. 87-7. Note the comparative size of the involute gear teeth in various diametral pitches.

461

They may be cut by milling, hobbing, or shaping. The basic dimension of a spur gear is the pitch diameter. The diametral pitch indicates the size of the tooth. Other terms employed in connection with spur gear teeth are given in Fig. 87-8.

MILLING A SPUR GEAR

The *spur gear* is frequently cut on the milling machine using standard involute gear cutters of the arbor-mounted type. The gear illustrated in Fig. 87-9 has an outside diameter of from 6.295 to 6.300 in. and is a 61-tooth, 10-pitch gear. The gear-blank stock is 1 in. thick and is made of AISI-3145 steel. The full depth of tooth is 0.225 in. (the depth of cut to be made). This information with spur gear teeth are given in Fig. 87-8.

ter. Note that the cutter must be a No. 2 involute gear cutter, having a 10-diametral pitch. This cutter has a 3 in. outside diameter and a 1¼-in. hole; it will cut gears having from 55 to 134 teeth.

MAKING THE SETUP

Install the dividing head (headstock and tailstock) on the table. Leave enough distance between them for a mandrel. Locate both the headstock and tailstock in the same table slot. Set the tailstock horizontally. Move the table as close to the column as possible. This will add to the rigidity of the setup. Install the cutter on the arbor. Make sure the cutter will revolve in the correct direction (to cut toward the head-

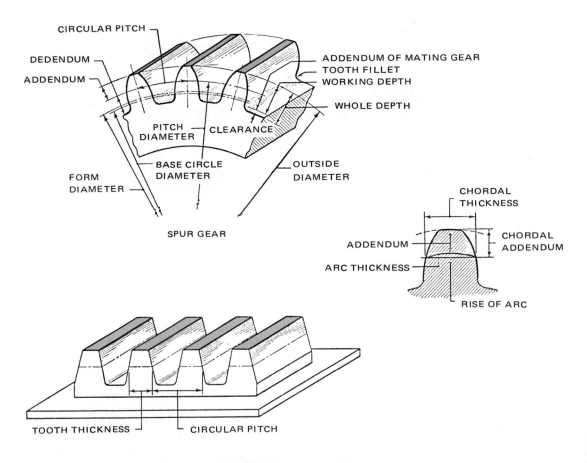

Fig. 87-8. Spur gear terminology.

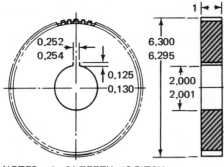

NOTES: 1. 61 TEETH, 10 PITCH
        2. AISI – 3145 STEEL
        3. TOOTH DEPTH EQUALS 0.225 IN.

Fig. 87-9. The dimensions of a 61-tooth, 10-pitch spur gear that will be machined.

stock). Move the dividing head directly under the cutter and accurately line up its center with the center of the cutter. Next lock the saddle in position so there can be no cross movement of the table. Put the gear blank on a mandrel and attach a milling machine dog to the large end of the mandrel. Lower the table and install the workpiece between centers with the large end of the mandrel toward the dividing head. Use a dial indicator to make sure the mandrel is level (Fig. 87-10).

USING THE DIVIDING HEAD

The dividing head is used to divide a gear accurately into an exact number of divisions (Fig. 87-11). One complete turn of the headstock crank will rotate the headstock spindle one-fortieth of a turn. Therefore, to divide a circle into 40 equal divisions, you would turn the crank once for each of the 40 divisions required. If 10 divisions were required, the crank would be turned four times for each division. The following formula is used to determine the number of crank turns for any number of divisions.

$$t = \frac{N}{D}$$

where t = number of turns of the index crank

$N = 40$

D = the number of divisions required in the workpiece.

Using a gear with 61 teeth as an example, $t = \frac{40}{61}$. A 61-hole circle would be required, and the crank would have to be moved a distance of 40 holes on this 61-hole circle. However, since an index plate with a 61-hole circle is not available, it is necessary to change $\frac{40}{61}$ to a new fraction whose denominator is equal to the number of holes found in a circle of a standard plate. For example, $\frac{40}{61} \times 3 = 120/183$. A check of Table 87-2 shows that side B of the high number index plate No. 1 includes a 183-hole circle. Therefore, this index plate is mounted on the dividing head. The crank is then adjusted so that its pin will drop into the holes of the 183-hole circle. The two adjustable *bronze sectors* on the front of the index plate may be used to position the crank pin. First, count off 120 spaces on the 183-hole circle (start with zero and count to

Fig. 87-10. Using a dial indicator to make sure the mandrel is level.

120). Next, fasten the sector arms so they move together and so the 120 holes are within the tapered sides of the sectors. Place the left sector arm firmly against the pin. To index, hold the left sector arm securely and move the crank pin to the inside of the right sector arm. Insert the pin in the hole and slide the two sector arms around for the next setting. It is a good idea to check the indexing by taking a very light cut completely around the gear blank (just enough to make nicks on one edge). In this way you can be absolutely sure that the divider head is

463

Table 87-2. Circles of holes in index plates.

CIRCLES OF HOLES IN STANDARD INDEX PLATE	
One Side	24—25—28—30—34—37—38—39—41—42—43
Other Side	46—47—49—51—53—54—57—58—59—62—66

CIRCLES OF HOLES IN HIGH NUMBER INDEX PLATES		
Plate No. 1	Side A	30—48—69—91—99—117—129—147—171—177—189
	Side B	36—67—81—97—111—127—141—157—169—183—199
Plate No. 2	Side C	34—46—79—93—109—123—139—153—167—181—197
	Side D	32—44—77—89—107—121—137—151—163—179—193
Plate No. 3	Side E	26—42—73—87—103—119—133—149—161—175—191
	Side F	28—38—71—83—101—113—131—143—159—173—187

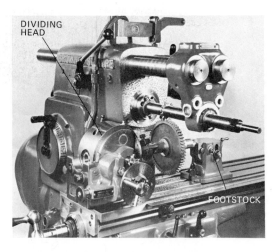

Fig. 87-11. A spur gear being cut. Note the sectors on the dividing head.

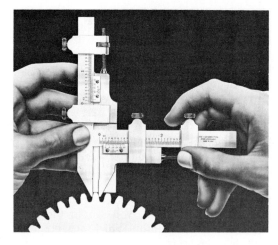

Fig. 87-12. Using a gear-tooth vernier caliper to check the width of the tooth at its pitch diameter.

set properly and will produce the number of teeth required.

SETTING THE DEPTH OF CUT

When you are positive that the divider head is correctly adjusted, turn on the power. Place a long, thin piece of paper over the gear blank and hold it in place. Slowly raise the table until the paper is just cut. Set the micrometer dial at zero.

The full depth of the tooth shown in Fig. 87-9 is 0.225 in. Since the gear must have a good finish, it is best first to rough cut, then finish cut to size. The roughing cut should equal full depth minus $\frac{1}{16}$ in., or about 0.163 in.

ROUGH MACHINING

The material used in the gear blank should be cut at about 50 surface feet per minute (sfpm). Since the cutter is 3 in. in diameter, the correct rpm (revolutions per minute) is approximately 63.

Make the first rough cut across the gear blank. Use a coolant both to lubricate the cutter teeth and to keep them cool. After the first cut is completed, stop the machine. Adjust the stops on the table feed to prevent the cutter from running into the dividing head. Return the table to the starting position and adjust the index plate for the next cut. Continue to machine until all teeth have been cut (Fig. 87–11).

FINISH MACHINING

Raise the table an additional 62 divisions (0.062 in.). Increase the speed and decrease the feed to improve the finish. Finish cut the first two teeth. Then check the thickness of the tooth with a gear-toothed vernier caliper (Fig. 87–12). Remember always to measure thickness on the pitch circle. If the thickness of the tooth is correct, finish cut completely around the gear. After the cutting is completed, disassemble the setup and return all tools to their proper places.

UNIT 88. The Vertical Milling Machine

The *vertical milling machine* is very versatile. With standard attachments, it can be used for vertical and horizontal milling, drilling, boring, cam milling, fly cutting, profiling, reaming, and slotting. With special attachments and accessories, the machine can do such unusual machining as three-dimensional duplicating and tracing (see Unit 90). In most machine shops, the vertical milling machine has completely replaced the shaper since it is faster and more efficient and can do all jobs that could be done on the shaper.

SIZE

Although there are no industrywide standards, vertical milling machines can generally be classified as small, medium, or large. The smaller types generally have a cylindrical ram that moves in and out and allows for the head to be adjusted to an angle (Fig. 88–1). Medium-size machines have a ram that moves in and out on ways, and a turret that allows the head to be revolved in a 180 degree (°) arc (Fig. 88–2). Some medium-size mills have a compound turret that can also be swiveled in and out. This allows its head to be set at a compound angle (Fig. 88–3). As an added feature, other medium-size ma-

chines have a column made in two parts. The upper part can swivel in a full circle (Fig. 88–4). Many of the larger milling machines do not have a ram or a turret. Instead only the head assembly can be moved up and down.

Fig. 88–1.   Small, vertical machine with the parts named. Note how the toolhead can swivel.

Fig. 88-2. A swivel head, turret-type, medium-size milling machine.

The *size* of the machine is dependent upon the following.

1. The overall size of the machine, including the overall height, depth, width, and weight.

2. The size and movement of the table. Tables are often available in several lengths for the same size machine. Larger tables allow for greater longitudinal travel and to some extent more cross travel.

3. The size of the electric motor used on the head assembly. These range from $\frac{1}{3}$ to $\frac{1}{2}$ horsepower (hp) for the smaller machines, from $\frac{1}{2}$ to 2 hp for medium-size machines, and 3 hp and up for the larger-size machines.

PARTS

The *column* is the real backbone and foundation of the vertical milling machine. It is generally a large, one-piece casting that is heavily ribbed for added strength. The front of the column is machined to hold the knee. The top of the column supports the turret.

The *knee* and *saddle* provide for vertical and cross travel. The knee is attached to the front of the column with clamping devices to hold it firmly in place when cutting is done. The saddle can be moved in or out. A *table* is mounted on top of the saddle and provides for longitudinal (back-and-forth) travel. The top of the table has T slots for clamping the vise and other holding attachments.

The *ram* and *turret* arrangement varies with the size and kind of machine. On smaller machines, the ram is a cylinder that can be moved in and out and turned so that the head can be positioned at an angle. On larger machines, the ram (or overarm as it is sometimes called) fits into dovetail ways located on the top of the column. The turret at the end of the ram can be rotated 180°. A *spindle head assembly* attached to the turret provides for the vertical movement of the cutting tool. It also supplies power to the tool (Fig. 88–5).

SPINDLE SPEED ADJUSTMENTS

Spindle speeds are adjusted as follows.

1. *V-belt pulleys.* By shifting the belt in the V pulleys, several speeds can be obtained. These speeds are almost always indicated on a plate mounted on the front of the spindle head.

2. *Variable speed.* A mechanical change in the driving and driven pulley's pitch diameters always results in a speed change. There is an almost unlimited number of speeds that are available within the range of the machine (Fig. 88–6).

3. *Quick-change gearbox.* Very large machines have a quick-change gearbox that allows for a selection of speeds. Usually two or more handles must be shifted to provide the desired speed.

FEED ADJUSTMENT

On most smaller vertical milling machines, feed adjustments are made manually (including the

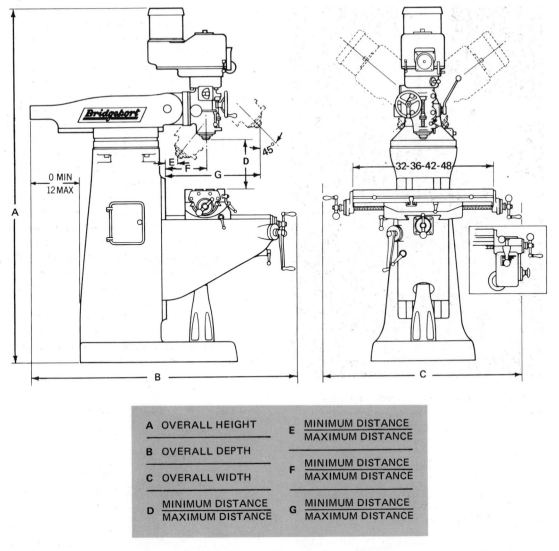

A	OVERALL HEIGHT	**E**	MINIMUM DISTANCE / MAXIMUM DISTANCE
B	OVERALL DEPTH	**F**	MINIMUM DISTANCE / MAXIMUM DISTANCE
C	OVERALL WIDTH		
D	MINIMUM DISTANCE / MAXIMUM DISTANCE	**G**	MINIMUM DISTANCE / MAXIMUM DISTANCE

Fig. 88-3. A turret miller, medium-duty machine.

table feed and the down feed). However, accessories are available to provide for power table feed and power down feed. On many medium-size machines, a power table feed is standard (Fig. 88-7). A few types are also equipped with a power down feed.

Recommended cutting speeds and feeds are listed in Table 88-1. Since the speeds shown are in feet per minute (fpm), it is necessary to de-termine revolutions per minute (rpm) before setting the spindle-head adjustment.

LUBRICATION

Lubrication requirements vary with the make and model of the machine used. You should consult the operator's manual to determine manufacturer's recommendations (Fig. 88-8).

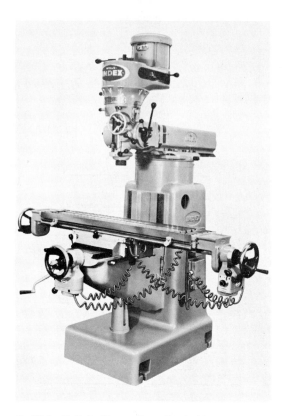

Fig. 88-4. Vertical milling machine equipped with extra attachments for power table and vertical feed.

Fig. 88-5. Head and spindle controls.

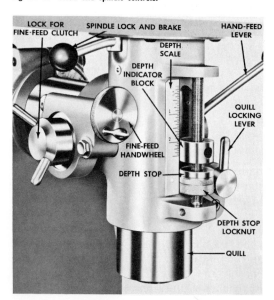

LOCK FOR FINE-FEED CLUTCH

SPINDLE LOCK AND BRAKE

HAND-FEED LEVER

DEPTH SCALE

DEPTH INDICATOR BLOCK

FINE-FEED HANDWHEEL

QUILL LOCKING LEVER

DEPTH STOP

DEPTH STOP LOCKNUT

QUILL

Fig. 88-6. A machine equipped with a variable-speed control.

Fig. 88-7. A power table feed is provided as an accessory on this machine.

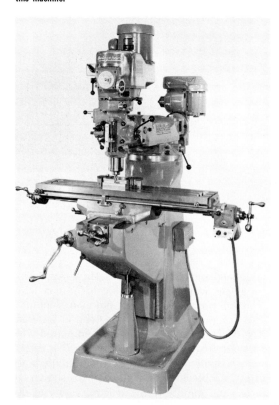

Table 88-1. Recommended cutting speeds and feeds.

GENERAL SPEED RECOMMENDATIONS

Material to be Cut	Feet Per Minute		
	Rough Cut	Rough and Finish	Light and Finish Cut
Cast Iron, Soft (Under 200 Brinnell)	70	80–90	120
Cast Iron, Medium (200–300 Brinnell)	55	60–70	90
Cast Iron, Hard (Over 200 Brinnell)	40	50–60	70
Steel (Chrome Nickel 40–45 Shore)	30	40	50
Steel (Stainless)	60	80	90
Steel (Low Carbon)	80	90	140
Steel (High Carbon)	40	50	70
Bronze (Medium)	90	120	150
Bronze (Hard)	65	90	130
Brass (Hard)	100	150	200
Copper	150	200	300
Duraluminum	400	–	600
Aluminum	600	–	1000

TABLE OF CUTTING SPEEDS AND FEEDS

Feet Per Minute	15	20	25	30	40	50	60	70	80	90	100
Diameter, Inches	Revolutions Per Minute										
$\frac{1}{16}$	917	1222	1528	1833	2445	3056	3667	4278	4889	5500	6112
$\frac{1}{8}$	458	611	764	917	1222	1528	1833	2139	2445	2750	3056
$\frac{3}{16}$	306	407	509	611	815	1019	1222	1426	1630	1833	2037
$\frac{1}{4}$	229	306	382	458	611	764	917	1070	1375	1375	1528
$\frac{5}{16}$	183	244	306	367	489	611	733	856	978	1100	1222
$\frac{3}{8}$	153	204	255	306	407	509	611	713	815	917	1019
$\frac{7}{16}$	131	175	218	262	349	437	524	611	698	786	873
$\frac{1}{2}$	115	153	191	229	306	382	458	535	611	688	764
$\frac{5}{8}$	91	122	153	183	244	306	367	428	489	550	611
$\frac{3}{4}$	76	102	127	153	204	255	306	357	407	458	509
$\frac{7}{8}$	65	87	109	131	175	218	262	306	349	393	437
1"	57	76	95	115	153	191	229	267	306	344	382
$1\frac{1}{8}$	50	67	84	102	136	170	204	238	272	306	340
$1\frac{1}{4}$	45	61	76	91	122	153	183	214	244	275	306
$1\frac{3}{8}$	41	55	69	83	111	139	167	194	222	250	278
$1\frac{1}{2}$	38	50	63	76	102	127	153	178	204	229	255
$1\frac{5}{8}$	35	47	58	70	94	118	141	165	188	212	235
$1\frac{3}{4}$	32	43	54	65	87	109	131	153	175	196	218
$1\frac{7}{8}$	30	40	50	61	81	102	122	143	163	183	204
2"	28	38	47	57	76	95	115	134	153	172	191

Fig. 88-8. Recommended lubrication for a typical turret milling machine.

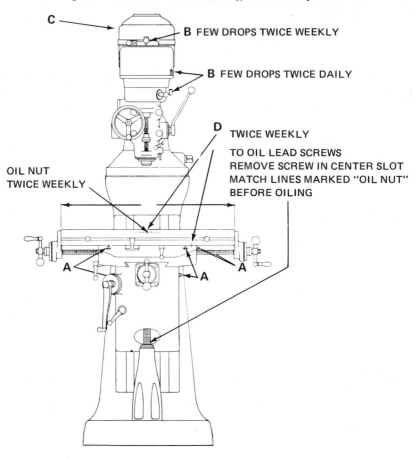

C

B FEW DROPS TWICE WEEKLY

B FEW DROPS TWICE DAILY

D TWICE WEEKLY

TO OIL LEAD SCREWS
REMOVE SCREW IN CENTER SLOT
MATCH LINES MARKED "OIL NUT"
BEFORE OILING

OIL NUT
TWICE WEEKLY

A

A

A

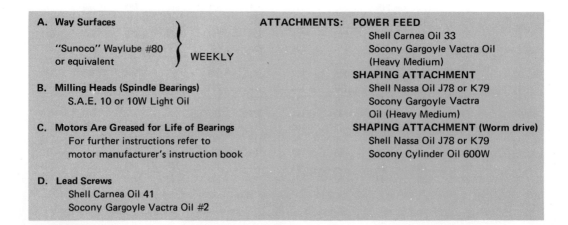

A. Way Surfaces

"Sunoco" Waylube #80
or equivalent } WEEKLY

B. Milling Heads (Spindle Bearings)
S.A.E. 10 or 10W Light Oil

C. Motors Are Greased for Life of Bearings
For further instructions refer to
motor manufacturer's instruction book

D. Lead Screws
Shell Carnea Oil 41
Socony Gargoyle Vactra Oil #2

ATTACHMENTS: POWER FEED
Shell Carnea Oil 33
Socony Gargoyle Vactra Oil
(Heavy Medium)
SHAPING ATTACHMENT
Shell Nassa Oil J78 or K79
Socony Gargoyle Vactra
Oil (Heavy Medium)
SHAPING ATTACHMENT (Worm drive)
Shell Nassa Oil J78 or K79
Socony Cylinder Oil 600W

Fig. 88-9. A measuring attachment designed to provide the utmost accuracy in the coordinate location of holes.

Fig. 88-10. A shaping attachment used for shaping and slotting operations.

STANDARD ACCESSORIES

Many kinds of standard accessories can be purchased for use on the vertical milling machine. The more common ones include:

1. *Power table feed.* Normally this unit is powered by an electric motor. A wide range of feed rates, in inches per minute (ipm), is possible with this accessory.

2. *Power down feed.* This unit can be attached to the spindle-head assembly. It is set to provide a specific down-feed rate in inches per minute.

3. *Measuring attachment.* The measuring attachment is used to locate hole coordinates accurately (Fig. 88-9). This unit really converts the vertical milling machine into a jig borer.

4. The *vertical shaping head* can be used to do a variety of slotting operations (Fig. 88-10).

5. An attachment to convert the vertical milling machine into a horizontal machine is also available.

6. Other attachments include *coolant* and *lubrication* systems.

HOLDING CUTTERS

Milling-machine manufacturers agreed on the American Standard steep tapers standard in 1927, but they have not followed this standard on vertical milling machines. The method of holding face and end mills in the spindle varies with the type of taper and size of machine (Fig. 88-11). Manufacturers often allow a choice of one of the following standard tapers, Brown and Sharpe, Morse or American, and Standard Steep Machine Taper (Milling Machine Taper). Other

Fig. 88-11. The type of toolholders, adaptors, and other machine holding accessories used will depend on the kind of taper the machine has. These toolholders are designed to hold straight-shank tools in a spindle having an American Standard steep machine taper. The holder is secured by a draw-in bar.

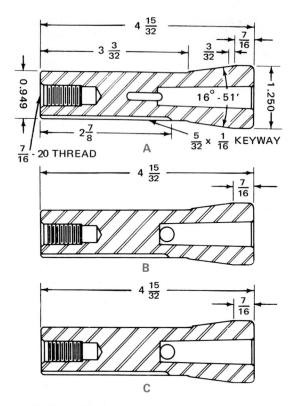

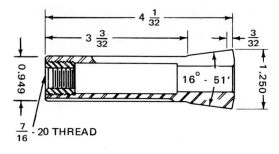

Fig. 88-13. This collet is used to hold straight-shank end mills.

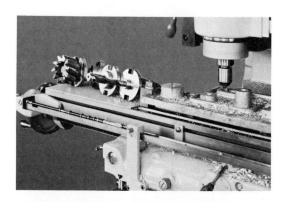

Fig. 88-12. These adaptors all fit a No. 8 Bridgeport taper on the outside. Their inside tapers are as follows: (A) No. 2 Morse, (B) No. 5 Brown and Sharpe, and (C) No. 7 Brown and Sharpe.

Fig. 88-14. A machine equipped with a quick-change spindle nose. Any of the tools shown can be installed with a simple twist of the toolholder collar.

tapers available include Bridgeport, Erickson, and quick change.

End milling cutters are held in the spindle in various ways. Those with a Brown and Sharpe taper have a threaded end which is fastened to a draw-in bar or bolt. On certain taper spindles, an adaptor with a threaded end is fastened in the spindle so that a Brown and Sharpe or Morse taper end mill can be installed (Fig. 88-12). Straight-shank end mills are often held in a collet chuck (Fig. 88-13). They can also be held in a toolholder that has a straight hole. To do this, a flat is machined on the tool shank which is clamped in the holder with a setscrew.

In industrial production, a *toolholder* is often fastened permanently in the machine spindle. The one toolholder can accommodate all tool adaptors (Fig. 88-14). Some of the tool adaptors include the straight-shank adaptor, the boring-head adaptor, the Jacobs-chuck adaptor, the taper-shank adaptor, the fly-cutter adaptor, and the shell-end mill cutter adaptor.

UNIT 89. Using a Vertical Milling Machine

The vertical milling machine is a versatile machine that can be used to perform a variety of operations including facing, end milling, drilling, boring, reaming, cutting a keyseat or slot, and many others (Fig. 89-1). Setting up a vertical milling machine is a relatively simple job.

CUTTERS FOR VERTICAL MILLING

End mills and face mills are used on the vertical milling machine. *End mills* are used to mill flat, vertical, and horizontal surfaces or an angle surface such as a bevel, chamfer, or taper. End mills are also used to produce a two-step surface or to machine a slot, groove, or keyway. When larger diameter shell end mills are used to machine a flat surface, it is very similar to face milling. Face milling, however, is more of a production operation done with cutters having a diameter of from $5\frac{1}{2}$ to 15 inches. End mills, on the other hand, vary in diameter from $\frac{1}{8}$ to 2 in. (Fig. 89-2). Shell end mills vary from $1\frac{1}{4}$ to 6 in. Whereas end milling can be done on a horizontal milling machine, it is better to use a vertical milling machine if one is available.

Always use small cutters for small work (Fig. 89-3). This allows more of the cutting-edges to be in simultaneous contact with the work and shortens the distance the workpiece must travel.

Other cutting tools commonly used on the vertical milling machine include straight- and taper-shank drills, adjustable boring bars, reamers, and fly cutters. A *fly cutter* is a single-point cutting tool which has been formed to a certain shape. Such a tool is held in and rotated by an arbor (Fig. 89-4).

SELECTION OF END MILLS

Single-end mills are preferred for general-purpose work which does not entail long production runs. For production milling, the double-end type is usually more economical.

The choice of high-speed steel or a carbide end mill depends upon the machinability, hardness and structure of the workpiece. The general shape of the workpiece and the type of milling to be done are also factors affecting this choice. High-speed steel end mills are low in cost when compared with carbide-tipped or solid-carbide end mills. They are also available in a much greater variety of sizes and styles. Carbide end mills are used for production milling of nonferrous, nonmetallic, or highly abrasive materials, where adequately powered equipment is employed.

Fig. 89-1. Common types of cuts that can be made on the vertical milling machine.

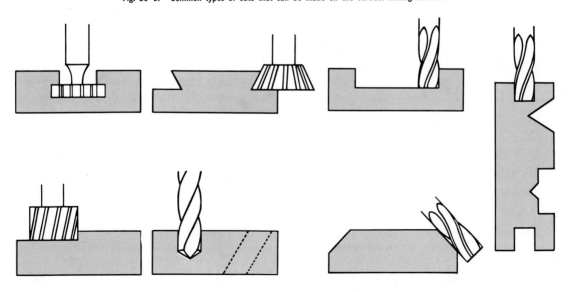

473

Fig. 89-2. Using a small end milling cutter on a medium-size milling machine.

Fig. 89-3. To improve efficiency, small cutters should be used for small work.

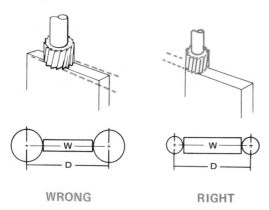

WRONG   RIGHT

USING SMALL CUTTERS FOR SMALL WORK ALLOWS MORE OF THE CUTTER'S TEETH TO BE SIMULTANEOUSLY IN CONTACT WITH THE WORK AND SHORTENS THE NEEDED TRAVEL.

Fig. 89-4. Using a fly cutter to cut a recess in the bottom of a machine part.

TWO-FLUTE VERSUS MULTIPLE-FLUTE

The question of whether to use a two-flute or a multiple-flute end mill must be decided on the basis of several factors. These factors include type of cut, chip space, production rate, and surface finish required. A two-flute end mill has greater chip space than does an end mill having four or more flutes. It is also capable of milling to greater depths and taking heavier cuts. Two-flute end mills are center cutting and therefore may be used for axial plunge cutting (drilling). A multiple-flute end mill must be of special center-cutting design in order to do this.

When two-flute and multiple-flute end mills are run at the same revolutions per minute (rpm) and feed, the multiple-flute end mills will have a better tool life and will produce finer finishes than will the two-flute-type. This is due to the lower chip load per tooth. (It is possible to approach these finer work finishes by running the two-flute end mill at a reduced feed per tooth, but this is often uneconomical, particularly on long production runs.) For production end milling where either two-flute or multiple-flute end mills can perform the required cut, it is more economical to use the multiple-flute end mill.

WORK-HOLDING DEVICES

The same types of work-holding devices are used on the vertical mill as on the drill press and milling machine. Remember that in making a setup for vertical milling, the cut should be taken against the solid side of the vise or supporting fixture (Fig. 89–5).

INSTALLING THE CUTTER

The method in which a cutter is held in the spindle depends on the kind of cutter, the kind of spindle taper, and the kind of toolholder, collet, adaptor, or arbor used. Many different combinations of spindles, toolholding devices, and milling cutters are possible. Several examples follow.

1. If the machine has a No. 9 Brown and Sharpe taper spindle, a No. 9 Brown and Sharpe threaded taper end mill is used as shown in Fig. 89–6A.

2. If the machine has an R-8 Bridgeport taper, and a No. 5 Brown and Sharpe taper end mill is used, an adaptor is needed. It should have a No. 8 Bridgeport taper on its outside and a No. 5 Brown and Sharpe taper on its inside (Fig. 89–6B).

3. If the machine has a No. 9 Brown and Sharpe taper and a straight end mill is used, then a collet with an outside taper to match the spindle and a straight inside hole can be used (Fig. 89–6C).

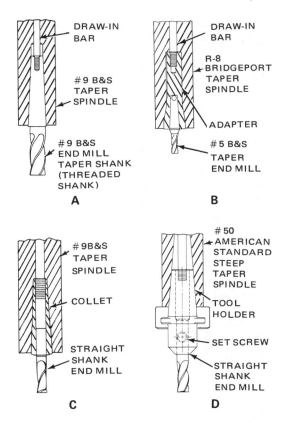

Fig. 89-6. Common methods of holding end mills in the spindle. The standard taper used on the spindle determines the outside size and shape of the tool adaptor, toolholder, arbor, or collet that must be used.

4. If a machine has a No. 50 American Standard steep machine taper, and a straight-shank mill is used, a toolholder with the correct outside taper is needed. A setscrew holds the cutter securely (Fig. 89–6D).

5. If a face or shell end mill is used, a short or stub arbor having the same taper as the spindle is needed.

6. If many different types of cutters are used in rapid succession, then a quick-change toolholder with the correct outside taper is permanently fastened in the spindle. All other tools are held in *adaptors* that fit this holder.

Note that the tooling needed for a machine will always require that the outside taper match the taper of the spindle, and that the inside opening fit the size (diameter or taper number)

Fig. 89-5. If the cutter rotates clockwise as viewed from the top, the cut will be made against the fixed jaw of the vise.

475

and type (straight or taper) of the cutting tool. All straight-shank end mills have a flat milled on their shanks. A setscrew is used to hold these mills solidly in place (Fig. 89-7).

MACHINING A FLAT SURFACE—
FACE MILLING

1. Measure the width of the surface to be machined. Select an end mill that is slightly larger in diameter than the width of the cut. If the cutter is not wide enough, more than one cut can be made across the surface.

2. Mount the milling cutter in the spindle.

3. Check to see if the milling head is at right angles to the table.

4. Mount the vise to the table with the jaws parallel to the T slots.

5. Fasten the workpiece securely in the vise. Make sure it is supported on parallels.

6. Adjust for correct speed and feed. If the machine has power feed, adjust the stop dogs on the front of the table.

7. Check the *hand* of the cutter and the direction of spindle rotation. A right-hand cutter should rotate clockwise.

8. Position the workpiece directly under the cutter.

9. Turn on the power, and then raise the knee until the cutter just touches the workpiece surface.

10. Adjust the micrometer collar on the knee crank to zero.

11. Move the table to the right, and then raise the knee about 0.015 in.

12. Move the table by hand until the cutting starts, and then use the power feed. If the machine does not have power feed, turn the table crank slowly, making a cut across the surface (Fig. 89-8).

13. Check the thickness of the workpiece with a steel rule or micrometer.

14. Use the micrometer collar on the knee crank to set for additional cutting to reach the proper depth of cut.

15. If considerable stock must be removed, make several cuts.

Fig. 89-7. Installing an end mill in a collet.

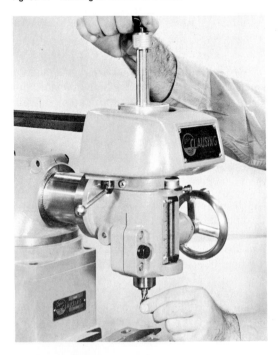

Fig. 89-8. Machining a flat surface with the work fastened directly to the table.

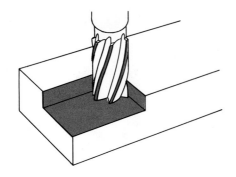

Fig. 89-9. Machining a step surface.

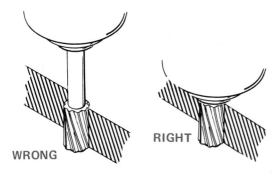

WRONG　　**RIGHT**

Fig. 89-10. When cutting with the side of an end mill, the tool should be held as close to the spindle head as possible.

MACHINING A STEP OR MULTILEVEL SURFACE

1. Draw a layout line along the edge and across the face of the workpiece to show the location of the step. If there is more than one level, lay out each across the face. Also mark the various depths of cut along the edge of the workpiece (Fig. 89-9).

2. Position the workpiece so that the cutter is directly over the deepest cut. Avoid overloading the end mill. If necessary, take several light cuts. Also keep the cutter as close to the spindle head as possible (Fig. 89-10).

3. Make the deep cuts first and then the shallow cuts.

4. Check the depth of each cut with a micrometer.

MACHINING A BEVEL, CHAMFER, OR TAPER

1. Mark a layout line on either side of the workpiece to show the location of the bevel, chamfer, or taper.

2. Fasten the workpiece to the table in a vise. Make sure the layout clears the top of the vise jaws.

3. Set the head at the correct angle for the cut. For example, to machine a chamfer, turn the head at a 45-degree (°) angle (Fig. 89-11).

4. Position the table and make one or more cuts to the layout line.

5. A tapered surface is milled by holding the workpiece at an angle (Fig. 89-12).

ANGULAR MILLING

An angle slot or a concave surface can be cut by adjusting the milling head to the required angle (Fig. 89-13).

Fig. 89-11. Note how the head is adjusted at a 45° angle for a chamfer cut.

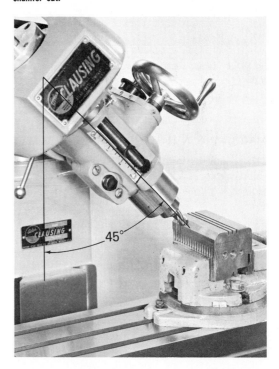

45°

Fig. 89-12.   A hammer head held in the vise at the correct angle for cutting the tapered surface.

Fig. 89-13.   Cutting a concave surface with the toolhead at an angle.

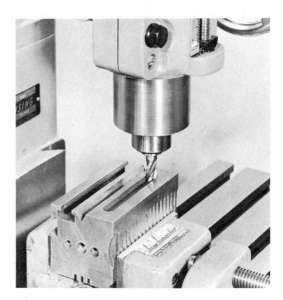

Fig. 89-14.   Machining a closed-end slot.

MACHINING A SLOT OR KEYWAY

1. Locate the center of the slot or keyway on the workpiece. A keyway is usually cut in a shaft (round workpiece).

2. Fasten the workpiece in a vise or to the table.

3. Select an end mill equal in diameter to the width of the slot. If it is a closed-end slot or keyway, use a *two-lip end mill* (Fig. 89-14).

4. Mount the cutter in the spindle.

5. Move the workpiece near but to one side of the cutter. Raise the table until the end of the cutter is below the center of the workpiece.

6. Put a thin sheet of tissue paper around the workpiece. Then carefully move the table until the side of the cutter just touches the paper. Set the micrometer collar at zero.

7. Lower the table.

8. To center the cutter, move the saddle an amount equal to half the diameter of the cutter, plus half the diameter of the workpiece, plus 0.001 in. (thickness of tissue paper). For example, if the diameter of the end mill is $\frac{1}{4}$ in. and the diameter of the workpiece is $\frac{3}{4}$ in., then the table must be moved 0.501 in. ($\frac{1}{2}$ of 0.250 + $\frac{1}{2}$ of 0.750 + 0.001) (Fig. 89-15).

9. A second method is first to center the cutter approximately. Then place a square against either side of the workpiece. Measure from the square to the cutter on either side. Adjust the cross-slide saddle until the distances are equal.

10. Always measure the depth of a keyway from the side of the slot.

11. Mill the slot. If the cutter is a two-lip end mill, it can be fed directly into the metal the same as a drill (Fig. 89-16).

12. The end mill can also be used to machine an internal opening, such as an elongated slot or open-end groove.

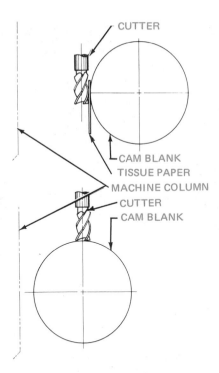

Fig. 89-15. Centering the end mill to machine a keyway.

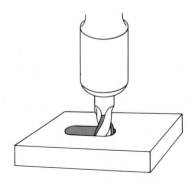

Fig. 89-16. Using a two-lip end mill to machine an elongated slot.

FINISHING A BOSS

A *boss* is a raised, reinforced area on a casting or other metal part (Fig. 89-17). There is often a hole through the center of the boss for a shaft or bolt. The top of the boss must be smooth and square with the hole, so that a washer, bolt head, or nut can be seated properly. Select an end mill equal in diameter to the diameter of the boss. Mill the boss as you would any flat surface.

Fig. 89-17. Machining a boss.

Fig. 89-18. Setup for machining a T slot.

CUTTING A T SLOT OR DOVETAIL

A T-slot cutter can be used to mill a T slot as shown in Fig. 89-18. A straight slot must be milled first before the T-slot cutter can be used. For the standard T-slot dimensions see *The New American Machinist's Handbook* or *Machinery's Handbook*. A dovetail is cut with a dovetail end mill (Fig. 89-19).

DRILLING, BORING, AND REAMING

Holes can be drilled, bored, and reamed on a vertical milling machine. Because the vertical

Fig. 89-19. Machining a dovetail.

Fig. 89-20. Accurate drilling operations can be done on the milling machine. The hand lever operates the spindle much like a drill press.

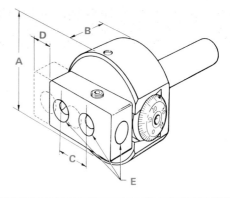

SPECIFICATIONS (in.)			
		#1	#2
A		$2\frac{1}{4}$	$3\frac{3}{8}$
B		$1\frac{1}{4}$	$1\frac{3}{4}$
C		$\frac{3}{4}$	$1\frac{3}{16}$
D	Adjustment	$\frac{3}{8}$	$\frac{1}{2}$
E	Size tool taken	$\frac{3}{8}$	$\frac{5}{8}$

Fig. 89-21. An adjustable boring head can be used to bore various-side holes.

Fig. 89-22. Using the shaping attachment to cut a keyway in a simple cast iron part.

milling machine is a precision tool, it can often serve as a jig borer when this machine tool is not available.

Fasten the workpiece to be drilled, bored, or reamed in a vise. Make sure there is plenty of clearance below the workpiece for the tool to go completely through. Center-punch the hole.

CAUTION

Always lock the knee, saddle, and table before making the cut.

If it is a small hole, fasten a Jacobs-chuck adaptor to the spindle and use a straight-shank drill (Fig. 89-20). It may be necessary first to drill a small hole before a larger one can be accurately made.

Boring with an adjustable boring bar permits holes of various diameters to be machined accurately (Fig. 89-21). Reaming can also be done in the same manner as on the drill press.

USING A VERTICAL SHAPING OR SLOTTING ATTACHMENT

The vertical shaping or slotting attachment can be used to produce a variety of shapes using a standard set of tool bits and holders (Fig. 89-22). With this attachment, round slots and keyways can be cut and other internal and external shapes can be made.

UNIT 90. Milling Machines in Industry

A variety of milling machines are utilized in industry. These can be divided into four groups, the column-and-knee type, like those you have been studying, the manufacturing or bed type used largely in production work, the planer type used for large work, and the special type, developed for special milling operations.

COLUMN-AND-KNEE MACHINES

1. The plain milling machine is commonly found in many metalworking plants. Larger models have mechanical or hydraulic power controls. These are also capable of rapid traverse action (fast travel) so that all movements can be made quickly. This saves time when returning the table to its starting position.

2. The universal milling machine is the same as the plain horizontal machine with one added feature. The table can be swiveled on the saddle, usually up to 45 degrees (°). This makes it possible to machine helical work such as reamers, drills, and milling cutters.

3. The vertical milling machine has a spindle that is held vertically. All larger models are equipped for power operation. Many have rapid traverse for quickly moving the workpiece into cutting position. Several attachments are available for use on vertical milling machines to perform special functions. These include the tracer-profiler, the profiler-duplicator, and the optical scanner.

a. The *tracer-profiler* may be a specially designed mill or a tracer attachment that is added to a standard vertical milling machine (Fig. 90-1). The tracer mill operates as follows. A pattern is first placed under the tracer attachment. The cutting tool is then mounted in the spindle, and the workpiece positioned under it. Movement of the tracer head over the pattern controls table movement and one or more spindle heads. Parts produced in this manner are exact duplicates of the pattern used (Fig. 90-2).

b. The *profiler-duplicator* is similar to the tracer-profiler except that it can duplicate a part in three dimensions (Fig. 90-3). Duplicators may be operated manually, electronically, hydraulically, or by a combination of methods (Fig. 90-4). A typical electronic hydraulic unit is made up of three sections, a control section, a processing section, and a drive section (Fig. 90-5). The command section consists of a tracer head, a stylus, and an operator's control panel. Movement of the stylus over the template is converted into electrical signals which are transmitted to the processing section. After processing, command signals are sent to the drive section which is made up of hydraulic motors, cylinders, and valves. These parts then move the machine axis according to the command information received. A large machine similar to a profiler is called a *die-sinking machine* (Fig. 90-6).

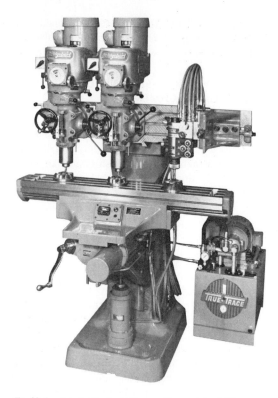

Fig. 90-1. A hydraulic duplicating machine used for 360° profiling and contouring.

Fig. 90-2. This tracer can follow a pattern and cut two identical shapes.

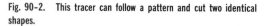

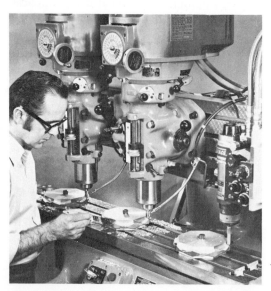

Fig. 90-3. Sometimes called a duplicating machine, this profiler-duplicator can reproduce irregularly shaped parts and pieces that have a three-dimensional machining requirement.

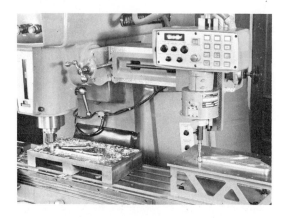

Fig. 90-4. A duplicator attachment.

c. The *optical scanner* is an attachment that permits duplication of flat parts directly from a line drawing, sketch, or print. In practice, a clean drawing of the part is laid on the scanning table and held in position with magnets to prevent accidental movement. The scanner generates electrical signals by scanning the line on the drawing and feeding these signals to the circuitry that controls the table movement. Since the scanning head is mounted on the same support that carries the milling tool, part reproduction is faithful and extremely accurate. An optical scanner can follow a

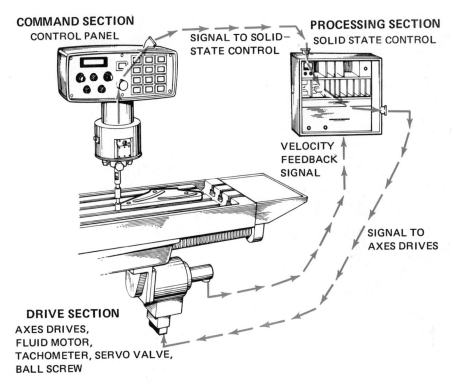

COMMAND SECTION
CONTROL PANEL

SIGNAL TO SOLID-
STATE CONTROL

PROCESSING SECTION
SOLID STATE CONTROL

VELOCITY
FEEDBACK
SIGNAL

SIGNAL TO
AXES DRIVES

DRIVE SECTION
AXES DRIVES,
FLUID MOTOR,
TACHOMETER, SERVO VALVE,
BALL SCREW

Fig. 90-5. Operation of the tracer controlled unit.

Fig. 90-6. In the die sinking machine, a metal finger traces the contours of a die cavity model at the top, causing matching impressions to be sunk automatically in the die block below.

sharp black line within ± 0.001 in. (Fig. 90-7).

MANUFACTURING OR BED-TYPE MACHINES

The *manufacturing* or *bed-type machine* is one of the simplest millers used in industry. It has a fixed table support or bed that can be moved longitudinally. The machine spindle is mounted in a special boxlike carrier that can be adjusted up and down. "In" and "out" adjustment of the cutter is possible because the spindle is mounted in a quill. This adjustment is used only for setup, however. Once the machine is ready, the operation is either partially or fully automatic. Bed-type millers are designed principally for large-scale, heavy-production work, involving simple machining operations. Some bed-type milling machines have a column and spindle located on the sides of the table (Fig. 90-8). With this arrangement, it is possible to mill two different surfaces on a workpiece with one pass of the table. The cycles of table movement on these machines are designed for automatic control.

Fig. 90-7. An optical scanner.

PLANER-TYPE MILLING MACHINES

The *planer-type milling machine* is used for the heaviest kinds of jobs. It looks somewhat like a planer but has milling-machine heads mounted on the crossrail and at the sides (Fig. 90-9). This type of machine is used to make several cuts at the same time on large or extremely long workpieces.

HORIZONTAL BORING MACHINES

The *horizontal boring machine* is a special type of milling machine designed primarily for boring, drilling, and milling large holes and surfaces (Fig. 90-10). Many different operations can be performed on this type of machine with but a single table setting of the workpiece. Boring machines may have either horizontal or vertical spindles; however, the horizontal is most common. Boring machine spindles differ from those of the conventional milling machine in that they are mounted in a quill and are capable of considerable travel in the direction of their long dimension. In this respect they closely resemble the drill press.

Fig. 90-8. A double-head bed-type milling machine.

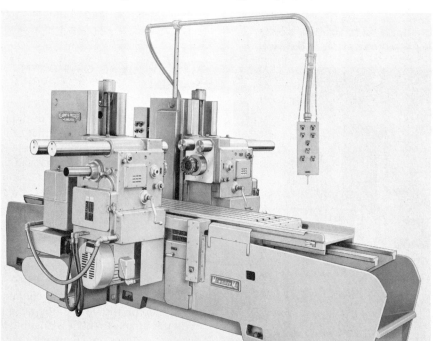

Fig. 90-9.   A planer-type milling machine used to mill castings.

Fig. 90-10.   A horizontal boring mill is being used to drill and bore holes in this large piece of equipment.

Fig. 90-11.   A jig borer. This machine is an extremely accurate drill press with a base similar to a milling machine.

JIG BORERS

Jig borers, although classified as milling machines, are in many respects more like a drilling machine than a miller (Fig. 90–11). Jig borers are not for the production line. They are used primarily in the manufacture of jigs and fixtures (see Unit 40).

MACHINING CENTERS

Machining centers are the most complicated of all machine tools (Fig. 90–12). They are so called because they can be utilized for almost every type of machining operation. They are often equipped with automatic tool-control systems that fit tools into the spindle automatically. All

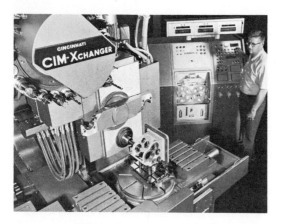

Fig. 90–12. One type of machining center. Notice how different types of cutters can be fed automatically into the spindle to do a wide variety of machining operations.

Fig. 90–13. Note the multiple spindles and hydraulically controlled fixtures used to mill duplicate parts.

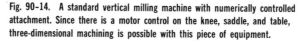

Fig. 90–14. A standard vertical milling machine with numerically controlled attachment. Since there is a motor control on the knee, saddle, and table, three-dimensional machining is possible with this piece of equipment.

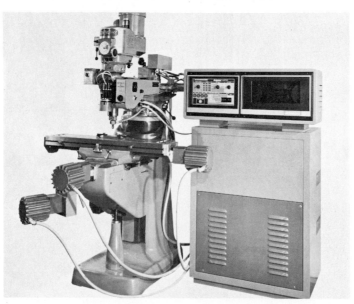

operations can be programmed on a numerical-control unit. In addition, the workpiece can be moved in any direction so that all the machining can be done in one setup.

PRODUCTION MACHINES

A large number of specialized milling machines have been developed for special uses on the production line. Many production-type milling machines have multiple spindle heads so that several parts can be machined simultaneously (Fig. 90-13).

NUMERICALLY-CONTROLLED (N/C) MACHINES

Every type of milling machine can be equipped with a numerical-control unit (Fig. 90-14). Once directions have been fed into this unit, the machine will perform the operations automatically

(Fig. 90-15). It is recommended that Unit 101 be reviewed to get a better understanding of how numerical-control units operate.

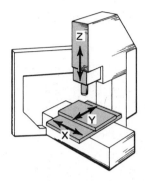

Fig. 90-15. On most N/C vertical milling machines, the Z axis denotes vertical tool movement, the X axis longitudinal table movement, and the Y axis refers to the cross movement of the table.

UNIT 91. Discussion Topics and Problems

1. What is the basic type of milling machine?

2. Describe the difference between a horizontal milling machine and a vertical milling machine.

3. What are the three movements on a plain milling machine?

4. What are the basic steps in all milling operations?

5. List five ways of identifying a milling cutter.

6. How do arbors for large and small milling machines differ?

7. List several ways of caring for milling cutters.

8. What is the difference between *upcutting* and *climb cutting*? Which can be done on smaller milling machines?

9. What is cutting speed on a milling machine?

10. What factors affect cutting speed?

11. At what speed should the milling machine operate when using a 6-in. high-speed milling cutter on copper?

12. What is feed on a milling machine?

13. What are cutting fluids used for on the milling machine?

14. Describe a dividing head.

15. What is another name for plain milling?

16. Describe the procedure for milling a flat surface.

17. What is face milling?

18. Name four types of side-milling cutters.

19. What is straddle milling?

20. How can sawing be done on a milling machine?

21. List some other operations performed on the milling machine.

22. What is the difference between end milling and face milling?

23. Why is end milling best done on a vertical milling machine?

24. List the steps in milling a slot.

25. What is a boss and how is it machined?

26. Why is safety so important when operating a milling machine?

27. What kind of tool is used on a vertical milling machine?

28. Describe the operation of the tracer-profiler.

29. What is a planer-type milling machine?

30. How does an optical scanner work?

31. Does an N/C vertical milling machine provide automatic control of more than one axis? Explain.

SECTION 9

GRINDERS AND ABRASIVE MACHINING

UNIT 92. Abrasive Machining and Grinding

Primitive man first removed chips from a workpiece by means of an abrasive stone. As time went on, he learned to make grinding materials that were even harder than steel. He also developed grinding machines on which to use these materials (Fig. 92-1). Today, modern industrial production depends to a large degree on grinding machines (Fig. 92-2).

It is important that you understand the difference between grinding and abrasive machining. *Grinding* is done primarily to smooth and finish a product. Very little metal is removed. *Abrasive machining,* on the other hand, is used primarily to remove metal and to shape the product (Fig. 92-3). Abrasive machines use both grinding wheels and coated abrasive belts (Fig. 92-4). Some advantages of abrasive machining over other machining methods such as turning, milling, planing, and shaping include faster removal of metal, requirement of fewer fixtures, completion of rough and finished machining in one pass, and reduction in machining costs.

GRINDING WHEELS

Grinding wheels are made up of thousands of abrasive grains. Each grain is actually a very small cutting tool. As the abrasive grains come in contact with the workpiece, they cut away very small pieces of the material called *chips*. These are very similar to the chips produced by a milling cutter.

The way a grinding wheel performs depends a good deal on how fast the wheel is turning and how fast the workpiece passes under it. If either the workpiece or the wheel moves too fast, the abrasive grains get very little chance to do any cutting. In this case, the wheel gives the impression of being hard. If the workpiece or the wheel moves too slowly, the abrasive grains cut for a longer time. Then the wheel seems to be soft.

The right grinding wheel for a job is one that has:

1. The correct coarseness of abrasive grains.

2. Abrasive grains spaced far enough apart to remove the right amount and kind of chips and to keep the wheel from clogging.

Fig. 92-1. This large numerically controlled grinder is typical of the specialized equipment used in industry today.

3. The proper bond to produce the desired smoothness of finish. A perfect grinding wheel is one that continually sharpens itself. As each abrasive grain becomes dull, it breaks off from the wheel to expose a new, sharp grain.

Grinding, like all other operations, produces heat. In production grinding, therefore, a continuous supply of coolant is always used. Cutting fluids are useful in preventing heat formation and in helping to carry the chips away.

KINDS OF GRINDING AND ABRASIVE MACHINING

The two major types of grinding are *offhand grinding* and *precision grinding*.

Offhand grinding is done by applying the grinding wheel manually to the work or by applying the work offhand to the grinding wheel. It is used to snag castings, grind wells, and sharpen tools. Offhand grinding cannot be done when close tolerances are required (Fig. 92-5).

Precision grinding includes a variety of

Fig. 92-2. (A) Cylindrical grinding is one of the more common kinds of grinding. The grinding wheel actually cuts chips. (B) Compare this with the surface grinder, which removes small chips.

A

B

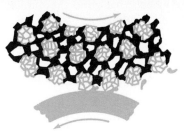

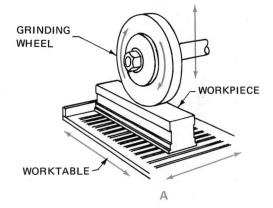

GRINDING WHEEL

WORKPIECE

WORKTABLE

A

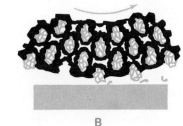

B

grinding operations done to machine work to extremely close tolerances. There are six basic precision grinding operations. Some grinding machines are capable of performing just one of these six, and others may do as many as five.

1. *Cylindrical grinding* produces a straight or tapered surface on a workpiece. The workpiece must be rotated (on centers) as it passes lengthwise across the face of a revolving grinding wheel.

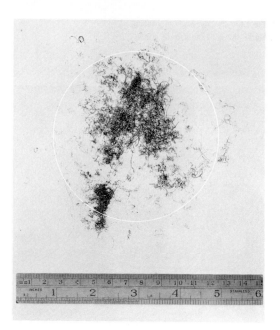

Fig. 92-3. Several sizes of chips removed by an abrasive machine. These are very similar to the chips formed by cutting.

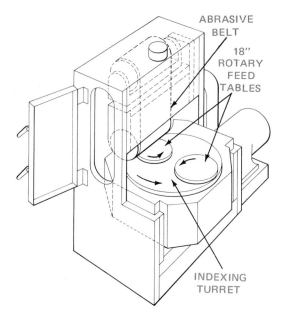

Fig. 92-4. This abrasive belt grinding machine is designed specifically for abrasive machining.

Fig. 92-5. Offhand grinding.

2. *Plunge-cut grinding* produces a straight, tapered, or formed surface on a workpiece as the grinding wheel moves into the workpiece.

3. *Form grinding* is done with specially shaped grinding wheels that grind the formed surface as in thread grinding.

4. *Internal grinding* is done to shape a cylindrical hole.

5. *Surface grinding* produces a flat surface.

6. *Centerless grinding* is a kind of cylindrical grinding in which the workpiece does not have to be held on centers. It is passed or fed between two wheels. One wheel is a grinding wheel and the other is a regulating wheel.

KINDS OF GRINDING MACHINES

There are many kinds of grinding machines. A few of the more common ones are:

1. *Plain center-type cylindrical grinder.* This machine is used to grind the outside of cylindrical parts (Figs. 92-6 and 92-7). The parts may be straight, tapered, or formed (Fig. 92-8).

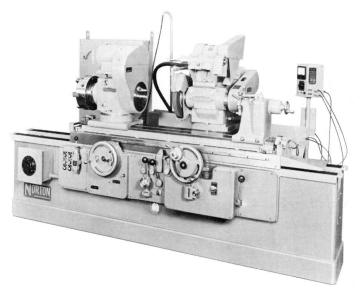

Fig. 92-6.　Plain cylindrical grinder of the type used in industry.

Fig. 92-7.　Operation of a center-type grinder.

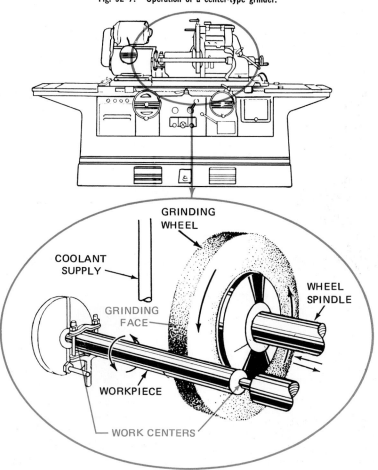

GRINDING WHEEL

COOLANT SUPPLY

GRINDING FACE

WHEEL SPINDLE

WORKPIECE

WORK CENTERS

The table fastened to the bed of this machine is capable of back-and-forth (reciprocating) movement and can also be swiveled about 10 degrees (°) on either side of the center line. Both headstock and footstock are mounted on this table. The workpiece to be ground is held between centers and must have center holes (Fig. 92-9). A dog is used to drive the workpiece. The grinding wheel is mounted on a spindle so that it can be moved to and from the workpiece.

Both the grinding wheel and the workpiece rotate during the machining operation. The grinding wheel turns rapidly—825 to 1,250 revolutions per minute (rpm), or 5,500 to 6,500 surface feet per minute (sfpm). The workpiece turns at a much slower rate—100 to 400 rpm. Also, the grinding wheel and the workpiece move in opposite directions at their line of contact (Fig. 92-10). The table is used to move the workpiece across the front of the wheel.

Generally, a workpiece is machined about 0.004 to 0.030 in. oversize, hardened, and then machined to final size. On very long, thin workpieces, more material is left for grinding. When grinding such workpieces, steady rests are used to support the stock (Fig. 92-11).

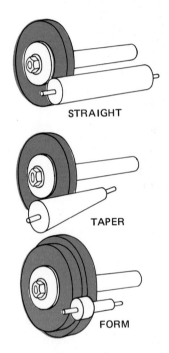

STRAIGHT

TAPER

FORM

Fig. 92-8.   Kinds of grinding that can be done on a plain grinding machine.

Fig. 92-9.   The centers on the grinder and the center holes on the workpiece must be exactly 60°. After heat-treating, recheck center holes before mounting the workpiece on the grinder.

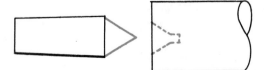

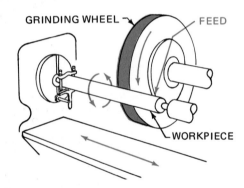

GRINDING WHEEL — FEED

WORKPIECE

Fig. 92-10.   Movements of the machine and the workpiece on a plain center-type grinding machine. The workpiece rotates and moves longitudinally (back and forth). The grinding wheel rotates and moves transversely (in and out) from the workpiece (infeed).

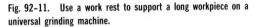

Fig. 92-11.   Use a work rest to support a long workpiece on a universal grinding machine.

Fig. 92-12. A universal grinding machine. The frame-type internal grinding fixture is in a raised position. The head can also be swiveled.

Fig. 92-13. A centerless cylindrical grinding machine.

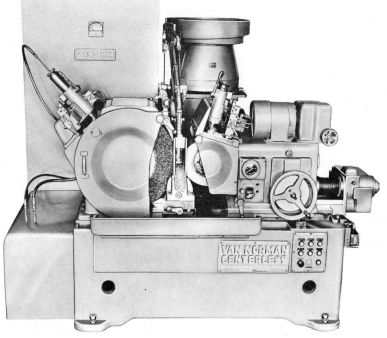

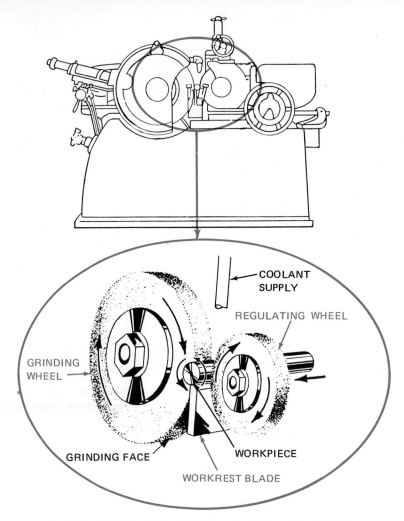

Fig. 92-14. A typical centerless grinder. The enlarged diagram shows the relative positions of the workpiece being ground.

2. *Universal grinding machine.* This machine is similar to the plain center-type cylindrical grinder. However, because its headstock and/or wheel head can be swiveled, it is capable of both straight and taper grinding (Fig. 92-12). Extra accessories make it possible to do internal and surface grinding with this type of machine.

3. *Centerless grinding machine.* The centerless grinder, as its name implies, does not use centers to hold the workpiece (Figs. 92-13 and 92-14). Instead, the workpiece rests on a *work-rest plate* (a narrow steel plate) which is positioned between two wheels (Fig. 92-15). The larger of the two wheels is the *grinding wheel.* It rotates at a rather high speed. The smaller is

a *regulating wheel* which operates at a slower speed. Notice that both these wheels rotate in the same direction (clockwise). The regulating wheel is usually made of a rubber-bonded abrasive. It serves to drive the workpiece, rotating it at a constant and uniform surface speed. There are four principal ways in which centerless grinding is accomplished.

a. *Thrufeed grinding* requires that the workpiece move from one side of the wheels to the other. This results in the production of straight cylindrical surfaces (Fig. 92-16).

b. *Infeed grinding* is similar to plunge or form grinding. This is done when the work-

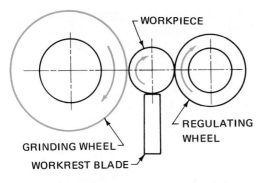

Fig. 92-15. The workpiece is supported behind the grinding wheel and the regulating wheel.

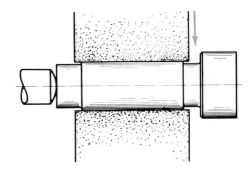

Fig. 92-17. Infeed grinding.

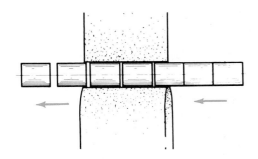

Fig. 92-16. Thrufeed grinding on a centerless grinding machine.

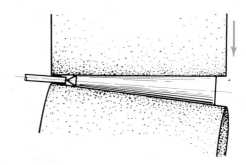

Fig. 92-18. End-feed grinding done to produce a tapered part.

piece has a shoulder or head or some other part that is larger than the part to be ground (Fig. 92-17).

c. *End-feed grinding* is done to produce tapers. The grinding wheel, regulating wheel, and blade (plate) are set at the correct angles to produce the taper on the workpiece (Fig. 92-18).

d. A *combination of infeed and thrufeed* is used to produce parts that require some of each type of grinding.

The centerless grinder is a production machine. If many parts of the same diameter must be manufactured, they can be put into the centerless grinder and finished to size in a short time. There is no need to worry about center holes or about mounting the workpiece in a holder of any kind (Fig. 92-19).

4. *Internal grinding machine.* Internal grinders are used to finish straight, tapered, or formed

holes to the correct size, shape, and finish (Fig. 92-20). Operating the internal grinder is much like boring on a lathe except that a grinding wheel serves as the cutting tool. In the most common type of internal grinding machine, the workpiece is mounted in a rotating chuck. The grinding wheel is mounted on a rotating spindle and can be moved in and out of the hole in the workpiece. Another type of machine employs a stationary spindle. The workpiece is moved back and forth over the grinding wheel. On a third type, the workpiece moves back and forth but does not rotate. Instead, the wheel spindle rotates about its own axis and also revolves in a planetary path.

5. *Surface grinding machine.* Surface grinding is the process of producing and finishing flat surfaces with a grinding machine. With special fixtures, angular and form surfaces can also be ground. For all types of precision surface grinding, the grinding wheel revolves on a spindle and the workpiece is brought in contact with

Fig. 92-19. An abrasive belt is used on a centerless grinder.

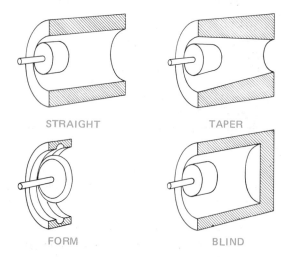

STRAIGHT

TAPER

FORM

BLIND

Fig. 92-20. Kinds of internal grinding.

the grinding wheel by means of a moving table. There are four basic types of surface grinders.

a. *Horizontal spindle reciprocating table machine.* These machines are built in a wide range of sizes for convenient, flat grinding (Fig. 92-21). This type of surface grinder is most common and will be described in detail in Unit 94.

b. *Horizontal spindle rotary table machine.* These machines are equipped with a rotary table (Fig. 92-22).

c. *Vertical spindle reciprocating table machine.* This machine is illustrated in Fig. 92-23. The column supporting the wheel head may be fixed or it may slide laterally for handling work wider than the grinding wheel.

d. *Vertical spindle rotating table machine* (Fig. 92-24).

6. *Tool and cutter grinding machine.* The universal tool and cutter grinding machine is used to sharpen all kinds of cutters (Fig. 92-25). It is a very versatile machine. Tools for sharpening may be mounted on a mandrel, in a chuck or collet, or on a fixture. Both the headstock assembly and the unit that holds the grinding wheel can be adjusted to any angle. Figure 92-26A illustrates the typical setup for grinding a reamer. Figure 92-26B shows the setup for grinding a face-milling cutter.

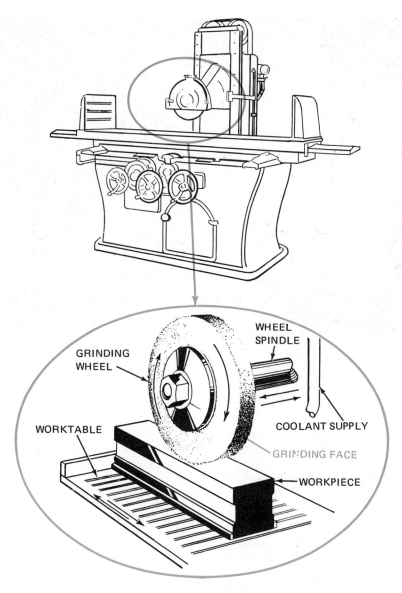

Fig. 92-21. Operation of a typical horizontal spindle surface grinder.

SAFETY AND CARE OF GRINDING MACHINES

Grinders present a different kind of hazard to the operator than other types of cutting tools. Grinding wheels are fragile tools and will not stand rough use. To prevent accidents and injuries it is most important that you learn the rules of safety that pertain to grinding machines.

1. You must always wear safety glasses of the correct type. Regular eyeglasses are not a substitute for safety glasses.

2. When you first start a grinding wheel or mount a new wheel, stand aside for a minute. The wheel may be cracked or damaged. If so, it may fly apart when it reaches full speed.

3. Work must never be forced against a wheel.

4. Learn how to test a wheel for soundness before mounting it.

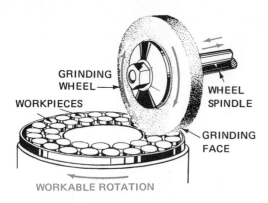

Fig. 92-22. Operation of an industrial-type horizontal spindle grinding machine equipped with a rotary table.

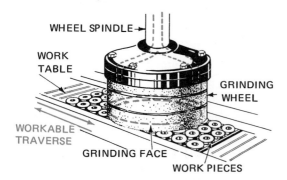

Fig. 92-23. Operation of a surface grinder with a vertical spindle and reciprocating table.

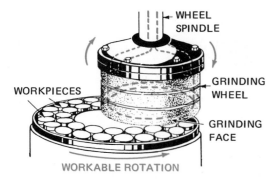

Fig. 92-24. Operation of a vertical spindle surface grinder with a rotating table.

Fig. 92-25. A typical tool and cutter grinder.

5. Never attempt to measure work near a revolving wheel.

6. Keep your fingers away from turning wheels. A grinding wheel is a cutting tool and it removes skin fast.

7. Make certain the work is held securely. Loose work is the cause of many injuries.

8. Make sure the wheel is clear of the work before starting a machine.

9. When holding work on magnetic chucks, always check the workpiece to make certain it is tight. Do this by gripping it with your hand or hands to see if it is loose or movable.

10. Magnetic chucks must be clean and smooth. Never place work with a rough finish on a magnetic chuck.

11. Always fill and adjust the oil cups on grinding-machine spindles. High-speed spindles require a light oil continuously while revolving. The wrong type or a heavy oil can soon ruin the bearings.

12. Be sure the correct type of wheel is securely mounted on the spindle. If in doubt, ask your instructor.

13. Work must never be placed in a grinding machine or on a magnetic chuck while the wheel is turning.

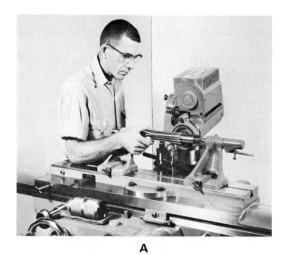 

A   B

Fig. 92-26. (A) Grinding a tapered reamer. (B) Grinding a milling-machine cutter.

14. Wheel guards must be kept in place over the wheels. If a wheel should break, the guard helps prevent the pieces from flying about the shop.

15. When a grinding machine is equipped with feed reverse and trip dogs, always test the movement first by using the hand feed. If the table does not reverse at the right moment, the wheel may be broken.

16. Remove all wrenches and other tools from the table before starting the grinding machine.

17. Never lay or drop tools or workpieces on the accurate table surfaces.

18. Small mounted wheels are just as dangerous as large wheels. Use them carefully.

UNIT 93. Grinding Wheels

Grinding wheels are multitoothed cutting tools (Fig. 93-1). They are made of crushed abrasive held together with a bonding material. Grinding wheels operate on the same general principle as all other cutting tools. As each tiny particle of abrasive passes over the metal surface, it cuts off a very small amount of metal, leaving a smooth, accurate finish (Fig. 93-2). As the abrasive grains become dull, they break away from the wheel to expose new, sharp cutting-edges. As the wheel wears and becomes duller, it must be dressed with a diamond dressing tool. This makes the wheel cut smoother and easier.

COMPOSITION OF GRINDING WHEELS

Every grinding wheel has two components, the *abrasive* which does the actual cutting and the *bond* which supports the abrasive grains while they cut. The arrangement of these two components gives a definite characteristic known as *structure* to the wheel (Fig. 93-3).

1. *Type of abrasive.* The ideal abrasive for grinding is one which has the ability to fracture when a serious dullness is reached. It should also exhibit a high resistance to point wear. There are two types of manufactured abrasives used in the production of wheels, *silicon carbide* and *aluminum oxide*. Silicon carbide is used for grinding materials of low tensile

strength such as aluminum, copper, ceramics, and cast iron. Aluminum oxide is for materials of high tensile strength such as heat-treated parts, all kinds of steels, and alloys of tough bronze.

2. *Grain*. Grain size selected is determined by the amount of material to be removed, the kind

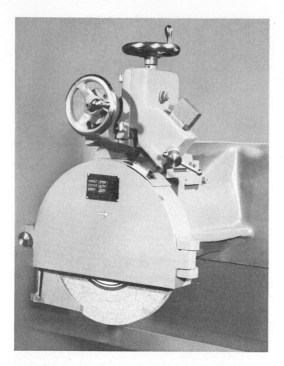

Fig. 93-1. To assure good grinding results, it is important to select the correct kind of wheel.

Fig. 93-2. An enlargement showing metal chips produced by a grinding wheel.

Fig. 93-3. Standard marking system for wheels.

STANDARD MARKING SYSTEM

SEQUENCE PREFIX	1 ABRASIVE TYPE	2 GRAIN SIZE	3 GRADE	4 STRUCTURE	5 BOND TYPE	6 MANUFACTURER'S RECORD
51	A	36	L	5	V	23

MANUFACTURER'S SYMBOL INDICATING EXACT KIND OF ABRA-SIVE (USE OPTIONAL)

MANUFACTURER'S PRIVATE MARKING TO IDENTIFY WHEEL

(USE OPTIONAL)

COARSE	MEDIUM	FINE	VERY FINE
10	30	70	220
12	36	80	240
14	46	90	280
16	54	100	320
20	60	120	400
24		150	500
		180	600

DENSE TO OPEN
1	9
2	10
3	11
4	12
5	13
6	14
7	15
8	ETC.

(USE OPTIONAL)

V—VITRIFIED
S—SILICATE
R—RUBBER
B—RESINOID
E—SHELLAC
O—OXYCHLORIDE

ALUMINUM OXIDE—A

SILICON CARBIDE—C

SOFT   MEDIUM   HARD

A B C D E F G H I J K L M N O P Q R S T U V W X Y Z

GRADE SCALE

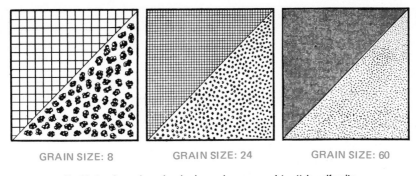

GRAIN SIZE: 8   GRAIN SIZE: 24   GRAIN SIZE: 60

Fig. 93-4. Comparison of grain sizes and screens used to attain uniformity.

of finish needed, and the kind of workpiece to be ground. Common grain sizes range from coarse to very fine. Grain sizes from 6 to 24 are classed *coarse;* from 30 to 60, *medium;* from 70 to 180, *fine;* and from 220 to 600, *very fine.* Fine grain sizes are used for fine-finish and small-diameter workpieces. Coarse grains are used for heavy cuts and workpieces of larger diameters.

Grain sizes are determined by the size of the screen opening through which they can be sifted. For example, 30-grit size will pass through a screen with 27 openings per inch and will be held on a screen having 33 openings per inch. The most common grit sizes are in the range of 24 to 80 (Fig. 93-4).

3. *Bond.* This refers to the material and process used to hold the abrasive grains together. There are five kinds of adhesives used, vitrified, silicate, shellac, rubber, and resinoid. About 75 percent of all wheels have a *vitrified* bond. This type of bond results when clay is baked in a kiln at a high temperature. In the kiln, the clay, which is mixed with abrasive grains, fuses into molten glass. On cooling, the glass cements the abrasive grains together. A vitrified bond is strong and porous. It is not affected by water, acid, or oils.

4. *Grade.* Grade is determined by the strength of the bond which holds the abrasive grains together. It is used to denote the relative hardness of the wheel. If the grains break away easily, it is a soft grade wheel. The more bonding material in the wheel, the harder the grade; less material indicates a soft grade. Softer wheel grades make for rapid cutting and are used for

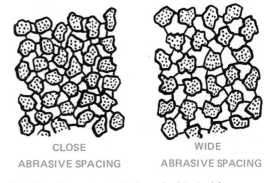

CLOSE   WIDE
ABRASIVE SPACING   ABRASIVE SPACING

Fig. 93-5. The spacing of abrasive grains (structure) is designated by a number. When the grains are close together relative to their size, the wheel has a dense structure.

hard materials and larger diameters. Harder wheel grades are for softer workpieces, for smaller diameters, and for grinding certain kinds of shapes. In wheel markings, the grade letters range from A to Z in the order of increasing hardness.

5. *Structure.* This refers to the way in which the abrasive grains are distributed through the bond (Fig. 93-5). Grain spacing may be close (dense), medium, or open (wide).

Grinding-wheel manufacturers have agreed on a standard marking system to include the above five factors (see Fig. 93-3). With this system it is easy to identify a wheel. For example, a marking "51A36-L5V23" means that the wheel

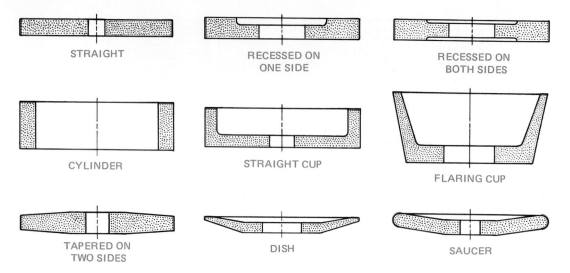

STRAIGHT   **RECESSED ON ONE SIDE**   **RECESSED ON BOTH SIDES**

CYLINDER   **STRAIGHT CUP**   **FLARING CUP**

TAPERED ON TWO SIDES   **DISH**   **SAUCER**

Fig. 93-6. Nine shapes of grinding wheels. The straight wheel is the most common.

is aluminum oxide abrasive, 36-grain size (medium), L grade (medium), No. 5 structure number, and vitrified bond (V). The 51 at the start and the 23 at the end refer to the manufacturer's catalogue records. These numbers may not be shown on all grinding wheels.

SHAPES AND FACES OF GRINDING WHEELS

Wheels are made in nine standard shapes and twelve standard faces (Figs. 93-6 and 93-7). These are used to do all kinds of grinding on all types of grinding machines. In addition to the standard wheel faces, there are many shapes of mounted points that are used for internal grinding and for grinding with a portable grinding tool or flexible shaft.

WHEEL SELECTION

The seven factors to consider when selecting a grinding wheel are:

1. *The material to be ground and its hardness.* This affects the selection of the abrasive. Use aluminum-oxide abrasives for steel and steel alloys. Use silicon-oxide abrasives for cast iron, nonferrous, and nonmetallic materials.

a. Use a fine grit for hard, brittle materials and coarse grit for soft, ductile materials.

b. The *grade* should be hard for easily penetrated materials and soft for hard materials.

2. *The amount of stock to be removed and the finish required.* This affects the choice of grit size.

a. Use a coarse grit for rapid stock removal as in rough grinding.

b. Use a fine grit for high finish.

c. Use a vitrified bond for fast cutting and commercial finish.

d. Use resinoid, rubber, and shellac for highest finish.

3. *Whether the grinding is done wet or dry.* This affects the choice of the grade. Wet grinding, as a rule, permits use of wheels at least one grade harder than for dry grinding without danger of burning the workpiece.

4. *The wheel speed.* This affects the choice of the bond. Standard vitrified wheels should not be used for speeds over 6,500 surface feet per minute (sfpm). Standard organic bonded wheels (resinoid, rubber, or shellac) are used for most applications over 6,500 sfpm.

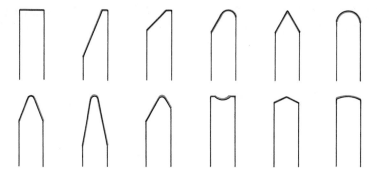

Fig. 93-7. Standard grinding wheel faces.

5. *The area of grinding contact.* This affects the choice grit size. The smaller the area of contact, the harder the wheel should be.

    a. Use coarse grit for large area of contact.

    b. Use fine grit for small area of contact.

6. *The severity of the grinding operation.* This affects the choice of abrasive.

    a. Use a tough abrasive for grinding steel and steel alloys under severe conditions.

    b. Use a mild abrasive for light grinding on hard steels.

    c. Use an intermediate abrasive for jobs of average severity.

7. *The horsepower of the machine.* This affects the choice of grade. Harder grades of wheels are used on the higher horsepower machines.

SAFETY

Grinding wheels must be handled, mounted, and used carefully. Be sure to follow these basic instructions.

Mounting the Wheel

1. Select the correct wheel for your operation. *Ring* the wheel to be sure it is not cracked (Fig. 93-8).

2. Never exceed maximum safe speed established for each wheel. Be sure machine speed is not excessive.

Fig. 93-8. Make the "ring" test before installing the grinding wheel. Suspend the wheel from your index finger. Tap it gently with a nonmetallic tool such as a screwdriver or mallet handle. A sound wheel will give a clear ring. If cracked, there is a dead sound.

3. Never alter the hole in the wheel or force the wheel on the spindle.

4. Use clean, recessed matching flanges that are at least one-third the wheel diameter.

5. Place one clean, smooth blotter under each flange.

6. Tighten the nut only enough to hold the wheel firmly.

CAUTION

. Adjust the wheel guard and put on safety glasses before starting.

Using the Wheel

1. Adjust the dust hood and coolant nozzle. On a bench or floor grinder, keep the work rest adjusted within $\frac{1}{8}$ in. of the wheel face.

2. Stand aside and allow the wheel to run idle a full minute before starting to grind.

3. True the wheel if necessary.

4. Make grinding contact without bumping or impact.

5. Grind only on the face of a straight wheel. *Use disk wheels for side grinding.* Light side grinding is permitted on a cup or saucer wheel.

6. Never force the grinding. The motor should not slow noticeably, and the workpiece should not get hot.

7. Protect the wheel when not in use. Store it safely when it is removed from the grinding machine.

UNIT 94. Surface Grinder

The surface grinder produces finished flat surfaces by means of a revolving abrasive wheel (Fig. 94–1). The most common type has a rectangular worktable that moves back and forth (reciprocates) under the abrasive wheel. The wheel is mounted on a horizontal spindle. The machine may be operated manually or with mechanical-hydraulic controls. Workpieces are usually held on a magnetic table (Fig. 94–2).

SIZE

The size of a surface grinder is determined according to its capacity to grind a workpiece (Fig. 94–3). For example, a 6 × 18-in. machine will have a cross-feed of 6 in. and a table that travels longitudinally a distance of at least 18 in. The vertical distance from the top of the table to the bottom of the standard wheel is also a determining factor.

PARTS

The major parts of a surface grinder are shown in Fig. 94–4. The *table* is mounted on a *saddle* and can be moved in and out (cross-feed) and back and forth (longitudinal feed). The table top is machined with T slots for fastening a chuck, vise, or any other work-holding device. Power longitudinal feed is available on most machines. Some machines are equipped with power cross-feed as well. The *wheel head* provides support for the grinding-wheel spindle and its bearings.

Three handwheels are used to control the grinder's movements (Fig. 94–5). The *elevating handwheel* moves the grinding wheel vertically (up or down) and controls the depth of cut. The *cross-feed handwheel* moves the table in and out (transverse movement). On some models there is a cross-feed direction control lever for power operation of the cross-feed. The *table handwheel* is used to move the table longitudinally (back and forth) by hand. The power-feed table handle, or lever, engages the power feed.

GRINDING CONDITIONS

Table Speeds. Table speeds may range up to 150 surface feet per minute (sfpm). In general, two

Fig. 94–1. Surface grinding a fine finish on a hard material.

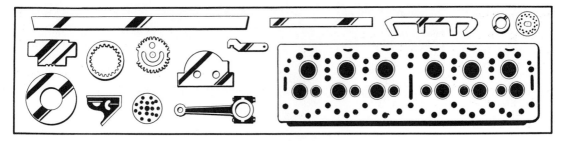

Fig. 94-2. Examples of the kinds of parts that can be ground on a surface grinder.

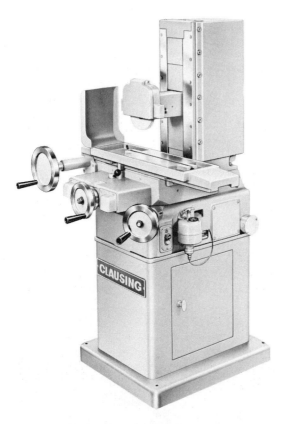

Fig. 94-3. A small dry-type surface grinder equipped with power table feed.

speed ranges are used, under 35 sfpm and over 35 sfpm. Machines operating in the latter range are known as *high reciprocation machines.*

Cross-feed. Feed is determined by the width of the wheel and the finish desired. Cross-feed should not exceed one-half the wheel face per revolution. The lower the cross-feed for any given width of wheel face, the greater the depth of cut that can be taken. When producing extremely high finishes, lower than average cross-feeds should be used.

Infeed. Infeed or depth of cut is controlled by the amount of metal to be removed, the finish desired, and the power and rigidity of the grinding machine. Depth of cut will determine, to a great extent, the pressures that are built up between wheel and work during the grinding operation. High working pressure creates heat and can result in distortion of the workpiece and/or burning. Thin stock requires reduced infeeds and lighter cuts. Dry grinding operations necessitate lighter cuts than if the operation were performed wet.

Coolants. Surface grinding operations are performed dry or with coolants (Fig. 94-6). Coolants are used to dissipate the heat generated during the grinding operation (Fig. 94-7A).

Particular attention must be given to the direction and flow of the coolant. The nozzle of the coolant pipe should be adjusted so that coolant is directed into the contact area between the wheel and the workpiece (Fig. 94-7B).

Wheel Speeds. Wheel speeds, for satisfactory operation on machines with table speeds of approximately 35 sfpm, should range from 4,500 to 5,500 sfpm. Most grinders have a fixed spindle speed of between 2,000 and 3,000 revolutions per minute (rpm). Wheel speed in sfpm can be determined using the following formula:

Wheel speed = rpm of spindle
$\times$ circumference of wheel (in feet).

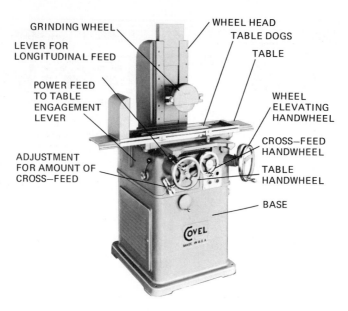

GRINDING WHEEL

LEVER FOR
LONGITUDINAL FEED

POWER FEED
TO TABLE
ENGAGEMENT
LEVER

ADJUSTMENT
FOR AMOUNT OF
CROSS—FEED

WHEEL HEAD
TABLE DOGS

TABLE

WHEEL
ELEVATING
HANDWHEEL

CROSS—FEED
HANDWHEEL

TABLE
HANDWHEEL

BASE

Fig. 94-4. Parts of a surface grinder.

Fig. 94-5. This cross-feed handwheel has graduations of 0.0002 in.

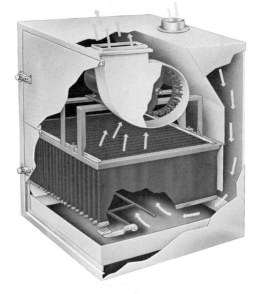

Fig. 94-6. An exhaust attachment should be used when grinding without a coolant. It removes grit and dust from the grinding operation and returns clean air.

WORK-HOLDING DEVICES

Many of the work-holding devices used on the surface grinder are the same as those described for the drill press, shaper, and milling machine (Fig. 94-8). Most grinders, however, are equipped with either a *permanent magnet* or *electromagnet-type chuck*. The permanent magnet chuck uses permanent magnets to hold the work firmly on the table. The electromagnetic

chuck is designed so that its magnetism can be turned on and off by means of a switch. These operate on either 110 or 220 volts (V) and must be energized with direct current. A magnetic

Fig. 94-7. The coolant is directed between the cutting wheel and the workpiece.

Fig. 94-8. Note the number of identical parts that can be held on the magnetic chuck.

V-block that can be used to hold round or irregular-shaped pieces is also available. Nonmagnetic materials such as brass, copper, or aluminum can be held on a magnetic chuck by placing them between two magnetic materials.

When mounting a magnetic chuck, make sure that its bottom surface is aligned with the machine table. Otherwise, it may distort the table's surface. To allow for expansion and contraction, the chuck should be rigidly held on one end only. (Its other end should be clamped tightly to the table.)

GRINDING WHEELS

Select a wheel of the correct grain size, grain structure, and bond. Aluminum-oxide wheels are used for grinding carbon steel, alloy steel, and high-speed steel. Silicon-carbide wheels are used primarily for cast iron, brass, bronze, and aluminum.

Before mounting the wheel, make sure that it is balanced and not defective. Mount it on the spindle as follows.

A. Open the guard and remove the old wheel (Fig. 94-9).

B. Place the inner flange against the shoulder of the spindle. Place a blotter-paper washer against the flange.

C. Slip the grinding wheel on the spindle. Make sure the hole in the wheel fits the spindle properly. Replace the washer, outer flange, and nut (Fig. 94-10).

D. Tighten the nut firmly, but not so much that you set up excessive strain in the wheel.

WHEEL TRUING

The wheel on a surface grinder may be dressed as follows.

Place a diamond wheel dresser on the chuck (Fig. 94-11). Adjust the table to bring the diamond slightly to the left of center under the wheel. Lower the spindle to a point where the high spots of the grinding wheel barely contact the diamond. By means of the hydraulic crossfeed, pass the diamond back and forth across the face of the wheel. Now use the elevating

Fig. 94-9. Grinding wheel and guard.

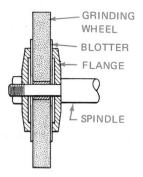

GRINDING WHEEL
BLOTTER
FLANGE
SPINDLE

Fig. 94-10. A correctly mounted wheel has a flange on either side. The two flanges are of equal diameter and must be recessed for proper support.

Fig. 94-11. Truing a grinding wheel for flat surface grinding.

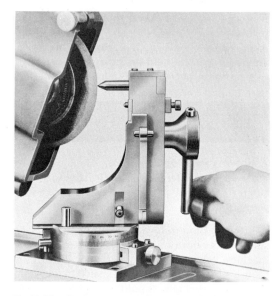

Fig. 94-12. Shaping a convex surface on the wheel. This kind of attachment is needed when doing form grinding on the surface grinder.

mechanism to feed the wheel down a distance of approximately 0.001 in. Pass the diamond completely across and beyond the edges of the wheel. Repeat the operation until the sound of the wheel in contact with the diamond indicates that the face of the wheel is true. A special wheel-dressing attachment is available when it is necessary to shape the wheel for form grinding (Fig. 94-12).

GRINDING THE WORKPIECE

1. Wipe the magnetic chuck clean.

2. Center the workpiece on the chuck, and turn on the switch to hold it in place with magnetism.

3. Adjust the table reverse dogs so the wheel will clear the ends of the workpiece by 2 in.

4. If coolant is used, turn it on at this time. If dry grinding, start the dust collector.

5. Set the speed control.

6. Adjust the rate of table feed.

7. Turn on the power.

8. Move the table in by hand feed until the workpiece is under the grinding wheel.

9. Turn on the power table feed (table control knob).

10. Turn the wheel down until it is near the work surface. Move the table cross-feed as you continue to feed the wheel down. Stop when it just touches the workpiece. This should be the highest spot on the work surface. To make sure, feed the work entirely under the wheel. Then feed the wheel down 0.002 or 0.003 in. and continue the grinding (Fig. 94-13).

11. Turn the cross-feed out about one-fourth the width of the grinding wheel just as the table changes direction.

12. Grind the entire surface. Measure the height.

13. Dress the wheel. For a high finish, the last grinding should not remove more than 0.001 in.

Fig. 94-13. The operator is carefully adjusting the wheel to grind a slot in this workpiece.

14. A method of grinding to finish size in one pass is as follows. Position one edge of the work under the wheel. Feed the wheel to the work until sparks appear. Then set the elevating dial according to the amount of stock to be removed.

UNIT 95. Cylindrical Grinding

Many machine shops use a small- or medium-size universal cylindrical grinder for external and internal grinding (Fig. 95-1). A universal grinder has several features that make it very versatile. For example, its table can be adjusted at an angle for grinding a taper (Fig. 95-2). Its headstock spindle can also be swiveled to do a variety of grinding operations. During these operations, the workpiece can be held in a chuck or spindle or between centers.

WHEEL SPEED

The grinding wheel is held on a rotating shaft or spindle. The speed at which this spindle revolves is indicated in revolutions per minute (rpm).

Spindle speed must not be confused with wheel speed. *Wheel speed* is a measure of how far one abrasive grain on the surface of a grinding wheel will travel in a given period of time. In other words, wheel speed is equal to the distance traveled in one minute by any point on a wheel. Wheel speed is indicated in surface feet per minute (sfpm).

Calculating Wheel Speed. To find the surface speed of the wheel in feet per minute (fpm), multiply the wheel's circumference (in feet) by the number of revolutions the wheel makes per minute (rpm).

Wheel speed (sfpm)
= diameter of the wheel (in inches)
$$\times \frac{3.1416 \times \text{spindle speed (rpm)}}{12}$$

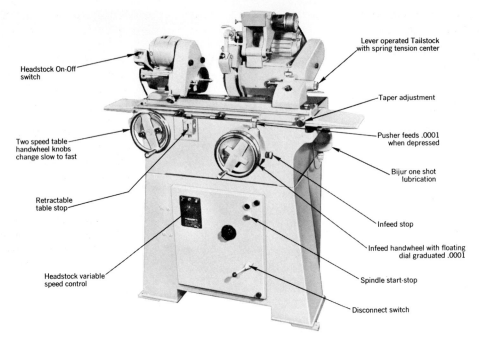

Fig. 95-1. Parts of a universal cylindrical grinder.

Headstock On-Off switch

Two speed table handwheel knobs change slow to fast

Retractable table stop

Headstock variable speed control

Lever operated Tailstock with spring tension center

Taper adjustment

Pusher feeds .0001 when depressed

Bijur one shot lubrication

Infeed stop

Infeed handwheel with floating dial graduated .0001

Spindle start-stop

Disconnect switch

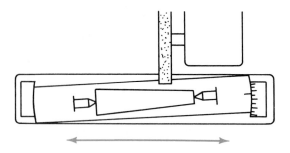

Fig. 95-2. The worktable moves back and forth while the grinding wheel remains in a fixed position. The worktable can also be swiveled for grinding tapers.

WORK SPEED

Work speed refers to speed at which the workpiece is moving. It is determined by the diameter of the workpiece and the rate at which it revolves (rpm). Work speed is indicated in surface feet per minute.

RATE OF TRAVERSE

The speed at which the grinding wheel moves across the workpiece is called the *rate of tra-*

verse. Many smaller machines have only two rates of traverse—slow and fast.

INFEED

Infeed refers to the movement of the grinding wheel in a plane perpendicular to and into the surface of the work being ground. The amount of infeed determines the depth of cut.

Fig. 95-3. The workpiece can be held between centers to do cylindrical grinding. Note the similarity to turning on the lathe. The grinding wheel replaces the cutting tool.

GRINDING ON A PRECISION CYLINDRICAL GRINDER

Mounting the Workpiece. The workpiece is mounted on a cylindrical grinder in much the same way as it would be on a lathe. For example, it can be held between centers (Fig. 95-3) or in a chuck (Fig. 95-4). The workpiece can also be placed directly in the machine's spindle V (Fig. 95-5).

Adjusting the Table. The table has a taper attachment with a graduated scale at either end. The scale at the right is graduated in degrees, and the scale at the left is in inches per foot. For straight grinding, the table should be set at zero degrees (°).

Checking the Headstock. The headstock is powered by a direct current motor having a variable-speed control. Speeds can be varied from 70 to 400 rpm. The speed selected, together with the diameter of the work being ground, will determine the actual work speed (in sfpm). For example, if the headstock is set at 70 rpm and the diameter of the workpiece is 3 in., then the work speed will be equal to approximately 55 sfpm. Generally, steel and other hardened materials are ground at the slower work speeds, and nonferrous alloys and soft metals are ground at the higher work speeds. Also, work speeds for rough grinding work may be higher than for finish grinding. Note too that low work speeds will permit increased depth of cut or infeed.

Adjusting Rate of Traverse. The traverse speed of a table should be in proportion to the width of the wheel and the finish desired. Use a slow table speed for the fine finishes and a faster table feed for roughing cuts. For rapid stock removal, table traverse should be about three-fourths of the wheel width for each revolution of the work. Also, set table dogs so that no more than one-third of the wheel runs off the work.

Adjusting the Infeed. The infeed handwheel is used to control the depth of cut. Dry grinding should be done with light cuts. If coolants are used, slightly heavier cuts can be taken (Fig. 95-6). If a coolant is used, make sure that its flow is directed between the wheel and workpiece. Never apply so much pressure that the workpiece becomes overheated and distorted.

INTERNAL GRINDING

An internal grinding attachment may be permanently mounted on the cylindrical grinding machine (Fig. 95-7). Hinged brackets are used to hold its direct motor-driven spindle. A clamp is used to lock the spindle in position for internal grinding. The spindle speed of the internal grinding unit can be adjusted to obtain a wide variety of work speeds (Fig. 95-8).

Fig. 95-4. This workpiece is held in a three-jaw chuck.

Fig. 95-5. The lathe center is held directly in the spindle by a reducing sleeve.

Fig. 95-6. A good supply of coolant will allow grinding at higher speeds with a greater depth of cut.

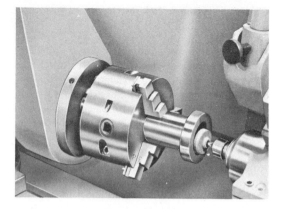

Fig. 95-8. A setup for internal grinding.

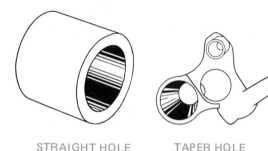

STRAIGHT HOLE   TAPER HOLE

Fig. 95-7. Both straight and tapered holes can be internally ground.

EXTERNAL GRINDING ON THE LATHE

A tool post grinder can be used for both external and internal grinding on the lathe (Fig. 95-9).

Mounting the Grinder. Remove the tool post. Clean both the grinder base and tool post slot, then clamp the grinder in the slot. Remove the grinder belt guard and loosen the clamp on the elevating screw. Align the center of the grinder spindle with the lathe tailstock center by adjusting the elevating screw. Retighten the clamp on the elevating screw and replace the belt guard.

When grinding a surface parallel to the lathe center line, set the compound rest at zero degrees and feed the carriage back and forth by hand or with the power feed. When grinding at an angle, the compound rest is set at the proper angle and the grinder is fed back and forth with the compound-rest feed. A taper attachment can be used to simplify taper grinding.

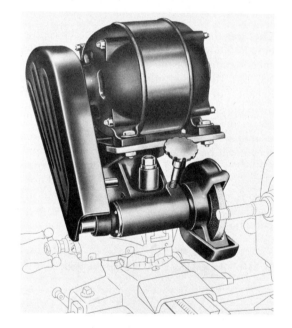

Fig. 95-9. The tool post grinder is a valuable accessory for a machine shop that is not equipped with a universal cylindrical grinder.

Remember, the workpiece must always turn in a direction opposite to that of the grinding wheel at the point of contact.

Protecting the Lathe. Grinding dust is a mixture of abrasive dust and fine particles of steel. This dust is extremely harmful when allowed to fall and remain on the lathe bed ways and cross slide.

Always cover the bed ways and the cross slide during grinding operations.

Paper, oilcloth, or canvas make a good cover. If a cloth is used, make sure it is closely woven. After the grinding operation, clean the bed ways and carriage dovetails thoroughly. Then apply plenty of clean oil (Fig. 95–10). A pan of oil or water placed directly under the grinding wheel can also be used to catch most of the abrasive dust.

Dressing the Grinding Wheel. After the grinder has been mounted in position and the lathe properly protected, the grinding wheel should be dressed. To do this, a dressing tool is mounted in a holder and clamped to the lathe bed (Fig. 95–11). The wheel is then moved *slowly* across the diamond with the same feed as will be used in the grinding operation. Light cuts are taken as the wheel is moved back and forth. This continues until the diamond cuts evenly and the glazed surface has been removed from the wheel. For a fine, accurate finish, the grinding wheel must be dressed before every operation and while it is in the exact position in which it will be used.

Fig. 95–10. Make sure you cover as much of the lathe as possible in order to keep abrasive dust off the ways.

Adjusting Speeds and Direction of Rotation. Step pulleys provide the grinder with two spindle speeds. Always use the lower speed for external grinding and the higher speed for internal grinding.

In grinding operations, the work must turn in a direction opposite that of the grinding wheel. The rotation of the lathe spindle must be clockwise (backward) for external grinding and counterclockwise (forward) for internal grinding (Fig. 95–12). A dependable reversing switch is essential for grinding and polishing operations.

Grinding the Workpiece. Adjust the lathe to a slow speed and medium feed. Switch on the power and adjust the cross-feed until the grinding wheel just touches the surface of the workpiece. Too fast or heavy a cut will result in overheating and possible warpage of the workpiece. Continue to grind until the workpiece is 0.001 to 0.002 in. oversize. Before making the last cut, be sure to dress the grinding wheel. Often a last pass is taken without advancing the feed.

Grinding 60° Lathe Centers. Dress the grinding wheel with the compound rest set at the exact angle required. Fasten the center in the lathe spindle. A slow spindle speed should be used for this operation. Be sure the spindle is turning in a direction opposite that of the grinding wheel. Feed up to the center with the carriage handwheel and lock the carriage in position.

Fig. 95–11. In truing a grinding wheel the diamond dresser should be mounted at a 10 to 15° angle to the wheel face (drag angle). The angle must point in the same direction the grinding wheel travels. Take light cuts of about 0.001 in. at each pass.

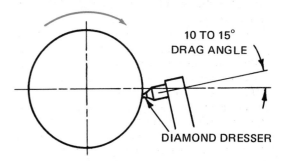

10 TO 15°
DRAG ANGLE

DIAMOND DRESSER

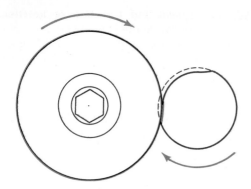

Fig. 95-12. The workpiece and grinding wheel must turn in opposite directions at the point of contact.

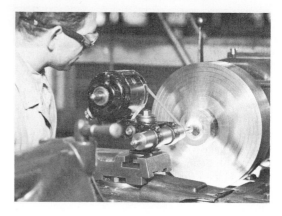

Fig. 95-14. Internal grinding on the lathe.

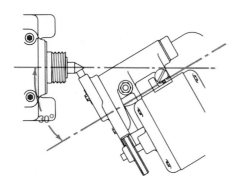

Fig. 95-13. Grinding a lathe center.

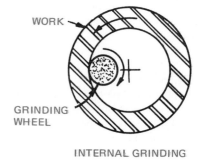

INTERNAL GRINDING

Fig. 95-15. In internal grinding, the workpiece turns counterclockwise, as in turning on a lathe. The grinding wheel turns clockwise.

Take light cuts using the compound rest to feed the wheel slowly across the lathe center (Fig. 95-13).

INTERNAL GRINDING ON THE LATHE

Internal grinding can be done on the lathe using a tool post grinder (Fig. 95-14).

A quill is used to hold the grinding wheel for internal work. It is threaded and tapered to fit inside the grinder spindle after the external wheel has been removed. The grinding wheel itself should be dressed before using.

It is necessary to use slow feeds and to take light cuts during internal grinding operations. After the last cut has been completed, it is common practice to allow the wheel to pass back and forth across the workpiece without advancing the feed. This is called *sparking out* and indicates whether or not the cut is complete. When no more sparks can be seen, the wheel is no longer cutting (Fig. 95-15).

UNIT 96. Discussion Topics and Problems

1. Why is grinding so important in modern production?

2. Describe how grinding shapes and finishes a metal surface.

3. What are the six kinds of grinding?

4. What is the difference between a plain grinding machine and a centerless grinding machine?

5. Describe in detail how an internal grinder operates.

6. What operations can be done on a universal grinder?

7. What kind of shops use tool and cutter grinders?

8. Define a grinding wheel.

9. Describe the difference between grinding and abrasive machining.

10. What kind of abrasive would be used to grind soft brass? Alloy steel? Give the reasons for your choices.

11. What kind of bond is used in about 75 percent of the grinding wheels?

12. Describe this wheel: C-46M-3V.

13. Name the parts of a surface grinder.

14. What precaution must be taken in mounting a wheel?

15. What is the most common kind of chuck used to hold workpieces on the surface grinder?

16. Describe how a surface grinder is used.

17. What kind of grinding can be done on the lathe?

18. What are the safety precautions you must take when using the grinding machine?

SECTION 10

MATERIALS

UNIT 97. Metals and Alloys

Metals are one of nature's most common elements (Fig. 97–1). Iron, copper, and aluminum are some examples. An *alloy* is a mixture of two or more metals. Usually it consists of a *base* metal (the largest part of the alloy) and a smaller amount of other metals. Brass, for instance, is an alloy of copper (the base metal) and zinc. Steel is an alloy of iron and carbon. In the machine shop, metals and alloys are usually called *metals*. Metals are divided into two groups, the *ferrous,* which contain a large percentage of iron, and the *nonferrous,* which contain no iron.

PROPERTIES OF METAL

The most important characteristics of metal are its *mechanical* properties, *magnetic* properties, and *chemical* properties.

Mechanical Properties. Mechanical properties are the characteristic responses of a material to applied forces. These properties fall into five broad categories, strength, hardness, elasticity, ductility, and toughness.

1. *Strength* is the ability of a material to resist applied forces. Bridge girders, elevator cables, and building beams all must have this property.

2. *Hardness* is the ability of a material to resist penetration and abrasion. Cutting tools, files, and drills must resist abrasion, or wear. Armor plate, crushing machinery, and metal rolls for steel mills all must resist penetration.

3. *Elasticity* is the ability to spring back to original shape. Auto bumpers and all springs should have this quality.

4. *Ductility* is the ability to undergo permanent changes of shape without rupturing. Our modern, deep-formed auto bodies and fenders, washing machines, and other stamped and formed products must have this property.

5. *Toughness* is the ability to absorb mechanically applied energy. Strength and ductility determine a material's toughness. Toughness is needed in railroad cars, automobile axles, hammers, rails, and similar products.

Fig. 97-1. This giant ladle is "charging" molten iron into one of the basic oxygen furnaces. After the vessel has been charged with scrap metal and molten iron, pure oxygen is blown into the charge to refine it into quality steel.

Magnetic Properties. Magnetic properties of metal are those which have to do with reactions to magnetic or electrical forces. Some metals are attracted by magnets, some are not. Certain high-carbon and alloy steels retain magnetism and are used to make permanent magnets. The magnetic properties of a metal often determine whether or not the metal can be used in a particular situation.

Chemical Properties. Chemical properties of metal pertain to its resistance to corrosion and oxidation. The melting temperature of a metal also falls into this category. Chemical properties often determine a metal's suitability for a specific purpose.

IRON AND STEEL

Iron is one of the basic elements in manufacturing. Steel is an alloy of iron and carbon. Steels are grouped as *carbon* steels, *alloy* steels, etc. Carbon steels are classified according to the amount of carbon by weight they contain. The

amount of carbon is given in *points* (100 points equal 1 percent) or as a *percentage*. Alloy steels include, in addition to iron and carbon, one or more other elements. These are added in order to impart a wanted quality to the metal.

Steels are classified in two ways, by the way they are made and by what they contain.

HOW STEEL IS MANUFACTURED

Steel production is one of the largest and most important industries in the United States. More than 3 billion tons of steel have been produced in this country in the past 100 years.

The iron ore used to make steel comes from open-pit and underground mines. It is moved by boat and rail to steelmaking centers located chiefly in Indiana, Ohio, and Pennsylvania. At these centers, the iron ore is transformed into a variety of kinds and grades of steel (Fig. 97-2).

Blast Furnace. The blast furnace is basically a huge steel shell, lined with firebrick. Some are almost as high as a ten-story building.

Ore processing begins in the blast furnace. A mixture of iron ore, coke, and limestone is first brought to the top of the furnace and dumped into it. This mixture is called the *charge*. Air that has been dried and heated to about 1250°F is then blown into the furnace near its base. As the coke burns in this air, it generates heat and gases which melt the charge. Impurities in the charge are absorbed by the limestone and form a substance known as *slag*. The temperature at the base of the furnace rises to approximately 3500°F and the iron and slag in this area become liquified. Since molten slag is lighter than the molten iron, it floats on top of the iron.

Tapping or removing the molten iron from the furnace is done every 4 or 5 hours. From 150 to 300 tons of pig iron (the type of iron produced in the blast furnace) can be drawn off at a time. It is interesting to note that it takes almost 2 tons of ore, 1 ton of coke, nearly $\frac{1}{2}$ ton of limestone, and a little less than 4 tons of air to make just 1 ton of pig iron.

PURIFYING PROCESSES

The molten pig iron that is tapped from the blast furnace still contains some impurities. To change

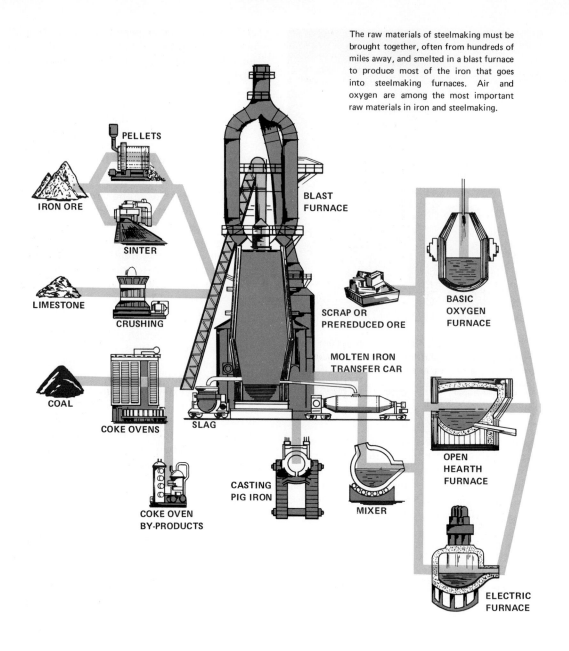

The raw materials of steelmaking must be brought together, often from hundreds of miles away, and smelted in a blast furnace to produce most of the iron that goes into steelmaking furnaces. Air and oxygen are among the most important raw materials in iron and steelmaking.

PELLETS

IRON ORE

SINTER

LIMESTONE

CRUSHING

COAL

COKE OVENS

SLAG

COKE OVEN BY-PRODUCTS

CASTING PIG IRON

BLAST FURNACE

SCRAP OR PREREDUCED ORE

MOLTEN IRON TRANSFER CAR

MIXER

BASIC OXYGEN FURNACE

OPEN HEARTH FURNACE

ELECTRIC FURNACE

Fig. 97-2. A simplified flow chart illustrating how steel is made. Each stop along the route from raw materials to mill products contained in this chart can itself be charted. From this overall view, one major point emerges: Many operations—involving much equipment and large numbers of men—are required to produce civilization's principal and least expensive metal.

Molten steel must solidify before it can be made into finished products by the industry's rolling mills and forging presses. The metal is usually formed first at high temperature, after which it may be cold-formed into additional products.

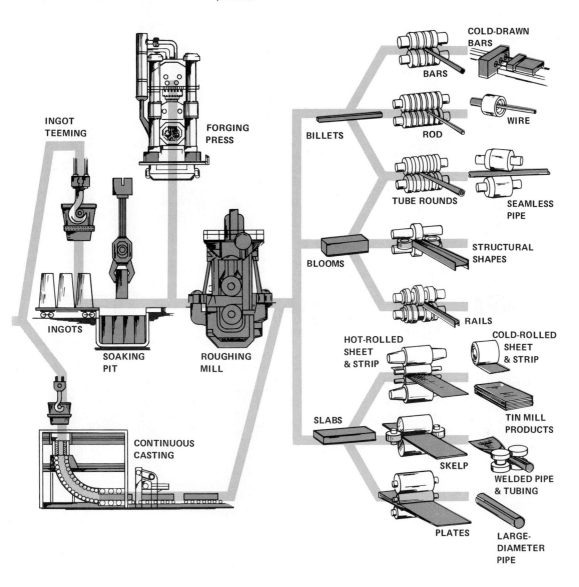

INGOT
TEEMING

FORGING
PRESS

INGOTS

SOAKING
PIT

ROUGHING
MILL

CONTINUOUS
CASTING

BILLETS

BLOOMS

SLABS

BARS

COLD-DRAWN
BARS

ROD

WIRE

TUBE ROUNDS

SEAMLESS
PIPE

STRUCTURAL
SHAPES

RAILS

HOT-ROLLED
SHEET
& STRIP

COLD-ROLLED
SHEET
& STRIP

TIN MILL
PRODUCTS

SKELP

WELDED PIPE
& TUBING

PLATES

LARGE-
DIAMETER
PIPE

pig iron into steel, these impurities must be removed. This is done in one of three kinds of furnaces: open-hearth, basic-oxygen, or electric.

Open-hearth Furnace. This furnace is used to convert molten pig iron, iron ore, and scrap iron into steel. Between 8 and 12 hours of intense heat are required before purified molten steel can be run from the furnace into a ladle.

Basic-oxygen Furnace. In this furnace, 80 tons of scrap and molten iron are changed into steel in just 40 to 60 minutes. The furnace is first tipped on its side and charged with molten iron and iron scrap. It is then rotated into an upright position. Oxygen, blown into the furnace at high speed, burns out the impurities. Limestone, converted into burnt lime, is also added at the same time as the oxygen.

Electric Furnace. This furnace is used to produce high grade carbon and alloy steels. Powerful electric currents are sent through three large rods (electrodes) that pass through the top of the furnace. When sparks from these electrodes strike the iron charge, they generate an intense heat. This heat is sufficient to melt the charge and burn out any impurities.

FROM MOLTEN TO FINISHED FORM

Teeming Ingots. The ladle of freshly made steel is held by a crane above a row of ingot molds. A valve in the bottom of the ladle is opened and the steel flows into each mold, filling it to the top (Fig. 97–3).

Stripping Ingots. After the liquid steel has solidified, the molds are lifted or stripped off. The first solid form of steel is called an *ingot*.

Soaking Pits. The ingots are placed in pits and *soaked* in heat until brought to a uniform rolling temperature (Fig. 97–4).

Rolling Mills. White-hot steel is fairly soft and can be squeezed into various shapes by passing it through a rolling mill. The mill contains powerful steel rolls, which work somewhat like a clothes wringer (Fig. 97–5). Ingots first go to a semifinishing mill, where they are rolled into blooms, slabs, and billets. These three semi-

Fig. 97–3. Steel is poured or "teemed" from the ladle into the ingot mold where it solidifies.

Fig. 97–4. This ingot is being hoisted from the soaking pit. The ingot has been heated in the soaking pit for several hours to bring the steel up to rolling temperature.

Fig. 97-5. Ingots are rolled into slabs.

finished shapes then go to finishing mills where they are formed into plate, sheet, strip, rails, rods, bars, and other shapes.

HOW STEELS ARE CLASSIFIED

Steels can be classified into five groups, carbon, alloy, high-strength low alloy, stainless, and tool-and-die. Here are some things you should know about steels.

1. *Carbon steel*

    a. Low-carbon steel contains from 0.04 to 0.30 percent of carbon (4 to 30 points). This steel does not contain enough carbon to be hardened. It can be heat-treated, however. It is used for projects and products in which an easily worked metal is needed. These are sometimes called *soft* or *mild steels.* Low-carbon steel is easily welded, machined, and formed.

    b. Medium-carbon steel has from 0.30 to 0.60 percent of carbon. A ton of medium-carbon steel contains 60 to 120 pounds of carbon. It is used for many standard machine parts such as bolts, nuts, and screws. It is also used for projects such as hammer heads and clamp parts that will be case-hardened.

    c. High-carbon steel contains from 0.60 to 1.70 percent of carbon. It is used for items that must be hardened and tempered. High-carbon steel is sometimes called *carbon tool steel.*

2. *Alloy steels.* The automobile contains about 100 different kinds of alloy steel. Each alloy steel has a "personality" all its own. Most steels contain some carbon, phosphorus, sulfur, and silicon. Alloy steels also contain very small quantities of other elements. Each alloy steel has special properties which are determined by the amount of these other materials (Fig. 97-6). Common alloying elements include:

    a. Nickel is added to increase strength and toughness. It also helps to prevent the steel from rusting.

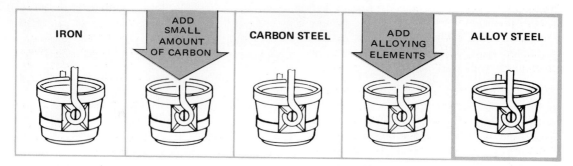

Fig. 97-6. Steps in making alloy steel.

b. *Chromium* adds hardness, toughness, and resistance to wear. Gears and axles are often made of chrome-nickel steel because of the greater strength of this steel.

c. *Manganese* is used in steel to produce a clean metal. It also adds to the strength of the metal and helps in heat-treating.

d. *Silicon* is used to make steel more elastic. Springs are made of silicon steel.

e. *Tungsten* is combined with chromium, vanadium, molybdenum, or manganese to produce *high-speed steel* used in cutting tools.

f. *Molybdenum* is used to add toughness and higher strength to steel. Some high-speed cutting tools are made from molybdenum steel.

g. *Vanadium* improves the grain of steel. It is used with chromium to make chrome-vanadium steel. This type of steel is very strong and has excellent shock resistance. Gears and shafts are often made of chrome-vanadium steel.

h. *Boron* is added to intensify the degree of hardening (the depth to which a steel can be hardened by heat treatment). Amounts as small as five ten-thousandths of 1 percent (0.0005 percent) are sufficient to reduce the quantities of more expensive or scarcer elements needed to obtain results.

i. *Cobalt* is used in magnet steels and permanent-magnet alloys, in special alloys for severe high-temperature service, and for tool steels that hold a cutting-edge at high temperatures. Cobalt steel is also used to put a hard surface on parts of equipment that must resist wear.

j. *Columbium* is added to increase the strength of some of the superalloys that are used in high-temperature service. Columbium is also added to prevent undesirable changes in the structure of certain grades of stainless steels when they are used at high temperatures or welded.

k. *Copper* may be added to some grades of steel in small amounts, usually under 0.5 percent, to retard rusting. Copper is added to steel as pure metal or as copper-bearing scrap.

l. *Titanium* is added to prevent undesirable changes in the structure of some stainless and heat-resisting steels when they are used at high temperatures or welded. Titanium is also used as an alloying element to increase the strength of some of the superalloys for severe high-temperature service.

The quantities of alloying ingredients added to steels vary according to the properties required. Amounts may range from as little as 0.005 percent of boron in boron alloy steels to as much as 26.0 percent chromium in certain stainless steels. The variations in percentages and combinations of different alloying elements that can be added to steel are almost limitless. This makes it possible for today's metallurgists to make a steel suitable for almost any purpose.

3. *Stainless steel.* Stainless steels are those that contain from about 10 percent to 26 percent

chromium. Nickel is often added to assure better corrosion resistance. The 18-8-type (18 percent chromium, 8 percent nickel) is widely used in soda fountains, steam cooking and pasteurizing equipment, dye kettles, and similar devices.

4. *Tool-and-die steels*. These steels, which include the high-speed steels (HSS), contain considerable amounts of alloying elements such as tungsten, molybdenum, cobalt, manganese, and chromium, as well as a normal amount of carbon. When brought to their particular hardening heat, these alloy steels harden by cooling in air. They are the most widely used steels in the cutting tool industry. All have the ability to retain red hardness and toughness at elevated temperatures. Unlike carbon tool steels, tool-and-die steels can cut while dull red (in the neighborhood of 1000° F.), without loss of hardness. The higher the cobalt content the greater the red hardness factor, thus allowing the tool to be used at higher cutting speeds.

CAST IRON

Cast iron is used in the heavy part of many machines. It is the most common material used in making castings. Cast iron is low in cost and wears well, but is very brittle and cannot be hammered or formed. It contains from 2 to 4 percent of carbon.

The basic kinds of cast iron are white iron, gray iron, and malleable iron. *Malleable iron* is a particular kind of cast iron that has been made more malleable by an annealing procedure (heated to a high temperature, then slowly cooled). Malleable-iron castings are not so brittle or so hard as cast iron. They have a harder outer surface and a softer interior. They can stand a great deal of hammering. *Nodular iron* is a kind of cast iron that has even more desirable qualities to withstand shock, blows, and jerks.

ROLLED STEELS

Steel bars, steel rods, and steel beams are produced by rolling the steel into these shapes. The steel is squeezed into shape, much as clothes are squeezed through a wringer. *Hot-rolled steels* are formed into shape while the metal is red hot. The metal goes through a series of rollers, each a little closer together. As the steel comes through the last rollers, hot water is sprayed over it, forming a *bluish scale*. This steel is fairly uniform in quality and is used for many different kinds of parts. The best quality hot-rolled bars are used to produce cold-finished steels.

Cold-finished steels are used when great accuracy, better surface finish, and certain mechanical properties are needed. There are several ways of producing cold-finished bars. The most common are two procedures that result in what is called *cold-worked steel*. In both, scale from the hot-rolled bars is first removed. The *cold-drawing technique* consists of drawing the bars through a series of dies, each a few thousandths inch smaller than the preceding one. The second method is very similar. The steel is rolled cold to the exact size. This is called *cold-rolling*. Both procedures change the properties of hot-rolled steel.

IDENTIFYING STEELS

There are three methods used to identify steels:

1. *Number system*. A number system for identifying *carbon* and *alloy* steels has been developed by the Society of Automotive Engineers (SAE) and the American Iron and Steel Institute (AISI). The system is based on the use of numbers composed of four or five digits:

a. The first digit tells the kind of steel: 1 shows carbon steels, 2 is nickel steel, 3 is nickel-chromium steel, 4 is molybdenum steel, etc.

b. The second digit in alloy steels shows the approximate percent by weight of alloy elements. For example, 2320 shows a nickel steel with about 3 percent nickel.

c. The last two (and sometimes three) digits show the carbon content in points (100 points equal 1 percent by weight). For example, AISI and SAE 1095 would be a carbon steel with 95 points of carbon.

Another letter and number system is used to identify *tool-and-die steels*.

The American Iron and Steel Institute has also developed a system for indicating the kind of furnace in which the steel was made:

A—Basic open-hearth alloy steel
B—Acid bessemer carbon steel
C—Basic open-hearth carbon steel
D—Acid open-hearth carbon steel
E—Electric-furnace steel

The letter is often placed before (as a prefix) the number of the steel. Complete information about each of the above systems can be found in *The New American Machinist's Handbook* and *Machinery's Handbook*.

2. *Color code.* Most manufacturers paint each different kind of steel a different color. Some paint only the ends. Others paint all along the bar. This is done to keep from confusing the steel bars in the steel racks. If a certain steel is painted red, it may mean that it is high-carbon steel. Each company has a different color code. Low- and medium-carbon steels are not identified in this way.

3. *Spark test.* This method of identification is rather inaccurate. The test is made by observing the sparks given off when the metal is ground. The kind, frequency, position, and color of the sparks are all considered in making the identification. Figure 97–7 shows sparks given off by various metals.

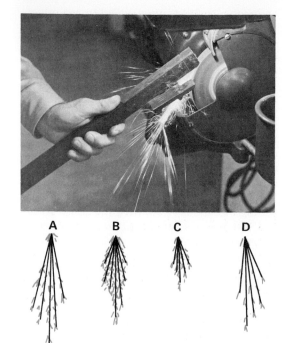

A—LOW CARBON (MACHINE)
B—HIGH CARBON (TOOL)
C—CAST IRON
D—STAINLESS

Fig. 97–7. The spark test is often helpful in identifying steels.

COMMON KINDS OF STEELS

The following are examples of some kinds of carbon steels that might be used for shop projects:

1. Hot-rolled

a. *SAE-AISI C1018.* This is a low-carbon, general-purpose steel that is used for hammer forging. It can be case-hardened. It would be good steel to use for general repair work or machine parts. It is made in the open-hearth furnace.

b. *SAE-AISI C1035.* This is an intermediate-carbon steel. It is higher in strength and hardness than low-carbon steel. It might be used for studs, bolts, and shafts that do not require too much strength.

c. *SAE-AISI 1045.* This is a higher-carbon machinery steel than can be used for projects or parts that require great strength and

hardness. This steel can be forged. It can also be heat-treated. It can be used for machinery parts, screwdrivers, bits, hammer heads, vise parts, and other items.

d. *SAE-AISI 1095.* This is a high-carbon spring steel. It is a less expensive material that may be used to make parts for later hardening and tempering.

2. Cold-finished

a. *SAE-AISI 1018.* This is a low-carbon steel made by the open-hearth method. It is quite easy to machine. It can also be bent cold. It is good to use for projects that must be brazed or welded. This steel can be used for any project not requiring great strength.

b. *SAE-AISI 1042.* This is a medium-carbon steel made in the open hearth. This steel will machine to a very fine finish. It can be heat-treated. It can be used for projects requiring a good deal of strength.

3. Tool-and-die steel. *SAE-AISI W 2-1.00 carbon*. This is an all-purpose, water-hardening carbon tool steel with a small amount of vanadium. It is easy to machine. The steel is best to use because of its excellent hardness and toughness. It can be hardened in water after heating to about 1400 to 1450°F. The tempering range is from 300 to 600°F. This steel should be used for making all kinds of tools with cutting-edges that require sharpening. It can be used for such items as knives, punches, chisels, cutters, and other general shop tools.

UNIT 98. Machinability of Steels

Machinability relates to the relative ease (or difficulty) with which a metal can be machined. The cost of any finished piece is influenced considerably by this characteristic. Materials difficult to machine must be worked at slower feeds and speeds and with shorter tool life. Often the selection of a relatively expensive material, which is readily machinable, may be more economical than a low-priced material that is difficult and slow to cut.

MACHINABILITY RATINGS

Tables which use a numbering system as an index of relative machinability are available for most common materials. The relative machinability ratings for AISI and SAE steels are shown in Table 98–1. Note that these ratings are approximate and will vary according to the particular machining operation involved. Note also that 1112 steel with a sulfur content of about 0.200 percent is given an arbitrary machinability rating of 100, and the cutting quality of other metals is rated against it. Tables like this, although approximate, have value in the machine shop because they aid in the selection of material, the determination of machining rates, and the estimation of production costs.

THE STRUCTURE OF STEEL

Maximum machinability of steel is generally obtained by a critical balance of alloy content and structure. The machining characteristics of the constituents of steel thus have to be closely examined. The hardness of the constituents is important since it provides an approximate indication of the abrasive action on the cutting tool during the machining operation.

Ferrite is a soft ductile form of iron. Despite its low strength, ferrite cannot be cut cleanly and a fine finish is not possible. Most alloying elements strengthen ferrite but do not materially decrease its ductility.

Carbides are extremely hard and are not cut by the tool but rather are pushed aside during cutting. The size of the particles is important. For example, larger carbide spheroids are generally an indication of superior machinability. *Cementite* is a compound of iron and carbon, known as *iron carbide*.

Pearlite comprises alternate layers of iron carbide and ferrite. It is relatively hard and can be cut cleanly. Considerable power is required in machining, however, and pearlite tends to abrade the tool.

Spheroidite is a structure of ferrite and carbide-cementite spheroids. The platelike form of carbide in pearlite is altered to a spherical shape by heat treatment. For any given carbon content, spheroidite is softer than a ferrite-pearlite structure. Steels containing unfavorable ferrite-pearlite ratios can be heat-treated so that partial or complete spheroidization takes place. By this means, machinability is enhanced.

Sulfides are about as hard as ferrite. In addition, these inclusions are plastic at fairly low temperatures and act to lubricate the tool-chip interface.

Oxide inclusions may be mildly to severely abrasive depending on their hardness. The oxides of aluminum and silicon are particularly undesirable from the standpoint of machinability.

Table 98-1. Approximate relative machinability of AISI steels.

Kind of Steel			Relative Machinability Based on 1112 as 100%
Free Machining Steels		1112	100
		1113	135
		1115	81
		1120	78
		1212	100
		1213	135
Carburizing Steels	Carbon Steels	1020	63
		1015	53
		1010	53
		1025	53
	Alloy Steels	3115	53
		3120	53
		5120	51
		2317	51
		4615	51
		4620	51
		8617	51
Heat Treating Steels	As Rolled	1030	62
		1035	62
		1040	60
		1045	48
		1050	45
		3130	41
		3135	38
		2330	35
		3140	32
		2345	30
	Annealed for Machinability	1045	60
		4340	58
		1050	57
		4130	55
		3130	55
		4140	50
		3135	48
		4150	45
		3140	45
		2330	45
		3145	43
		5140	42
		3150	40
		6150	40
		9260	40
		5150	40
		2340	38
		2345	37
		1095	30
		52100	30

Grain size affects machinability in much the same way as does spheroidite. Coarse grains help the cutting qualities of high-carbon steels; fine grains, on the other hand, are preferred in grades which are normally too soft to be machined cleanly.

IMPROVING MACHINABILITY

Steel producers use two basic methods, either singly or in combination, to provide the machinability that users demand. These are finishing methods (such as control of hot-rolling and cold-drawing operations) and chemical composition control.

Finishing Method. Cold finishing can substantially improve the mechanical and machining properties of a hot-rolled steel bar. Cold-finished bars are free of scale. They are also smoother, brighter, straighter, and more accurate in size than hot-rolled material. The cold-drawing process also increases the strength of the metal.

Chemical Composition. Nonresulfurized low-carbon steels are not generally used for machining, since their structure is predominantly ferrite with only small quantities of pearlite. The machinability rating of such steels ranges from 50 to 60. However, the machining properties of low-carbon steels can be improved by cold finishing. Steels with carbon contents of about 0.30 percent (such as grade 1030) contain approximately 65 percent ferrite and 35 percent pearlite. Cleaner cutting action results from the greater presence of pearlite and such materials are rated at about 75.

In high-carbon steels, the control of structure for maximum machinability is influenced greatly by the nature and severity of the machining process. Thus, simple turning calls for softer material than does broaching or drilling.

The effect of chemicals on machining performance is complex. Although the majority of additions react unfavorably, the addition of certain elements such as sulfur, selenium, tellurium, bismuth, lead, phosphorus, and nitrogen make it possible to produce steels which are *free-machining* (such steels are designed to provide optimum machinability).

UNIT 99. Heat Treatment and Testing

Heat treatment is a term applied to a variety of procedures for changing the characteristics of metal by heating and cooling. By proper heat treatment, it is possible to obtain certain characteristics in metal such as *hardness, tensile strength* (ability to resist stretching), and *ductility*. Heat treatment can be a simple process requiring few tools. In industry, it is a highly scientific and complicated procedure requiring much equipment.

The processes of heat treatment are not strictly a part of the machinist's trade. However, many of the projects or products made in the machine shop have little or no value until they are heat-treated. This unit includes only the most elementary information about the heat treatment of steel. For more specific information on how to heat-treat a particular kind of steel, refer to *The New American Machinist's Handbook*. Heat treatment can also be done on many of the nonferrous metals such as aluminum, copper, and brass. The procedures are different, however, and will not be considered here.

The beginner in machine shop should be acquainted with (1) hardening, (2) tempering, (3) annealing, and (4) case hardening.

HARDENING

Hardening is a process of heating and cooling steel to increase its hardness and tensile strength, to reduce its ductility, and to obtain a fine grain structure. The procedure includes heating the metal above its critical point or temperature, followed by rapid cooling. As steel is heated, a physical and chemical change takes place between the iron and carbon. The *critical point,* or *critical temperature,* is the point at which the steel has the most desirable characteristics. When steel reaches this temperature—somewhere between 1400 and 1600°F—the change is ideal to make for a hard, strong material if it is cooled quickly. If the metal cools slowly, it changes back to its original state. By plunging the hot metal into water, oil, or brine (*quenching*), the desirable characteristics are retained. The metal is very hard and strong and less ductile than before. The exact critical temperature and quenching procedure for each different kind of steel will be found in *The New American Machinist's Handbook*.

Heating is done in a furnace fired by gas, oil, or electricity (Fig. 99–1). A device called a *pyrometer* is attached to the furnace. This accurately registers the exact temperature in the furnace (Fig. 99–2). The temperature of the metal can also be determined by observing its color. Figure 99–3 indicates approximate colors for the different temperatures. You can make use of the colors when heat-treating simple metal parts and tools. Colors are not very accurate, however. Even the expert heat-treater will be off as much as 20°F from the true temperature.

HARDENING PROCEDURE

1. Light the furnace, and allow it to come to the right temperature.

2. Place the metal in the furnace, and heat it to the critical temperature. For carbon tool

Fig. 99–1. This is a typical small heat-treating furnace.

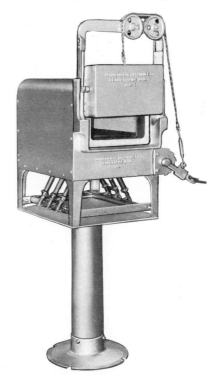

steels, allow about 20 to 30 minutes per inch of thickness for coming up to heat. Allow about 10 to 15 minutes per inch of thickness for soaking at hardening temperature.

3. Select the correct cooling solution. Some steels can be cooled in water, and others must be cooled in oil or brine. *Water* is the most widely used material for quenching carbon steels because it is inexpensive and effective. *Brine* is usually made by adding about 9 percent of common salt to the water. Brine helps to produce a more uniform hardness. The brine

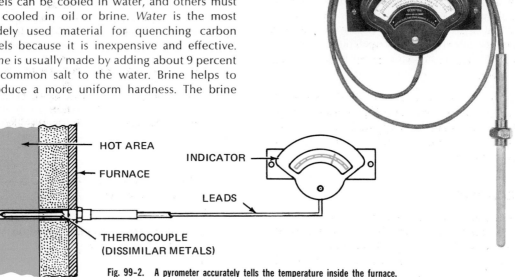

Fig. 99-2. A pyrometer accurately tells the temperature inside the furnace.

Fig. 99-3. This chart shows the colors that can be followed in the hardening process. Using colors is not a very accurate method.

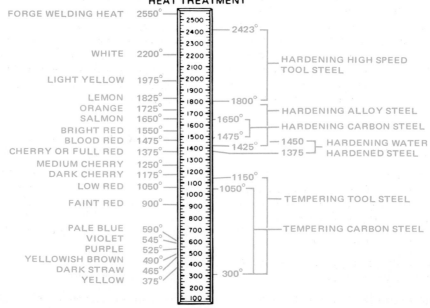

TEMPERATURE CHART
(FAHRENHEIT DEGREES)
HEAT TREATMENT

FORGE WELDING HEAT	2550°	2500		
		2400	2423°	
		2300		
WHITE	2200°	2200		HARDENING HIGH SPEED TOOL STEEL
		2100		
LIGHT YELLOW	1975°	2000		
		1900		
LEMON	1825°	1800	1800°	
ORANGE	1725°	1700		HARDENING ALLOY STEEL
SALMON	1650°		1650°	HARDENING CARBON STEEL
BRIGHT RED	1550°	1600		
BLOOD RED	1475°	1500	1475°	1450 — HARDENING WATER
CHERRY OR FULL RED	1375°	1400	1425°	1375 — HARDENED STEEL
MEDIUM CHERRY	1250°	1300		
DARK CHERRY	1175°	1200		
LOW RED	1050°	1100	1150°	
		1000	1050°	
FAINT RED	900°	900		TEMPERING TOOL STEEL
		800		
PALE BLUE	590°	700		TEMPERING CARBON STEEL
VIOLET	545°	600		
PURPLE	525°	500		
YELLOWISH BROWN	490°	400		
DARK STRAW	465°	300	300°	
YELLOW	375°	200		
		100		

cools the parts all over more quickly. *Oil* is used for a somewhat slower speed of quenching. Most oils used for quenching are mineral oils.

4. Remove the hot metal with tongs, and plunge it into the cooling solution. Agitate (move it about in a figure 8) so that the metal cools quickly and evenly. If it is a thin piece (like a knife or blade), cut the cooling solution with the object so it won't warp. If one side cools faster than the other, there will be some warping.

5. A properly hardened piece of steel will be hard and brittle and have high tensile strength. It will also have internal strain. If left in this state, these internal strains could cause the metal to crack.

TEMPERING

Tempering is a process of reducing the degree of hardness and strength and increasing the toughness. It removes the brittleness from a hardened piece. It is a process that follows the hardening procedure and makes the metal as hard and tough as possible. To *draw* means the same as to *temper*. Tempering is done by reheating the metal to low or moderate temperature, followed by quenching or by cooling in air. As the metal is heated for tempering, it changes in color. These colors are called *temper colors*. You can watch these colors to know when the correct heat is reached. A more accurate method, of course, is to watch the pyrometer. Many parts and projects are completely tempered. Others are tempered in one section, and the rest remains in the hardened state. Table 99–1 shows the correct temper colors for various parts.

TEMPERING PROCEDURE

1. To temper the entire piece, place it in the furnace. Reheat to the correct temperature to produce the hardness and toughness you want. Remove the metal and cool it quickly.

2. To temper small cutting tools:

   a. Harden the entire tool. Clean off the scale with abrasive cloth.

   b. Heat a scrap piece of metal red hot.

Table 99-1. Tempering colors.

Degrees Fahrenheit	Color	Use
375	Yellow	Punches, scrapers, and centers
425	Light straw	Hammers and tool bits
465	Dark straw	Dies, drills, hacksaw blades, taps, and reamers
490	Yellowish brown	Wood chisel, axes, and drifts
525	Purple	Axes, needles, and cold chisels
590	Pale blue	Picks and screwdrivers

c. Place the tool on the metal with the point extending beyond the hot piece of metal.

d. Watch the temper colors. When the correct color reaches the point of the tool, quench it.

HARDENING AND TEMPERING SMALL TOOLS

To do both hardening and tempering on small tools, first heat the tool to the critical temperature. Plunge only the point of the tool in the quenching bath. Move it around for uniform cooling. Remove the tool, and clean the point with abrasive cloth. *Remember that the handle of the tool will be very hot.* Now watch the temper colors move toward the point. When the correct color reaches the point, quench the entire tool.

HARDENING AND TEMPERING WATER-HARDENING CARBON STEEL

This steel is used to make small tools that must have a good cutting-edge, such as center punches, prick punches, and cold chisels.

1. Heat the tool to 1475 to 1500°F.

2. Quench it in water.

3. Reheat to 425 to 590°F.

4. Cool in water or as described above.

HARDENING AND TEMPERING TOOL-AND-DIE STEEL

This is another steel used for small tools.

1. Heat the metal to 1400 to 1450°F.

2. Quench it in water or brine.

3. Reheat to 300 to 650°F for tempering.

4. Cool in water.

ANNEALING

Annealing is the process of softening steel to relieve internal strain. This makes the steel easier to machine. The metal is heated above the critical temperature and cooled slowly. The most common method is to place the steel in the furnace and heat it thoroughly. Then turn off the furnace, allowing the metal to cool slowly. Another method is to pack the metal in clay, heat it to the critical temperature, remove it from the furnace, and allow it to cool slowly.

It may be necessary to anneal a hardened metal part that needs to be reworked in the machine shop. For example, you may want to anneal an old file or a spring before machining the metal for some other purpose.

CASE HARDENING

Case hardening is a process of hardening the outer surface or case of ferrous metal. By adding a small amount of carbon to the case of the low-carbon steel, it can be heat-treated to make the case hard. At the same time the center, or core, remains soft and ductile.

There are many methods of case hardening. In industry, molten cyanide is used (this is called *cyaniding*). Another industrial method is *carburizing*. This is a case-hardening procedure in which carbon is added to steel from the surface inward by one of the following methods: (1) pack method, (2) gas method, or (3) liquid-salt method. In the school shop the most common method is to use a nonpoisonous coke compound (pack method) such as Kasenit.

To case-harden the project:

1. Pack it in the material in an open *metal box* or *pot*.

2. Put the covered box in a furnace, and heat to about 1650°F.

3. Leave the box in the furnace from 15 minutes to 1 hour, depending on the depth of case required (Fig. 99–4). The steel will absorb carbon to a depth of as much as 0.015 in.

4. Take the object out of the Kasenit.

5. Quench it in water. Only the case will be hardened. The inside, or core, remains soft.

This process can be done on such items as hammer heads, piston pins, and other items that must stand a good deal of shock and wear. It can never be used on anything that must be sharpened by grinding.

TESTING FOR HARDNESS

There are four common ways to determine the degree of hardness of heat-treated steel.

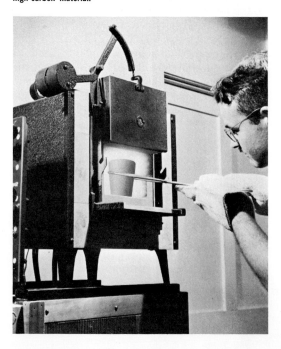

Fig. 99–4. Placing an object in the furnace to case harden it. The parts are packed in a container filled with some kind of high-carbon material.

Fig. 99-5. A Brinell hardness tester.

Fig. 99-6. A Rockwell hardness tester.

Fig. 99-7. A Shore scleroscope hardness tester.

1. Old-timers used to press a new file across the corner of the work. They could tell about how hard it was by the appearance of the scratch. The three scientific ways are with hardness testers.

2. The *Brinell tester* has a round ball that is forced into the metal (Fig. 99-5). The width of the dent is measured through a microscope. The degree of hardness is related to the width of the dent. The higher the number, the harder the metal. The wider the dent, the softer the metal and the lower the number. This tester is best for soft and medium-soft materials.

3. *Rockwell testers* measure the amount of penetration of a point in the metal (Fig. 99-6). The greater the penetration, the softer the metal. This tester has a dial gage that gives a direct reading to show the degree of hardness.

4. The *Shore scleroscope* has a diamond-tipped hammer that drops on the metal (Fig. 99-7). The amount of rebound indicates the degree of hardness.

UNIT 100. Discussion Topics and Problems

1. What is the difference between a metal and an alloy?

2. Name the five mechanical properties of metal.

3. What are the three basic furnaces used to produce steel?

4. What does teeming mean?

5. How many points of carbon are there in low-carbon steel?

6. What is meant by alloy steel?

7. Name some of the elements used in alloying steel.

8. What does the C mean in AISI C1035 steel?

9. To what does the term machinability refer?

10. How does the machinability of AISI or SAE 1040 steel compare with 1112?

11. What is meant by the term heat treatment?

12. List the basic steps involved in hardening steel.

13. Describe the basic steps involved in tempering steel.

14. For what purpose is annealing done?

15. How is a metal case-hardened?

16. What is the simplest method of testing for hardness?

17. Name three kinds of hardness testing machines.

SECTION II

RELATED MACHINING PROCEDURES

UNIT 101. Numerical Control

Numerical control is simply a means of directing some or all the functions of a machine automatically from coded instructions. Numerical control, commonly denoted N/C, is the automatic control of machines by means of electrical devices which receive operating instructions from a prepared tape (usually a punched tape) instead of from a human operator. This tape supplies, in coded form, dimensional data taken from a drawing of the part to be produced (Fig. 101-1).

With N/C, additional steps have been inserted between the preparation of an engineering drawing and machining of the part. These steps are programming and tape preparation (Fig. 101-2). *Programming* is another name for writing down every move the machine is to make in producing a part. It requires a man who knows good machining and tooling practices and who is familiar with the cutting characteristics of the material from which the part will be made. He must think through each step in machining the part, determine speeds and feeds,

specify the path the tool is to take, instruct the machine to turn on coolant or turn it off, and do all the other operations that a good machinist would do. His instructions, called a *format*, are written in a special way so that they can be readily converted into punched tape. This punched tape, in turn, is *read* by a control unit that operates the machine according to the instructions it sees.

Numerical-control equipment is not only capable of doing complex and accurate work, but also offers many economic advantages. Tooling and fixture requirements are minimized. Machine flexibility is increased. Changing workpieces may only require changing to a new tape.

WHAT IS N/C?

Numerical control of machine tools was developed in response to the aerospace industry's need for machining techniques that could produce the complicated components of modern planes and spacecraft more accurately, faster, and at less cost than was possible with conventional metalworking techniques. One way to understand N/C is to compare it with the con-

535

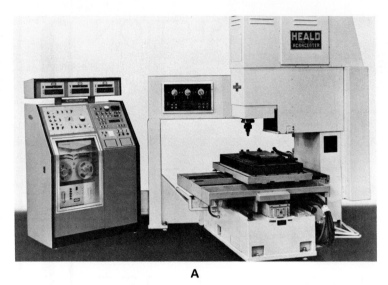

A

B

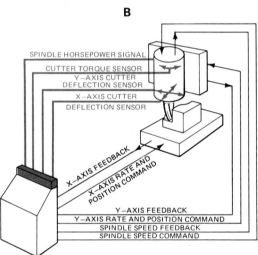

SPINDLE HORSEPOWER SIGNAL

CUTTER TORQUE SENSOR

Y—AXIS CUTTER
DEFLECTION SENSOR

X—AXIS CUTTER
DEFLECTION SENSOR

X—AXIS FEEDBACK

X—AXIS RATE AND
POSITION COMMAND

Y—AXIS FEEDBACK

Y—AXIS RATE AND POSITION COMMAND

SPINDLE SPEED FEEDBACK

SPINDLE SPEED COMMAND

Fig. 101-1. (A) This vertical milling machine is designed specifically for numerical control. (B) The numerical control unit operates table movement and also controls the action of the cutting tool.

trol of conventional machine tools and specialized pieces of equipment.

The man who runs a standard general-purpose machine tool such as a turret lathe, drill press, or milling machine is expected to produce a part that conforms to a drawing or print. How-to-do-it instructions are given in the job sheet. It is the operator's responsibility to determine the speeds and feeds at which to run the machine and to make continuing machine ad-justments. Specialized machine tools, on the other hand, are guided by electromechanical devices. They are able to do a fixed set of operations necessary to produce items of one design. Machines that turn out engine blocks by the thousands, with little human assistance, are examples of special-purpose machine tools.

Numerical control of machine tools is achieved through coded instructions either on punched cards or on magnetic or paper tape.

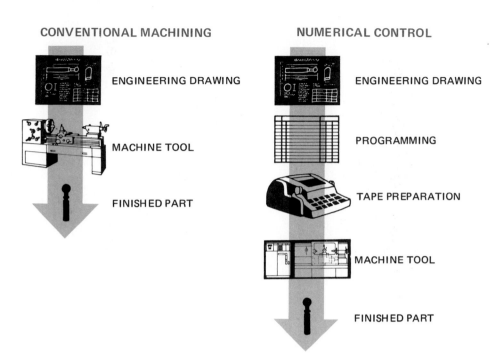

CONVENTIONAL MACHINING
- ENGINEERING DRAWING
- MACHINE TOOL
- FINISHED PART

NUMERICAL CONTROL
- ENGINEERING DRAWING
- PROGRAMMING
- TAPE PREPARATION
- MACHINE TOOL
- FINISHED PART

Fig. 101-2. Conventional machining compared to N/C.

These instructions control the sequence of machining operations, the selection of the proper tool, the speed and feed of the machine, the flow of coolant, and the position of the workpiece. The margin for human error in operation is largely eliminated since the operator's manipulation of the control system is limited to placing a roll of tape or a deck of punched cards in the control unit. The operator's duties in an N/C setup are to watch the tool for wear or malfunction, load and unload the work, start and stop the machine, and change instructions (tapes or cards) in the control unit.

USING N/C ON MACHINE TOOLS

Preparation for N/C begins during the design stage. The part must be designed and drawings dimensioned for ease of production on N/C equipment. Beginning with a blueprint, the steps in carrying out an N/C program are shown in Fig. 101-3.

POSITIONING FOR N/C

It is possible to define the location of a point in space with reference to another point by considering three mutually perpendicular axes commonly called X, Y, and Z (Fig. 101-4). The X and Y axes represent horizontal table motion, and the Z axis represents vertical motion of the cutting tool, such as on a drill press or milling machine. Figure 101-5 illustrates how the idea works in two dimensions. Note how points A and B can be described in terms of their distance from the X and Y axes. Provided you know where the origin of the two axes lies (the O setup point, or origin) and where they cross, you can define the location of A, B, or any other two-dimensional point by stating its two coordinates. The location of any point in space, therefore, can be indicated by stating its X, Y, and Z coordinates.

POSITIONING SYSTEMS

Two positioning systems are used by the programmer, namely, the *point-to-point system* and the *continuous-path,* or *contouring, system.* Point to point is the simplest of the two systems. Positioning is always along one axis or at a 45 degree (°) angle. Such a system is ideal for controlling straight-line cutting or milling and for applications such as drilling wherein work is

537

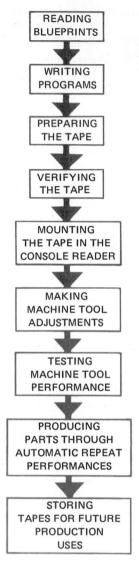

Fig. 101-3. Steps in using numerical control.

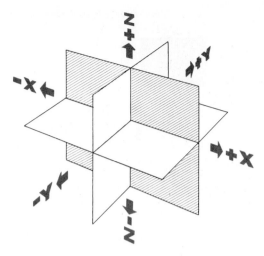

Fig. 101-4. The X and Y axes represent horizontal table movements. The Z axis denotes vertical tool or table movement.

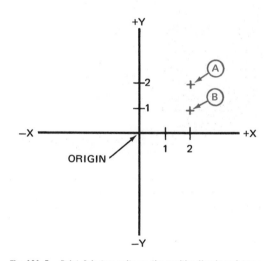

Fig. 101-5. Point A is two units on the positive Y axis and two units on the positive X axis, and point B is one unit on the positive Y axis and two units on the positive X axis.

performed after positioning. Programming does not require use of a computer and can be accomplished by anyone having a basic knowledge of machining practices and the ability to read and understand engineering drawings. Point-to-point positioning may be either incremental or absolute. With *incremental positioning,* each positioning movement is programmed from the last position. With *absolute positioning,* each machining location is given in relation to a zero point or origin.

Continuous-path positioning allows for the simultaneous control of two or more machine axis motions. This feature permits the programmer to instruct the N/C unit to process any contour within the capability of the machine and its working tool.

PREPARING A TAPE PROGRAM

Before preparing a tape program, the programmer must know whether the program is being

Fig. 101-6. The program information is transferred to tape by means of a tape-punching machine, which is a special type of typewriter.

3. Select the first tool change point where the finished part will be unloaded and a new part inserted at the completion of the tape program. This location can be at the setup point or, if necessary, at a second point to allow sufficient clearance when removing and inserting the parts.

4. Determine a sequence of operations and select any additional tool change points required. Be sure the tool will not hit the fixturing or the workpiece during any positioning motion.

5. Record the sequence of operations together with any operator's instructions on a program sheet. The program sheet layout must be compatible with the tape format to be used. When the programmer has completed the program sheet, a copy of the sheet is given to a typist who transfers the program information onto tape with a tape-punching machine (Fig. 101-6).

Figure 101-7 shows a simple point-to-point drilling program that might be used to produce the part shown in Fig. 101-8. If we assume that the program will be used on an incremental positioning controller, a sketch of the part having dimensions changed to point-to-point increments must be made (Fig. 101-9). Note that the setup point has been added and the holes numbered to show the order in which they will be drilled. Arrows indicate the plus direction for the X and Y axes.

Figure 101-10 shows a completed program sheet for the drilling program. Since the holes do not require center drilling and are all the same diameter, no tool changes are needed. Each horizontal line of information on the sheet makes up one sequence or block of operations. It contains the information for one positioning movement, together with any miscellaneous functions such as tool changes required. In this program, the drilling is performed by the controller after positioning has been completed. No code is required for tool movement since this controller automatically starts the tool after positioning unless inhibited in the tape program.

In order, starting from zero, each line of information is assigned a sequence number which is entered on the first column on the left of the sheet (Fig. 101-10). The zero sequence

prepared for an incremental or an absolute positioning system. He should also be familiar with the required tape format and codes. It is often helpful to make a rough sketch of the part, redimensioning as required for purposes of programming and showing tool changes. Essentially, the following steps are required to produce a tape program.

1. Determine the fixturing required to locate and hold the part on the table.

2. Select a setup point. This point may be located at a corner of the part, at a reference point on the holding fixture, or at some other convenient reference point.

EIA STANDARD RS-244 KEYBOARD SYMBOLS	ALTERNATE KEYBOARD SYMBOLS	CODE ON TAPE									SYSTEM FUNCTION
		CHANNEL NUMBERS									
		1	2	3	•	4	5	6	7	8	
TAPE FEED	SPACE, BUZZ, FEED										LEADER
	RWST, %, $										RWS (REWIND STOP)
TAB											TAB
+											+ (OPTIONAL)
−											−
1											1
2											2
3											3
4											4
5											5
6											6
7											7
8											8
9											9
0											0
CAR. RET. OR EOB											EOB (END OF BLOCK)
DELETE	TAPE FEED										DELETE

Channel numbers: 1 2 3 • 4 5 6 7 8

Fig. 101-7. A typical tape code for a numerical controller employing the tab-sequence format.

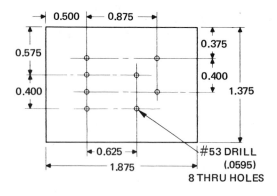

Fig. 101-8. Drawing of a metal component board having eight holes.

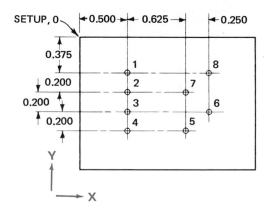

Fig. 101-9. A programmer's "sketch" of the drawing that is shown in Fig. 101-8.

contains no positioning information; only the required rewind-stop instructions to the tape reader and the end-of-block (EOB) code are entered here. With the tab-sequential format, X-axis positioning commands follow the first tab, and Y-axis positioning commands follow

the second tab. Therefore, a tab should be entered in the second column and the direction (+ or −) and magnitude of the desired X increment entered in the third and fourth columns. A tab is entered in the fifth column to indicate that the X-axis command is complete and the

SLO-SYN TAPE CONTROLLED INDEXER PROGRAM

COMPANY NAME *Acme Precision Products* ADDRESS *Clark St. Podunk, Conn.*

PREPARED BY *LH* DATE *1-26-66* CK'D BY *BmL* DATE *1-27-66* SHEET *1* OF *1* DEPT *18* TAPE NO *105*	PART NAME *Component Board* REMARKS: *NCIR24 w/Backlash Compensation* *Bridgeport 72421 Machine* *#53 Drill 8 Thru Holes*	PART NO. *BL11365*	OPER. NO. —

SEQ NO.	TAB OR EOB	. OR	X INCREMENT	TAB OR EOB	. OR	Y INCREMENT	TAB OR EOB	M FUNCT	EOB	INSTRUCTIONS
	E									
%	E									LOAD START
1	T		500	T	–	375	E			
2	T			T	–	200	E			
3	T			T	–	200	E			
4	T			T	–	200	E			
5	T		625	E						
6	T		250	T		200	E			
7	T	–	250	T		200	E			
8	T		250	T		200	E			
9	T	–	1375	T		375	T	02	E	

Fig. 101-10.   A program sheet for the part shown in Fig. 101-8.

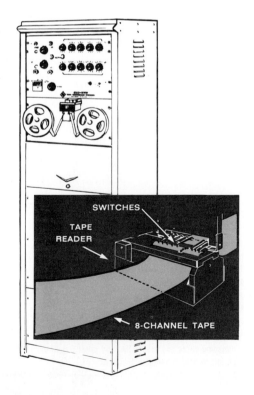

SWITCHES

TAPE READER

8-CHANNEL TAPE

Fig. 101-11.   The eight-channel tape goes through a tape reader which operates the controller. This, in turn, operates the movements of the machine just as a machinist would do with manual controls.

Y-axis command is to follow. The appropriate Y-axis commands are entered in the sixth and seventh columns, and a tab code is placed in the eighth column. Rewind, tool change, and any other miscellaneous function codes required are entered in the ninth column. An EOB code is placed in the tenth column to tell the controller that the block of information is complete.

In sequence 1 on the program sheet, the program calls for movements of 0.500 in. toward the plus direction along the X axis and 0.375 in. toward the minus direction along the Y axis. Upon completion of the positioning phase, the control will actuate the tool to drill the first hole. In the same manner, the remaining seven holes will be drilled. When all eight holes have been drilled, the control returns the work to the setup point and rewinds the tape. The machine is then ready for the completed part to be removed and a new part inserted. The 02 code in sequence 9 is the numerical code for rewind.

USING THE TAPE

Once the tape has been prepared and checked for errors it is given to the machinist. After the machine is set up according to the written instructions, the tape is threaded into the tape reader (Fig. 101–11). The workpiece is mounted on the table and a test is made of the machine's performance by running the tape through without doing any actual cutting. Sometimes a cutting test is made on a piece of soft plastic or wood to make sure the program is correct. This is followed by a trial run on an actual part. If correct, the parts are produced through automatic repeat performance.

UNIT 102. Electrical Machining

Most of the electrical machining processes have come about due to the development of space-age metal alloys that are tough and hard to machine. Grinding, cutting, and shaping with cutting tools are exacting, time-consuming, and expensive processes on such alloys. In some cases, machining with conventional equipment is almost impossible. A material like tungsten carbide, for example, is very difficult to machine even with diamond cutting tools.

On standard machine tools, electrical energy is converted by an electric motor into motion that is transmitted through a series of shafts, pulleys, belts, and gears to a cutting tool. In contrast, the electrical machining processes make direct use of electrical energy. This results in certain abilities that are unique to these processes. These include machining metals of any hardness, machining without cutting forces, machining without tool rotation or without touching the workpiece, machining odd shapes, and machining dissimilar metals without loading the tool.

Three major electrical machining processes are EDM (electrical discharge machining), ECM (electrochemical machining), and ECG (electrochemical grinding) (Table 102–1). Other processes are ECD (electrochemical deburring), electroforming, and AJM (abrasive jet machining).

THE EDM PROCESS

Electrical discharge machining is a form of metal removal in which pulsating direct current is ap-

Table 102-1. Electrical machining processes.

EDM	ECM
Machining of:	Machining of:
1) Dies (stamping, cold heading, forging, injection molding)	1) High temperature alloy forgings
2) Carbide forming tools	2) Turbine wheels with integral blades
3) Tungsten parts	3) Jet engine blade airfoils
4) Burr-free parts	4) Jet engine blade cooling holes
5) Odd-shaped holes and cavities	5) Deburring of all kinds of parts
6) Small diameter deep holes	6) Odd-shaped holes and cavities
7) High strength and high hardness materials	7) Small deep holes
8) Narrow slots (0.002″ – 0.012″ width)	8) Honeycomb cores and assemblies and other fragile parts
9) Honeycomb cores and assemblies and other fragile parts	9) High strength high hardness materials

Fig. 102-1. A medium-size EDM machine. Note how it resembles a drill press or vertical milling machine.

plied to a shaped tool (electrode) and a workpiece, both of which are capable of conducting electricity (Fig. 102-1). The two are held in close proximity with a dielectric (nonconducting) fluid serving as an insulator between them. When a voltage high enough to break down the insulator is reached, a spark jumps the gap between the tool and the workpiece. This spark removes a small portion of material. In EDM, spark discharges occur at frequencies ranging from 500 to 1,000,000 pulses per second. Material is removed from the workpiece in the form of melted or vaporized particles (Fig. 102-2).

The EDM process is frequently used to make dies and molds (Fig. 102-3A, B). It is also used to cut odd-shaped openings in supertough alloys (Fig. 102-4).

Fig. 102-2. A diagram showing the operation of an EDM machine.

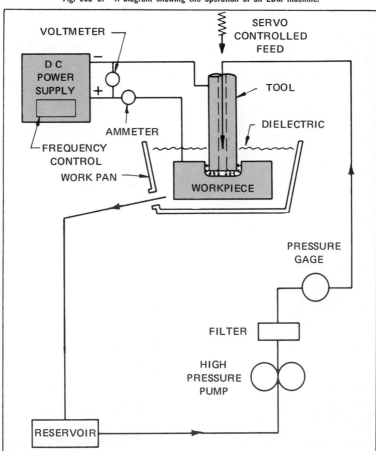

To the average person, an EDM machine looks something like a drill press or a vertical milling machine. The twist drill, however, has been replaced by precision-shaped electrodes (Fig. 102-5). In practice, a ram advances the

Fig. 102-3. (A) A rough set and a finished set of electrodes. These will be used to produce the dies shown in part B. Electrodes can be made out of several materials including copper and graphite. (B) This set of dies was made by the EDM process. Each is opposite in shape to the electrode used to machine it.

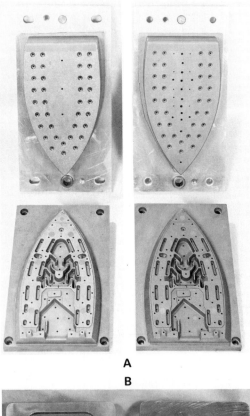

A

B

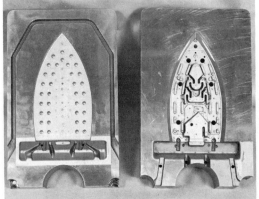

Fig. 102-4. Shapes such as these can be produced by electrical discharge machining. An electrode of the correct shape must first be produced.

electrode close to the workpiece (to within five-thousandths of an inch). As the electrode nears the workpiece, sparks, which look very much like miniature lightning bolts, are produced. Temperatures up to 10,000° F vaporize the metal. In addition to serving as a dielectric barrier between electrode and workpiece, the dielectric is needed to cool the workpiece and also to flush away particles as they are produced.

The surface finish of a part produced on an EDM machine is dependent upon the size of the sparks generated between it and the electrode. Figure 102-6 illustrates how big, powerful sparks produce a rough surface and small, less powerful sparks produce a smooth surface. Metal removal rates and surface finish are controlled by the frequency and intensity of the spark. High-frequency, low-intensity sparks result in a low metal removal rate and produce a smooth finish. Low-frequency, high-intensity sparks result in rapid metal erosion and a coarse finish.

THE ECM PROCESS

In the electrochemical machining process, electrical energy is used to bring about a chemical reaction which causes metal to dissolve from a workpiece and go into an electrolytic solution (Fig. 102-7).

Figure 102-8 illustrates how an ECM machine operates. Basically, the tool (cathode) is brought very close to the workpiece (anode). The distance between the tool and workpiece may range from less than 0.001 to 0.010 in. A low-voltage, high-density, electrically conductive electrolyte solution is then pumped between the tool and workpiece. This solution is under high pressure and is generally maintained at a temperature of 100°F. The current that passes through the electrolyte solution is usually quite high (currents as high as 20,000 amperes are not uncommon). As this current passes from the workpiece to the tool, metallic particles on the surface of the workpiece (ions) are caused to go into solution because of the electrochemical reaction. As they do, however, they are swept away by the rapidly flowing electrolyte.

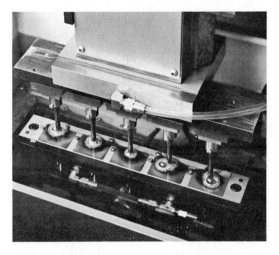

Fig. 102-5. Cutting five odd-shaped holes at the same time using an EDM machine. Note how the sparks cause bubbling of the dielectric.

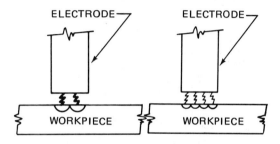

Fig. 102-6. Large, powerful sparks (left) create a rough surface. Smaller sparks (right) produce a smoother surface.

Fig. 102-7. A machine for doing electrochemical machining.

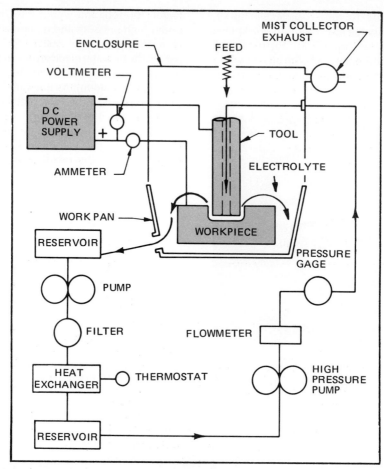

Fig. 102-8. A typical ECM system.

Fig. 102-9. Aluminum airplane fuselage parts with recessed sections that have been produced by chemical milling.

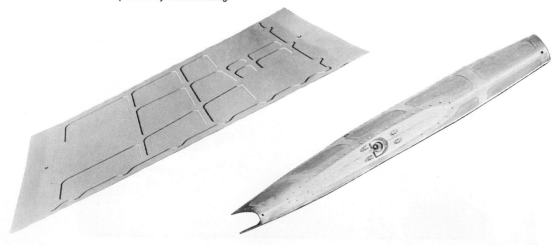

The ECM process is used primarily for removing metal from the surface of castings, forgings, and extrusions (Fig. 102-9). It is especially suitable when the parts are contoured, when alloys that are hard and tough must be shaped, when thin sections must be cut away, and when metal must be removed across a wide area to a very shallow depth (see Table 102-1). Electrochemical milling is practiced extensively throughout industry, particularly in aerospace manufacturing.

THE ECG PROCESS

Electrochemical (electrolytic) grinding is very much like electrochemical machining. The process is the same; only the application is different (Fig. 102-10A). Metal is removed from the surface of the workpiece by a combination of electrochemical decomposition and the action of abrasive particles embedded in a metal-bonded wheel. Briefly, here is what happens. Both wheel and work are connected to a source

Fig. 102-10. A diagram showing the operation of an electrochemical grinding unit.

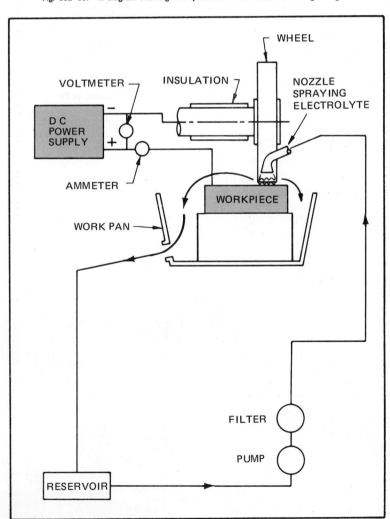

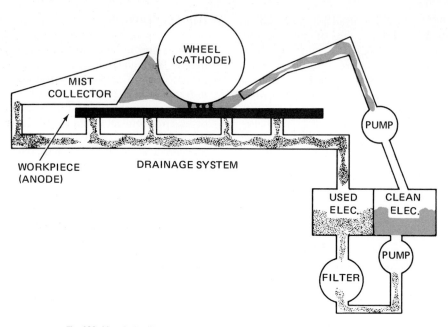

WHEEL
(CATHODE)

MIST
COLLECTOR

PUMP

WORKPIECE
(ANODE)

DRAINAGE SYSTEM

USED
ELEC.

CLEAN
ELEC.

PUMP

FILTER

Fig. 102-11. A simplified drawing showing how the wheel doesn't quite touch the workpiece. Metal that has been removed from the material is eliminated by the drainage system.

of direct-current power (Fig. 102–10B). They are separated from each other by the abrasive particles protruding from the wheel. These particles maintain the necessary gap between the metal of the wheel and the metal of the workpiece, and at the same time form thousands of little pockets which are filled with an electrically conductive fluid, or electrolyte. As current flows from the workpiece (anode) through the electrolyte to the wheel (cathode), the pockets of fluid act as electrochemical cells, decomposing the metal on the surface of the work. The rate of decomposition is determined by the amount of current flowing from work to wheel. Approximately 90 percent of the metal removed is the result of this electrochemical action; the remaining 10 percent is removed by the abrasive particles which, while scrubbing away the decomposed material, remove metal by abrasive grinding (Fig. 102–11).

Electrochemical grinding offers a number of advantages over conventional grinding. Among the most important of these is ECG's ability to grind difficult-to-machine materials rapidly and economically (Fig. 102–12). Electrochemical

grinding is also more accurate and much faster than conventional grinding. Because of the dissolving action and the absence of both heat and wheel contact, the ECG process is ideal for grinding fragile parts.

Fig. 102-12. Sharpening a carbide-tipped milling cutter on an electrochemical grinder. A complete cut for each tooth can be made with one pass across the grinding wheel.

UNIT 103. Careers in Machine Shop

What will be your future in the world of work (Fig. 103–1)? Some of you may decide on a career in the metal-cutting industries, particularly machine shop. This is a good choice, since ours is an industrial nation. The foundation of every production line is the precision machinist or tool-and-die maker. Machine tools make mass production possible. It takes a great many people to design, build, and operate these machines. Whether the product is a small metal toy or a new car, manufacturing depends on the skill of the machinist who makes it.

There are approximately three-quarters of a million people who work directly as machinists or machine operators. There are several million more who can profit by a knowledge of machine shop.

LEARNING ABOUT THE TRADES AND PROFESSIONS

A *trade* is a job requiring great skill and knowledge. Usually from 2 to 5 years of special training are needed. A *profession* requires formal education, at least a bachelor's degree. Between the trade and the profession is a new group called *technicians*. These are people who have had the equivalent of a trade education but, in addition, have had some education in science, mathematics, and business related to that area of work. They qualify to hold more responsible jobs in industry than the tradesmen. For example, the engineer is a professional man. He designs and supervises the planning, building, and operating of machines and mechanical equipment. The skilled tradesman (machinist, for example) performs highly skilled work. Technicians do the work that ranges between that of the engineer and the skilled tradesman.

It is not easy to explain exactly what a technician does because a technician's job depends on the particular industry or the particular product that is being manufactured. Here are a few examples of what he might do.

1. Act as a liaison (go-between) man between the engineering department and the production department.

2. Sell and service the equipment as a technical salesman.

3. Act as a liaison man between his company and another company. His company might be making a subassembly for a larger product manufactured by the other company—or the reverse might be true.

4. Write the technical bulletins for the product being manufactured.

Before you make a choice of a trade, technical position, or profession, study the jobs that interest you. Find out all you can about them. Some of the questions you should find answers to are these:

1. Where will I work?

2. What will I do?

3. How much will I earn?

4. Do I meet the physical requirements?

5. What are the chances of promotion?

6. Where can I learn the trade or profession? How long will it take?

7. Do I have the mental ability to finish the course of training?

Fig. 103-1. Deciding what you are going to do for a living is one of the most important decisions you will ever make.

8. Is this job something I will enjoy doing?

Many of the answers to these questions can be found by reading and studying and by asking the people already doing the work.

OPPORTUNITIES IN THE SKILLED TRADES

A *machine tool operator* (sometimes called a *machine hand*) is a semiskilled person who can operate only one machine or do only a few operations. His job is a routine one. He does the same thing over and over again everyday. Machine operators are employed in large production shops where it is necessary to have many machines of the same type (Fig. 103-2).

The *all-around machinist* is one who can set up and operate all the machine tools. He must be able to read prints, use precision measuring tools, and make adjustments. He is a highly skilled worker who might be employed in a small job shop, in the toolroom of a large manufacturing concern, or in a large production shop (Fig. 103-3).

Tool-and-die makers are highly skilled machinists. They design, make, and repair the tools, dies, fixtures, and jigs that are used in the manufacture of all types of products. The toolmaker must have qualifications that make him the best of the skilled metalworkers, above all others in the plant in prestige as well as pay.

Fig. 103-2. The machine operator uses only one machine all day long. He does a repetitive type of work.

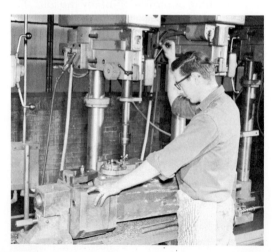

Layout men are skilled machinists who read prints and transfer measurements to metal. These are the men who get the parts ready to be machined. They must know mathematics. They must also know how to read blueprints and use precision measuring devices.

Setup men are skilled machinists who get the machines ready (do the setups) for the machine operator. They must be able to sharpen

Fig. 103-3. The all-around machinist must know how to use all kinds of hand and machine tools. Today's machinist must be skilled not only in machine tool operation but also in the use of precision inspection equipment.

Fig. 103-4. Inspection offers many opportunities for the appropriately trained person.

cutting tools, set and adjust the machine, and check it to make sure it will make the part exactly as shown on the print.

Inspectors are trained to use all types of precision measuring tools and gages to check finished workpieces for accuracy (Fig. 103-4).

Foremen and supervisors are the skilled machinists who have been promoted to positions of responsibility. They supervise the work of other men in the shop.

OPPORTUNITIES IN THE PROFESSIONS

The *mechanical engineer* must know how to design, build, and supervise the operation of machine tools. He must know the mathematics, mechanics, drawing, and science necessary to do this job. The mechanical engineer is one of the most important people in industry.

Industrial teachers (industrial arts and industrial, vocational, and technical education) teach machine shop in high schools and trade, vocational, and technical schools (Fig. 103-5).

Tool designers have a thorough knowledge of machine shop plus the training and ability to do designing. They design the tools, dies, and fixtures needed to manufacture new products (Fig. 103-6).

HOW TO OBTAIN TRAINING IN MACHINE SHOP

There are two principal ways of learning the machinists' trades. The first method is to enter a trade, vocational, or technical school. Here you would spend 2 or 3 years learning the fundamentals of the trade and related information about science, mathematics, and drawing. This will give you a good start in learning the trade (Fig. 103-7). The second method is to become an *apprentice* in a company shop. An apprentice is a young man who agrees to work with an experienced tradesman (machinist) for 4 years to learn the trade. The apprentice works in the company shop part time and studies the related subjects part time.

You can become a technician by enrolling in a technical education program. Technicians work on teams with engineers, scientists, supervisors, and skilled craftsmen converting theories and ideas into products and processes. There are two main types of technicians, namely, the engineering technician and the industrial technician. *Engineering technology* is that part of the engineering field which requires the application of scientific and engineering knowledge and methods combined with technical skills in support of engineering activities. It lies in the occu-

Fig. 103-5. Teaching is a rewarding career if you like to work with people.

Fig. 103-6. The tool designer must have creative ability as well as a sound technical background.

Fig. 103-7. A good way to get into the machine trades is to take a course in machine shop in a vocational school.

Fig. 103-8. The technician must be able to do scientific work as well as skilled activities.

Fig. 103-9. The graduate of a four-year industrial engineering program must be able to use all kinds of scientific equipment.

pational area between the craftsman and the engineer, at the end of the area closest to the engineer. The *industrial technician* exhibits similar competencies within a narrower range of industry in such areas as drafting, tool-and-die design, and machine tools. Technical programs are normally offered in technical institutes and/or community-junior colleges. Special attention is given to the technical and related phases of the metal trades. You will usually have to take courses in time-and-motion study and production problems, as well as in the basic subjects of English, mathematics, science, and shop (Fig. 103-8).

Four- or five-year college programs are required to qualify for some technical positions and for all professional positions in the metal trades. In addition to such engineering programs as mechanical and industrial engineering, there are college-degree programs in *industrial distribution, industrial supervision,* and *industrial engineering.* These degree programs combine education in the metal trades with many courses in business, management, and psychology (Fig. 103-9).

TYPES OF SHOPS

The *production shop* is the place where finished parts and products are manufactured in quantity. It is usually a very large concern in which all types of machine tools are used. Many of the machines are automatic. The production shop employs men with varying qualifications. These include many machine operators, machinists, tool-and-die makers, layout men, engineers, tool designers, and other tradesmen with related skills.

A *job shop* is a small shop in which dies, tools, fixtures, and small quantities of one part are made. The basic machine tools are used mostly by all-around machinists and tool-and-die makers.

UNIT 104. Discussion Topics and Problems

1. Define numerical control.

2. What are the two positioning systems used in numerical control?

3. Who plans the information that is put on a tape by a special typewriter?

4. What are three electrical machining techniques?

5. What is the greatest value of the EDM process?

6. What is the difference between EDM and ECM?

7. What is the difference between a jig and a fixture?

8. What is a technician? Describe what kind of work he does.

9. Name four skilled divisions in the machine-shop trades. Tell what each requires.

10. Describe two ways to get training in machine-shop work.

11. What professions require persons with experience in machine shop?

12. What is the difference between a production shop and a job shop?

INDEX

2 3 4 5 6 7 8 9 10 VHVH 82 81 80 79 78 77 76 75 74